AN INTRODUCTION TO INTERNATIONAL ECONOMICS

New Perspectives on the World Economy

This book is designed for a one-semester or two-semester course in international economics, primarily targeting non-economics majors and programs in business, international relations, public policy, and development studies. It has been written to make international economics accessible to wide student and professional audiences. The book assumes a minimal background in microeconomics and mathematics and goes beyond the usual trade–finance dichotomy to give equal treatment to four "windows" on the world economy: international trade, international production, international finance, and international development. It takes a practitioner point of view rather than a standard academic view, introducing students to the material they need to become effective analysts in international economic policy. The website for the text is found at http://iie.gmu.edu.

Kenneth A. Reinert is Professor of Public Policy in the School of Public Policy at George Mason University, where he won a Distinguished Teaching Award. He held past positions at Kalamazoo College, Wellesley College, and the U.S. International Trade Commission. He has published more than 60 articles and book chapters in the areas of trade, development, and environmental policy. In addition to the first release of this book, *Windows on the World Economy: An Introduction to International Economics*, his books include *The Princeton Encyclopedia of the World Economy* (co-edited with Ramkishen Rajan, 2009), *Globalization for Development* (co-authored with Ian Goldin, 2006; revised edition, 2007), and *Applied Methods for Trade Policy Analysis* (co-edited with Joseph Francois; Cambridge University Press, 1998).

AN INTRODUCTION TO INTERNATIONAL ECONOMICS

New Perspectives on the World Economy

KENNETH A. REINERT
School of Public Policy
George Mason University

CAMBRIDGE UNIVERSITY PRESS
Cambridge, New York, Melbourne, Madrid, Cape Town,
Singapore, São Paulo, Delhi, Tokyo, Mexico City

Cambridge University Press
32 Avenue of the Americas, New York, NY 10013-2473, USA

www.cambridge.org
Information on this title: www.cambridge.org/9780521177108

First published 2012

Printed in the United States of America

A catalog record for this publication is available from the British Library.

Library of Congress Cataloging in Publication data

Reinert, Kenneth A.
An introduction to international economics : new perspectives on the world economy / Kenneth A. Reinert. – 2nd ed.
p. cm.
Rev. ed. of: Windows on the world economy / Kenneth A. Reinert. 2005.
Includes bibliographical references and index.
ISBN 978-1-107-00357-6 (hardback) – ISBN 978-0-521-17710-8 (paperback)
1. International economic relations. 2. International trade. 3. International finance.
I. Reinert, Kenneth A. Windows on the world economy. II. Title.
HF1411.R4198 2012
337–dc22 2011015937

ISBN 978-1-107-00357-6 Hardback
ISBN 978-0-521-17710-8 Paperback

Additional resources for this publication at http://iie.gmu.edu

To Gelaye, Oda, and Ayantu

Summary Contents

Detailed Contents

Preface

I have written *An Introduction to International Economics: New Perspectives on the World Economy* for one- and two-semester courses in international economics, primarily targeting non-economics majors and programs in business, international relations, public policy, and development studies. The book assumes a *minimal* background in microeconomics, namely, familiarity with the supply and demand diagram and the production possibilities frontier diagram, along with basic algebra. It goes beyond the usual trade–finance dichotomy to give equal treatment to four "windows" on the world economy: international trade, international production, international finance, and international development. It also takes a practitioner point of view rather than a standard academic view. In one semester, there won't be time to cover all the book's chapters. In this case, the instructor can use the following table as a rough guide to choosing among chapters.

I have written the book to make international economics accessible to a wider student and professional audience than has been served by many international economics texts. I hope I have at least partially succeeded in this effort.

The book has an informal website to which I will be posting occasional updates as events and new research inevitably move forward. I would invite the reader to visit this website periodically: http://iie.gmu.edu.

SUGGESTED CHAPTER USE BY PROGRAM

Chapter	Economics	Business	International Studies	Development Studies
1 Windows on the World Economy	X	X	X	X
Part I International Trade				
2 Absolute Advantage	X	X	X	X
3 Comparative Advantage	X	X	X	X
4 Intra-Industry Trade	X	X		
5 The Political Economy of Trade	X	X	X	X
6 Trade Policy Analysis	X	X	X	X
7 The World Trade Organization	X		X	X
8 Preferential Trade Agreements	X	X	X	X
Part II International Production				
9 Foreign Market Entry and International Production		X		
10 Foreign Direct Investment and Intra-Firm Trade		X		
11 Managing International Production		X		
12 Migration			X	X
Part III International Finance				
13 Accounting Frameworks	X	X	X	X
14 Exchange Rates and Purchasing Power Parity	X	X	X	X
15 Flexible Exchange Rates	X	X	X	X
16 Fixed Exchange Rates	X	X	X	X
17 The International Monetary Fund	X		X	X
18 Crises and Responses	X	X	X	X
19 Monetary Unions	X		X	
Part IV International Development				
20 Development Concepts	X		X	X
21 Growth and Development	X		X	X
22 International Production and Development		X		X
23 The World Bank			X	X
24 Structural Change and Adjustment				X

Acknowledgments

I would like to express my sincere appreciation to Scott Parris for his suggestion that I publish the second edition of this book with Cambridge University Press and for his assistance in the revision process. I would like to thank the following individuals who have supported *An Introduction to International Economics* as a critical user or as a reviewer over the years: Sisay Asefa, Richard Blackhurst, Robert Blecker, Iva Bozovic, Barbara Craig, Desmond Dinan, Gerald Epstein, Diane Flaherty, Sasidaran Gopalan, Joe Joyce, Leo Kahane, Tony Lima, Jon Nadenichek, Carl Pasurka, Willard Posko, Ramkishen Rajan, Chris Rodrigo, Farhad Sabetan, Ralph Sonenshine, Wendy Takacs, Dominique van der Mensbrugghe, the late Tony Wallace, and Jonathan Wight. Apologies to anyone I have missed here.

I would also like to thank a few international economists who have directly influenced my thinking over the years: Christopher Clague, Joseph Francois, Ian Goldin, Arvind Panagariya, Ramkishen Rajan, David Roland-Holst, and Clinton Shiells.

I would finally like to thank Gelaye, Oda, and Ayantu for their patience and support during the revision process. This book is dedicated to them!

Acronyms

AANZFTA	ASEAN-Australia-New Zealand Free Trade Area
ACP	African, Caribbean, and Pacific
AD	Antidumping
AFTA	ASEAN Free Trade Area
AGE	Applied general equilibrium
AIDS	Acquired immune deficiency syndrome
ALBA	Bolivarian Alternative for the Americas
AMC	American Motor Corporation
AMS	Aggregate measure of support
ASEAN	Association of Southeast Asian Nations
ATC	Agreement on Textiles and Clothing
BAW	Beijing Auto Works
BIS	Bank for International Settlements
BIT	Bilateral investment treaty
CAMA	Central African Monetary Area
CAP	Common Agricultural Policy
CBD	Convention of Biological Diversity
CDF	Comprehensive Development Framework
CEC	Commission on Environmental Cooperation
CEPT	Common effective preferential tariff
CET	Common external tariff
CFA	Communauté Financière Africaine
CIG	Capital-intensive goods
CINDE	Coalición Costarricense de Initiativas para el Desarrollo/Costa Rican Investment Board
CIP	Covered interest rate parity
CITES	Convention on International Trade in Endangered Species of Wild Fauna and Flora
CMA	Common Monetary Area of Southern Africa
CMO	Contract manufacturing organization
CO	Certificate of origin
CPIA	Country Policy and Institutional Assessment
CRTA	Committee on Regional Trade Agreements
CTE	Committee on Trade and the Environment
CTH	Change in tariff heading

CU	Customs union
CVD	Countervailing duties
DD	Demand diagonal
DPL	Development policy lending
DSB	Dispute Settlement Body
DSU	Dispute Settlement Understanding
EC	European Community
ECB	European Central Bank
ECF	Extended Credit Facility
ECOFIN	European Council of Ministers of Economics and Finance
ECSC	European Coal and Steel Community
ECU	European currency unit
EEC	European Economic Community
EFF	Extended Fund Facility
EFSF	European Financial Stability Facility
EKC	Environmental Kuznets curve
EMI	European Monetary Institute
EMIT	Working Group on Environmental Measures and International Trade
EMS	European Monetary System
EMU	European Monetary Union
EPZ	Export processing zone
ESCB	European System of Central Banks
EU	European Union
FAO	United Nations Food and Agriculture Organization
FCL	Flexible credit line
FDI	Foreign direct investment
FEER	Fundamental equilibrium exchange rate
FOGS	Functioning of the GATT system
FTA	Free trade agreement
FTAA	Free Trade Agreement of the Americas
GAB	General Agreement to Borrow
GATS	General Agreement on Trade in Services
GATT	General Agreement on Tariffs and Trade
GDI	Gender-related development index
GDP	Gross domestic product
GEM	Gender empowerment measure
GNI	Gross national income
GNP	Gross national product
GPN	Global production network
GTAP	Global Trade Analysis Project
GTC	General trading company
HDI	Human development index
HDR	*Human Development Report*
HICP	Harmonized index of consumer prices
HIPC	Highly indebted poor country
HIV	Human immunodeficiency virus
HPI	Human poverty index

HSM	High-skilled migration
IBRD	International Bank for Reconstruction and Development
ICSID	International Center for Settlement of Investment Disputes
ICT	Information and communication technology
ICU	International Clearing Union
IDA	International Development Agency (World Bank)
IDA	Industrial Development Authority (Ireland)
IDM	Integrated device manufacturer
IFC	International Finance Corporation
IFIAC	International Financial Institutions Advisory Commission
IFSC	International Financial Services Center (Ireland)
IIA	International investment agreement
ILO	International Labor Office
IMF	International Monetary Fund
IOM	International Organization for Migration
IP	Intellectual property
ISF	International Stabilization Fund
ITO	International Trade Organization
JV	Joint venture
LIG	Labor-intensive goods
LOLR	Lender of last resort
LSM	Low-skilled migration
M&A	Mergers and acquisitions
MAI	Multilateral Agreement on Investment
MAL	Minimum access level
MBS	Mortgage-backed security
MDG	Millennium Development Goals
MEA	Multilateral environment agreements
MFN	Most favored nation
MIGA	Multilateral Investment Guarantee Agency
MNE	Multinational enterprise
MPI	Multidimensional poverty index
MTN	Multilateral trade negotiation
NAAEC	North American Agreement on Environmental Cooperation
NAALC	North American Agreement on Labor Cooperation
NAB	New Agreement to Borrow
NAFTA	North American Free Trade Agreement
NATO	North Atlantic Treaty Organization
NGBT	Negotiating group on basic telecommunications
NIC	Newly industrializing country
NT	National treatment
NTB	Nontariff barrier
NTM	Nontariff measure
OECD	Organization for Economic Cooperation and Development
OLI	Ownership, location, and internalization
OTDS	Overall trade distortion support
PC	Personal computer

PIIGS	Portugal, Italy, Ireland, Greece, and Spain
PNDC	Provisional National Defense Council (Ghana)
PPF	Production possibilities frontier
PPP	Purchasing power parity
PRGF	Poverty Reduction and Growth Facility
PRS	Poverty Reduction Strategy
PTA	Preferential trade agreement
QPC	Quantitative performance criteria
R&D	Research and development
RCF	Rapid Credit Facility
REER	Real effective exchange rate
REEs	Rare earth elements
RIT	Regional investment treaty
ROO	Rule of origin
RORE	Rate of return to education
RTA	Regional trade agreement
RVC	Regional value content
SAB	South African Breweries
SACU	Southern African Customs Union
SAL	Structural adjustment lending
SBA	Standby Arrangement
SCF	Stand-By Credit Facility
SDR	Special drawing rights
SITC	Standard international trade classification
SLIG	Skilled labor–intensive goods
SOE	State-owned enterprise
SPS	Sanitary and phyto-sanitary
SRF	Supplemental Reserve Facility
STR	Standards and technical regulations
TBT	Technical barriers to trade
TEU	Treaty on European Union (Maastricht Treaty)
TNI	Transnationality index
TRIMS	Trade-related investment measures
TRIPS	Agreement on Trade-Related Aspects of Intellectual Property Rights
TRQ	Tariff rate quota
TSMC	Taiwan Semiconductor Manufacturing Company
UIP	Uncovered interest rate parity
ULIG	Unskilled labor–intensive goods
UN	United Nations
UNCTAD	United Nations Conference on Trade and Development
UNDP	United Nations Development Program
UNESCO	United Nations Educational, Scientific and Cultural Organization
UNICEF	United Nations Children's Fund
URR	Unremunerated reserve requirement
U.S.	United States
USITC	United States International Trade Commission
VDR	Variable deposit requirement

VEAM	Vietnam Engine and Agricultural Machinery Corporation
VER	Voluntary export restraint
VNM	Value of nonoriginating materials
WAMU	West African Monetary Union
WEO	World Environmental Organization
WTO	World Trade Organization

Symbols

A	Technology factor
B	Grubel-Lloyd index
BI	Belassa index of revealed comparative advantage
C	Household consumption or conditions
D	Demand or distance
DD	Demand diagonal
Δ	Change in
e	Nominal exchange rate or exports as a percent of GDP
E	Exports or emigration
ES	Emigration supply
F	Fixed costs or flow of trade/foreign direct investment
G	Government expenditures
h	Ratio of total human capital to total labor (human capital-labor ratio)
H	Total human capital
I	Investment
ID	Immigration demand
k	Ratio of total physical capital to total labor (capital-labor ratio)
K	Physical capital
L	Labor, liquidity, or loans
M	Money
n	Natural rate of population growth
P	Price or price level
Q	Quantity
r	Interest rate or crude birth/death rate
R	Total return on asset
re	Real exchange rate
rw	Relative wage
S	Supply
S_F	Foreign savings
S_G	Government savings
S_H	Household savings
t	Ad valorem tariff
T	Specific tariff or taxes
θ	Constant

V	Variable costs
w	Wage
y	Real gross domestic product
Y	Nominal gross domestic production or gross national income
Z	Imports

1 Windows on the World Economy

In the late 1990s, I met an anthropology student who had just returned from a year in Senegal. As soon as she learned that I was an international economist, she asked, "Can you tell me about the CFA franc devaluation? Why was it necessary? It has made life very difficult in Senegal." Some years later, I met a religion student who had just returned from a semester of working in a health clinic in Haiti. As soon as he learned that I was an international economist, he asked, "Can you tell me about structural adjustment programs? I'm concerned about how they are being applied to Haiti." More recently, my son's school bus driver quizzed me about the Doha Round of multilateral trade negotiations.

These are not rare incidents. I receive such inquiries on a routine basis from all sorts of people. Increasingly, it seems, more and more of us – religion students, bus drivers, as well as economics and business students – need to know something about the world economy. Why is this? Put simply, the world economy impacts us all in increasingly significant ways. It has become very difficult to take shelter in our academic majors and professions without being knowledgeable about the fundamentals of international economics. Increasingly, trade flows, exchange rates, and multinational enterprises matter to us all, even if we would prefer that they did not. The global financial crisis that began in 2007 made this apparent in the most dramatic way.

As a consequence of these changes, students and professionals, and, more broadly, citizens now have significant concerns about "globalization." Shortly before the failed Seattle Ministerial Meeting of the World Trade Organization (WTO) in December 1999, for example, I received a phone call from a former student. She was about to travel to Seattle to join in the protests against the WTO. She knew that I had spent a brief amount of time at the WTO and, before she set off, she wanted to raise her concerns about globalization and the impact it was having on rural economies in the United States with me. The Seattle Ministerial was a failure, in part because of the efforts of my former student and her fellow protesters. The same was true of the Cancún Ministerial Meeting of 2003.

Were my student's concerns well placed? Is globalization the evil that some contend it to be? Or, is it the unmitigated good that others contend it is? Most likely, the actualities of globalization are more variegated than the good–evil dichotomy that is often invoked. For example, in an analysis of the effects of various globalization processes on the developing world, Goldin and Reinert (2007) stated that, "The relationship between globalization and poverty is not well understood. . . . By examining both the processes through which globalization takes place and the effects that each of these processes has on global poverty alleviation, current discussions can be better informed" (p. 1).

Better informing students and professionals about globalization is an important component of this book; exploring key aspects of globalization is one of the tasks we take up here. We will try to explore the world economy and globalization in as balanced a manner as possible. This will help us develop informed views and opinions, whatever they might be. Developing informed views and opinions requires a serious study of international economics. This field of study is typically divided into two parts: international trade and international finance. Indeed, these two parts often constitute the only two courses in a standard "core-course" series. In this book, however, we approach things differently. Acknowledging the diverse interests of students and professionals, as well as the diverse aspects of the world economy, we explore four different *windows* on the modern world economy. These are international trade, international production,

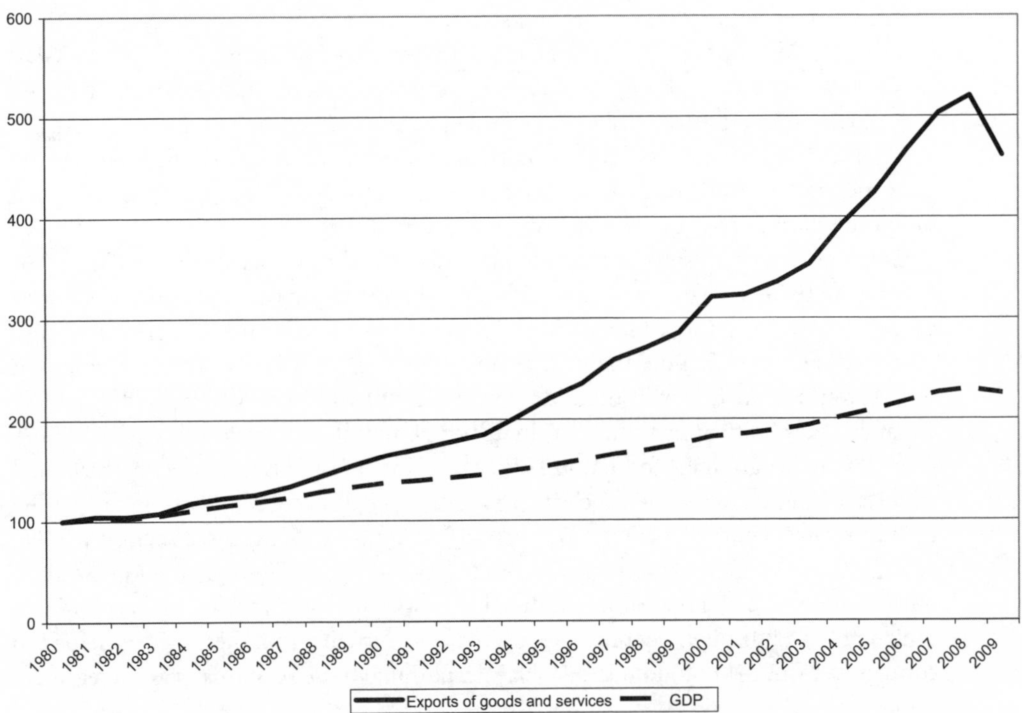

Figure 1.1. Gross Domestic Product and Exports in the World Economy, 1980 to 2009 (1980 = 100). *Source:* World Bank, World Development Indicators and author calculations

international finance, and international development. Let us briefly consider each of these in turn.

INTERNATIONAL TRADE

Our first window on the world economy is **international trade.**[1] International trade refers to the exchange of goods *and* services among the countries of the world. In the previous sentence, the "and" between "goods" and "services" is important. We typically picture international trade as involving only *goods*, such as steel, automobiles, wine, or bananas. However, this view is incomplete. It is important to acknowledge that a significant portion of world trade is composed of trade in *services*. Financial services, architectural services, and engineering services are all traded internationally. In fact, trade in services is about one-fourth the volume of trade in goods.[2]

International trade in goods and services is playing an increasing role in the world economy. Consider the data presented in Figure 1.1. This figure plots two series of data for the years 1980 to 2009. The first series, represented by a dashed line, is inflation-adjusted world **gross domestic product** (GDP), a measure of world output. It has been normalized so that the value in 1980 is 100, and the values for each subsequent year are

[1] Every time you encounter a term in **bold face** in this book, you can find its definition in the glossary.

[2] It is sometimes said that the word "goods" refers to things you can drop on your toe. Therefore, "services" refers to things you *cannot* drop on your toe! More formally, goods are tangible and storable, whereas services are intangible and non-storable. On trade in services, see Francois and Hoekman (2010).

measured relative to 1980. The second series, represented by a solid line, is inflation-adjusted world exports.[3] This series has been normalized in the same way as the GDP series. As you can see in this figure, over the decades considered, trade activity increased faster than production activity in the world economy. This is one of the main features of globalization, namely the expansion of exchange of goods and services among the countries of the world. You can also see that trade decreased more quickly in 2009 than did production in response to the global recession of that year.

There are many reasons for the expansion of world trade, as shown in Figure 1.1. During the 1970s, a revolution in global goods shipping began with the use of containers; ships built to carry thousands of increasingly standardized, 20-foot containers; and ports redesigned to handle these ships and containers efficiently. This was followed by a revolution in information and communications technology (ICT) that greatly enhanced the ability of firms to coordinate both international trade logistics and, more generally, international production systems. Advances in ICT also greatly facilitated some types of services trade via electronic commerce. ICT subsequently enhanced the development of container shipping to such an extent that, to paraphrase Levinson (2006, p. 267), the container, combined with the computer, opened the way to globalization. Furthermore, an era of trade liberalization began with the lowering of tariff barriers both unilaterally and through regional and multilateral initiatives. All these factors helped to contribute to a world economy in which international trade relations grew increasingly important.

You will begin to understand the major factors underlying international trade in Part I of this book. We will apply standard microeconomic thinking in analyzing both trade and trade policies. You will also be introduced to a set of key policy issues surrounding the management of international trade, including issues pertaining to the WTO and to **preferential trade agreements** such as the North American Free Trade Agreement (NAFTA) and the Association of Southeast Asian Nations (ASEAN). A full understanding of the factors underlying international trade, however, also requires an understanding of international production, which is discussed in Part II of this book.

INTERNATIONAL PRODUCTION

Our second window on the world economy is **international production**. Production patterns in the modern world economy can be relatively complex. For example, when my children were toddlers, one of their favorite books was *Bear's Busy Family*, published by Barefoot Books. Featured in *Inc. Magazine* in 2006, Barefoot Books was founded in 1993 by Tessa Strickland and Nancy Traversy. It was initially run from their homes in the United Kingdom (where burgeoning inventory broke a table), but subsequently expanded with a flagship store in Cambridge, Massachusetts, in the United States. In the case of *Bear's Busy Family*, the color separation was done in Italy and the actual printing in Malaysia. So the book my children held with such interest in their hands was a result of a production process that took place in four countries. Production of a product in multiple countries is what we mean by international production.

[3] Note that world imports track world exports very closely, so we can use the level of exports as a proxy for the overall level of world trade.

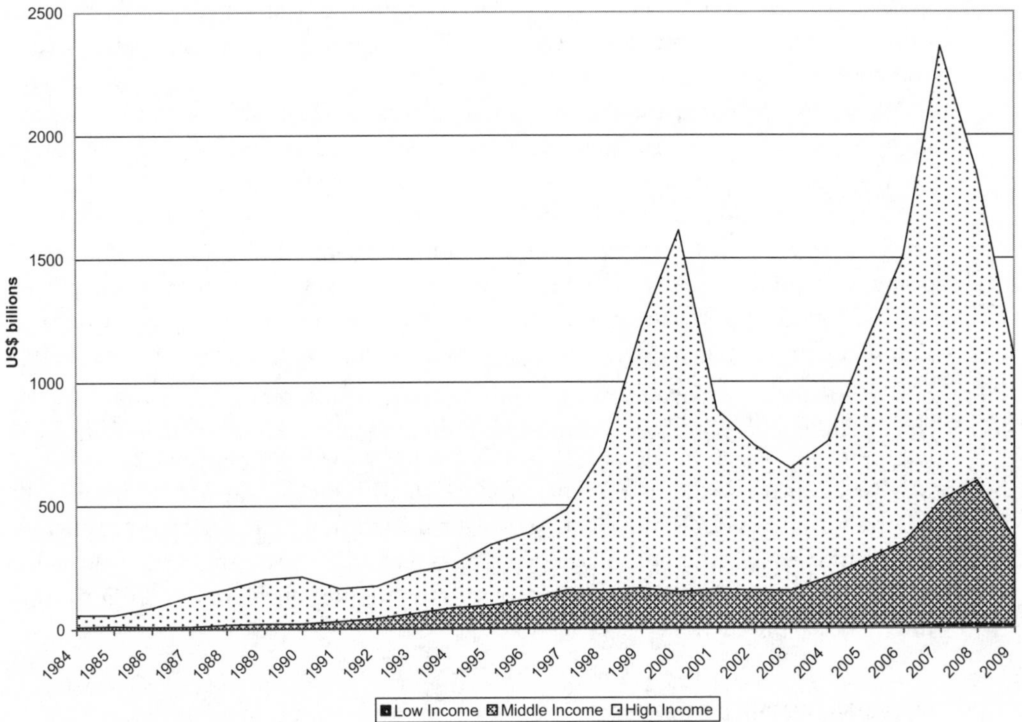

Figure 1.2. Nominal FDI Inflows to Low, Middle, and High Income Countries, 1984 to 2009. *Source:* World Bank, World Development Indicators

At the broadest level, international production can take place through two modes: contracts (international licensing and franchising) and **foreign direct investment** (FDI) undertaken by **multinational enterprises** (MNEs). Contracting is an arm's length relationship across national boundaries that can be described as a low-commitment–low-control option. FDI involves firms based in one country, owning at least 10 percent of a firm producing in another country and thereby exerting management influence. It can be described as a high-commitment–high-control option. MNEs are now a major component of the world economy. To see this, consider the following facts:

1. MNEs account for approximately one-fourth of world GDP.
2. The sales of foreign affiliates of MNEs now exceed the volume of world trade.
3. MNEs are involved in approximately three-fourths of all world trade.
4. Approximately one-third of world trade takes place *within* MNEs.
5. MNEs account for approximately three-fourths of worldwide civilian research and development.

A series of data on global FDI inflows from 1984 to 2009 is provided in Figure 1.2. The inflows are broken down among low-income, middle-income, and high-income countries that host the FDI. It is clear that the 1990s experienced a large surge of FDI flows, mostly into high-income countries and partly reflecting an upturn in mergers and acquisitions activity. What is also clear, however, is that the middle-income countries of the world are hosting a growing amount of FDI. FDI inflows into low-income countries are both very low and stagnant, with these members of the global economic community largely excluded from this important part of economic globalization. Finally, as a result of the financial crisis and global recession, FDI flows decreased substantially in 2008 and 2009.

What has accounted for the long-term increase in FDI activity in middle- and high-income countries? Two relevant factors mentioned earlier in our discussion of international trade include improvements in transportation and ICT. Add to these factors an expansion of global mergers and acquisition activity, particularly in the services sector (finance, transport, and communications). Indeed, services began to account for approximately half of FDI flows in the 1990s. Furthermore, many countries in the developing world began to shift from a policy posture of antipathy toward FDI inflows to one of relative friendliness. For example, this accompanied the well-known rise of FDI flows into China.

As the preceding facts and data indicate, the operation of MNEs is another main feature of globalization. In Part II of this book, you will gain an understanding of MNEs and their role in international production. This includes an appreciation of the relatively complex decisions facing global firms, the function of **global production networks** (GPNs), and the management issues that arise when firms are spread across international borders. You will also gain an appreciation of the role of **migration** in international production.

INTERNATIONAL FINANCE

Our third window on the world economy is **international finance**. Whereas international trade refers to the exchange of goods and services among the countries of the world, international finance refers to the exchange of **assets** among these countries. Assets are financial objects characterized by a monetary value that can change over time. They make up the wealth portfolios of individuals, firms, and governments. For example, individuals and firms around the world conduct international transactions in currencies, equities, government bonds, corporate bonds (commercial paper), and even real estate as part of their management of portfolios. The way in which the prices of these assets change in response to these international transactions affects the countries of the world in important ways. Additionally, as we will see, these transactions can provide a source of savings to countries over and above the domestic savings of their households and firms.

International finance plays an increasingly important role in the world economy. We can see this by considering foreign exchange transactions. Foreign exchange transactions are much larger than trade transactions. For example, Figure 1.3 plots two variables for 3-year intervals between 1989 and 2010. The first variable, plotted as the vertical bars in reference to the lefthand scale (lhs), is daily foreign exchange turnover as measured by the Bank for International Settlements (BIS) in its triennial April surveys. Despite a downturn in 2001, the total foreign exchange turnover increased substantially over time. Observers were amazed when it broke US$1 trillion in 1995, but in 2010 it reached US$4 trillion!

The second variable plots the annualized foreign exchange turnover (assuming constant turnover each day) as a multiple of total world exports in reference to the right-hand scale (rhs), but only up to 2007. As you can see, foreign exchange turnover is *60 to 70 times* the value of exports. This makes it strikingly clear that, on an annual basis,

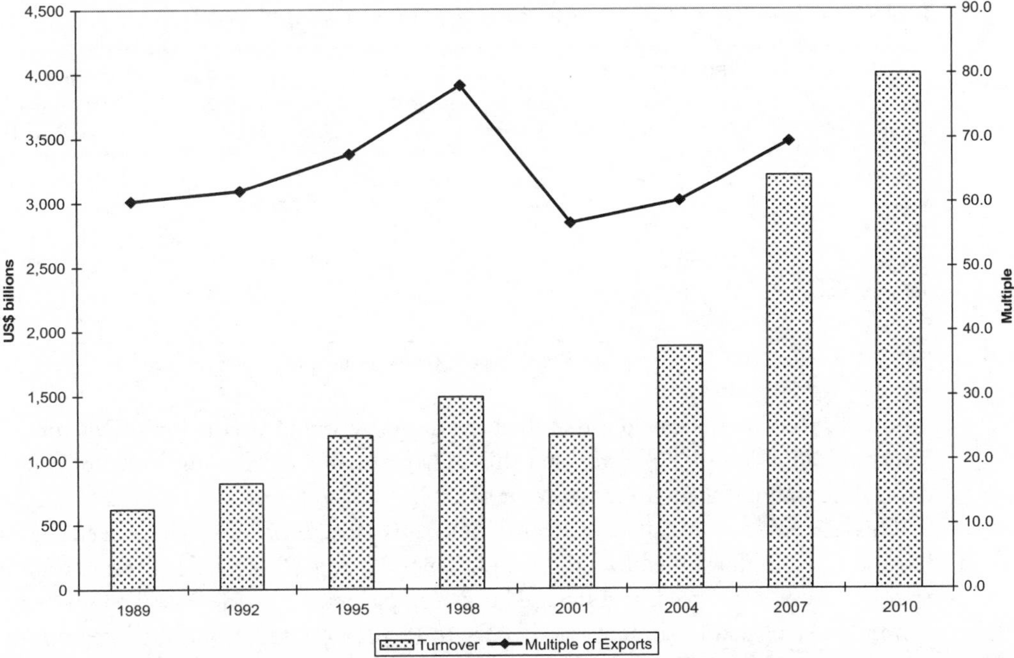

Figure 1.3. Daily Foreign Exchange Market Turnover and Annualized Multiple of Exports (billions of U.S. dollars on lhs and multiple of exports on rhs). *Sources:* Bank for International Settlements Triennial Central Bank Surveys and World Bank, World Development Indicators. *Note:* The multiple of exports assumes a constant foreign exchange turnover each day of the year.

global transactions in foreign exchange dwarf global trade transactions. International finance matters.

Another important feature of international finance has emerged in recent years. A typical expectation in the field of international finance is that developing countries will naturally receive net inflows of capital and invest them at relatively high rates of return, with this capital being supplied by developed countries with relatively low rates of return. Since 2000, however, this pattern has been reversed. Largely as a result of deficits in the United States (U.S. citizens spending in excess of national savings), the developing world is now a significant exporter of financial capital rather than an importer. As of 2008, the capital exports of the developing world exceeded US$500 billion. This is a major new development in international finance.

The importance of international finance, seen in Figure 1.3, became very evident in the later part of the 1990s. During this time, investors quickly sold assets in Mexico, Thailand, Indonesia, the Philippines, Russia, and Brazil, causing **balance of payments** and financial crises. This was a process known as **capital flight**. Capital flight involves investors selling a country's assets and reallocating their portfolios into other countries' assets. Beginning in mid-2008, the power of international finance again became evident in the form of a global crisis with roots in the United States housing market. Losses in housing mortgages were transmitted around the globe via a pyramid of financial instruments related to this sector. This was the result of banks taking loans that would have traditionally remained on their books, repackaging them in the form of asset-based securities, and trading these securities internationally. This provided a mechanism for a crisis involving new financial products that originated in one country to take on a global

Table 1.1. Measures of living standards (2008, except where indicated)

Country	PPP GDP per capita (U.S. dollars)	Life expectancy (years)	Adult literacy (percent)	Human development index (0 to 1)
Ethiopia	869	55	36 (2004)	0.414
India	3,032	64	63 (2006)	0.612
China	6,195	73	91 (2000)	0.772
Costa Rica	11,250	79	95 (2000)	0.854
South Korea	26,875	80	..	0.937
United States	47,210	79	..	0.956

Source: World Bank, World Development Indicators and United Nations Development Program

profile that has yet to be resolved at the time of this writing. As noted in the *Financial Times* in 2008, "The global system has shifted from financing anything, however crazy, to refusing to finance anything, however sensible."

This crisis did not just affect the United States. Its most severe effects have been felt in Europe – first in the United Kingdom, and then in Portugal, Italy, Ireland, Greece, and Spain. The crises in Greece and Ireland have been particularly acute, and the European Union has struggled to contain the damage to its political and economic integration. Watching the United States and the European Union succumb to financial instability has given many experts and policymakers pause.

As we can see, international finance is a realm of increasing importance in the modern world economy. You will enter into this realm in Part III of this book. You will learn about open-economy accounting, exchange rate determination, the international monetary system, and financial crises. Throughout Part III, the asset considerations that set international finance apart from international trade will be paramount.

INTERNATIONAL DEVELOPMENT

The fourth and final window on the world economy is **international development**. The processes of international trade, international production, and international finance reflect the many goals of their participants. From a public policy perspective, however, it is hoped that these three processes will contribute to improved levels of welfare and standards of living throughout the countries of the world. Two major issues are involved here. The first is how we conceptualize levels of welfare or standards of living. The second is how the processes of international trade, production, and finance support or undermine international development.

One inclusive, although not uncontroversial, measure of these differences in living standards is the **human development index** (HDI) measured by the United Nations Development Program (UNDP). For our purposes here, suffice it to say that the HDI reflects per capita income (adjusted for cost of living), average life expectancy, and average levels of education. Some data on these measures for the year 2005, as well as on the HDI itself, are presented for a small sample of countries in Table 1.1.

As we can see from the data presented in Table 1.1, there is a wide range in measures of well-being among the countries of the world. GDP per capita ranges from less than US$1,000 in Ethiopia to approximately US$47,000 in the United States, a factor of

50 in this standard measure of economic development.[4] Life expectancies range from 55 years in Ethiopia to 80 in South Korea (and even 83 in Japan). Low life expectancies often reflect high mortality among infants and children – sadly, nearly 10 million of whom perish each year. Literacy rates range from less than 40 percent of the population in Ethiopia to near-universal literacy in other countries. When combined into the single measure of the HDI, we see a wide variance as well, with a variation of approximately 0.41 to 0.96. However we view development (income, health, or education), its level *varies widely* among the countries of the world.

The variation in development indicators reflects the fact that economies around the world differ in their productive capacities. For example, Florida (2005) constructed a world map that proxies productive capacities with nighttime light emissions in which higher emission levels appear as raised surfaces above the earth. Florida described the result as follows: "U.S. regions appear almost Himalayan on this map. From their summits one might look out on a smaller mountain range stretching across Europe, some isolated peaks in Asia, and a few scattered hills throughout the rest of the world" (p. 49). Florida refered to this pattern of development as "spiky globalization," a pattern that confronts the world with a significant and persistent development challenge to raise productive capacities.

You will begin to understand how the activities of international trade, production, and finance affect international development in Part IV of this book. In Part IV, we consider alternative concepts of development, the way trade can contribute to economic growth, the process of hosting MNEs, and the role of the World Bank and structural adjustment in developing countries. These intersections of our windows on the world economy are critical for improving the well-being of (literally) billions of individuals worldwide.

CONNECTING WINDOWS

Each of our four windows on the world economy – trade, production, finance, and development – offers a view, but each has a frame. That is, each window offers some insight into the world economy, an insight that needs to be supplemented by one or more of the other windows. Let me give you an example. In 1991, I was working for the U.S. International Trade Commission (USITC) in Washington, DC. At that time, most of my efforts were dedicated to analyzing the *trade* effects of the North American Free Trade Agreement (NAFTA). Based on the narrow trade window, I was excited about Mexico's prospects. One day, the USITC received a delegation from Mexico, and I had an hour-long appointment with a Mexican economist accompanying the delegation. As it turned out, he was as worried about Mexico's prospects, even as I was excited. During our conversation, he said, "I am very worried about the future. All of the excitement over NAFTA is causing an inflow of portfolio investment. It is very short term, and it is financing a large trade deficit. It could turn around in a day! And then where will we be?"

As it turned out, this Mexican economist was right. The portfolio investment did turn around and cause a crisis in late 1994 and early 1995. My window on the Mexican

[4] The GDP per capita measures are purchasing power parity measures, which adjust for differences in costs of living among countries (see Chapter 20).

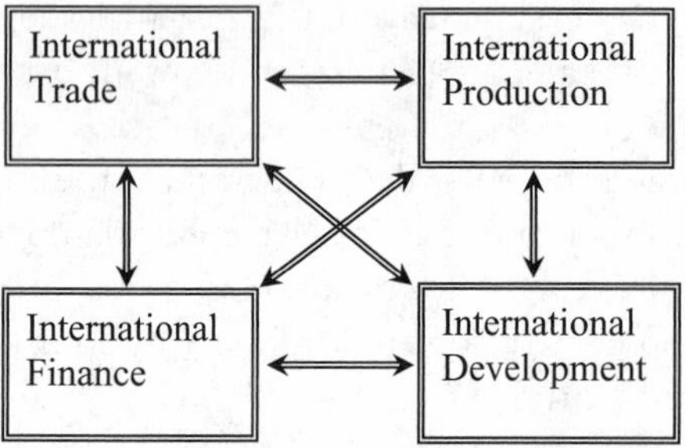

Figure 1.4. Connecting Windows

economy was insufficient to allow me (and many other trade economists) to appreciate where Mexico was heading. The Mexican economist was more attuned to the realities of the Mexican economy because he was viewing it through more than one window. He was using the window of international finance as well.

I want to suggest that you take the integrated view illustrated in Figure 1.4. In the figure, the four windows of our book are represented with four boxes. More important, there are six *connections* among the windows, represented by double-headed arrows. These are the connections among our four windows that we must keep in mind. NAFTA was an agreement for liberalizing trade and investment among the countries of North America, but its effects went beyond the trade and production windows to the finance window. The financial crises of the 1990s took place in the realm of international finance, but the effects were strongly transmitted to the realm of international development: standards of living fell. So as you proceed through the remainder of this book, it will be important for you to identify connections among the four windows.

Figure 1.4 helps us to be cognizant of the connections among the four aspects of international economics that you will explore in this book; however, we must keep in mind that there are additional realms that affect the way in which the world economy evolves over time. These are *technology, politics, culture*, and the *environment*. At various points in the book, we discuss how these factors play important roles. It is fair to say that the boxes and arrows in Figure 1.4 should be thought of as being strongly influenced by technological, political, cultural, and environmental factors. The accompanying box takes up technology in the form of ICT. We must also say a few words about politics, culture, and the environment.

ICT in the World Economy

As a dynamic, driving force for global economic change, technology is central. Indeed, a large part of the globalization process can be attributed to revolutions in information and communication technologies (ICT). It is ICT that allows an employee of Philips, the Dutch consumer-electronics firm, to use the Internet in order to adjust a television assembly line process in the Flextronics factory in Guadalajara, Mexico. It is ICT that allows a fund manager in London to quickly buy or sell equities on the Johannesburg stock exchange. Most recently, new ICT technologies in the area of "telepresence" (e.g., Hewlett-Packard's Halo system) allow teleconferencing to move into a new era in which it appears that participants half a world away are sitting across the table, greatly enhancing global coordination and reducing the need for international travel.

In the realm of international production, ICT has had a somewhat unusual impact of moving production in two opposing directions: toward greater global integration and toward selective disintegration of production systems. Communication and coordination costs of multinational production have long been a deterrent to FDI, requiring that MNEs possess offsetting advantages before engaging in successful foreign production. Advances in ICT have lowered these costs, contributing to increased integration of global production systems. Swissair, for example, has set up an accounting subsidiary in Mumbai, India. Because close of business in Switzerland corresponds to morning in Mumbai, this accounting work is done on an overnight basis from the Swiss standpoint. This is an example of services being globalized but remaining *internal* to the firm.

At the same time, however, a second process has been at work. Improvements in ICT have resulted in firms *contracting out* on a global basis functions that they used to carry out in-house. This process has become known as "outsourcing." For example, many U.S. firms now contract their software development to Indian firms, notably to Tata Consultancy Services and Tata Unysys Ltd. Also, a number of hospitals in the United States now contract with Indian firms for medical transcription services, making use of satellite technology. These are example of services being globalized while being *external* to the firm.

Both of the preceding scenarios, FDI and outsourcing, are made possible by advances in ICT that are only a few decades old. These advances are causing a global reconfiguration of the way work is carried out. This is a process that has not yet reached its final destination point but has already had revolutionary impacts on the world economy.

Sources: Dicken (2007) and *The Economist* (2000, 2007)

In an ideal world, countries would interact with one another within the multilateral framework of international law, committed to dispute resolution procedures, conflict prevention, transparency, and respect for human rights. We do not live in this ideal world: country governments do not always respect international law, and armed, non-state actors exert their own influence across national boundaries. Consequently, *political events* of all magnitudes continually impact the world economy. Civil and international conflicts dramatically affect the supply sides of national economies, bias government expenditures toward armaments, and promote the role of militaries in national governments. These national governments themselves are of varying degrees of strength and capability, from effective to outright failed. Political instability in struggling states affects all four windows on the world economy, but impinges on international development most strongly and negatively. Consequently, the best-intentioned developments in the world of international economic policy can come to naught in our less-than-ideal political world.

Culture is as real as it is difficult to define, and we usually do not notice it until our own cultural norms have been seriously violated. It is popular to depict cultural clashes as inevitable and growing in strength in the form of a "clash of civilizations" and to further define this clash as one that is occurring between Islam and Christianity. Many of these claims do not stand up to close scrutiny. For example, Sen (2006) noted that India is considered to be central to the "Hindu world," but has more Muslim citizens than most of the countries classified as part of the "Muslim world." That said, it is nevertheless important to recognize that the extent to which cultural conflicts are managed (at the level of international politics or within a single MNE) matters a great deal to the evolution of the world economy. We should not discount the importance of culture.

The *environmental* issue as it relates to the world economy has developed along a number of tracks. There are global issues such as climate change, regional issues such as the environmental impacts of NAFTA, and local issues related to globalization such as toxic waste dumping. A common theme related to the politics of environmental issues is the importance of a multilateral approach to environmental problems, which is embodied in "multilateral environmental agreements," or MEAs.[5] MEAs include the Convention on International Trade in Endangered Species of Wild Fauna and Flora (CITES), the Montreal Protocol on Substances that Deplete the Ozone Layer (Montreal Protocol), the Convention on Biological Diversity (CBD), the Kyoto Protocol to the UN Framework Convention on Climate Change (Kyoto Protocol), and the Convention on Biological Diversity (CBD). The hope of many working in this realm is that MEAs will help the world economy avoid the dangers of serious and irreversible environmental harm.

It is important for us to appreciate the extent to which the political, cultural, environmental, and economic can be deeply entwined. I once had the opportunity to talk at length with Dr. Owens Wiwa, the brother of Ken Saro-Wiwa, a member of the Ogani people of the Niger delta. Dr. Wiwa informed me of his brother's campaign against the environmental damage resulting from oil exploration in the Niger delta for which he was eventually executed by the Nigerian government. One particular fact pressed upon me by Dr. Wiwa was that the gas flaring within the region takes place *horizontally* across the ground rather than vertically, as is typical practice. Despite being a handy way to dry laundry, this has had severe environmental and health impacts. Today, one can view these gas flares on Google Images, and the Niger delta is in a near civil war. Global production of petroleum has gravely affected the politics, culture, and environment of this particular region of the world economy. Other examples of the way political, cultural, and environmental issues interact are common around the globe.

ANALYTICAL ELEMENTS

As we begin to examine the four windows of the world economy, we will utilize a number of *analytical elements* to improve our understanding of many complex processes. These are simultaneously actual elements at work in the real world economy and conceptual elements of the various models used by researchers to understand the world economy. We will rely on seven such analytical elements:

1. *Countries.* These are the states of the world economy, their national governments, serving as "home" to both firms and residents.
2. *Sectors.* These are categories of production defined largely in terms of final goods. An example is the automotive sector.
3. *Tasks.* On occasion, we are going to need to recognize that production in a particular sector involves a number of steps or separate tasks. Automobile production moves from a chassis to engine mounting to body mounting, for example.
4. *Firms.* Production in any sector of a country is undertaken by firms, either purely local or MNEs.
5. *Factors of production.* Production in any sector of a country undertaken by a firm makes use of various factors of production. Automobile production uses labor and physical capital.

[5] On MEAs, see Runge (2009).

6. *Currencies.* Most (not all) countries in the world economy have a separate currency in which transactions with other countries take place through foreign exchanges.
7. *Financial assets.* Both countries and firms issue various types of financial assets, denominated in a particular currency, that can be bought to be part of wealth management portfolios by other countries, other firms, and residents of any country.

These are the seven analytical elements that we will draw upon in various combinations as we move through the chapters of this book. In each chapter, I will let you know at the beginning what elements we are going to use.

CONCLUSION

It is becoming increasingly difficult for us to ignore the important realities of the world economy. Students and professionals of many types are finding that a basic understanding of international economics is necessary for them to operate successfully in the world. Perhaps you have the same experience. A thorough understanding of the world economy involves the study of four realms of international economics: international trade, international production, international finance, and international development. These are the four windows on the world economy that we explore in this book.

International trade is increasing faster than global production. International production, meanwhile, is taking on more and more complex forms, involving both contractual arrangements and FDI. FDI is undertaken by multinational enterprises, and these organizations play a critical role in the world economy that cannot be ignored. However, as we have seen, viewing the world through trade and production windows is also incomplete. The realm of international finance is paramount, with foreign exchange transactions dwarfing trade transactions.

It is hoped that international trade, international production, and international finance will contribute positively to international development, improving welfare and living standards. Understanding how this occurs (or does not occur) provides an important fourth window on the world economy.[6]

These four windows – trade, production, finance, and development – must be seen as connected. Furthermore, these four windows are strongly affected by the realms of technology, politics, culture, and the environment. The task of understanding how these four windows and the four larger realms (technology, politics, culture, and the environment) evolve over time in a system of globalization is not, to say the least, an easy one. Indeed, it takes us far beyond the scope of this book. However, with persistence and some patience, you will begin to build an intellectual foundation for understanding this system in the remaining chapters.

REVIEW EXERCISES

1. Why are you interested in international economics? What is motivating you? How are your interests, major, or profession affected by the world economy?
2. What are the four windows on the world economy?
3. What is the difference between trade in goods and trade in services?

[6] On this important issue, see Goldin and Reinert (2007).

4. What is the difference between international trade and foreign direct investment?
5. What is the difference between international trade and international finance?
6. Identify one way in which the activities of international trade, finance, and production could *positively* contribute to international development. Identify one way in which these activities could *negatively* contribute to international development. How could you demonstrate that the activities have either a positive or negative impact on development?

FURTHER READING AND WEB RESOURCES

Osterhammel and Petersson (2005) present a concise history of globalization accessible to a broad audience. Dicken (2007) and Dunning and Lundan (2008) look at foreign direct investment in recent decades, and Prahalad and Lieberthal (2008) provide a short, interesting assessment of FDI in developing countries. On international trade, see Hoekman and Kostecki (2009). Eichengreen (2008) gives an excellent history of international finance, and the *Financial Times* (2008) takes a brief look at its recent failure. Szirmai (2005) and Goldin and Reinert (2007) examine the relationship of a number of aspects of globalization to development and poverty alleviation, Sen (2006) effectively addresses cultural issues in a global perspective, and Speth and Haas (2006) address global environmental issues. Finally, Reinert et al. (2009) have edited a comprehensive encyclopedia of the world economy directly relevant to the four windows on the world economy examined here.

The Peterson Institute for International Economics in Washington, DC, provides timely and readable analyses of many issues in international economics. Its website is www.iie.com. Two quality sources on international economic developments are *The Economist* and *The Financial Times.* Their websites are www.economist.com and www.ft.com. Important institutions of the world economy include the World Trade Organization (www.wto.org), the World Bank (www.worldbank.org), and the International Monetary Fund (www.imf.org).

REFERENCES

Dicken, P. (2007) *Global Shift: Mapping the Changing Contours of the World Economy*, Guilford.

Dunning, J.H. and S.M. Lundan (2008) *Multinational Enterprises and the Global Economy*, Edward Elgar.

The Economist (2000) "Have Factory, Will Travel," February 12.

The Economist (2007) "Behold, Telepresence," August 24.

Eichengreen, B. (2008) *Globalizing Capital: A History of the International Monetary System*, Princeton University Press.

Financial Times (2008) "The Year the God of Finance Failed," December 26.

Florida, R. (2005), "The World Is Spiky," *Atlantic Monthly*, October.

Francois, J.F. and B. Hoekman (2010) "Services Trade and Policy," *Journal of Economic Literature*, 48:3, 642–92.

Goldin, I. and K.A. Reinert (2007) *Globalization for Development: Trade, Finance, Aid, Migration and Policy*, World Bank.

Hoekman, B.M. and M. Kostecki (2009) *The Political Economy of the World Trading System*, Oxford University Press.

Levinson, M. (2006) *The Box: How the Shipping Container Made the World Smaller and the World Economy Bigger*, Princeton University Press.

Osterhammel, J. and N.P. Petersson (2005) *Globalization: A Short History*, Princeton University Press.

Prahalad, C.K. and K. Lieberthal (2008) *The End of Corporate Imperialism*, Harvard Business Press.

Reinert, K.A., R.S. Rajan, A.J. Glass, and L.S. Davis (eds.) (2009) *The Princeton Encyclopedia of the World Economy*, Princeton University Press.

Runge, C.F. (2009) "Multilateral Environmental Agreements," in K.A. Reinert, R.S. Rajan, A.J. Glass, and L.S. Davis (eds.), *The Princeton Encyclopedia of the World Economy*, Princeton University Press, 795–9.

Sen, A. (2006) *Identity and Violence: The Illusion of Destiny*, Norton.

Speth, J.G. and P. M. Haas (2006) *Global Environmental Governance*, Island Press.

Szirmai, A. (2005) *The Dynamics of Socio-Economic Development*, Cambridge University Press.

I INTERNATIONAL TRADE

2 Absolute Advantage

Throughout most of the 1980s, Vietnam imported rice. In 1989, however, Vietnam *exported* more than 1 million tons of rice. In the 1990s, its annual rice exports increased to more than 3 million tons. Despite a fall in rice exports in 2004, Vietnam was expected to export 6 million tons of rice in 2009. As discussed in Goldin and Reinert (2007, Chapter 3) and Heo and Doanh (2009), despite being the staple consumption crop in Vietnam, the expansion of rice exports helped to alleviate poverty in that country through increased employment and wage income. This beneficial increase in rice exports represents one important aspect of Vietnam's entry into the world economy through the process of trade expansion we discussed in Chapter 1.

Why does a country export or import a particular good? This chapter takes a first step in helping you answer this fundamental question by utilizing a framework that should be familiar to you from your introductory economics class: the supply and demand diagram. We will use this diagram to illustrate an important concept in international economics, that of **absolute advantage**. Absolute advantage refers to the possibility that, due to differences in supply conditions, one country can produce a product at a lower price than another country.[1] In this chapter, we consider the product rice and the fact that Vietnam can produce rice more cheaply than Japan. This situation causees rice to be exported from Vietnam to Japan. It also involves what international economists call the **gains from trade**, which benefit *both* Vietnam *and* Japan. These gains are what motivate countries to take part in trading relationships.

Analytical elements for this chapter:
Countries, sectors, and *factors of production.*

SUPPLY AND DEMAND IN A DOMESTIC MARKET

Throughout the world, rice is exchanged in markets. Although these markets are international, let's assume for a moment that we can analyze a single domestic market in isolation. This will help orient you to the supply and demand model. Figure 2.1 illustrates such a market. The diagram has two axes. The horizontal axis plots the quantity (Q) of rice in tons per year. The vertical axis plots the price (P) of rice per ton. There are two curves in the diagram identified by the symbols S and D. S is the supply curve and represents the behavior of domestic rice-producing firms. D is the demand curve and represents the behavior of domestic consumers of rice, both firms and households.[2]

There are a number of properties of the supply and demand curves in Figure 2.1 that are important to understand. Let's consider the supply curve first. It is upward sloping, and this indicates that firms supply more rice to the market as the price increases. Consequently, changes in price are represented in the diagram by *movements along* the supply curve. These movements are known as **changes in quantity supplied**. There are two additional supply-side factors relevant to the supply curve. These are input or factor prices and technology. Reductions in input prices and improvements in technology shift the supply curve to the right. This means that producers supply more rice than before at every price. Increases in input prices and technology setbacks shift the supply curve

[1] For an alternative approach, see Van Marrewijk (2009).

[2] Firms consuming rice use it as an intermediate product to produce a final product such as rice flour or a restaurant meal.

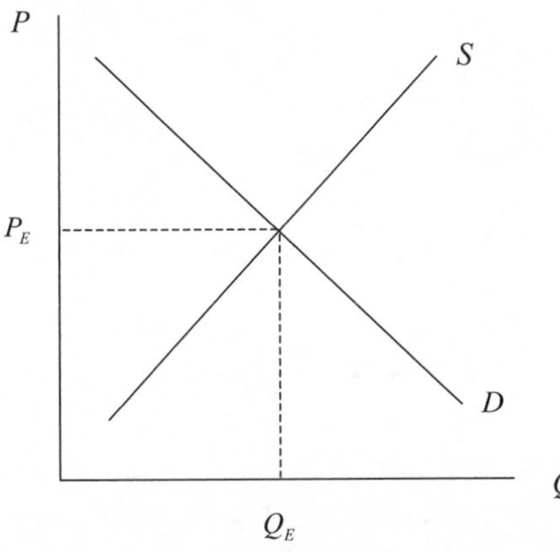

Figure 2.1. A Domestic Rice Market

to the left. This means that producers supply less rice than before at every price. We can see that changes in input prices and technology are represented by *shifts of* the supply curve. These shifts are known as **changes in supply**.

Now let's take a look at the rice demand curve. It is downward sloping, and this indicates that consumers demand less rice from the market as the price increases. Consequently, changes in price are represented in the diagram by *movements along* the demand curve. These movements are known as **changes in quantity demanded.** There are a number of additional demand-side factors relevant to the demand curve. Two important ones are incomes and preferences.[3] Increases in incomes and increased preference for rice consumption shift the demand curve to the right. This means that consumers demand more rice than before at every price. Decreases in incomes and decreased preference for rice consumption shift the demand curve to the left. This means that consumers demand less rice than before at every price. Consequently, changes in incomes and preferences are represented by *shifts of* the demand curve. These shifts are known as **changes in demand.**

Finally, the intersection of the supply and demand curves in Figure 2.1 determines the equilibrium in the domestic rice market. In this diagram, the equilibrium price is P_E, and the equilibrium quantity is Q_E. Given what was just stated about the role of input prices, technology, incomes, and preferences in shifting the two curves in Figure 2.1, you can see that any such shifts will change the equilibrium price and quantity for rice by shifting the demand or supply curves. These sorts of changes are natural parts of market processes.

As we stated above, rice markets are actually international. Therefore, we cannot analyze them effectively using Figure 2.1. We need to consider how to account for the international character of rice markets in the supply and demand framework, an important initial step in understanding international trade.

ABSOLUTE ADVANTAGE

Rice is produced in many countries, but to simplify, suppose we consider just Vietnam and Japan. To help us analyze the international rice market that arises between these

[3] Other demand-side factors are prices of related products, wealth, and expectations. Changes in these factors shift the demand curve, as do changes in income and preferences.

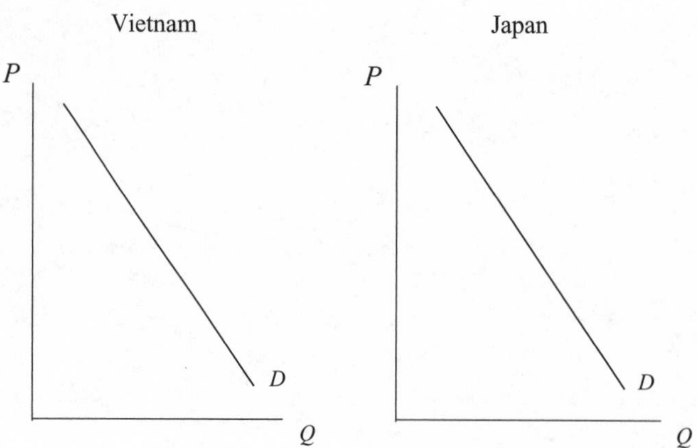

Figure 2.2. Demand for Rice in Vietnam and Japan

two countries, we will make a simplifying assumption about the demand side of the rice market in both Vietnam and Japan. More specifically, we assume that *demand conditions are exactly the same in both countries.* That is, there are no differences in preferences, incomes, or the way demand responds to price changes in Vietnam and Japan. This implies that the demand curves for rice in the two countries are exactly the same, as illustrated in Figure 2.2.

The reason we make this simplifying demand-side assumption is that trade often arises due to differences in supply conditions rather than in demand conditions. Indeed, most of the field of trade theory is based on various explanations for these supply-side differences among countries. Therefore, we will allow supply conditions for rice to differ between Vietnam and Japan. In particular, we will assume that the supply curve for Vietnam is farther to the right than the supply curve for Japan, which means that at every price, Vietnam supplies more rice than Japan.

Why might this be? One possibility is that Vietnam produces rice using *technology* superior to that of Japan so that labor productivity in rice production in Vietnam is higher than in Japan. This possibility, however, is not relevant to rice production in these two countries.[4] Another possibility is that the prices for *inputs* used in rice production are lower in Vietnam than in Japan. This, in turn, could reflect the fact that Vietnam is more abundantly endowed with rice production factors (available land and agricultural labor) than Japan. It is this latter factor that is relevant in the current case.

This situation is depicted in Figure 2.3. The upward sloping supply curves reflect the positive relationship between price and quantity supplied. The difference in supply conditions positions Vietnam's supply curve farther to the right than Japan's supply curve. The intersections of the supply and demand curves determine the equilibrium prices of rice in the two markets. The two prices are recorded as P^V and P^J in the figure. Because no trade is involved, these two prices are known in international economics as **autarky** prices. Autarky is a situation in which a country has no economic relationships with other countries.

[4] For a case where technology is relevant, see the box on p. 25 on Japan's advantage in industrial robots.

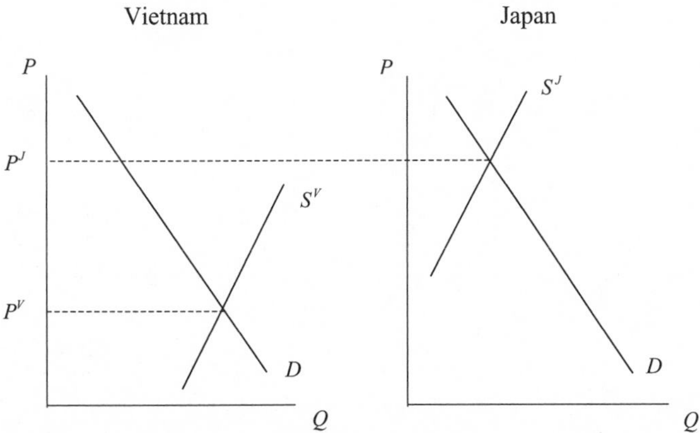

Figure 2.3. Absolute Advantage in the Rice Market

Figure 2.3 depicts a situation in which the autarky price of rice is lower in Vietnam than in Japan. That is:

$$P^V < P^J \tag{2.1}$$

In international trade theory, this situation is interpreted as Vietnam having an **absolute advantage** in the production of rice vis-à-vis Japan. This absolute advantage reflects the differences in supply conditions in the two countries. The presence of absolute advantage makes international trade a possibility.

INTERNATIONAL TRADE

The idea of absolute advantage was first stated in Adam Smith's *Wealth of Nations*, published in 1776. Adam Smith (1937) stated the following: "If a foreign country can supply us with a commodity cheaper than we ourselves can make it, better buy it of them with some part of the produce of our own industry, employed in a way in which we have some advantage" (p. 424). In other words, a pattern of absolute advantage implies a potential pattern of trade. How does this apply to our example? If the two countries move out of autarky and begin to trade, the world price of rice P^W will be somewhere between the two autarky prices, as follows:

$$P^V < P^W < P^J \tag{2.2}$$

This situation is depicted in Figure 2.4. In the movement from autarky to trade, Vietnam experiences an increase in the price of rice to the world level (from P^V to P^W). Quantity supplied will increase, whereas quantity demanded will decrease. The amount by which quantity supplied exceeds quantity demanded in Vietnam at P^W constitutes its *exports* of rice, E^V. Japan experiences a decrease in the price of rice to the world level (from P^J to P^W). Here, quantity supplied will decrease, whereas quantity demanded will increase. The amount by which quantity demanded exceeds quantity supplied in Japan at P^W constitutes its *imports* of rice, Z^J.[5] The country that has an absolute advantage (Vietnam) expands its quantity supplied and exports the good in question,

[5] We use a Z to denote imports throughout this book. Why Z? As we will see, I is used in economics to denote investment, and M is used to denote money. Therefore, we cannot use either of the first two letters of the word "imports."

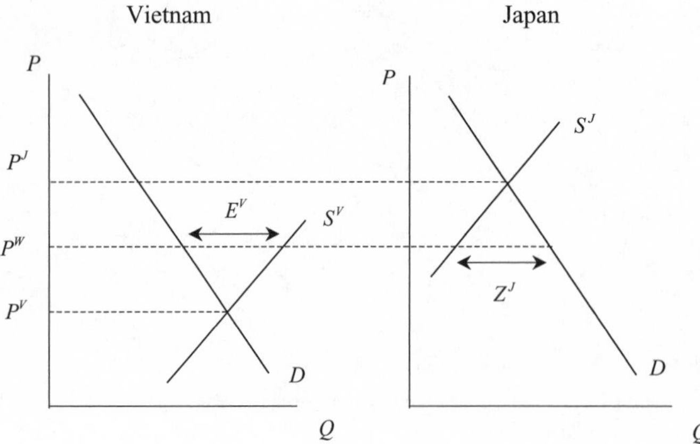

Figure 2.4. Trade in the Rice Market

whereas the trading partner (Japan) contracts its quantity supplied and imports the good.

The associations you should have in your mind from the preceding discussion are presented in Figure 2.5. The starting points are comparative levels of technological proficiency and endowments of factors used in the production of the sector's product. The latter affects the relevant input prices for a sector in a country. Vietnam, for example, has lower domestic prices for rice-growing land and labor. Technological and factor characteristics determine a pattern of absolute advantage between two countries. This pattern of absolute advantage, in turn, can generate a pattern of trade. Vietnam tends to export rice, whereas Japan tends to import rice. Another example in which Japan's technological proficiency in the production of industrial robots leads to exports is given in the accompanying box.

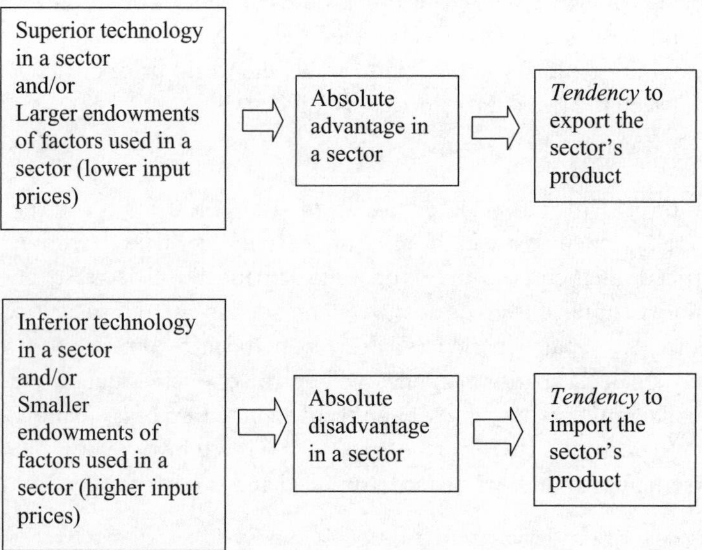

Figure 2.5. A Schematic View of Absolute Advantage

Japan's Advantage in Industrial Robots

The word *robot* first appeared in 1921 in a Czech play written by Karel Čapek, based on the Czech word "robota," meaning *drudgery.* The world's first industrial robot was built in the United States by the industrialist Joseph Engelberger, who founded the company Unimation in 1956 and installed the first industrial robot in 1961. Engelberger had a moment of fame in 1966 when one of his robots appeared on Johnny Carson's *Tonight Show,* opening and pouring a can of beer. In 1967, Engelberger was invited to Japan and addressed 600 Japanese scientists and business executives. As a result, Japan imported its first industrial robots from the United States. In 1969, robot production began in Japan under a licensing agreement with Unimation. In 1972, the Japan Robot Association was founded. Thus began Japan's involvement with what has been called "the most important manufacturing innovations of recent times" (Mansfield, 1989, p. 19).

Japan's first exports of industrial robots began in 1975. Thereafter, exports grew slowly but steadily. By the end of the 1980s, Japan became the leader in most areas of the robotics industry, such as numerical controllers, machine tools, motors, and optical sensors. It accounted for one-half of the world production of industrial robots. The technological nature of Japan's advantage in robot production was captured by Porter (1990): "The pace of innovation and new product introduction among the Japanese firms was feverish. Product innovations were soon imitated or upstaged by other producers. For example, the American firm Adept Technology introduced the world's first commercially successful direct-drive robot near the end of 1984. Less than a year later, seven Japanese firms, including Yamaha, Matsushita, and FANUC, introduced direct drive robots" (p. 235). Along with faster innovation times, Japanese firms benefited from lower innovation costs. There is some evidence that Japan's faster innovation times and lower innovation costs were due to a greater emphasis on manufacturing over marketing in the innovation process in comparison with the United States.

Accompanying and contributing to Japan's technological lead in industrial robots was the degree of competition in the Japanese industrial robots industry. With fewer than 10 firms in 1968, the industry expanded to nearly 300 firms by 1987 and declined to approximately 150 firms in 2000. Another important factor has been *intra-firm diffusion,* where firms requiring the use of robots (e.g., the electronic equipment industry) begin producing robots for their own use. A final factor pushing the use of robots in Japan has been the presence of significant labor shortages in many areas; robots replaced humans where these shortages appeared. As of 1997, Japan used one robot for every 36 manufacturing employees, whereas the United States used only one robot for every 250 manufacturing employees. Currently, one-half of the world's industrial robots are installed in Japan.

Despite these long-term positive factors, the Japan Robot Association (2001) pointed to some weaknesses. The industry has had difficulty moving out of large industrial applications into biotech, medical, and consumer applications as well as leveraging venture capital. In contract to past models of technological innovation characterizing Japan, the Japan Robot Association called for a focus on small business and greater openness. This, it was hoped, would position the industry for a different set of robotic applications with promising future growth prospects.

Sources: The Economist (1980), Horiuchi (1989), Mansfield (1989), Porter (1990), Tanzer and Simon (1990), and Japan Robot Association (2001)

It is important to stress here that Figure 2.5 is only a *preliminary* look at international trade. In the real world, international trade is actually determined by **comparative advantage** rather than absolute advantage. This is why we use the word *tendency* in the far right-hand boxes of the figure. Consequently, you will not have a full appreciation of how international trade is determined until you complete Chapter 3. Nevertheless, our discussion in this chapter is useful in order to understand how the traditional supply and demand framework must be modified to account for trading relations and to understand the gains from trade.[6]

A question that often arises in students' minds is: What ensures that the amount exported by Vietnam is the same as the amount imported by Japan? The answer is that, if E^V were smaller than Z^J, there would be excess demand or a shortage in the world market for rice. As we know from introductory microeconomics, excess demand causes the price to rise. As P^W rose, exports of Vietnam would increase and imports of Japan would decrease until the excess demand in the world market disappeared. Similarly, if E^V were larger than Z^J, P^W would fall to bring the world market back into equilibrium.

Before moving on to discuss the gains from trade, another key concept in international economics, let's summarize what we have shown thus far in a box:

> Differences in supply conditions among the countries of the world can give rise to complementary patterns of absolute advantage. These patterns of absolute advantage, in turn, make possible complementary patterns of international trade.

GAINS FROM TRADE

Up to this point, we have seen that, given a pattern of absolute advantage, it is possible for a country to give up autarky in favor of importing or exporting. Japan can import rice, and Vietnam can export rice. But *should* a country actually do this? We can answer this question by examining Figure 2.4 from the standard economic point of view using **consumer surplus** and **producer surplus.**[7] This is done in Figure 2.6. If you do not recall the consumer surplus and producer surplus concepts from your introductory microeconomics course, please consult the appendix to this chapter.

Let us first consider Vietnam. In its movement from autarky to exporting in the rice market, producers experience both an increase in price and an increase in quantity supplied along the supply curve. This should be good for producers, and as you can see in Figure 2.6, there has been an increase in producer surplus of area $A + B$ as a result of the movement from autarky to trade. Consumers, on the other hand, experience an increase in price and a decrease in quantity demanded along the demand curve. This should harm consumers, and you can see in Figure 2.6 that there has been a decrease in consumer surplus of area A.

What do these effects mean for Vietnam? Producers have gained area $A + B$, whereas consumers have lost area A. The gain to producers exceeds the loss to consumers.

[6] As we will see in Chapter 6, the supply and demand framework is also used to conduct trade policy analysis.

[7] There are alternatives to the standard economic view of welfare. These are discussed in Chapter 20 and very briefly in the appendix to this chapter.

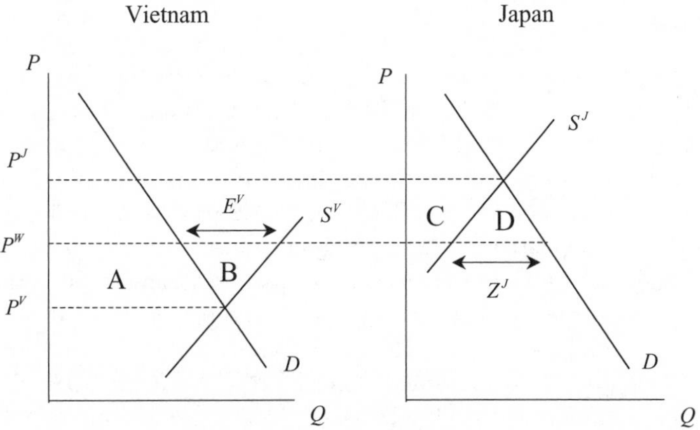

Figure 2.6. Gains from Trade in the Rice Market

For the economy as a whole, then, there is a *net welfare increase* of area B. Vietnam gains from its entry into the world economy as an exporter.[8]

Next, consider Japan. In its movement from autarky to importing in the rice market, producers experience a decrease in price and a decrease in quantity supplied along the supply curve. This should harm these producers, and you can see in Figure 2.6 that there has been a decrease in producer surplus of area C. Consumers, on the other hand, experience a decrease in price and an increase in quantity demanded. These contribute to an increase in consumer surplus of area $C + D$.

What do these effects mean for Japan? Consumers have gained $C + D$, whereas producers have lost area C. The gain to consumers exceeds the loss to producers. For the economy as a whole, then, there is a net welfare increase of area D. Japan gains from its entry into the world economy as an importer.[9]

You can see that moving from autarky to either importing or exporting involves a net increase in welfare for the country involved. This net increase in welfare is known as the **gains from trade**. Not only is it possible for a country to give up autarky in favor of importing or exporting, but it makes sense to do so in most instances from the standpoint of overall welfare.

The notion of gains from trade is an important concept. To judge from the tone and content of many popular writings on the world economy, trade relationships are a win-lose proposition for the countries involved. To export is to win; to import is to lose. The gains from trade idea, however, tells us that trade can be *mutually* beneficial to the countries involved. For this reason, we need to be cautious in our assessment of some popular writing of the win-lose variety. Although there are specific instances in which trade can be a win-lose proposition, this is not the case for trade in general.[10] For the peculiar case of international advantages in rare earth elements, see the accompanying box.

[8] Area A can be viewed as a transfer from consumers to producers in Vietnam.

[9] Area C can be viewed as a transfer from producers to consumers in Japan.

[10] This point was emphasized some time ago by Krugman (1996). Krugman stated that "The conflict among nations that so many policy intellectuals imagine prevails is an illusion; but it is an illusion that can destroy the reality of mutual gains from trade" (p. 84).

Rare Earth Elements

Rare earth. No, not the rock band. Rather, 17 chemical elements collectively known as "rare earth elements," or REEs. REEs are key components in some of the information and communication technology (ICT) discussed in Chapter 1 as drivers of globalization. These include liquid-crystal displays, fiber-optic cables, communication system magnets, wind turbines, solar panels, and rechargeable batteries used in hybrid cars. REEs are not actually rare, however. Some of them, for example, are much more common than gold. Despite this abundance, REEs are not usually concentrated enough for commercial mining, and there are consequently only a few sources. From 1965 to 1980, most REEs came from the Mountain Pass mine in the Mojave Desert in the United States. Beginning in 1985, advantage switched to the Inner Mongolia region of China. *The Economist* (2009) noted that Communist Party Leader Deng Xiaoping, "declaring rare earths to be the oil of China, encouraged the development of mines in the mid-1980s. Prices fell dramatically and existing mines in America were priced out of business." Currently, China supplies 95 percent of the global market for REEs, and the Mountain Pass mine closed in 2002.

As China's own demand for REEs has grown, concern has arisen about the security of supplies. *The Economist* (2009) reported: "sales of (REEs) add up to less than $2 billion each year. But without them, industries worth trillions of dollars would grind to a halt." In response to this situation, there has been even talk in the Chinese government about a ban of exports of some important REEs. Consequently, attention has turned to alternative supply possibilities with Western Australia, North America (Alaska and Quebec), and South Africa.

In 2010, REEs became part of a dispute between Japan and China over the Senkaku (Japanese) or Diaoyu (Chinese) islands in the East China Sea, which are claimed by both countries. China barred exports of REEs to Japan as a result. Consequently, the U.S. Congress began discussions of reopening Mountain Pass mine. The matter was also taken up in the World Trade Organization (WTO) dispute settlement process (see Chapter 7), which ruled against China in 2011.

Sources: Bradsher (2010), *The Economist* (2009), and U.S. Geological Survey (2002)

LIMITATIONS

The notion of absolute advantage, first suggested by Adam Smith in his *Wealth of Nations*, is useful to understanding international trade in the context of the familiar supply and demand framework. It is also useful to understanding that trade can improve overall welfare for the countries involved. The concept has its limits, however. In particular, it suggests the possibility that a country could not have an absolute advantage in *anything*, and therefore would have nothing to export at all. This, it turns out, is unlikely. To understand why, we must turn to a more sophisticated notion of trade, **comparative advantage**. We do this in the next chapter.

The notion of the gains from trade also has its limits. It suggests that countries *as a whole* mutually gain from trade. It does not suggest, however, that *everyone within* a country will gain from trade. As you have already seen in the example of this chapter, producers of rice in Japan lose from trade, and consumers of rice in Vietnam lose from trade. We will take up the subject of the winners and losers from trade in earnest in Chapter 5 on the political economy of trade.

CONCLUSION

Autarky refers to a situation in which a country does not engage in either imports or exports. It is a rare situation. More commonly, countries engage in both importing and exporting relationships with other countries of the world economy. In this chapter, you have begun to understand why. Absolute advantage reflects differences among countries in technology or factor conditions. A country with better technology and larger endowments of the factors necessary to produce an item is more likely to have absolute advantage in the production of that item. It is also more likely to export that item. Patterns of absolute advantage in the world economy also make possible mutual gains from trade in which the overall welfare of the countries involved increases.

The notion of absolute advantage has its limits. First, it suggests that a country might not have anything to export at all. This, as we will see in the next chapter on comparative advantage, is an unlikely outcome. Second, it does not suggest that all persons in a country will gain from trade. Within any country, there can be both winners and losers from international trade.

REVIEW EXERCISES

1. Use Figure 2.1 to consider the following changes: a fall in incomes due to a recession; an increased preference for rice consumption; an increase in input prices for rice production; and an improvement in rice production technology. Use diagrams to analyze the effects of these changes on equilibrium price and quantity.
2. Create an example of an absolute advantage model by choosing two countries and a single product.
   a. Draw a diagram describing *autarky* and a *pattern of absolute advantage* for your example.
   b. Show the transition from autarky to trade in your diagram, label the trade flows, and demonstrate the *gains from trade.*
   c. In a new diagram, and starting from a trading equilibrium, show what would happen to the world price if *income increased* by exactly the same, small amount in both countries.
3. Can you recall from introductory microeconomics the notions of the price elasticity of demand and price elasticity of supply? If so, can you say what would happen to the gains from trade as supply *and* demand in Vietnam *and* Japan become more and more *inelastic*?

FURTHER READING AND WEB RESOURCES

The idea of absolute advantage was first discussed in Chapter II, Book IV of Smith (1937). This book is available in the nonfiction section of www.bibliomania.com. A much more recent overview can be found in Van Marrewijk (2009). A blog about global rice trade can be found at *rice-trade.blogspot.com.*

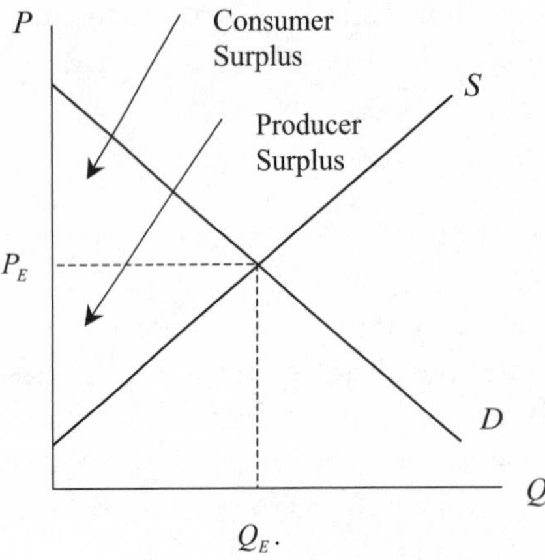

Figure 2.7. Consumer and Producer Surplus

APPENDIX: CONSUMER AND PRODUCER SURPLUS

Our discussion of the gains from trade in this chapter utilized the notions of consumer surplus and producer surplus. These concepts are illustrated in Figure 2.7. This figure considers equilibrium in a single market. The equilibrium price is P_E, and the equilibrium quantity is Q_E. The height of the demand curve shows consumers' maximum *willingness to pay* for the good in question. For quantities between zero and Q_E, however, the willingness to pay is *greater than* what consumers actually pay. That is, the height of the demand curve is greater than the market price. This gives the consumers a premium on each unit up to Q_E, and the sum of the consumer premia is the upper triangle in the figure, consumer surplus.

The height of the supply curve shows the producers' minimum *willingness to accept* for the good in question. For quantities between zero and Q_E, however, the willingness to accept is *less than* what the producers actually receive. That is, the height of the supply curve is less than the market price. Producers too, then, receive a premium on each unit up to Q_E. The sum of the producer premia is the lower triangle in the figure, producer surplus.

In demonstrating the gains from trade in Figure 2.6, we considered the *changes* in consumer and producer surplus that result from the price changes brought on by the move from autarky to trade. This analysis of the gains from trade is based on the standard view of economic welfare. As discussed in Reinert (2004) and in Chapter 20, this standard view does impose some limitations. It restricts our consideration of welfare to income per capita or, more formally, what economists term *the utility of consumption*. Alternative views, such as in the form of human capabilities as argued by Sen (1987), are advocated by some economists.

REFERENCES

Bradsher, K. (2010) "Amid Tension, China Blocks Crucial Exports to Japan," *New York Times*, September 22.

The Economist (1980) "Robots," October 17.

The Economist (2009) "The Hunt for Rare Earths," October 8.

Goldin, I. and K.A. Reinert (2007) *Globalization for Development: Trade, Finance, Aid, Migration and Policy*, World Bank.

Heo, Y. and N.K. Doanh (2009) "Trade Liberalization and Poverty Reduction in Vietnam," *World Economy*, 32:6, 934–964.

Horiuchi, T. (1989) "Development Process of Robot Industries in Japan," *Rivista Internazionale di Scienze Economiche e Commerciali*, 36:12, 1089–1108.

Japan Robot Association (2001) *Summary Report on Technology Strategy for Creating a Robot Society in the 21st Century.*

Krugman, P. (1996) "The Illusion of Conflict in International Trade," in *Pop Internationalism*, MIT Press, 69–84.

Mansfield, E. (1989) "Technological Change in Robotics: Japan and the United States," *Managerial and Decision Economics*, Special Issue, 19–25.

Porter, M.E. (1990) *The Competitive Advantage of Nations*, The Free Press.

Reinert, K.A. (2004) "Outcomes Assessment in Trade Policy Analysis: A Note on the Welfare Propositions of the 'Gains from Trade,'" *Journal of Economic Issues*, 38:4, 1067–1073.

Sen, A. (1987) *The Standard of Living*, Cambridge University Press.

Smith, A. (1937) *The Wealth of Nations*, Modern Library (first published in 1776).

Tanzer, A. and R. Simon (1990) "Why Japan Loves Robots and We Don't," *Forbes*, 145:8, April 16, 148–153.

United States Geological Survey (2002) *Rare Earth Elements: Critical Resources for High Technology*, USGS Fact Sheet 087–02.

Van Marrewijk, C. (2009) "Absolute Advantage," in K.A. Reinert, R.S. Rajan, A.J. Glass, and L.S. Davis (eds.) *The Princeton Encyclopedia of the World Economy*, Princeton University Press, 1–3.

3 Comparative Advantage

In Chapter 2, we used the concept of **absolute advantage** to examine trade in rice between Vietnam and Japan. For Vietnam, rice is a significant component of the country's total production and an important component of domestic consumption. As incomes have increased in Vietnam, however, there is another product that many Vietnamese think about buying. That product is a motorcycle. Indeed, motorcycles have been all the rage in Vietnam. Originally, the most desirable motorcycle was the aptly named Honda Dream, but subsequently, attention turned to the Honda Wave. These brands are so popular that copies of them are made in China and exported to Vietnam. Hundreds of new motorcycles are registered daily in the city of Hanoi alone, and tourists visiting this city report being overwhelmed by the chaos of motorcycle traffic. In this chapter, we place motorcycles alongside rice so that you can begin to understand the powerful concept of **comparative advantage** and its role in generating patterns of trade among the countries of the world.

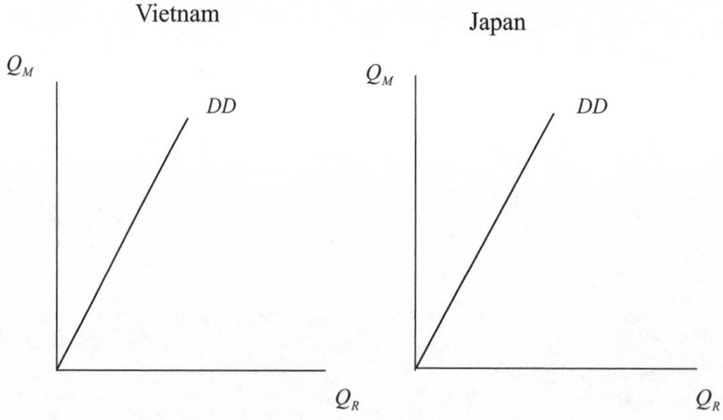

Figure 3.1. Demand Diagonals in Vietnam and Japan

In order to understand comparative advantage, we will use the concept of a **production possibilities frontier** (PPF). The PPF should be familiar to you from an introductory microeconomics course. If it is not, please see the appendix to this chapter for a brief introduction.

> Analytical elements for this chapter:
>
> *Countries, sectors* and *factors of production.*

AUTARKY AND COMPARATIVE ADVANTAGE

Consider again our two countries, Vietnam and Japan. Both of these countries produce two goods, rice and motorcycles. To help us in our analysis of comparative advantage, we will assume that demand for rice and motorcycles in both Vietnam and Japan are such that these two goods are consumed in the *same, fixed proportions.*[1] This assumption is depicted in Figure 3.1. In the diagrams for Vietnam and Japan, the quantity of rice

[1] We use this assumption to simplify the presentation of comparative advantage for the introductory student. However, this assumption can be relaxed without changing any of the results of this chapter. Indeed, this is exactly what is done in more advanced texts in trade theory such as Markusen et al. (1995) and Brakman et al. (2006).

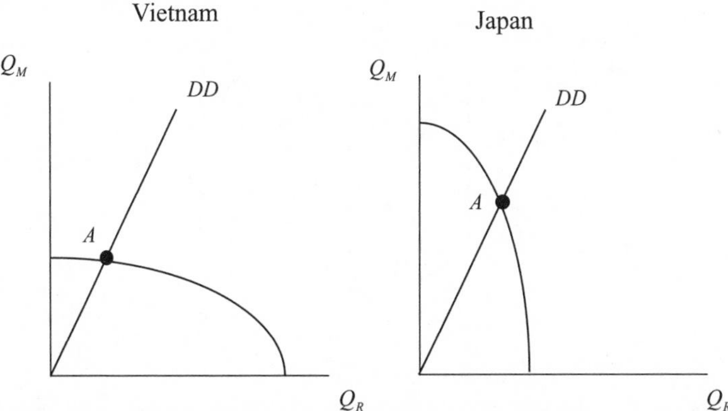

Figure 3.2. Demand and Production Possibility Frontiers in Vietnam and Japan

(Q_R) is measured on the horizontal axes, and the quantity of motorcycles (Q_M) is measured on the vertical axes. Because demand for these two goods is in the same, fixed proportions, we can represent it by diagonal lines from the origins. We label both of these lines DD for "demand diagonal." Any change in preferences for the two products would rotate the demand diagonal lines either up or down, maintaining the intercept at the origin. Changes in income would move a country up and down a given demand diagonal.[2] As we will see next, movements up and down a demand diagonal can also be viewed as changes in economic welfare.

As we learned in Chapter 2, trade often arises due to differences in supply conditions. Therefore, we once again allow supply conditions to differ between Vietnam and Japan. In particular, we assume that resource or technology conditions in Vietnam give it a **production possibilities frontier** (PPF) that is biased toward rice, whereas resource or technology conditions in Japan give it a PPF that is biased toward motorcycles. Why might this pattern arise? Vietnam might have superior technology in rice production, and Japan might have superior technology in motorcycle production. Alternatively, Vietnam might be better endowed in rice production factors (land and labor), and Japan might be better endowed in motorcycles production factors (physical capital). Whatever the reason, the PPFs take on complementary shapes, as depicted in Figure 3.2.[3] We label the intersection of the PPFs with our demand lines with the letter A.

In our discussion of absolute advantage in Chapter 2, we were able to determine the price of rice by the intersections of supply and demand curves in Vietnam and Japan. What do we do when we have two goods as in Figures 3.1 and 3.2? The DD lines represent the demand sides of the two economies, and the PPFs represent the supply sides of the two economies. How do we determine prices, though? The slope of the PPFs shows how many motorcycles must be given up to produce an additional unit of rice. Recall from introductory microeconomics that this slope measures the **opportunity**

[2] Some caution is necessary here. The DD lines in Figure 3.1 are *not* demand curves. Demand curves show a relationship between price and quantity demanded, but no price appears on an axis in Figure 3.1. Furthermore, demand curves are downward-sloping, not upward-sloping as the DD curves are. We take the DD approach here to avoid using indifference curves, with which many students are not familiar. The results we obtain are the same as those derived with the more advanced indifference curve concept.

[3] The technology explanation of comparative advantage is associated with what is known as the Ricardian model (e.g., Deardorff, 2009), whereas the factor endowment explanation is associated with what is known as the Heckscher-Ohlin model (e.g., Panagariya, 2009). We consider the Heckscher-Ohlin model in Chapter 5.

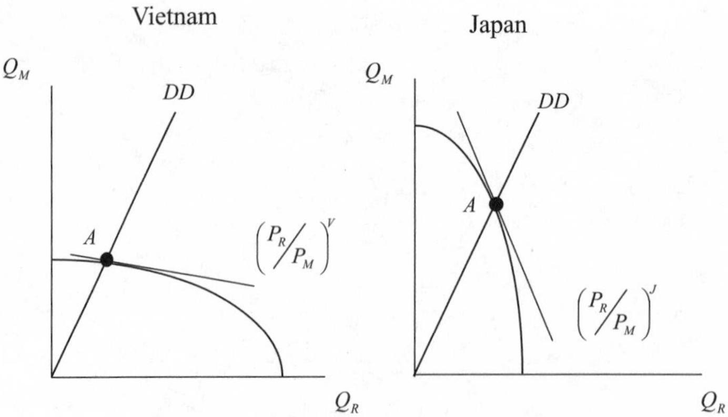

Figure 3.3. Relative Prices in Vietnam and Japan under Autarky

cost of producing the item on the horizontal axis, rice, expressed in terms of how many units of the item on the vertical axis, motorcycles, must be given up or not produced because resources have switched to rice.

In a system of freely operating markets, perfect competition, and full employment of production factors, opportunity costs are fully reflected in *relative* prices. Therefore, the slope of the PPFs where the demand diagonal crosses it is the relative price of rice, $(\frac{P_R}{P_M})$. We represent this in Figure 3.3 by drawing in the *tangent* lines to the PPFs where the demand lines cross them at points A.[4] Points A in the two PPFs of Figure 3.2 represent the two countries under **autarky** in isolation from the rest of the world economy.

Looking at points A in Figure 3.3, you can see that the tangency line giving relative prices is flatter in Vietnam than in Japan. That is, the opportunity cost of rice is lower in Vietnam than in Japan. In other words, under autarky:

$$\left(\frac{P_R}{P_M}\right)^V < \left(\frac{P_R}{P_M}\right)^J \tag{3.1}$$

This equation says that the relative price of rice is lower in Vietnam than in Japan. Because Vietnam is the country that has a supply advantage in producing rice, Equation 3.1 makes sense. This inequality is an expression of a pattern of **comparative advantage**. Differences in economy-wide supply conditions cause differences in relative autarky prices and, thereby, a pattern of comparative advantage. It is these differences that make trade possible.

We need to note one very important thing about Equation 3.1. This comparative advantage inequality involves *four prices* rather than *two prices*, as in the absolute advantage inequality of Equation 2.1. This difference has an immediate and important implication: a country can have a *comparative advantage* in a good in which it has an *absolute disadvantage*.[5] This is one reason why the comparative advantage concept is more powerful than the absolute advantage concept.

[4] We discuss this further in the appendix to this chapter.

[5] The reader who is not convinced of this can work with the following example: $P_R^V = 2$, $P_R^J = 1$, $P_M^V = 4$, $P_M^J = 1$. Here, you will see that Japan has an *absolute* advantage in producing both goods ($P_R^J < P_R^V$ and $P_M^J < P_M^V$), but Vietnam has a *comparative* advantage in producing rice.

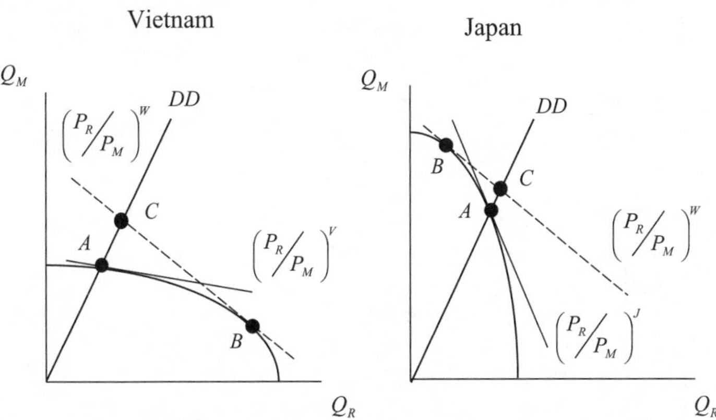

Figure 3.4. Autarky and Comparative Advantage in Vietnam and Japan

The concept of comparative advantage was first introduced in 1817 by David Ricardo in his *Principles of Political Economy and Taxation* (Ricardo, 1951). In a footnote in Chapter 7 of that book, Ricardo stated: "It will appear . . . that a country possessing very considerable advantages in machinery and skill, and which may therefore be enabled to manufacture commodities with much less labour than her neighbors, may, in return for such commodities, import a portion of its corn required for its consumption, even if its land were more fertile, and corn could be grown with less labour than in the country from which it was imported" (p. 36). This country, in our example, is Japan, whose endowments of "machinery and skill" might in principle give it an absolute advantage in producing both rice and motorcycles. Corn in Ricardo's time was the word for "grain," and in our example, this is rice. Ricardo therefore suggests that, given its *comparative* advantage in motorcycles, Japan can import rice even if it has an *absolute* advantage in rice production.

INTERNATIONAL TRADE

If Vietnam and Japan abandon autarky in favor of trade, the world relative price of rice $(\frac{P_R}{P_M})^W$ will be somewhere between the two autarky price ratios:

$$\left(\frac{P_R}{P_M}\right)^V < \left(\frac{P_R}{P_M}\right)^W < \left(\frac{P_R}{P_M}\right)^J \tag{3.2}$$

This situation is depicted in Figure 3.4. The world price ratio here is depicted with dashed lines that have the slope $(\frac{P_R}{P_M})^W$. These lines are steeper than the autarky price line in Vietnam and flatter than the autarky price line in Japan, as is indicated in Equation 3.2. The tangencies of these world price lines with the PPFs determine the new production points in Vietnam and Japan. These points are labeled B. In Vietnam, the movement along the PPF from A to B involves an increase in the production of rice, whereas in Japan, this movement involves an increase in the production of motorcycles. This is known as *specialization in production.* The important lesson you should understand here is that moving from autarky to trade restructures an economy's production toward the good in which the country has a comparative advantage. This is one reason why opening economies up to trading relations with the rest of the world

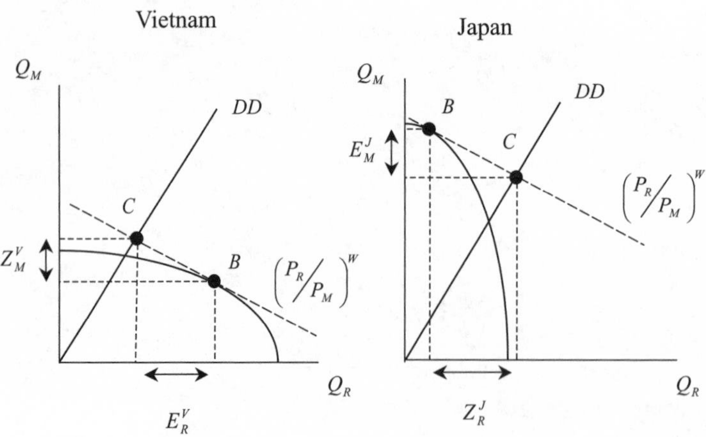

Figure 3.5. Trade between Vietnam and Japan

can be difficult for the countries involved. Workers and other resources must be moved from one sector of the economy to another in the process.[6]

Consumption points for Vietnam and Japan must be along our demand diagonal lines. These points, labeled C in Figure 3.4, occur where the dashed world price lines intersect the demand lines. Why is this? Both consumption and production must respect world prices. That is, *both* points B and C must be on the world price lines. In contrast to autarky, consumption and production points are now different. How can this be so? Through trade.

Look at Figure 3.5, which removes the autarky points and autarky price lines. In Vietnam, production of rice exceeds consumption of rice, and the difference is exported (E_R^V). Production of motorcycles, however, falls short of consumption of motorcycles, and this shortfall is imported (Z_M^V).[7] In Japan, production of motorcycles exceeds consumption of motorcycles, and the difference is exported (E_M^J). Production of rice, however, falls short of production, and this shortfall is imported (Z_R^J). What we see in Figure 3.5 is that a pattern of comparative advantage, based on differences in supply conditions between two countries, gives rise to a complementary pattern of trade.

What ensures that the quantities imported and exported in Figure 3.5 balance? Suppose that E_R^V were smaller than Z_R^J. If this were the case, there would be excess demand for (or a shortage of) rice in the world market. As we saw in our absolute advantage model of Chapter 2, excess demand for rice would cause P_R^W to rise. Therefore, the $(\frac{P_R}{P_M})^w$ lines in Figure 3.5 would become steeper. This would direct production in both countries along the PPFs toward rice, alleviating the excess demand.[8]

We mentioned in Chapter 2 that the absolute advantage concept can leave the impression that a country could lack an advantage in anything, and therefore have nothing to export. The concept of comparative advantage clears up this problem. Having an *absolute* disadvantage in a product does not preclude having a *comparative* advantage in that product. Vietnam could have an absolute disadvantage in rice, but still export this product because of its comparative advantage. This is why comparative

[6] We take up the political economy implications of these resource movements in Chapter 5.

[7] As in Chapter 2, we use Z to denote imports, since the symbols I and M are taken up by investment and money, respectively.

[8] In more advanced treatments (e.g., Markusen et al., 1995), adjustments also occur on the demand side.

advantage is a more powerful concept than absolute advantage. Indeed, comparative advantage is perhaps the most central concept in international economics. The empirical application of the concept in the form of *revealed comparative advantage* is discussed in the accompanying box.

Before moving on to discuss the gains from trade, another key concept in international economics, let's summarize what we have shown thus far in a box:

> Differences in supply conditions among the countries of the world give rise to complementary patterns of comparative advantage. These patterns of comparative advantage, in turn, make possible complementary patterns of international trade.

Revealed Comparative Advantage

How is the notion of comparative advantage applied in practice? Beginning with Belassa (1965), the standard practice is to examine actual trade flows of a country to understand what is known as *revealed comparative advantage.* This is done in relative terms to a set of comparison countries or to a single comparison country. What has come to be known as the *Belassa index* (BI) is calculated for country i in sector j as follows:

$$BI_j^i = \frac{\textit{share of sector } j \textit{ in country } i\textit{'s exports}}{\textit{share of sector } j \textit{ in reference country exports}}$$

Comparative advantage is said to be "revealed" when BI_j^i is greater than one. As is evident in this formula, however, a key question is what country or countries to use as a point of reference in the denominator. Another issue is how to handle *intra*-industry trade, a topic discussed in Chapter 4. Despite these problems, revealed comparative advantage has been used for a long time by a number of researchers to understand evolving patterns of comparative advantage in the world economy.

Sources: Belassa (1965) and Van Marrewijk (2002)

GAINS FROM TRADE

To this point, we have seen that, given a pattern of comparative advantage, it is possible for a country to give up autarky in favor of importing and exporting. But should a country actually do this? We can answer this question by examining Figure 3.4 once again. Notice that the post-trade consumption points C are up and to the right ("northeast") of the autarky consumption points A. This directional relationship between points A and C means that the movement from autarky to trade increases consumption of *both* rice *and* motorcycles. Increased consumption of both goods, in turn, implies that economic welfare has increased. Vietnam and Japan have experienced mutual **gains from trade** based on comparative advantage.[9]

As in Chapter 2, a few caveats are in order. First, the gains from trade occur for the country as a whole. The fact that a country as a whole benefits in the aggregate from trade does not mean that every individual or group within the country benefits. Indeed, as you will see in Chapter 5, there are good reasons to expect that there will be groups

[9] Our implicit assumption here is the standard one in economics, namely that welfare is determined by consumption levels. For a well-known challenge to this assumption, see Sen (1987). We return to this issue in the context of development in Chapter 20.

that *lose* from increased trade. These groups will oppose increased trade despite the overall gains to their country. To foreshadow our discussion in Chapter 5, for example, rice producers in Japan have a long history of opposing imports of rice.

Second, in recent years, there has also been a great deal of discussion of the impacts of trade based on comparative advantage on the environment. It is sometimes alleged that international trade is almost always detrimental to the environment. However, the situation is not always this straightforward. Both theoretical and empirical results demonstrate that increased trade can be either good or bad for the environment, and that we need to approach the trade and environment issue on a case-by-case basis. This issue is discussed in the accompanying box.

Third, some goods are traded that do not contribute to increased welfare. Land mines, heroin, and prostitution services are all traded internationally, but their consumption significantly reduces welfare rather than increases it. For this reason, you need to be careful not to generalize the gains from trade concept too far.[10]

Comparative Advantage and the Environment

Given the steady advance of the volume of trade discussed in Chapter 1 and the growing concern about environmental issues worldwide, it is natural to ask what role trade and comparative advantage play in levels of pollution and other forms of environmental degradation. Although this issue is largely empirical, trade and environmental economists have identified three means through which trade can have positive or negative environmental impacts: a scale or growth effect, an activity composition effect, and a technique effect.

The *scale or growth effect* refers to the possibility that trade can stimulate the overall level of economic activity that can, in turn, have environmental repercussions. This effect holds constant the composition of economic activity and production technology. For example, trade might stimulate the overall use of scarce natural resources or the overall level of pollution. It is here that we encounter the "inverted U" hypothesis that environmental degradation first increases and then decreases with the level of economic activity, or gross domestic product (GDP). This inverted U relationship is sometimes also known as the environmental Kuznets curve, or EKC.

The *activity composition effect* refers to something that we have seen in this chapter, namely that trade changes the location of countries on the PPF. This effect holds constant the overall level of economic activity and the production technology. Depending on the pattern of comparative advantage, pollution intensive sectors such as chemicals and metals can either increase or decrease their share in the total output of a country. López and Islam (2009) state a general rule of thumb that physical capital and natural resource intensive sectors tend to be more polluting than human capital intensive sectors.

The *technique effect* holds constant both the overall level of economic activity and the sectoral composition of that activity. It refers to the possibility that the pollutant intensity of a given level of output in a sector can change, sometimes for the better. López and Islam (2009 note that "The technique effect of trade has been found to reduce certain pollutants, particularly air pollutants, but the effects on other environmental factors (are) less significant." The technique effect also becomes applicable in the spread of green or environmentally friendly technologies on which much hope has been placed in recent years.

[10] See, for example, Reinert (2004).

The *net effect* of trade on the environment is, as we stated above, an empirical issue, and the case of NAFTA and the environment is discussed in a box in Chapter 8. But in principle, this net effect would reflect the combined impacts of the scale or growth effect, the activity composition effect, and the technique effect. These are the lenses through which economists view the trade and environment issue.

Sources: Beghin and Potier (1997) and López and Islam (2009)

CONCLUSION

Differences in technology and/or factor endowments among the countries of the world can generate patterns of comparative advantage. Although patterns of comparative advantage can be *influenced* by patterns of absolute advantage, they are not *determined* by patterns of absolute advantage. Indeed, a country can have a comparative advantage in a good in which it has an absolute disadvantage. Patterns of comparative advantage determine patterns of trade in the world economy and generate mutual gains from trade.

As with our analysis of absolute advantage in Chapter 2, it is important to remember that the gains from trade arising from comparative advantage are for countries as a whole and not for all individuals and groups within a country. Within any country, there can be both winners and losers from international trade. This is the issue of the political economy of trade that we take up in Chapter 5.

REVIEW EXERCISES

1. What is the difference between *absolute* and *comparative* advantage?
2. Create an example of a comparative advantage model by choosing two countries and two products.
   a. Draw a diagram describing *autarky* and a *pattern of comparative advantage* for your example.
   b. Show the transition from autarky to trade in your diagram, label the trade flows, and demonstrate the *gains from trade.*
3. Can you think of any patterns of comparative advantage and trade in the world economy that might have some significant environmental impacts? What are they?

FURTHER READING AND WEB RESOURCES

A concise introduction to comparative advantage can be found in Maneschi (2009) and a historical perspective can be found in Maneschi (1998). A more advanced treatment can be found in Chapter 5 of Markusen et al. (1995) and in Chapter 3 of Brakman et al. (2006). Krugman (1998) has also written an interesting essay on comparative advantage entitled "Ricardo's Difficult Idea" that is very much worth reading. *The Economist* maintains a set of research tools on its website, including a set of terms, at http://www.economist.com/research/economics. You can read their entry on comparative advantage using their search facility. On motorcycle use in Vietnam, see Truitt (2008).

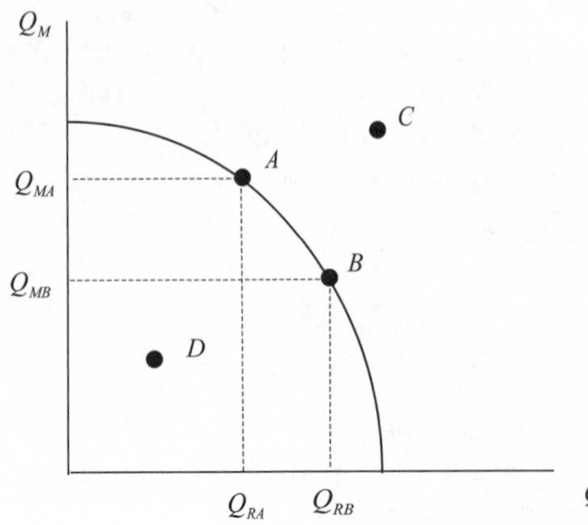

Figure 3.6. The Production Possibilities Frontier

APPENDIX: THE PRODUCTION POSSIBILITIES FRONTIER

Consider an economy that produces two goods, rice and motorcycles. The quantities in these two sectors we will call Q_R and Q_M, respectively. We will depict the supply side of this economy using a **production possibilities frontier** (PPF) diagram. The PPF depicts the combinations of output of rice and motorcycles that the economy can produce given its available resources and technology. The PPF is depicted in Figure 3.6. The PPF is depicted as *concave* with respect to the origin in this figure. Given the available resources and technology, the economy can produce anywhere on or inside the PPF. Point A on the PPF itself is one such point. If the economy were at point A on the PPF, it would be producing Q_{RA} of rice and Q_{MA} of motorcycles. If the economy were to move from point A to point B, the output of rice would increase from Q_{RA} to Q_{RB}. However, the output of motorcycles would *fall* from Q_{MA} to Q_{MB}. The fall in motorcycles output is an example of a very general and very important concept in economics: **opportunity cost.** Opportunity cost is what must be forgone when a particular decision is made. If this economy chooses to move from point A to point B, then the decreased production of motorcycles is the opportunity cost of the increased production of rice.

Point C is another production point in Figure 3.6. It is more desirable than either points A or B, because point C provides more of both rice and motorcycles compared with A and B. Point C, however, is infeasible given the resources and technology of the economy. Point D, inside the PPF, is feasible. However, in comparison to points A and B, it offers less of both rice and motorcycles. Points A and B are said to be *efficient* in that, at these points, the economy is getting all it can from its scarce resources. This is not true at point D, and consequently, point D is *inefficient.*[11]

How are the relative prices we use in this chapter determined in a PPF? We consider this in Figure 3.7 using the following steps:

Step 1. The slope of the PPF ($\frac{\Delta Q_M}{\Delta Q_R}$) is the opportunity cost of the good on the horizontal axis, rice. It indicates how many motorcycles must be given up to produce an additional unit of rice.

[11] Recall that the concept of efficiency in economics refers to *allocative efficiency*, not technological efficiency.

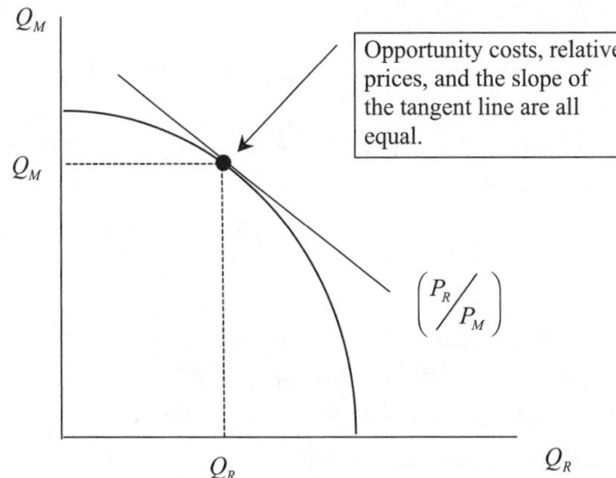

Figure 3.7. Relative Prices and the Production Possibilities Frontier

Step 2. In a perfectly competitive, market system, when resources are fully employed and firms maximize profits, the opportunity costs are fully reflected in relative prices. The relative price of rice, the good on the horizontal axis, is $(\frac{P_R}{P_M})$.

Step 3. A tangent line to the PPF shares the same slope of the PPF, namely $(\frac{\Delta Q_M}{\Delta Q_R})$.

Step 4. Given steps 1, 2, and 3, we can see that a tangent line to the PPF has a slope equal to the relative price of the good on the horizontal axis, $(\frac{P_R}{P_M})$.

This is the result we use in this chapter and indicated in Figure 3.7.

Does the result of step 4 that the slope of a tangent line represents the relative price of rice, the good on the horizontal axis, make any sense? Let's look at this a bit further in Figure 3.8. Suppose that, from point A, we want to *increase* the output of rice from Q_{RA} to Q_{RB}. Because there are opportunity costs of production represented by the PPF, this implies a *decrease* in the output of motorcycles from Q_{MA} to Q_{MB}. As production moves from point A to point B, the slope of the PPF increases, reflecting increasing opportunity costs of rice production. To offset these increasing opportunity costs, the relative price of rice must rise. Therefore, increasing the output of rice requires increasing its relative price from $(\frac{P_R}{P_M})_A$ to the steeper $(\frac{P_R}{P_M})_B$. This supply relationship, equivalent to the upward-sloping rice supply curve of Chapter 2, indeed makes economic sense.

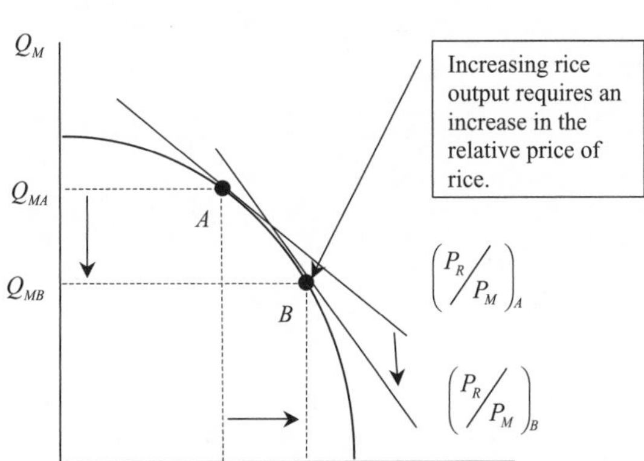

Figure 3.8. An Increase in Rice Output

REFERENCES

Beghin, J. and M. Potier (1997) "Effects of Trade Liberalisation on the Environment in the Manufacturing Sector," *The World Economy*, 20:4, 435–456.

Belassa, B. (1965) "Trade Liberalization and 'Revealed' Comparative Advantage," *Manchester School of Economic and Social Studies*, 33:2, 92–123.

Brakman, S., H. Garretsen, C. van Marrewijk, and A. van Witteloostuijn (2006) *Nations and Firms in the Global Economy: An Introduction to International Economics and Business*, Cambridge University Press.

Deardorff, A.V. (2009) "Ricardian Model," in K.A. Reinert, R.S. Rajan, A.J. Glass, and L.S. Davis (eds.), *The Princeton Encyclopedia of the World Economy*, Princeton University Press, 973–980.

Krugman, P. (1998) "Ricardo's Difficult Idea," in G. Cook (ed.), *Freedom and Trade: The Economics and Politics of International Trade*, Volume 2, Routledge, 22–36.

López, R. and A. Islam (2009) "Trade and the Environment," in K.A. Reinert, R.S. Rajan, A.J. Glass, and L.S. Davis (eds.), *The Princeton Encyclopedia of the World Economy*, Princeton University Press, 1103–1108.

Maneschi, A. (1998) *Comparative Advantage in International Trade: A Historical Perspective*, Edward Elgar.

Maneschi, A. (2009) "Comparative Advantage," in K.A. Reinert, R.S. Rajan, A.J. Glass, and L.S. Davis (eds.), *The Princeton Encyclopedia of the World Economy*, Princeton University Press, 198–205.

Markusen, J.R., J.R. Melvin, W.H. Kaempfer, and K.E. Maskus (1995) *International Trade: Theory and Evidence*, McGraw-Hill.

Panagariya, A. (2009) "Heckscher-Ohlin Model," in K.A. Reinert, R.S. Rajan, A.J. Glass, and L.S. Davis (eds.), *The Princeton Encyclopedia of the World Economy*, Princeton University Press, 591–597.

Reinert, K.A. (2004) "Outcomes Assessment in Trade Policy Analysis: A Note on the Welfare Propositions of the 'Gains from Trade,'" *Journal of Economic Issues*, 38:4, 2004, 1067–1073.

Ricardo, D. (1951) "On the Principles of Political Economy and Taxation," in P. Sraffa (ed.), *The Works and Correspondence of David Ricardo*, Volume I, Cambridge University Press (first published in 1817).

Sen, A. (1987) *The Standard of Living*, Cambridge University Press.

Truitt, A. (2008) "On the Back of a Motorbike: Middle-Class Mobility in Ho Chi Minh City, Vietnam," *American Ethnologist*, 35:1, 3–19.

Van Marrewijk, C. (2002) *International Trade and the World Economy*, Oxford University Press.

4 Intra-Industry Trade

Once, while visiting the World Trade Organization in Geneva, I took a three-day side trip to Cleremont-Ferrand, France, in order to visit some students who were on study abroad there. At my first buffet breakfast in the hotel, I noticed an exceptional-looking blue cheese. It was as exceptional to eat as to look at, and upon my inquiry, I learned that this was the famed *blue d'Auvergne* from the surrounding region.[1] I sampled it as often as I could during my short trip, and upon my return to the United States, began to purchase it whenever possible. In this way, I contributed to the total volume of cheese imports of the United States. It turns out, however, that the United States also *exports* cheese, especially what is known as "food-service" cheese (admittedly less exceptional than the *blue d'Auvergne*). Thus the United States *both* imports *and* exports cheese, a phenomenon known as **intra-industry trade**.

In this chapter, you will begin to appreciate this important type of trade. You will also understand how it differs from **inter-industry trade**, why it occurs, and its role in the world economy. We begin by contrasting inter- and intra-industry trade.

Analytical elements used in this chapter:
Countries, sectors, tasks, firms, and *factors.*

INTRA-INDUSTRY AND INTER-INDUSTRY TRADE

In Chapter 3, we discussed the important concept of comparative advantage. In our example in that chapter, we saw that Japan imported rice and exported motorcycles, whereas Vietnam exported rice and imported motorcycles. This is an example of how comparative advantage is associated with inter-industry trade. In inter-industry trade, a country *either* imports *or* exports a given product. Our example above of U.S. cheese trade is quite different. The United States *both* imports *and* exports cheese. Therefore, you should have the following associations in mind when distinguishing intra-industry trade from inter-industry trade:

Inter-industry trade ⇔ either / or
Intra-industry trade ⇔ both / and

As we just mentioned, and as indicated in Table 4.1, inter-industry trade has its source in comparative advantage, in the differences in technology and factor endowments of countries. Intra-industry trade and its sources are different, and there are actually two types of intra-industry trade. The example of trade in cheese varieties is a case of *horizontal* intra-industry trade and has its source in **product differentiation**. The term *horizontal* refers to the fact that the products exchanged are at the same level of processing. That is, both the exported variety (food-service cheese) and the imported variety (*blue d'Auvergne*) are final goods. The role of product differential here is that the two varieties of cheese are different from one another. The final product *blue d'Auvergne* is not the same kind of product as food-service cheese or Wisconsin cheddar. Similarly, the final product Ford Focus is not exactly the same kind of product as a Honda Civic.[2]

[1] The term *blue d'Auvergne* is one example of what is known as a *regional indicator* in international trade law. We will encounter regional indicators in our discussion of intellectual property in Chapter 7.

[2] As stated by van Marrewijk (2002), "A satisfactory theoretical explanation (of intra-industry trade) should . . . be able to distinguish between goods and services which are close, but imperfect substitutes" (p. 183).

Table 4.1. Types of trade

Type of trade	Phrase	Meaning	Source
Inter-industry	Either/or	*Either* imports *or* exports in a given sector of the economy	Comparative advantage
Horizontal intra-industry	Both/and/same	*Both* imports *and* exports in a given sector of the economy and at the *same* stage of processing	Product differentiation
Vertical intra-industry	Both/and/different	*Both* imports *and* exports in a given sector of the economy and at *different* stages of processing	Fragmentation (comparative advantage in some instances)

The second type of intra-industry trade is *vertical* intra-industry trade and has its source in fragmentation (again, see Table 4.1). For example, China imports computer components and assembles them into the final product, computers. The imported computer components are at a previous stage of processing than the exported computers, but from the point of view of computer products, this is intra-industry trade. The reason this has occurred is that firms have decided to break up the production process of computers into tasks or fragments and distribute them across national boundaries. This fragmentation is an example of what we called international production in Chapter 1, and vertical intra-industry trade is one area where the windows of international trade and international production interact in an important way. Indeed, another term for fragmentation is *international production sharing*.[3] This is a relatively new phenomenon and has shown up in the increased volumes of parts and components in international trade flows.

There is another subtle issue associated with vertical intra-industry trade. Some types of fragmentation take place so that final assembly will occur where there is abundant, inexpensive labor.[4] This sounds a lot like the comparative advantage story we discussed in Chapter 3. Although these issues are still being fully worked out by trade theorists, there is agreement that some part of fragmentation is comparative advantage working in a *new way*, within the realm of parts and components rather than final goods. So, although comparative advantage is not much help in explaining *horizontal* intra-industry trade, it is of help in explaining some types of *vertical* intra-industry trade.[5]

[3] See, for example, Arndt (2009). Arndt rightly notes that there are important connections between fragmentation and foreign direct investment. Indeed, some vertical intra-industry trade can also be intra-firm trade within a multinational enterprise. As the OECD (2002) stated: "The combination of rising intra-industry trade and high foreign direct investment inflows (in some countries) is consistent with the increasing extent to which multinational firms have located parts of their production operations in these countries" (p. 162).

[4] As Brakman et al. (2006) noted, "technological and communication advances have enabled many production processes to be subdivided into various phases which are physically separable, a process known as fragmentation. This enables a finer and more complex division of labor, as the different phases of the production process may now be spatially separated and undertaken at locations where costs are lowest" (p. 37).

[5] One reason why comparative advantage does not explain all vertical intra-industry trade is that, for this kind of trade involving a series of tasks located in different countries, proximity to transportation and logistics hubs can also be important.

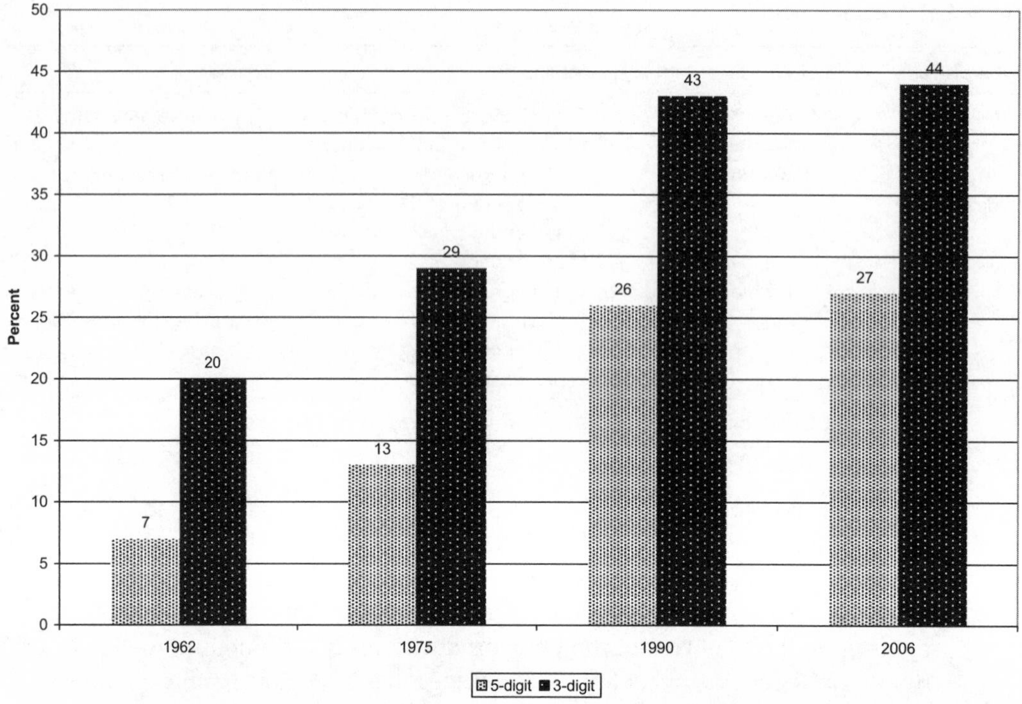

Figure 4.1. The Evolution of Intra-Industry Trade at the 5- and 3-Digit SITC Levels (percent of total trade). *Source:* Brülhart (2009). *Note:* SITC refers to Standard International Trade Classification.

Globally, intra-industry trade is becoming more important over time. In the next section, we will examine the global pattern of this type of trade. Then we will consider more formal explanations of how and why this type of trade occurs.

GLOBAL PATTERNS OF INTRA-INDUSTRY TRADE

Estimates of the amount of intra-industry trade vary and depend both on the measurement technique and the level of disaggregation of the trade data. As discussed in the appendix, the more disaggregated are the trade data, the less the measured amount of intra-industry trade. One comprehensive assessment of global intra-industry trade is that of Brülhart (2009). His estimates are presented in Figure 4.1. This figure shows that, measured at the five-digit Standard Industrial Trade Classification (SITC) level, intra-industry trade increased from 7 percent of world trade in 1962 to 27 percent of world trade in 2006. Measured at the three-digit SITC level, intra-industry trade increased from 20 percent of world trade in 1962 to 44 percent of world trade in 2006. Based on this evidence, it would be appropriate to state that approximately one-third of world trade is intra-industry trade.

It is also clear that intra-industry trade is especially prominent in trade in manufactured goods, particularly as the degree of sophistication of the manufacturing process increases. Increased sophistication of the manufacturing process allows for both greater differentiation of final products in horizontal intra-industry trade and greater scope of fragmentation in vertical intra-industry trade.[6] For some countries and manufactured products, intra-industry trade can exceed 70 percent of trade.

Intra-industry trade was first analyzed in the context of trade among the countries of Western Europe, as well as trade between the United States and Europe. The early study by Grubel and Lloyd (1975) focused on intra-industry trade among 10 original countries of the Organization for Economic Cooperation and Development (OECD), an organization consisting of mostly high-income countries. These 10 countries were Australia, Belgium, Canada, France, Italy, Japan, the Netherlands, the United Kingdom, the United States, and West Germany (before integration with East Germany). These authors developed an index used to measure the degree of intra-industry trade that is explained in the appendix to this chapter. Using this index, they noted an increase in intra-industry trade among these 10 countries during the 1960s. Subsequent studies found that this trend continued into the 1970s and beyond.

It turns out, however, that it was a mistake to envision intra-industry trade as taking place exclusively among high-income countries. I mentioned in Chapter 1 that I spent the early years of the 1990s analyzing NAFTA for the U.S. International Trade Commission. As part of this analysis, I developed a database of trade among the countries of North America for the year 1988.[7] What struck me at the time was the decidedly intra-industry character of the trade flows between Mexico and the United States even before NAFTA went into effect. With the few exceptions of petroleum, nonmetallic minerals, and nonelectrical machinery, trade between these two countries was very balanced. I realized at that time that intra-industry trade could take place between low- and high-income countries as well as between high-income countries.

At about the same time, Globerman (1992) published results indicating substantial increases in intra-industry trade between the United States and Mexico between 1980 and 1988. Ruffin (1999) analyzed trade between Mexico and the United States for 1998, a decade later than the year of my database, and concluded that it was nearly 80 percent of bilateral trade. The OECD (2002) also noted Mexico's role in intra-industry trade, estimating it at more than 70 percent of that country's trade during the 1996 to 2000 period. Clearly, intra-industry trade is not confined to developed countries alone.

Evidence of increases in intra-industry trade in Asia also surfaced. As indicated in the accompanying box, intra-industry trade in Asia appears to be most important among the newly industrialized countries (Singapore, Hong Kong, and South Korea) and the newly exporting countries (Malaysia, Thailand, the Philippines, and Indonesia). However, evidence emerged of increasing intra-industry trade between Japan and other Asian countries (e.g., Wakasugi, 1997), as well as in the trade of China and its major trading partners (e.g., Hu and Ma, 1999). Hence we can view intra-industry trade as a multiregional process that is increasing over time.[8] However, there are regions that have been left out of this trend. Evidence suggests that Western Asia (including the Middle East) and most of Africa participate very little in intra-industry trade.[9] This is one of the main distinctions between these two regions and the rest of the world with regard to international trade characteristics.

[6] See OECD (2002).
[7] See Reinert, Roland-Holst, and Shiells (1993).
[8] We revisit the case of China in the appendix to this chapter.
[9] See, for example, Brülhart (2009).

Intra-Industry Trade in East Asia

The phenomenon of intra-industry trade was first noticed in the expansion of trade among the countries of Western Europe and between Western Europe and the United States that occurred after World War II. Later, however, researchers recognized its importance for the countries of East Asia, including China, Hong Kong, Indonesia, Japan, Malaysia, the Philippines, Singapore, South Korea, Taiwan and Thailand. Early on, Hellvin (1994) provided estimates of intra-industry trade in East Asia that exceeded 20 percent in the mid-1980s. Subsequent analysis was provided by Thorpe and Zhang (2005) and Ando (2006). Thorpe and Zhang (2005) suggested that intra-industry trade increased from approximately 25 percent to approximately 50 percent between the mid-1970s and the mid-1990s. They also suggested that vertical intra-industry trade increased to about 30 percent during this period. Evidence from the machinery sector presented by Ando (2006) suggested that these trends continued through at least 2000.

The East Asian region remains a very important one for the world economy, setting trends that are later experienced in other regions. What can now be called decadal evidence on the expansion of East Asian trade suggests that intra-industry trade in general and vertical intra-industry trade in particular are going to be increasingly important for this region of the world economy.

Sources: Ando (2006), Hellvin (1994), and Thorpe and Zhang (2005)

The increasing extent of intra-industry trade in the world trading system has some important implications for the adjustment of economies to increasing trade. Recall from Chapters 2 and 3 that increases in inter-industry trade based on absolute or comparative advantage involve import sectors contracting and export sectors expanding. This, in turn, requires that productive resources, most notably workers, shift from contracting to expanding sectors in order to avoid unemployment. Workers in Vietnam must shift from the motorcycle sector to the rice sector. Workers in Japan must shift from the rice sector to the motorcycle sector. This is not always an easy process, and as we will discuss in Chapter 5, it often gives rise to calls for protection.

The adjustment process in the case of intra-industry trade can be quite different. A given sector experiences increases in imports and exports *simultaneously*. Therefore, workers are less likely to need to shift between sectors of their home economy. In the case of horizontal intra-industry trade, the labor market adjustment is across product market niches. For example, workers in the U.S. cheese sector can adjust to the expansion of imports of cheese by expanding exports of a different cheese variety. In the case of vertical intra-industry trade, the labor market adjustment is across tasks or stages of production. For example, workers in a computer sector might need to shift from producing both computer components and final, assembled computers to just producing certain components.[10]

The potential for intra-industry trade to provide smoother trade trajectories from an adjustment point of view has been dubbed the "smooth adjustment hypothesis"

[10] Empirical evidence of intra-industry trade reducing demand for trade protection was first given in Marvel and Ray (1987). Subsequently, the same point was made by Grimwade (1989) and Thom and McDowell (1999). Ruffin (1999) also noted that: "One of the great benefits of intra-industry trade is that international trade need not cause the dislocations associated with inter-industry trade" (p. 7).

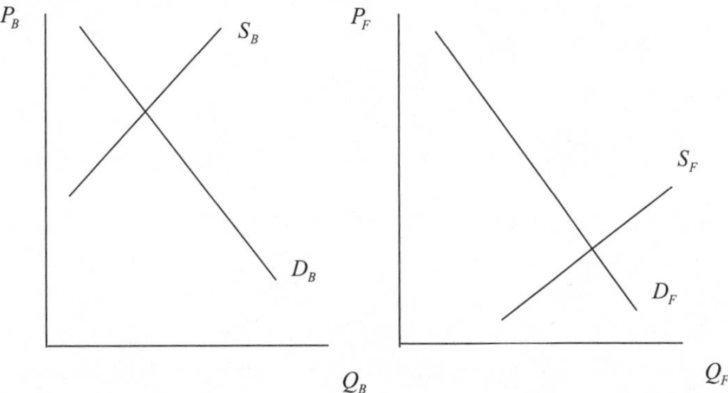

Figure 4.2. Markets for Blue and Food-Service Cheese

by Brülhart (2009). If we were to rank the *smoothness* of adjustment across the three types of trade, it would be as follows:

Inter-industry trade:	Low (not at all smooth)
Vertical intra-industry trade:	Medium (somewhat smooth)
Horizontal intra-industry trade:	High (smooth)

Engagement with the world trading economy is therefore easier from labor and political points of view in the case of intra-industry trade than in the case of inter-industry trade.

AN EXPLANATION OF INTRA-INDUSTRY TRADE

We are now going to develop an explanation of horizontal intra-industry trade using the example of U.S. trade in cheese. As suggested previously, in order to do this, we are going to have to allow for product differentiation among types of cheese. To keep things simple, we will restrict ourselves to two types of cheese: blue cheese (denoted by *B*) and food-service cheese (denoted by *F*). Because there are two distinct products, there are two distinct markets, each with its own price and quantity. This situation is represented in Figure 4.2.

Figure 4.2 depicts the two cheese markets from the perspective of the United States. There are two sets of axes, one for each type of cheese, with prices (P_B and P_F) on the vertical axes and quantities (Q_B and Q_F) on the horizontal axes. U.S. households consume both types of cheese, and U.S. firms produce both types of cheese. U.S. demand curves for the two types of cheese are denoted D_B and D_F, and these are downward sloping. U.S. supply curves for the two types of cheese are denoted S_B and S_F, and these are upward sloping. The U.S. supply curve for food-service cheese is farther to the right than its supply curve for blue cheese. This reflects the presence of more firms producing food-service cheese than blue cheese.

The trade implications of these supply and demand relationships are illustrated in Figure 4.3. To simplify the situation for ourselves, we are going to assume that the United States cannot influence the world price of either type of cheese.[11] Thus, in Figure 4.3,

[11] This comprises what international economists call the "small country assumption." For the case of the United States in world cheese markets, this might not always be a good assumption. We use it here, however, to simplify our analysis of intra-industry trade.

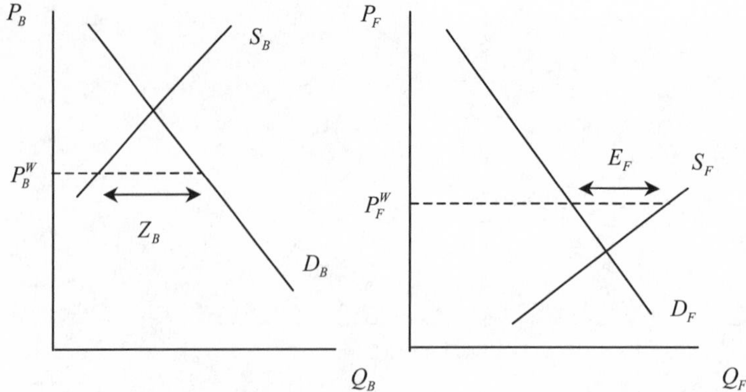

Figure 4.3. U.S. Intra-Industry Trade in Cheese

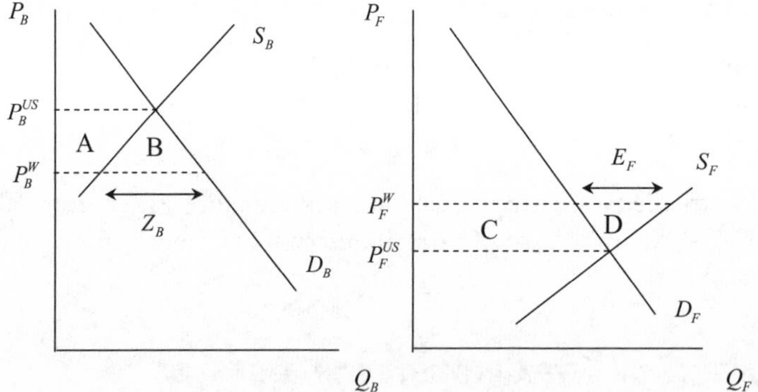

Figure 4.4. The Gains from Intra-Industry Trade

the United States cannot affect the values of either P_B^W or P_F^W along the vertical axes. Therefore, even with quality differences implying that the world price of food-service cheese is below the world price of blue cheese ($P_F^W < P_B^W$), the United States exports E_F of food-service cheese and imports Z_B of blue cheese. In this way, the United States engages in intra-industry trade in cheese, *both* importing *and* exporting cheese. An alternative example of vertical intra-industry trade in computer products is provided in the accompanying box.

Does intra-industry trade in cheese benefit the United States? We take up this issue in Figure 4.4. This figure is the same as Figure 4.3, but it includes autarky prices for the United States (P_B^{US} and P_F^{US}). Consider first the blue cheese market. You can see that, as the United States moves from autarky to trade, the gain in U.S. consumer surplus $(A + B)$ exceeds the loss in U.S. producer surplus (A) by area B.[12] Next consider the food-service cheese market. You can see that as the United States moves from autarky to trade, the gain in U.S. producer surplus $(C + D)$ exceeds the loss in U.S. consumer surplus (C) by area D. Therefore, the movement from autarky to intra-industry trade entails a total gain of areas B and D. There are gains from intra-industry trade as well as from inter-industry trade.

[12] Recall that there is an appendix to Chapter 2 reviewing the consumer surplus and producer surplus ideas. Please refer to it if you need to refresh your memory.

Computer Products Trade

As noted by Curry and Kenney (2004), the personal computer is a highly modular product. This fact has ensured that personal computer assembly is one that supports vertical intra-industry trade via fragmentation and production sharing. The tasks involved in building a personal computer stretch out along what is known as the value chain, ranging from raw materials to many kinds of component manufacturing to final assembly and sales. Various raw materials such as ceramics, metals, and chemicals are used to produce a large range of components such as the microprocessor, circuit boards, display panel, and many others. Compared with component manufacturing, assembly is very straightforward. Indeed, Curry and Kenney (2004) state that: "Modularity and international standardization has [sic] proceeded to such an extent that an assembler with minimal training can assemble a PC in fifteen minutes with little more equipment than a screwdriver and a socket set" (p. 118). Consequently, computer assembly is more of a logistics operation than a manufacturing operation.

In recent years, a great deal of computer assembly has been taken on by Taiwanese firms operating in China. These firms often need to import computer components (particularly the high-end components such as microprocessors) that are then used to assemble the final computer. Despite a growing PC market in China, most of the assembled computers are then exported to major markets outside of China. Thus China imports computer products at one stage of processing (components) and exports computer products at another stage of processing (the final, assembled computer). This is vertical intra-industry trade in computer products.

Sources: Curry and Kenney (2004) and McIvor (2005)

CONCLUSION

In Chapters 2 and 3, we considered models of *inter*-industry trade. However, approximately one-third of world trade consists of *intra*-industry trade. This breaks down into two types: *horizontal intra*-industry trade based on product differentiation, and *vertical intra*-industry trade based on fragmentation and potentially on comparative advantage. If, as you proceed through this book, you have trouble distinguishing inter-industry and intra-industry trade, be sure to refer back to Table 4.1. We also noted that adjustment to trade can be smoother in the case of intra-industry trade than in the case of inter-industry trade.

We have used the supply and demand diagram to develop a simple analysis of horizontal intra-industry trade. Our description of vertical intra-industry trade made preliminary use of the **value chain** and the notion of *tasks* in a preliminary description of international production. We will return to these ideas more fully in Part II of the book.

REVIEW EXERCISES

1. In your own words, please explain the difference between *inter*-industry and *intra*-industry trade.
2. How is the phenomenon of horizontal intra-industry trade related to product diversification?

3. Create your own example of a horizontal intra-industry trade model by choosing a country and a product. Draw a diagram equivalent to Figure 4.3 describing intra-industry trade for your example. Next, draw a diagram equivalent to Figure 4.4 describing the gains from intra-industry trade.
4. Create your own example of vertical intra-industry trade and explain how it is related to fragmentation.
5. Explain why the adjustment process stemming from intra-industry trade is easier for a country to accommodate than the adjustment process stemming from inter-industry trade.

FURTHER READING AND WEB RESOURCES

The original work on intra-industry trade was by Grubel and Lloyd (1975), and an early review was by Greenaway and Torstensson (1997). For concise, more recent reviews, see Chapter 10 of van Marrewijk (2002), OECD (2002), Chapter 4 of Brakman et al. (2006), and van Marrewijk (2009). For a longer, empirical review, see Brülhart (2009).

APPENDIX: THE GRUBEL-LLOYD INDEX

We mentioned in this chapter that Grubel and Lloyd (1975) completed the first important study of intra-industry trade. In this study, these authors developed what is now a well-known index for measuring the degree of intra-industry trade, the **Grubel-Lloyd index**. This appendix introduces you to this index and provides a brief example of its application to China.

The Grubel-Lloyd index looks at a given product category denoted by the letter *i*. The index of intra-industry trade in this product category is usually denoted by B_i. B_i is calculated based on the level of imports of product *i* (denoted Z_i) and the level of exports of product *i* (denoted E_i). The Grubel-Lloyd index is calculated as:

$$B_i = \left[1 - \frac{|E_i - Z_i|}{(E_i + Z_i)}\right] \cdot 100$$

Recall that $|E_i - Z_i|$ refers to the *absolute value* of the difference between exports and imports of product *i*. This value is always positive. The best way to make sense of the Grubel-Lloyd index is to consider the case where intra-industry trade is at its maximum.

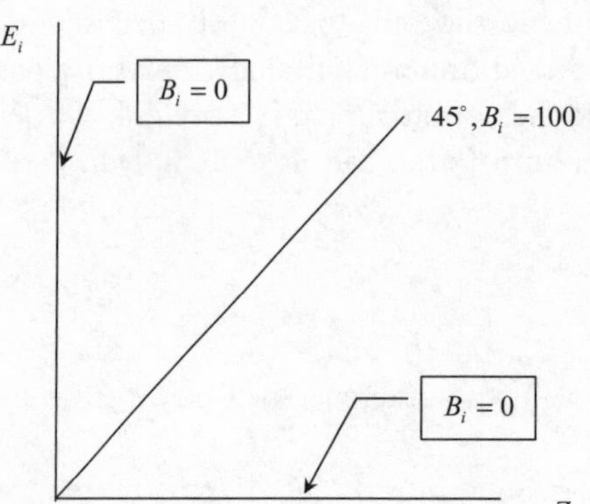

Figure 4.5. Visualizing the Grubel-Lloyd Index

Table 4.2. Measuring China's intra-industry trade using the Grubel-Lloyd index

Year	3-digit SITC or 237 Sectors	2-digit SITC or 67 Sectors	1-digit SITC or 10 Sectors
1980	20	30	63
1985	20	29	44
1990	36	45	60
1995	38	48	67
2000	39	48	57
2005	42	49	58

Source: Van Marrewijk (2009). Note: SITC refers to standard international trade classification. The Grubel-Lloyd indices reported here are average, trade-weighted indices.

That is where exports and imports of product *i* are *exactly equal* to one another. In this case, $|E_i - Z_i| = 0$ and $B_i = (1 - 0) \cdot 100 = 100$. Therefore, the Grubel-Lloyd index ranges from 0 to 100. As the index increases from 0 to 100, the amount of intra-industry trade in product category *i* increases.

We can visualize this using Figure 4.5. In cases where $E_i = Z_i$, a particular trading economy will be on the 45-degree line in this figure and $B_i = 100$. As the trading economy diverges in either direction from the 45-degree line, B_i will decline from 100. If the import and export values are such that one is zero (the pure inter-industry trade case), then the economy will be on one of the two axes and $B_i = 0$.

Table 4.2 reports a few measures of intra-industry trade for China using the Grubel-Lloyd index calculated by Van Marrewijk (2009). Van Marrewijk rightly draws three conclusions from the results presented in this table. First, as we disaggregate further (moving right to left in the table), the amount of trade classified as intra-industry declines. Second, despite this decline, intra-industry trade does not disappear.[13] Third, as discussed in this chapter, the amount of intra-industry trade increases over time.

REFERENCES

Ando, M. (2006) "Fragmentation and Vertical Intra-Industry Trade in East Asia," *North American Journal of Economics and Finance*, 17:3, 257–281.

Arndt, S.W. (2009) "Fragmentation," in K.A. Reinert, R.S. Rajan, A.J. Glass, and L.S. Davis (eds.), *The Princeton Encyclopedia of the World Economy*, Princeton University Press, 498–502.

Bergstrand, J.H. (1982) "The Scope, Growth, and Causes of Intra-Industry International Trade," *New England Economic Review*, September-October, 45–61.

Brakman, S., H. Garretsen, C. van Marrewijk, and A. van Witteloostuijn (2006) *Nations and Firms in the Global Economy: An Introduction to International Economics and Business*, Cambridge University Press.

Brülhart, M. (2009) "An Account of Global Intra-industry Trade, 1962–2006," *World Economy*, 32:3, 2009.

[13] Van Marrewijk (2009) notes that "This is a general characteristic of current trade flows as intraindustry trade exists for very detailed sector classifications" (p. 710). For examples of the detailed sector classifications for the case of China, see Hu and Ma (1999).

Curry, J. and M. Kenney (2004) "The Organization and Geographic Configuration of the Personal Computer Value Chain," in M. Kenney (ed.), *Locating Global Advantage: Industry Dynamics in the International Economy*, Stanford University Press, 113–141.

Globerman, S. (1992) "North American Trade Liberalization and Intra-industry Trade," *Weltwirtschaftliches Archiv*, 128:3, 487–497.

Greenaway, D. and J. Torstensson (1997) "Back to the Future: Taking Stock on Intra-industry Trade," *Weltwirtschaftliches Archiv*, 133:2, 249–269.

Grimwade, N. (1989) *International Trade: New Patterns of Trade, Production, and Investment*, Routledge.

Grubel, H.G. and P.J. Lloyd (1975) *Intra-Industry Trade: The Theory and Measurement of International Trade in Differentiated Products*, John Wiley.

Hellvin, L. (1994) "Intra-Industry Trade in Asia," *International Economic Journal*, 8:4, 27–40.

Hu, X. and Y. Ma (1999) "International Intra-industry Trade of China," *Weltwirtschaftliches Archiv*, 135:1, 82–101.

Marvel, H.P. and E.J. Ray (1987) "Intraindustry Trade: Sources and Effects on Production," *Journal of Political Economy*, 95:6, 1278–1291.

McIvor, R. (2005) *The Outsourcing Process: Strategies for Evaluation and Management*, Cambridge University Press.

Organization for Economic Cooperation and Development (2002) "Intraindustry and Intrafirm Trade and the Internationalisation of Production," *OECD Economic Outlook*, 71:1, 159–170.

Reinert, K.A., D.W. Roland-Holst, and C.R. Shiells (1993) "Social Accounts and the Structure of the North American Economy," *Economic Systems Research*, 5:3, 295–326.

Ruffin, R.J. (1999) "The Nature and Significance of Intra-Industry Trade," *Federal Reserve Bank of Dallas Economic and Financial Review*, 4th Quarter, 2–9.

Thom, R. and M. McDowell (1999) "Measuring Marginal Intra-Industry Trade," *Weltwirtschaftliches Archiv*, 135:1, 48–61.

Thorpe, M. and Z. Zhang (2005) "Study of the Measurement and Determinants of Intra-Industry Trade in East Asia," *Asian Economic Journal*, 19:2, 231–247.

Van Marrewijk, C. (2002) *International Trade and the World Economy*, Oxford University Press.

Van Marrewijk, C. (2009) "Intraindustry Trade," in K.A. Reinert, R.S. Rajan, A.J. Glass, and L.S. Davis (eds.), *The Princeton Encyclopedia of the World Economy*, Princeton University Press, 708–712.

Wakasugi, R. (1997) "Missing Factors of Intra-Industry Trade: Some Empirical Evidence Based on Japan," *Japan and the World Economy*, 9:3, 353–362.

5 The Political Economy of Trade

In Chapter 3, you learned that it was possible for countries to move from autarky to inter-industry trading relationships based on patterns of comparative advantage. So, for example, Japan can export motorcycles to Vietnam while importing rice from Vietnam. You also learned that such movements from autarky to trade involve improvements in welfare for the countries involved. In other words, both Japan and Vietnam can experience gains from trade. In point of fact, however, Japan has a long history of *restricting* imports of rice. This reluctance to import rice has been explained by the Consulate General of Japan in San Francisco:

> Rice has been the staple of the Japanese for over 200 years and can be considered the most important element in the evolution of the Japanese culture and social structure. Therefore, a significant segment of the Japanese population express cultural concerns over rice imports. In addition, many Japanese rice producers have historically been strongly opposed to accepting rice imports for both economic security and cultural reasons.

Indeed, during the Uruguay Round of multilateral trade negotiations, the Japanese Diet (Parliament) passed three resolutions opposing the proposed partial liberalization of the Japanese rice market. At the very end of the Uruguay Round negotiations (in 1994), Japan was given "special treatment" to continue to restrict rice imports. To this day, Japan offers significant protection to its domestic rice sector such that the domestic price is approximately twice as high as the world price.[1]

Welcome to the political economy of trade policy. In Chapters 2 and 3, we were careful to mention that the improvement in overall welfare in a country that occurs due to the gains from trade does not necessarily imply an improvement in welfare for *every* individual and group in that country. In this chapter, you will learn that it is both possible and likely that, in countries moving from autarky to trade, certain groups actually *lose* from this change.[2] Japanese rice producers are one such politically powerful group. The fact that there are both winners and losers from international trade gives rise to the political economy of trade. This is a realm where the field of international trade begins to merge somewhat into political science and public policy, a very exciting prospect for many researchers and practitioners.

We begin in this chapter by considering different approaches to the political economy of trade, including country-based, factor-based, sector-based, and firm-based. We then revisit the model of comparative advantage developed in Chapter 3. This will be the means through which we explore factor-based and sector-based approaches to the political economy of trade. First, we consider the role of factors of production in comparative advantage as described by the **Heckscher-Ohlin model** of trade and take up the associated **Stolper-Samuelson theorem**. Second, we examine the application of this theorem to the topic of North-South trade. Finally, we consider the role of sectors in the specific factors model of the political economy of trade. An appendix to the chapter considers a model of **endogenous protection**.

Analytical elements for this chapter:
Countries, sectors, firms, and *factors of production.*

[1] See Fukuda, Dyck, and Stout (2003), for example.

[2] As in the cases of Chapters 2 and 3, we are working in this chapter within the standard economic view of welfare. We do need to recognize that there are other views that can lead to different interpretations of trade issues.

Table 5.1. Approaches to the political economy of trade

Focus	Name	Insight
Country-based	Realism	There are security externalities associated with international trade that need to be managed by country governments.
Country-based	Institutionalism	Institutional structures within country governments affect trade policy outcomes.
Factor-based	Heckscher-Ohlin model Stolper-Samuelson theorem	Under factor mobility within a country, different factors can win or lose from increased trade.
Sector-based	Specific factors model	With sector-specific factors, whether factors win or lose can depend on whether they are specific to an export- or import-oriented sector.
Firm-based	Firm-based	The exposure of firms to trade or international capital mobility can influence the posture of these firms to trade liberalization.

Source: Adapted from Walter and Sen (2009)

APPROACHES TO THE POLITICAL ECONOMY OF TRADE

Research on the political economy of trade provides a framework of a *market for protection* that draws our attention to supply-side and demand-side factors in this market.[3] The supply of protection is provided by national governments, and we have two country-based approaches in the field of international relations and political science that offer alternative perspectives of this side of the protection markets. As shown in Table 5.1, these are the perspectives of *realism* and *institutionalism.* Realism is a school of thought in international relations that stresses the lack of global government and the consequence that inherently anarchic relations must be addressed via the projection of power by leading countries.[4]

Realism views trade through the lens of power, emphasizing the security and technology aspects of trade and the need to harness these to promote national "strength." For example, trade in certain defense-related products can dissipate power and consequently be tightly controlled within established alliances. High technology can be "dual-use," potentially having defense-related characteristics. It too can be tightly controlled. Finally, access to hydrocarbons and minerals is often viewed through a realist lens by national governments, as in the case of rare earth elements (REEs), discussed in Chapter 2. Protection is often offered by governments in support of these ends, and more generally, these governments often view trade relations through a lens of security alliances.

Institutionalism is associated with most branches of the social sciences and focuses on the "rules of the game" within a particular sociopolitical or socioeconomic system. In the realm of the political economy of trade, institutional analysis emphasizes the importance of certain key aspects of national governments in supplying protection.[5] The distribution of decision-making power within a national government apparatus can be important, as well as the relationship of executive and legislative branches with

[3] See, for example, Rodrik (1995) and Milner (1999).
[4] For a more thorough treatment of realism, see Donnelly (2000).
[5] See, for example, Milner (1997). For empirical evidence, see Henisz and Mansfield (2006).

regard to trade policy. To generalize a bit, the contrast with realism is to view national governments as nonunitary actors rather than as unitary actors in the realm of global power politics. A central insight of institutional analysis is that trade policy changes are more likely the more centralized is decision-making power within the institutional framework of a government.

Other approaches to the political economy of trade emphasize the role of demand for protection in the form of what is sometimes referred to as *pressure group models.* It is here that international economists have made their most important contribution to analyzing the political economy of trade, and the rest of this chapter considers these contributions. One approach is factor-based in that pressure comes from classes composed of one factor of production or another that lose as a result of trade liberalization. Later, we will consider the **Heckscher-Ohlin model** and its **Stolper-Samuelson theorem** as a factor-based theory of the demand for protection. A second approach is that pressure comes from sectors rather than classes (sector interests can cut across classes), and here we encounter what is known as the **specific factors model**. Together, the Stolper-Samuelson theorem and the specific factors model represent economists' contribution to the political economy of trade.

There is another strand in the analysis of the political economy of trade that focuses on specific firms and their exposure to trade and international capital mobility. This *firm-level analysis* was inspired by Milner (1988), who argued that firms that are more export-oriented and "multinationalized" in their production and/or ownership tend to be less protectionist in their lobbying efforts. This is a plausible hypothesis in many circumstances, but might fall short of a general principle.[6]

Table 5.1 reveals that the political economy of trade is not straightforward, but is rather subject to a number of influences at the levels of nations, factors, sectors, and firms. In the remainder of this chapter, we will focus on factor-based and sector-based explanations, but we should not lose sight of the fact that specific cases could be more complex than suggested by these frameworks.

COMPARATIVE ADVANTAGE REVISITED

In order to begin talking more specifically about the factor and sector approaches to the political economy of trade, it is useful to revisit the model of comparative advantage we developed in Chapter 3. Figure 5.1 reproduces Figure 3.3 from that chapter. Recall that Vietnam has a comparative advantage in the production of rice (denoted R), and Japan has a comparative advantage in the production of motorcycles (denoted M). As these two economies move from autarky to trade, production in each country expands in the direction of the sector in which it has comparative advantage. In the movement from points A to B along the production possibility frontiers in Figure 5.1, rice production expands in Vietnam, and motorcycle production expands in Japan. The purpose of this chapter is to analyze these processes much more carefully.

What determines the pattern of comparative advantage illustrated in Figure 5.1? Recall from Chapters 2 and 3 that there are two broad determinants: technology and factors of production. A factor-based analysis of the political economy of trade policy

[6] For a critique of the hypothesized relationship between firms with "multinationalized" ownership and less protectionist orientations, see Hiscox (2004).

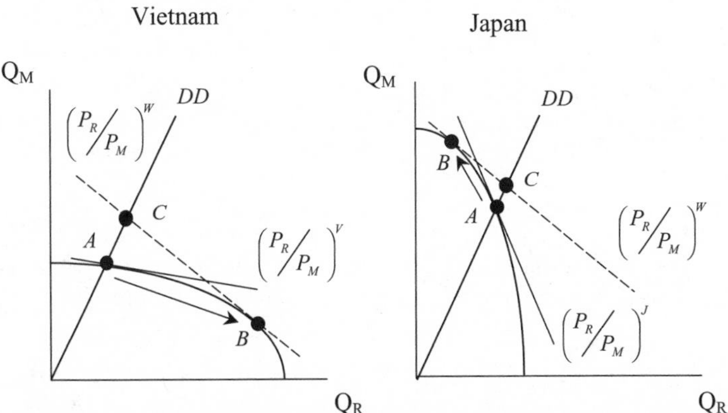

Figure 5.1. Autarky and Comparative Advantage in Vietnam and Japan

takes up the latter determinant and examines the implications of the movement from points *A* to *B* in Figure 5.1 for factors of production in Vietnam and Japan.

TRADE AND FACTORS OF PRODUCTION

Suppose that the pattern of comparative advantage illustrated in Figure 5.1 is based on different *endowments* of factors of production. More specifically, suppose that Vietnam's comparative advantage in rice reflects the fact that it has a relatively large endowment of land. In the language of international trade theory, Vietnam is relatively *land abundant.* By this, we mean that the ratio of land to physical capital is larger in Vietnam than in Japan. This relative abundance of land gives Vietnam a comparative advantage in producing the *land-intensive* good, rice. Similarly, suppose that Japan's comparative advantage in motorcycles reflects the fact that it has a relatively large endowment of physical capital. In the language of international trade theory, Japan is relatively *capital abundant.* By this, we mean that the ratio of physical capital to land is larger in Japan than in Vietnam. This relative abundance of capital gives Japan a comparative advantage in producing the *capital-intensive* good, motorcycles.[7]

We must pause here for a moment. In the previous paragraph, we associated the term *endowments* with countries (Vietnam, Japan) and the term *intensities* with sectors or goods (rice, motorcycles). It is very easy to forget these associations, so we must keep them firmly in mind. Here is something you can refer to as you read the remainder of this section:

Factor endowments ⇔ Countries
Factor intensities ⇔ Sectors or goods

As mentioned previously, the explanation of comparative advantage in terms of factor endowments is associated with the Heckscher-Ohlin model of international trade.[8] This model is one of the most famous models in trade theory. The logic of the Heckscher-Ohlin model is illustrated in the top six boxes of Figure 5.2. The top two

[7] We need to interpret these statements with care. We are saying that Vietnam is relatively land abundant *in comparison* to Japan. In comparison to its own population, land is indeed scarce in Vietnam. See *The Economist* (2002b).

[8] This model originated in the work of Heckscher (1949) and Ohlin (1933).

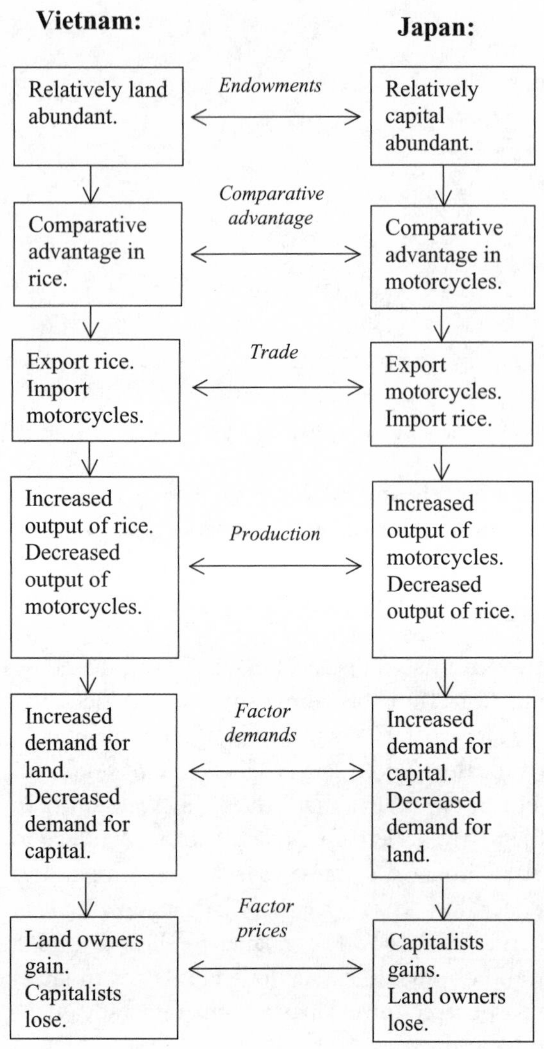

Figure 5.2. The Heckscher-Ohlin Model and the Stolper-Samuelson Theorem

boxes of this figure concern factor endowments. Vietnam is relatively land abundant, and Japan is relatively capital abundant. The next two boxes concern the pattern of comparative advantage. Vietnam has a comparative advantage in rice (land intensive), and Japan has a comparative advantage in motorcycles (capital intensive). The third level of boxes in Figure 5.2 concerns trade flows. In accordance with the pattern of comparative advantage, Vietnam exports rice to Japan, and Japan exports motorcycles to Vietnam.

More generally, the Heckscher-Ohlin model of international trade gives the following result with regard to trade:

> A country exports the good whose production is intensive in its abundant factor. It imports the good whose production is intensive in its scarce factor.

The implication of Figure 5.2 for the political economy of trade policy is addressed in the bottom six boxes. In Vietnam, the comparative advantage in rice causes an increase in the output of rice at the expense of motorcycles. Consequently, there is an increase in demand for land and a decrease in demand for physical capital. These factor demand changes have the result that landowners in Vietnam gain from trade, whereas Vietnamese capital owners (capitalists) lose from trade.[9]

In Japan, the comparative advantage in motorcycles causes an increase in the output of motorcycles at the expense of rice. Consequently, there is an increase in demand for physical capital and a decrease in demand for land. These changes cause Japanese capital owners to gain from trade and Japanese landowners to lose from trade.

Given the results of Figure 5.2, we would expect that landowners in Vietnam and capital owners in Japan would support trade. Political opposition to trade or demand for protection would come from capital owners in Vietnam and landowners in the Japan. Thus we can see why the strong and persistent opposition to rice imports in Japan discussed in the introduction to this chapter arises and persists. It is due, at least in part, to the political clout of Japanese landowners. The reason, however, is not "economic security and culture." Rather, it is income loss.[10]

Let's summarize these results in more general terms. In both Vietnam and Japan, the sector intensive in the country's abundant factor expands, whereas the sector intensive in the country's scarce factor contracts. This, in turn, causes an increase in the demand for the abundant factor in each country and a decrease in demand for the scarce factor in each country. These changes in demand, in turn, have implications for the returns to or incomes of the factors in question and hence the demand for protection.

The Heckscher-Ohlin model thus has an important implication for the political economy of trade, and this implication is summarized in a central result of international trade theory, the Stolper-Samuelson theorem.[11] In general terms, this theorem can be stated as follows:

> As a country moves from autarky to trade, the country's abundant factor of production (used intensively in the export sector) gains, whereas the country's scarce factor of production (used intensively in the import sector) loses. Opposition to trade or demand for protection therefore arises from the scarce factor of production.

The Stolper-Samuelson theorem thus locates the potential opposition to increased trade (and support for protection) in the scarce factor of production in a country. This key insight composes the lens through which many international economists and policymakers view the political economy of trade. An extension of the model to the issue of endogenous protection is presented in the appendix. The Stolper-Samuelson theorem cannot be applied blindly, however. It applies only to *inter*-industry trade based on different endowments in factors of production. *Intra*-industry trade and trade based on differences in technology can mitigate the effects described by the theorem.

[9] Given that Vietnam is a socialist country, we need to be careful here. Institutions of ownership can be very different than in fully market-oriented countries.

[10] The historical relevance of this result can be seen in the work of Anderson and Hayami (1986). Walter and Sen (2009) noted that "an electoral system that gives representation to rural districts, as in Japan, can entrench protectionist policies in agriculture" (p. 82). For proposed changes to this system, see *The Economist* (2011).

[11] This theorem originated in a famous article by Wolfgang Stolper and Paul Samuelson (1941). In the words of Deardorff (1998), "One might have thought and hoped that the broader gains from trade . . . might have allowed both abundant and scarce factors to gain from trade. . . . But alas no, Stolper and Samuelson showed this is not the case" (p. 364). Another theorem of the Heckscher-Ohlin model, the Rybczynski theorem, is presented in the appendix to Chapter 24.

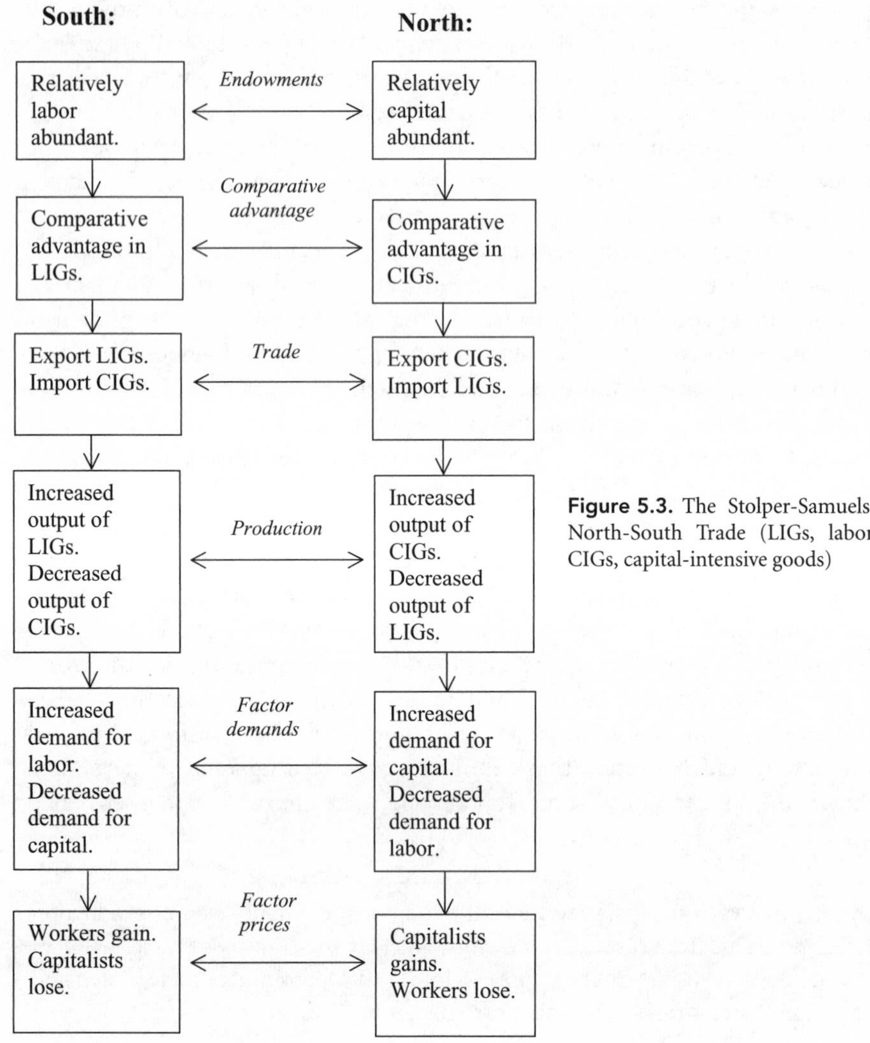

Figure 5.3. The Stolper-Samuelson Theorem and North-South Trade (LIGs, labor-intensive goods; CIGs, capital-intensive goods)

These alternative considerations arise in the application of the theorem to the issue of North-South trade and wages.

NORTH-SOUTH TRADE AND WAGES

There is an application of the Stolper-Samuelson theorem that has generated a great deal of recent interest and controversy. This is the question of North-South trade and wages. The term *North* refers to the high-income or "developed" countries of the world, whereas the terms *South* refers to the low- and middle-income or "developing" countries of the world. High-income countries tend to be relatively capital abundant, whereas developing countries tend to be relatively labor abundant. The implications of these relative factor endowments are illustrated in Figure 5.3. The Heckscher-Ohlin model of trade would suggest that the North has a comparative advantage in capital-intensive goods (CIGs) and that the South has a comparative advantage in labor-intensive goods (LIGs). This is illustrated in the top six boxes of Figure 5.3. Furthermore, the Stolper-Samuelson theorem would suggest that *labor in the North* will *lose* as a result of trade. This is illustrated in the bottom six boxes of Figure 5.3. The possibility of Northern labor losing as a result of trade has led labor interests in the North to be, in many instances, opposed to increased trade. For example, the U.S. labor movement opposed both the North American Free Trade Agreement (NAFTA) and the formation of the World Trade Organization (WTO).

Although the possibility of Northern labor as a whole losing as a result of increased international trade with the South is in itself of some interest, there is a more subtle issue in the ongoing debate concerning North-South trade and wages that is very much worth emphasizing here. There is evidence that developing countries in the South have comparative advantage in *unskilled*-labor–intensive goods and that developed countries in the North have comparative advantage in *skilled*-labor–intensive goods. If this is indeed true, then according to the Stolper-Samuelson theorem, the Northern workers who lose as a result of increased North-South trade are actually *unskilled* workers. This possibility, first introduced by Wood (1994), is of a great deal of interest and concern. For example, since the early 1980s in the United States, unskilled workers have seen their wages decline relative to skilled workers, with negative impacts for the overall income distribution. Perhaps increased North-South trade has caused this relative wage decline.[12]

Since the early 1990s, these concerns have prompted ongoing empirical investigation into the effects of trade on Northern wages (see the box on Southern wages in the case of Latin America). The number of studies is too large, and the technical issues too detailed, for a review here.[13] However, we can note the important empirical result that there are two (not one) main causes for the decline in relative wages of Northern unskilled workers: trade and technology.

The trade impacts are those suggested by the Stolper-Samuelson theorem, namely, that Northern unskilled workers lose because the North has a comparative advantage in *skilled*-labor-intensive goods. These effects, however, tend to be smaller than the Stolper-Samuelson theorem would suggest. Why is this? First, there is some evidence that export-oriented industries in the North tend to pay higher wages than other industries. Consequently, the labor reallocations caused by increased trade tend to boost average wages.[14] Second, some North-South trade is based on higher labor productivity (better technology) in the North rather than differences in factor endowments. Third, some North-South trade is *intra*-industry in nature and might therefore offer more adjustment opportunities to Northern workers than *inter*-industry trade.[15] For these reasons, although important, trade is not the only source of the decline in relative wages of Northern unskilled workers. Technology matters as well, and intra-industry trade might mitigate the standard Stolper-Samuelson effects.

[12] In the case of the United States, the concern was summarized some years ago by Krugman and Lawrence (1996) as follows: "The conventional wisdom holds that foreign competition has eroded the U.S. manufacturing base, washing out the high-paying jobs that a strong manufacturing sector provides. . . . And because imports increasingly come from Third World countries with their huge reserves of unskilled labor, the heaviest burden of this foreign competition has ostensibly fallen on less educated American workers" (p. 35).

[13] For reviews, see Freeman (1995), Richardson (1995), Deardorff (1998), Wood (2002), and Krugman (2008).

[14] See Bernard and Jensen (1995).

[15] See Reinert and Roland-Holst (1998) for the example of the North American Free Trade Agreement.

Let's turn to the technology effects of North-South trade on Northern unskilled workers. There appears to be an ongoing process of technological change in the North that increases demand for skilled workers and makes these workers more productive, relative to unskilled workers.[16] This is the process we mentioned in Chapter 1 in the box entitled "ICT in the World Economy." Some time ago, Deardorff (1998) aptly summarized the relevance of this process to wage changes:

> The computer revolution has made it possible for highly skilled workers, manipulating their environments with electronic devices, to produce far more than equally skilled workers could have previously, also replacing to a large extent the unskilled workers whose tasks are taken over increasingly by intelligent machines. As a result, the productivity and wages of skilled workers rise, while those of unskilled workers do not (p. 368).

There are policy analysts in the North, with well-grounded concerns about the plight of unskilled Northern workers, who call for trade restrictions to address the effects of North-South trade on unskilled wages in the North. For a number of reasons, this is probably not the best policy approach. First, technology appears to be as important a factor as trade, and few policy analysts call for limiting technological change. Second, trade restrictions will suppress overall gains from trade in both the North and South. Third, such restrictions could violate multilateral commitments made in the WTO (see Chapter 7). Fourth, trade restrictions might harm unskilled workers in the South who are in more dire straits than their Northern counterparts. A more long-term and productive policy approach would be to offer other forms of support to unskilled Northern workers. These could be income supports (including trade adjustment assistance) and, more importantly, support to increase human capital assets (education, training). If there is one factor contributing to wage and income inequality in the North, it is the failure to complete secondary (high school) education. Remedying educational failures is an important, and neglected, policy imperative in Northern countries as well as in Southern countries.

Trade and Wages in Latin America

In our preceding discussion, we suggested that developing countries in the "South" have a comparative advantage in *unskilled*-labor–intensive goods. As suggested by the Heckscher-Ohlin model, this is a result of these countries being abundant in unskilled labor. If this is the case, then according to the Stolper-Samuelson theorem, increased trade would benefit unskilled labor in developing countries, relative to skilled labor. It turns out, however, that in some Latin American countries, the opposite appears to have been the case. For example, trade liberalization in a number of Latin America countries has been accompanied by decreases in the relative wages of unskilled workers. Why would the Stolper-Samuelson theorem be wrong?

One reason is trade in physical capital. As some Latin American countries liberalized their trading regimes, firms imported more physical capital (machines) in order to

[16] This appears to be part of the shift toward flexible manufacturing systems discussed in Chapter 9 and has had the effect of suppressing blue-collar wages. In addition, globally, multinational enterprises often serve as conduits of technological change through their foreign direct investment activities. Therefore, it is possible that MNEs can contribute to changing wage patterns via technology.

remain competitive. Embodied in these machines was a newer technology level that demanded relatively more skilled workers than the old technology that had been in use. Consequently, as trade was liberalized, the technology effects overpowered the Stolper-Samuelson effects, and the net result was that unskilled workers lost relative to skilled workers as a result of trade.

Here, then, is another important case of the political economy of trade. Given that the majority of workers in Latin America are unskilled and Latin American counties already have severe inequality problems, the above results are of some cause for concern. They indicate that trade can, in some instances, exacerbate existing inequalities and, thereby, contribute to political tensions.

Sources: Gindling and Robbins (2001), Robbins and Gindling (1999), and Wood (1997)

THE ROLE OF SPECIFIC FACTORS

As we saw in Table 5.1, a sector-based approach to the political economy of trade is associated with what is called the specific factors model. A central assumption of the Heckscher-Ohlin model and its Stolper-Samuelson theorem is that resources or factors of production such as labor, physical capital, and land can move effortlessly among different sectors of trading economies. So, for example, Japanese resources are assumed to be able to shift back and forth between rice and motorcycle production. The same is assumed to be true for Vietnam. For some types of analysis, particularly that applying to the *long run*, this "perfect factor mobility" assumption is reasonable. In other instances, the assumption can be at odds with reality. Instead, factors of production can be *sector specific*, and it is this phenomenon that motivates the specific factors model and its approach to the political economy of trade.[17]

The presence of specific factors requires a modification of the Stolper-Samuelson theorem. To see this, let's consider the example of steel production in the United States. The United States is, without a doubt, relatively abundant in physical capital. The Stolper-Samuelson theorem would therefore suggest that capital owners in the United States would *gain* as a result of increased trade. But here is the puzzle. In its 2000 annual report, the U.S.-based Weirton Steel Corporation drew attention to what it called an "import crisis" and pledged to fight the "import war." It said it planned to "aggressively seek changes in Washington (DC) to stop the devastation caused by unfair trade." This hardly sounds like capitalists gaining from trade.

Why would capitalists in a capital-abundant country oppose increased trade in violation of the Stolper-Samuelson theorem? As it turns out, the notion of specific factors helps us to address this puzzle. Weirton Steel Corporation, and many other U.S. steel firms, are owners of large amounts of specific factors in the form of steel mills, some of them very large, "integrated" facilities.[18] These facilities cannot move into the production of other products such as semiconductors. They are *specific* to the production of steel.

[17] von Haberler (1937) first emphasized the role of specific factors in models of international trade, but this model was formalized by Jones (1971).

[18] Blecker (2009) noted that "Steel production, especially in integrated mills, is capital intensive and has large economies of scale, which create a tendency toward the existence of excess capacity (except in times of strong demand)" (p. 1032). In the short run, the large amount of capital in integrated mills constitutes a sector-specific factor.

A modification of the Stolper-Samuelson theorem in the face of such specific factors is important to understanding the U.S. steel and other similar cases. This modification is as follows:

> Factors of production that are specific to import sectors tend to lose as a result of trade, whereas factors of production specific to export sectors tend to gain as a result of trade.

Thus Weirton steel's actions are not difficult to understand. It is a company in an import sector that is characterized by sector-specific physical capital (and perhaps even labor). The owners of Weirton steel therefore stand to lose as a result of increased trade. Consequently, as described in the box, "U.S. Steel Protection," the firm entered the "import war" to attempt to reduce imports and protect the incomes of its specific factors.

It is not always easy to keep the difference between specific and mobile factors in mind when assessing the political economy of trade. For this reason, we need a box to help us:

> *Mobile factors of production:* The Stolper-Samuelson theorem applies. The abundant factor of production (used intensively in the export sector) gains, whereas the scarce factor of production (used intensively in the import sector) loses.
>
> *Specific factors of production:* The Stolper-Samuelson theorem does *not* apply. The factor of production specific to the export sector gains, whereas the factor of production specific to the import sector loses. The fate of mobile factors is uncertain.

When you come upon a political economy of trade issue, in any country of the trading world, it will be very helpful to your understanding if you were to first pause for a moment and try to identify the mobile or specific factors of production involved. Then glance up at the above box. The political economy of trade issue should be very much clarified by this process. If not, it is probably the case that technology, not factors of production, drives the trade involved.

U.S. Steel Protection

In September 1998, 12 U.S. steel companies, including Weirton Steel mentioned previously, filed cases with the U.S. government alleging that the hot-rolled steel exports of Russia, Japan, and Brazil had been unfairly "dumped" or sold at "less than fair value" in U.S. markets. The U.S. International Trade Commission (USITC) found in favor of the U.S. steel industry, and protection to offset the dumping was applied. In June 1999, seven U.S. steel companies, again including Weirton Steel, filed follow-up cases involving cold-rolled steel exports of China, South Africa, Turkey, Brazil, Argentina, Thailand, Russia, Venezuela, Japan, Indonesia, Slovakia, and Taiwan. The USITC found in favor of the U.S. steel industry in the cases of Indonesia, Slovakia, and Taiwan. Next, in October 1999, Weirton Steel filed an antidumping case against Japan's exports of tin mill products, and the USITC found in Weirton's favor.

Despite these results, capping two decades of special protection, the U.S. steel industry felt that a more comprehensive solution was required to support the incomes of its sector-specific factors. Under the banner "Stand Up for Steel" (U.S.-manufactured steel, that is), the industry pressed on with a campaign for further protection. This campaign, in which Weirton played a leading role, included petitions, lobbying, and even motorcycle rallies ("Ride for Steel"). The efforts were best organized in Weirton's home state, West Virginia, a state that helped secure George W. Bush's position as U.S. president through switches in party loyalties.

In June 2001, President Bush's administration instructed the USITC to undertake a *global safeguard investigation* of U.S. steel imports. Such an investigation does not require a finding of "unfair" trade or "dumping," nor is it targeted to specific countries. In December 2001, the USITC found that the U.S. steel industry had been subject to injury as a result of imports and recommended certain remedies. In March 2002, the Bush administration imposed a number of protection measures, including "safeguard" tariffs of up to 30 percent, on US$30 billion worth of steel imports. The European Union and Japan, both of whom were targets in the protection, appealed to the World Trade Organization (WTO) in Geneva. In 2003, the WTO found against the United States and ruled that the tariffs were incompatible with WTO principles.

Sources: The Economist (2002a), Blecker (2009), and Weirton Steel Corporation

CONCLUSION

Support for trade is not universal, and protection from trade is common. Country-based explanations of the supply of protection can be found in realism and institutionalism. Explanations of the demand for protection can be found in factor-based and sector-based insights from trade theory. In this chapter, we have seen that the movement from autarky to trade in any country can hurt some groups of people in that country. According to the Stolper-Samuelson theorem of the Heckscher-Ohlin model, this can be as a result of owning a factor of production that is scarce in their country. Alternatively, it can also be a result of owning a factor specific to an import sector. Suppose that these losing groups become unhappy with the level of trade in their country. What might they do? It is possible that they would lobby their government to intervene in the trade relationship, as we saw in the case of the U.S. steel industry. This is demand for protection. It turns out that such trade policy interventions are common. Despite the gains from trade described in Chapters 2, 3, and 4, governments usually intervene in free trade in some way in response to political pressures from constituencies. This is supply of protection. Interactions in the market for protection constitute the political economy of trade.

We mentioned in Chapter 1 that there are important cultural issues that affect the world economy. At times, opposition to trade and demand for protection can be an expression of cultural issues. This is evident in the quote at the beginning of this chapter. It is important to recognize that cultural and economic factors work side-by-side in many national contexts. The analysis of this chapter helps us understand the economic factors.

What are the effects of the protective policies that develop in the market for protection? We will find out in the next chapter.

REVIEW EXERCISES

1. Consider the trade between Germany and the Dominican Republic. Germany is a capital-abundant country, and the Dominican Republic is a labor-abundant

country. There are two goods: a capital-intensive good, chemicals, and a labor-intensive good, clothing.

a. Draw a comparative advantage diagram such as Figure 5.1 for trade between Germany and the Dominican Republic, labeling the trade flows along the axes of your diagrams.
b. Using the Stolper-Samuelson theorem, describe who will support and who will oppose trade in these two countries. Use a flow chart diagram like that of Figure 5.2 to help you in your description

2. In the early 1800s in England, a debate arose in Parliament over the Corn Laws, restriction on imports of grain into the country. David Ricardo, the father of the comparative advantage concept, favored the repeal of these import restrictions. Consider the two relevant political groups in England at that time: land owners and capital owners. Who do you think agreed with Ricardo? Why?
3. Use daily newspapers to identify a political economy of trade issue. Can you also identify the factors of production involved in this issue? Are they mobile factors as in the Heckscher-Ohlin model, or are they specific factors? Alternatively, are there any elements of technology involved?

FURTHER READING AND WEB RESOURCES

An excellent review of the subject of this chapter can be found in Chapter 3 of Walter and Sen (2009). Another very useful starting point for the reader interested in the political economy of trade is Baldwin (1989). A concise introduction to the Heckscher-Ohlin model is provided by Panagariya (2009), and a volume dedicated to the Stolper-Samuelson theorem has been edited by Deardorff and Stern (1994). For a review of the trade and wages debate, see Marjit and Archaryya (2009). An interesting discussion of fairness in the political economy of trade can be found in Davidson, Matusz, and Nelson (2006).

You can follow one aspect of the market for protectionism in the United States via the website for the U.S. International Trade Commission at www.usitc.gov. For the case of the European Union, see *ec.europa.eu/trade.*

APPENDIX: ENDOGENOUS PROTECTION

The factor-based approach to the political economy of trade as represented by the Heckscher-Ohlin model can be extended to a concept known as **endogenous protection.** This is a formal explanation of why the demand for and supply of protection interact in such a way to result in positive levels of protection, particularly but not exclusively in the form of tariffs (see Chapter 6). Suppose that there are 100 individuals in a country described by the Heckscher-Ohlin model and that each of these individuals has one unit of labor (herself or himself). The other factor of production or resource in the Heckscher-Ohlin economy is physical capital. For each individual, the relative endowment of physical capital is the ratio of the individual's physical capital to labor. Because the labor endowment is just "1," the ratio is just the amount of physical capital they own. For example, for individual 10:

$$\frac{K_{10}}{L_{10}} = \frac{K_{10}}{1} = K_{10} \tag{5.1}$$

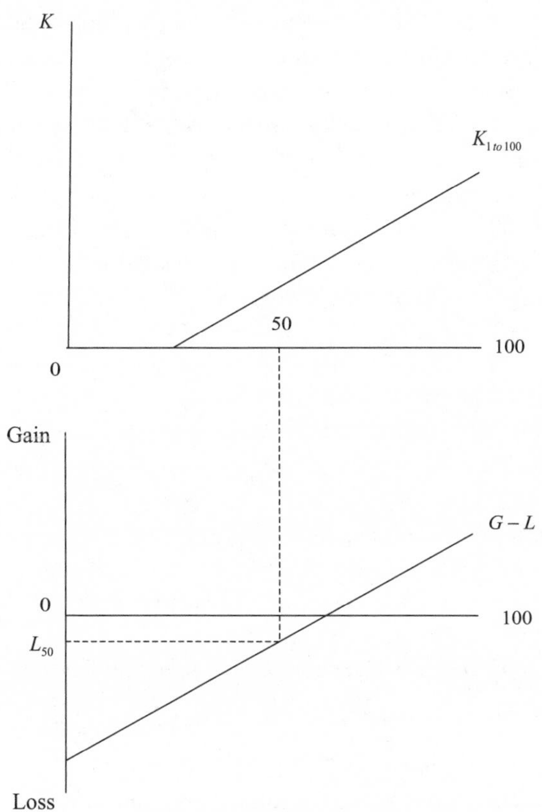

Figure 5.4. Endogenous Protection: Capital Ownership among 100 Residents

We then rank our individuals from the lowest amount of physical capital owned to the highest amount, as follows:

$$K_1 \leq K_2 \leq K_3 \leq \cdots \leq K_{100} \tag{5.2}$$

We graph these ownership ratios in the upper graph in Figure 5.4. Note that many individuals own no physical capital at all and are therefore at "0" in this graph.

If we place these 100 individuals in the Heckscher-Ohlin framework developed in this chapter, then a significant result emerges. Suppose that this is a capital-abundant country that will export the capital-intensive good. Then Mayer (1984) showed that losses will occur for those individuals who own less capital and that gains will occur for those individuals who own more capital.[19] We get a gain/loss ($G - L$) graph something like that in the lower graph of Figure 5.4. All the individuals with "0" capital lose, but so do those with only a little capital, as well as the median individual. Gains are reserved for those with larger amounts of capital.[20]

The presence of losses for the majority of the individuals represents a significant demand for protection due to the Mayer/Stolper/Samuelson effects. But that is not all. There is a basic insight in public choice theory due to Black (1948) that politicians who want to maximize their number of votes will abide by the policy preference of

[19] The actual measure here is with respect to the overall capital/labor ratio for the economy.

[20] Suppose that instead of 100 individuals, there were only five with relative endowments of 0, 0, 1, 2 and 3. The median individual has an endowment of 1, but the mean endowment is 1.2. Because our median individual has less than the mean endowment, he or she would lose as a result of trade, as is the case for individual 50 in Figure 5.42732.

the median voter.[21] This is voter or individual "50" in our model, and this individual suffers losses under free trade in this capital-abundant country. There is thus a bias in this framework toward protectionism. Supply of protection meets demand.

The model considered here combines a factor-based approach to the demand for protection with an explanation of the supply of protection that is a very particular and narrow example of institutionalist considerations. The model is not universal. Not all economies are best described by the Hecksher-Ohlin model; as we have seen in this chapter, specific factors matter as well. Also, politics is more complicated than that described by Black (1948). Nevertheless, the model illustrates one possibility that is commonly recognized by many trade policy analysts.

REFERENCES

Anderson, K. and Y. Hayami (eds.) (1986) *The Political Economy of Agricultural Protection: East Asia in International Perspective*, Allen and Unwin.

Baldwin, R.E. (1989) "The Political Economy of Trade Policy," *Journal of Economic Perspectives*, 3:4, 119–135.

Bernard, A.B. and J.B. Jensen (1995) "Exporters, Jobs and Wages in U.S. Manufacturing: 1976–1987," *Brookings Papers on Economic Activity*, 67–112.

Black, D. (1948) "On the Rationale of Group Decision-Making," *Journal of Political Economy*, 56:1, 23–34.

Blecker, R.A. (2009) "Steel," in K.A. Reinert, R.S. Rajan, A.J. Glass, and L.S. Davis (eds.), *The Princeton Encyclopedia of the World Economy*, Princeton University Press, 1030–1035.

Davidson, C., S. Matusz, and D. Nelson (2006) "Fairness and the Political Economy of Trade," *The World Economy*, 29:8, 989–1004.

Deardorff, A.V. (1998) "Technology, Trade, and Increasing Inequality: Does the Cause Matter for the Cure?" *Journal of International Economic Law*, 1:3, 353–376.

Deardorff, A.V. and R.M. Stern (1994) *The Stolper-Samuelson Theorem: A Golden Jubilee*, University of Michigan Press.

Donnelly, J. (2000) *Realism in International Relations*, Cambridge University Press.

The Economist (2002a) "Steel: Rust Never Sleeps," March 9.

The Economist (2002b) "Vietnam: Land and Freedom," June 15.

The Economist (2011) "Electoral Reform in Japan: Breaking the Backs of Farmers," January 29.

Freeman, R.B. (1995) "Are Your Wages Set in Beijing?" *Journal of Economic Perspectives*, 9:3, 15–32.

Fukuda, H., J. Dyck, and J. Stout (2003) "Rice Sector Policies in Japan," Economic Research Service, U.S. Department of Agriculture.

Gindling, T.H. and D. Robbins (2001) "Patterns and Sources of Changing Wage Inequality in Chile and Costa Rica during Structural Adjustment," *World Development*, 29:4, 725–745.

Heckscher, E. (1949) "The Effect of Japan Trade on the Distribution of Income," in H.S. Ellis and L.A. Metzler (eds.), *Readings in the Theory of International Trade*, Irwin, 1950, 272–300.

Henisz, W. and E.D. Mansfield (2006) "Votes and Vetoes: The Political Determinants of Commercial Openness," *International Studies Quarterly*, 50:1, 189–211.

Hiscox, M.J. (2004) "International Capital Mobility and Trade Politics: Capital Flows, Political Coalitions, and Lobbying," *Economics and Politics*, 16:3, 253–285.

[21] This is referred to as "Black's Theorem" or the "median voter model." It is not a perfect model, but it illustrates one possibility.

Jones, R.W. (1971) "A Three-Factor Model in Theory, Trade, and History," in J.N. Bhagwati et al., *Trade, Balance of Payments and Growth*, North Holland, 3–21.

Krugman, P. (2008) "Trade and Wages, Reconsidered," *Brookings Papers on Economic Activity*, Spring, 103–138.

Krugman, P. and R.Z. Lawrence (1996) "Trade, Jobs, and Wages," in P. Krugman, *Pop Internationalism*, MIT Press.

Marjit, S. and R. Archaryya (2009) "Trade and Wages," in K.A. Reinert, R.S. Rajan, A.J. Glass, and L.S. Davis (eds.), *The Princeton Encyclopedia of the World Economy*, Princeton University Press, 1108–1112.

Mayer, W. (1984) "Endogenous Tariff Formation," *American Economic Review*, 74:5, 970–985.

Milner, H.V. (1988) *Resisting Protectionism: Global Industries and the Politics of International Trade*, Princeton University Press.

Milner, H.V. (1997) *Interests, Institutions, and Information*, Princeton University Press.

Milner, H.V. (1999) "The Political Economy of International Trade," *Annual Review of Political Science*, 2, 91–114.

Ohlin, B. (1933) *International and Inter-Regional Trade*, Harvard University Press.

Panagariya, A. (2009) "Heckscher-Ohlin Model," in K.A. Reinert, R.S. Rajan, A.J. Glass, and L.S. Davis (eds.), *The Princeton Encyclopedia of the World Economy*, Princeton University Press, 591–597.

Reinert, K.A. and D.W. Roland-Holst (1998) "North-South Trade and Occupational Wages: Some Evidence from North America," *Review of International Economics*, 6:1, 74–89.

Richardson, J.D. (1995) "Income Inequality and Trade: How to Think, What to Conclude," *Journal of Economic Perspectives*, 9:3, 33–55.

Rodrik, D (1995) "Political Economy of Trade Policy," in G.M. Grossman and K. Rogoff (eds.), *Handbook of International Economics*, Vol. III, Elsevier, 1457–1494.

Robbins, D. and T.H. Gindling (1999) "Trade Liberalization and the Relative Wages for More-Skilled Workers in Costa Rica," *Review of Development Economics*, 3:2, 140–154.

Stolper, W. and P.A. Samuelson (1941) "Protection and Real Wages," *Review of Economic Studies*, 9:1, 58–73.

von Haberler, G. (1937) *The Theory of International Trade*, Macmillan.

Walter, A. and G. Sen (2009) *Analyzing the Global Political Economy*, Princeton University Press.

Wood, A. (1994) *North-South Trade, Employment, and Inequality: Changing Fortunes in a Skill-Driven World*, Oxford University Press.

Wood, A. (1997) "Openness and Wage Inequality in Developing Countries: The Latin American Challenge to East Asian Conventional Wisdom," *World Bank Economic Review*, 11:1, 33–57.

Wood, A. (2002) "Globalization and Wage Inequalities: A Synthesis of Three Theories," *Weltwirtschaftliches Archiv*, 138:1, 54–82.

6 Trade Policy Analysis

In Chapter 5, you saw that there are reasons to expect that landowners in Japan might oppose the import of rice from Vietnam or, for that matter, from any other country. This opposition to imports exists despite the overall gains to Japan from these imports due to a loss in landowners' income as a result of trade. Whether for these economic reasons, or for cultural reasons, demands for protection are common. For example, Ikuo Kanno, a fourth-generation Japanese rice farmer stated: "I believe that the value of agriculture can't be measured just by an economic yardstick. Japan has been a farming country for centuries, and rice farming is embedded in the culture. It should be preserved."[1] Indeed, as we discussed in Chapter 5, rice farming in Japan has been supported a great deal through various stringent limits on imports.

For an international affairs professional or a trade policy analyst, knowing that factor conditions lead to the demand for import protection is not enough. These individuals are often called on to assess, both qualitatively and quantitatively, the numerous impacts of government interventions in international trade. If you pursue an international economic affairs career, it is likely that you will either be involved in making these assessments or in interpreting the assessments made by someone else. Therefore, it is important for you to understand how the assessments are made. This is the purpose of the present chapter.

We begin our discussion of trade policy analysis by revisiting the model of absolute advantage in rice between Japan and Vietnam that we developed in Chapter 2. Next, we consider the large variety of trade policy measures available to governments. Then we analyze what happens when Japan introduces a **tariff** on its imports of rice. We also consider the **terms-of-trade effects** of this tariff. Next, we consider what happens when Japan introduces a **quota** on its imports of rice. Tariffs and quotas compose the basic means of protecting domestic markets from competition. It is important that you are familiar with both of these policies. Finally, we briefly take up trade policy analysis using the comparative advantage model of Chapter 3. For the interested reader, appendices to the chapter consider the case of the imperfect substitutes model, used in many kinds of trade policy analysis, and the case of tariff rate quotas (TRQs) used to protect the Japanese rice sector and other agricultural sectors.

Analytical elements used in this chapter:

Countries, *sectors*, and *factors of production*.

ABSOLUTE ADVANTAGE REVISITED

In Chapter 2, we developed a model of absolute advantage and applied it to trade in rice between Vietnam and Japan. This model is summarized in Figure 6.1. Recall from Chapter 2 that we assume the demand conditions in the two countries to be exactly the same. Consequently, we can use the same demand curve in both the diagrams of this figure. We also assume that supply conditions in the two countries are such that Vietnam's supply curve for rice is farther to the right than Japan's supply curve. Consequently, the autarky price of rice in Vietnam, P^V, is lower than the autarky price of rice in Japan, P^J. This gives Vietnam an absolute advantage in producing rice.

[1] Planet Rice (2000).

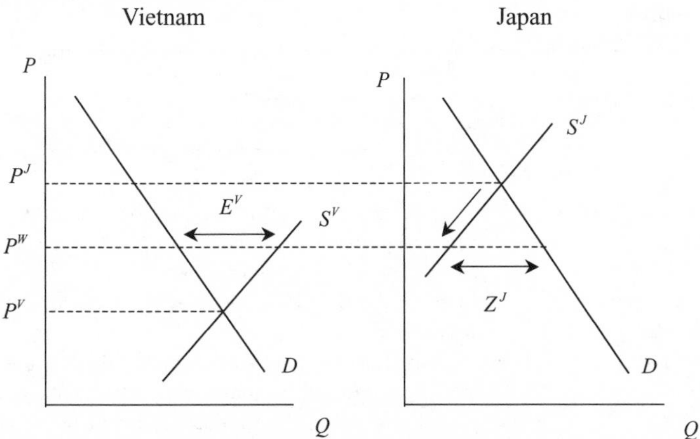

Figure 6.1. Absolute Advantage and Trade in the Rice Market

The world price settles between the two autarky prices. Vietnam exports rice, whereas Japan imports rice. The world price will adjust to ensure that Vietnam's exports are the same as Japan's imports.

Note that, in moving from autarky to trade in Figure 6.1, there is a reduction in domestic quantity supplied in Japan, as indicated by the downward arrow along S^J. It is possible that the firms producing rice in Japan would lobby the Japanese government to oppose this decrease in domestic quantity supplied, demanding protection from Vietnam exports. This is exactly what has happened in Japan, given the political voice of people like Ikuo Kanno mentioned previously. More generally, though, demands for protection are nearly universal. Indeed, because protective policies are so widespread in the world economy, analyzing them is an important sub-field of international economics.

TRADE POLICY MEASURES

When a country seeks to grant import protection to a sector of its economy, it can choose among a number of measures that can be broadly classified as either *tariffs* or *nontariff measures.* A tariff is a tax on imports. It is a very common trade policy used by almost all countries. There are two primary kinds of tariffs. A *specific tariff* is a fixed tax per physical unit of the import, and an *ad valorem* tariff is a percentage tax applied to the value of the import. Governments in the world trading system employ both types of tariffs.[2]

From the point of view of many trade policy analysts and the World Trade Organization (WTO), the ideal trading system would consist of only tariffs. Tariffs, particularly ad valorem tariffs, are seen as the most transparent kind of trade policy and one that is least susceptible to political manipulation and corruption. However, tariffs are far from the only type of trade policy. Therefore, the second category of trade policy measures we need to consider is the inclusive and large collection of **nontariff measures** (NTMs).[3]

[2] Bacchetta (2009) notes that there are three additional kinds of tariffs. A *compound tariff* has both an ad valorem component and a specific component. A *mixed tariff* takes on an ad valorem or a specific form, depending on which is higher. Finally, a *technical tariff* depends on the product's content and inputs.

[3] You might come across an older, less inclusive term of *nontariff barriers*, or NTBs.

Table 6.1. Nontariff measures

Category	Measure	Description
Tax-like measures	Anti-dumping (AD) duties	Tariff-like charges imposed on imports that are deemed by the imposing government to have been "dumped" or sold at "less than fair value" by the exporter.
	Countervailing duties (CVDs)	Tariff-like charges imposed on imports that are deemed by the imposing government to have been "unfairly" subsidized by the exporting country government.
	Temporary import surcharges	Extra import tariffs imposed in "emergency" circumstances of various kinds.
	Variable levies	Import tariffs whose size depends on the price of the imported good. They are usually imposed to help maintain a certain level of domestic price, particularly in agricultural sectors.
Cost-increasing measures	Standards and technical regulations (STRs) or technical barriers to trade (TBTs)	A large set of measures including certification guidelines, performance mandates, testing procedures, and labeling requirements designed to contribute to consumer safety, environmental protection, national security, product interoperability, and other goals.
	Sanitary and phytosanitary (SPS) requirements	Technical barriers to trade in the agricultural arena designed to protect plant, animal, and human health.
	Prior import deposits	Non–interest-bearing deposits equal to a percentage of the value of an imported good that must be deposited into a central bank for a specified amount of time.
	Customs procedures	Inspection and customs clearance procedures that can increase costs of imports and impose delays.
	Reference or minimum import prices	Official prices used to calculate import tariffs.
Quantitative measures	Import quota	A maximum import quantity set for a particular good.
	Tariff rate quota (TRQ)	Involves two tariff levels: a lower tariff for levels of imports within the quota and a higher tariff for levels of imports above the quota.
	Voluntary export restraint (VER)	An export quota that is "voluntarily" applied by the exporting country.
	Import licensing	The requirement that a license be obtained from the importing country government before a product can be imported.
	Foreign exchange controls	The allocation of foreign exchange by the importing country government among potential importers as a way to limit imports.
	Sanctions and embargoes	Export bans and trade embargoes imposed on countries for political reasons.
	Local or domestic content requirements	A requirement that imported goods must contain a minimum amount of intermediate products from the importing country.
	Import or export balancing requirements	A requirement that a firm importing intermediate products must export a certain amount.
Government procurement practices		The myriad processes that governments employ in determining their contract procurements and the posture of these contracts toward imported goods.

Sources: Takacs (2009) and Laird (1997)

The range of these NTMs is limited only by the imaginations of policymakers, and the particularly strange case of used automobile imports in Latin America is discussed in the accompanying box.

To get a handle of the numerous kinds of NTMs, we can follow Takacs (2009) and distinguish among four categories: tax-like measures, cost-increasing measures, quantitative trade restrictions, and government procurement policies. A number of examples of these are presented in Table 6.1. *Tax-like measures* include anti-dumping (AD) duties, countervailing duties (CVDs), temporary import surcharges, and variable levies. Dumping involves the price of an exported good being lower than the price of the same good in the exporting country, and AD duties can be applied in certain circumstances when dumping takes place. CVD measures "countervail" subsidies by exporters and again can be applied in certain circumstances. AD and CVD measures are together often referred to as "administrative protection" and form a veritable industry of trade policy analysis spanning national governments and trade policy law firms attempting to assure that trade is "fair."[4]

Cost-increasing measures include what is known both as standards and technical regulations (STRs) and technical barriers to trade (TBTs), sanitary and phytosanitary (SPS) requirements, prior import deposits, customs procedures, and reference or minimum import prices. STRs and TBTs are a growing area of trade policy activity and analysis.[5] It is one area where there are clear cases in which increasing protection can improve welfare in instances such as consumer health and safety. However, it is also an area where barriers are put in place simply for their protective effect. Customs procedures is another area that has received increased attention. This is for two reasons. First, there is a concern that slow customs clearance procedures in developing countries can be wasteful. Second, customs clearance, particularly in a "post-9/11" context, can be a real barrier for developing country exporters trying to enter developed country markets. Consequently, there is a concern with capacity building for developing country exporters in this area.

Used Automobile Protection in Latin America

In the wake of the debt crises of the early 1980s, Latin America embarked on a process of significant trade liberalization, reducing tariffs and removing quotas. In the case of used automobiles, however, this liberalization has not, in general, taken place. Many Latin American countries retain significant restrictions on the imports of used automobiles, even as liberalization has occurred in the new automobiles sector. What is more, the protective measures applied to used automobile imports have been rather creative.

As of 1999, seven relatively small Latin American countries imposed only minimal restrictions on imports of used automobiles. These countries were Bahamas, Barbados, Belize, Bolivia, El Salvador, Guatemala, and Panama. Some of these countries used "reference prices" to value the used automobiles. These reference prices were either domestically generated or published "Kelley Blue Book" values.

Five relatively small countries imposed clear restrictions on the imports of used automobiles. These countries were Costa Rica, Dominican Republic, Haiti, Honduras, and Nicaragua. A popular measure here was capped depreciation. For example, the

[4] For a review of AD and CVD measures from a legal perspective, see Chapters 10 and 11 of Matsushita, Schoenbaum, and Mavroidis (2006).

[5] See Wilson (2009).

Dominican Republic accepted invoices as the value of new automobiles, but it did not do so for used automobiles. Instead, the value of a used automobile was calculated using a depreciation schedule based on the price of an equivalent, new automobile in the current year. However, given the depreciation schedule, the price of the used automobile could not fall below 50 percent of the new automobile. As we know, the market prices of used automobiles are often substantially below 50 percent of equivalent, new automobiles, so this represented a discriminatory measure.

Jamaica, Peru, and Trinidad and Tobago imposed relatively severe protection measures against imports of used automobiles. Trinidad and Tobago required that used automobiles be *disassembled* before importation! Engines were often removed from used vehicles before importation and shipped separately. Peru and Jamaica both had age-delimited bans. Beginning in 1996, Peru banned automobiles over five years old and commercial vehicles over eight years old. Furthermore, imported used automobiles with fewer than 24 seats faced a "selective consumption tax" of 45 percent, whereas similar new automobiles faced a rate of only 20 percent. In 1998, Jamaica's motor vehicle policy was tightened to allow only licensed used automobile dealers to import automobiles no older than four years old and light commercial vehicles no older than five years old.

Finally, in 1999, nine of the largest Latin American countries prohibited imports of used automobiles altogether. These countries were Argentina, Brazil, Chile, Colombia, Ecuador, Mexico, Paraguay, Uruguay, and Venezuela. In the cases of Argentina, Brazil, Paraguay, and Uruguay, this import ban was part of the Mercosur preferential trade agreement (see Chapter 8). It is clear that, when it comes to used automobiles, even "free trade" countries such as Chile chose the most severe form of protection.

Source: Pelletiere and Reinert (2002)

Quantitative measures is a large group of NTMs including import quotas, tariff rate quotas (TRQs), voluntary export restraints (VERs), import licensing, foreign exchange controls, sanctions and embargoes, local or domestic content requirements, and import or export balancing requirements. As will be discussed in Chapter 7, for many years, import quotas were the norm in agriculture, textiles, and clothing trade. This is no longer the case among WTO members, but can still exist in nonmember countries. TRQs, however, are still in use in agricultural sectors, including the Japanese rice sector. These involve two tariff levels: a lower tariff for levels of imports within the quota (the within-quota tariff) and a higher tariff for levels of imports above the quota (the out-of-quota tariff). These complexities make it complicated to administer and analyze.[6] Sanctions and embargoes are a perennial topic with regard to their effectiveness in influencing regimes deemed to be unacceptable (e.g., Apartheid South Africa or present-day Myanmar).

Government procurement practices concern the processes that governments employ in determining their contract procurements and the posture of these contracts toward imported goods. Takacs (2009) reminds us that "In most countries, regardless of the stage of development, government is the single largest purchaser of goods and services" (p. 845). That makes the government procurement processes and their specific posture toward imports an important matter.

From this discussion and the content of Table 6.1, it is clear that trade policies are numerous. We are going to simplify greatly in this chapter and focus on the basic

[6] See Hertel and Martin (2000), de Gorter (2009), and the appendix to this chapter.

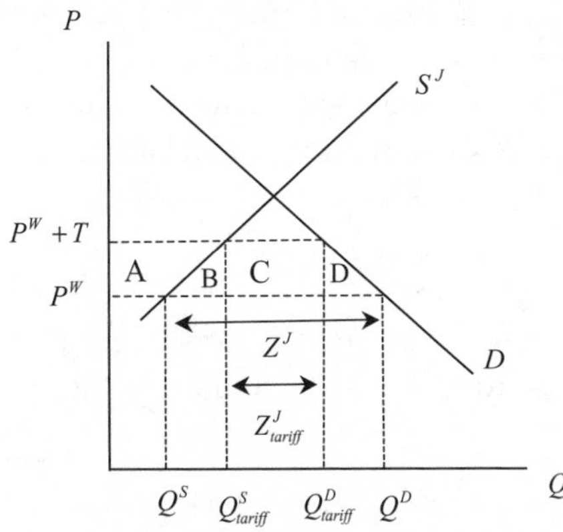

Figure 6.2. A Tariff on Japan's Imports of Rice

analysis of a tariff and quota within the absolute advantage framework. We begin with the case of a tariff.

A TARIFF

As mentioned earlier, there are two kinds of tariffs, a specific tariff and an ad valorem tariff. For our graphical analysis in this chapter, it is much simpler to consider a specific tariff, so that is what we will do. The basic results you will learn here, however, will also apply to an ad valorem tariff. Let's introduce a specific tariff on Japan's imports of rice. This policy is depicted in Figure 6.2. The world price is P^W. At this price, Japanese rice suppliers choose to supply Q^S, and Japanese consumers demand Q^D. The difference, $Q^D - Q^S = Z^J$, is imported from Vietnam.

Suppose then that the Japanese government imposes a specific tariff of T on its imports of rice from Vietnam. This raises the domestic price of the imported product above the world price to $P^W + T$. In the case of Japanese rice, the domestic price is many times larger than the world price. The increase in the domestic price of rice above the world price has a number of effects. Japan's production of rice expands from Q^S to Q^S_{tariff}. This expansion in output is what the Japanese rice farmers hoped to gain from the tariff. Domestic consumption of rice falls from Q^D to Q^D_{tariff}. Imports fall from Z^J to Z^J_{tariff}. The tariff has suppressed the importing relationship of Japan with Vietnam.[7]

In addition to the quantity effects of a tariff, there is also a set of welfare and revenue effects. These involve Japan's households, firms, and government. What has happened to the consumer surplus of Japanese households in Figure 6.2?[8] Examining this diagram carefully, you should be able to see that the tariff has caused consumer surplus to fall by area A+B+C+D. Because Japanese rice consumers are paying more and consuming less, this fall in consumer surplus makes sense.

What has happened to the producer surplus of Japanese firms? Again examining the diagram carefully, you should be able to see that producer surplus has increased by area A. Japanese rice producers are better off as a result of the tariff; their welfare

[7] This makes sense. A tariff is a tax, and a tax on any activity causes the amount of that activity to decrease. In this case, the taxed activity is rice imports by Japan.

[8] Remember that the concepts of consumer and producer surplus are covered in the appendix to Chapter 2. Please review this appendix if necessary.

has increased. Because Japanese producers are receiving more for their product and producing more as well, this increase in producer surplus makes sense.

What about the Japanese government? It is receiving revenue from the import tax. How much revenue? The tariff is T, and the post-tariff import level is Z^J_{tariff}. Therefore, the tariff revenue is $T \times Z^J_{tariff}$, or area C in Figure 6.2.[9]

Economists or trade policy analysts are often asked to assess the *net welfare effect* of a trade policy. This standard measure summarizes the welfare impact of the policy for the country as a whole. What would the net welfare effect be? In this case, we take the gains to firms and the government and subtract the losses to households. Doing this, we have:

$$N = A + C - (A + B + C + D) = -(B + D) \qquad (6.1)$$

Area A is a transfer from consumers to producers, whereas area C is a transfer from consumers to the government. These areas cancel out with each other in Equation 6.1. That leaves areas B and D. There is a net welfare *loss* of the tariff equal to areas B+D. From an economic standpoint, the tariff hurts the Japanese society as a whole. Although it benefits producers and government, the losses imposed on consumers outweigh these benefits. The two triangles B and D are similar to the "deadweight loss" triangle of a monopoly you learned about in introductory microeconomics. They represent economic or allocative inefficiency. In certain situations, tariffs do not necessarily cause a net welfare loss. One such situation, a *terms-of-trade* gain, is explored in the next section.

Please note one more thing. Figure 6.2 gives us information on what happens to Japanese rice output as a result of the tariff. As we stated above, Japanese rice output increases from Q^S to Q^S_{tariff}. Given information on the employment/output ratio in this sector, we could translate the change in output into a change in employment. From the point of view of Japan politicians, this employment effect is important. Therefore, trade policy analysts often include an estimate of the employment effects of tariffs and other trade policies.

TERMS-OF-TRADE EFFECTS

In some important cases, the analysis of the preceding section is incomplete. Why? We have showed that, when Japan imposes a tariff on its imports from Vietnam, the amount of these imports decreases. Looking at Figure 6.1, however, we can see that, as Japan's imports of rice decrease, there will be excess supply in the world market for rice. As we discussed in Chapter 2, this excess supply of rice will cause the world price to fall. Because Japan is importing rice, this is a good thing for this country. The fall in the price of an import good is one kind of terms-of-trade effect. It is depicted in Figure 6.3.

The main difference between Figure 6.3 and Figure 6.2 is that, in Figure 6.3, the world price does not stay constant as the Japanese government places a tariff on imports of rice. The world price before the tariff is P^W. After the tariff, the world price falls to

[9] There is an important public finance lesson here. An increase in the import tax (tariff) from zero to T reduces the potential *tax base* from Z^J to Z^J_{tariff}. All increases in taxes decrease the base on which the tax is assessed. For many developing countries, tariffs are an important source of government revenue, so this tax base reduction can be important.

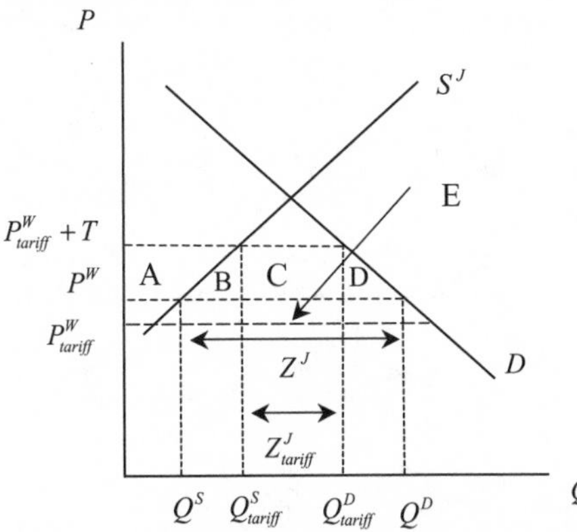

Figure 6.3. The Terms-of-Trade Effect of Japan's Tariff

P^W_{tariff}, and the tariff is placed on top of this lower world price. Therefore, after the tariff is in place, the domestic price is $P^W_{tariff} + T$. The fall in the world price of rice affects the welfare analysis of the tariff. Consumer surplus in Japan falls by (A+B+C+D), as in Figure 6.2. Producer surplus in Japan rises by A, as in Figure 6.2. Japan government revenue, however, is now area C + E. Therefore, the net welfare effect is:

$$N = A + (C + E) - (A + B + C + D) = -(B + D) + E \quad (6.2)$$

The net welfare effect in Figure 6.3 is different than in Figure 6.2. There is still the efficiency loss of B+D as in the previous case. Now, however, there is a *terms-of-trade gain* of area E in equation 6.2. For this reason, we cannot say whether the tariff hurts welfare in Japan or not. If the world price falls by a lot, E could be very large, even larger than (B+D). However, we should not jump to the conclusion that, given large terms-of-trade effects, tariffs are good for countries. This is because Vietnam would probably not sit idly by when Japan imposes a tariff on imports of rice. Vietnam could instead *retaliate* by imposing a tariff on a product that Japan exports. This tariff would lower the world price of Japan's export good, which would hurt Japan's welfare. Japan might further retaliate in turn. This tit-for-tat retaliation process in often known as a *trade war*, and it is always welfare reducing in the end. It is to prevent such trade wars that the General Agreement on Tariffs and Trade (GATT) was drawn up after World War II. We discuss the GATT and its successor, the World Trade Organization (WTO), in Chapter 7.

A QUOTA

An import **quota** is a quantitative restriction on imports and one important type of NTM. When the Japanese government imposes a quota on rice imports, it says to rice exporters and domestic importers, we will allow imports up to this amount, and no more! Suppose that instead of imposing a tariff as in Figures 6.2 and 6.3, Japan imposes a quota. We examine this in Figure 6.4.

Before the quota, rice imports are $Z^J = Q^D - Q^S$. For political economy of trade reasons, the Japanese government is not satisfied with this outcome. It decides to restrict imports to a smaller amount $Z^J_{quota} = Q^D_{quota} - Q^S_{quota}$. This policy induces a shortage of rice relative to the initial situation without the quota. The domestic price of rice in Japan rises from P^W to P_{quota}. The difference between these two prices is known as the

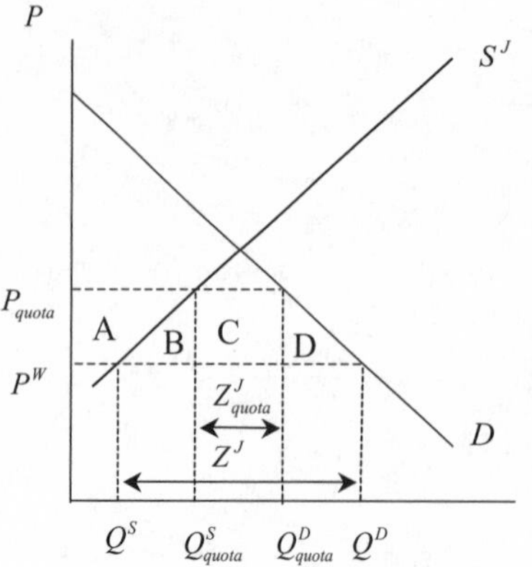

Figure 6.4. A Quota on Japan's Rice Imports

quota premium. As with the case of a tariff, consumer surplus falls by area A+B+C+D, and producer surplus increases by area A. The new matter we must deal with in the case of a quota is the nature of area C.

The quota policy is typically administered via a system of **import licenses.** In effect, the quota policy has restricted the supply of import licenses in the world. The area C represents the extra value of the right to import amount Z^J_{quota}. It is known as **quota rents.**[10] Who receives the rents depends on how the quota licenses are allocated. There are two common possibilities[11]:

1. Import licenses are *allocated to domestic (Japanese) importers.* Here, the quota rents accrue to the importers, so they remain within the country. They are a *gain to Japan.*
2. Import licenses are *allocated to foreign (Vietnamese) exporters.* Here, the quota rents accrue to these exporters, so they leave the country. They are a *loss to Japan.*

With the above in mind, we can address the question of the net welfare effect of the quota. In the case of import licenses allocated to *domestic* importers, the area C is a transfer from domestic consumers to domestic importers. Area C is a loss to consumers and a gain to importers for a net effect of zero for Japan as a whole. Our net welfare effect is just like a specific tariff, equal to the quota premium $P_{quota} - P^W$, that results in an import level of Z^J_{quota} (known as the *equivalent tariff*):

$$N = A + C - (A + B + C + D) = -(B + D) \tag{6.3}$$

In the case of import licenses allocated to *foreign* exporters, area C is a transfer from domestic consumers to these foreign exporters. It is no longer a net loss of zero, because the loss to consumers is not offset by a gain to domestic importers. Our net welfare effect is simply the gain to firms less the loss to consumers:

$$N = A - (A + B + C + D) = -(B + C + D) \tag{6.4}$$

In this case, the quota is worse than a tariff that results in an import level of Z^J_{quota}.

[10] Corden (1997) noted that "(T)here will be quota profits . . . received by the lucky people who obtain the import licenses. These quota profits are *rents* because they are not received as payments for any services, and any reduction in these profits would not affect the supply of any resource" (p. 127).

[11] There is a third possibility in which the import licenses are auctioned to the highest bidder by the government. Because the quota auction proceeds accrue domestically (to the government), the welfare properties of this case are like that of the case in which the import licenses are allocated to domestic importers.

Given what we have just said, suppose you were a government official administering quota policy. Which of the above two alternatives would you choose: a quota allocated to domestic importers or a quota allocated to foreign exporters? Your answer is probably the quota allocated to domestic importers because these have the smaller welfare loss. Now, here is a puzzle: when quotas were in active use, many governments chose a foreign allocated quota.[12] Why? One possibility is that they were uninformed about the economic implications of their choices. Another possibility is that political considerations caused such a choice. For some reason, governments found it beneficial from a political point of view to assist foreigners, particularly developing countries. A better approach from the viewpoint of developing country exporters, however, would have been to remove the quota altogether.

In this and the previous two sections, we have discussed four trade policy possibilities: a tariff, a tariff with terms-of-trade effects, a domestic-allocated quota, and a foreign-allocated quota. Before moving on to briefly discuss comparative advantage analyses of trade policies, let's summarize these four possibilities in a box:

Tariff: unambiguous net welfare loss due to consumer surplus loss outweighing gains in producer surplus and government revenue

Tariff with terms-of-trade effects: ambiguous net welfare effect due to terms of trade gain (fall in world price) potentially outweighing the efficiency loss

Domestic-allocated quota: unambiguous net welfare loss due to consumer surplus loss outweighing gains in producer surplus and quota rents

Foreign-allocated quota: unambiguous net welfare loss that exceeds that of the domestic-allocated quota case and equivalent tariff

COMPARATIVE ADVANTAGE MODELS

Our analysis of trade policies in this chapter has been based on the absolute advantage model of Chapter 2. The absolute advantage model has taken us quite far. We have shown how one can examine trade policies to make estimates of production, consumption, trade, employment, and welfare impacts. In many instances, however, the effects of trade policies go beyond a single sector. Protecting a large sector such as automobiles can draw resources from other sectors into the protected automobile sector. Perhaps workers in the metal furniture sector will move into the automobile sector as it expands under protection. Also, protecting a large intermediate product sector, like petroleum or steel, can raise costs for other sectors that use petroleum or steel in their production processes.

In these cases, trade policy analysts turn to models of comparative advantage such as those we discussed in Chapter 3. As you recall, the comparative advantage model analyzes more than one sector simultaneously (e.g., rice and motorcycles). In some instances, this is an important feature. Such models are much more complicated than the absolute advantage models we considered in this chapter, and we will not formally discuss them here. You should, however, be aware of their use. At the level of basic

[12] For example, this was the case for quotas in textiles and clothing until they were phased out at the end of 2004.

theory, the central insight of the comparative advantage approach includes the fact that a protective measure in one sector acts as an implicit tax on production in other sectors, reducing their output levels. This is the result of the opportunity costs of production we discussed in Chapter 3.[13]

Given the importance of the comparative advantage perspective in many trade policy issues, trade policy analysts have turned to mathematical models of comparative advantage known as applied general equilibrium (AGE) models.[14] These combine the insights of the comparative advantage model of Chapter 3 with the framework of the imperfect substitutes model discussed in the appendix to this chapter. Some years ago, constructing an AGE model for trade policy analysis was a substantial undertaking. More recently, however, a few standard models have eased the difficulty of using them. We discuss one such standard model in the accompanying box. We will also encounter AGE models again in Chapter 8 in the context of preferential trade agreements (PTAs).

The Global Trade Analysis Project

The Global Trade Analysis Project (GTAP) began in 1993 and is based at Purdue University. It has evolved into a global network of trade policy analysts conducting research in an applied general equilibrium (AGE) framework. At its core, GTAP is a source for a database of global production and trade that is combined with a standard GTAP AGE model. Around this core is a global network of users, developers, and contributors who use the database and the model or just the database and their own model. At the time of this writing, the latest version of the database is GTAP 7, describing the world economy in 2004 with 113 regions/countries and 57 sectors. The latest version of the model was GTAP 6.2a, released in 2007.

The GTAP network of trade policy analysts convene each year in an annual conference, and short courses on using the GTAP database and model are held around the world. This effort has advanced the use of AGE models of trade policy in both national governments and global organizations such as the United Nations. In addition, multilateral financial institutions often rely on the GTAP model or database for their own trade policy analysis. For example, the World Bank's Linkage model, used to simulate the Doha Round of multilateral trade negotiations (see Chapter 7), relies on the GTAP database.

Efforts such as GTAP have contributed immensely to the ease and widespread use of the comparative advantage framework in trade policy analysis. They are a central tool for trade policy analysis.

Sources: Hertel (1997), van der Mensbrugghe (2005), and https://www.gtap.agecon.purdue.edu

CONCLUSION

In order to help protect the losers of increased international trade, most countries of the world engage in trade policies. The supply and demand analysis of the absolute advantage model allows us to discover the effects of these trade policies on production,

[13] See Chapters 15 and 16 of Markusen et al. (1995).

[14] On AGE models in general, see Reinert (2009) and references therein.

consumption, trade, welfare, and employment. In this chapter, we have analyzed tariffs, tariffs with terms-of-trade effects, and quotas. The appendix considers the important cases of the imperfect substitutes model and tariff rate quotas. In addition, we briefly mentioned trade policy analysis based on comparative advantage models of trade. In general, the intervention in free trade reduces the overall welfare of the country intervening. However, certain groups might benefit from these policies, which is why they are usually implemented.

This chapter has engaged in formal, economic analysis of trade policies. In Chapter 7, we will engage in a more institutional or legal analysis of trade policies when we examine the World Trade Organization. In practice, trade policy analysis is a combination of formal economic analysis and institutional or legal analysis. The marriage of these two perspectives is what allows for a full appreciation of trade policies.

REVIEW EXERCISES

1. Consider Figure 6.2. For a given T, what would be the impact of an *increase in supply* (a shift of the supply curve to the right) on government revenue? What would be the impact of an *increase in demand* (a shift of the demand curve to the right)?
2. In Figure 6.3, we introduced the terms-of-trade effects of Japan's tariff on imports of rice. The terms-of-trade effect (area E in the diagram) was positive for Japan. In a new diagram similar to Figure 6.1, show that these terms-of-trade effects adversely affect the welfare of Vietnam.
3. Consider our diagram of a quota in Figure 6.4. Suppose the government reduced the quota to below Z^J_{quota}. What would happen to the *quota premium*? Can you say with certainty what would happen to the total *quota rent*? What would this depend on?
4. Trade protection is often used to maintain employment in a sector. Given our analysis, what do you think of this approach to maintaining employment? Can you think of any other measures that might also maintain employment in a sector?

FURTHER READING AND WEB RESOURCES

For some fundamental introductions to trade policy analysis, see Vousden (1990), Corden (1997), and Francois and Reinert (1997). For the analysis of additional trade policies using the absolute advantage framework, see the appendix to Hoekman and Kostecki (2009). See Anderson (2005) for the role economics has played in trade policy analysis in the post–World War II era and an excellent set of references. Goode (2003) provides an excellent dictionary of the plethora of trade policy terms. You can visit the Global Trade Analysis Project website at https://www.gtap.agecon.purdue.edu.

APPENDIX A: THE IMPERFECT SUBSTITUTES MODEL

The absolute advantage model used in this chapter assumes that the imported good and domestic competing goods are perfect substitutes. In a number of instances, however, trade policy analysts want to allow for the possibility that the imported and domestic

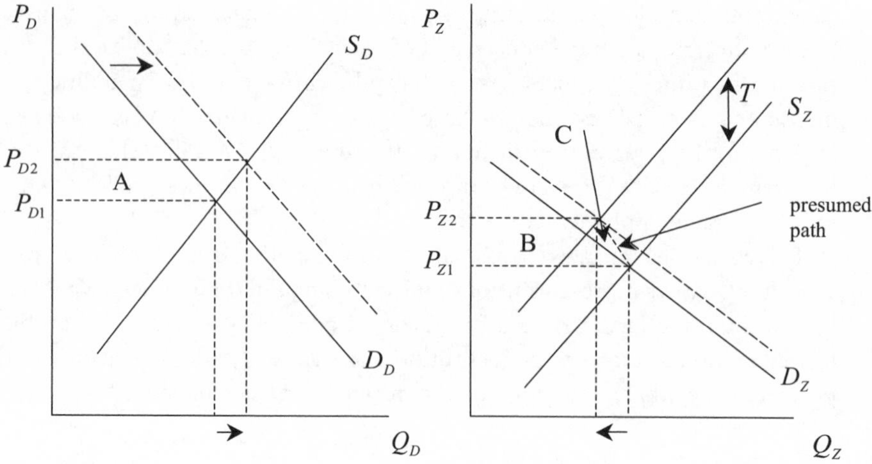

Figure 6.5. The Imperfect Substitute Model

competing goods are *imperfect* substitutes.[15] This leads us to what is now known as the imperfect substitutes model depicted in Figure 6.5.[16] This figure allows for the terms-of-trade effects described in this chapter.

The important difference between Figure 6.5 and those previously considered in this chapter is that there are now *two* closely related markets, one for the imported good Z and another for a domestic competing good D. The demand curves for these two markets are related through the cross-price elasticity of demand between the two goods. The initial equilibrium in the absence of a tariff results in the two prices P_{Z1} and P_{D1}. The imposition of a specific tariff T on imports of good Z causes the supply curve of this good to shift upward by the amount of the tariff, raising the domestic price of the imported good along the demand curve. The increase in the price of good Z affects the demand for good D, shifting the curve out as households substitute toward the domestic good. This increases the domestic price of good D, which in turn causes a substitution toward good Z and a shift out of the demand curve for imports. These two substitution effects are *simultaneous*, and the resulting, new prices are P_{Z2} and P_{D2}.

We next consider the welfare effects of the tariff in this imperfect substitutes framework. In the market for the domestic good, there is an increase in producer surplus along the supply curve equal to trapezoid A (extending from the vertical price axis all the way to the supply curve). This entire area, however, comes as a cost to the consumers, with the producer gain and the consumer loss exactly offsetting each other. In the market of the imported good, there are no domestic producers to account for. The estimation of the consumer welfare effect is troubled by the fact that both the supply curve and the demand curve in the market for good Z have shifted. The standard approach to this is to measure the change in consumer surplus along the presumed path between the initial and final equilibria points. The resulting consumer surplus loss is the trapezoid B+C. Rectangle B represents an increase in tariff revenue, so the entire net welfare effect in Figure 6.5 is just triangle C.

[15] This is one type of product differentiation known as *product differentiation by country of origin* that is related to explanations of intra-industry trade we discussed in Chapter 4. An early contribution to this approach was Armington (1969).

[16] The original contribution on this model was Baldwin and Murray (1977). A more explicit version was provided by Rouslang and Suomela (1988).

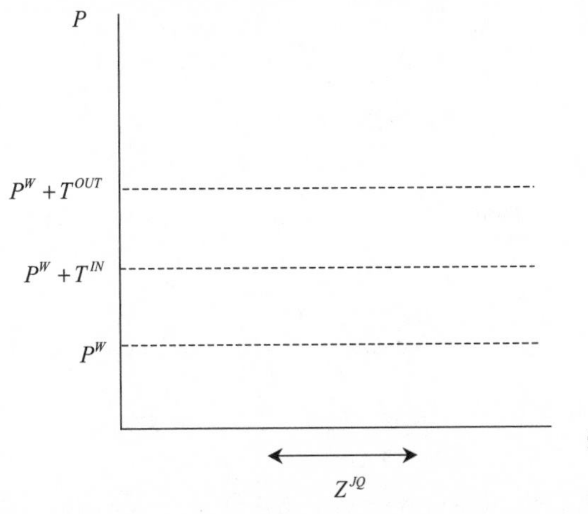

Figure 6.6. Framework for Analyzing Japan's Tariff Rate Quota on Rice

One important aspect of Figure 6.5 is that, discounting for the effect of the shift of the demand curve, the rise in the domestic price of the imported good is less than the tariff. This is because there is a movement in world quantity supplied down S_Z and a resulting decline in the border price of the imported good. This is the terms-of-trade effect we discussed in this chapter. The terms-of-trade effect has the property of reducing the height of the net welfare triangle C and is present unless the import supply curve S_Z is horizontal or perfectly elastic.

This might seem to be a more complicated approach to trade policy analysis than the perfect substitutes case of Figures 6.2 and 6.3. However, the approach is *widely used*, particularly in the analysis of AD and CVD cases by national governments. For this reason, it is very much worth understanding.

APPENDIX B: A TARIFF RATE QUOTA

In Chapter 7, we will discuss the Uruguay Round of multilateral trade negotiations and its Agreement on Agriculture. One implication of the Agreement on Agriculture is that many developed countries and some developing countries now impose **tariff rate quotas** (TRQs) on imports of agricultural goods.[17] A TRQ involves two tariff levels: a lower tariff for levels of imports within the quota and a higher tariff for levels of imports above the quota. Suppose Japan were to impose a TRQ on imports of rice. This policy can be stated as follows. Up to the quota amount Z^{JQ}, Japan applies a *within-quota tariff rate* of T^{IN}. Above the quota amount Z^{JQ}, Japan applies a larger, *out-of-quota tariff rate* of T^{OUT}. To analyze this policy, it is best to consider three cases:

Case I: $Z^J < Z^{JQ}$
Case II: $Z^J = Z^{JQ}$
Case III: $Z^J > Z^{JQ}$

We are going to consider each of these three cases in turn. For each, we are going to use a diagram set out along the lines illustrated in Figure 6.6. The quota amount, Z^{JQ}, is plotted along the horizontal axis, and this distance is indicated with a double-headed arrow. Along the vertical axis, there are three prices indicated. The first, lowest

[17] See Hertel and Martin (2000) and de Gorter (2009).

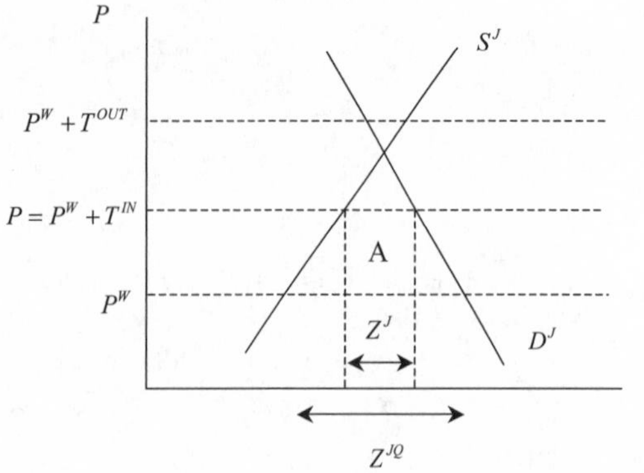

Figure 6.7. Case I of Japan's Tariff Rate Quota on Rice

price is the world price of imported rice, P^W. To simplify our analysis here, we assume that Japan cannot affect this world price. That is, there are none of the terms-of-trade effects we discussed in this chapter. The second, higher price is the world price plus the within-quota tariff rate of T^{IN}. The third, higher price is the world price plus the out-of-quota tariff rate of T^{OUT}.

We are going to use the framework depicted in Figure 6.6 to analyze the three cases mentioned above. Case I is presented in Figure 6.7. Here the level of rice imports is within the quota amount. Therefore, the domestic price P is determined by the lower tariff value, T^{IN}, and the tariff revenue collected by the government is area A.

Case II is presented in Figure 6.8. Here the level of rice imports is exactly equal to the quota amount. In this case, the domestic price is somewhere between the two tariff-inclusive prices. That is, $P^W + T^{IN} \leq P \leq P^W + T^{OUT}$. As in Case I, the tariff revenue collected by the government is area A. However, if the positions of the Japanese supply and demand curves for rice cause the domestic price P to be above $P^W + T^{IN}$, then there are also quota rents equal to area B.

Case III is presented in Figure 6.9. Here the level of rice imports exceeds the quota amount. Therefore, the domestic price P is determined by the higher tariff value. The total tariff revenue collected by the government is composed of three areas. Area A represents the tariff revenue collected on the imports that are within quota. Areas C and D represent the additional tariff revenue collected on the imports that are above

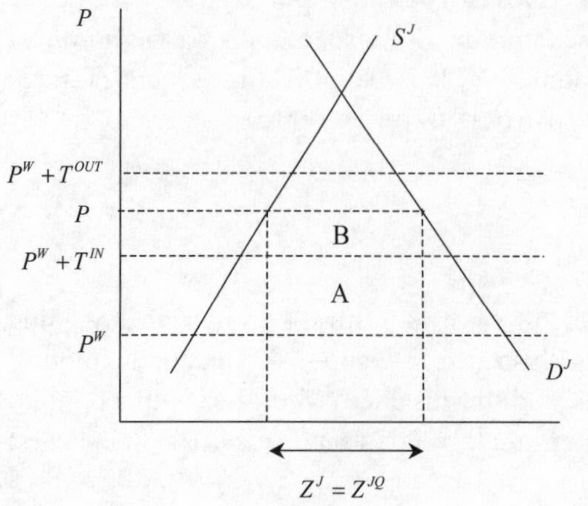

Figure 6.8. Case II of Japan's Tariff Rate Quota on Rice

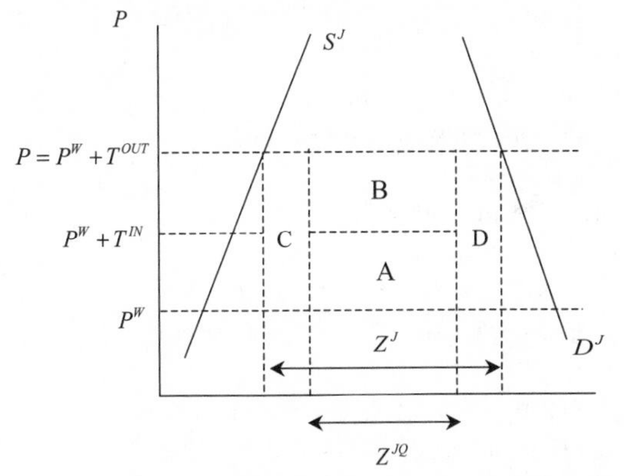

Figure 6.9. Case III of Japan's Tariff Rate Quota on Rice

quota. In addition, as in Case II, there are quota rents on the quota amount equal to area B.

Readers of this appendix will no doubt get the impression that the analysis of TRQs is a bit complicated. Unfortunately, it is simply a reality of the modern world trading system and requires some patience and persistence on the part of the student or professional. The world is a complex place, and our analysis of it often needs to be complex as well.

REFERENCES

Anderson, K. (2005) "Setting the Trade Policy Agenda: What Role for Economists?" *Journal of World Trade*, 39:2, 341–381.

Armington, P. (1969) "A Theory of Demand for Products Distinguished by Place of Production," *IMF Staff Papers*, 16:3, 159–176.

Bacchetta, M. (2009) "Tariffs," in K.A. Reinert, R.S. Rajan, A.J. Glass, and L.S. Davis (eds.), *The Princeton Encyclopedia of the World Economy*, Princeton University Press, 1063–1067.

Baldwin, R.E. and T. Murray (1977) "MFN Tariff Reductions and Developing Country Trade under the GSP," *Economic Journal*, 87:345, 30–46.

Corden, W.M. (1997) *Trade Policy and Economic Welfare*, Oxford University Press.

de Gorter, H. (2009) "Tariff Rate Quotas," in K.A. Reinert, R.S. Rajan, A.J. Glass, and L.S. Davis (eds.), *The Princeton Encyclopedia of the World Economy*, Princeton University Press, 1060–1063.

Francois, J.F. and K.A. Reinert (eds.) (1997) *Applied Methods for Trade Policy Analysis: A Handbook*, Cambridge University Press.

Goode, W. (2003) *Dictionary of Trade Policy Terms*, Cambridge University Press.

Hertel, T.W. (1997) *Global Trade Analysis: Modeling and Applications*, Cambridge University Press.

Hertel, T.W. and W. Martin (2000) "Liberalising Agriculture and Manufactures in a Millennium Round: Implications for Developing Countries," *The World Economy*, 23:4, 455–469.

Hoekman, B.M. and M.M. Kostecki (2009) *The Political Economy of the World Trading System*, Oxford University Press.

Laird, S. (1997) "Quantifying Commercial Policies," in *Applied Methods for Trade Policy Analysis: A Handbook*, Cambridge University Press, 27–75.

Markusen, J.R., J.R. Melvin, W.H. Kaempfer, and K.E. Maskus (1995) *International Trade: Theory and Evidence*, McGraw-Hill.

Matsushita, M., T.J. Schoenbaum, and P.C. Mavroidis (2006) *The World Trade Organization: Law, Practice, and Policy*, Oxford University Press.

van der Mensbrugghe, D. (2005) *Linkage Technical Reference Document*, World Bank.

Pelletiere, D. and K.A. Reinert (2002) "The Political Economy of Used Automobile Protection in Latin America," *The World Economy*, 25:7, 1019–1037.

Planet Rice (2000) "Japan to USA: Rice Farming is Our Culture: Don't Interfere," http://www.planetrice.net, November 26.

Reinert, K.A. (2009) "Applied General Equilibrium Models," in K.A. Reinert, R.S. Rajan, A.J. Glass, and L.S. Davis (eds.), *Princeton Encyclopedia of the World Economy*, Princeton University Press, 74–79.

Rouslang, D.J. and J.W. Suomela (1988) "Calculating the Welfare Costs of Import Restrictions in the Imperfect Substitutes Model," *Applied Economics*, 20:5, 691–700.

Takacs, W. (2009) "Nontariff Measures," in K.A. Reinert, R.S. Rajan, A.J. Glass, and L.S. Davis (eds.), *The Princeton Encyclopedia of the World Economy*, Princeton University Press, 843–847.

Vousden, N. (1990) *The Economics of Trade Protection*, Cambridge University Press.

Wilson, J.S. (2009) "Technical Barriers to Trade," in K.A. Reinert, R.S. Rajan, A.J. Glass, and L.S. Davis (eds.), *The Princeton Encyclopedia of the World Economy*, Princeton University Press, 1067–1070.

7 The World Trade Organization

Geneva is a beautiful city, and walking along Lake Geneva is an activity enjoyed by many of its residents and tourists. If you begin in downtown Geneva and proceed along the northwestern shore of Lake Geneva, you will have a grand view of the beautiful water jet in the middle of the lake. *Quai du Mont Blanc* turns into *Quai Wilson*, and you will then proceed by a number of statues and pleasant, open parks. Next, you will enter into the wooded *Parc Mon Repos* and proceed by the Graduate Institute of International and Development Studies. Finally, you will walk between a large, gray building and the lake. If you turn to face this building, you will be looking at the **World Trade Organization** (WTO), an organization both lauded and vilified with equal intensity by various groups with concerns about trade policy.

Although many individuals and groups have strong opinions about the World Trade Organization, most know very little about it. This chapter is dedicated to making sure you understand the key aspects of this important institution of world trade. Later in the book, you will also be introduced to the International Monetary Fund and the World Bank, important institutions of international finance and international economic development, respectively. To develop your understanding of the WTO, we first take up its precursor, the **General Agreement on Tariffs and Trade** (GATT). Here we undertake a historical examination of the GATT and introduce the principles it established for the conduct of international trade in goods. Next, we turn to the WTO itself, as established by the 1994 Marrakesh Agreement. Here we cover the main provisions of the Marrakesh Agreement in the areas of goods, services, intellectual property, and dispute settlement. We also consider the issue of trade and the environment within the WTO. Finally, we take up the current round of **multilateral trade negotiations** in the form of the Doha Round.

Nobel Laureate Douglass North (1990) defined institutions as "humanly devised constraints that shape human interaction" (p. 3). A less formal definition is as "the rules of the game." As an institution of international trade, the WTO sets out the rules of the global trading game. These rules have force as international economic law, and a careful study of the WTO takes place on the boundary of economics and law. This, in turn, involves a subtle change in vocabulary that may appear odd or unnecessary at first. Trust that it is indeed necessary. The terms we introduce here are widely accepted and utilized in the field of international trade among economists, lawyers, and policy analysts.

> Analytical elements used in this chapter:
>
> *Countries* and *sectors*.

THE GENERAL AGREEMENT ON TARIFFS AND TRADE

During World War II, the United States and Britain began developing the outlines of a set of post-war, economic institutions. The specifics of the plan were negotiated in July 1944 at the Bretton Woods Conference in Bretton Woods, New Hampshire. The conference set up the International Bank for Reconstruction and Development (World Bank) and the International Monetary Fund, discussed in Chapters 23 and 17, respectively. The conference also noted, however, that there should be a third international organization in the realm of international trade.

Table 7.1. GATT/WTO rounds of multilateral trade negotiations

Name of round	Years	Number of countries	Auspices
Geneva	1947	23	GATT
Annecy	1949	29	GATT
Torquay	1950–1951	32	GATT
Geneva	1955–1956	33	GATT
Dillon	1960–1961	39	GATT
Kennedy	1963–1967	74	GATT
Tokyo	1973–1979	99	GATT
Uruguay	1986–1994	117	GATT
Doha Round	2001–	Over 150	WTO

Source: World Trade Organization, www.wto.org

In 1945, the United States indeed attempted to launch the idea of an International Trade Organization (ITO), and this proposal was taken up by the United Nations Economic and Social Council in a 1946 meeting in London to begin work on an ITO charter. In early 1947, a draft General Agreement on Tariffs and Trade (GATT) based on the commercial language of the draft ITO charter was prepared at a meeting in the United States. This led to a later meeting that year in Geneva, where 23 countries (13 developed and 10 developing) signed the Final Act of the GATT. The ITO charter itself was finalized at a 1948 meeting in Havana, Cuba. However, in 1950, the U.S. government announced that it would *not* seek U.S. congressional ratification of the Havana Charter, effectively terminating the ITO plan. Consequently, the vehicle for post-war trade negotiations became the GATT.[1]

Between 1946 and 1994, the GATT provided a framework for a number of "rounds" of multilateral trade negotiations, the most recently concluded being the Uruguay Round. These rounds, along with the WTO-sponsored Doha Round, are listed in Table 7.1. The GATT-sponsored rounds reduced tariffs among member countries in many (but not all) sectors. As a result, the weighted average tariff on manufactured products imposed by industrial countries fell from approximately 20 percent to approximately 5 percent.[2] Despite these successes, the Geneva-based GATT Secretariat could not always effectively enforce negotiated agreements without the legal standing of the ITO. This and other "constitutional defects" noted by Jackson (1990) limited its effectiveness. These limitations were finally addressed in 1994 with the Uruguay Round negotiations ending in a signing ceremony that took place in Marrakesh, Morocco. The **Marrakesh Agreement** provided for the creation of the World Trade Organization (WTO), which took up the vision of the ITO for enforceable trade agreements among its members. This section of the chapter will focus on the GATT, whereas the following sections focus on the WTO.

What does the GATT entail? Its most important principle is that of **nondiscrimination**. As illustrated in Figure 7.1, nondiscrimination has two important subprinciples, namely **most favored nation** (MFN in GATT Article I) and **national treatment**

[1] The decision to not seek ratification was in response to pressures from isolationist members of the U.S. Congress. Formally, the GATT was able to exist without the ITO due to what was called the Protocol of Provisional Application, which had standing under international law. The 23 Geneva signatories became "contracting parties" to the GATT rather than "members" of the ITO. Jackson (1990) noted that "Since the ITO did not come into being, a major gap was left in the fabric intended for post-World War II international economic institutions – the Bretton Woods system" (p. 15).

[2] See Hoekman and Kostecki (2009), p. 138.

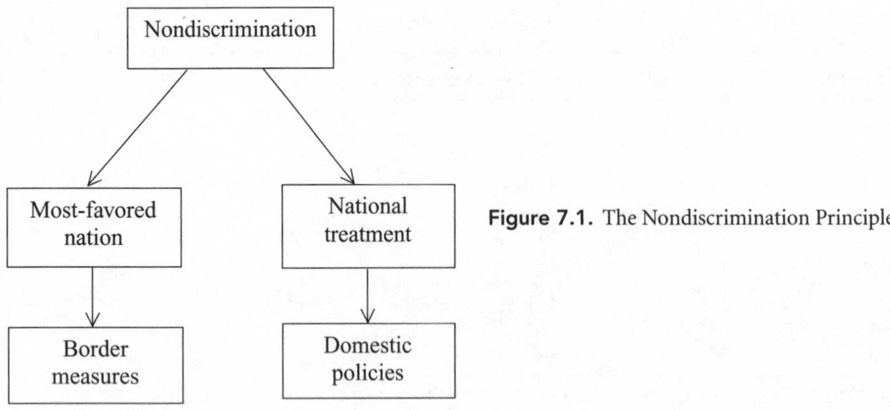

Figure 7.1. The Nondiscrimination Principle

(NT in GATT Article III). Under MFN, each member must grant treatment to all other members as favorable as it extends to any individual member country. If Japan lowers a tariff on Indonesia's exports of a certain product, it must also lower its tariff on the exports of that product from all other member countries for "like products." The MFN treatment has special importance for developing countries, because they will benefit from tariff reductions negotiated among developed countries. Exceptions to MFN treatment are allowed in the case of certain preferential trade agreements (see Chapter 8) and preferences granted to developing countries.

Whereas MFN addresses border measures, NT addresses internal, domestic policies such as taxes. NT specifies that foreign goods within a country should be treated no less favorably than domestic goods with regard to tax policies and other regulations (e.g., technical standards), again for "like products." Together, MFN and NT compose the nondiscrimination principle.

A second important GATT principle is the general prohibition of quotas or quantitative restrictions on trade. This reflects a longstanding view that price distortions (tariffs) are preferred to quantity distortions in international markets. It also reflects the history of GATT. During its birth, quantitative restrictions were one of the most significant impediments to trade. As always, there are exceptions allowed. Temporary quantitative restrictions on trade can be used in the case of balance of payments difficulties, but these must be implemented with the nondiscrimination principle of Figure 7.1 in mind.

For many years, there were additional, sector-specific exceptions to the general prohibition of quotas in the GATT. The first was the case of agricultural products and applied when certain domestic programs were in place. This exception was granted to address U.S. agricultural programs.[3] This exception was used for decades to reduce U.S. imports of sugar, dairy products, and peanuts. In addition, the United States insisted that export subsidies, prohibited in general by the GATT, be allowed for agriculture. Despite the early role of the United States in these violations of GATT principles in agriculture, it was the European Union that became the most vociferous supporter of these exemptions in the 1980s and 1990s under its Common Agricultural Policy (CAP).[4] The second important exemption to quota prohibition was for textiles and

[3] See Hathaway (1987), p. 109.

[4] On the EU Common Agricultural Policy, see Hathaway (1987), Hathaway and Ingo (1996), and chapter 11 of Dinan (2010).

clothing. These began in the early 1960s and were in place through the end of 2004, the 1995 to 2004 period being under the auspices of the World Trade Organization.[5]

Exceptions to the quota prohibitions of the GATT in the areas of agriculture, textiles, and clothing generated negative feelings on the part of developing countries with regard to the world trading system. Why? Agriculture, textiles, and clothing are three groups of products that countries first turn to in their trade and development process. The fact that these three groups of products were taken out of the GATT framework at the insistence of developed countries (led by the United States and Western Europe) left the developing countries wondering how they could have a fair chance to participate in the trade and development process. These sentiments have not entirely disappeared.

A third important GATT principle is that of **binding**. GATT- and WTO-sponsored reductions in tariff levels have been based on the practice of binding tariffs at agreed-upon levels, often *above* applied levels. Once set, tariff bindings may not in general be increased in the future. Applied rates that are below bound rates, however, may be increased. Although there are provisions made for some re-negotiation of bound tariffs, such re-negotiations must be accompanied by compensation. The general purpose of the binding principle is to introduce a degree of predictability into the world trading system.[6]

A final important GATT principle is that of "fair trade." In the interest of promoting "fair" competition in the world trading system, the GATT introduced a number of stipulations with regard to subsidies, countervailing duties (CVD), and antidumping duties (AD). The use of subsidies is not supposed to harm the trading interests of other members. When subsidies are shown to cause "material injury" or "threat thereof" to a domestic industry of another country, that other country is authorized to apply countervailing duties or tariffs on its imports of the product from the subsidizing country. The GATT leaves room for different interpretations, especially in the case of production as opposed to export subsidies. This, combined with differing national laws, leaves a great deal of room for controversy. "Dumped" goods are defined as exports sold at a price below those charged by the exporter in its domestic market. As in the case of countervailing duties, a country can impose antidumping duties when the dumping is shown to cause "material injury" or "threat thereof" to a domestic industry. The determination of dumping and injury is not straightforward in practice, but these forms of protection have been, at times, widely used among GATT and WTO members.[7]

THE WORLD TRADE ORGANIZATION

As discussed previously, the initial Bretton Woods vision of an ITO failed to materialize. However, when the Uruguay Round was launched in 1986, there was recognition that the GATT had inherent institutional flaws. Consequently, the Uruguay Round included

[5] The 1961 quotas were in the form of what was called the Short Term Arrangement Regarding International Trade in Cotton Textiles. The 1962 to 1973 period was under the Long Term Arrangement Regarding International Trade in Cotton Textiles. The 1974 to 1994 period was under a series of Multifiber Arrangements (MFAs) that expanded quota coverage across countries and fibers.

[6] It is important to note that the MFN principle applies to *both* applied *and* bound tariff rates. Gaps between bound and applied rates are known as "water in the tariff."

[7] A succinct legal review of antidumping and countervailing duties can be found in Chapters 10 and 11 of Matsushita, Schoenbaum, and Mavroidis (2006).

a negotiating group on the "function of the GATT system," or FOGS. Then John Jackson (1990), a preeminent trade lawyer, suggested that the Uruguay Round consider establishing a World Trade Organization, or WTO. In 1991, the Director General of GATT, Authur Dunkel, released a draft agreement for the Uruguay Round that became known as "the Dunkel text." The Dunkel text included a draft charter for the WTO. By the end of 1993, the text of the Uruguay Round contained a final charter for a WTO.

The Marrakesh Agreement is actually the "Marrakesh Agreement Establishing the World Trade Organization." Therefore, the stipulations of this agreement are formally an element of the WTO, and the new GATT (known as GATT 1994) has been folded into the institutional structure of the WTO. The Marrakesh Agreement and the WTO are sometimes referred to as a "tripod" in that it primarily addressed the following three areas:

Trade in Goods, governed by GATT 1994, including an Agreement on Agriculture and an Agreement on Textiles and Clothing
Trade in Services as specified in the General Agreement on Trade in Services (GATS)
Intellectual Property as specified in the Agreement on Trade-Related Aspects of Intellectual Property Rights (TRIPS)

The Marrakesh Agreement also included a WTO charter. It established the WTO as a legal international organization and stipulated that "The WTO shall provide the common institutional framework for the conduct of trade relations among its members."[8] The charter also defined the functions of the WTO, including to facilitate the implementation, administration, and operation of the multilateral trade agreements; to provide a forum for negotiations among members concerning multilateral trade relations; to administer disputes among members; and to cooperate with the International Monetary Fund and World Bank.

The administrative aspects of the WTO are summarized in Table 7.2. Members of the WTO send representatives to a Ministerial Conference that meets at least once every two years and carries out the functions of WTO. The Ministerial Conference appoints a Director General of the WTO Secretariat who, in turn, appoints the staff of the Secretariat. The Ministerial Conference adopts "regulations setting out the powers, duties, conditions of service and term of office of the Director General." Between meetings of the Ministerial Conference, the General Council meets to conduct the affairs of the WTO. The General Council establishes rules and procedures, discharges responsibilities of the Dispute Settlement Body, and discharges the responsibilities of the Trade Policy Review Body.

When possible, the Ministerial Conference and the General Council make decisions by *consensus.* Consensus is defined to be a situation in which "no member, present at the meeting when the decision is taken, formally objects to the proposed decision." Therefore, consensus does not necessarily imply unanimity, but only the absence of formally expressed objection. This definition of consensus proves to be important in the dispute settlement process of the WTO (to be discussed later in this chapter). When consensus cannot be reached, the WTO makes decisions through a process of majority voting (one vote per member).[9]

Let's now turn to a few important aspects of the WTO.

[8] All quotations without citations are taken from GATT Secretariat (1994).
[9] This is in contrast to the International Monetary Fund and World Bank where voting is weighted.

Table 7.2. Administrative structure of the WTO

Body	Composition	Function
Ministerial Conference	Representative of all members.	Meets at least once every two years. Carries out functions of WTO. Makes decisions and takes actions.
General Council	Representative of all members.	Meets between the meetings of the Ministerial Conference. Establishes rules and procedures. Discharges responsibilities of the Dispute Settlement Body. Discharges responsibilities of the Trade Policy Review Body.
Council for Trade in Goods	Representative of all members.	Oversees the functioning of the multilateral agreements of Annex 1A.
Council for Trade in Services	Representative of all members.	Oversees the functioning of the multilateral agreements of Annex 1B.
Council for Trade-Related Aspects of Intellectual Property Rights	Representative of all members.	Oversees the functioning of the multilateral agreements of Annex 1C.
Dispute Settlement Body	Representative of all members.	Establishes panels, adopts panel and Appellate Body reports, maintains surveillance of implementation of rulings and recommendations.
Dispute Settlement Panels	Three or five well-qualified governmental and/or nongovernmental individuals.	Assist the dispute settlement body by making findings and recommendations in dispute settlement cases.
Appellate Body	Seven persons, three of whom serve on any one case.	Hears appeals from panel cases.
Secretariat	Director General and staff.	Provides support for the activities of the member countries.

TRADE IN GOODS

The section of the Marrakesh Agreement related to trade in goods contains GATT 1994, an update of the original GATT, as well as an Agreement on Agriculture and an Agreement on Textiles and Clothing. The Agreement on Agriculture addresses three outstanding issues concerning international trade in agricultural goods: market access, domestic support, and export subsidies. In the case of *market access*, the Agreement on Agriculture replaced a quota-based system with a system of bound tariffs and tariff-reduction commitments. The conversion of quotas into equivalent tariffs is a process known as **tariffication**. In this aspect, the Agreement on Agriculture represents a significant change of regime. Nontariff measures (quotas) are now prohibited. Further, developed country members must have reduced average agricultural tariffs by 36 percent by 2001, and developing country members must have reduced average agricultural tariffs by 24 percent by 2005. Least-developed country members are not required to reduce their tariffs.[10] In practice, the current tariff regime includes **tariff rate quotas**, discussed in the Appendix to Chapter 6.

[10] The 50 least developed countries are recognized by the United Nations based on criteria of low income, low human resource development, and economic vulnerability.

In the case of *domestic support*, a distinction is made between non–trade-distorting policies, known as "green box" measures, and trade-distorting policies, known as "amber box" measures. Green box measures are exempt from any reduction commitments. Amber box measures are not exempt, and these commitments are specified in terms of what are known as "total aggregate measures of support" (total AMS). Developed country members must have reduced total AMS by 20 percent by 2001, and developing country members must have reduced total AMS by 13 percent by 2005. Least-developed country members are not required to reduce their total AMS.

Finally, in the case of *export subsidies*, use has *not* been eliminated. Rather, it has been limited to specified situations. Developed country members must have reduced export subsidies by 36 percent by 2001, and developing country members must have reduced export subsidies by 24 percent by 2005. Least-developed country members are not required to reduce their export subsidies. The persistence of developed-country export subsidies represents a major distortion in global agricultural trade.

Despite these specified reduction commitments, the Agreement on Agriculture is best viewed as a *change in rules* rather than as a significant program for the liberalization of trade in agricultural products.[11] The hope is that further liberalization of the new tariffied quotas will take place in the current (as of this writing in early 2011) Doha Round of trade negotiations (discussed later).

The Agreement on Textiles and Clothing (ATC) required that, in four stages of a 10-year transition period beginning in 1995, countries reintegrate their textile and clothing sectors back into the GATT framework (GATT 1994). At the end of the 10-year period, all quotas on textile and clothing trade were removed. This represented a reintegration of the textile and clothing sector into the GATT-WTO principles from which it had been removed for a half-century.

TRADE IN SERVICES

As we discussed in Chapter 1, trade in services composes more than 20 percent of total world trade and has at times grown faster than trade in goods.[12] The General Agreement on Trade in Services (GATS) represents the first time that services have been brought into a multilateral trade agreement. For these reasons, the GATS was a significant outcome of the Uruguay Round. The negotiations on GATS, however, were difficult. Contributing to this difficulty was the fact that trade in services is less tangible than trade in goods. To provide a structure to trade in services, GATS defined trade in services as occurring in one of four modes:

Mode 1: cross-border trade
Mode 2: movement of consumers
Mode 3: commercial presence or foreign direct investment (FDI)
Mode 4: movement of natural persons

Let's consider each of these in turn. Cross-border trade is a mode of supply that does not require the physical movement of producers or consumers. For example, Indian

[11] Hathaway and Ingco (1996) supported this view.
[12] For the role of services in the world economy, see Francois and Hoekman (2010).

firms provide medical transcription services to U.S. hospitals via satellite technology. Movement of consumers involves the consumer traveling to the country of the producer and is typical of the consumption of tourism services. Commercial presence or FDI is involved for services that require a commercial presence by producers in the country of the consumers and is typical of financial services. Finally, the movement of natural persons involves a noncommercial presence by producers to supply consulting, construction, and instructional services.[13]

Another difficulty in negotiating the GATS was that there was resistance to it on the part of a number of developing countries. The United States and the European Union were in favor of it, however, and prevailed upon developing countries to allow negotiations to move forward. The GATS includes the principle of nondiscrimination previously discussed. Each member was allowed to specify nondiscrimination exemptions on a "negative list" of sectors upon entry into the agreement that lasted for 10 years.

For those sectors a member country specifies on a "positive list," the GATS prohibits certain market access restrictions. Six types of limitations were prohibited: the number of service suppliers, the total value of service transactions, the total number of operations or quantity of output, number of personnel employed, the type of legal entity in the case of FDI, and the share of foreign ownership in the case of FDI.

The GATS contains an understanding that periodic negotiations would be required to incrementally liberalize trade in services. These negotiations have resulted in the following protocols to the GATS[14]:

Second GATS Protocol: Revised Schedules of Commitments on Financial Services, 1995.

Third GATS Protocol: Schedules of Specific Commitments Relating to Movement of Natural Persons, 1995.

Fourth GATS Protocol: Schedules of Specific Commitments Concerning Basic Telecommunications, 1997.

Fifth GATS Protocol: Schedules of Specific Commitments and Lists of Exemptions from Article II Concerning Financial Services, 1998.

The Second and Fifth Protocols on financial services were a significant outcome of the post-Marrakesh negotiations, although the negotiation process was contentious. As a result, beginning in 1999, a total of 102 WTO Members entered into multilateral commitments in the areas of insurance, banking, and other financial services. The Fourth Protocol on telecommunications is discussed in the accompanying box. The Third Protocol on the movement of natural persons (Mode 4 defined previously) was not significant, involving only a few countries. This is a disappointment to developing countries because, as stressed by Mattoo (2000) and others, Mode 4 services trade is where developing countries possess an important comparative advantage.[15]

[13] GATS Mode 4 is often referred to as the *temporary* movement of natural persons, but as Matsushita, Schoenbaum, and Mavroidis (2006) noted, "nowhere does . . . GATS state that the movement of natural persons under Mode 4 is intended to be temporary."

[14] The list begins with the "Second Protocol" because the first protocol was the GATS itself.

[15] As Winters et al. (2003) demonstrated, the gains for developing countries from an increase of only 3 percent in their temporary labor quotas would exceed the value of total aid flows and be similar to the expected benefits from the Doha Round of trade negotiations, with most of the benefits to developing countries coming from increased access of unskilled workers to jobs in developed countries.

Telecommunication Services in the GATS

As we discussed in Chapter 1, information and communication technology (ICT) has been an important driver of globalization processes. Nevertheless, the Marrakesh Agreement of 1994 contained no agreement on trade in telecommunication services. Negotiations on telecommunication services had begun in 1989 at the instigation of the United States. These negotiations broke down, however, because the United States was unsatisfied with the size of the market access concessions made by other countries of the world. The Marrakesh Agreement did contain a commitment to convene a Negotiating Group on Basic Telecommunications (NGBT) with a deadline of concluding an agreement in 1996.

Despite this commitment, telecommunications negotiations broke down in the spring of 1996, again with the United States being dissatisfied with market access commitments. Further negotiations proved to be successful, and in early 1997, they resulted in an Agreement on Basic Telecommunications among 69 countries that composed the Fourth Protocol of the GATS, involving commitments by 69 countries. The agreement contains general provisions on nondiscrimination. It also contains specific commitments in the areas of market access and domestic regulation. The latter regulatory principles are contained in an associated Reference Paper.

The Agreement on Basic Telecommunications addresses telecommunications trade in 14 telecom sectors and came into effect in 1998. By that time, it included three additional signatories for a total of 72 WTO members. In principle, the Fourth Protocol applies to all forms of basic telecommunications services, all modes of transmission, and all modes of supply. As WTO members that have committed themselves to the GATS, the 72 signatories have already committed themselves to MFN treatment and transparency. But as Fourth Protocol signatories, they have also committed themselves to market access and national treatment commitments and the regulatory principles of the Reference Paper. Subsequent accession agreements and unilateral actions have led to commitments of one type or another by 77 WTO members at the time of this writing.

Sources: Bronckers and Larouche (1997), Cowhey and Klimenko (2000), Fredebeul-Krein and Freytag (1999), and World Trade Organization

The GATS committed signatories to begin a new round of GATS negotiations beginning in the year 2000, now known as GATS 2000. The WTO Services Council launched these negotiations in February of that year. On the agenda of GATS 2000 are subsidies, safeguard measures, government procurement, and additional market access. Progress in these negotiations was slow throughout the year, and it took the launch of the Doha Round in 2001 to revive the service negotiations. In 2006, plurilateral requests and offers were tabled as part of the Doha Round, but overall progress in the round has been held up at the time of this writing (discussed later).[16]

INTELLECTUAL PROPERTY

The most contentious aspect of the Marrakesh Agreement is to be found in the Agreement on Trade-Related Aspects of Intellectual Property Rights (TRIPS). Intellectual

[16] The 2006 requests and offers fell under four categories: the addition of sectors that are not included in current schedules, the removal of existing limitations or reducing levels of restrictiveness, requests for additional commitments that relate to matters not falling within the scope of market access and national treatment, and the removal of MFN exemptions.

property, or IP, is an asset in the form of rights conferred on a product of invention or creation by a country's legal system.[17] The TRIPS agreement defined intellectual property as belonging to any of six categories: copyrights, trademarks, geographical indications, industrial designs, patents, and layout designs of integrated circuits.[18] It is thus quite comprehensive.

The trade-relatedness of IP refers to the fact that "theft" of intellectual property suppresses trade of the goods in question. For example, if India takes a new drug invented in the United States, analyzes its chemical constitution, and produces its own version of that drug, ignoring the U.S. patent, it will import substantially less of the patented drug. If it agrees to honor the U.S. patent, it would import the drug from the United States or have its domestic market supplied via FDI by the U.S.-based company holding the patent. Or, if a jeweler in Dubai sells counterfeit Cartier watches in place of authentic Cartier watches, this trademark violation will suppress the imports of authentic Cartier watches from France or Switzerland. No one takes this possibility more seriously than Cartier itself, which has crushed counterfeit watches with steamrollers and maintains its Middle East headquarters in Dubai.

The United States and the European Union pushed for the inclusion of IP in the Uruguay Round. Developing countries, led by India and Brazil, opposed it. The United States and the European Union prevailed, and the TRIPS became a part of the WTO. The ensuing disagreements, which have continued to this day, were well summarized by Barton et al. (2006):

> Conclusion of the TRIPS agreement has had important legal and political implications. As a legal matter, it has taken the GATT/WTO system into uncharted territory, covering not merely border measures, but also mandating threshold national regulatory standards and means of enforcing those standards. Politically, it has placed WTO rules and negotiations into the center of domestic political battles over the appropriate scope of IP protection, and has been responsible more than any other issue area for exacerbating North-South acrimony in Geneva (pp. 140–141).

The TRIPS agreement applied the principle of nondiscrimination to IP. Any advantage a WTO member grants to any country with regard to IP must now be granted to all other members. If India agrees to honor UK pharmaceutical patents, it must honor U.S. pharmaceutical patents as well. This aspect of the TRIPS agreement must have been implemented by 1996.

The TRIPS agreement also sets out obligations for members structured around the six IP categories listed above:

1. *Copyrights.* Members must comply with the 1971 Berne Convention on copyrights. Computer programs are protected as literary works under the Berne convention, and the unauthorized recording of live broadcasts and performances is prohibited. The term of this protection is to be 50 years.
2. *Trademarks.* Trademarks of goods and services are to be protected for a term of no less than seven years. Provisions for the registration of trademarks must be made and are renewable indefinitely.

[17] See Maskus (2000).

[18] Geographical indications are defined as: "indications which identify a good as originating in the territory of a Member, or a region or locality in that territory, where a given quality, reputation or other characteristic of the good is essentially attributable to its geographic origin." We saw an example of this in Chapter 4 in the form of *blue d'Auvergne* cheese.

3. *Geographical indications.* Members must provide legal means to prevent the false use of geographical indications.
4. *Industrial designs.* Members must protect "independently created industrial designs that are new or original." This protection does not apply to "designs dictated essentially by technical or functional considerations." The protection of industrial designs must last at least 10 years.
5. *Patents.* The Agreement states, "patents shall be available for any inventions, whether products or processes, in all fields of technology, provided that they are new, involve an inventive step and are capable of industrial application." Exceptions to this do exist and include the protection of public order, and human, animal, and plant life. Patents are to be extended for at least 20 years, representing a harmonization to the high-income country standard.
6. *Layout designs of integrated circuits.* The distribution of protected layout designs, as well as integrated circuits embodying protected layout designs, is forbidden. This protection is to extend for at least 10 years.

Currently, citizens and firms in developed countries own most of the world's IP. It is also the case that developing countries currently often have less IP protection than developed countries, especially in the case of patents. Therefore, the TRIPS agreement raises the cost of many goods and services to developing countries. India and other developing countries will have to pay more for drugs as a result of the TRIPS agreement, and this will have an adverse effect on welfare in these countries, especially the welfare of the poor. In the short term, then, the TRIPS agreement represents a transfer from developing country consumers to developed country producers.

The intellectual case in favor of multilateral *trade* liberalization of the kind embodied in the Marrakesh Agreement is the improvement of welfare that generally, although not always, accompanies the liberalization. In the case of the TRIPS agreement, however, such welfare gains can be absent, especially in short to medium time frames. Indeed, some prominent trade economists from developing countries (e.g., Jagdish Bhagwati and Arvind Panagariya) consider the TRIPS to be a welfare-worsening, "nontrade" agenda item that has no place in the WTO. These economists view TRIPS as lacking in the efficiency gains that characterize trade (see Chapters 2 and 3) and as inappropriately restricting the freedom of countries to choose the intellectual property regime that is best for them.[19]

Can developing countries expect any benefits from the TRIPS Agreement? Prominent trade economist Keith Maskus (2000) argued that they can. These come in the form of increased inward FDI and technology transfer, as well as in the form of increased domestic innovation. Thus the TRIPS Agreement imposes short-term costs in the hopes of generating long-term benefits. Whether this tradeoff has been made in an appropriate manner by TRIPS is an issue on which there is still much disagreement.

Access to Medicines

If there is one area in which the TRIPS agreement has been most contentious, it is in the area of access to medicines. With the advent of the new TRIPS regime in 1995, the U.S. government put a great deal of pressure on the governments of Brazil, India, and South

[19] See, for example, Panagariya (2004).

Africa to honor U.S. patents on HIV/AIDS drugs, thus raising the costs of these drugs to AIDS patients in these countries. In 2001, WTO members gathered in Doha Qatar for the fourth Ministerial Conference of the WTO. At this meeting, developing countries pushed back. As a result, the members issued a special Declaration on the TRIPS Agreement and Public Health. This declaration included the statement that "the TRIPS Agreement does not and should not prevent Members from taking measures to protect public health." More specifically, the declaration reaffirmed four "flexibilities" with regard to TRIPS and public health. For example: "Each member has the right to determine what constitutes a national emergency or other circumstances of extreme urgency, it being understood that public health crises, including those related to HIV/AIDS, tuberculosis, malaria and other epidemics, can represent a national emergency or other circumstances of extreme urgency."

These flexibilities also included the production of generic drugs under **compulsory licensing** arrangements under Article 31 of TRIPS. However, Article 31(f) limited the use of these generic drugs to the domestic markets of the producing countries. Matthews (2004) noted that this had "the practical effect of preventing exports of generic drugs to countries that do not have significant pharmaceutical industries themselves.... For countries with insufficient manufacturing capacity, the only realistic sourcing mechanism is importation" (p. 78).

Unfortunately, importation of this kind was restricted under TRIPS Article 31(f). A WTO "decision" on this issue was adopted in August 2003 that allowed least-developed WTO members to import off-patent, generic drugs. However, it was not yet clear that these provisions ensured that existing knowledge would be effectively deployed to confront some of the most serious health crises of modern times. First, the August 2003 decision was procedurally demanding. Second, deliberations at the TRIPS Council regarding the application of the decision could be lengthy. Third, there was a concern that developed countries with pharmaceutical industries will take unilateral action against developing countries making use of the decision. Fourth, there was evidence of bilateral, TRIPS-plus activity that might be extended to rights under the decision.

The 2003 WTO decision also directed the WTO TRIPS Council to prepare an *amendment* based "where appropriate" on the decision. An agreement regarding this amendment was reached in 2005 and is in the process of being ratified by member countries. It remains, however, both for supporting legislation in WTO member countries to be fully enacted and for the provisions of the amendment to be tested in practice. Indeed, Matthews (2006) noted that "it is perhaps surprising that no developing country has yet used the new mechanism to allow the importation of generic medicines following the issuance of a compulsory license in a developed country prior to patent expiry" (p. 130). Rwanda became the first country to do this in 2007 in order to import HIV/AIDS antiretroviral drugs from Canada.

It has become clear that capacity building is necessary to support use of the system, and the World Bank has been active in this regard. Hopefully, the compulsory licensing option will be helpful in harnessing knowledge in the form of pharmaceuticals to alleviate health crises and promote human development. Another avenue, however, is to improve productive capacities for key pharmaceuticals in developing countries, and the German government has been active in this area. Whatever the mechanism, a sustained commitment by all parties will be necessary.

Sources: Abbott and Reichman (2007) and Matthews (2004, 2006)

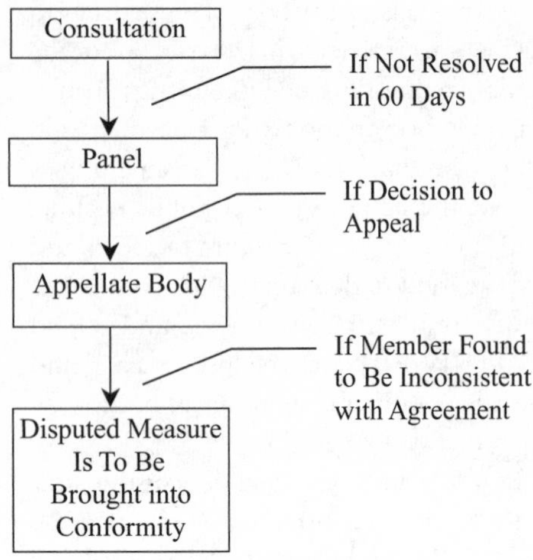

Figure 7.2. Dispute Settlement in the WTO

DISPUTE SETTLEMENT

The Marrakesh Agreement included an Understanding on Rules and Procedures Governing the Settlement of Disputes. The original GATT had been somewhat unclear about the resolution of disputes, and in establishing the WTO, the Marrakesh Agreement attempted to clarify dispute settlement procedures. As shown in Table 7.2, the WTO includes councils on trade in goods and services as well as a council on TRIPS. These councils should help to minimize the occurrence of disputes, but they certainly have not eliminated them. In the event of disputes, the WTO turns to a Dispute Settlement Body (DSB), whose function is to administer the dispute settlement rules and procedures (see Table 7.2). The DSB makes decisions by "consensus." As with the WTO in general, consensus for the DSB exists "if no Member, present at the meeting of the DSB when the decision is taken, formally objects to the proposed decision."

The dispute settlement procedure is summarized in Figure 7.2. If a member of the WTO has a complaint against another member, the first step in settling this dispute is a *consultation* between the members involved. If the consultation process fails to settle a dispute within 60 days, the complaining member *may* request the establishment of a *panel.*[20] This request also must be submitted in writing. Panels are composed of three or five "well-qualified governmental or non-governmental individuals." The function of the panel is to assist the DSB in the dispute settlement process. It consults the parties involved and provides the DSB with a written report of its findings. The DSB then has 60 days to adopt the report by consensus unless a party to the dispute decides to appeal.

The appeal of a panel report is referred to an *Appellate Body*, composed of seven persons "of recognized authority, with demonstrated expertise in law, international trade and the subject matter of the covered agreements generally." The Appellate Body reviews the appeal and submits its report to the DSB. At this point, it is stipulated that the Appellate Body report "shall be adopted by the DSB and unconditionally accepted by the parties to the dispute unless the DSB decides by consensus *not* to adopt the Appellate Body report within 30 days following its circulation to the members." Therefore, given

[20] The word "may" here is important. As noted by Hoekman and Kostecki (2009, p. 93), the average consultation process lasts more than 200 days.

the definition of consensus for the DSB, *any DSB member can effectively insist on the adoption of the Appellate Body report.* Renowned international trade lawyer John Jackson (1994) referred to this appellate body procedure as "ingenious" and noted that "the result of the procedure is that appellate report will in virtually every case come into force as a matter of international law" (p. 70). The way in which this dispute settlement process evolved in the famous Bananas Dispute is presented in the accompanying box.

The "Bananarama" Dispute

Perhaps the most controversial of all dispute settlement proceedings of the WTO is the famous "bananas dispute" between five Latin American countries and the European Union. Its roots actually go back to the GATT era when, in 1993, Costa Rica, Colombia, Nicaragua, Guatemala, and Venezuela invoked GATT dispute resolution proceedings against the newly created European Union (EU; then European Community) harmonized banana regime. This regime was put into place to support the banana exports of former colonies in the African, Caribbean, and Pacific (ACP) group recognized by the EU and consisted of a discriminatory tariff rate quota system (see appendix to Chapter 6). The ensuing GATT panel found against the EU, citing the regime's violation of MFN and quantitative restriction principles. However, the EU and the ACP blocked the adoption of the panel under GATT's positive consensus rule on panel reports. A similar result followed a second GATT panel requested by the five Latin American countries that addressed the specific rules of the EU banana regime, but it was again blocked.

Under the new WTO regime, which came into effect in 1995, the United States joined the Latin American claimants in support of U.S.-based banana multinationals. Having acceded to the WTO in early 1996, Ecuador also joined in asking for a panel that year. The panel issued its report in 1997, again finding against the EU. The EU appealed, and an Appellate Body was also set up, but it did not significantly change the panel's findings. The WTO's negative consensus rule ensured that the Appellate Body's findings were adopted in September 2007. The EU subsequently obtained an arbitration finding allowing it 15 months to bring its banana regime into conformity.

As a result of this, a *new* EU banana regime replacing country-specific measures began in 1999. Not satisfied, the United States, the original five Latin American countries, Ecuador, and Panama initiated further consultations with the EU. The United States was planning to retaliate against the EU under its own domestic trade legislation, and a WTO arbitration decision set the value of this retaliation in April 1999. This complicated consultative process, and further subsidiary disputes, finally resulted in a *revised*, new EU banana regime in May 2001. Initially, this appeared to satisfy all parties by phasing in a tariff-only regime by 2006.

What the EU put in place in 2006, however, maintained duty-free access for ACP countries, while imposing a tariff of €176 per ton of bananas from non-ACP sources. In 2007, both Ecuador and the United States initiated new dispute settlement proceedings against the EU. In 2007, a panel again found against the EU. Parties to the dispute met in 2008 to attempt to resolve their disagreements, but it took until the end of 2009 for the matter to be resolved with a drop of the tariff from €176 per ton to €114 per ton in 2017. With the approval of this compromise by the European Parliament in early 2011, the "Bananarama" dispute finally came to an end.

Sources: Herrmann, Kramb, and Monnich (2003) and Salas and Jackson (2000)

The dispute settlement procedure outlined earlier and in Figure 7.2 applies to all aspects of the Marrakesh Agreement. It improves significantly the procedures of the old GATT and therefore makes a significant contribution to the conduct of international trade.[21] However, the effectiveness of the procedures depends on members' commitment to it. A country has the option of ignoring the outcome of the dispute settlement process. In this case, the complaining member has the right to impose retaliatory tariffs on a volume of imports from the other country determined by the DSB, as in the Banana Dispute.

THE ENVIRONMENT

In 1991, the GATT reactivated a long-dormant Working Group on Environmental Measures and International Trade (EMIT). Not coincidentally, this was the year that a GATT dispute resolution panel issued its controversial opinion in the now-famous tuna–dolphin case. The panel ruled against a U.S. law banning imports of Mexican tuna that involved dolphin-unsafe fishing practices, issued in response to the U.S. Marine Mammal Protection Act. The panel argued that the import ban violated the general prohibition against quotas and that the United States had not attempted to negotiate cooperative agreements on dolphin-safe tuna fishing. The U.S. environmental community reacted strongly against the GATT panel ruling, casting the GATT as antienvironment, and the trade-environment issue has loomed large over the WTO ever since.[22]

With the advent of the WTO in 1995, EMIT was replaced by the Committee on Trade and the Environment (CTE). Most developing country members of the WTO have taken a dim view of the work of the CTE, fearing the possibility of further protection against their exports on environmental grounds, what they term "green protection." These members often view environmental matters as nontrade issues that have no place in the trade policy agenda of the WTO. The subsequent polarization of views has inhibited the effectiveness of the CTE.[23]

Many trade economists (e.g., Anderson, 1996 and Hoekman and Kostecki, 2009, Chapter 13) are broadly supportive of the developing-country view that environmental issues represent an "intrusion" into the WTO trade agenda. These trade economists suggest, perhaps correctly, that the environmental agenda could result in an inappropriate "one size fits all" approach to environmental policies across WTO members. As Hoekman and Kostecki (2009) noted, "Countries may have very different preferences regarding environmental protectionism, reflecting differences in the absorptive capacity of their ecosystems, differences in income levels (wealth), and differences in culture" (p. 614). The limitation of this argument is that it could just as easily be (and sometimes is) applied to the TRIPS agreement discussed previously. Consequently, many trade economists appear to be inconsistent on these matters.

[21] For more on the WTO dispute settlement procedures, see Kuruvila (1997), Davey (2000), Hoekman and Mavroidis (2000), and Brown (2009).

[22] For a review of the tuna–dolphin case, see Chapter 4 of Runge (1994). Posters at the time, issued by U.S.-based environmental groups, depicted GATT as "GATTzilla," a monster destroying national environmental sovereignty. In actuality, as pointed out by Matsushita, Schoenbaum, and Mavroidis (2006), the realities of the dispute settlement procedure under the GATT made the tuna–dolphin finding nonbinding.

[23] See Shaffer (2001). This author notes that "In light of the immense challenge developing countries face in meeting the basic needs of the majority of their human populations, southern constituencies typically place less weight on the social value of environmental preservation than on economic and social development and poverty eradication" (p. 87).

In 1999, the WTO took up the trade and environment issue formally with the publication of a "special studies" report on this subject (Nordström and Vaughan, 1999). As with Runge (1994) and others, this report argued that increased trade can have both positive and negative impacts on the environment. The report emphasizes, however, that trade-driven growth cannot always be counted on to deliver improvements in environmental quality through increased incomes, as many economists claim. Consequently, these higher incomes must be "translated into higher environmental quality" through the mechanism of international cooperation. As emphasized by Barrett (1999), designing environmental treaties to include the appropriate combination of incentives and threats to achieve international cooperation on environmental matters is not always easy. This has been shown in the case of the Kyoto Protocol on greenhouse (global warming) gasses. The WTO report also emphasized that government subsidies to polluting and resource-depleting sectors such as agriculture, fishing, and energy can exacerbate the environmental consequences of trade.

The role of the WTO in trade and environment matters will continue to be both important and controversial. The decade of the 1990s ended with another difficult case regarding the impact of shrimp fishing on sea turtles.[24] The Appellate Body report on this case stressed the importance of international environmental agreements in reconciling trade and the environment. Further, as noted by Esty (2001), the WTO has reached such a position of prominence that it will find it very difficult to avoid scrutiny on environmental issues. To some degree, then, the success of the WTO depends on the willingness and ability of its members to enter into **multilateral environmental agreements** (MEAs).[25] Some observers (e.g., Runge, 1994) have gone further to suggest that the CTE be replaced by a World Environmental Organization (WEO) to stand alongside the WTO. Runge (2009) has suggested that the WEO be modeled on the North American Commission on Environmental Cooperation (CEC). The WEO could bring a sense of rationality to the large set of existing MEAs and could potentially provide a dispute settlement mechanism for environmental disagreements. Although currently not a global, political reality, the WEO proposal is one that will not go away.

DOHA ROUND

As mentioned in Chapter 1, the Seattle Ministerial Conference of the WTO that took place in December 1999 was not successful. This was, in part, due to the protests of young people against the WTO as an agent of globalization. It was also due to a lack of agreement between developed and developing WTO member countries on a number of issues discussed in this chapter. For both these reasons, WTO members were not able to launch the hoped-for new round of multilateral trade talks.

A second attempt to launch a new round took place in Doha, Qatar, in 2001 at the next Ministerial Conference. This attempt was successful, although disputes between developing and developed countries still simmered beneath the surface. Although, as mentioned above, progress was made on the TRIPS/AIDS issue, the European Union (EU) maintained its intransigent position with regard to agricultural trade

[24] This finding overturned a number of the findings of the tuna–dolphin case.

[25] Some existing MEAs include the Convention on International Trade in Endangered Species (CITES), the Montreal Protocol on Substances that Deplete the Ozone Layer (Montreal Protocol), and the Convention of Biological Diversity (CBD). There are many others.

liberalization, and the developing countries were displeased with the introduction of new agenda items such as investment and competition policy.[26]

The progress in what has come to be called the Doha Round of multilateral trade negotiations has been very uneven. A focus point was the Cancún Ministerial Meeting of 2003. The EU had insisted that the so-called Singapore issues (competition policy, transparency in government procurement, trade facilitation, and investment) be included in the negotiations. Further, the EU and the United States had just issued a draft text on the agricultural negotiations. Coalitions of developing countries emerged to oppose both of these. In the case of agriculture, a representative of the Brazilian government stated:

> The real dilemma that many of us had to face was whether it was sensible to accept an agreement that would essentially consolidate the policies of the two subsidizing superpowers... and then have to wait for another 15 to 18 years to launch a new round, after having spent precious bargaining chips.[27]

A new bargaining group of developing countries emerged at Cancún. Known as the G20 and led by Argentina, Brazil, China, India, and South Africa, this group accounted for more than two-thirds of the world population and more than 60 percent of its farmers. It adamantly opposed the EU/US agricultural text, proposing more strenuous liberalization in agricultural markets. Despite predictions to the contrary, the group held firm during the negotiations. The ministerial statement coming out of Cancún was only one-half page long. It noted that "more work needs to be done in some key areas to enable us to proceed towards the conclusion of the negotiations in fulfillment of the commitments we took at Doha." In the polite language of trade diplomacy, this was an admission of failure.

Some progress appeared in July 2004 with the "July 2004 Package" that reaffirmed the Doha Ministerial commitments in agriculture and acknowledged in some specific ways the concerns of the developing countries (e.g., cotton subsidies). Most important was the adoption of a "tiered approach" to reductions in domestic support and tariffs and the commitment to eliminate exports subsidies by an unspecified date. Despite this progress, the next deadline for progress in agricultural negotiations, July 2005, was missed. The next small breakthrough occurred in October 2005 with proposals for domestic support being tabled using the tiered framework. In July 2006, negotiations among the United States, the EU, Japan, Brazil, India, and Australia regarding the Doha Round broke down, and the WTO Director General Pascal Lamy suspended further discussions, noting that "We have missed a very important opportunity to show that multilateralism works." Further failed talks were held in the summer of 2008 and resulted in what became known as the "July 2008 Package."[28] Sufficient progress to conclude the round, however, has not yet been made at the time of this writing in mid-2011. The 2009 Ministerial Meeting in Geneva largely ignored the Doha Round, and a March 2010 "stocktaking" meeting was reportedly one in which there was "no stock to take." However, at the end of 2010, Lamy announced a "final countdown" to finish the Doha Round by the end of 2011.

[26] See chapter 13 of Hoekman and Kostecki (2009).

[27] See Narlikar and Tussie (2004), p. 951.

[28] The July 2008 package specified tariff cut tiers in agricultural market access, as well as agricultural domestic support reductions, the latter in terms of an Overall Trade Distortion Support (OTDS) measure.

The Doha Ministerial statement of 2001 stated that: "International trade can play a major role in the promotion of economic development and the alleviation of poverty. We recognize the need for all our peoples to benefit from the increased opportunities and welfare gains that the multilateral trading system generates. The majority of WTO members are developing countries. We seek to place their needs and interests at the heart of the Work Program adopted in this Declaration." This vision has largely been lost due to the politics of trade in the United States and the EU.[29]

CONCLUSION

The WTO came into being in 1995, completing the Bretton Woods vision of a global trade institution. Since its birth, it has both demonstrated the importance of a multilateral approach to managing trade issues and stirred up controversies in a number of areas. All evidence suggests that the WTO will continue, as stated in the introduction to this chapter, to be "both lauded and vilified with equal intensity by various groups with concerns about trade policy." In general, a common fault line exists across many issues within the WTO between developed and developing countries.

With regard to the old GATT agenda of trade in goods, developing countries are still at a market access disadvantage in textiles, clothing, and agriculture. Their exports must contend with higher than normal tariff levels in the developed world and, in the case of agriculture, with the massive domestic and export subsidies of the United States and the European Union that exceed US$100 billion per year. The ongoing controversies over TRIPS also have a similar fault line. In the short term, developing countries will generally lose from intellectual property protection through the higher prices they will have to pay for goods and services. This short-term cost will have to be accepted by the developing world, waiting for the hoped-for, long-term benefits of increased inward FDI and domestic innovation. Finally, ongoing disputes concerning environmental issues often pit developed and developing countries against one another. Developing countries fear a surge of "green protection," exacerbating their disadvantages in other areas.

These fissures within the WTO deserve attention. Unfortunately, years of negotiating energy have been put into the Doha Round, with (as of this writing in mid-2011) little to show for it. The WTO faces a crisis of legitimacy that can only be overcome through greater commitment to it by its leading members. Whether this commitment will be forthcoming remains to be seen.

REVIEW EXERCISES

1. What is meant by *nondiscrimination* in international trade agreements? Be as specific as you can.
2. One criticism of the Agreement on Agriculture is that it involves something known as *dirty tariffication*. Dirty tariffication involves quotas being converted into tariffs that are larger than the actual tariff equivalent of the original tariff. Draw a diagram like that of Figure 6.4, illustrating dirty tariffication.

[29] The appendix to this chapter puts the Doha Round negotiation process in some context. For a recent summary of the Doha Round, see Martin and Mattoo (2010).

3. The chapter mentioned the four modes by which trade in services can occur: cross-border trade, movement of consumers, foreign direct investment, and personnel movement. Try to give an example of each of these modes. The more specific the better.
4. The chapter also gave an example of the way that the "theft" of intellectual property in the case of pharmaceuticals suppresses trade in this product. Try to give another example of such trade suppression.
5. Can you think of any ways in which trade issues and environmental issues interact?

FURTHER READING AND WEB RESOURCES

Concise introductions to the GATT and the WTO can be found in Blackhurst (2009a, 2009b). The reader interested in further pursuing an understanding of the GATT/WTO system can start with the works by Hoekman and Kostecki (2009) and Barton, Goldstein, Josling, and Steinberg (2006). A more legal approach can be found in Jackson (1997) and Matsushita, Schoenbaum, and Mavroidis (2006). Journals covering the subjects of this chapter include the *Journal of World Trade*, *World Trade Review*, and the *Journal of International Economic Law*. The controversy over TRIPS is analyzed by Maskus (2000), and case studies of developing countries in trade negotiations can be found in Odell (2006).

To keep up with the work of the WTO, including the Doha Round, the reader should visit its website, www.wto.org. Perhaps the most useful link here is the one to "trade topics." However, the document dissemination facility at this website is a particularly useful resource. The reader should monitor the Centre for Trade and Sustainable Development at www.ctsd.org, a very important resource on issues of trade and sustainable development broadly defined.

APPENDIX: WTO MEMBERSHIP AND MULTILATERAL TRADE NEGOTIATIONS

Multilateral trade negotiations (MTNs) are trade negotiations that occur under the auspices of the previous GATT and current WTO in the form of *rounds*, as documented in Table 7.1. In MTNs, there is much reference to what are termed *modalities*, or the rules of the negotiations. In the first five rounds through the Dillon Round, the central modality was a *principal supplier* or *request-and-offer* method. Here, requests for market access were made by the principal supplier of a product to other members' markets in what was really a bilateral negotiation over *concessions*. Concessions were generalized across the membership through the MFN principle. The exchange of concessions is known as *reciprocity*.

The Kennedy Round introduced a new modality in the form of linear or proportional, across-the-board tariff reductions. This modality can be represented as:

$$t_1 = a\, t_0 \quad 0 \leq a \leq 1 \tag{7.1}$$

where t_1 is the final tariff, and t_0 is the initial or base tariff. If, for example, $a = 0.8$, then all tariffs would be reduced by 20 percent.

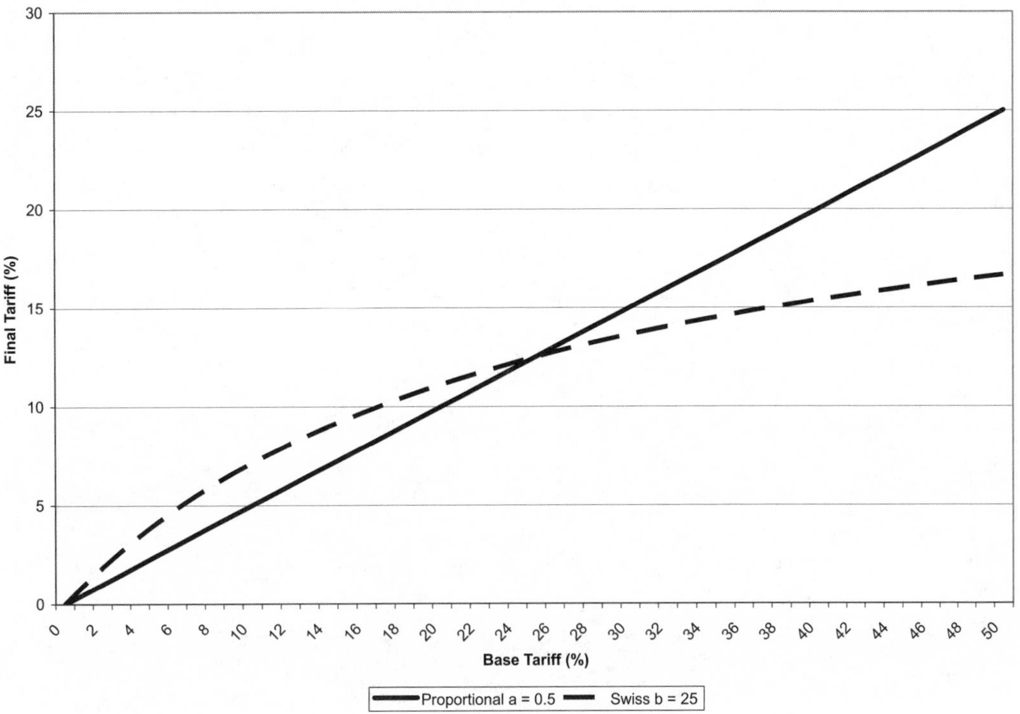

Figure 7.3. Proportional Swiss Formula Comparison. *Source:* Author's calculations

The Tokyo Round introduced a new modality innovation in the form of the "Swiss formula," which can be represented as:

$$t_1 = \frac{b\,t_0}{b + t_0} \qquad 0 \leq b \leq 100 \tag{7.2}$$

where b is the ceiling tariff.

The purpose of the Swiss formula is to reduce higher base tariffs by a greater proportion than lower base tariffs. This can be seen in Figure 7.3, which translates base tariffs along the horizontal axis into final tariffs along the vertical axis. The linear formula is presented as the solid line for a proportional reduction of 50 percent or $a = 0.50$. So, you can see in the figure that a base tariff of 50 percent is reduced to a final tariff of 25 percent. The Swiss formula is presented as the dashed line with a ceiling of 25 percent or $b = 25$. Here, for each base tariff of more than 25 percent, the reduction of the base tariff is greater than in the linear case. Further, as you can see, the gap between the proportional and Swiss reductions over the 25 percent base tariff increases as the base tariff increases.

How long do MTNs last? Figure 7.4 plots the eight rounds of multilateral trade negotiations previous to the Doha Round. The surprisingly linear relationship between number of members and years of negotiations (explaining 98 percent of the variance in the latter) indicates that, given the current WTO membership, the Doha Round should last approximately a decade. If we put our faith in such statistical relationships (and there are reasons not to do so), the Doha Round should not end before 2011.

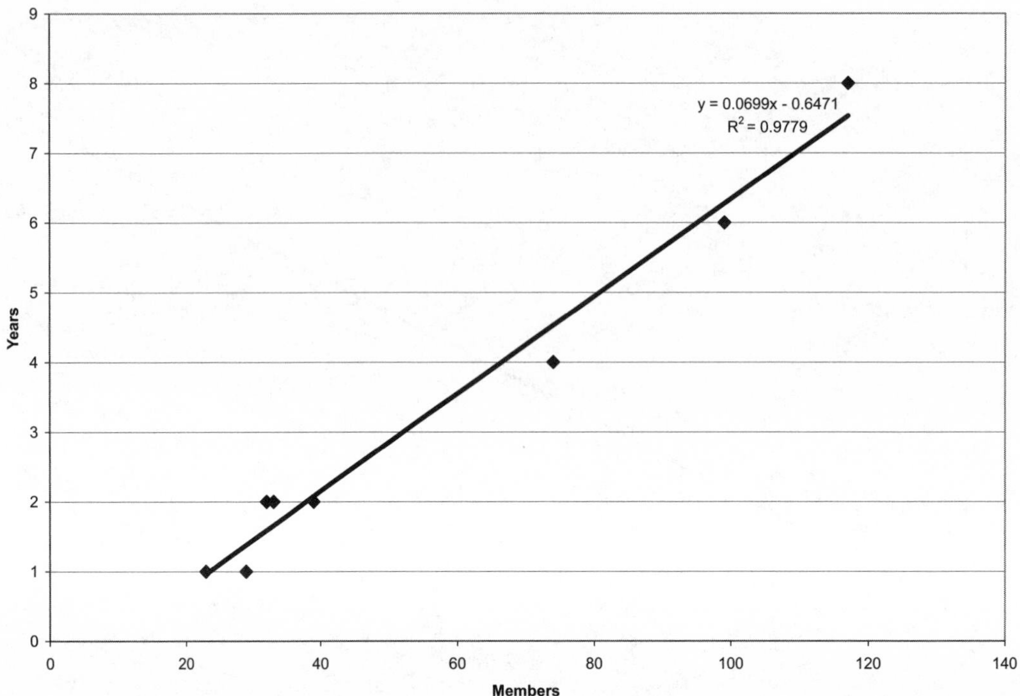

Figure 7.4. Members and Years to Conclude GATT/WTO Rounds. *Source:* World Trade Organization and author's calculations

REFERENCES

Abbott, F.M. and J.H. Reichman (2007) "The Doha Round's Public Health Legacy: Strategies for the Production and Diffusion of Patented Medicines under the Amended TRIPS Provisions," *Journal of International Economic Law*, 10:4, 921–987.

Anderson, K. (1996) "The Intrusion of Environmental and Labor Standards into Trade Policy," in W. Martin and L.A. Winters (eds.), *The Uruguay Round and the Developing Countries*, Cambridge University Press, 1996, 435–462.

Barrett, S. (1999) "Montreal versus Kyoto: International Cooperation and the Global Environment," in I. Kaul, I. Grunberg, and M.A. Stern (eds.), *Global Public Goods: International Cooperation in the 21st Century*, Oxford University Press, 192–219.

Barton, J.H., J.L. Goldstein, T.E. Josling, and R.H. Steinberg (2006) *The Evolution of the Trade Regime: Politics, Law, and Economics of the GATT and the WTO*, Princeton University Press.

Blackhurst, R. (2009a) "General Agreement on Tariffs and Trade (GATT)," in K.A. Reinert, R.S. Rajan, A.J. Glass, and L.S. Davis (eds.), *The Princeton Encyclopedia of the World Economy*, Princeton University Press, 521–528.

Blackhurst, R. (2009b) "World Trade Organization," in K.A. Reinert, R.S. Rajan, A.J. Glass, and L.S. Davis (eds.), *The Princeton Encyclopedia of the World Economy*, Princeton University Press, 1185–1191.

Bronckers, M.C.E.J. and P. Larouche (1997) "Telecommunications Services and the World Trade Organization," *Journal of World Trade*, 31:3, 5–47.

Brown, C.P. (2009) *Self-Enforcing Trade: Developing Countries and WTO Dispute Settlement*, Brookings Institution.

Cowhey, P. and M.M. Klimenko (2000) "Telecommunications Reform in Developing Countries after the WTO Agreement on Basic Telecommunications Services," *Journal of International Development*, 12:2, 265–281.

Davey, W.J. (2000) "The WTO Dispute Settlement System," *Journal of International Economic Law*, 3:1, 15–18.

Dinan, D. (2010) *Ever Closer Union: An Introduction to European Integration*, Lynne Rienner.

Esty, D.C. (2001) "Bridging the Trade-Environment Divide," *Journal of Economic Perspectives*, 15:3, 113–130.

Francois, J.F. and B. Hoekman (2010) "Services Trade and Policy," *Journal of Economic Literature*, 48:3, 642–692.

Fredebeul-Krein, M. and A. Freytag (1999) "The Case for a More Binding WTO Agreement on Regulatory Principles in Telecommunication Markets," *Telecommunications Policy*, 23:9, 625–644.

GATT Secretariat (1994) *The Results of the Uruguay Round of Multilateral Trade Negotiations: The Legal Text.*

Hathaway, D.E. (1987) *Agriculture and the GATT: Rewriting the Rules*, Institute for International Economics.

Hathaway, D.E. and M.D. Ingco (1996) "Agricultural Liberalization and the Uruguay Round," in W. Martin and L.A. Winters (eds.), *The Uruguay Round and the Developing Countries*, Cambridge University Press, 30–57.

Herrmann, R., M. Kramb, and C. Monnich (2003) "The Banana Dispute: Survey and Lessons," *Quarterly Journal of International Agriculture*, 42:1, 21–47.

Hoekman, B.M. and M. Kostecki (2009) *The Political Economy of the World Trading System: From GATT to WTO*, Oxford University Press.

Hoekman, B.M. and P.C. Mavroidis (2000) "WTO Dispute Settlement, Transparency and Surveillance," *The World Economy*, 23:4, 527–542.

Jackson, J.H. (1990) *Restructuring the GATT System*, Royal Institute of International Affairs.

Jackson, J.H. (1994) "The World Trade Organization, Dispute Settlement and Codes of Conduct," in S.M Collins and B.P. Bosworth (eds.), *The New GATT*, Brookings Institution.

Jackson, J.H. (1997) *The World Trading System*, MIT Press.

Kuruvila, P.E. (1997) "Developing Countries and the GATT/WTO Dispute Settlement Mechanism," *Journal of World Trade*, 31:6, 171–207.

Martin, W. and A. Mattoo (2010) "The Doha Development Agenda: What's on the Table?" *Journal of International Trade and Economic Development*, 19:1, 81–107.

Maskus, K.E. (2000) *Intellectual Property Rights in the Global Economy*, Institute for International Economics.

Matsushita, M., T.J. Schoenbaum, and P.C. Mavroidis (2006) *The World Trade Organization: Law, Practice, and Policy*, Oxford University Press.

Matthews, D. (2004) "WTO Decision on Implementation of Paragraph 6 of the Doha Declaration on the TRIPS Agreement and Public Health: A Solution to the Access to Essential Medicines Problem?" *Journal of International Economic Law*, 7:1, 73–107.

Matthews, D. (2006) "From the August 30, 2003 WTO Decision to the December 6, 2005 Agreement on Amendments to TRIPS: Improving Access to Medicines in Developing Countries," *Intellectual Property Quarterly*, 10:2, 91–130.

Mattoo, A. (2000) "Developing Countries in the New Round of GATS Negotiations: Towards a Pro-Active Role," *The World Economy*, 23:4, 471–489.

Narlikar, A. and D. Tussie (2004) "The G20 and the Cancún Ministerial: Developing Countries and Their Evolving Coalitions in the WTO," *World Economy*, 27:7, 947–966.

Nordström, H. and S. Vaughan (1999) *Trade and the Environment*, World Trade Organization.

North, D.C. (1990) *Institutions, Institutional Change and Economic Performance*, Cambridge University Press.

Odell, J.S. ed. (2006) *Negotiating Trade: Developing Countries in the WTO and NAFTA*, Cambridge University Press.

Panagariya, A. (2004) "TRIPS and the WTO: An Uneasy Marriage," in K. Maskus (ed.), *The WTO, Intellectual Property Rights and the Knowledge Economy*, Edward Elgar, 42–53.

Runge, C.F. (1994) *Freer Trade, Protected Environment*, Council of Foreign Relations.

Runge, C.F. (2009) "Multilateral Environmental Agreements," in K.A. Reinert, R.S. Rajan, A.J. Glass, and L.S. Davis (eds.), *The Princeton Encyclopedia of the World Economy*, Princeton University Press, 795–799.

Salas, M. and J.H. Jackson (2000) "Procedural Overview of the WTO EC-Banana Dispute," *Journal of International Economic Law*, 3:1, 145–166.

Shaffer, G.C. (2001) "The World Trade Organization under Challenge: Democracy and the Law and Politics of the WTO's Treatment of Trade and Environmental Matters," *Harvard Environmental Law Review*, 25:1, 1–93.

Winters, L.A., T.L. Walmsley, Z.K Wang, and R. Grynberg (2003) "Liberalizing the Temporary Movement of Natural Persons: An Agenda for the Development Round," *The World Economy*, 26:8, 1137–1161.

8 Preferential Trade Agreements

I once attended a talk by a Canadian trade negotiator who made the following potent statement: "When multilateralism falters, regionalism picks up the pace." His use of the term *multilateralism* referred to the GATT/WTO system described in Chapter 7 and its multilateral trade negotiations. His use of the term *regionalism* referred informally to the possibility of pursuing what are formally known as **preferential trade agreements** (PTAs). Recall that one of the founding principles of the GATT/WTO system is **nondiscrimination**, and that nondiscrimination, in turn, involves the **most favored nation** (MFN) and **national treatment** (NT) sub-principles. Under MFN, each WTO member must grant to each other member treatment as favorable as they extend to any other member country. PTAs are a *violation of the nondiscrimination principle* in which one member of a PTA discriminates in its trade policies in favor of another member of the PTA and against nonmembers.[1] This discrimination has been allowed by the GATT/WTO under certain circumstances. These circumstances include the well-known cases of **free trade areas** (FTAs), **customs unions** (CUs), and interim agreements leading to a FTA or CU "within a reasonable length of time."[2]

Before we begin, we need to clarify an issue of terminology. Originally, FTAs and CUs were collectively known as *regional trade agreements* (RTAs), and this is the term commonly employed by the WTO. However, since the 1990s, an increasing number of FTAs have been between or among countries that are *not geographically contiguous*, such as the Canada-Chile and Japan-Mexico FTAs. Consequently, a number of leading economists and trade lawyers have recommended that the RTA nomenclature be replaced with that of PTAs.[3] In the spirit of greater accuracy, we use this term here, but it is likely that you will encounter both terms and their acronyms.

As suggested by the comment of the trade minister above, regionalism (or, more accurately, preferentialism) and multilateralism represent two alternative trade policy options available to the countries of the world. When the larger countries of the world lose commitment to the multilateralism option, multilateralism "falters." However, this is when countries often turn their attention to the preferential option, and regionalism "picks up the pace." Indeed, nearly every member of the WTO is also a member of at least one PTA, and 290 PTAs are in force at the time of this writing in 2010.[4] PTAs are therefore a central feature of the world trading system.

This chapter will introduce you to various types of PTAs and their economic effects. These effects are analyzed in international economics in terms of the concepts of **trade creation** and **trade diversion**. We then consider some examples of PTAs, namely the European Union, the North American Free Trade Agreement, Mercosur and the Free Trade Area of the Americas, and the ASEAN Free Trade Area. Finally, we consider in more detail the relationship of regionalism to multilateralism.

[1] The history of PTAs is often traced back to the establishment of the German Customs Union (Zollverein) in 1834.

[2] All quotations without citations are from GATT Secretariat (1994).

[3] For example, Matsushita, Schoenbaum, and Mavroidis (2006) stated: "The term 'regional integration', which is often used in the literature, is probably misleading: in essence, what the term aims to capture are preferential schemes that deviate from the obligation not to discriminate. Not all such schemes are regional, in the sense of geographical proximity. One third of the free trade areas (FTAs) currently under investigation are among countries that are not in geographical proximity" (pp. 548–549).

[4] This 290 figure was the official WTO figure at the end of 2010. As we explain later, there is actually some double counting involved in the way the WTO records PTAs.

Analytical elements for this chapter:

Countries, *sectors*, and *tasks*.

Table 8.1. Types of preferential trade agreements

Type of PTA	Description	Number in force in 2010
GATT Article XXIV (FTA)	An agreement on the part of a set of countries to *eliminate* trade restrictions among themselves.	160
GATT Article XXIV (CU)	An agreement on the part of a set of countries to eliminate trade restrictions among themselves and to adopt a *common external tariff*.	15
Enabling Clause	Allows PTAs in goods trade among developing countries.	31
GATS Article V	An agreement to reduce barriers to trade in services among a set of countries.	84
		Total: 290

Source: World Trade Organization. *Note:* Consult the WTO website for current information.

PREFERENTIAL TRADE AGREEMENTS

Under the WTO and as listed in Table 8.1, there are four ways in which a PTA can occur. Under Article XXIV of the General Agreement on Tariffs and Trade (GATT 94) covering trade in goods, a PTA can be notified as either a free trade area (FTA) or as a customs unions (CU). As noted in Table 8.2, both of these PTA types involve the member countries *eliminating* trade restrictions among themselves. The difference between the FTA and CU options is that the latter involves member countries establishing a *common external tariff* (CET). Article XXIV of the GATT requires that WTO members who wish to form FTAs or CUs must meet certain requirements. First, trade barriers against

Table 8.2. Steps to regional integration

Type	Description
Free trade area	An agreement on the part of a set of countries to *eliminate trade restrictions among themselves.*
Customs union	An agreement on the part of a set of countries to eliminate trade restrictions among themselves and to *adopt a common external tariff.*
Common market	An agreement on the part of a set of countries to eliminate trade restrictions among themselves, to adopt a common external tariff, and to allow the *free movement of labor and physical capital* among member countries.
Monetary union	A common market that adopts a *common currency* and adopts a *common monetary policy.*
Economic union	A monetary union that adopts a process of *domestic policy harmonization* in areas such as tax and spending policies and domestic regulation.

nonmembers cannot be "higher or more restrictive than" those in existence prior to the FTA or CU. Second, the FTA or CU must be formed "within a reasonable length of time." Third, the FTA or CU must eliminate trade barriers on "substantially all the trade" among the members. As can be seen in Table 8.1, the number of FTAs notified to the WTO greatly exceeds the number of CUs.

A third way in which a PTA can occur under the WTO is known as the "enabling clause." This 1979 decision (currently part of GATT 94) allows PTAs in goods trade among developing countries. According to this decision, the pursuit of a PTA within the enabling clause is for the "mutual reduction or elimination" of tariffs and nontariff measures. There is thus less emphasis on eliminating trade restrictions than in the case of FTAs and CUs. As can be seen in Table 8.1, there are more enabling clause PTAs than CUs, but significantly fewer than FTAs.

The fourth and final way in which a PTA can occur under the WTO is under Article V of the General Agreement on Trade in Services (GATS). FTAs or CUs under the GATS must involve "substantial sectoral coverage," language that differs from trade in goods. Importantly, most PTAs (other than enabling clause PTAs) notified to the WTO since its inception in 1995 have been under both GATT Article XXIV and GATS Article V. Therefore, there is *double-counting* in the WTO PTA system that is reflected in Table 8.1.[5]

Whether notified under trade in goods or both trade in goods and services, oversight of PTAs by the WTO is difficult. This is because the phrases "higher or more restrictive than," "within a reasonable length of time," "substantially all trade," and "substantial sectoral coverage" are simply too vague. As part of the Uruguay Round of trade negotiations leading up to the Marrakesh Agreement and the establishment of the WTO, there was an agreed-on "understanding" on PTAs. This understanding specified that the relevant measure to assess restrictiveness against nonmembers is a weighted average of tariff rates and that the length of time allowable for the elimination of trade barriers within FTA and CUs is to be no more than 10 years.

Even with this understanding, however, there is room for differing interpretations.[6] Further, despite the institutional structure present in the WTO to govern PTAs, the unfortunate fact is that there has never been any serious evaluation or enforcement of PTAs under either the GATT or the WTO. As noted by Matsushita, Schoenbaum, and Mavroidis (2006), most PTAs are of "dubious WTO-consistency." However, no WTO member has the incentive to challenge PTAs through WTO dispute settlement because nearly all important WTO members are themselves members of at least one PTA. This "cooperative equilibrium" has proven to be quite durable. Some small steps toward increased transparency have been taken by the WTO's Committee on Regional Trade Agreements (CRTA) in the form of an improved database of FTAs and CUs (see Further Reading and Web Resources at the end of this chapter), but transparency is not enforcement.[7]

[5] In the words of the WTO, its statistics on PTAs "are based on notification requirements rather than on physical numbers" of PTAs. Thus, for any PTA including both goods and services, the WTO counts two notifications (one for goods and the other services) rather than one.

[6] See Serra et al. (1997).

[7] Matsushita, Schoenbaum, and Mavroidis (2006) stated: "The ultimate conclusion from our analysis is that PTAs, in their overwhelming majority, have not even been properly evaluated by the WTO. As a result, there is an abundance of PTAs, the consistency of which with the WTO rules is simply put, unknown" (p. 554).

Although many PTAs are not regional, a number of PTAs are true attempts to build regional integration among contiguous countries. When this is the case, PTAs can be seen as steps along a continuum of increased regional integration. This continuum is described in Table 8.2. Here we see that FTAs and CUs are the first two steps toward a common market in which the regional membership has allowed for the free flow of both labor and physical capital. A common market can proceed further to a monetary union with a common currency and common monetary policy. Finally, an economic union is characterized by members attempting to harmonize domestic policies concerning the areas of taxation and spending, domestic regulation, competition, and other areas of interest. The most notable case of an economic union is the European Union, discussed later.

One issue that inevitably arises in the design of PTAs in the form of FTAs is how to determine whether a product is from a partner country. In an FTA, a product can be imported into a low-tariff member and then resold in a high-tariff member, a process known as *tariff rate arbitrage*.[8] To protect against tariff rate arbitrage, FTA members usually establish **rules of origin** (ROOs).[9] As outlined by Krishna (2009), ROOs can be defined using four criteria. The first of these is the amount of *domestic content* of the good, measured either in terms of value added or in direct, physical terms. The second is in terms of a *change in tariff heading* (CTH) where the good must move from one tariff category to another during a production process in an FTA member country. The third is in terms of *specified processes* (or tasks) that outline the actual production processes that must take place within the FTA.[10] The fourth approach is in terms of *substantial transformation*, a loosely defined term that can vary from one instance to another. In many respects, FTAs are defined by their ROOs, and an understanding of them is therefore a key part of understanding any particular FTA. Further, empirical evidence suggests that they have significant impacts.[11] The case of automobile ROOs in the North American Free Trade Agreement (NAFTA) is considered in the accompanying box.

NAFTA Automobile ROOs

Under the North American Free Trade Agreement (NAFTA), exporters must fill out a NAFTA Certificate of Origin (CO) based on NAFTA ROOs. In general, the origination of a product is defined in terms of *substantial transformation*, and substantial transformation is, in turn defined in terms of a *change in tariff heading* (CTH). This requirement can be relaxed, however, under a *de minimis rule* if nonoriginating materials make up less than 7 percent of the total value of the product. There is also the alternative of demonstrating sufficiently high *regional value content* (RVC). RVC, in turn, can be defined in two ways: in terms of transactions value or in terms of net cost. Even this superficial view of the NAFTA ROOs indicates that they are not a model of simplicity.

[8] As noted by Tarr (2009), CUs do not need rules of origin because goods from outside the CU enter any CU member under the same tariff regime. This is one advantage of a CU over an FTA.

[9] In terms of global governance, ROOs are covered under the International Convention on the Simplification and Harmonization of Customs Procedures (the Kyoto Convention, 1974, revised in 1998).

[10] Clearly, this can be very close to the CTH approach. Krishna (2009) noted that "The difference between this and the CTH criterion is only that the latter is based on some commonly used description such as the tariff code, whereas the specified process definition is defined in terms of production processes specific to each industry" (p. 980).

[11] See, for example, Anson et al. (2005) for the case of NAFTA.

Automobiles have special provisions for a NAFTA CO. Here, the RVC must be calculated using the net cost method. The NAFTA automobile RVC calculation includes the *value of nonoriginating materials* (VNM), and this is, in turn, calculated using one of two sets of tracing rules for materials used in the manufacturing process, one for "heavy-duty" goods (engines and transmissions) and another for "light-duty" goods. Heavy-duty goods are required to include the total value of *all* nonoriginating materials in the VNM. Light-duty goods, on the other hand, only need to include the value of nonoriginating materials specified on a light-duty tracing list.

Preparation of a NAFTA CO is complicated in general, which is why Friedman (2003) advised: "It is imperative that producers and exporters asked to complete a NAFTA CO understand and properly apply the NAFTA Rules of Origin before certifying merchandise or relying on a CO from a supplier.... Consequently, advice concerning a specific circumstance should come from a qualified customs attorney." The exporter or producer of an automotive product needs to be particularly concerned that it has adequately addressed the complicated ROOs governing this kind of trade in North America.

Sources: Trade Information Center, U.S. Department of Commerce, and Friedman (2003)

THE ECONOMIC EFFECTS OF PREFERENTIAL TRADE AGREEMENTS

What are the economic effects of PTAs? Jacob Viner (1950) first addressed this question in a famous book entitled *The Customs Union Issue.* In this book, Viner distinguished between the concepts of trade creation and trade diversion in PTAs. Trade creation occurs when the formation of a PTA leads to a switching of imports from a high-cost source to a low-cost source. Trade diversion occurs when imports switch from a low-cost source to a high-cost source. As we will soon see, trade creation tends to improve welfare, whereas trade diversion tends to worsen welfare. Let's summarize trade creation and trade diversion in a box:

Trade creation: switching of imports from a high-cost source to a low-cost source. Tends to improve welfare.

Trade diversion: switching of imports from a low-cost source to a high cost source. Tends to worsen welfare.

We are going to illustrate the concepts of trade creation and trade diversion using the absolute advantage model we developed in Chapter 2. We are going to consider two countries that are members of a PTA, Brazil (B) and Argentina (A). We are also going to refer to a third country, El Salvador (S), which is an excluded nonmember. A PTA that involves *trade creation* is presented in Figure 8.1. In this figure, we take the perspective of Brazil. S^B is Brazil's supply curve of some good, and D^B is Brazil's demand curve for the same good. Brazil can import the good from Argentina at price P^A and from El Salvador at price P^S. The crucial point here is that Argentina is the lower cost producer in comparison with El Salvador.

Before the PTA, Brazil has in place a specific (per unit) tariff of T on imports from *both* Argentina and El Salvador. Because $P^A + T < P^S + T$, Brazil imports the good from Argentina, and the initial import level is Z^B. Once Brazil joins the PTA with Argentina, the tariff is removed on imports from Argentina. Clearly, $P^A < P^S + T$,

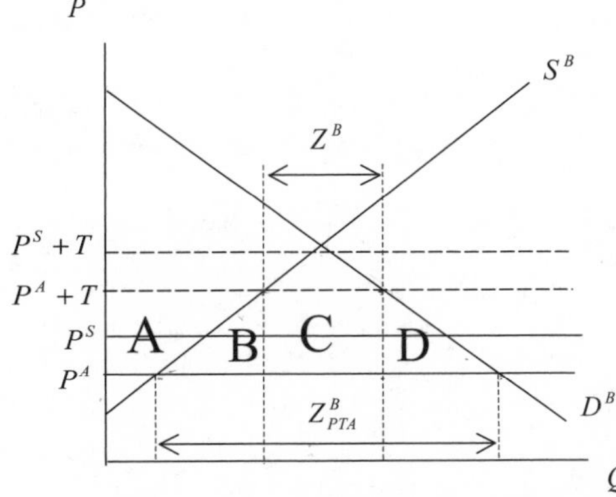

Figure 8.1. A Trade-Creating PTA between Brazil and Argentina Note: Areas A, B, C, and D extend vertically between P^A and $P^A + T$.

so the good continues to be imported from Argentina. The imports, however, expand from Z^B to Z^B_{PTA} as the price falls from $P^A + T$ to P^A.

As a result of the PTA with Argentina, consumer surplus in Brazil increases in Figure 8.1 by area A + B + C + D. Producer surplus falls by A, and government tariff revenue falls by C.[12] The net increase in welfare due to trade creation is B + D. Let's summarize this:

Consumer surplus:	A + B + C + D
Producer surplus:	−A
Government revenue:	−C
Net welfare:	B + D

The switch in "imports" in the trade-creating PTA described in Figure 8.1 is from a high-cost source, namely Brazil itself, to a low-cost source, Argentina, and takes place in the movement down the Brazilian supply curve. This trade-creating switch is what generates the increase in welfare in Brazil.

A PTA that involves *trade diversion* is presented in Figure 8.2. In this figure, and in contrast to Figure 8.1, El Salvador is now the lower cost producer in comparison with Argentina. That is, $P^S < P^A$. Because $P^S + T < P^A + T$, before the PTA, Brazil imports the good from El Salvador, and the initial import level is Z^B. Once Brazil joins a PTA with Argentina, however, $P^A < P^S + T$, so Brazil switches to Argentina as an import supplier. Imports expand to Z^B_{PTA} as the domestic price falls from $P^S + T$ to P^A.

As a result of the PTA with Argentina, consumer surplus in Brazil increases by area A + B + C + D in Figure 8.2. Producer surplus falls by A, and government revenue falls by C + E. The net increase in welfare is therefore B + D − E.

Let's summarize this:

Consumer surplus:	A + B + C + D
Producer surplus:	−A
Government revenue:	−C − E
Net welfare:	B + D − E

[12] Recall that the concepts of consumer and producer surplus were discussed in the appendix to Chapter 2. Please refer to that appendix if you need to.

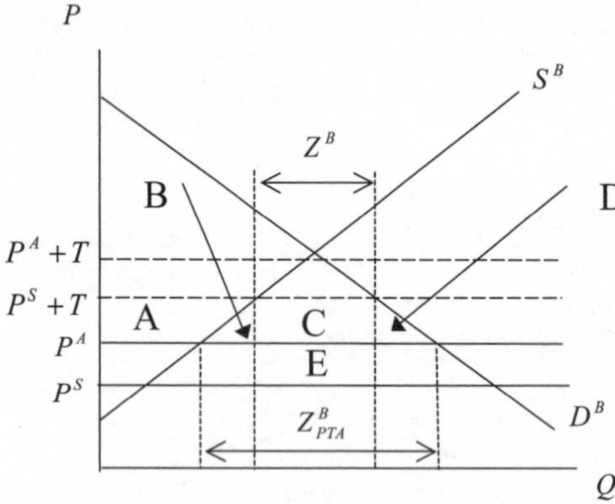

Figure 8.2. A Trade-Diverting PTA between Brazil and Argentina. *Note:* Areas A, B, C, and D extend vertically between P^A and $P^S + T$.

Whether the net welfare effect in Figure 8.2 is a positive or negative value depends on the relative sizes of B + D and E. Area B + D represents the trade-creating effects of switching "imports" from the higher cost source of Brazil to the lower cost source of Argentina. However, area E represents the trade-diverting effects of switching imports from the lower cost source of El Salvador to the higher cost source of Argentina. If the trade-diverting effects outweigh the trade-creating effects (if E > B + D), then the PTA will *reduce* welfare in Brazil.

What should you take from the preceding discussion of trade creation and trade diversion? Let's summarize it in a box:

PTAs can be either welfare-improving or welfare-worsening. Whether a PTA is welfare-improving or welfare-worsening is something that must be assessed on a case-by-case basis, based on evidence of the relative strengths of trade creation and trade diversion.

As a consequence of the above, assessments of PTAs are often made using more sophisticated and numerical versions of Figures 8.1 and 8.2. That is, trade economists are often called on to mathematically model the effects of PTAs.[13] If you are involved with the assessment of PTAs in any way, you might need to interpret the results of such modeling exercises. Each of the chapters in Part I of this book concerning our first window on the world economy, international trade, has contributed to your ability to do so. This issue is examined briefly in the appendix to this chapter.

THE EUROPEAN UNION

The European Union (EU) is the current name for a set of agreements among 27 (at the time of this writing) European countries in the realms of economics, foreign and security policies, and justice and home affairs. The evolution of the EU is summarized in Table 8.3. Its roots extend back to the Marshall Plan under which the United States aided in the reconstruction of Europe after World War II and promoted the liberalization of trade and payments among the European countries in its zone of influence. These liberalization processes were facilitated by the Organization for European Economic

[13] For the important case of the North American Free Trade Agreement, see Francois and Shiells (1997). This was one of the first instances where mathematical models played an important role in the actual policy deliberations surrounding a proposed PTA.

Table 8.3. The evolution of the European Union

Year	Initiative	Treaty	Members added
1951	European Coal and Steel Community	Treaty of Paris	Belgium France Germany Italy Luxembourg Netherlands
1958	European Economic Community	Treaty of Rome	
1973	Enlargement		Denmark Ireland United Kingdom
1981	Enlargement		Greece
1986	Enlargement		Portugal Spain
1992	European Union	Treaty on European Union (TEU), or the Maastricht Treaty	
1995	Enlargement		Austria Finland Sweden
1999	European Monetary Union		United Kingdom, Sweden, and Denmark not included
2002	Common EMU currency: the euro		United Kingdom, Sweden, and Denmark not included
2004	Enlargement		Cyprus Czech Republic Estonia Hungary Latvia Lithuania Malta Poland Slovakia Slovenia
2007	Enlargement		Bulgaria Romania
2007	EU Constitution	Lisbon Treaty	

Sources: Dinan (2010) and europa.eu

Cooperation and the European Payments Union.[14] In 1951, the Treaty of Paris was signed, and this led to the formation of the European Coal and Steel Community (ECSC) among Belgium, France, Germany, Italy, Luxembourg, and the Netherlands, countries that became known as The Six. The purpose of the ECSC was to liberalize trade and promote competition in the steel and coal sectors of the Western European economy.

[14] The Organization for European Economic Cooperation later became the Paris-based Organization for Economic Cooperation and Development (OECD).

In 1957, the Treaty of Rome was signed. This led to the formation of the European Economic Community (EEC) in 1958. The ultimate goal of the EEC was the creation of a common market. Initially, however, the EEC was a movement toward an FTA in a decade-long transitional period. The EEC took the step to a CU in 1968 with the introduction of a common external tariff. Between 1973 and 1986, its membership increased from six to 12 countries. The year 1992 marked the *official* completion of a common market in which barriers to labor and physical capital were to be removed (the *actual* completion of a common market will always be a work in progress). With the signing of the Maastricht Treaty in 1992, the EEC was joined by initiatives in the areas of foreign and security policy and justice and home affairs under what became known as the European Union. Austria, Finland, and Sweden joined the EU in 1995, bringing the membership to 15. An ambitious enlargement in 2004 added 10 more countries as EU members, and an enlargement in 2007 brought the total membership to 27.[15]

In recent years, the EU has ventured even beyond a common market to a monetary union with the launch of the euro in January 2002. We take up these important developments in Chapter 19. A current preoccupation of the EU is the issue of a constitution or constitutional treaty. At the time of this writing, the Lisbon Treaty is the active constitutional document, and it was ratified by all 27 EU members as of 2009.

In an early round of research, some economists (e.g., Hufbauer, 1990; Lawrence, 1991; and Sapir, 1992) argue that trade creation dominated trade diversion in the European Community and EU. Winters (1993) expressed a much more cautionary view, noting that, despite the common external tariff of the European Union CU, nontariff barriers (e.g., quotas) increased in sectors such as motor vehicles, VCRs, and footwear. He also noted that EU subsidies increased in sectors such as aircraft, steel, shipbuilding, and agriculture. An intermediate view was offered by Tsoukalis (1997), who pointed to overall trade creation in manufactured goods and overall trade diversion in agricultural goods. The latter has been largely the result of the Common Agricultural Policy (CAP), which has protected EEC/EU agriculture from foreign competition and has involved the heavy use of export subsidies. Protection levels for EU agriculture under the CAP remain high, but the WTO Agreement on Agriculture, discussed in Chapter 7, has introduced a modicum of discipline.[16]

More recent research has been provided by De Santis and Vicarelli (2007) and Gil, Llorca, and Martíniz-Serrano (2008). De Santis and Vicarelli (2007) examined the EU's trade patterns between 1960 and 2000 and accounted for its evolving network of PTAs with nonmembers. These authors found significant trade creation among EU members but only limited trade diversion due to the expanding set of external PTAs. Gil, Llorca, and Martíniz-Serrano (2008) focused on trade creation (but not trade diversion). These researchers carefully examined the evolution of the EU's trading relationships and trade flows over the years 1950–2004, accounting for its gradual expansion of members. They conclude that each successive enlargement has increased trade and that the deepening of the regional integration scheme from an FTA to CU to common market and monetary union also has had a positive effect on trade. Because this study did not account for trade diversion, it is not a welfare analysis as in Figures 8.1 and 8.2, but is significant nonetheless.

[15] At the time of this writing, candidate countries included Croatia, Macedonia, and Turkey.
[16] The EU CAP has also had implications for progress in the Doha Round. See Reinert (2007).

THE NORTH AMERICAN FREE TRADE AGREEMENT

In 1989, an FTA between Canada and the United States came into effect. Sometime thereafter, former Mexican President Carlos Salinas de Gortari approached a number of countries in Western Europe with the intent of convincing them to enter into trade liberalization with Mexico. On his trip to Europe, he found these countries to be distracted with the movement to the European Union described in the preceding section. As the story is now told, on a return flight from Europe, Salinas decided to pursue an FTA with the United States. In 1990, former U.S. president George H.W. Bush and Salinas announced their intention to begin negotiating an FTA. In 1991, however, they were joined by Canada to begin negotiations for a **North American Free Trade Agreement** (NAFTA) involving all three countries. The agreement was signed in 1992 and took effect in 1994.[17] It was fully phased in by 2009.

The NAFTA agreement was ambitious. Along with trade in goods, it addressed financial services, transportation, telecommunications, foreign direct investment, intellectual property rights, government procurement, and dispute settlement. With regard to trade in goods, NAFTA liberalized trade in the highly protected automobile, textile, and clothing markets. However, as discussed in the following box, it employed restrictive ROOs in these sectors as well. In agriculture, NAFTA phased out tariffs over a 10-year period and transformed quotas into tariff-rate quotas (see Chapter 6 Appendix), which were phased out over 10- to 15-year periods. Foreign direct investment was liberalized.[18] NAFTA also provided significant intellectual property protection in a manner similar to the TRIPs Agreement discussed in Chapter 7.

During the discussions and political deliberations surrounding the NAFTA negotiations, issues of trade and the environment and trade and labor rose quickly to the surface. Mathematical models of these issues are discussed in the accompanying box. Institutionally, however, NAFTA was innovative in that it responded to these concerns with the North American Agreement on Environmental Cooperation (NAAEC) and the North American Agreement on Labor Cooperation (NAALC). These are sometimes referred to as the NAFTA "side agreements." The NAAEC established the Border Environmental Cooperation Commission, the North American Development Bank, and the Commission for Environmental Cooperation, whereas the NAALC established the Commission for Labor Cooperation.

What does research on NAFTA tell us about its effects? Evidence suggests that FDI into Mexico did indeed respond positively to the presence of NAFTA, although there is a constitutional ban against FDI in Mexico's energy sector.[19] Despite arguments to the contrary, NAFTA's impacts on job losses in the United States have been small relative to overall employment trends in that country.[20] The NAFTA ROOs substantially limit market access for Mexico in all but textiles and clothing,[21] and the NAFTA agreement has had detrimental impacts on Mexico's corn producers.[22] Despite the ROOs, however,

[17] Since then, Mexico and the EU have signed an FTA.

[18] Despite the fact that NAFTA involves the removal of barriers to FDI, it is not a common market because it does not allow for the free movement of *labor* within North America.

[19] See Ramirez (2006).

[20] See Hufbauer and Schott (2005).

[21] See Anson et al. (2005).

[22] See Ramirez (2003). Martin (2005) noted that "Mexico had about 3 million corn farmers in the mid-1990s, but the 75,000 corn farmers in Iowa produced twice as much corn as Mexico at half the price" (p. 452). This is partly due to the heavy subsidization of corn in the United States.

automobile trade (both parts and finished automobiles) within North America has expanded rapidly.

NAFTA, Wages, and Industrial Pollution

The issues of trade and wages in general and of North-South trade and wages in particular have recently received a great deal of attention by economists and public policy analysts. Most of the discussion has taken place in terms of the Heckscher-Ohlin model of international trade and its associated Stolper-Samuelson theorem, discussed in Chapter 5. Reinert and Roland-Holst (1998) set out to address this issue in the context of the North American Free Trade Agreement (NAFTA).

These researchers constructed a 26-sector model of the North American economy, including Canada, the United States, and Mexico. They simulated the effects of expanding trade that would take place under NAFTA on five labor categories: professional and managerial, sales and clerical, agricultural, craft, and operators and laborers. In a number of different simulations under different labor supply assumptions, they found that real wages in the United States *increased* for all five types of workers. There was no downward pressure on wages in the United States, even for blue collar workers.

As suggested by Ruffin (1999) in another study, and as discussed in Chapter 4, these results reflect the presence of a great deal of *intra*-industry trade between the United States and Mexico that their model captures. In most sectors, trade expands in *both* directions between these two countries, something that is not possible in the strict Heckscher-Ohlin framework of *inter*-industry trade.

In 2000, the North American Commission for Environmental Cooperation (CEC) sponsored the First North American Symposium on Understanding the Linkages between Trade and Environment. In one contribution to this symposium, Reinert and Roland-Holst (2001) set out to assess the impacts of trade liberalization under NAFTA on industrial pollution in Canada, the United States, and Mexico. They used the same model of the North American economy described above, focusing on the manufacturing sectors in the model and utilizing pollutant data from the Industrial Pollution Projection System of the World Bank.

Reinert and Roland-Holst found that the most serious environmental consequences of NAFTA occur in the base metals sector. In terms of magnitude, the greatest impacts are in the United States and Canada, and this is the case for most of the pollutants considered. As alleged in the debate over NAFTA and the environment mentioned previously, the Mexican petroleum sector is a significant source of industrial pollution, particularly in the case of air pollution. For specific pollutants in specific countries, the transportation equipment sector and the chemicals sector are also important sources of industrial pollution.

Modeling results such as the above alert policymakers to likely labor market and pollution effects of PTAs and can be repeated for any new PTAs that come under negotiation.

Sources: Reinert and Roland-Holst (1998), Reinert and Roland-Holst (2001), and Ruffin (1999)

Truck transportation has been a sticking point in NAFTA. Full access to the U.S. trucking market was to have been granted by 2000, and a NAFTA arbitration panel ruled in Mexico's favor on this in 2001. Even the U.S. Supreme Court weighed in on the issue in favor of Mexico in 2004. But the U.S. Congress removed funding for even a successful pilot project in 2009, and Mexico consequently imposed retaliatory tariffs. This issue was resolved in mid-2011. Another sticking point has been migration. Despite hopes that NAFTA would decrease migration from Mexico to the United States, this has not been the case.[23] Hopes for development and environmental improvements along the U.S.-Mexican border have also been disappointed due to the lack of funding for the North American Development Bank.

MERCOSUR AND THE FTAA

A PTA among Argentina, Brazil, Paraguay, and Uruguay was launched in 1991 with the Treaty of Asunción, named after the capital city of Paraguay. This PTA, the Common Market of the South, or Mercosur, took on Chile and Bolivia as associate members in 1996 and 1997, respectively. Peru, Colombia, and Ecuador became associate members is 2003–2004. Venezuela signed a membership agreement in 2006, but at the time of this writing, finalization of this status is awaiting ratification in the Brazilian and Paraguayan parliaments. The name Mercosur is somewhat misleading, because it suggests that the PTA among the four core members is an actual common market with the free movement of labor and physical capital (see Table 8.2). This is not the case, however. Mercosur entered into force in 1995 as an FTA. A customs union was to be finalized by 2006. Free movement of labor and physical capital is a long way off.[24]

The formulation of Mercosur has had a positive impact on the amount of trade among its four core members, and the technology profile of traded goods is higher for trade within Mercosur than for trade between Mercosur and the rest of the world. That said, however, intra-Mercosur trade is low by world standards. Mercosur has also been troubled by two asymmetries. First, Argentina and Brazil dwarf Paraguay and Uruguay in economic size. Consequently, the smaller members find themselves somewhat sidelined from the core relationship between Argentina and Brazil. Second, for a number of years, there was a fundamental macroeconomic asymmetry between Argentina and Brazil. After its crisis of 1998, the Brazilian real became a freely floating currency, whereas until its crisis in 2002, the Argentine peso was rigidly pegged to the U.S. dollar under a currency board arrangement (see Chapter 16). These asymmetries caused a great deal of friction between Argentina and Brazil and complicated the functioning of Mercosur.[25]

The institutions of Mercosur have been described by a number of researchers as being "wide" but not "deep." These include a Council providing political leadership, an executive Common Market Group, a Commerce Commission, a Joint Parliamentary Commission, and a Secretariat in Montevideo, Uruguay. There have also been allegations that the PTA has become "politicized." This is largely due to the 2006 Córdoba Meeting in which Venezuelan president Hugo Chavez played a significant role, denouncing the United States and "neoliberalism." Despite all of these difficulties

[23] See Martin (2005). Of the approximately 8 million Mexican workers in the United States, approximately 6 million are illegal. We take up migration issues in Chapter 12.

[24] Politically, Mercosur is indeed an achievement. Its two main members, Brazil and Argentina, were estranged rivals as recently as the mid 1980s. Consider Reid (2002): "Until 1985, apart from a couple of border encounters, only three Brazilian presidents had ever visited Argentina, and only two Argentine rulers had made the trip the other way. The two countries' railway networks had been built to different gauges. As recently as the 1970s, Argentina and Brazil were engaged in a nuclear arms race" (p. 4).

[25] More recently, a conflict began in 2006 between Argentina and Uruguay over the issue of Uruguay's intent to site paper mills on the Uruguay River between the two countries. Despite adjudication of this issue by the International Court of Justice in the Hague in 2007, this issue remains unresolved.

and limitations, however, the achievements of Mercosur have been significant, and it could continue to play an important role in Latin America.

At the end of 1994, the governments of 34 countries in the Western Hemisphere met at the First Summit of the Americas. They agreed to pursue a Free Trade Area of the Americas (FTAA) with the goal of concluding such an agreement by 2005. Negotiations concerning the FTAA were launched at the Second Summit of the Americas in 1998. Nine negotiating groups were formed in the following areas: (1) Market Access, (2) Investment, (3) Services, (4) Government Procurement, (5) Dispute Settlement, (6) Agriculture, (7) Intellectual Property Rights, (8) Subsidies, Antidumping, and Countervailing Duties, and (9) Competition Policy. Draft agreements in each of these areas were concluded in 2001 and 2002. If it had been successful, the FTAA would have represented the largest free trade area in the world in terms of both market size and territory.

Beginning in 2002, the United States began to implement increased protection of its steel sector and increased subsidies for its agricultural sector. Within Latin America, these measures were seen as unfortunate and called into question the spirit of the FTAA process. The Brazilian government was particularly concerned about U.S. steel protection. Having at one time attempted to move up the FTAA negotiations deadline to the end of 2003, the United States eventually agreed to keep the original 2005 deadline. This deadline, though, was missed.

The 2004 Summit of the Americas, taking place in Monterrey, Mexico, proved unable to solve remaining issues. The most significant disagreement was between the United States and Brazil. The United States had insisted that issues related to agricultural subsidies and antidumping measures be excluded from the FTAA negotiations, to be pursued only in the ongoing *multilateral* trade negotiations taking place as part of the Doha Round. Brazil objected to these stipulations, as well as to the insistence of the United States that the FTAA negotiations include issues of government procurement and intellectual property.[26] In the end, what emerged from the 2004 Summit of the Americas was a far less ambitious "FTAA lite," with offers by the United States to pursue deeper agreements on a plurilateral basis with interested subsets of countries in the Americas.

The Fifth Summit of the Americas took place in 2005 in Mar del Plata, Argentina. It was hosted by President Néstor Kirchner, who formed an alliance with Venezuela's Hugo Chavez. At this Summit, Mercosur members plus Venezuela blocked any further FTAA progress. In its stead, Chavez pushed the Bolivarian Alternative for the Americas (ALBA). With only Venezuela, Cuba, Bolivia, and Nicaragua as members, however, this falls far short of regional integration in the Americas, which remains an unfulfilled goal.

ASEAN AND AFTA

PTAs have been proliferating in the Asia-Pacific region since the late 1990s. At the center of this proliferation is the Association of Southeast Asian Nations (ASEAN).

[26] Rivas-Campo and Juk Benke (2003) noted that: "Given the U.S. position . . . to encourage global instead of regional liberalization in agriculture, Latin American countries have underlined the minimal gains that an FTAA without agricultural liberalization would signify for developing and agriculture-dependent countries" (p. 669) and "As long as the U.S. remains reluctant to eliminate agricultural subsidies, Latin American countries may also be unwilling to favor substantial agricultural liberalization in the region" (p. 670).

ASEAN was formed in 1967 and currently includes 10 countries: Brunei, Cambodia, Indonesia, the Lao People's Democratic Republic, Malaysia, Myanmar, the Philippines, Singapore, Thailand, and Vietnam. Since the late 1970s, it has turned its attention from political cooperation to economic integration.[27] In 1992, the first six members of ASEAN (ASEAN-6) formed the ASEAN Free Trade Area (AFTA), but this PTA now includes all 10 members, although the ASEAN-4 (Cambodia, Lao PDR, Myanmar, and Vietnam) are not expected to be fully integrated until 2012.

The AFTA is an attempt to reduce intra-PTA tariffs and nontariff measures. This is done using what AFTA terms the Common Effective Preferential Tariff (CEPT). The CEPT is a means through which AFTA is in the process of reducing all intra-PTA tariffs to the 0–5 percent ad valorem range. ROOs are of course utilized to determine ASEAN origination. Efforts are underway to liberalize investment within ASEAN as well.

ASEAN is linking its AFTA to other countries in the region through a number of initiatives. For example, in the wake of the Asian financial crisis of 1997, ASEAN formed a relationship with the East Asian countries China, Japan, and South Korea. This has become known as the ASEAN+3. ASEAN+3 initially focused on financial issues, but there has been talk of this regional partnership evolving into a PTA. This was overshadowed by a number of "ASEAN+1" agreements, including ASEAN-China (2002), ASEAN-Japan (2002), ASEAN-India (2002), and ASEAN-Republic of Korea (2009). In 2009, there was also concluded an ASEAN-Australia-New Zealand Free Trade Area or (AANZFTA).[28]

One interesting and oft-noted fact characterizing AFTA is that its major trading partners are outside of ASEAN. Cabalu and Alfonso (2007) attribute this to helping suppress trade diversion effects. Indeed, they note that ASEAN's trade with the rest of the world grew by nearly 7 percent annually in real (inflation-adjusted) terms between 1980 and 2005. Cabalu and Alfonso examined the trade patterns of the ASEAN-6 and found significant trade creation in basic industrial goods. They note that this is "in keeping with AFTA's goal of turning the region into a single production base" (p. 15).

REGIONALISM AND MULTILATERALISM

Due to their discriminatory nature, the presence of PTAs in the world trading system sits uneasily with principles of multilateralism. As we stated in the introduction, regionalism and multilateralism represent two alternative trade policy options available to the countries of the world. In the 1950s and 1960s, there had been what is now called the "first wave" of PTAs in the developing world, particularly in Latin America. This was often in conjunction with protectionist policies against the rest of the world, particularly in Latin America.[29] For example, there had been an ill-fated Central American Common Market (CACM) launched at the end of the 1960s. Beginning in the 1980s, there began what is now called the "second wave" of PTAs, during which their numbers began to increase substantially. The question on many observers' minds is whether this second wave of PTAs complements the multilateral framework or works at cross-purposes to it.

[27] See Feridhanusetyawan (2005) and Tongzon (2009).

[28] These dates refer to the first official statements of intent, not of implementation.

[29] In the Latin American case, see Chapter 9 of Bulmer-Thomas (2003).

The (lengthy) policy discussion on the role of second-wave PTAs in the world trading system often addresses whether they are more appropriately described as "building blocks" or "stumbling blocks" to multilateral trade liberalization.[30] As building blocks, PTAs could evolve as ever-expanding systems that bring more and more countries into postures of trade liberalization. For example, Baldwin (2006) envisioned PTAs evolving into a form of "multilateralized regionalism." As stumbling blocks, PTA negotiations (and there are a lot of them) can take energy and focus away from multilateral trade negotiations. As Bhagwati (1993) stated many years ago, "the taking to two roads can affect adversely the travel down one" (p. 30).

There is also concern with regard to the overlapping and complex nature of PTAs and their ROOs. This has taken the form of what Bhagwati (1993) famously termed the "spaghetti bowl" of PTAs (sometimes called a "noodle bowl" in Asia). On this point, Bhagwati, Greenaway, and Panagariya (1998) warned of a movement toward "numerous and crisscrossing (PTAs) and innumerable applicable tariff rates depending on arbitrarily-determined and often a multiplicity of sources of origin" (p. 1139). Take, for example, the case of Mexico. As discussed previously, Mexico is a member of NAFTA, but it also is (at the time of this writing) a member of the following PTAs: Mexico-Chile, Mexico-Costa Rica, Mexico-EU, Mexico-European Free Trade Area, Mexico-Guatemala, Mexico-Honduras, Mexico-Israel, Mexico-Japan, and Mexico-Nicaragua. Mexico is connected to the United States via NAFTA, and the Central American countries in this list are connected to the United States via the Central American Free Trade Agreement. Simplicity this is not.

More positively, the perspective of international political economy suggests that trading blocs and customs unions (and their increased levels of trade and FDI) can have a role in reducing international conflict, including military conflict, a clear benefit.[31] There are also repeated calls for attempts to better leverage PTAs as building blocks to strengthened multilateralism on the grounds that trading blocs and customs unions are "here to stay." Economists, social scientists, and policymakers will no doubt debate these issues for some time to come. What is clear, however, is that proper oversight of these arrangements at the level of the WTO is a necessary condition for a positive relationship between PTAs and the multilateral trading system. As discussed previously, however, this oversight is missing.

The WTO could go further and tighten its requirements on the external protection of FTAs and CUs. To understand why this could be important, take a new look at the trade-diverting PTA between Brazil and Argentina as depicted in Figure 8.2. Suppose that the tariff on imports from El Salvador had been eliminated, along with the tariff on imports from Argentina. If this were the case, Brazil would continue to import from El Salvador, there would be no trade diversion, and welfare would unambiguously increase. This fact has led some analysts to argue that external tariffs ought to be reduced in a CU or FTA in order to mitigate against trade diversion. Analysts similarly call for common external tariffs in CUs to be set to the *lowest* of the pre-CU tariffs of the members.[32]

These considerations indicate that it is possible to lessen the tensions between regionalism and multilateralism. It is probably not possible to eliminate these tensions entirely.

[30] This terminology was first introduced by Bhagwati (1993).
[31] See, for example, Mansfield and Pevehouse (2000).
[32] See McMillan (1993), Bhagwati (1993), and Serra et al. (1997).

As stated at the beginning of this chapter, "when multilateralism falters, regionalism picks up the pace." It is the responsibility of all WTO members, but especially the larger WTO members, to ensure that multilateralism does not falter. Without this commitment to multilateralism, no amount of tinkering with WTO provisions on PTAs will help.

"New" or "Open" Regionalism

In the debate of the relationship between PTAs and multilateralism, you will sometimes come across the terms *new regionalism* and *open regionalism*. It was Ethier (1998, 2001) who first made a case for what he termed *new regionalism*. In his view, this new regionalism was distinct from the "old regionalism" of the 1950s and 1960s in both its environment and its content. Countries were engaging in PTAs while also committing to multilateral trade liberalization, with the membership of the WTO expanding steadily. Many PTAs also involve the liberalization of FDI (and harmonization of other policies) along with trade liberalization.

According to Ethier, "the new regionalism reflects the success of multilateralism – not its failure." Why? Small countries use PTAs as a means to secure the FDI inflows that make sustained trade liberalization possible. These FDI inflows are necessary to provide visible benefits to citizens that offset losses associated with trade liberalization. Note that our discussion of trade diversion and trade creation in Figures 8.1 and 8.2 said nothing about FDI flows. When it comes to the political economy of trade liberalization, these FDI flows can be important in maintaining political support for the multilateral trading system.

Sources: Ethier (1998, 2001)

CONCLUSION

The GATT and WTO have allowed for exceptions to the basic nondiscrimination principle in the case of four avenues to PTAs: FTAs, CUs, enabling clause arrangements, and GATS arrangements. These and other PTAs have been part of the world trading system for decades, and all evidence points to their continued presence. The evolution of PTAs in Europe, the Americas, and Asia are some prominent examples. PTAs may improve or worsen welfare depending on the balance between their trade creation and trade diversion effects. Trade policy faces the significant challenge of incorporating the preferential predilections of the WTO's member countries into a general multilateral evolution of world trade. This challenge can only be met by WTO oversight of active PTAs. Unfortunately, this important ingredient is missing.

REVIEW EXERCISES

1. What distinguishes a customs union from a free trade area? What distinguishes a common market from a customs union?
2. What is the difference between trade creation and trade diversion? Can you provide an example of each?
3. Do you support regionalism and PTAs as a legitimate trade policy option? Why or why not?

4. We mentioned earlier that the size of Brazil's tariff against El Salvador affects the amount of trade diversion that occurs in a PTA. Use a version of Figure 8.2 to demonstrate that the lower *T* is against El Salvador, the more likely it is that the PTA will improve welfare. Show that if the *T* on imports from El Salvador were eliminated, the PTA would unambiguously improve welfare.
5. Pay a visit to the WTO's website on regionalism. From www.wto.org, follow the link to "Trade Issues" and, from there, to "Regionalism." Spend some time perusing the WTO's materials on this issue.

FURTHER READING AND WEB RESOURCES

An early and important analysis of PTAs can be found in de Melo and Panagariya (1993a, 1993b). A more recent source on regional integration more broadly and its links to development is Schiff and Winters (2003). For a view from the perspective of the WTO, see Crawford and Fiorentino (2005). An important overview of the European Union can be found in Dinan (2010). For NAFTA, see Hufbauer and Schott (2005). For a critical review of Mercosur, see Malamud (2005). For a concise introduction to the FTAA, see Feinberg (2009). Readers who want to delve deeper into issues of the role of ASEAN and AFTA in Asian PTAs can consult Francois and Wignaraja (2008).

The WTO maintains a Regional Trade Agreements Information System (RTA-IS). To access this, go to www.wto.org and select: Trade Topics ⇒ Regional Trade Agreements ⇒ RTA Database. The European Union's website can be found at europa.eu. The NAFTA Secretariat's home page is www.nafta-sec-alena.org. The official Mercosur website is at www.mercosur.int, and the FTAA website is at www.alca-ftaa.org. Finally, the ASEAN Free Trade Area website is at www.aseansec.org.

APPENDIX: RULES OF THUMB IN EVALUATING PTAS

Despite the importance of multilateral trade negotiations, preferential trade agreements (PTAs) have been of growing importance in the world trading system. As shown in this chapter, the welfare effects of PTAs involve a degree of ambiguity. Consequently, trade policy analysts have turned to mathematical models known as applied general equilibrium (AGE) models to investigate the economic effects, including welfare effects, of this increasingly important component of the world economy.[33]

A large and increasing number of PTAs have been analyzed using the AGE methodology, and researchers Harrison, Rutherford, and Tarr (2003) identified a number of empirical regularities deriving from their simulations of PTAs in Chile, Brazil, Morocco, Tunisia, Turkey, Iran, and Kyrgyzstan. They refer to these empirical regularities as "rules of thumb" for evaluating PTAs. A few of these are as follows:

1. Countries excluded from a PTA almost always lose.
2. Market access is a key determinant of the net benefits of a PTA.
3. Lowering external tariffs against nonmembers of a PTA improves their desirability from a welfare standpoint.
4. Multilateral trade liberalization results in significantly larger gains to the world than a network of PTAs.

[33] On AGE models in general, see Reinert (2009). We mentioned the GTAP AGE model in Chapter 6.

5. For some countries, "additive PTAs" can be more beneficial than unilateral trade liberalization due to the market access gains involved in the former.
6. For developing countries, "North-South" PTAs can offer beneficial increases in competition in their home markets.

These are the sorts of insights available from AGE models of PTAs. For further examples of AGE modeling applied to PTAs, see Reinert and Roland-Holst (1998) and Francois and Wignaraja (2008).

REFERENCES

Anson, J., O. Cadot, A. Estevadeordal, J. de Melo, A. Suwa-Eisenmann, and B. Tumurchudur (2005) "Rules of Origin in North-South Preferential Trading Arrangements with an Application to NAFTA," *Review of International Economics*, 13:3, 501–517.

Bhagwati, J. (1993) "Regionalism and Multilateralism: An Overview," in J. de Melo and A. Panagariya (eds.), *New Dimensions in Regional Integration*, Cambridge University Press, 22–51.

Bhagwati, J., D. Greenaway, and A. Panagariya (1998) "Trading Preferentially: Theory and Policy," *The Economic Journal*, 108:449, 1128–1148.

Baldwin, R.E. (2006) "Multilateralising Regionalism: Spaghetti Bowls as Building Blocks on the Path to Global Free Trade," *World Economy* 29:2, 1451–1518.

Bulmer-Thomas, V. (2003) *The Economic History of Latin America since Independence*, Cambridge University Press.

Cabalu, H. and C. Alfonso (2007) "Does AFTA Create or Divert Trade?" *Global Economy Journal*, 7:4, Article 6.

Crawford, J.-A. and R.V. Fiorentino (2005) *The Changing Landscape of Regional Trade Agreements*, World Trade Organization.

de Melo, J. and A. Panagariya (eds.) (1993a) *New Dimensions in Regional Integration*, Cambridge University Press.

de Melo J. and A. Panagariya (1993b) "Introduction," in J. de Melo and A. Panagariya (eds.), *New Dimensions in Regional Integration*, Cambridge University Press, 3–21.

De Santis, R. and C. Vicarelli (2007) "The 'Deeper' and the 'Wider' EU Strategies of Trade Integration: An Empirical Evaluation of EU Common Commercial Policy Effects," *Global Economy Journal*, 7:4, Article 4.

Dinan, D. (2010) *Ever Closer Union: An Introduction to European Integration*, Lynne Rienner.

Ethier, W.J. (1998) "The New Regionalism," *The Economic Journal*, 108:449, 1149–1161.

Ethier, W.J. (2001) "The New Regionalism in the Americas: A Theoretical Framework," *North American Journal of Economics and Finance*, 12:2, 159–172.

Feinberg, F. (2009) "Free Trade Area of the Americas," in K.A. Reinert, R.S. Rajan, A.J. Glass, and L.S. Davis (eds.), *Princeton Encyclopedia of the World Economy*, Princeton University Press, 505–508.

Feridhanusetyawan, T. (2005) "Preferential Trade Agreements in the Asia-Pacific Region," *International Monetary Fund Working Paper* 149.

Francois, J.F. and C.R. Shiells (1997) *Modeling Trade Policy: Applied General Equilibrium Assessments of North American Free Trade*, Cambridge University Press.

Francois, J.F. and G. Wignaraja (2008) "Economic Implications of Asian Integration," *Global Economy Journal*, 8:3, Article 1.

Friedman, L.M. (2003) "NAFTA Rules of Origin," Barnes Richardson Global Trade Law at www.barnesrichardson.com.

GATT Secretariat (1994) *The Results of the Uruguay Round of Multilateral Trade Negotiations: The Legal Text.*

Gil, S., R. Llorca, and J.A. Martíniz-Serrano (2008) "Assessing the Enlargement and Deepening of the European Union," *World Economy*, 31:9, 1253–1272.

Harrison, G.W., T.F. Rutherford, and D.G. Tarr (2003) "Rules of Thumb for Evaluating Preferential Trading Arrangements: Evidence from CGE Assessments," *Cuadernos de Economia*, 40:121, 460–468.

Hufbauer, G.C. (ed.) (1990) *Europe 1992: An American Perspective*, The Brookings Institution.

Hufbauer, G.C. and J.J. Schott (2005) *NAFTA Revisited: Achievements and Challenges*, Institute for International Economics.

Krishna, K. (2009) "Rules of Origin," in K.A. Reinert, R.S. Rajan, A.J. Glass, and L.S. Davis (eds.), *Princeton Encyclopedia of the World Economy*, Princeton University Press, 980–982.

Lawrence, R. (1991) "Emerging Regional Agreements: Building Blocks or Stumbling Blocks," in R. O'Brien (ed.), *Finance and the International Economy*, Oxford University Press.

Malamud, A. (2005) "Mercosur Turns 15: Between Rising Rhetoric and Declining Achievement," *Cambridge Review of International Affairs*, 18:3, 421–436.

Mansfield, E.O. and J.C. Pevehouse (2000) "Trade Blocs, Trade Flows, and International Conflict," *International Organization*, 54:4, 775–808.

Martin, P. (2005) "Mexico-U.S. Migration," in G.C. Hufbauer and J.J. Schott, *NAFTA Revisited: Achievements and Challenges*, Institute for International Economics, 441–466.

Matsushita, M., T.J. Schoenbaum, and P.C. Mavroidis (2006) *The World Trade Organization: Law, Practice, and Policy*, Oxford University Press.

McMillan, J. (1993) "Does Regional Integration Foster Open Trade? Economic Theory and GATT's Article XXIV," in K. Anderson and R. Blackhurst (eds.), *Regional Integration and the Global Trading System*, Harvester Wheatsheaf, 292–310.

Ramirez, M.D. (2003) "Mexico under NAFTA: A Critical Assessment," *Quarterly Review of Economics and Finance*, 43:5, 863–892.

Ramirez, M.D. (2006) "Is Foreign Direct Investment Beneficial for Mexico? An Empirical Analysis," *World Development*, 43:5, 863–892.

Reid, M. (2002) *Mercosur: A Critical Overview*, Chatham House.

Reinert, K.A. (2007) "The European Union, the Doha Round, and Asia," *Asia Europe Journal*, 5:3, 317–330.

Reinert, K.A. (2009) "Applied General Equilibrium Models," in K.A. Reinert, R.S. Rajan, A.J. Glass, and L.S. Davis (eds.), *Princeton Encyclopedia of the World Economy*, Princeton University Press, 74–79.

Reinert, K.A. and D.W. Roland-Holst (1998) "North South Trade and Occupational Wages: Some Evidence from North America," *Review of International Economics*, 6:1, 74–89.

Reinert, K.A. and D.W. Roland-Holst (2001) "NAFTA and Industrial Pollution: Some General Equilibrium Estimates," *Journal of Economic Integration*, 16:2, 165–179.

Rivas-Campo, J.A. and R.T. Juk Benke (2003) "FTAA Negotiations: Short Overview," *Journal of International Economic Law*, 6:3, 661–694.

Ruffin, R.J. (1999) "The Nature and Significance of Intra-Industry Trade," *Federal Reserve Bank of Dallas Economic and Financial Review*, 4th Quarter, 2–9.

Sapir, A. (2000) "EC Regionalism at the Turn of the Millennium: Toward a New Paradigm," *World Economy*, 23:9, 1135–1148.

Sapir, A. (1992) "Regional Integration in Europe," *Economic Journal*, 102:415, 1491–1506.

Schiff, M. and L.A. Winters (2003) *Regional Integration and Development*, World Bank.

Serra, J. et al. (1997) *Reflections on Regionalism: Report of the Study Group on International Trade*, Carnegie Endowment for International Peace.

Tarr, D.G. (2009) "Customs Unions," in K.A. Reinert, R.S. Rajan, A.J. Glass, and L.S. Davis (eds.), *Princeton Encyclopedia of the World Economy*, Princeton University Press, 256–259.

Tongzon, J.L. (2009) "Association of Southeast Asian Nations," in K.A. Reinert, R.S. Rajan, A.J. Glass, and L.S. Davis (eds.), *Princeton Encyclopedia of the World Economy*, Princeton University Press, 87–89.

Tsoukalis, L. (1997) *The New European Economy Revisited*, Oxford University Press.

Viner, J. (1950) *The Customs Union Issue*, Carnegie Endowment for International Peace.

Winters, L.A. (1993) "The European Community: A Case of Successful Integration?" in J. de Melo and A. Panagariya (eds.), *New Dimensions in Regional Integration*, Cambridge University Press, 202–228.

II INTERNATIONAL PRODUCTION

9 Foreign Market Entry and International Production

In Chapter 3, we discussed the motorcycle market in Vietnam. We saw that the considerations of comparative advantage suggested that Japan would export motorcycles to the Vietnamese market while importing rice. Indeed, beginning in the 1990s, exports of Japanese motorcycles to Vietnam began to increase significantly. The companies involved were Honda, Suzuki, and Yamaha, but the favorite motorcycle in Vietnam was Honda. Indeed, Tiep (2007) noted that "For a long period of time, Honda had become a common name for every motorcycle. Whenever someone saw a motorcycle, he called it 'Honda'" (p. 302). However, in 1997, Honda began to produce motorcycles *in Vietnam itself.* This is not a possibility that we considered in Chapter 3. In that chapter, we implicitly assumed that there was only one means by which Japanese motorcycle manufacturers could serve the Vietnamese market, namely exporting. In practice, however, other means are available. As we begin to examine these other means, we move from the exclusive realm of trade to that of **international production**, the subject of Part II of this book.

As you will learn in this chapter, exports are one possible choice in a menu of options by which a firm can serve a foreign market. Another broad option is **foreign direct investment** (FDI). FDI involves the holding of *at least* 10 percent of the shares in a foreign productive enterprise, considered to be a threshold indicating management influence. A third broad option is **contracting** a foreign firm to carry out production in that country. Our first task in this chapter is to evaluate the three types of **foreign market entry**: exporting, contracting, and FDI. Our second task is to identify a set of *motivations* for international production. Our third task is to consider the entry mode choice decision. Finally, we provide a brief, historical overview of multinational enterprises (MNEs) and international production. This set of topics will give you the necessary background for the more detailed considerations of Chapters 10, 11, and 22.[1] An appendix to the chapter explicitly relates FDI to the comparative advantage model of Chapter 3.

Analytical elements for this chapter:
Countries, sectors, tasks, firms, and *factors of production.*

FOREIGN MARKET ENTRY

In Chapter 1, we saw that trade and foreign direct investment (FDI) were two of the main types of international economic activity. As we will see, trade and FDI are two generic parts of a *menu* of ways in which a firm in one country can interact with the world economy. This menu of options is presented in Table 9.1 and concerns the process of foreign market entry. Foreign market entry takes a close look at a firm's decision-making process with regard to how it is going to supply a foreign market. As indicated in Table 9.1, there are three broad categories of entry: exporting, contractual, and investment.

We begin considering a purely *domestic*, home-country firm. The entire sales of this firm are within its home-country base. At some point, it might begin to considering selling its output in foreign markets. How might it do this? One possible way of

[1] Chapter 22 on international economic development, in Part IV of the book, takes up a set of policy issues that arise when developing countries play host to MNEs.

Table 9.1. The foreign market entry menu

Category	Mode	Characteristics
Domestic	None	The home-country firm is a purely domestic firm relying solely on its home market for sales.
Exporting	Indirect Exporting	The home-country firm relies on another firm known as a sales agent or trading company to complete the export transaction.
Exporting	Direct Exporting	The home-country firm takes on the export transaction itself.
Contractual	Licensing	The home-country firm licenses a foreign firm to allow it to use the home-country firm's production process (including logos, trademarks, designs, and branding) in the foreign country.
Contractual	Franchising	The home-country firm licenses a foreign firm to allow it to use the home-country firm's production process in the foreign country but exerts more control over production and marketing to ensure consistency across foreign markets. The home-country firm also provides assistance to the foreign firm to ensure this consistency.
Contractual	Subcontracting	The home-country firm contracts with a foreign firm to produce a product to certain specifications (materials, processes, and quality). Also known as outsourcing and contract manufacturing.
Investment	Joint Venture (JV)	The home-country firm establishes a separate firm in the foreign country that is jointly owned with a foreign-country firm.
Investment	Mergers and Acquisitions (M&As)	The home-country firm buys part (merger) or all (acquisition) of the shares of an already existing production facility in the foreign country.
Investment	Greenfield Investment	The home-country firm establishes a brand-new production facility in the foreign country that it fully owns.

Source: Based on Root (1998) and Hill (2009)

entering foreign markets is via *exporting*. This might seem to be a simple decision, but as Bernard et al. (2007) emphasize, the extra costs of exporting to foreign markets can confine exporting activity to a relatively small set of firms. For example, they estimate that just 4 percent of firms based in the United States engage in exports. Even within the tradable industries of the United States, only 15 percent of firms export. So the decision to export is not as casual as we might first assume.

Exporting

How can the home-country firm begin its exporting activity? As suggested in Table 9.1, there are two basic approaches. If the firm has little experience with and knowledge of international trade, it might first enter foreign markets in an *indirect exporting* mode. Here it relies on another firm known as a sales agent or trading company to complete the export transaction.[2] This indirect mode of exporting can give the firm some experience with foreign market entry even if it is indirect experience. Alternatively, given this

[2] Hill (2009) noted that "Today's trading companies provide market contacts, trade expertise, commercial financing, foreign distribution, and quality control for traded goods. They vary considerably in size and in sophistication from small, independent operations (such as the Export Management and Export Trading Companies in the United States) to Japan's large *sogo shosha*, or general trading companies (GTCs)" (p. 403). For a historical view of the *sogo shosha*, see Yoshino and Lifson (1986).

experience, it can begin to make a commitment to a *direct exporting* mode. In this case, the firm undertakes the export transaction itself rather than relying on another specialized firm. In this case, the firm takes on the research, marketing, finance, and logistics requirements of the trade transaction. Despite these extra costs, there might be offsetting advantage in being able to develop and manage its own foreign market entry strategy.

Contractual

For a number of reasons, it is possible that our firm might grow dissatisfied with the exporting mode and begin to wish to actually *produce* abroad. As we mentioned previously, this was the case for Honda in Vietnam. The firm might be motivated by the perceived need to engage in some final product finishing, service, or sales to address local demand conditions in an export market. Or it might simply need to engage in some trade-related services itself in that country.[3] However, lack of experience in global production might make it wary of carrying out production itself in the foreign market. This would lead the firm to the *contractual* modes of foreign market entry listed in Table 9.1. The key characteristic of contractual entry modes is that, although they are one important mode of international production, the relationships involved are arm's length, market-based relationships, not ones of ownership

We can distinguish among at least three types of contractual foreign market entry. These are *licensing, franchising,* and *subcontracting.* In the licensing case, the home-country firm sells a license to a foreign firm to allow it to use the home-country firm's production process. This could include use of logos, trademarks, designs, and branding. In return, the foreign firm would pay royalties to the home-country firm for the license rights. In some cases, technology features prominently in decisions with regard to licensing. This is because, given the nature of the firm, the resulting licensing agreement is largely about licensed technology. This puts the firm in the realm of what is known as *technology licensing agreements* on which a great deal of research has taken place. The key issue with technology licensing agreements is that there is always a danger that the home-country firm could lose aspects of the licensed technology to the foreign firm. We will return to this issue below.[4]

In the franchising type of contractual foreign market entry, the home-country firm licenses a foreign firm to allow it to use the home-country firm's production process in the foreign country but exerts more control over production and marketing to ensure consistency across foreign markets. The home-country firm also provides assistance to the foreign firm to ensure this consistency. Franchising arrangements are more common in service and retail firms than in manufacturing, and we are usually most familiar with this type of mode through international hotel and fast food chains.

The third type of contractual foreign market entry is subcontracting, but it is also known as foreign outsourcing and contract manufacturing.[5] Here the home-country

[3] As Dunning and Lundan (2008) stated, "where a market has to be created for a product, where the product needs to be adapted to the requirements of the local buyers, where multiple products are being marketed and there are net benefits to coordinating the sales of these products, or where an efficient after-sales usage, repair and maintenance service is a key ingredient of the product's appeal, a firm may decide that the risk that a foreign sales agent will not adequately meet its needs is likely to outweigh any setting up cost of marketing and distributing facilities from the start" (p. 217).

[4] For a thorough review of technology licensing issues, see chapter 7 of Caves (2007).

[5] There is an important point here with regard to terminology. *Offshoring* refers to moving production to a foreign country but *retaining ownership* and therefore belongs in the *investment* mode. *Outsourcing* or *foreign*

firm contracts with a foreign firm to produce a product to certain specifications (materials, processes, and quality). This form of international production, while not new, has become increasingly important over time. Indeed, it is so significant in some sectors (e.g., clothing and electronics), that there are now contract manufacturing organizations (CMOs) that have evolved to facilitate the activity.

Investment

Contracting is not the only way to produce abroad. The home-country firm can also engage in foreign direct investment (FDI). As listed in Table 9.1, there are three modes of FDI to consider. These are *joint venture* (JV), *mergers and acquisitions* (M&As), and *greenfield investment.* In a JV, the home-country firm establishes a separate firm in the foreign country that is jointly owned with a foreign-country firm. Sometimes a JV is required by a foreign host country, whereas in other instances, a home-country firm will enter into a JV willingly in order to tap into local assets of the foreign partner. These local assets might include local market knowledge, existing production facilities, and knowledge of the local regulatory environment. A classic case of a JV and its foibles in the form of "Beijing Jeep" is discussed in the accompanying box.

Beijing Jeep

In 1983, the American Motors Corporation (AMC) formed a *joint venture* with the Beijing Auto Works (BAW) to build a Chinese version of the Jeep. The joint venture was called the Beijing Jeep Company, Ltd., and it involved both AMC and BAW owning large shares of the company's equity. The negotiations leading up to the joint venture took years to complete, but the resulting agreement was "the first major manufacturing joint venture set up after China opened its doors to foreign investment" (Mann, 1997, p. 25). The most important consideration on the part of AMC in entering into the joint venture was the large and growing market for automobiles in China. As Mann explained, "even those companies hoping to cut their production costs by manufacturing in China . . . were interested mainly because of the possibility of selling their output there. You could find cheap labor elsewhere in the world, but you couldn't find a billion consumers anywhere else" (p. 53).

The Chinese have a saying, *tong chuang yi meng.* It means "same bed, different dreams." There was a large measure of this in the AMC/BAW relationship. Cultural conflict, financial difficulties, and opposing business interests plagued the operation from the start. To the disappointment of the Chinese, the Beijing Jeep Company actually did *not* make a Chinese version of the Jeep. Instead, it assembled American Jeep Cherokees from imported kits. To the disappointment of the Americans, finding the foreign exchange (US dollars) to pay for these kits was a serious problem. The Americans thought the Chinese workers were lazy; the Chinese had great difficulty respecting American executives who used foul language.

The Beijing Jeep Company is still operating, and its factory has been modernized. Chrysler bought AMC in 1987. In 1995, two decades after the start of the joint venture, a Chrysler executive commented: "Our Beijing Jeep is starting to be a halfway decent little company, but there are going to be lots of ups and down in China." Many different firms who have invested in China would probably have concurred with that last observation.

outsourcing refers to moving production to a foreign country but *relinquishing ownership* through a contractual relationship and therefore belongs in the *contract* mode. See Feenstra and Jensen (2009).

As of 2005, the firm became known as the Beijing Benz-DaimlerChrysler Automotive Company. *Business Week* commented in 2007 on this new company, saying "It's been a long road for Chrysler in China, and an equally challenging path lies before the company. But after years of wandering aimlessly in the Middle Kingdom, we can say the company has finally chosen a new direction and is moving with a renewed sense of purpose." Despite that upbeat assessment, Chrysler and Daimler Benz parted ways in 2007, and Chrysler is in the process of merging with Fiat. We will see what role Beijing Jeep plays in the emerging Fiat-Chrysler corporate strategy.

Sources: Mann (1997) and Dunne (2007)

The second way of engaging in FDI is through M&As. Here the home-country firm buys part (merger) or all (acquisition) of the shares of an already existing production facility in the foreign country. As has been pointed out by many observers, M&A activity is the most prominent type of investment mode for foreign market entry. That is, M&As are the most common means of FDI.[6] For example, Dicken (2007) stated that the M&A vehicle "offers the attraction of an already functioning business compared with the more difficult, and possibly more risky, method of starting a firm from scratch in an unfamiliar environment" (p. 116). Interestingly, however, cross-border M&A activity is somewhat volatile and characterized by waves, such as occurred in the late 1990s.

The third means of engaging in FDI is through greenfield investment, or starting a subsidiary from scratch. Here the home-country firm establishes a brand-new production facility in the foreign country that it fully owns. This is clearly the investment option that requires the most commitment on part of the home-country firm but one that offers this firm the most control over the foreign-based production facility.

In the case of Honda in Vietnam, it hoped to move from a direct exporting mode of foreign market entry to a greenfield investment mode with a wholly owned factory. However, the Vietnamese government prevented Honda from pursuing this strategy and required that it enter the market as a JV with a Vietnamese firm. As a result, Honda Vietnam is only 70 percent owned by Honda. The Vietnam Engine and Agricultural Machinery Corporation (VEAM) owns the remaining 30 percent. This JV was established in 1997 outside of Hanoi producing the Super Dream motorcycle. It began producing the Future motorcycle in 1999 and the Wave Alpha motorcycle in 2001. In 2008, Honda Vietnam opened a second factory as well.

An important insight to be gained from Table 9.1 is that achieving market entry involves the firm incurring various sorts of costs. This insight is largely left out of the trade framework of Part I of this book. It is partly for this reason that the field of international production is often cast in terms of what are known as *transactions costs.* This perspective emphasizes the empirical reality that foreign market entry is not free.[7]

MOTIVATIONS FOR INTERNATIONAL PRODUCTION

Now that we have a sense of the means by which firms engage in international production, the next step is to say something about the *motivations* for these activities.

[6] As a rule of thumb, we can say that approximately three-fourths of FDI is of the M&A form.
[7] See, for example, Zhao, Luo, and Suh (2004).

Two central motivations that have emerged from international business research are *resource seeking* and *market seeking*. We consider each in turn.

A primary motivation for international production is **resource seeking**. Here, the home-country firm is trying to gain access to certain resources in a foreign country. The resources involved could be natural resources such as minerals or timber, as well as human resources such as inexpensive or specially trained labor. Despite the continued relevance of resource-seeking as a motivation for international production, the gradual shift over time away from resource seeking international production is one of the most important aspects of the history of MNEs. In the current era, therefore, use of a simple mental model in which MNEs locate production solely based on wage considerations is incomplete. For example, the province of Ontario, Canada, has been a destination of a great deal of foreign investment, and this province has wage rates and benefits packages that exceed even those of the United States.

A second, growing reason for international production is **market seeking**. A number of considerations can be active here. First, international production might be necessary to adopt and tailor products to local needs. Second, international production might be required to effectively deliver a product, as is the case for many financial services. Third, international production might be required for a firm supplying intermediate products to another firm opening up operations in a foreign country. For example, Japanese auto parts firms often follow Japanese auto companies to Europe and the United States. Finally, firms may simply locate where they expect demand to grow in the future. This certainly has been the case in China where, despite losses, many foreign firms maintain at least small operations. Why? A deputy chairman of a Malaysian conglomerate stated, "You cannot not be there" (*The Economist*, 1997). The reason for this statement was the anticipated growth of the market.[8]

Along with the two central motivations for international production of resource seeking and market seeking, there are two subsidiary motivations identified by Dunning and Lundan (2008). One of these is **efficiency seeking**. As expressed by these authors, the concern here "is to rationalize the structure of established resource-based or market-seeking investment in such a way that the investing company can gain from the common governance of geographically dispersed activities" (p. 72). These efficiencies may stem from economies of scale, economies of scope, and a concept we discuss in the next chapter called *firm-level economies*. The efficiency-seeking motivation is most important for large, mature MNEs with a great deal of international experience.

The next subsidiary motivation is **strategic asset seeking**. This motivation can be quite important for M&As in the current era but can also be difficult to comprehend. Strategic asset-seeking behavior tends to be part of the *strategic game* among competitors in oligopolistic sectors. Dunning and Lundan (2008) described a number of illustrative alternatives:

> One company may acquire or engage in a collaborative alliance with another to thwart a competitor from so doing. Another might merge with one of its foreign rivals to strengthen their joint capabilities *vis à vis* a more powerful rival. A third might acquire a group of suppliers to corner the market for a particular raw material. A fourth might seek to gain access over distribution outlets to better promote its own

[8] With the perspective of more than another decade's experience, it is clear that the lure of the Chinese market has disappointed many firms. See *The Economist* (2009), which noted that "Corruption, protectionism and red tape hamper foreigners in all fields" (p. 73).

> brand of products. A fifth might buy out a firm producing a complementary range of goods or services so it can offer its customers a more diversified range of products. A sixth might join forces with a local firm in the belief that it is in a better position to secure contracts from the host government, which are denied to its exporting competitors. (p. 73)

To take one example, some time ago the U.S.-based MNE Kodak established a film sales affiliate in Japan called Nagase. The purpose of Nagase was not limited to the market-seeking motivation. A further motivation was to *attack the profit sanctuary* of the Japanese film company Fujifilm. As alleged by a Kodak executive, "While Fuji competes with Kodak on a global basis, it makes virtually all of its profits in Japan, using those proceeds to finance low-price sales outside Japan" (Baron, 1997, p. 151). For Kodak, Nagase was a strategic asset.[9]

ENTRY MODE CHOICE

As we have seen in the preceding discussion, Table 9.1 identifies exporting, contractual, and investment as three categories of foreign market entry mode choice. What prompts a firm to choose one category over another? It turns out that the answer to this question is not as straightforward as we might like it to be. Both international economists and international business researchers would like to be able to effectively capture all of the relevant factors affecting firms' foreign market entry decision-making process. That is, they would like to accurately explain and predict firms' choices among the entry possibilities of Table 9.1. As it turns out, however, a fully satisfying explanation of this process has proved to be elusive. Instead, we have to make do with a set of possible explanations, each with its own relevance.

From a purely economic point of view, we can begin with the observation that a firm will chose the entry mode that will provide it with the greatest risk-adjusted or expected return on the entry investment.[10] Although this statement in itself is accurate, it is not entirely helpful because it does not specify the types or magnitudes of risks involved nor how returns would differ among the mode choices. Consequently, we need to take a slightly more applied approach, and there are a few of these we can consider.

The first approach to foreign market entry can be called the *sequential approach.*[11] The focus in the sequential approach is on the home-country firm's learning process. The foreign market and the entry process itself are largely unknown to the purely domestic home-country firm at the top of Table 9.1. This firm develops its understanding of the environment and process by slowly moving down Table 9.1 in a sequential or evolutionary process from indirect exporting to greenfield FDI. This approach makes some sense and captures some important features of the firm's decision-making process: learning is indeed important. Its limitation is that not all firms abide by it! Instead, they sometimes jump into foreign environments farther down Table 9.1 rather than moving sequentially.[12]

[9] Along with explaining some types of FDI, strategic asset-seeking behavior also helps to explain a number of *non*-FDI activities of MNEs, especially strategic alliances, which do not involve the exchange of equity. For more information on strategic alliances, see chapter 9 of John et al. (1997) and chapter 10 of Hill (2009).

[10] We will make a similar statement about the purely economic point of view on the migration decision in Chapter 12.

[11] It is also sometimes called the *evolutionary approach.*

[12] For example, Fima and Rugman (1996) examined the Upjohn pharmaceuticals company and found that "Upjohn (used) multiple entry modes at the same time. This (provided) flexibility in an industry which is very

Table 9.2. Factors influencing choice of foreign market entry mode

Mode	Degree of control	Level of resource commitment	Degree of dissemination risk
Trade	Low	Low	Low
Contractual	Low	Low	High
Investment – Joint Venture	Medium	Medium	Medium
Investment – M&A or greenfield	High	High	Low

Source: Adapted from Hill, Hwang, and Kim (1990)

Why might that be so? An answer can be found in a second approach to foreign market entry that can be called the **firm-specific asset approach**. The term *firm-specific assets* refers to tangible and intangible resources that the firm owns and that contribute to its competitiveness over time. It might be a patent on particular technology, or it might be a corporate product brand. It could even be some aspect of corporate culture that allows a firm to be more productive. Whatever the asset's form, its presence is the result of the firm incurring costs to acquire it, and it provides the firm with value in enhancing its competitiveness.

It is worth noting that, among all the different types of firm-specific assets that can exist, **knowledge capital** can play a particularly important role. Of course some knowledge is also embedded in individuals rather than firms in the form of human capital, but a lot of knowledge is also embedded in firms themselves in the form of knowledge capital or intellectual capital. Indeed, one of the well-known models of FDI behavior is known as the *knowledge capital model.*[13] The presence of knowledge capital as an important firm-specific asset leads to the issue of **dissemination risk**. Dissemination risk refers to the possibility of a foreign firm obtaining knowledge capital of the home-country firm and exploiting it for its own commercial advantage. This risk is especially prevalent in the licensing mode of entry.[14]

Given the possibility of dissemination risk for knowledge-intensive firms, FDI can be a favored means of entry. However, it also requires a greater degree of resource commitment on the part of the home-country firms. The way in which issues of control, resource commitment, and dissemination risk affect the choice of foreign market entry mode can be appreciated using Table 9.2. Suppose a firm's most important concern was the degree of control over the production and marketing process. This would draw the firm toward an investment mode of foreign market entry based on a subsidiary obtained either through M&A or greenfield investment. Alternatively, if a firm were concerned only with limiting resource commitment to low levels, it would consider either trade or contractual modes of foreign market entry. Finally, if a firm were solely concerned with maintaining a low degree of dissemination risk, then either trade or investment via a subsidiary would be the preferred mode of entry. In most instances, firms have more than one primary concern, so the entry strategy is less than clear-cut.

Due to the role of dissemination risk in pushing firms toward adopting FDI as a market entry process, a robust correlation between knowledge intensity and FDI

dependent on political factors and is often dictated to by changes in host-government regulations" (p. 211). Some firms also emerge with an international scope right from the beginning. On this phenomenon of being "born global," see Gabrielsson et al. (2008).

13 For an accessible review, see Urban (2009).

14 For example, Hill, Hwang, and Kim (1990) stated that: "Unfortunately, if a (firm) grants a license to a foreign enterprise to use firm-specific know-how to manufacture or market a product, it runs the risk of the licensee, or an employee of the licensee, disseminating that know-how, or using it for purposes other than those originally

emerges. In fact, one of the most common predictors of FDI in any particular sector is its research and development (R&D) spending. Recall from Chapter 1 that MNEs account for approximately three-fourths of worldwide civilian R&D. This is not by chance. Indeed, as has been emphasized by Caves (2007), the relationship between MNEs and knowledge intensity is two-way. MNEs are most likely to form in knowledge-intensive sectors, but once they do form, the network of subsidiaries in different countries helps the MNE to absorb and deploy new ideas more effectively than domestic firms. Consequently, MNEs find themselves at the center of global innovation.

THE RISE OF MULTINATIONAL ENTERPRISES AND INTERNATIONAL PRODUCTION

How have the preceding considerations played out historically? Early MNEs were part and parcel of the colonization efforts of the European powers during the sixteenth and seventeenth centuries. These included state-supported trading companies such as the British East India Company, the Dutch East India Company, and the Royal African Company. This period is often known as the age of **merchant capitalism**, and this name is a reflection of the international activities of these trading companies. With the advent of the industrial revolution in the nineteenth century, however, merchant capitalism gave way to what is now known as **industrial capitalism**. During the nineteenth century, there was a rise of British-based MNEs operating in India, China, Latin America, and South Africa. These firms were involved in mining, plantation agriculture, finance, and shipping. Their focus was the procurement of industrial inputs and the promotion of manufactured exports, often at the expense of host-country economies. Japan became involved in similarly motivated MNE activity toward the end of the nineteenth century after the Meiji Restoration. The companies involved here were industrial groups known as *zaibatsu*, and these were associated with trading companies known as *sogo shosha*, which still exist in various forms to the present day.[15]

In the twentieth century, industrial production grew more capital intensive. The role of the production line and associated economies of scale grew more important. The era of industrial capitalism gave way to what is now known as **managerial capitalism** or **Fordism**. Along with this shift, the center of innovative economic activity moved from Europe to the United States. Firm size increased, and business success became based on the ability to coordinate growing sets of complementary activities. World War I was a distinct blow to the global reach of European MNEs, and after the war, U.S.-based MNEs substantially increased their FDI in Canada, Latin America, and Europe.[16]

The world depression that began in 1929 and the Second World War hurt most forms of international economic activity, including FDI. The post-war recovery, however, further strengthened the role of U.S.-based MNEs in the world economy. Indeed, the

intended. For example, RCA once licensed its color TV technology to a number of Japanese companies. The Japanese companies quickly assimilated RCA's technology and then used it to enter the U.S. market" (p. 119).

[15] After World War II, Japan's *zaibatsu* were dismantled but re-established themselves as *kieretsu*. On the *sogo shosha*, see Yoshino and Lifson (1986).

[16] John et al. (1997) summarized this era quite well: "Over the course of the 1920s the book value of United States' foreign direct investment doubled and the amount of this FDI devoted to manufacturing grew by a still larger proportion. It has been argued that by the end of the 1920s the size of United States' investments in both Canada and Latin America exceeded those of British investors for the first time and that more than 1,300 companies or organizations in Europe were either owned or controlled by United States' capital. It was during this era that the American multinational truly first came of age" (p. 33).

Table 9.3. Leading sources of world FDI (percent of global, outward stocks)

Source	1960	1980	1990	2000	2008
United States	47[a]	43	24	22	20
United Kingdom	18[a]	16	13	15	9
Germany	1[a]	8	8	9	9
France	6[a]	4	6	7	9
Japan	1[a]	4	11	5	4
China	0	0	0	0	1
Brazil	0	0	2	1	1
All Developing	NA	3	8	14	15

[a]From the 1998 edition of Dicken (2007)
Source: UNCTAD, *World Investment Reports*, various years

technological advantage of U.S.-based MNEs during the early post-war period was the point of reference of an early theory of FDI developed by Vernon (1966) and known as the **product life-cycle theory**. This theory viewed production as being confined to the home base of an MNE during the early phases of a product life cycle due to the need for technologically sophisticated production techniques. During later phases of the production cycle, as the production of the good becomes more routine and established, production can move to subsidiaries in foreign countries in order to take advantage of lower labor costs.[17]

The 1970s brought another new change in global production with the rise of industrial output in the newly industrializing countries (NICs) of East Asia, especially Japan, Taiwan, and South Korea. Although there is still debate over this matter, many see the rise of industrial production in the NICs as a move into a new economic era known as *post-Fordism* or, to some, **Toyotism.**[18] In this era, economies of scale were replaced by *flexibility* as the progressive element in manufacturing. This was based on the application of information and communication technologies (ICT) to international production processes. Dicken (2007) summarized this era of **flexible manufacturing** as follows:

> The key to production flexibility in today's world lies in the use of *information technologies* in machines and operations. These permit more sophisticated control over the production process. With the increasing sophistication of automated processes and, especially, the new flexibility of electronically controlled technology, far-reaching changes in the process of production need not necessarily be associated with increased scale of production. Indeed, one of the major results of the new electronic and computer-aided production technology is that it permits rapid switching from one part of a production process to another and allows... the tailoring of production to the requirements of individual customers. (p. 96)

The importance of this change for our purposes here is that the rise of industrial output was followed by a rise in FDI on the part of East-Asian-based MNEs, especially those based in Japan. Consider the data presented in Table 9.3 on the leading sources of world

[17] In a later assessment of the product life-cycle theory, Vernon (1979) stated that it had been applicable during the historical period of 1900 to 1970 in explaining the activity of U.S.-based MNEs. However, his assessment was that its applicability declined significantly after 1970.

[18] An important and fascinating account of this ongoing transition can be found in Ruigrok and van Tulder (1995). For a critical review of the current generation of Japanese firms, however, see *The Economist* (2010b).

FDI. In 1960, as suggested by our previous discussion, the United States dominated global FDI, accounting for almost one-half of total outward FDI stocks. The United Kingdom accounted for much less, and Japan accounted for only 1 percent. By 1990, Japan accounted for 11 percent, although this decreased between 1990 and 2008. More generally, the share of the United States in global, outward stocks declined to 20 percent in 2008.

A further trend evident in Table 9.3 is what used to be called "the rise of Third World multinationals," that is, increasing FDI by MNEs with home bases in developing countries.[19] Observers began to take note of this trend beginning in the mid-1980s when the share of the developing world in global, outward stocks was only 3 percent. By 2008, this had increased to 15 percent, more than that of Japan. This trend reflected the fact that developing countries began, at that time, to relax restrictions on FDI capital outflows. For example, India maintained restrictions on FDI capital outflows until the end of the 1980s. As a result of this change, Indian firms began to engage in FDI in North America in the areas of engineering, consulting, and software services. Another notable example of this process is the Mexican-based cement firm Cemex, which now maintains a productive capacity outside Mexico that is two times as large as its Mexican capacity. In 2007, it ranked 45th among the largest nonfinancial MNEs measured by foreign assets. A further example from South Africa is given in the accompanying box.[20]

SAB and the Emergence of a South African MNE

Many of us think of South Africa in terms of the transition from the Apartheid regime. For beer drinkers worldwide, however, South Africa is an important country as the home base of an MNE in the brewing sector. Castle Breweries was founded in South Africa in 1895. It was listed as South Africa Breweries (SAB) on the Johannesburg Stock Exchange in 1897 and the London Stock Exchange a year later. In 1925, it acquired a stake in the British Schweppes beverage company. In 1964, it was granted the first license by the Irish brewery Guinness to produce outside of Ireland.

SAB's foreign market entry process began in earnest in the 1990s. In 1993 it acquired breweries in Tanzania (Tanzania Breweries) and Hungary (Dreher). Further acquisitions were made in other African countries as well as in Poland (Lech), Romania (Vultural, Ursus, and Pitber), Slovakia (Pivovar), Russia (Kaluga), the Czech Republic (Pilsner Urquell and Radegast) and China. In 2002, to the astonishment of beer drinkers in the United States, it acquired Miller brewers and became SABMiller. Further acquisitions followed in Italy (Birra Peroni) and the Ukraine (Sarmat). For 2007, it ranked as the 78th largest nonfinancial MNE by foreign assets with a transnationality index of nearly 80 percent.

Drawing on a long-standing philanthropic tradition, in recent years, the company has become quite active in HIV/AIDS and hunger in its South African home base. Consequently, both in commercial and human terms, SAB has made its market in the global brewing industry.

Sources: sabmiller.com, *The Economist* (1995, 2006)

[19] See, for example, Heenan and Keegan (1979).

[20] Another important change is the emergence of some developing countries as players in what has come to known as "frugal innovation." See *The Economist* (2010a).

Table 9.4. Leading destinations of world FDI (percent of global, inward stocks)

Destination	1980	1990	2000	2008
United States	16	20	22	15
United Kingdom	12	10	8	7
Germany	7	6	5	5
France	5	5	5	7
Japan	1	1	1	1
China	0	1	3	3
Brazil	3	2	2	2
All Developing	26	27	30	29

Source: UNCTAD, *World Investment Reports*, various years

The other side of these trends can be seen in Table 9.4 on leading destinations of global FDI. Here too, the United States plays an important role, with currently 15 percent of global, inward stocks. The developing world plays a more constant role with just under 30 percent of global, inward stocks. Within the developing world, China has emerged as a new destination, increasing its share from zero to three percent of global, inward stocks. The poorest counties of the world, however, are largely left out of this process.[21]

Who are the current main players in the world of MNEs? We can get a sense of this by looking at the top 25 nonfinancial MNEs as measured by foreign assets in Table 9.5. We see here that this group of firms is dominated by firms from Western Europe, the United States, and Japan. They are often in the electrical equipment, telecommunications, automobiles, petroleum, utilities, and electrical equipment sectors. For many of them, their home base still features prominently in their operations and sales. This is measured by UNCTAD's transnationality index (TNI), an average of three ratios expressed in percentage terms: foreign assets to total assets, foreign sales to total sales, and foreign employment to total employment. For many of the top 25 MNEs, this ratio is barely over 50 percent, indicating that the home base accounts for nearly one-half of operations and sales.

CONCLUSION

The economic activity of international trade is one of a number of modes of foreign market entry. The other modes of contracting and investment take us into the realm of international production. The choice among trade, contracting, and investment depends on balancing considerations of control, resource commitments, and dissemination risk. The motivations for international production include resource seeking, market seeking, efficiency seeking, and strategic asset seeking. Firms that engage in international production, multinational enterprises, have a long history. This history has moved from merchant capitalism, industrial capitalism, managerial capitalism or

[21] There are, however, some positive signs. Migiro (2009) noted that: "Emerging and developing economies invest differently. According to a recent UN estimate, 40 per cent of FDI from countries of the South goes to the highly vulnerable least-developed countries, many of which are just emerging from conflict. In countries such as the Democratic Republic of the Congo, Malawi and Lesotho, for example, about half of inward FDI comes from South Africa."

Table 9.5. The world's largest 25 nonfinancial MNEs, 2007

MNE	Home country	Sector	Total foreign assets (billions US $)	TNI (percent)[a]
General Electric	United States	Electrical equipment	420	51
Vodafone	United Kingdom	Telecommunications	231	87
Royal Dutch Shell	Netherland/ United Kingdom	Petroleum	197	71
British Petroleum	United Kingdom	Petroleum	185	80
Exxon/Mobil	United States	Petroleum	175	68
Toyota	Japan	Automobiles	153	52
Total	France	Petroleum	144	75
Electricité de France	France	Electricity, gas, and water	129	35
Ford	United States	Automobiles	128	51
E.ON	Germany	Electricity, gas, and water	123	54
ArcelorMittal	Luxembourg	Metals	119	89
Telefónica	Spain	Telecommunications	107	70
Volkswagen	Germany	Automobiles	104	57
ConocoPhillips	United States	Petroleum	103	44
Siemens	Germany	Electrical equipment	103	72
DaimlerChrysler	Germany/ United States	Automobiles	100	56
Chevron	United States	Petroleum	98	58
France Telecom	France	Telecommunications	97	52
Deutsche Telekom	Germany	Telecommunications	96	48
Suez	France	Electricity, gas, and water	91	69
BMW	Germany	Automobiles	84	56
Hutchison Whampoa	Hong Kong	Diversified	83	83
Honda	Japan	Automobiles	83	82
Eni	Italy	Petroleum	78	74
Eads	Netherlands	Aircraft	75	74

[a] UNCTAD calculates the TNI, or transnationality index, using three ratio measures: foreign assets to total assets, foreign sales to total sales, and foreign employment to total employment.
Source: UNCTAD, *World Investment Report*, 2009

Fordism, to Toyotism or post-Fordism. The last of these has accompanied a process known as flexible manufacturing, which, in turn, is based on information technologies.

In at least two important ways, our discussion in this chapter is very much incomplete. Being motivated to engage in international production does not mean that a firm can actually be successful in doing so. Indeed, a firm faces additional costs in operating in a foreign country compared with foreign country firms. For that reason, a firm operating in a foreign country must have command over some sort of scarce resource that gives it an advantage over foreign firms. This is the issue we take up in Chapter 10. Additionally, our brief history of MNE activity masks a great deal of historic controversy between MNEs and their host countries. This controversy has been particularly acute in the case of developing host countries. We take up this issue in Chapter 22 on international development in Part IV of the book.

REVIEW EXERCISES

1. Why should a firm move beyond trading relationships into international production? What is its motivation for doing so?

2. Suppose a firm's competitiveness was based on its proprietary knowledge, perhaps in the form of a patent on a product or process. What can you say about its considerations with regard to foreign market entry?
3. What key characteristics differentiate managerial capitalism or Fordism from Toyotism based on flexible manufacturing?
4. For each of the four motivations for international production, please provide an example. The more specific your example, the better.

FURTHER READING AND WEB RESOURCES

A recent review of foreign market entry is given in Chapter 9 of Hill (2009). Dunning and Lundan (2008, Chapter 6) and John et al. (1997, Chapter 1) offer very useful reviews of the rise of international production and multinational enterprises. For a study of Asian multinationals, see Mathews (2002). An interesting book that places international production within the broader context of a changing world economy is Dicken (2007). Doremus et al. (1998) also offer a useful, thematically arranged bibliography, and Caves (2007) provides an economic analysis of MNEs. A review of the political economy of FDI is also given in Chapter 6 of Walter and Sen (2009).

The United Nations Conference on Trade and Development (UNCTAD) publishes an annual *World Investment Report.* This is a good place to turn for data on and discussion of FDI in the world economy. Their web site is at http://www.unctad.org, and the *World Investment Report* is at http://www.unctad.org/wir/.

APPENDIX: FDI AND COMPARATIVE ADVANTAGE

In Chapter 3, we considered comparative advantage and its implications for inter-industry trade in rice and motorcycles between Vietnam and Japan. Recall that, given biases in production possibilities frontiers (PPFs), Vietnam had a comparative advantage in and exported rice, whereas Japan had a comparative advantage in and exported motorcycles. In Chapter 5, we also introduced the Heckscher-Ohlin model, explaining patterns of comparative advantage in terms of the resource or factor endowments of countries and the factor intensities of sectors. Japan's comparative advantage (and the bias of its PPF) in motorcycles was due to its relatively large endowment of physical capital and the physical capital intensity of motorcycle production.

FDI was absent in Chapters 3 and 5. So the question arises: What difference would FDI make to the comparative advantage story of those chapters? Figure 9.1 (a close copy of Figure 3.3) helps us answer this question. Recall that we evaluate comparative advantage by examining the relative price of rice to motorcycles or $(\frac{P_R}{P_M})$ in Vietnam and Japan. As we saw in Chapter 3, this price ratio was lower in Vietnam, indicating that Vietnam had a comparative advantage in rice and that Japan had a comparative advantage in motorcycles.

Now suppose that we allow for an FDI flow from Japan to Vietnam. To make matters simple, suppose that this is a full offshoring involving a closing of a motorcycle factory in Japan and the opening of a new motorcycle factory in Vietnam. This FDI flow changes the relative factor endowments of the two countries. Japan becomes less capital abundant and Vietnam becomes more capital abundant. These two changes have impacts on the PPFs of the two countries. The PPFs shift in a manner biased

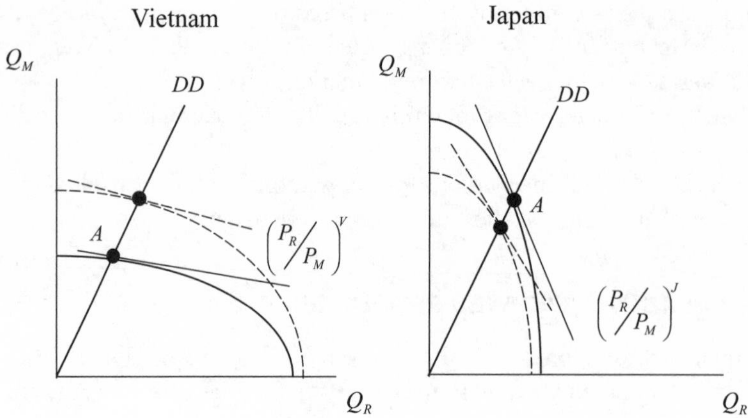

Figure 9.1. FDI and Comparative Advantage between Vietnam and Japan

toward the capital-intensive good, motorcycles. In Vietnam, with the inflow of capital, the PPF shifts *out* to the dashed concave curve, whereas in Japan, the PPF shifts *in* to the dashed curve. The new autarky points along the demand diagonals (DD) are such that the autarky price ratios change to the dashed lines. In Vietnam, $(\frac{P_R}{P_M})^V$ increases, whereas in Japan, $(\frac{P_R}{P_M})$ decreases. You can see this by examining the relative slopes of the solid and dashed price lines.

What do these changes in the autarky price ratios mean? It means that the gap between the two autarky price ratios is narrowing or that the pattern of comparative advantage is weakening. As we have examined the process here, it indicates that FDI can function as a *substitute* for trade.[22] However, recall from Chapter 5 that the assumption of the Heckscher-Ohlin model is that production technology is the same in each country of the world. This is not always the case, and where technologies differ, sometimes FDI can be a *complement* to trade. That is, with differing technologies, some types of FDI can strengthen patterns of comparative advantage.[23]

REFERENCES

Baron, D.P. (1997) "Integrated Strategy, Trade Policy, and Global Competition," *California Management Review*, 39:2, 145–169.

Bernard, A.B., J.B. Jenson, S.J. Redding, and P.K. Schott (2007) "Firms in International Trade," *Journal of Economic Perspectives*, 21:3, 105–130.

Caves, R.E. (2007) *Multinational Enterprise and Economics Analysis*, Cambridge University Press.

Dicken, P. (2007) *Global Shift: Mapping the Changing Contours of the World Economy*, Guilford.

Doremus, P.N., W.W. Keller, L.W. Pauly, and S. Reich (1998) *The Myth of the Global Corporation*, Princeton University Press.

Dunne, T. (2007) "Can Chrysler Rebound in China?" *Business Week*, November 2.

Dunning, J.H. and S.M. Lundan (2008) *Multinational Enterprises and the Global Economy*, Edward Elgar.

The Economist (1995) "Lion of Africa, Brewer to the People," September 9.

[22] This famous result was first pointed out by Mundell (1957).

[23] This modified result is due to Purvis (1972).

The Economist (1997) "The China Syndrome," June 21.

The Economist (2006) "South African Business: Going Global," July 15.

The Economist (2009) "Impenetrable: Selling Foreign Goods in China," October 17.

The Economist (2010a) "The World Turned Upside Down," April 17.

The Economist (2010b) "Into the Unknown: A Special Report on Japan," November 20.

Feenstra, R.C. and J. B. Jensen (2009) "Outsourcing/Offshoring," in K.A. Reinert, R.S. Rajan, A.J. Glass, and L.S. Davis (eds.), *The Princeton Encyclopedia of the World Economy*, Princeton University Press, 881–887.

Fima, E. and A.M. Rugman (1996) "A Test of Internalization Theory and Internationalization Theory: The Upjohn Company," *Management International Review*, 36:3, 199–213.

Gabrielsson, M., V.H.M. Kirpalani, P. Dimitratos, C.A. Solberg, and A. Zucchella (2008) "Born Globals: Propositions to Help Advance the Theory," *International Business Review*, 17:4, 385–401.

Heenan, D.A. and W.J. Keegan (1979) "The Rise of Third World Multinationals," *Harvard Business Review*, January-February, 101–109.

Hill, C.W.L., P. Hwang, and W.C. Kim (1990) "An Eclectic Theory of the Choice of International Entry Mode," *Strategic Management Journal*, 11:2, 117–128.

Hill, J.S. (2009) *International Business: Managing Globalization*, Sage.

Hymer, S.H. (1976) *The International Operations of National Firms: A Study of Direct Foreign Investment*, MIT Press.

John, R., G. Ietto-Gillies, H. Cox, and N. Grimwade (1997) *Global Business Strategy*, International Thompson Business Press.

Mann, J. (1997) *Beijing Jeep*, Westview Press.

Mathews, J.A. (2002) *Dragon Multinationals: A New Model for Global Growth*, Oxford University Press.

Migiro, A.R. (2009) "A New Spirit of Solidarity Rises in the South," *Financial Times*, December 8.

Mundell, R.A. (1957) "International Trade and Factor Mobility," *American Economic Review*, 47:3, 321–335.

Purvis, D.D. (1972) "Technology, Trade and Factor Mobility," *Economic Journal*, 82:327, 991–999.

Root, F.R. (1998) *Entry Strategy for International Markets*, Jossey-Bass.

Ruigrok, W. and R. van Tulder (1995) *The Logic of International Restructuring*, Routledge.

Tiep, N.D. (2007) "The Honda Motorcycle Business in the Vietnamese Emerging Market," *International Journal of Emerging Markets*, 2:3, 298–309.

Urban, D.M. (2009) "Knowledge-Capital Model of the Multinational Enterprise," in K.A. Reinert, R.S. Rajan, A.J. Glass, and L.S. Davis (eds.), *The Princeton Encyclopedia of the World Economy*, Princeton University Press, 719–723.

Vernon, R. (1966) "International Investment and International Trade in the Product Cycle," *Quarterly Journal of Economics*, 80:2, 190–207.

Vernon, R. (1979) "The Product Cycle Hypothesis in a New International Environment," *Oxford Bulletin of Economics and Statistics*, 41:4, 255–267.

Walter, A. and G. Sen (2009) *Analyzing the Global Political Economy*, Princeton University Press.

Yoshino, M.Y. and T.B. Lifson (1986) *The Invisible Link: Japan's Sogo Shosha and the Organization of Trade*, MIT Press.

Zhao, H., Y. Luo, and T. Suh (2004) "Transaction Cost Determinants and Ownership Entry Mode Choice: A Meta-Analytical Review," *Journal of International Business Studies*, 35:6, 524–544.

10 Foreign Direct Investment and Intra-Firm Trade

As we saw in Chapter 1, one of the great drivers of economic globalization is information and communication technology (ICT). At the center of ICT, in turn, we find the *semiconductor*. Semiconductors are the various devices and integrated circuits made using silicon that control the flow of electrical signals. These devices are included in personal computers, communications equipment including mobile phones, audiovisual equipment, automobiles, and many other types of modern machinery. The manufacturing of semiconductors is a global industry, but one broken up into discrete tasks connected together by a number of possible organizational forms, including foreign **direct investment** (FDI) and **intra-firm trade**, the subjects of this chapter.[1]

In this chapter, we introduce the basic frameworks of the **value chain** and the **global production network** (GPN). We will use these frameworks to understand key concepts related to the FDI process, namely **firm-specific assets** and **internalization**. These will help us to understand FDI and intra-firm trade. We will relate the internalization process to the standard cost analysis of microeconomics. Finally, we also introduce the well-known approach to the study of multinational enterprises (MNE) known as the OLI (Ownership, Location, Internalization) Framework. An appendix to the chapter briefly describes the gravity model of trade and FDI used for empirical research.

Analytical elements for this chapter:

Countries, *sectors*, *tasks*, and *firms*.

VALUE CHAINS AND GLOBAL PRODUCTION NETWORKS

Understanding international production in any industry requires use of the value chain concept. A value chain is a series of value-added processes involved in the production of any good or service. It proceeds in steps from beginning or upstream tasks to subsequent downstream tasks. The semiconductor value chain is very complex, but we can simplify it by considering the following tasks:

1. *Research, development, and design* leading up to details of the physical circuitry of the chip to be placed on the silicon.
2. *Fabrication* (or just *fab* in semiconductor jargon) in an advanced manufacturing process in which circuitry layouts are etched onto silicon wafers containing many die. This step also requires sophisticated equipment and materials. Plants engaged in fabrication are known as *foundries.*
3. *Assembly and testing* in which the die are cut from wafers and mounted or packaged into a functioning device with wire contacts and insulation.
4. *Final incorporation* in which the semiconductor is incorporated into the final piece of equipment, such as a personal computer or mobile phone.

These four stages are represented in Figure 10.1. An additional task in this figure is that of advanced equipment and materials crucial to the fabrication process.[2] Importantly, it is not necessary for a firm to be active across all stages of semiconductor manufacturing in Figure 10.1. The task scope of a firm in the industry is the result of a firm's

[1] Recall from Chapter 1 that approximately one-third of world trade takes place *within* MNEs in the form of intra-firm trade.

[2] On the role of Japanese firms in providing this equipment, see *The Economist* (2009a).

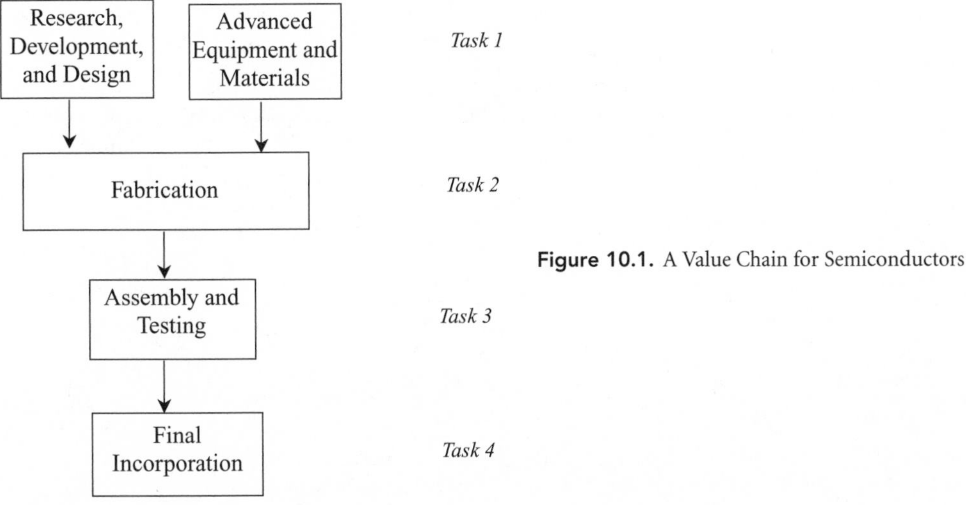

Figure 10.1. A Value Chain for Semiconductors

decision making with regard to what tasks to perform along the value chain. Not represented in Figure 10.1, but important nevertheless, is a reverse flow of information (from the bottom to the top in the diagram) as well as numerous supporting producer services such as accounting, transportation and logistics, legal services, human resource management, and the like. Indeed, sometimes the arrows in Figure 10.1 are referred to as service linkages.

Consider the case of perhaps the most famous semiconductor firm of them all, *Intel.* Intel is involved in the first three stages of the value chain: research, development, and design; fabrication; and assembly and testing. It is not involved in final incorporation, leaving that task to other firms. For example, one of its biggest customers is Dell computers, which incorporates Intel's semiconductors into its personal computers. Having integrated the first three tasks of the semiconductor value chain, however, Intel is known as an *integrated device manufacturer* (IDM). Other semiconductor firms approach the value chain differently. For example, some firms such as Nvidia operate only in the first task of research, development, and design but contract out fabrication and assembly. These firms are known as "fabless" semiconductor companies. Usually, the companies to which they contract out fabrication are fabrication-only companies known as *pure-play foundries,* the most famous of which is the Taiwan Semiconductor Manufacturing Company (TSMC).

The semiconductor firm could in principle be a purely domestic firm. If that were the case, the task decision would be the only value chain decisions it needs to make. However, there is another potential type of decision making involved as well, one related to our foreign market entry discussion of Chapter 9. This arises because value chains are potentially distributed across countries. When these international value chains are linked together in potential buyer–supplier or ownership relationships, they become known as **global production networks** (GPNs). An example of this is given in Figure 10.2. Here, we have only two countries, the United States and Costa Rica. In reality, of course, the GPN for semiconductors spans many countries around the world (particularly those of the Pacific Basin, but also those in Europe), but we want to keep

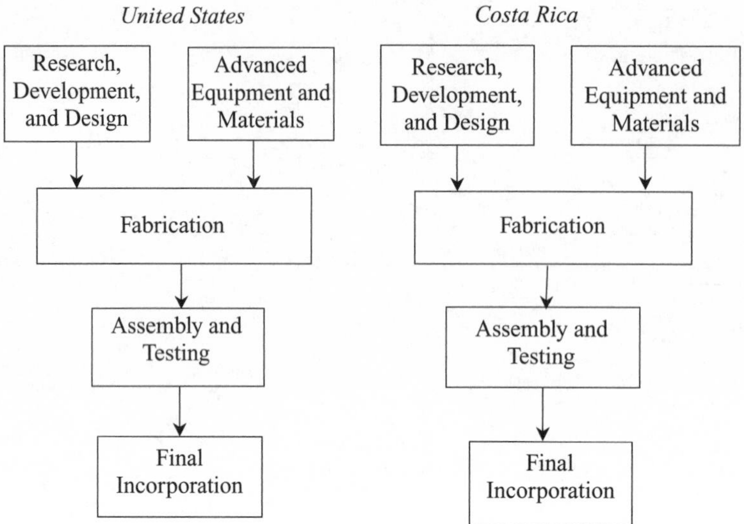

Figure 10.2. A Global Production Network for Semiconductors

things as simple as possible here.[3] Figure 10.2 alerts us to the fact that the semiconductor production decision is two-fold, namely the decision regarding what part of the value chain to take on and in which countries to do so. Thus there are both *task* and *location* decisions to consider.

There is another way to look at the GPN decision-making process. This is in terms of the distinction between what is known as the horizontal and vertical dimensions of GPNs. Movements up and down the value chains of Figure 10.2, whether in the United States or Costa Rica, are *vertical* movements. Movements from one country to another, from the United States to Costa Rica, for example, are *horizontal* movements. Further, movements up a value chain from subsequent to previous tasks are *backward vertical* movements, and movements down a value chain from previous to subsequent tasks are *forward vertical* movements. We will return to these distinctions when we take up the concept of internalization later, but for now we can see that the GPN decision that firms face involves both the vertical (task) and horizontal (location) dimensions.

FIRM-SPECIFIC ASSETS AND INTERNALIZATION

As is clear from the above discussion, firms can and do take more than one approach to the semiconductor value chain or GPN. Our next task is to try to understand *why* one approach might prevail over another in a particular instance. We will do this using Intel as an example. As we mentioned previously, Intel is an *integrated device manufacturer* (IDM). It maintains fabrication plants in the United States, its home base. It also has assembly and testing plants in a few other countries, including Costa Rica. We can therefore view its simplified GPN as in Figure 10.3. The dashed lines indicate potential areas where Intel has chosen not to operate, namely research, development, design, and fabrication in Costa Rica and final incorporation everywhere. Let's see how we can go about explaining the GPN configuration in Figure 10.3.

[3] For an excellent review of the GPN in semiconductors, see chapter 11 of Dicken (2007).

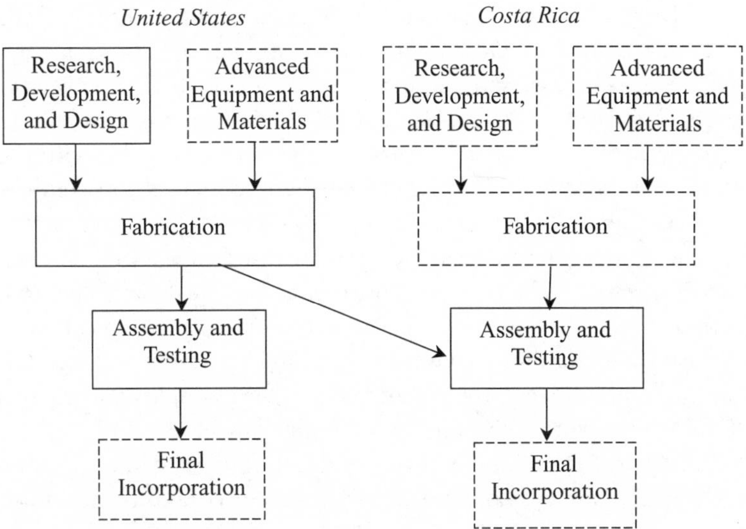

Figure 10.3. A Global Production Network for Semiconductors

To begin, suppose that Intel has a demonstrated competitive ability in research, development, and design in the United States and is successfully operating as a "fabless" semiconductor firm. What might explain this competitive success in this form? Corporate strategists typically point to the role of something we discussed in Chapter 9, namely **firm-specific assets**. These firm-specific assets can either be *tangible*, such as access to silicon and other advanced materials, or *intangible*, such as specialized knowledge, patented products or processes, organizational abilities, or brand distinctiveness and loyalty ("Intel Inside").[4]

Intel might begin to consider a move down the value chain in the United States to fabrication. Why might it do so? One answer, typically given by corporate strategists analyzing this kind of forward vertical integration, is that Intel might experience an *efficiency gain* by spreading the costs incurred in acquiring its firm-specific assets (both tangible and intangible) over more value chain stages. These efficiency gains are known as **firm-level economies.**[5] Given the vast amount of firm-specific assets in the form of intellectual property that Intel possesses, this explanation appears to be relevant to this specific case.

The concept of firm-level economies is very helpful. However, it is not, in general, sufficient to explain the preceding integration process. Why? Because Intel always had the option (discussed in Chapter 9) of *licensing* its firm-specific assets to other fabrication producers. That is, Intel could draw up a contract to rent its firm-specific assets to a fabrication firm for a specific period of time in return for which it would receive payment. Indeed, in one specific instance, Intel has done just that, using TSMC as a pure-play foundry. Therefore, part of the explanation of forward or backward integration must answer the question: Why did Intel choose *not* to exercise the licensing option? Or, to state it another way: Why did Intel choose not to engage in a market transaction for its assets, but rather chose to *internalize* this asset market within itself?

[4] Chapter 1 of Caves (2007) provides a description of the role of intangible assets in MNEs. See also Toubal (2009).
[5] The concept of firm-level economies was discussed by Markusen (1995).

Corporate strategists suggest that a firm's decision to internalize the firm-specific asset market reflects *market failure*.[6] That is, for a number of reasons, it has difficulty in selling its firm-specific assets in a contractual arrangement. This explanation can be relevant for all sorts of firm-specific assets, but has been shown to be particularly relevant for the case of intangible assets. In the case of tangible assets, such as specific production techniques, Intel or any other firm might be reluctant to incur the **dissemination risk** we discussed in Chapter 9. In the case of intangible assets, such as management practices or reputation, it might be the case that the assets are inseparable from the firm's human resources or organization. How do you license reputation? Such market failures are what sometimes lead firms with competitive success in one task of a value chain to internalize an adjacent task via forward or backward vertical integration. It could certainly be of relevance to Intel and its many firm-specific assets. One example of intangible assets in the case of the MNE Toyota is given in the accompanying box.

The concepts of firm-specific assets, firm-level economies, and internalization help us to explain why Intel operates as an IDM across the first three tasks of the semiconductor value chain in the United States. But what of the relationship of this value chain and the one in Costa Rica illustrated in Figure 10.3? We take up this issue in the next section.

Intangible Assets: "Team Toyota" and "The Toyota Way" in Kentucky

As an MNE, Toyota became such a touchstone in the evolution of FDI and corporate history that (as we discussed in Chapter 9) it became synonymous with flexible production success in the era of "Toyotism." Behind its early rise was the corporate philosophy of *kaizen* or continuous improvement, and the crowning jewel of its corporate history was the Toyota Lexus, an icon to manufacturing excellence.

In 1985, Toyota announced that it would begin to produce the Toyota Camry at a new plant in North America, the chosen location being Georgetown, Kentucky. Early on in the process of planning this greenfield FDI project, Toyota identified its key intangible asset: an organizational culture based on team membership. According to Toyota, the Georgetown plant maintained quality by encouraging team members to play an active role in quality control, utilizing team members' ideas and opinions, and practicing *kaizen*. In Toyota's words: "Toyota team members treat the next person on the production line as their customer and will not pass a defective part to that customer. If a team member finds a problem with a part or the automobile, the team member stops the line and corrects the problem before the vehicle goes any farther down the line." This was an attempt to transfer the *kaizen* concept from Japan to the United States.

According to an early study by Besser (1996), the team concept at the Kentucky plant took place at three levels: the work team, the company team, and the corporate team. The last of these, the corporate team, included "all members of the Toyota corporation, including, but not limited to, manufacturers in the United States and Japan, their suppliers, various other subsidiaries, and the semi-independent marketing and sales corporations affiliated with the corporation" (p. 51). Thorough hiring processes ensured that the Kentucky plant employed only those who could be good team members.

One former team member quoted by Besser (1996) commented: "You'll be expected to kill yourself for Toyota and you'll be paid a decent living wage. If you can take it, you'll be taken care of for the rest of your life. When they say you start at 6:30, they don't

[6] This insight is part of what is known as transaction cost economics and has its root in the work of Williamson (1975) on what is known as the boundary of the firm.

mean 6:31. You start at 6:30 and you kill yourself for two hours, take a ten-minute break and kill yourself for two more hours. So if someone wants to do that in exchange for the money and security, go for it" (p. 47). Many local workers have, but a significant number have also left the company complaining of "slave labor" and "management by stress."

In 2001, a new theme emerged in Toyota's North American subsidiary, namely the "Toyota Way." The Toyota Way consists of 14 principles that include *kaizen* and teamwork among them. Key employees from North America travel to Toyota City in Japan to attend the Toyota Technical Skills Academy to be schooled in the Toyota Way. There is concern among auto industry analysts, however, that the Toyota Way is not being disseminated evenly throughout the Toyota GPN. As an analyst at JPMorgan in Tokyo puts it: "Toyota is growing more quickly than the company's ability to transplant its culture to foreign markets. This is a huge issue for Toyota, one of the biggest it will face in coming years."

Meanwhile, the Toyota plant in Kentucky now produces a number of different Toyota vehicles and engines including Camry hybrids. It is Toyota's largest production facility outside of Japan, having produced more than five million vehicles. To some degree then, Team Toyota and the Toyota Way had indeed taken root in the United States.

The challenges to the Toyota Way emerged dramatically in 2010 in the face of a series of well-publicized safety recalls in the United States and elsewhere. There is evidence that the roots of this crisis had its origins in the company's decision in 2002 to pursue an increase in global market share from 11 to 15 percent. This necessitated that Toyota begin to work with suppliers with whom it did not have long-term relationships. It will take some time for the company to regain its complete commitment to the Toyota Way.

Sources: Besser (1996), Fackler (2007), *The Economist* (2009b), and *The Economist* (2010)

INTRA-FIRM TRADE

In 1996, to the surprise of many observers, Intel decided to locate an assembly and testing plant in Costa Rica for the Pentium processor. The significance of this decision for Costa Rica can be appreciated by the fact that, at the time, the sales of Intel were twice that of Costa Rica's gross domestic product (GDP). The strategic thinking that motivated Intel to engage in this expansion of its GPN included a search for a relatively low-cost but technical and highly trainable workforce.[7] Whatever the strategic reasons, however, we know from Chapter 9 that Intel could have *contracted* for the assembly and testing processes. It decided against this, opting instead for greenfield FDI (see Table 9.1). As we discussed previously, contracting in the presence of dissemination risk and intangible, firm-specific assets can be difficult. Some of these considerations that are relevant to the Intel case have been listed by Clausing (2009):

> For example, there may be a need to control the quality of the product, accompanied by difficulties in the formation of contracts at arm's length to ensure the reputation of the firm. Also, proprietary firm-specific knowledge can make it difficult to appropriate the gains from production via licensing, as it is difficult to charge the appropriate fee for knowledge without revealing the knowledge itself, thus lowering the incentive to pay for it. (p. 707)

[7] See Multilateral Investment Guarantee Agency (2006). Costa Rica had been promoted for some time by the Coalición Costarricense de Initiativas para el Desarrollo (CINDE), which approached Intel beginning in 1993. We will return to this case in Chapter 22.

Table 10.1. Industry and firm dimensions of trade

	Firm Dimension	
Industry Dimension	**Inter-firm**	**Intra-firm**
Inter-industry	Trade that takes place between two different industries and two different firms.	Trade that takes place between two different industries and within a single firm.
Intra-industry	Type of trade that takes place within a single industry and between two different firms.	Trade that takes place within a single industry and within a single firm.

With the GPN of Figure 10.3 established, we can observe a pattern of *intra-firm trade.* As we see in that figure, Intel exports fabricated die from its home base to its subsidiary in Costa Rica. This is not an arm's-length, market-based transaction that takes place at world prices. Rather, it is a trade transaction within Intel itself at a price set by it. The FDI depicted in Figure 10.3 is known as *forward vertical* FDI because the FDI links fabrication in the United States to the next stage in the value chain, assembly and testing in Costa Rica. If, instead, Intel had sourced dies in Costa Rica for assembly and testing in the United States (not likely!), this would be a case of *backward vertical* FDI. Finally, if Intel only engaged in assembly and testing in both the United States and Costa Rica without any intra-firm trade, this would be an example of *horizontal* FDI.

Recall that, in Chapter 4, we made an important distinction between *inter-industry* trade and *intra-industry* trade. We now have also distinguished between *inter-firm* trade and *intra-firm* trade. Things are becoming a bit complicated! To help you sort all this out, please consult Table 10.1. This table characterizes international trade along two dimensions: industry and firm. Along the industry dimension (rows), it distinguishes between inter-industry and intra-industry. Along the firm dimension (columns), it distinguishes between inter-firm and intra-firm. This gives us four cells in the table.

Down the inter-firm column of Table 10.1, we have the types of trade considered in Chapters 3 and 4 of Part I of this book, that is, inter-firm trade that can be either between or within industries. Down the intra-firm column of the table, we have the types of trade considered in this chapter, that is, intra-firm trade that can take place either between or within industries. Consider Figure 10.3. Given an industry classification of "computer products," the trade depicted there would be intra-firm and intra-industry. However, if we distinguish between "semiconductor fabrication" and "semiconductor assembly and testing" as two separate industries, the trade depicted there would be intra-firm and inter-industry. This gives you an appreciation of how the degree of detail in industry classification determines the extent of inter-industry and intra-industry trade.[8]

The tools of value chains and GPNs allow us to understand how FDI and intra-firm trade arise. The example of FDI flows in Asia that result from the considerations developed in this and the previous chapters is taken up in the accompanying box.

[8] Recall Table 4.2 in the appendix to Chapter 4.

FDI Flows in Asia

In Chapter 9, we considered data on the *stocks* of FDI globally across a number of decades. It is also important to examine the *flows* of FDI among countries, that is, the value of the inflow into or outflow from a particular country. Hattari and Rajan (2009) did this for developing Asia in order to better understand FDI processes in this region. They found that 35 percent of FDI flows to developing Asia came from the region itself, mostly from Hong Kong, the People's Republic of China, Singapore, and Taiwan. The top 10 flows from source to destination were:

Hong Kong to China
China to Hong Kong
Singapore to China
Singapore to Hong Kong
Singapore to Malaysia
Singapore to Thailand
Malaysia to China
Hong Kong to Malaysia
Hong Kong to Thailand
Korea to Hong Kong

These researchers went on to model FDI flows among countries in developing Asia using the *gravity model* described in the appendix to this chapter. Among a large set of findings were the following: market size as measured by GDP, particularly of destination countries, positively affects FDI flows; joint membership in a preferential trade area (PTA) as described in Chapter 8 positively affects FDI flows; distance between countries negatively affects FDI flows even when controlling for PTA membership; and exports from the source country to the destination country positively affect FDI flows, showing that for developing Asia, trade and FDI are complements as opposed to substitutes, as discussed in the appendix to Chapter 9.

On this last result, the authors note that "This may indicate that exporting to a country first leads to greater market familiarity, which in turn facilitates greater FDI flows to that country" (p. 87). Most importantly, though, the whole investigation by Hattari and Rajan shows that it is indeed possible to successfully analyze FDI flows empirically.

Source: Hattari and Rajan (2009)

A COST VIEW OF INTERNALIZATION

The preceding discussion considers a number of issues that relate to firm decision making with regard to GPNs. We have seen that GPN decisions are two-fold, involving both the decisions regarding what part of the value chain to take on and in which countries to do so. Thus there are both task and location decisions to consider. As it turns out, some standard economic analysis can help in GPN decision making. Recall from your microeconomics course that, when considering the costs of a firm, we can distinguish between fixed and variable costs. Suppose that a home-country firm faces a fixed cost of setting up a production facility in country j of FP_j. Suppose also that the firm faces a *smaller* fixed cost of establishing a contractual relationship with a firm from country j of FC_j. There are also variable costs associated with these two options

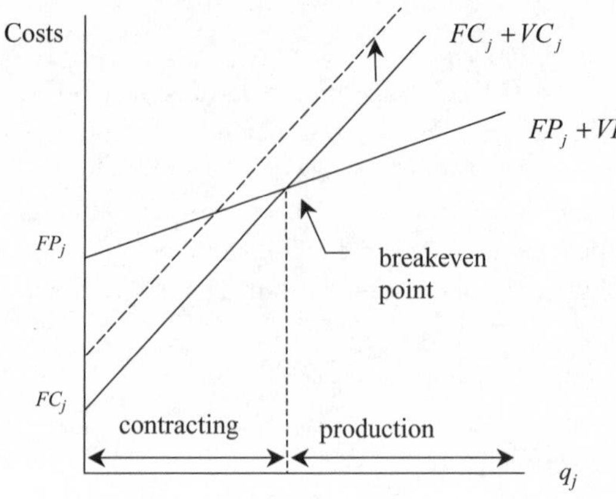

Figure 10.4. A Cost Analysis of Production and Contracting

of VP_j and VC_j. The variable costs of international contracting are *larger* than the variable costs of international production due to the firm-specific assets that give it an advantage over the potential contracting partner. In other words, the firm itself knows how to make its product more easily than other firms.

These considerations lead us to Figure 10.4. Here, the solid $FP_j + VP_j$ graph begins at the vertical axis intercept equal to the fixed cost of production and increases from there with a slope equal to the variable costs of production. The solid $FC_j + VC_j$ graph begins at a lower vertical axis intercept equal to the lower fixed cost of contracting and increases from there with a slope equal to the variable costs of contracting. The two solid lines intersect at a "breakeven point" that establishes a boundary between quantities where it would be better for the firm to engage in contracting and quantities where it would be better for the firm to engage in production. This analysis is useful because it allows us to see that the contracting/production decision might be related to the volume of output the firm has in mind.

Dissemination risk involved in contracting can be included in this diagram in a simplified way. It increases the fixed cost of contracting and moves the solid contracting graph upward to the dashed line. This moves the breakeven point to the left and reduces the range of quantities where contracting is to be preferred.

TYING THINGS TOGETHER: THE OLI FRAMEWORK

If an MNE decides to engage in FDI in a foreign country, it likely that it will be at a disadvantage in some important areas vis-à-vis local firms in that foreign country. The home-country MNE will have to incur the additional costs of operating its business internationally, including increased transportation, communication, and coordination costs. Therefore, if the home-country MNE is indeed able to successfully engage in business in the foreign country, there must be some other advantages that offset the additional costs of conducting business internationally.[9] In what now is a well-known framework, Dunning (1988) outlined three basic advantages: ownership (or O) advantages, location (or L) advantages, and internalization (or I) advantages.[10]

[9] This insight was originally due to Hymer (1976) who, it can be argued, originated the modern, firm-based analysis of the MNE.

[10] See Dunning and Lundan (2008) and Markusen (1995).

Table 10.2. The OLI framework

Symbol	Meaning	Contribution
O	Ownership advantage	Explains how a firm's tangible and intangible assets help it to overcome the extra costs of doing business internationally. Explains why a home-country firm, rather than a foreign firm, produces in the foreign country.
L	Location advantage	Explains why a home-based MNE chooses to produce in a foreign country rather than in its home country.
I	Internalization advantage	Explains why a home-based MNE chooses FDI rather than licensing to achieve production in a foreign country.

Ownership or O advantages refer to ownership of tangible or intangible firm-specific assets the home-country MNE owns and that provide it with a competitive edge over the foreign firms. As summarized by Markusen (1995), "Whatever its form, the ownership advantage confers some valuable market power or cost advantage on the firm sufficient to outweigh the disadvantage of doing business abroad" (p. 173). As we discussed previously, by deploying these assets over a larger range of activities, the home-country MNE can realize cost advantages over its rivals through firm-level economies. The role of the O advantage is to explain why the MNE engages in the production of a good for the foreign market instead of a foreign firm.

Location or L advantages are associated with the foreign country. The L advantages could include input costs, transportation costs, import restraints, foreign government promotional policies, or access to foreign consumers. L advantages often closely relate to the first two motivations for international production discussed in Chapter 9: resource seeking and market seeking. The role of the L advantage is to explain why the home-country MNE chooses to produce in the foreign country rather than the home country.

Finally, as we saw previously, internalization or I advantages explain why the home-country MNE chooses FDI over the contracting option. The I advantages are therefore related to all the reasons why contracting might not be a viable option. In Dunning's view, and in the view of other researchers deploying this framework, all three advantages are necessary to explain the presence of FDI. What has come to be called the OLI Framework is summarized in Table 10.2.

CONCLUSION

Approximately one-third of world trade is intra-firm trade, taking place within MNEs. This trade occurs within global production networks. As we have seen, firms offset the extra costs of doing business internationally through their tangible or intangible assets, which provide ownership advantages to them and generate firm-level economies. Firms choose to operate abroad because various foreign countries offer location advantages to them, and they choose investment modes of foreign market entry over contractual modes because there are advantages to internalization. Some of these issues can be examined using cost analysis, but the full set of these issues can be summarized in the OLI framework.

REVIEW EXERCISES

1. Choose any production process that might be of interest to you. Both merchandise and services are appropriate. As best you can, draw a value chain for this production process.
2. Next, for this production process, choose two countries. Place the value chains for these two countries side by side in a GPN. Show how FDI by a firm based in the first country in the second country can be depicted for the cases of horizontal FDI, backward vertical FDI, and forward vertical FDI.
3. Make a list of as many firm-specific assets you can think of, both tangible and intangible.
4. For each of ownership advantages, location advantages, and internalization advantages, state how it helps you to understand why firms engage in FDI rather than trade or contractual modes of foreign market entry.

FURTHER READING AND WEB RESOURCES

For very useful reviews of the global semiconductor industry, see Dibiaggio (2007), chapter 11 of Dicken (2007), and Macher, Mowery, and Simcoe (2002). For a concise review of intra-firm trade, see Clausing (2009). For a review of value chains and GPNs, respectively, see chapter 5 of McIvor (2005) and Coe, Dicken, and Hess (2008). An excellent introduction to global corporate strategy is Verbeke (2009). The OLI Framework is discussed in chapter 4 of Dunning and Lundan (2008) and in Markusen (1995). A global political economy view of some of the issues discussed in this chapter can be found in chapter 6 of Walter and Sen (2009).

The United Nations Conference on Trade and Development is an organization that has dedicated itself to the analysis of FDI and its role in economic development. Their website is http://www.unctad.org. Of particular interest is their annual *World Investment Report*, which is highlighted at http://www.unctad.org/wir/.

APPENDIX: THE GRAVITY MODEL

Gravity models utilize the gravitational force concept as an analogy to explain the volume of trade or FDI among the countries of the world. For example, gravity models establish a baseline for trade or FDI *flows* as determined by gross domestic product (GDP), population, and distance.[11] The effect of policies on trade or FDI flows can then be assessed by adding the policy variables to the equation and estimating deviations from the baseline flows. In many instances, gravity models have significant explanatory power, leading Deardorff (1998) to refer to them as a "fact of life."

Gravity models begin with Newton's Law for the gravitational force (GF_{ij}) between the two objects *i* and *j*. In equation form, this is expressed as:

$$GF_{ij} = \frac{M_i M_j}{D_{ij}} \quad i \neq j \tag{10.1}$$

[11] The emphasis on *flows* here is to remind us that the gravity model does not explain FDI stocks such as those reported in Chapter 9. Distance is sometimes expanded conceptually to include linguistic and cultural distance. The origins of the gravity model go back to Tinbergen (1962).

In this equation, the gravitational force is directly proportional to the masses of the objects (M_i and M_j) and indirectly proportional to the distance between them (D_{ij}).

Gravity models are estimated in terms of *natural logarithms*, denoted " ln." In this natural log form, what is multiplied in Equation 10.1 becomes added, and what is divided becomes subtracted, translating Equation 10.1 into a linear equation:

$$\ln GF_{ij} = \ln M_i + \ln M_j - \ln D_{ij} \quad i \neq j \tag{10.2}$$

Gravity models of international trade and FDI implement Equation 10.2 by using trade flows or FDI flows from county i to country j (F_{ij}) in place of gravitational force, with arbitrarily small numbers sometimes being used in place of any zero values. Distance is often measured using "great circle" calculations. The handling of mass in Equation 10.2 takes place via at least two alternatives. In the *first alternative* with the most solid theoretical foundations, mass in Equation 10.2 is associated with the gross domestic product (*GDP*) of the countries. In this case, Equation 10.2 becomes:

$$\ln F_{ij} = \alpha + \beta_1 \ln GDP_i + \beta_2 \ln GDP_j + \beta_3 \ln D_{ij} \tag{10.3}$$

In general, the expected signs here are $\beta_1, \beta_2 > 0$, and $\beta_3 < 0$.

In the *second alternative*, mass in Equation 10.2 is associated with *both* GDP *and* population (*POP*). In this case, Equation 10.2 becomes:

$$\ln F_{ij} = \varphi + \gamma_1 \ln GDP_i + \gamma_2 \ln POP_i + \gamma_3 \ln GDP_j + \gamma_4 POP_j + \gamma_5 \ln D_{ij} \tag{10.4}$$

With regard to the expected signs on the population variables, these are typically interpreted in terms or market size and are therefore positive ($\gamma_2, \gamma_4 > 0$).

REFERENCES

Besser, T.L. (1996) *Team Toyota: Transplanting the Toyota Culture to the Camry Plant in Kentucky*, State University of New York Press.

Caves, R.E. (2007) *Multinational Enterprise and Economics Analysis*, Cambridge University Press.

Clausing, K.A. (2009) "Intrafirm Trade," in K.A. Reinert, R.S. Rajan, A.J. Glass, and L.S. Davis (eds.), *The Princeton Encyclopedia of the World Economy*, Princeton University Press, 706–708.

Coe, N.M., P. Dicken, and M. Hess (2008) "Global Production Networks: Realizing the Potential," *Journal of Economic Geography*, 8:3, 271–295.

Deardorff, A.V. (1998) "Determinants of Bilateral Trade: Does Gravity Work in a Neoclassical World?" in J.A. Frankel (ed.), *The Regionalization of the World Economy*, University of Chicago Press.

Dibiaggio, L. (2007) "Design Complexity, Vertical Disintegration and Knowledge Organization in the Semiconductor Industry," *Industrial and Corporate Change*, 16:2, 239–267.

Dicken, P. (2007) *Global Shift: Mapping the Changing Contours of the World Economy*, Guilford.

Dunning, J.H. (1988) *Explaining International Production*, Unwin Hyman.

Dunning, J.H. and S.M. Lundan (2008) *Multinational Enterprises and the Global Economy*, Edward Elgar.

The Economist (2009a) "Briefing: Japan's Technology Champions," November 7.

The Economist (2009b) "Briefing Toyota: Losing Its Shine," December 12.

The Economist (2010) "Toyota's Overstretched Supply Chain," February 27.

Fackler, M. (2007) "The 'Toyota Way Is Translated for a New Generation of Foreign Managers," *New York Times*, February 15.

Hattari, R. and R.S. Rajan (2009) "Understanding Bilateral FDI Flows in Developing Asia," *Asian-Pacific Economic Literature*, 23:2, 73–93.

Hymer, S.H. (1976) *The International Operations of National Firms: A Study of Direct Foreign Investment*, MIT Press.

Macher, J.T., D.C. Mowery, and T.S. Simcoe (2002) "E-Business and Disintegration of the Semiconductor Industry Value Chain," *Industry and Innovation*, 9:3, 155–181.

Markusen, J.R. (1995) "The Boundaries of Multinational Enterprise and the Theory of International Trade," *Journal of Economic Perspectives*, 9:2, 169–189.

McIvor, R. (2005) *The Outsourcing Process: Strategies for Evaluation and Management*, Cambridge University Press.

Multilateral Investment Guarantee Agency (2006) *The Impact of Intel in Costa Rica*, World Bank.

Tinbergen, J. (1962) *Shaping the World Economy: Suggestions for an International Economic Policy*, The Twentieth Century Fund.

Toubal, F. (2009) "Intangible Assets," in K.A. Reinert, R.S. Rajan, A.J. Glass, and L.S. Davis (eds.), *The Princeton Encyclopedia of the World Economy*, Princeton University Press, 638–640.

Verbeke, A. (2009) *International Business Strategy: Rethinking the Foundations of Global Corporate Success*, Cambridge University Press.

Walter, A. and G. Sen (2009) *Analyzing the Global Political Economy*, Princeton University Press.

Williamson, O.E. (1975) *Markets and Hierarchies*, The Free Press.

11 Managing International Production

In Chapter 10, we considered the semiconductor firm Intel and its decision making with regard to a two-country global production network (GPN). This was a vast, if useful simplification. At the time of this writing, Intel has 15 fabrication plants located in the United States, Ireland, and Israel. It also maintains seven assembly and testing plants in China, Costa Rica, Malaysia, the Philippines, and Vietnam. Reflecting the nature of the semiconductor industry, the company maintains research and development (R&D) facilities in the United States, China, Mexico, India, and Europe (Ireland, Spain, Germany, Russia, France, Belgium, United Kingdom, Poland, and Switzerland). Intel's GPN is significantly more complicated than Chapter 10 suggests.

With semiconductor production facility costs denominated in billions of U.S. dollars, it is unlikely that Intel and other semiconductor firms locate these plants willy-nilly. The same would hold, if perhaps to a lesser degree, for multinational enterprises (MNEs) in other sectors as well. There must be some logic to the organization of MNEs and their GPNs, and this chapter summarizes that logic. We begin by considering a set of issues that arise in organizing the MNE's international operations, both with regard to intra-firm design and inter-firm relationships, and look at the particular case of joint ventures. We then consider a set of issues related to the MNE's home base. This leads naturally to a consideration of spatial clusters and their relationship to MNEs. We conclude by considering MNE management of R&D functions within their GPNs.

Analytical elements for this chapter:

Countries, *sectors*, *tasks*, and *firms*.

ORGANIZING THE MNE

As we saw in Chapter 10, the MNE faces the two-fold decision regarding what *tasks* in which *countries* to include within its corporate boundaries. The result of this two-fold decision is the task and geographic extent of the MNE that we illustrated with solid lines in Figure 10.3 for the case of Intel's GPN and reproduce here as Figure 11.1.

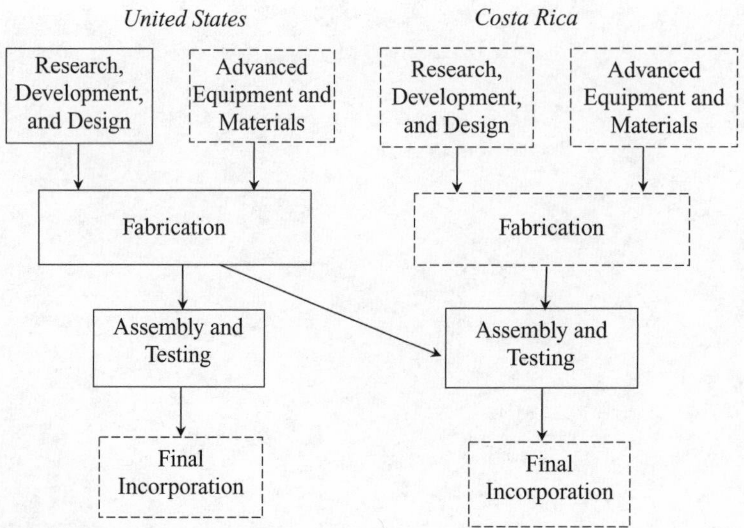

Figure 11.1. Intel's Global Production Network for Semiconductors

Table 11.1 Generic types of intra-firm MNE design

MNE characteristics	MNE intra-firm design
Single product, single country	Functional divisions
Single product, few countries	Single, foreign division
Single product, multicountry	Country/regional divisions
Multiproduct, few countries	Product divisions
Multiproduct, multicountry	Mixed structure based on matrix management or "heterarchy"

Recall that, within the solid lines of the MNE's boundaries, *intra*-firm trade can take place. Outside these boundaries, the MNE can be involved in *inter*-firm trade. Considering the GPN in its vertical dimension, beyond the upstream extent of the firm's boundary are (with dotted lines) relationships with suppliers, potentially involving imports if those suppliers are abroad. Similarly, beyond the downstream extent of the firm's boundary are (again with dotted lines) relationships with buyers, potentially involving exports if those buyers are abroad. Consequently, organizing the MNE involves both intra-firm design and inter-firm relationship considerations.

As it turns out, the issue of intra-firm design is not straightforward. Before the process of foreign market entry considered in Chapter 9, the firm might consist of *functional divisions* (management, finance, research and development, production, sales) all reporting to the head office or chief executive. As is shown in Table 11.1, this is typical for single-product, single-country firms. With foreign market entry via foreign direct investment (FDI), the question arises regarding what functions to locate abroad: just production and sales, or more? Initially, it might be just production and sales occurring in a *foreign division*, but as foreign operations develop and mature, there is a tendency to locate a greater number of corporate functions abroad. The MNE moves beyond the "single product, few countries" row of Table 11.1.

As global presence increases, pressures build on the foreign division. It has more countries and functions to look after, and eventually, something needs to give way. As noted by Caves (2007), "A single international division is seldom used if the firm makes 40 percent or more of its sales abroad" (p. 79). One option that is generically associated with single-product, multicountry MNEs is that of a *country/regional division*, where each country or region covered by the MNE has its own division responsible for all functions. Another option that is generically associated with multiproduct but few-country MNEs is that of *product divisions*, where each of the firm's products has its own corporate division for global production and sales. The most complicated but relevant generic case is that of the multiproduct, multicountry MNE. Here, a standard approach is that of *matrix management*, where there are both product and country/regional dimensions to reporting lines.[1]

If we were to generalize a bit from the generic types of organizational design listed in Table 11.1, we can identify two general tendencies. First, the narrower the range of its products, the more likely the MNE will adopt a country/region divisional structure. Second, the wider the range of its products, the more likely the MNE will adopt a

[1] The problems of matrix management were summarized by Dunning and Lundan (2008), who stated that "because it made for a more intensive network of intra-firm communication, the matrix structure created its own organizational challenges, notably those that arose from ambiguities over the locus of management responsibility, and a conflict of goals and strategies of the members of the network" (p. 248).

product divisional structure.[2] These are rather limited statements, and the truth of the matter is that there is no complete set of principles that can guide MNE organizational design.

In response to the lack of guidance regarding MNE design, a last option has emerged that is also mentioned at the bottom of Table 11.1, that of *heterarchy*. Heterarchy involves information sharing and informal ways of circumventing the limitations of formal organizational design. This shift of thinking had many sources, but one important one was the work of Bartlett and Ghoshal (2002). These international business researchers noted that MNEs face three strategic challenges: global efficiency, local responsiveness, and global innovation. *Global efficiency* is obtained from economies of scale and scope that can occur as the MNE rationalizes production within the GPN. *Local responsiveness* involves using local facilities and personnel to tailor goods and services to the needs and preferences of local consumers. Finally, *global innovation* refers to the combined and complementary use of innovations from many parts of the multinational value network. In these authors' view, "more and more businesses are being driven by *simultaneous* demands for global efficiency, national responsiveness, and worldwide leveraging of innovations and learning" (p. 33).[3]

Bartlett and Ghoshal argued in favor of a model of global management that they describe as "flexible centralization/coordination" or as an "integrated network." These are examples of heterarchy that we can characterize in three ways. First, the role of subsidiaries is differentiated throughout the GPN, taking on different roles in different countries or regions. One subsidiary might only be involved in sales, whereas another subsidiary is involved in locally relevant R&D. Second, coordination of the MNE is achieved using multiple methods. For example, flows of goods can be coordinated through centralization, flows or resources can be coordinated through formalization, and flows of information can be coordinated through corporate socialization. In the last case, socialization, Bartlett and Ghoshal advocate the rotation of personnel throughout the MNE in order to facilitate information flows within the social networks that develop. Finally, the disparate elements of the MNE are tied together in a coherent mission through the use of vision and innovative human resource development policies. Some of these issues in the context of emerging markets are considered in the accompanying box.

The End of Corporate Imperialism?

Prahalad and Lieberthal (2008) emphasized the growing importance of a few large, emerging markets to MNEs long-term corporate strategy. The countries they had in mind were the likes of Brazil, China, India, and Indonesia. They warned against what they termed the "imperialist mind-set" of many MNE executives in which these large emerging markets are just seen as an extension of their operations in their Western home bases. Instead, these researchers emphasized that the bulk of the household markets in

[2] See chapter 8 of Dunning and Lundan (2008).

[3] The tensions among these objectives were alluded to in the following advertisement by Citibank: "These days, everybody says they're 'global.' But saying you're global isn't the same as 'being' global. It's not just where you are, it's how you are there. To us, being global means being completely local. Entirely at home. The way we are in 100 countries around the world. Our job is to understand a country by its people, not just by its airports" (in *The Economist*, July 4, 1998).

these economies are relatively low income and that this has an impact on the preferences of the households. In addition, local responsiveness needs to consider relationships to suppliers, distribution system design, and the political environments. In the view of Prahalad and Lieberthal, MNEs need to rethink their approach to product design, the distribution system, supplier relationships, and personnel policies.

One area of challenge is the role of MNEs' expatriate managers. For example, Prahalad and Lieberthal stated that "In the early stages of market development, expatriates are the conduits for information flow between the multinational's corporate office and the local operation. But while headquarters staffs usually recognize the importance of sending information to the local operation, they tend to be less aware that information must also be received from the other direction" (p. 30). Lines of communication can be very complicated. Reporting on an expatriate MNE representative in China, these researchers stated that "as the head of his company's China effort, he has to coordinate with the company's regional headquarters in Japan, report to international headquarters in Europe, and maintain close contact with corporate headquarters in North America" (pp. 37–38). This is the practical difficulty of "heterarchy."

These management issues become all the more acute as the emerging markets themselves are no longer just destinations for innovations occurring in the corporate headquarters but are sources of innovation in themselves. The authors emphasized that "the imperialist assumption that innovation comes from the center will gradually fade away and die" (p. 45). Product development innovations will start to flow from the periphery to the center instead. Prahalad and Lieberthal warned that "success in the big emerging markets will surely change the shape of the modern multinational as we know it today" (p. 43).

The Economist (2010) took this argument one stage further, stating that developing countries "are reinventing systems of production and distribution, and they are experimenting with entirely new business models. All the elements of modern business, from supply-chain management to recruitment and retention, are being re-jigged or reinvented in one emerging market or another" (p. 3). Western MNEs should take note.

Sources: Prahalad and Lieberthal (2008) and *The Economist* (2010)

With regard to inter-firm relationships, an important issue is that of vertical connections to supplying firms. Here, Gereffi, Humphrey, and Sturgeon (2005) emphasized that some of the considerations of Chapter 10 that lead MNEs with firm-specific assets (and in particular, intangible assets) to pursue FDI modes of foreign market entry (rather than contractual modes) can be overcome in certain kinds of relationships that we might describe as *contractual plus.* Contractual plus arrangements consist of "repeated transactions, reputation, and social norms that are embedded in particular geographic locations or social groups" (p. 81). These features can help overcome the difficulties of the contractual mode in the presence of intangible assets and dissemination risk.

These researchers go on to distinguish among four types of relationships between an MNE and its suppliers: market, modular, relational, and captive.[4] The *market model* consists of standard contractual relationships, but these can be augmented by trust and normality developed through repeated transactions. The *modular model* occurs when

[4] See also chapters 4 and 5 of Ruigrok and van Tulder (1995) for a political economy view of buyer-supplier relationships.

the product and production process in question are standard and generic, and the suppliers are coalesced around specific breakpoints in GPNs. We saw this in the semiconductor case with "fabless" semiconductor firms contracting with pure-play foundries, but this situation usually occurs in sectors that are less technologically advanced, such as clothing and footwear.[5] In the *relational model*, MNE-supplier interactions are more complex, described by Gereffi, Humphrey, and Sturgeon (2005) as "mutual dependence." This can be associated with ethnic ties or geographic proximity. We will return to this model when we consider spatial clusters below. Finally, in the *captive model*, we find an asymmetric relationship in which the MNE is dominant over its suppliers. The example usually cited in this case is Toyota. The captive model has been part of the success of Japanese-style, flexible manufacturing at the heart of "Toyotism."

What is clear from this brief discussion is that MNE management in both intra-firm design and inter-firm relationship components is a relatively complex and difficult task. There is no single approach that can be grasped as the "answer" to multinational management. Rather, there is an ongoing learning process that takes place, with varying degrees of success, within the historical trajectories of MNEs. This is what makes global corporate strategy such an interesting and dynamic field.

JOINT VENTURES

In Chapter 9, we considered three types of FDI, namely, joint ventures (JVs), mergers and acquisitions (M&As), and greenfield, noting that M&As are the most common type. It is worthwhile to spend some time examining JVs, however, because they pose a set of challenges not generally encountered in M&A and greenfield FDI.[6] Recall that, in a JV, the home-country firm establishes a separate firm in the foreign country that is jointly owned with a foreign-country firm. The motivation for a JV usually reflects the presence of complementary, firm-specific assets in the two firms involved. Raff (2009) summarizes this very well[7]:

> A joint venture is a mechanism for combining complementary assets owned by separate firms. These assets can be tangible, such as machinery and equipment, or intangible, such as technological know-how, production or marketing skills, brand names, and market-specific information. (p. 714)

So the advantage of JVs comes from the presence of complementary, firm-specific assets. JVs can be a particularly desirable mode of FDI when the home-country firm is unsure about the qualities of the foreign-country firm's assets and wants the opportunity to study them up close before moving on to a full M&A or when the home-country firm is only interested in a subset of the foreign-country firm's assets, so M&A does not make sense. JVs also occur in large, resource-extraction FDI projects where both firms are interested in risk sharing and achieving large-scale economies. Finally, in some circumstances, the foreign-country government chooses to require JVs to ensure profit-sharing.[8]

[5] Some researchers refer to this as the "Lego" or "turnkey" model of MNE-supplier relationship. See chapter 5 of Dicken (2007).
[6] We touched on this in the box on Beijing Jeep in Chapter 9.
[7] A more extensive consideration can be found in Choi and Beamish (2004).
[8] See chapter 3 of Caves (2007).

We spent some time in Chapter 10 trying to understand how *intra-firm trade* takes place within GPNs. As it turns out, the likelihood of a JV appears to be negatively related to the amount of intra-firm trade present. Desai, Foley, and Hines (2004) found that the greater the amount of intra-firm trade in MNEs, the less likely they are to pursue JVs. The explanation here is that the large amounts of intra-firm transactions are best handled through wholly owned subsidiaries. But when intra-firm transactions are not prominent, JVs become a possible FDI mode.

Despite advantages in some circumstances, JVs are notoriously unstable and relatively short-lived.[9] This is due to the difficulty of managing two firms together, clashes of organizational culture, and clashes of national culture. This is probably why Hill (2009) reported that successful JVs usually involve up to 2 years of preliminary negotiations in the areas of technology transfer, asset valuation, divisions of management responsibility, financial policy, and strategic objectives. Ironically, cultural distance is one additional reason why JVs are considered in the first place. The home-country firm might not feel confident enough to execute an M&A when cultural differences loom large and therefore opt for a JV to lessen resource exposure and engage in cultural learning. Indeed, the JV irony is larger than that. They tend to form due to differences between the firms involved, but these very differences make them difficult to manage. Despite these difficulties, JVs remain an important component of international production.

THE HOME BASE

Outside of the "born global" firms mentioned in Chapter 9, MNEs must start in one country or another in what is known as the **home base**. Recall our discussion of UNCTAD's transnationality index (TNI) from Chapter 9. We saw in that chapter that, for many of the top nonfinancial MNEs, home bases often account for nearly one-half of total operations and sales. This alone suggests that home bases are more than convenient addresses. To begin, the home base of an MNE is in almost all cases the location of *corporate headquarters*.[10] As it turns out, headquarters are important from the point of view of intra-firm design, and home base environments can be important for the competitiveness of MNEs.

Although the role of headquarters can vary from one MNE to another, there are a few generalizations we can make about them. There is a tendency for certain functions in the MNE to be centralized within the headquarters in the home base. These functions include finance, corporate control, and R&D. We mentioned in Chapter 1 that MNEs are responsible for approximately three-fourths of global, civilian R&D. The location decisions of these MNEs with regard to R&D facilities therefore have tremendous impacts on the global technology capabilities of countries.[11] Financial functions also tend to be located in corporate headquarters, creating a sort of patron–client relationship with subsidiaries. Production, marketing, and sales, on the other hand, tend to be dispersed outward within the global GPN.

[9] Evidence on this goes far back, but one example is Park and Ungson (1997). For an early and important analysis of JVs, see Kogut (1988).

[10] For a review of corporate headquarters, see Young et al. (2000).

[11] Despite the tendency toward centralization of R&D within corporate headquarters, there can be certain R&D functions that MNEs do choose to decentralize toward subsidiaries in the form of regional R&D units. We will discuss this issue later.

International business research has also explored the role of the home base in supporting MNE competitiveness. It is possible for these home bases to support the firm-specific assets that drive MNEs into international production. This was the argument made, for example, by Michael Porter in his well-known book *The Competitive Advantage of Nations* (1990), who asked the question: "Why are firms based in a particular nation able to create and sustain competitive advantage against the world's best competitors in a particular field?" (p. 1). Porter's answer was in terms of four determinants of competitive advantage: factor conditions; demand conditions; related and supporting industries; and firm strategy, structure, and rivalry.[12] We consider each in turn.

Factor conditions. In Chapters 2 and 3, we discussed the role of factor endowments in determining absolute and comparative advantage. The factors we considered (labor, land, natural resources, and physical capital) are what Porter called *basic factors* that are largely *inherited.* More important from Porter's point of view are *advanced factors* that are *created.* These advanced factors include such things as sophisticated infrastructure, labor educated and trained in very specific ways, and focused research institutions. Porter also made a distinction between *generalized factors* and *specialized factors.* Generalized factors can be used in a number of different industries, whereas specialized factors are tailored for use in specific industries. Porter argued that sustained competitive advantage has its basis in the creation of advanced and specialized factors.

Demand conditions. Porter stressed three aspects of demand conditions in the home base. These are demand composition, demand size and pattern of growth, and degree of internationalization. Porter argued that sophisticated, demanding, and anticipatory home demand contributes to firms' success. To take one example, Porter argued that the low gasoline prices in the United States (by global standards) have contributed to domestic demand that is out of step with global demand trends for fuel-efficient cars. This can help to explain the long-term competitive issues that have plagued "Detroit." As a second example, Porter pointed to the small living quarters and sophistication with electronic goods in Japan as contributing positively to competitive success in the Japanese electronic keyboard industry.[13]

Related and supporting industries. Porter stressed the important role played by supplying industries in the home base. He argued that these suppliers can provide the MNE with better developed inputs that reflect ongoing coordination between the MNE and its suppliers and that this coordination also supports innovation and upgrading for both the MNE and its suppliers. This possibility points to the importance of the relational model of inter-firm relationships we discussed previously. Porter and others have emphasized the gains to competitiveness that arise from the presence of *clusters* of competitive, domestic suppliers. We will take up this issue later.

Firm strategy, structure, and rivalry. Porter recognized that one country differs from another with regard to managerial systems and philosophies and with regard to capital market conditions. He suggested that institutional environments that allow firms to take a *long-term view* contribute positively to competitiveness. Also important, however, is the presence of a large number of competing firms or rivals in the domestic industry. Porter claimed: "Among the strongest empirical findings from our research is

[12] These four aspects of the home base are often represented graphically in a diamond format that became known as the *Porter diamond.* Two other subsidiary determinants are chance and government policy.

[13] These two examples can be related. A Japanese person once remarked to me (a U.S. citizen): "Your cars are bigger than our apartments!"

the association between vigorous domestic rivalry and the creation and persistence of competitive advantage in an industry" (p. 117). We know from introductory microeconomics that competition among firms is necessary for *allocative efficiency* in a market system, but Porter also stressed the role of domestic rivalry in contributing to *dynamic, technological efficiency*. This was the case, for example, in the Japanese industrial robot sector discussed in Chapter 2.

In Chapter 10, we discussed Intel's decision to locate an assembly and testing plant in Costa Rica. There is a good deal of evidence that Costa Rican officials, particularly those in the Costa Rican Investment Board (*CINDE* in Spanish), were in communication with Michael Porter during the years leading up to Intel's decision. This was to help promote a "focused development" in Costa Rica in the area of computer products that proved to be quite successful. We next turn to some aspects of focused development in the form of spatial clusters.

SPATIAL CLUSTERS

In Chapter 9, we mentioned the recent rise of **flexible manufacturing** and its contributions to the competitive success of some MNEs, especially those based in Japan. In this chapter, we have stressed the potential role of the *home base* in contributing to the competitive success of MNEs. It turns out that the flexibility and home base concepts converge in a phenomenon we mentioned in the previous section, that of spatial clustering.

Variously referred to as clusters, networks, centers of excellence, and industrial districts, what we will term **spatial clusters** first came to be noticed in Silicon Valley in the United States (semiconductors again!), in what is now known as the Third Italy, in Southern Germany, and in East Asia. Malmberg, Sölvell, and Zander (1996) defined a spatial cluster as "a set of interlinked firms/activities that exist in the same local and regional milieu, defined as to encompass economic, social, cultural and institutional factors" (p. 91). Putting aside for a moment the role of the milieu, spatial clusters evolve because of the nature of the innovation process.

As emphasized by Kogut and Zander (1992), much productive knowledge cannot be codified into explicit forms. Rather, this *tacit knowledge* must be communicated via a social process of face-to-face interaction over a relatively long period of time. Consequently, innovation and learning comprise a spatially located, social, and collective process among a group of firms.[14] As Malmberg, Sölvell, and Zander (1996) pointed out, "the very nature of the innovation process tends to make technological activity locally confined" (p. 90). A particular case of this in Pakistan is discussed in the accompanying box.

Why can spatial clusters contribute to the productivity of firms? First, the concentrated communication made possible by a cluster increases learning and innovation. This, in turn, contributes to the dynamic, technological efficiency of firms in the cluster. Second, trust increases over time, and this facilitates contracting and exchange among firms (the relational model discussed earlier). Third, a common business culture develops, and this reduces uncertainty. These processes are particularly important in flexible

[14] See also Scott (1995). Spatial clusters are one example of *positive externalities* that can exist among firms.

manufacturing systems because these are "strongly externalized" or "transactions-intensive" (Scott, 1995). That is, much of the activity in flexible production systems takes place *among firms*, especially between core firms and their suppliers. The dotted lines of GPNs such as those in Figure 11.1 can be as important as the solid lines, and the inter-firm relational model discussed previously can be extended to whole sets of suppliers within a spatial cluster.

A cluster exists within a **milieu**. The milieu consists of the cluster's firms, the knowledge embedded within the cluster, its institutional (e.g., legal) environment, and the ties of the cluster's firms to customers, research institutions, educational institutions, and local government (Malmberg, Sölvell, and Zander, 1996). The milieu supports the cluster with rules and norms for business activity, social cohesion, business culture, and government support.

Porter (1990) suggested that government policies can address spatial clusters when considering investments in education, research, and infrastructure. In the realm of education, specialized training closely tied to spatial clusters can be very important. This specialized training can be provided by technical institutes or professional associations. Government can play a direct, albeit limited, role in "the testing of materials, inspection and certification of quality control standards, calibration of measurement instruments, establishment of repositories of technical information, patent registration, research and design, and technical training" (Battat, Frank, and Shen, 1996, p. 22).[15] Finally, competition policies can restrict horizontal collusion while fostering vertical communication and collaboration.

What is the importance of spatial clusters and milieux to the MNE? In its home base, an MNE obviously has the possibility of contributing to the local cluster and milieu. This is the message of Porter in his emphasis on the home base discussed previously. Porter overemphasized the role of the home base, however, in underestimating the potential of foreign suppliers to support an MNE's competitive advantage. Indeed, it is possible that an MNE can tap into selected *foreign* clusters and milieux. For these reasons, spatial clusters can be important in *both* the home base *and* in the foreign operations of MNEs.

The Surgical Instruments Cluster in Pakistan

It might be surprising to some readers, but the second-largest exporter of stainless steel surgical instruments in the world is Pakistan, a country that has been making surgical instruments for more than a century. The advent of surgical instrument manufacturing is traced back to the 1890s when local ironsmiths began repairing the instruments of a local hospital. Now the surgical instruments sector in Pakistan is in the form of a cluster, centered in the city of Sialkot and consisting of 350 firms and 30,000 workers making thousands of different types of instruments.

Our preceding discussion of clusters and milieux emphasized their social nature. The research of Nadvi (1999) showed that this is certainly a key characteristic of the Sialkot cluster. Nadvi commented that "Social networks can have an important impact

[15] As an example, Porter (1990) cited a materials testing institute linked to the German cutlery cluster in the city of Solingen. Battat, Frank, and Shen (1996) cited the Singapore Institute of Standards and Industrial Research. Brenton et al. (2009) stressed the importance of metrology, testing, and conformity assessment facilities in helping potential exporters meet evolving standards.

on the workings of local firms. They can provide a basis for regulating inter-firm relations, thereby mediating local competition and co-operation, and facilitate the historical sedimentation of 'tacit,' sector-specific knowledge" (p. 143). Nadvi also noted that communication within the Sialkot cluster is intense, taking place both within and outside of the official trade association. The social networks along which the communication takes place are supported by systems of kinship (*biraderi*), extended families (most firms are family firms), and localness in geographic, cultural, and historical senses. Consequently, "Trust, reputation and honour in business relationships are intertwined with the social relations that agents have with each other and their overall social standing" (p. 156). Despite these social ties, however, rivalry is intense among firms, especially at the marketing end of value chains, and this rivalry promotes competitiveness.

Much less positively, the Sialkot surgical instruments cluster has been implicated in the use of child labor in the making of surgical instruments. The Pakistani government itself estimated that there are a few thousand children employed in the Sialkot cluster. The International Labor Organization has been collaborating with the United Nations Children's Fund (UNICEF) and the Pakistani government to attempt to remove children from the cluster and to enroll them in schools.

The most important surgical instruments cluster in the world is that in Tuttlingen, Germany. Navdi and Halder (2005) examined the relationship between the Sialkot and Tuttlingen clusters. They found that the Sialkot cluster specializes in more mature products, whereas the Tuttlingen cluster specializes in the development of new products and that actors in the Tuttlingen cluster are involved in supporting technical development and equipment upgrading in Sialkot. The reason for this is that the Tuttlingen cluster relies on the Sialkot cluster for outsourced work. A constraint on the Sialkot cluster is a very shallow milieu that forces it to rely on Tuttlingen for technical upgrading. Recognizing this, actors in the Sialkot cluster have invested directly in the Tuttlingen cluster. Inter-firm relationships, therefore, can exist between clusters separated by great distances in the world economy.

Sources: Nadvi (1999), Navdi and Halder (2005), International Labor Organization, and Government of Pakistan

RESEARCH AND DEVELOPMENT

In our consideration of the home base above, we stated that there is a tendency to centralize R&D functions in the home base country or even in the corporate headquarters.[16] That is fine as a general rule. But we have also seen that Intel has chosen to locate R&D in a number of countries outside of its home base. Given MNEs' involvement in approximately three-fourths of global, civilian R&D, the way in which MNEs configure R&D within their GPNs matters enormously to global technological capabilities. To obtain a perspective on the magnitudes involved, consider Figure 11.2. This figure reports R&D expenditures for five of the MNEs listed in Table 9.5 (Ford, DaimlerChrysler, Toyota, Volkswagen, and Honda) and five emerging markets (Taiwan, Brazil, Russia, India, and Mexico). What is clear from this figure is that MNE R&D expenditures are on the same order of magnitude as those of many significant countries in the world economy. Given these magnitudes, where MNEs choose to locate their R&D is no small matter. There is

[16] For example, UNCTAD (2005) reported that "R&D is among the least internationalized segments of the (MNE's) value chain; production, marketing and other functions have moved abroad much more quickly" (p. 121).

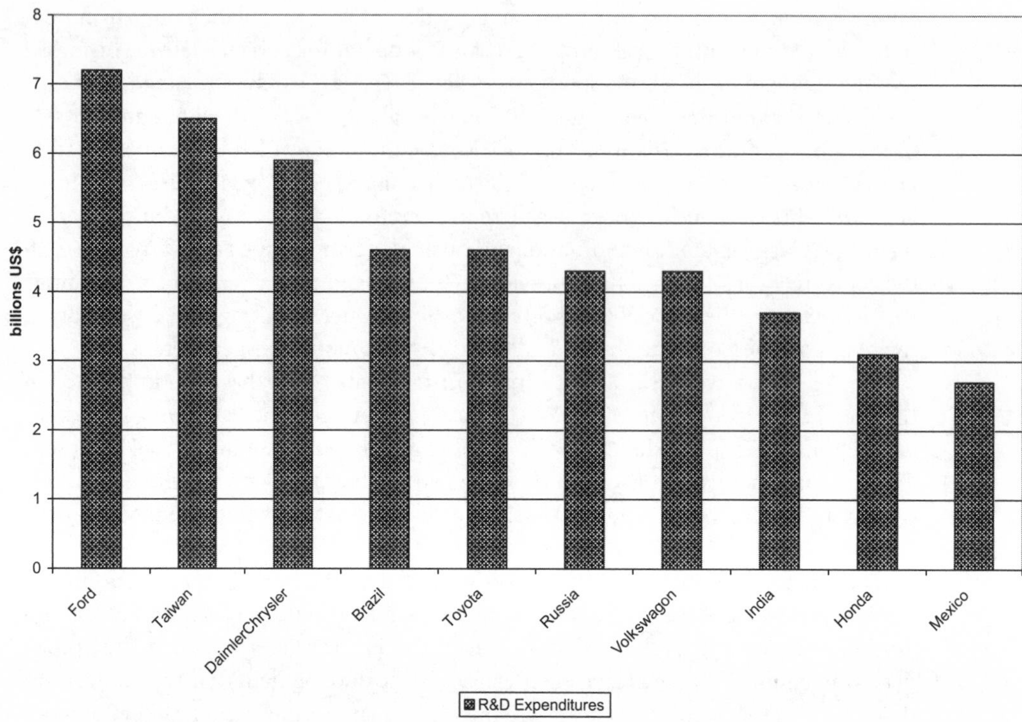

Figure 11.2. R&D Expenditures of Selected MNEs and Countries, 2002 (billions of US$). *Source:* UNCTAD (2005)

a historical element to the R&D issue. Throughout the era of Fordism and early in the era of Toyotism (see Chapter 9), the tendency to conduct R&D in the home base was strong. Hill (2009) described this era in the following terms:

> In those days, the role of foreign R&D amenities was straightforward: to adapt products and services to the needs of regional and individual markets. Basic R&D was performed in the home market to gain research scale economies, safeguard new product ideas, and facilitate communication with core functional areas such as marketing and manufacturing. (p. 424)

This historical pattern of R&D in MNE GPNs is now undergoing a change. Part of the reason is due to the information and communication (ICT) developments discussed in Chapter 1. A second reason was identified in the preceding box on the "end of corporate imperialism," namely the rise of emerging markets and the need to better tailor products to these markets. A third reason, however, might be the most fundamental of all. As we saw in Chapter 9, the list of largest MNEs in the world is dominated by firms from Western Europe, the United States, and Japan. But the talent and creativity for effective R&D is no longer confined to these three areas. To name just two countries, China and India have emerged as sources of scientific and engineering talent.[17] MNEs that want to tap into this talent can either recruit it by bringing it to their home bases and other R&D sites (a possibility we will discuss in Chapter 12) or begin to relocate their R&D. Many MNEs have chosen to relocate some aspects of their R&D.

[17] See, for example, Yusuf, Nabeshima, and Perkins (2006).

From an economic perspective, relocating R&D to these new sources of scientific and engineering talent can make a great deal of sense. As reported by Khurana (2006), "both China and India offer dramatic cost advantages of 30–60 percent, even after accounting for training and coordination costs" (p. 50). These realities have forced MNEs to rethink the role of R&D in their GPNs, choosing to locate specific kinds of R&D outside of the home base and developing *regional R&D facilities* that they link together in coordinated networks. If a trend can be identified, it is for basic research (the R in R&D) to remain in the home base, with more applied research (the D in R&D) moving abroad.[18]

Dicken (2007, chapter 5) noted that the R&D element most likely to be dispersed throughout MNEs GPNs is the *support laboratory*. The purpose of this R&D unit is to "adapt parent company technology to the local market and to provide technical backup" (p. 144). There is a tendency to locate these in association with production facilities. Less often, but increasingly, MNEs choose to set up the aforementioned regional R&D laboratories with more responsibilities than support laboratories, including a focus on new product development. Asia is a common location for these laboratories.[19] The potential role of intellectual property in these changes is discussed in the accompanying box.

TRIPS and International Production

In Chapter 7, we considered the World Trade Organization's Agreement on Trade-Related Intellectual Property Rights (TRIPS) and noted that this was a new and powerful area of operation for the WTO. In Chapter 9, we considered the three general modes of market entry (exporting, contractual, and FDI) and noted that the choice was influenced by dissemination risk and the role of firm-specific assets. One key type of firm-specific asset is intellectual property, so the question arises regarding whether increased intellectual property protection might have an impact on the mode of international production.

There are many ambiguities involved in this issue, but one thing is clear. To the extent that increased protection of intellectual property occurs under the TRIPS and recourse to WTO dispute settlement grows with dispute settlement cases in this area, dissemination risk should decrease. As dissemination risk decreases, we should see a switch from FDI to contractual modes of entry, particularly that of licensing. We can call this a *switching effect* of TRIPS on international production.

In addition to the switching effect, there might also be a *volume effect*. That is, increased intellectual property protection might increase the overall amount of international production through all modes: exporting, contractual, and FDI. In the case of exports, evidence suggests that stronger enforcement of intellectual property rights does lead to increased exporting overall. Two caveats to this result appear, however. The result is strongest for middle-income export destinations where the threat of dissemination risk is greater. Also, the result is less strong for high-technology exports, for which FDI and licensing appear to be preferred modes of foreign market entry.

[18] See, for example, chapter 7 of Caves (2007) and the many references therein.

[19] *The Economist* (2010) wrote that "the world's biggest multinationals are becoming increasingly happy to do their research and development in emerging markets. Companies in the *Fortune* 500 list have 98 R&D facilities in China and 63 in India. Some have more than one" (p. 4).

In the case of contracting, there also seems to be a volume effect that reinforces the switching effect. It is possible that this can have a positive impact on technology transfer in the case of technology licenses, but this particular possibility needs further investigation and case studies.

For volume effects in the case of FDI, the results are more mixed. Intellectual property protection does seem to matter for FDI flows to middle-income countries, but less so for low-income countries. As Fink and Maskus put it: "A poor country hoping to attract inward FDI would be better advised to improve its overall investment climate and business infrastructure than to strengthen its patent regime sharply, an action that would have little effect on its own" (2005, p. 7). Given the ongoing controversies regarding TRIPS, further research to investigate potential volume effects will always be welcome.

Sources: Fink and Maskus (2005) and Nicholson (2007)

CONCLUSION

The design and management of GPNs, and the role of MNEs within them, are a complex process. The process can be considered as having two aspects: intra-firm design and inter-firm relationships. There are no specific models of either intra-firm design or inter-firm relationships that can be identified as optimal. Rather, there are ranges of options available to MNEs and their suppliers that can vary from sector to sector and firm to firm. Heterarchy often serves as an important mode of operation in the face of multiple demands placed on MNEs, but it too involves management challenges.

The home base has been shown to play a particularly important role for MNEs and can be analyzed in terms of factor conditions, demand conditions, related and supporting industries, and firm strategy, structure, and rivalry. Both home-base and foreign spatial clusters can provide benefits to competitiveness. The paradox between the local emphasis of spatial clusters considered in this chapter and the global emphasis of the OLI framework considered previously is simply a part of the dynamics of the world economy. Both need to be reckoned with. So does the ongoing issue of how to best disperse various R&D functions within GPNs in light of new, growing markets and emerging talent outside of traditional MNE home bases.

REVIEW EXERCISES

1. Please provide specific examples of an *intra-firm design* issue and an *inter-firm relationship* issue, the latter in the context of an MNE and a supplier.
2. What is the difference between a *basic factor* of production and an *advanced factor* of production? What is the difference between a *generalized factor* of production and a *specialized factor* of production? Please give specific examples of these.
3. Please use an Internet search engine to identify a joint venture that is currently in operation. Can you gain some insight into the motivation for this JV?
4. In our discussion of the surgical instruments cluster in Pakistan, we raised the issue of child labor. In your view, is this a cultural issue to which an international manager must be sensitive, or is it a violation of global norms that the manager should confront head on?

FURTHER READING AND WEB RESOURCES

An important journal covering the subjects of this chapter is the *Journal of International Business Studies*. The books by Caves (2007) and Dicken (2007) are also important here, as in Chapters 9 and 10. Although slightly dated now, Bartlett and Ghoshal (2002) is still very much worth reading. So is the encyclopedic book by Dunning and Lundan (2008). One of Porter's more recent works on clusters is Porter (1998).

REFERENCES

Bartlett, C.A. and S. Ghoshal (2002) *Managing across Borders: The Transnational Solution*, Harvard Business School Press.

Battat, J., I. Frank, and X. Shen (1996) *Suppliers to Multinationals: Linkage Programs to Strengthen Local Companies in Developing Countries*, Foreign Investment Advisory Service Occasional Paper 6, The World Bank.

Brenton, P., R. Newfarmer, W. Shaw, and P. Walkenhorst (2009) "Breaking into New Markets: Overview," in R. Newfarmer, W. Shaw, and P. Walkenhorst (eds.), *Breaking into New Markets: Emerging Lessons for Export Diversification*, World Bank, 1–35.

Caves, R.E. (2007) *Multinational Enterprise and Economics Analysis*, Cambridge University Press.

Choi, C.-B. and P.W. Beamish (2004) "Split Management Control and International Joint Venture Performance," *Journal of International Business Studies*, 35:3, 201–215.

Desai, H.A., C.F. Foley, and J.R. Hines (2004) "The Costs of Shared Ownership: Evidence from International Joint Ventures," *Journal of Financial Economics*, 73:2, 323–374.

Dicken, P. (2007) *Global Shift: Mapping the Changing Contours of the World Economy*, Guilford.

Dunning, J.H. and S.M. Lundan (2008) *Multinational Enterprises and the Global Economy*, Edward Elgar.

The Economist (2010) "The World Turned Upside Down," April 17.

Fink, C. and K.E. Maskus (2005) "Why We Study Intellectual Property Rights and What We Have Learned," in C. Fink and K.E. Maskus (eds.), *Intellectual Property and Development: Lessons from Recent Economic Research*, World Bank and Oxford University Press, 1–15.

Gereffi, G., J. Humphrey, and T. Sturgeon (2005) "The Governance of Global Value Chains," *Review of International Political Economy*, 12:1, 78–104.

Hill, J.S. (2009) *International Business: Managing Globalization*, Sage.

Khurana, A. (2006) "Strategies for Global R&D," *Research Technology Management*, 49:2, 48–57.

Kogut, B. (1988) "Joint Ventures: Theoretical and Empirical Perspectives," *Strategic Management Journal*, 9:4, 319–332.

Kogut, B. and U. Zander (1992) "Knowledge of the Firm, Combinative Capabilities, and the Replication of Technology," *Organizational Science*, 3:3, 383–397.

Malmberg, A., Ö. Sölvell, and I. Zander (1996) "Spatial Clustering, Local Accumulation of Knowledge and Firm Competitiveness," *Geografiska Annaler*, 76B: 2, 85–97.

Nadvi, K. (1999) "Shifting Ties: Social Networks in the Surgical Instrument Cluster of Sialkot, Pakistan," *Development and Change*, 30:1, 141–175.

Navdi, K. and G. Halder (2005) "Local Clusters in Global Value Chains: Exploring Dynamic Linkages between Germany and Pakistan," *Entrepreneurship and Regional Development*, 17:5, 339–363.

Nicholson, M.W. (2007) "The Impact of Industry Characteristics and IPR Policy on Foreign Direct Investment," *Review of World Economics*, 143:1, 27–54.

Park, S.H. and G.R. Ungson (1997) "The Effect of National Culture, Organizational Complementarity, and Economic Motivation on Joint Venture Dissolution," *Academy of Management Journal*, 40:2, 279–307.

Porter, M.E. (1990) *The Competitive Advantage of Nations*, The Free Press.

Porter, M.E. (1998) "Clusters and the New Economics of Competition," *Harvard Business Review*, November-December, 77–90.

Prahalad, C.K. and K. Liberthal (2008) *The End of Corporate Imperialism*, Harvard Business Press.

Raff, H. (2009) "Joint Ventures," in K.A. Reinert, R.S. Rajan, A.J. Glass, and L.S. Davis (eds.), *The Princeton Encyclopedia of the World Economy*, Princeton University Press, 714–717.

Ruigrok, W. and R. van Tulder (1995) *The Logic of International Restructuring*, Routledge.

Scott, A.J. (1995) "The Geographical Foundations of Industrial Performance," *Competition and Change*, 1:1, 51–66.

Sölvell, Ö. and I. Zander (1995) "Organization of the Dynamic Multinational Enterprise," *International Studies of Management and Organization*, 25:1–2, 17–38.

United Nations Conference on Trade and Development (2005) *World Investment Report: Transnational Corporations and the Internationalization of R&D.*

Young, D., M. Goold, G. Blanc, R. Bühner, D. Collis, J. Eppink, T. Kagono, and C. Jiménez Seminario (2000) *Corporate Headquarters: An International Analysis of their Roles and Staffing*, Pearson.

Yusuf, S., K. Nabeshima, and D.H. Perkins (2006) "China and India Reshape Industrial Geography," in S. Yusuf and L.A. Winters (eds.), *Dancing with the Giants: China, India and the Global Economy*, World Bank, 35–66.

12 Migration

As described in Chapters 9, 10, and 11, international production occurs when firms either form contractual relationships across national borders or when they engage in foreign direct investment (FDI), stretching the firm's own boundary across national borders in the latter case. But there is a third means by which international production can take place, namely the *movement of people* across national borders in the form of temporary or permanent **migration**. At the time of this writing, this mode of international production involves approximately 200 million migrants, or 3 percent of the world's population. As such, migration is an important component of the world economy.

As we discussed in Chapter 1, the world economy has experienced significant liberalization of trade, FDI, and financial flows. These are the processes that have characterized economic globalization. Not so with labor, however. As barriers to the movements of goods, services, direct investment, and finance transactions have fallen over time, barriers to the movement of people have largely remained in place or even increased. This has caused some international economists (e.g., Pritchett, 2006) to refer to "everything but labor" globalization. That said, some specific types of labor flows have increased over time, and it is very much worthwhile to examine these in some detail.

We begin our consideration of migration by examining types of migration. We then consider the migration decision in its economic aspects. We take up high-skilled and low-skilled migration and then turn to the issues of remittances and migration policy. Finally, in an appendix, we consider the relationship between comparative advantage and migration.

Analytical elements for this chapter:
Countries, firms, and *factors of production.*

TYPES OF MIGRATION

There are many types of international migration with different degrees of relevance to the issue of international production. To take one possible categorization, Beath, Goldin, and Reinert (2009) distinguished among nine different types of international migration. We briefly consider each of them here:

- *Permanent high-skilled migration* involves permanent residence and is sometimes granted in countries such as Australia, New Zealand, Canada, the United States, and the European Union. It is granted to high-skilled migrants often at the urging of hiring corporations such as the multinational enterprises (MNEs) we discussed in Chapters 9 through 11. Leading source countries include China and India.
- *Temporary high-skilled migration* is similar in motivation to permanent high-skilled migration but can be more politically palatable in some cases where there is political resistance to granting permanent residence.
- *Temporary low-skilled migration* is more important in volume than temporary high-skilled migration. Temporary low-skilled migration includes migrant workers in the areas of manual labor, construction, domestic service, and nursing.
- *Family migration* allows permanent residence to the families of those who have already gained this residence. Beath, Goldin, and Reinert (2009) note that

"family migration is among the largest channels of migration and represents a disproportionate share of flows from low- and middle-income countries to high-income countries" (p. 766).

- *Coethnic and national priority migration* exists in some countries and involves granting permanent residence based on ethnic background, religious affiliation, and national origin. The most famous and controversial is Israel's "Law of Return."
- *Asylum seekers* are granted certain rights by the 1951 Geneva Convention addressing persons with well-founded fears of persecution.
- *Refugees* are those who flee to neighboring countries to escape war, famine, or environmental catastrophes. They become the responsibility of the United Nations High Commissioner for Refugees. The International Organization for Migration (IOM) estimates that there are about 16 million refugees.
- *Undocumented migration* involves both voluntary and nonvoluntary (trafficked) illegal migrants. In some regions (e.g., North America and part of Africa), these flows can be quite significant. The IOM estimates that there are about 25 million undocumented migrants.
- *Visa-free migration* relates to our discussion of common markets in Chapter 8 that involve the free movement of both labor and capital. The European Union is a prime example of visa-free migration, but this arrangement also exists between Australia and New Zealand, for example.

All of these nine types of migration are important from political, human rights, and public policy perspectives, but not all of them are relevant to international production. In this chapter, we focus on high-skilled and low-skilled migration. Before we take on these specific types of migration, however, we need to consider the migration decision itself.

THE MIGRATION DECISION

Just as we need to know what considerations are involved for firms in the foreign market entry decision (Chapter 9), so we need to know what motivates migrants in their decision making. We will focus on the economic decision making of potential migrants, understanding that in some cases, such as refugees considered in the preceding section, noneconomic issues might be more potent. In focusing on the economic decision making of migration, we will identify a set of factors that influence the decision-making process. To set the stage, consider the following summary from de Haas (2007):

> In reality, migration is a selective process. The poorest tend to migrate less than those who are slightly better off. This seems particularly true for relatively costly and risky international migration. . . . Labor migrants generally do not flee from misery but move deliberately in the expectation of finding a better or more stable livelihood, and of improving their social and economic status. Moreover, in order to migrate, people need the human, financial and social resources as well as the aspiration to do so. (p. 832)

Let's see how we might capture these considerations analytically by identifying *five factors* that influence migration decisions of potential migrants from Morocco (M) to the European Union (EU). These factors are relative wages, youth population growth, financial resources, education levels, and migrant networks. We consider each of these

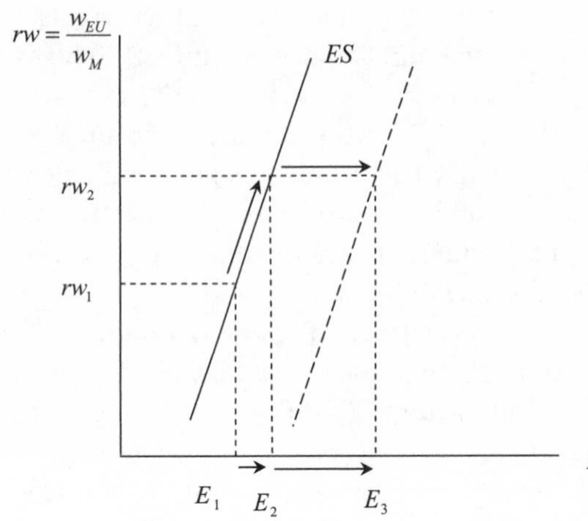

Figure 12.1. The Migration Decision

factors in turn using Figure 12.1. The first factor (relative wages) and the following four factors (youth population growth, financial resources, education levels, and migrant networks) affect Figure 12.1 differently. Relative wages will be a "movement along" factor, whereas the other four will be "shift" factors.[1]

Relative wages. One central variable that influences migration is relative wages (rw), particularly relative unskilled wages, and we measure the wage in the EU to that in Morocco as $rw = \frac{w_{EU}}{w_M}$. The larger is this relative wage measure, the greater the number of Moroccans who would like to emigrate to the European Union. As rw increases or decreases, there is a movement along (up or down) an "emigration supply" (*ES*) curve in Figure 12.1. For example, an increase of the relative wage from rw_1 to rw_2 will increase the desired emigration from E_1 to E_2.

Despite the importance of the relative wage as a factor in the migration decision, other factors can be even more important. Indeed, Hatton and Williamson (2009) emphasized that wage gaps among countries "will not by themselves explain emigration" (p. 17). The other four factors in our list each have the effect of *shifting* the *ES* curve in Figure 12.1.

Youth population growth. Population growth in Morocco will increase the number of individuals who are considering emigrating from Morocco to the EU. Particularly important here is growth of the *youth* population. The young are more prone to be risk-takers, and because the net benefits of migration can take a long time to accrue to the individual migrant, the young are more likely to have the years ahead of them for net benefits to become positive. The age structure of populations can therefore influence the migration decision. An increase in the youth population will have the effect of shifting the *ES* curve in Figure 12.1 to the right.

Financial resources. The cost of emigration can be substantial and include not just the direct costs of (legally or illegally) traveling from one country to another, but also the opportunity costs of leaving the home country with its family and friends and the risks involved in settling in a new country. A consequence of these costs is that, despite the desire to migrate, many poor people cannot finance migration. Reflecting this, there is a tendency for the effective *ES* curve of Figure 12.1 to move to the right as per-capita

[1] This will be similar to "movement along" and "shift" factors affecting the demand and supply curves of Chapter 2.

income or gross domestic product (GDP) rises from low- to middle-income levels and improves the ability of potential migrants to finance the move. This is why de Haas (2007) stated earlier that "The poorest tend to migrate less than those who are slightly better off" (p. 832).

Education levels. An increase in education levels in Morocco will have the effect of increasing the aspirations of Moroccans and making them more aware of economic and social possibilities abroad. Increased education also allows Moroccans to better absorb and process information flows from the EU in order to assess opportunities there. Increased education levels have the effect of shifting the *ES* curve in Figure 12.1 to the right.

Migrant networks. Beath, Goldin, and Reinert (2009) noted that "the willingness of people to migrate will increase with the quantity and quality of information that is available" (p. 170). The information in question is that related to the destination country. The potential migrant in Morocco needs to know something about the economic and social environment in the EU. In many cases, this information is provided by preceding migrants. Migrant networks are conduits of information back to potential migrants in origin countries. As migrant networks develop, quality information flows increase and the *ES* curve of Figure 12.1 again shifts to the right.

Historical evidence suggests that shifts of the *ES* curve in Figure 12.1 can be more significant than movements along the curve.[2] What is more, the four shift factors can work together as origin countries develop. Suppose we turn the clock back a bit to a time when per-capita GDP in Morocco was much lower than it is today. As GDP per capita increases from this initial low level, infant mortality decreases, whereas education levels and youth population increase. The increase in GDP per capita, youth population, and education levels shifts the *ES* curve to the right. As the first Moroccan migrants succeed in establishing lives in the EU, quality information flows increase and the *ES* curve shifts even farther to the right.

The approximate correlation of all these four shift factors in time can lead to a phenomenon known as the *migration hump.*[3] A highly stylized migration hump is presented in Figure 12.2. This figure shows that, as GDP per capita increases from low to medium levels, emigration increases. As GDP per capita increases further from medium to high levels, economic opportunities expand in Morocco relative to the EU, youth population begins to shrink in Morocco, and emigration decreases.[4] It is for these reasons that some observers (e.g., de Hass, 2007) see the migration hump as simply a part of the socioeconomic development process in source countries.

What is the significance of the migration hump for understanding global migration patterns? First, it alerts us to the fact that, barring political or ecological impetus, relatively little international migration occurs from low-income countries. Rather, most of it is from middle-income countries. Second, the migration flows that occur near the peak of the migration hump can persist for some time (perhaps a decade or two) as source countries move through the middle-income range of GDP per capita. Third, as pointed out by de Haas (2007), economic development from relatively low levels of GDP per capita will *increase* rather than decrease outward migration flows in distinct

[2] See Hatton and Williamson (2009).

[3] See, for example, Zelinsky (1971), Martin and Taylor (1996), Olesen (2002), and Goldin and Reinert (2007).

[4] The sharp-eyed reader will begin to see a link here to the idea of a *demographic transition* in development and population studies.

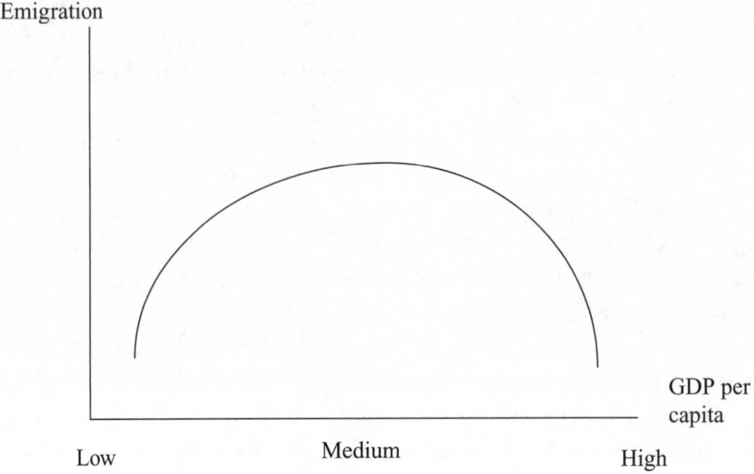

Figure 12.2. A Highly Stylized "Migration Hump"

contrast to some claims. Globalization in some forms might support development of low-income countries, but this development will spur outward migration.

HIGH-SKILLED MIGRATION

In Chapter 11, we discussed the recent phenomenon of MNEs beginning to locate some types of research and development (R&D) facilities in countries with emerging science and engineering talent. However, it is also possible for this science and engineering talent to itself move. And so it does in the form of **high-skilled migration** (HSM), both temporary and permanent. Hart (2006) and others provided warnings that data on HSM are both scarce and unreliable, but nevertheless some patterns are discernible. For example, HSM has been on an upward trend for some time now. The increase in demand for HSM appears to be related to skills-based technological change in high-income destination countries that is related to the information and communication technology (ICT) advances we discussed in Chapter 1. There is increasing evidence that the demand for HSM will not abate.[5] For example, the *Financial Times* (2010) reported that, even for the U.S. manufacturing sector that shed more than 2 million jobs between 2008 and 2010, skilled shortages are acute.

Evidence presented in Bauer and Kunze (2004), although incomplete, suggests that the types of firms that hire HSM tend to be larger firms that are more internationalized via foreign ownership and exports. However, firms active in HSM face volatile policy regimes. For example, for the case of the U.S. H1-B visa that supports HSM into the United States, the baseline quota is only 65,000. This jumped up to 115,000 in 1999 and 2000, and then to 195,000 in 2001, 2002, and 2003. Then it was abruptly decreased back to 65,000 in 2004. This is not the sort of environment conducive to long-range human resource planning on the part of high-technology firms in the United States.[6]

As emphasized by Goldin and Reinert (2007), "today's skilled migrants are not typical of the communities they leave behind, as they often have been trained at substantial cost

[5] Bauer and Kunze (2004) noted that the rising relative wage for high-skilled workers indicates that, despite the rise of HSM, there is an increasing demand for these kinds of workers.

[6] See *The Economist* (2010b).

to the taxpayers of source countries with the expectation that they would serve their communities" (p. 172). That they have not done so to the extent expected is related to the phenomenon of **brain drain**. Brain drain refers to the loss of human capital in low-income source countries due to the migration of citizens to foreign destination countries.[7] For example, El-Khawas (2004) pointed out that there are more Ethiopian doctors in Europe and North America than in Ethiopia. This example is significant because brain drains in the health sector can be particularly severe. Particularly in low-income countries with HIV/AIDS and other health crises, the loss of trained doctors and nurses can be traumatic.[8]

Recently, return migration back to home countries has begun, and these new flows have at times transferred technology and entrepreneurial skills back to the origin countries. For example, Saxenian (2002) emphasized the role of Chinese and Indian return migrants in developing high-technology clusters in Taiwan, China, and India. She regards these "transnational communities" as players in their own right in the world economy, global actors along with MNEs and national governments.[9] Return migration flows have potential consequences for brain drain. There is a hope that the phenomenon of brain drain can evolve into "brain circulation" in which expatriates from developing countries return either temporarily or permanently to contribute to what might be called "intellectual remittances." For example, Saxenian (2005) described some of these return migrants as follows:

> When foreign-educated venture capitalists invest in their home countries, they transfer first-hand knowledge of the financial institutions of the new economy to peripheral regions. These individuals, often among the earliest returnees, also typically serve as advisers to domestic policymakers who are anxious to promote technology growth. As experienced engineers and managers return home, either temporarily or permanently, they bring worldviews and identities that grow out of their shared professional and educational experiences. These cross-regional technical communities have the potential to jump-start local entrepreneurship. (p. 36)

As shown by Docquier and Lodigiani (2010), these return migrants can even have a subsequent, positive effect on inflows of FDI. The return migration and subsequent enterprise development act as a signal to foreign MNEs that conditions are ripe for FDI by enhancing the location advantages we discussed in Chapter 10. To the extent that these reverse HSM flows can assist in the development of home countries, they are to be welcomed and encouraged.

LOW-SKILLED MIGRATION

Although HSM might be the more interesting subject from a technological perspective, it actually encompasses a minority of global migrants. More migrants fall into the category of **low-skilled migration** (LSM). LSM is also often subject to the most political controversy, involving individuals who might seem more unlike the original or current

[7] As stated by OECD (2005), "emigration of highly skilled workers may adversely affect small countries by preventing them reaching a critical mass of human resources, which would be necessary to foster long-term economic development."

[8] Approaches to deal with the difficult issue of brain drain of health professionals were discussed in Martineau, Decker, and Bundred (2004).

[9] Saxenian (2002) also explored the role of these "technical communities" in the development of global production networks or GPNs discussed in Chapters 10 and 11.

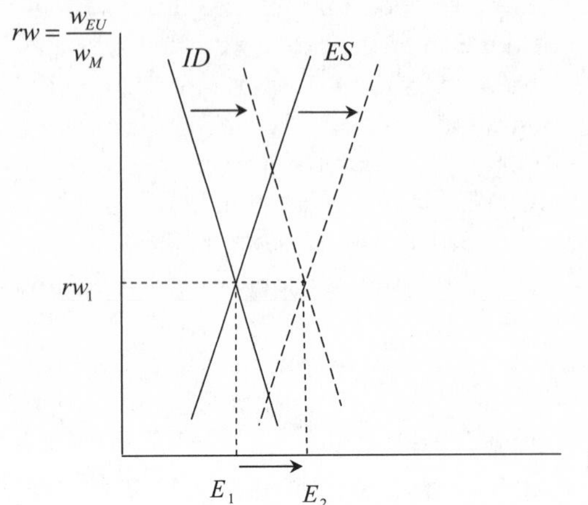

Figure 12.3. The Market for Low-Skilled Migration

populations of host countries. Nevertheless, there are fundamental economic forces at play in LSM, forces that show no signs of abating. The supply side of LSM can be roughly described using our previous discussion of Figure 12.1. But there are also interesting characteristics of the demand side in destination countries. The first of these relates to demographic trends in some destination countries, notably those in the EU, but also Japan. Italy, Germany, France, the United Kingdom, and Japan are all experiencing or are about to experience absolute declines in their populations as fertility rates fall below "replacement" levels. This is sometimes referred to as the "birth dearth."[10] The evolving birth dearth can cause an increase in demand for migrants.

A second fundamental demand-side characteristic involves what Pritchett (2006) referred to as "productivity-resistant, low-skill, hard-core non-tradable services." It has long been recognized that some types of services are resistant to productivity growth. This has been associated with the work of William Baumol and is known as the "Baumol effect" or "cost disease."[11] In a case often mentioned, it is difficult to increase the productivity of haircuts, for example. This is also true of other low-skilled services, and these are often nontradable services. The persistence of these kinds of services in the structures of modern economies, as well as their nontradable nature, ensures that there will always be increasing demand for migrants to perform them. As Pritchett noted, "although the future belongs to greater and greater levels of technology, information revolution, and capital-labor substitution, the future of employment belongs to haircuts" (p. 35).

These two demand-side characteristics, combined with supply-side changes discussed previously, ensure that LSM is an important component of the modern world economy. LSM has been a part of the European Union countries and the United States for decades now, but recent demand for LSM has emerged in the Middle East and East Asia. LSM has therefore become a key feature of many important parts of the world economy. We can get a graphical sense of these changes using Figure 12.3. This figure combines the emigration supply (*ES*) graph of Figure 12.1 with an immigration demand (*ID*) graph. For reasons we have discussed here, both of these graphs shift to

[10] One important exception to this is the United States, also a key LSM destination country. On the birth dearth in Japan, see *The Economist* (2010c). On Germany, see Dempsey (2011).

[11] This goes back to Baumol (1967).

the right. As they do, low-skilled emigration from Morocco to the EU increases. As this graph is drawn, the relative unskilled wage remains the same, but it could either increase or decrease.

LSM is much more likely than HSM to also fall into the categories of *refugees* and *undocumented migration* mentioned at the beginning of this chapter. For example, *The Economist* (2010a) reported that there are up to 3 million low-skilled migrants in Thailand and that many of these are undocumented workers who are refugees from Myanmar. The illegal nature of much LSM makes it politically volatile but also economically attractive to firms hiring them since the workers have no bargaining power. Illegality also makes the migrants open to exploitation and abuse. For example, as stated by Goldin and Reinert (2007), "In source countries, recruitment agencies and brokers may demand large sums up front from prospective migrants.... Some migrants evidently consider this to be a price worth paying, although few are offered any reciprocal guarantees that the conditions of employment will be as promised" (pp. 162–163). In many cases, they are not. As documented in the accompanying box, tragedy can also ensue.

Migration Gone Wrong: The Morecambe Bay Cockle Tragedy

In February 2004, Chinese migrants were working in Morecambe Bay of the United Kingdom, collecting cockles. The workers were illegal, unskilled migrants, most from the Fujian province of China. Many of them had migrated with the financial help of family and village members with the hopes that they would send remittances back home. Most of the workers paid criminal "snakehead" gangs in order to migrate to the United Kingdom. Consequently, their work in the United Kingdom was overseen by a "gang-master."

The Morecambe Bay is notorious for its swift tides and quicksands. The Chinese migrants were tragically cut off from the shore by a rising tide. They tried to place a distress call with the words "sinking water," but due to the language barrier, this was not successful. Twenty-three of the cockle gatherers drowned. Realizing the danger he was in, one migrant, Guo Bin Long, was able to use his mobile phone to call his wife in China. He said to her, "I am in great danger. I am up to my chest in water. Maybe I am going to die." He did.

Here we have a small piece of globalization, a migrant financed by his village to the extent that he was equipped with a mobile phone, utilizing advanced ICT to communicate with his wife in China. At that level, globalization was operating with sophistication. However, Guo Bin Long was operating under the cover of illegality and a gang-master who eventually went to jail for the incident. At that level, globalization was acting in tragic form. As a survivor reported, "We worked in conditions of hell, we had rotten food, rotten accommodation and worked in very cold conditions and dark, risking our lives trying to make a living in this country."

This tragedy of migration became immortalized in a 2006 British film "Ghosts." The UK Guardian newspaper described the film as a "harsh, in-your-face movie that should have audiences worrying that something must be done about the issue it raises." Advocates for low-skilled and illegal migrants worldwide would agree.

Sources: British Broadcasting Corporation (BBC) and UK *Guardian*

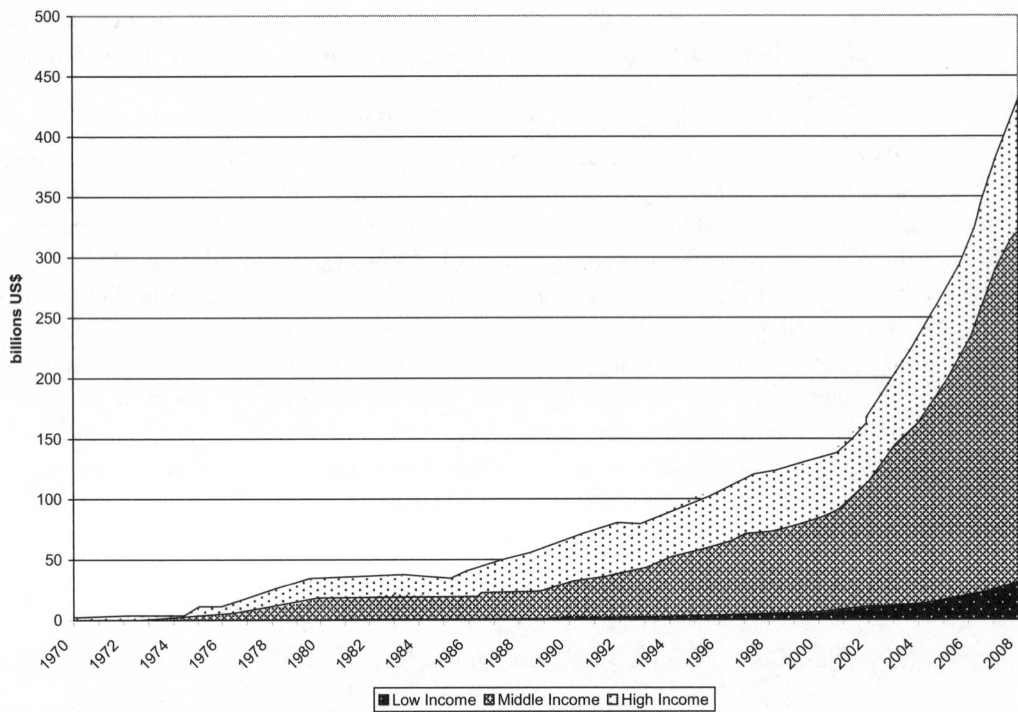

Figure 12.4. Remittances, 1970 to 2008. *Source:* World Bank, World Development Indicators

REMITTANCES

When migrants begin working in foreign countries, they don't abandon all ties to their home country. Particularly in an era of calling cards and electronic money transfers, maintaining ties with family and friends in one's home country is easier now that in past decades. One part of maintaining ties with the home country involves migrants sending money back to family members in the form of what are known as **remittances.** These flows have become increasingly important in the world economy.

Data on remittance flows going back to 1970 are presented in Figure 12.4. As is clear from these data, remittance flows have increased dramatically since the mid-1990s. What is also clear is that most of the increase in remittances has been to middle-income countries.[12] In some countries and regions, remittance inflows now exceed FDI inflows. Remittances to the developing (low- and middle-income) world in 2008 were $328 billion dollars. This was more than double the amount of official development assistance (ODA) in that year. As emphasized by *The Economist* (2009), these flows can have significant and positive impacts in developing countries by directly transferring income more efficiently than foreign aid.[13]

The positive role that remittances (and therefore international production via migration) can play in source countries seems to be related to something we considered at the beginning of this chapter, namely migrant networks. For example, Woodruff and

[12] This parallels the increase in FDI flows to middle-income countries we discussed in Chapter 1. See Figure 1.2 of that chapter.

[13] Pozo (2009) noted that "Previously, little effort was expended to measure and analyze (remittance) flows because they were thought to be small in magnitude and of little significance for most countries. Evidence to the contrary has motivated policymakers and others to pay closer attention to the measurement, determinants, and impact of remittances" (pp. 963–964).

Zenteno (2007) provided evidence that migrant networks between the United States and Mexico have helped channel remittance flows to microenterprise development in Mexico. Similar efforts have taken place in El Salvador. There is also evidence that remittances can act as a risk-management strategy for poor households in developing countries through income source diversification and can contribute to human capital investments in some cases, offsetting to some extent brain drain effects.[14] Further, Dadush and Falcau (2009) noted that "the availability of foreign exchange through remittances increases the food security of drought-prone countries and enables countries to import medicines and other technologies" (p. 2).

Remittance flows are then a potentially positive result of international production based on migration. They are not international production *per se*, but harnessing them for development outcomes shows a great deal of promise. This is one area where the windows of international production and international development can interact with largely happy outcomes.

MIGRATION POLICY

Unlike in the realms of international trade (the World Trade Organization), international finance (the International Monetary Fund), and international development (the World Bank), there is no multilateral organization for migration policy. In most cases, the policy locus of international migration policy is the nation-state based on the principle of *sovereignty*. In contrast to the "pro-market" orientations of policy regimes in trade, finance, and development policy, intervention and coercion are the order of the day in migration policy.[15] There are international governance mechanisms applying to refugees in the form of a 1951 Geneva Convention and a few International Labor Organization (ILO) conventions. There is also the International Organization for Migration (IOM) that provides for intergovernmental coordination in some areas related to migration policy. But by and large, it is sovereignty that rules in migration policy.

Beginning in 2001, the Berne Initiative involved extensive consultations on the possibility of developing nonbinding guidelines for best practices in migration policy. The Berne Initiative was followed by the Global Commission on International Migration (GCIM), established in 2003 by the United Nations Secretary-General. In 2005, the GCIM suggested that greater multilateral coordination of migration policies would be a good idea. The GCIM was followed by the United Nations High-Level Dialogue (HLD) on International Migration and Development in 2006. As assessed by Martin, Martin, and Cross (2007), the HLD was an important event for furthering multilateral communication on migration issues, but it did not translate into specific action items for increased global governance of migration. Some observers (e.g., Bhagwati, 2003 and Goldin and Reinert, 2007) have suggested that such a multilateral organization would be a good idea. One area for movement in trade-related migration policy is Mode 4 of the WTO's General Agreement on Trade in Services (GATS) discussed in the accompanying box.

[14] See Maimbo and Ratha (2005).

[15] Pritchett (2006) was very frank here: "People with guns apply force to prevent people from crossing borders. People with guns force people to leave if discovered in a country without permission. The fact that this coercive force is (usually) exercised with domestic political legitimacy, restraint, or even prudence in rich countries should not mask the fact that it is coercion" (p. 63). For the way these policies have been strengthened in recent years, see *The Economist* (2008).

GATS Mode 4: The Temporary Movement of Natural Persons

Recall from Chapter 7 that the WTO's General Agreement on Trade in Services (GATS) defined trade in services in four ways: cross-border trade (Mode 1); movement of consumers (Mode 2); foreign direct investment (FDI) (Mode 3); and movement of natural persons (Mode 4). The movement of natural persons involves a temporary, noncommercial presence by individuals to supply any sort of service in another country. Although there exists a protocol under the GATS for Mode 4 service delivery, this is largely to address the transfer of personnel within MNEs to support FDI. In other words, it is designed to benefit developed rather than developing countries and high-skilled migrants rather than low-skilled migrants.

There have been calls to establish a multilateral system to identify individuals seeking temporary Mode-4 migration, providing national security clearance to them, and granting *multi-entry* GATS visas to them. This would be a step toward harnessing temporary migration for development and would require a new GATS protocol dedicated to the issue. As Winters et al. (2003) demonstrated, the gains for developing countries from an increase of only 3 percent in their temporary labor quotas would exceed the value of total aid flows and be similar to the expected benefits from the Doha Round of trade negotiations, with most of the benefits to developing countries coming from increased access of unskilled workers to jobs in developed countries.

Given these development benefits, it is interesting that Mode-4 migration has not been an active part of the Doha Round in the form of the Doha Development Agenda. This appears to be another example of an "everything but labor" approach to economic liberalization.

Sources: Bhatnager (2009), Goldin and Reinert (2007), and Winters et al. (2003)

Not everyone is convinced that multilateral approaches to migration policy are the best. For example, Pritchett (2006) explicitly stated that, given political realities, migration policy advances can best be achieved *bilaterally*. He stated: "In the end, domestic politics will dictate that each country have control over who may or may not enter its borders, and that this will not be part of any general international or multilateral binding commitment.... Pushing for multilateral agreements along the lines of the WTO is unlikely to be successful" (p. 121).

This might well be true, but does not rule out the pursuit of limited, basic principles at the multilateral level. For example, the IOM oversees an International Dialogue on Migration that it describes as "an opportunity for governments, inter-governmental and non-governmental organizations and other stakeholders to discuss migration policy issues, in order to explore and study policy issues of common interest and cooperate in addressing them." This policy can move forward at both the bilateral and multilateral levels.

CONCLUSION

Migration is an important component of globalization in general and international production in particular. However, it is one aspect of globalization that has experienced less liberalization than others. Migration comes in a relatively large number of varieties with important political, human rights, and public policy considerations. Economic migration considered here includes both low-skilled and high-skilled varieties and has significant influences on global patterns of international production. It also has development implications, positive in the case of remittances and negative in the case of brain drain. Migration policy is an evolving, complex, and crucial area of global public policy that will be near the top of global policy agendas for the foreseeable future.

REVIEW EXERCISES

1. Do you know any migrants? To what extent and how does their experience fit into the discussion of this chapter? To what extent and how does it differ?
2. Can you identify reasons why the liberalization of the trade, FDI, and finance components of economic globalization has proceeded much faster than for labor migration?
3. We discussed the political economy of trade policy in Chapter 5. Can you identify any insights from that chapter that could be used in thinking about the political economy of migration policy?
4. Can you identify any benefits for relaxing sovereignty in favor of multilateral policy coordination of migration?

FURTHER READING AND WEB RESOURCES

An excellent and concise overview of migration issues can be found in de Hass (2007). For a more thorough review, see Goldin, Cameron, and Balarajan (2011). See Pritchett (2006), Ozden and Schiff (2006), and Goldin and Reinert (2007) for a consideration of migration issues from a development perspective. A review of remittances can be found in Maimbo and Ratha (2005). For a concise review of migration policy, see Martin (2009) and Dadush and Falcau (2009). For a striking story about Mexican migrants in the United States, see *The Economist* (2010d).

A multilateral organization dedicated to migration issues is the International Organization for Migration (www.iom.int). See also the International Migration Institute at Oxford (www.imi.ox.ac.uk) and the Institute for the Study of International Migration (http://isim.georgetown.edu). The IOM and the ISIM jointly publish the *International Migration Journal.*

APPENDIX: MIGRATION AND COMPARATIVE ADVANTAGE

In Chapter 3, we considered comparative advantage and its implications for inter-industry trade in rice and motorcycles between Vietnam and Japan. Recall that, given biases in production possibilities frontiers (PPFs), Vietnam had a comparative advantage in and exported rice, whereas Japan had a comparative advantage in and exported motorcycles. In Chapter 5, we also introduced the Heckscher-Ohlin model, explaining patterns of comparative advantage in terms of the resource or factor endowments of countries and the factor intensities of sectors. In Chapter 5 we saw that Japan's comparative advantage in motorcycles (and the bias of its PPF) was due to its relatively large endowment of physical capital and the physical capital intensity of motorcycle production. Similarly, Vietnam's comparative advantage in rice (and the bias of its PPF) was due to its relatively large endowment of labor and the relative labor intensity of rice

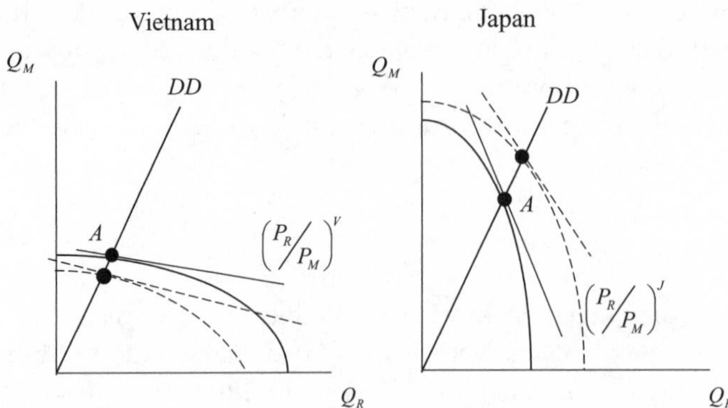

Figure 12.5. Migration and Comparative Advantage between Vietnam and Japan

production. Finally, in an appendix to Chapter 9, we examined the influence of FDI on patterns of comparative advantage.

Migration was absent in Chapters 3, 5, and 9, so the question arises: what difference would migration make to the comparative advantage story of those chapters? Figure 12.5 (a close copy of Figure 3.3) helps us answer this question. Recall that we evaluate comparative advantage by examining the relative price of rice to motorcycles or $(\frac{P_R}{P_M})$ in Vietnam and Japan. As we saw in Chapter 3, this price ratio was lower in Vietnam under autarky, indicating that Vietnam had a comparative advantage in rice and that Japan had a comparative advantage in motorcycles.

Now suppose that we allow for a migration flow from Vietnam to Japan.[16] This migration flow changes the relative factor endowments of the two countries. Japan becomes more labor abundant (less capital abundant), and Vietnam becomes less labor abundant (more capital abundant). These two changes have impacts on the PPFs of the two countries in a manner affecting the labor-intensive sector, rice, most strongly. In Vietnam, with the outflow of labor, the PPF shifts *in* to the dashed concave curve, whereas in Japan the PPF shifts *out* to the dashed curve. The new autarky points along the demand diagonals (DD) are such that the autarky price ratios change to the dashed lines. In Vietnam, $(\frac{P_R}{P_M})^V$ increases, whereas in Japan, $(\frac{P_R}{P_M})^J$ decreases. You can see this by examining the relative slopes of the solid and dashed price lines.

What is the implication of these changes in the autarky price ratios? It means that the gap between the two autarky price ratios is narrowing or that the pattern of comparative advantage is weakening. As we have examined the process here, it indicates that migration (as well as FDI considered in the appendix to Chapter 9) can function as a *substitute* for trade.[17] However, recall from Chapter 5 that the assumption of the Heckscher-Ohlin model is that production technology is the same in each country of the world. This is not always the case, and where technologies differ, sometimes migration can be a *complement* to trade. That is, with differing technologies, some types of migration can strengthen patterns of comparative advantage.[18]

[16] Pritchett (2006) estimated the relative wage between Japan and Vietnam to be approximately nine and notes that this is higher than relative wages prevalent during the "Great Migration" of the late nineteenth and early twentieth centuries. In fact, however, Japan has well-developed mechanisms to ensure that this would never occur in any meaningful way despite its significant "birth dearth" problems.

[17] This famous result was first pointed out by Mundell (1957).

[18] This modified result is due to Purvis (1972).

Next, we can consider some linkages from the political economy of trade to migration. Recall from Chapter 5 our discussion of the **Heckscher-Ohlin model** and its **Stolper-Samuelson theorem**. As Japan and Vietnam engage in trade, labor in Vietnam (the labor-abundant country) experiences real income gains. This can help provide the resources for labor to migrate to Japan.[19] In Chapter 5, we also considered North-South trade, and in that case, labor in the South (the labor-abundant region) experiences real income gains. This can help to provide the resources for labor to migrate from North to South. In the long run, these migration flows lessen the pattern of comparative advantage among trading countries or regions.

REFERENCES

Beath, A.L., I. Goldin, and K.A. Reinert (2009) "International Migration," in K.A. Reinert, R.S. Rajan, A.J. Glass, and L.S. Davis (eds.), *The Princeton Encyclopedia of the World Economy*, Princeton University Press, 764–770.

Bauer, T.K. and A. Kunze (2004) "The Demand for High-Skilled Workers and Immigration Policy," *Brussels Economic Review*, 47:1, 1–19.

Baumol, W.J. (1967) "Macroeconomics of Unbalanced Growth: The Anatomy of Urban Crisis," *American Economic Review*, 42:3, 415–426.

Bhagwati, J. (2003) "The World Needs a New Body to Monitor Migration," *Financial Times*, October 24.

Bhatnagar, P. (2009) "Temporary Movement of Natural Persons," in K.A. Reinert, R.S. Rajan, A.J. Glass, and L.S. Davis (eds.), *The Princeton Encyclopedia of the World Economy*, Princeton University Press, 1081–1084.

Dadush, U. and L. Falcau (2009) "Migrants and the Global Financial Crisis," *Carnegie Endowment for International Peace, Policy Brief* 83.

de Haas, H. (2007) "Turning the Tide? Why Development Will Not Stop Migration," *Development and Change*, 38:5, 819–841.

Dempsey, J. (2011) "As Germany Booms, It Faces a Shortage of Workers," *New York Times*, February 4.

Docquier, F. and E. Lodigiani (2010) "Skilled Migration and Business Networks," *Open Economies Review*, 21:4, 565–588.

The Economist (2008) "Migration: A Turning Tide?" June 28.

The Economist (2009) "Migration and Development: The Aid Workers Who Really Help," October 10.

The Economist (2010a) "Inhospitality: Migrant Workers in Thailand," February 27.

The Economist (2010b) "Skilled Immigration: Green Card Blues," October 20.

The Economist (2010c) "Into the Unknown: A Special Report on Japan," November 20.

The Economist (2010d) "Fields of Tears," December 18.

El-Khawas, M.A. (2004) "Brain Drain: Putting Africa between a Rock and a Hard Place," *Mediterranean Quarterly*, 15:4, 37–56.

Financial Times (2010) "U.S. Manufacturers Face Skills Shortages," February 28.

Goldin, I., G. Cameron, and M. Balarajan (2011) *Exceptional People: How Migration Shaped our World and Will Define our Future*, Princeton University Press.

Goldin, I. and K.A. Reinert (2007) *Globalization for Development: Trade, Finance, Aid, Migration and Policy*, World Bank.

[19] See, for example, Schiff (1994).

Hart, D.M. (2006) "Managing the Global Talent Pool: Sovereignty, Treaty, and Intergovernmental Networks," *Technology in Society*, 28:4, 421–434.

Hatton, T.J. and J.G. Williamson (2009) "Emigration in the Long Run: Evidence from Two Global Centuries," *Asian-Pacific Economic Literature*, 23:2, 17–28.

Maimbo, S.M. and D. Ratha (eds.) (2005) *Remittances: Development Impacts and Future Prospects*, World Bank.

Martin, P. (2009) "Migration Governance," in K.A. Reinert, R.S. Rajan, A.J. Glass, and L.S. Davis (eds.), *The Princeton Encyclopedia of the World Economy*, Princeton University Press, 770–775.

Martin, P., S. Martin, and S. Cross (2007) "High-Level Dialogue on Migration and Development," *International Migration*, 41:1, 7–25.

Martin, P. and J.E. Taylor (1996) "The Anatomy of a Migration Hump," in J.E. Taylor (ed.), *Development Strategy, Employment, and Migration: Insights from Models*, Organization for Economic Cooperation and Development, 43–62.

Martineau, T., K. Decker, and P. Bundred (2004) "Brain Drain of Health Professionals: From Rhetoric to Responsible Action," *Health Policy*, 70:1, 1–10.

Mundell, R.A. (1957) "International Trade and Factor Mobility," *American Economic Review*, 47:3, 321–335.

Olesen, H. (2002) "Migration, Return and Development," *International Migration*, 40:5, 125–150.

Organization for Economic Cooperation and Development (2005) *Trends in International Migration – 2004*.

Ozden, C. and M. Schiff (eds.) (2006) *International Migration, Remittances and the Brain Drain*, World Bank.

Pozo, S. (2009) "Remittances," in K.A. Reinert, R.S. Rajan, A.J. Glass, and L.S. Davis (eds.), *The Princeton Encyclopedia of the World Economy*, Princeton University Press, 963–968.

Pritchett, L. (2006) *Let Their People Come: Breaking the Gridlock On Global Labor Mobility*, Center for Global Development.

Purvis, D.D. (1972) "Technology, Trade and Factor Mobility," *Economic Journal*, 82:327, 991–999.

Saxenian, A. (2002) "Transnational Communities and the Evolution of Global Production Networks," *Industry and Innovation*, 9:3, 183–202.

Saxenian, A. (2005) "From Brain Drain to Brain Circulation: Transnational Communities and Regional Upgrading in India and China," *Studies in Comparative International Development*, 40:2, 35–61.

Schiff, M. (1994) *How Trade Aid and Remittances Affect International Migration*, World Bank.

Winters, L.A., T.L. Walmsley, Z.K Wang, and R. Grynberg (2003) "Liberalizing the Temporary Movement of Natural Persons: An Agenda for the Development Round," *The World Economy*, 26:8, 1137–1161.

Woodruff, C. and R. Zenteno (2007) "Migration Networks and Microenterprise in Mexico," *Journal of Development Economics*, 82:2, 509–528.

Zelinsky, W. (1971) "The Hypothesis of Mobility Transition," *Geographical Review*, 61:2, 219–249.

III INTERNATIONAL FINANCE

13 Accounting Frameworks

In this chapter, we begin to develop your understanding of our third window on the world economy, international finance. Recall from Chapter 1 that, whereas international trade refers to the exchange of goods and services among the countries of the world economy, international finance refers to the exchange of **assets** among these countries. Recall also that the global exchange of assets in the world economy is between 60 and 70 times larger than the exchange of goods and services. This is one central reason why international finance is such an important subject.

There is a basic principle in economics that can be informally stated as "things add up." In the realm of international economics, this principle is a very important one. If you forget it, you can find yourself making claims that are simply incorrect. If you remember the principle and know how to use it, you will have a powerful tool in your hands for analyzing economies and their relationships to the larger world economy. The consideration of the way "things add up" takes us into the realm of economic accounting, the subject of this chapter. We take a simple approach to the accounting issue, and the insights you will gain will be crucial to your understanding of the world economy.

We begin with a consideration of **open-economy accounts**, taking as our starting point the **circular flow diagram**. Next, we consider the **balance of payments** as a more detailed look at one important relationship in the open-economy accounts, namely the interactions of an economy with the rest of the world. For the interested reader, we consider the subject of *accounting matrices* in the appendix to this chapter. A second appendix presents a simple *open-economy macroeconomic model.*

> Analytical elements for this chapter:
>
> *Countries, currencies,* and *financial assets.*

OPEN-ECONOMY ACCOUNTS

In your introductory economics course, it is very likely that you came across a graphical description of an economy called the **circular flow diagram**. We are going to use this diagram to initiate our analysis of open-economy accounts. We want to view an economy as being aggregated into one giant sector. To make things more concrete, let's take the example of Mexico. To begin, we treat the Mexican economy as being composed of two accounts: a "Firm" account and a "Household" account. The relationships between these two accounts are summarized as a circular flow diagram of a *simple, closed economy* in Figure 13.1. The term *simple* refers to the absence of capital (savings/investment) and government considerations, whereas the term *closed* refers to the absence of any

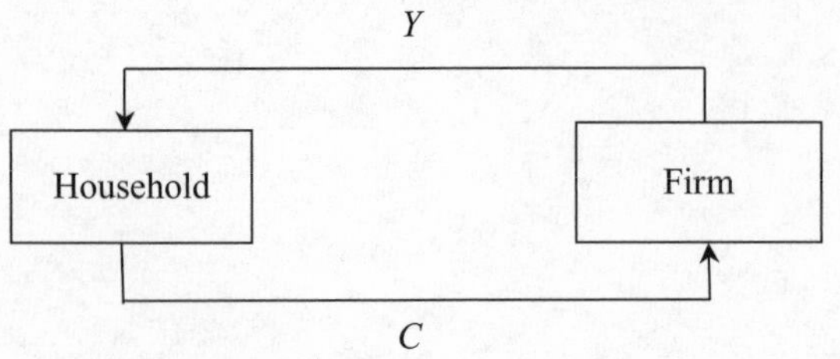

Figure 13.1. A Circular Flow Diagram for a Simple, Closed Economy

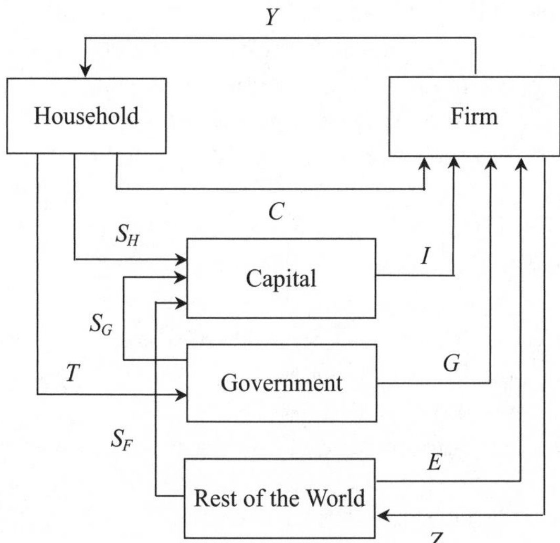

Figure 13.2. An Open Economy with Government, Savings, and Investment

trade and financial interactions with the rest of the world economy. In Figure 13.1, the production process of the Firm generates income that accrues to the Household. This income is denoted as *Y* and consists of wages, salaries, and payments for the use of property assets. Given the simple assumptions of this chapter, *Y* is also equal to both the nominal **gross domestic product** (GDP) and the nominal **gross national income** (GNI) of Mexico.[1] The consumption process of the Household generates consumption expenditures that accrue to the Firm. This consumption is denoted as *C* in the figure.

Figure 13.1 corresponds to the circular flow diagrams found in introductory textbooks, but it is exceedingly simple and begs for more realism. For our purposes in this chapter, we need to add three new accounts. The first we will call "Capital," and this account acts as a financial intermediary in the savings-investment process. These financial intermediaries are composed of institutions such as banks, mutual funds, and brokers that receive funds from savers and use these funds to make loans or buy assets, thereby placing the funds in the hands of investors. The term *capital* used here does not refer to physical capital such as machinery and buildings. Instead, it refers to *income not consumed*, which is available for use in investment. The second new account is "Government," and the third is "Rest of the World." The Rest of the World account captures the interactions of the Mexican economy with the other countries of the world.

Including these three new institutions results in a circular flow diagram for an *open economy with government, savings, and investment*. This is illustrated in Figure 13.2. As in Figure 13.1, the production process of the Firm generates income that accrues to the Household. Now, however, the Household has three types of expenditures. The first of these is consumption of goods and services, *C*. The second expenditure type is household savings, which is denoted S_H. Through the work of financial intermediaries, Household savings accrue as income to the Capital account. The third expenditure

[1] Differences between GDP and GNI arise in practice due to the presence of international factor payments. We discuss this distinction in the appendix to Chapter 20.

is taxes paid to Government and is denoted T.[2] Government makes two alternative expenditures: government spending (denoted G) and government savings (denoted S_G). In many cases, government savings are negative (a government deficit), and the flow is reversed, from Capital to Government. You can treat these cases as a negative S_G. Finally, Capital has a single expenditure, I, which consists of funds provided to firms for investment purposes.

The Rest of the World interacts with the Mexican economy in three ways. First, the Rest of the World makes an expenditure that accrues to the Firm account in the form of its purchases of Mexico's exports. We denote these total exports as E. Second, the Rest of the World receives income in the form of Mexico's purchases of imports. We denote these total imports as Z. Finally, the Rest of the World makes an expenditure that accrues to Capital in the form of **foreign savings**, denoted S_F.

To begin your understanding of the open economy, we are going to focus on the Capital and Rest of the World accounts of Figure 13.2. Let's consider the Capital account first. The Capital account has a single expenditure, depicted by an arrow leaving the Capital box in Figure 13.2. This is the expenditure on domestic investment. The Capital account also has three types of receipts, depicted by arrows entering the Capital box. These are all savings flows, namely, household, government, and foreign savings. The first two of these, household and government savings, together give us *domestic savings.* In the introduction to this chapter, we stated that a basic principle of economics is that "things add up." The application of this principle here is that expenditures must equal receipts for the Capital account.[3] Expressing this as an equation gives us:

$$I = (S_H + S_G) + S_F \tag{13.1a}$$

In words:

$$\text{Domestic Investment} = \text{Domestic Savings} + \text{Foreign Savings} \tag{13.1b}$$

It is helpful to rearrange this equation by subtracting domestic savings from both sides. This gives us:

$$I - (S_H + S_G) = S_F \tag{13.2a}$$

Or:

$$\text{Domestic Investment} - \text{Domestic Savings} = \text{Foreign Savings} \tag{13.2b}$$

The fact that "things add up" for the Capital account implies that any gap between domestic investment and domestic savings is made up for by an inflow of foreign savings. We will discuss this further in just a moment.

Next, let's turn our attention to the Rest of the World account. This account has two expenditures, depicted by arrows leaving the Rest of the World box in Figure 13.2. These expenditures are Mexico's exports and foreign savings. The Rest of the World account

[2] To simplify matters for ourselves, we ignore corporate taxes.

[3] Reinert and Roland-Holst (1997) stated that "Economic accounting is based on a fundamental principle of economics: For every income or receipt there is a corresponding expenditure or outlay" (p. 95).

also has a single receipt in the form of Mexico's imports, depicted by an arrow entering the Rest of the World box. The equation expressing the equality between expenditures and receipts for the Rest of the World account is:

$$E + S_F = Z \tag{13.3a}$$

Or, in words:

$$\text{Exports} + \text{Foreign Savings} = \text{Imports} \tag{13.3b}$$

In this and subsequent chapters, we want to place foreign savings (S_F) on equal footing with the two sources of domestic savings (S_H and S_G). We therefore solve Equation 13.3a for S_F to obtain:

$$S_F = Z - E \tag{13.4a}$$

Or:

$$\text{Foreign Savings} = \text{Trade Deficit} \tag{13.4b}$$

The fact that "things add up" for the Rest of the World account implies that any gap between imports and exports (any trade deficit) has a counterpart in and inflow of foreign savings. We will discuss this further later.[4]

Take a look at the Capital account of Equation 13.2a and the Rest of the World account of Equation 13.4a. Notice that both of these equations have foreign savings on one side. This means that we can combine them into a single relationship that we call the **fundamental accounting equation** for open economies. This equation is:

$$I - (S_H + S_G) = S_F = Z - E \tag{13.5a}$$

Or:

$$\text{Domestic Investment} - \text{Domestic Savings} = \text{Foreign Savings} = \text{Trade Deficit} \tag{13.5b}$$

The fundamental accounting equation is also written in a different form, obtained by multiplying it by the number −1. This form is:

$$(S_H + S_G) - I = -S_F = E - Z \tag{13.6a}$$

Or:

$$\text{Domestic Savings} - \text{Domestic Investment} = \text{Foreign Investment} = \text{Trade Surplus} \tag{13.6b}$$

In Equations 13.6a and 13.b, foreign investment (minus S_F) refers to Mexico's *capital outflows*, that is, its investment in foreign countries. It is just the reverse of foreign savings (S_F) being capital inflows.

[4] As we will see in the next section of the chapter on balance of payments, the trade deficit will correspond to the current account of the balance of payments, whereas foreign savings will correspond to the capital/financial account of the balance of payments.

Table 13.1. Domestic savings, domestic investment, foreign savings, and the trade balance

Domestic investment and domestic savings	Foreign savings	Trade balance	Explanation
Domestic investment exceeds domestic savings	Foreign savings is positive	Trade deficit	Domestic savings is too small to finance domestic investment. Therefore, the country requires an inflow of foreign savings to make up the difference. This inflow of foreign savings finances the trade deficit.
Domestic savings exceeds domestic investment	Foreign savings is negative or foreign investment is positive.	Trade surplus	Domestic savings exceeds the requirements of domestic investment. Therefore, the country lends the difference to the Rest of the World. This outflow of foreign investment generates a trade surplus.

Depending on the source, you might find the fundamental accounting equations expressed in either Equation 13.5a,b form or Equation 13.6a,b form. They communicate the same important accounting insight that we repeat in the following box for emphasis:

Fundamental Accounting Equations

Domestic Investment – Domestic Savings = Foreign Savings = Trade Deficit

Domestic Savings – Domestic Investment = Foreign Investment = Trade Surplus

What do the fundamental accounting equations tell us? Let's study them very carefully with the help of Table 13.1. There are two cases to consider, one for each equation. First, suppose that Mexico's domestic investment exceeds its domestic savings. This case is explained by the first equation in the preceding box. The shortfall in domestic savings is made up for by a positive inflow of foreign savings. Then, according to the first equation, there must be a trade deficit. Does this make sense? A trade deficit means that the Mexican economy is importing more goods and services in value terms than it is exporting. Therefore, Mexico must sell something else other than goods and services to the rest of the world to make up the difference. This "something else" turns out to be assets: government and corporate bonds, corporate equities, and even real estate. The purchase of Mexican assets by the Rest of the World is the very thing that generates the inflow of foreign savings into Mexico. The first equation therefore makes sense.

Next, suppose that Mexico's domestic savings exceeds its domestic investment. This case is explained by the second equation in the box above. An excess of domestic savings generates a positive outflow of foreign investment by Mexico. Then, according to the second equation, there must be a trade surplus. Does this make sense? A trade surplus means that the Mexican economy is exporting more goods and services in value terms than it is importing. Therefore, Mexico must buy something else other than goods and services from the rest of the world to make up the difference. That "something else" again is assets. The purchase of foreign assets by Mexico generates the outflow of foreign investment to the Rest of the World. The second equation also makes sense.[5]

It is often the case that the accounts of this section are expressed in the form of *accounting matrices.* This possibility is considered in the first appendix to this chapter. Also, the accounts can be utilized in a basic *open-economy macroeconomic model*, and this is described in the second appendix to this chapter.

The field of international finance is concerned with the *international* aspects of economies as aggregate entities. Therefore, a focus is often placed on the previous Rest of the World account equation (Equation 13.4a,b) in the form of a more detailed set of accounts know as the **balance of payments** accounts. We take up these important accounts next.

BALANCE OF PAYMENTS ACCOUNTS

The **balance of payments** accounts of any country focus exclusively on the relationship of the country with the rest of the world. Recall from the previous section that the open-economy accounts were divided into five sub-accounts, namely Firm, Household, Capital, Government, and Rest of the World. The purpose of the balance of payments accounts is to examine in more detail the final, Rest of the World account, almost like holding up a magnifying glass to it. This examination is in its own style of accounting, however, with a terminology that is not entirely consistent with the open-economy accounts previously discussed. Consequently, the balance of payments accounts sometimes require a bit of patience on the part of the user.

We begin our discussion of the balance of payments accounts by considering a summary account for Mexico in 2007. This is presented in Table 13.2. The balance of payments in this table has five parts, each with a heading in italics. These parts are the current account, the capital/financial account, official reserve transactions, errors and omissions, and the overall balance. The current account of the balance of payments records transactions that create earnings and generate expenditures between Mexico and the Rest of the World. These *do not* involve the exchange of assets. The capital/financial account of the balance of payments records transactions between Mexico and the Rest of the World that *do* involve the exchange of assets. The official reserve transactions also involve the exchange of assets between Mexico and the Rest of the World, but these are governmental (central bank and treasury) transactions rather than the private transactions of the capital/financial account. Finally, there are inevitably errors and omissions.[6]

The starting point for understanding the balance of payments is to recognize that the overall balance must be zero. This is another example of the principle that

[5] Some time ago, Krugman (1996) wrote of "the disturbingly difficult ideas of people who know how to read national accounts or understand that the trade balance is also the difference between savings and investment" (p. ix). You are now one of these people.

[6] High (2009) noted that "Although balance of payments accounts are constructed using sophisticated accounting principles . . . , a country's cross-border transactions are not measured with the accuracy of a corporation's accounts. Balance of payments figures are statistically estimated based on sampling data gathered by government agencies . . . . Although these agencies do their utmost to provide reliable estimates, of necessity the accounts contain errors; the statistical estimates are based on data that are incomplete and otherwise imperfect" (p. 102).

Table 13.2. Mexican balance of payments, 2007 (billions of U.S. dollars)

Item	Gross	Net	Major Balance
Current Account			
1. Goods exports	271.9		
2. Goods imports	−281.9		
3. Goods trade balance		−10.0	
4. Service exports	17.6		
5. Service imports	−24.1		
6. Goods and services trade balance		−16.5	
7. Net income		−18.3	
8. Net transfers		26.4	
9. Current account balance			−8.4
Capital/Financial Account			
10. Direct investment		18.8	
11. Portfolio investment		11.3	
12. Other investment		−10.6	
13. Capital/financial account balance			19.5
Official Reserve Transactions			
14. Official reserves balance			−10.3
Errors and Omissions			
15. Errors and omissions			−0.8
Overall Balance			
16. Overall balance			0

Source: International Monetary Fund, International Financial Statistics

"things add up." Consequently, we can think of the balance of payments in the following terms:

$$\text{Current Account} + \text{Capital/Financial Account} + \text{Official Reserve Transactions} + \text{Errors and Omissions} = 0 \tag{13.7}$$

Now let's consider the balance of payments accounts of Table 13.2 in some detail. As we just mentioned, the first section of the balance of payments in known as the *current account* and includes items 1 through 9. Some of these items are reported in gross terms, some in net terms, and one as a major balance.[7] We consider them one at a time. Item 1 is Mexico's total goods exports. It is reported in gross terms at a 2007 value of US$271.9 billion. Similarly, item 2 is Mexico's total goods imports, reported in gross terms at a value of −$281.9 billion. You can see here that goods exports, generating a receipt for Mexico, have a positive value, whereas goods imports, generating a payment for Mexico, have a negative value. The net of these two items is known as the *goods trade balance* and is reported in net terms of −$10.0 billion.[8]

Services trade is reported separately in items 4 and 5 of the balance of payments in Table 13.2. Service exports are reported in gross terms in item 4 as $17.6 billion,

[7] Items reported in *gross* terms record the inflow or outflow separately. Items reported in *net* terms record the *difference* between the inflow and the outflow.

[8] We need to be careful here. The International Monetary Fund awkwardly refers to the "goods trade balance" as the "trade balance." However, this "trade balance" is actually only the balance on goods trade and ignores services trade.

and service imports are reported in gross terms in item 5 as −$24.1 billion. Again we see that service exports, generating a receipt for Mexico, have a positive value, whereas service imports, generating a payment for Mexico, have a negative value. Item 6 gives our second net balance, namely the *goods and services trade balance* of −$16.5 billion.[9] This value corresponds to the $E - Z$ value in the open economy accounts considered previously.

Items 7 and 8 in Table 13.2 are *new* items that we have not yet encountered. Furthermore, they are the two items that cause a difference between the goods and services trade balance and the current account balance. Item 7 is *net income.* It requires a little explanation. Residents of Mexico, either households or firms, own factors of production located in the Rest of the World. That is, a Mexican firm might own a factory in a foreign country. This firm receives income or profits from this factory during the year in question, and this is income receipts or income credits. Alternatively, residents of foreign countries own factors of production located in Mexico, and they receive payments from Mexico. From Mexico's point of view, these are income payments or income debits. Item 7 of Table 13.2 records the *net* of income receipts and income payments. Income payments exceed income receipts, and net income is −$18.3 billion.

Item 8 is *net transfers* and includes foreign aid, foreign remittances (discussed in Chapter 12), and international pension flows. For Mexico in 2007, inward transfers exceeded outward transfers by $26.4 billion, and it is this net figure that is entered into the balance of payments.

The sum of the net items 6 through 8 composes the *current account balance* and is entered into the accounts as a major balance in item 9 of Table 13.2. In 2007, Mexico had a current account *deficit* of $8.4 billion. Because the accounts between Mexico and the rest of the world must balance ("things add up," once again), it must be the case that there were other transactions in the balance of payments offsetting the current account deficit.

As mentioned previously, whereas the current account records earnings and expenditure transactions that do not involve the exchange of assets, the *capital/financial account* has the distinguishing feature of consisting of transactions that involve the exchange of assets.[10] The type of asset exchanged and who exchanges them determine the capital/financial account item in which a transaction is recorded. For example, item 10 in Table 13.2 is *direct investment,* which is just the **foreign direct investment** (FDI) we discussed in previous chapters. As we discussed in Chapter 1, the assets involved in direct investment contain an element of management influence reflected in shares amounting to at least 10 percent of the enterprise in question. In the case of Mexico in 2007, there was a net inward flow of direct investment of $18.8 billion.

The second capital account item is *portfolio investment.* Portfolio investment includes government bonds of various maturities, corporate equities, and corporate

[9] The International Monetary Fund records the "goods and services trade balance" as the "balance on goods and services."

[10] The International Monetary Fund actually breaks up this account into separate capital and financial accounts, but we do not do that here. The financial account is where the actual capital flows are recorded and is therefore more important in most cases. The capital account includes other items, such as revaluation.

bonds. Unlike direct investment, portfolio investment does *not* involve an element of management influence.[11] As we see in item 11 in Table 13.2, in the case of Mexico in 2007, there was a net inward flow of portfolio investment of $11.3 billion.

The third capital/financial account item is *other investment*. This includes commercial bank lending and other residual items. As we see in item 12 of Table 13.2, in the case of Mexico in 2007, there was a net outward flow with an entry of −$10.6 billion.[12]

The sum of the net items 10 through 12 composes the *capital/financial account balance* and is entered into the accounts as a major balance in item 13 of Table 13.2. In 2007, Mexico had a capital account *surplus* of $19.5 billion, more than offsetting the current account deficit of $8.4 billion. This value corresponds most closely to the S_F value in the open-economy accounts considered earlier.

The third component of the balance of payments accounts is *official reserve transactions*, reported in net terms as a major balance in Table 13.2. It is an item that did not appear in the open-economy accounts relationship of the preceding balance of payments equation. The official reserves balance is recorded as item 14 at a value of −$10.3 billion in 2007. The official reserves balance reflects the actions of the world's *treasuries and central banks*. Central banks need to hold reserves of foreign exchange. They hold these in the form of other countries' government bonds and in accounts at foreign central banks. Transactions on the official reserves balance occur in four instances:

1. When Mexico's central bank sells foreign exchange holdings, this generates an inward flow of funds and income or receipts on Mexico's official reserves balance (positive entries).
2. When Mexico's central bank buys foreign exchange holdings, this generates outlays or expenditures on the official reserves balance (negative entries).
3. When foreign central banks sell their reserves of Mexico's currency, this generates an outward flow of funds and an outlay or expenditure on Mexico's official reserves balance (negative entries).
4. Finally, when foreign central banks buy reserves of Mexico's currency, this generates an income or receipts on Mexico's official reserves balance (positive entries).

Let's take stock of our balances up to this point: the current account balance is −$8.4 billion, the capital/financial account balance is $19.5 billion, and the official reserves balance is −$10.3 billion. Adding these three balances gives us $0.8 billion. The balance of payments accounts address this kind of difference through the *errors and omissions* entry. This entry, item 15 in Table 13.2 of −$0.8 billion, ensures that the overall balance of payments in item 16 is indeed zero. "Things add up."

[11] Portfolio investment can be broken up further into *long-term capital* and *short-term capital*. This distinction is important because short-term capital is more volatile than long-term capital. For example, some time ago *The Economist* (2002) noted that "The volatility of portfolio finance – its tendency to pour in when investors are confident, and flee just as suddenly – is the main reason for growing skepticism about the whole process of foreign borrowing by emerging market economies" (p. 64). For a detailed discussion of this, see Goldin and Reinert (2005).

[12] Along with short-term components of portfolio investment, commercial bank lending recorded in other investment can be quite volatile. Again, see Goldin and Reinert (2005).

ANALYZING THE BALANCE OF PAYMENTS ACCOUNTS

With this understanding of the balance of payments accounts in hand, we can now turn to how we might use the accounts in a more analytical fashion. As we saw in Equation 13.7, the sum of the current account, the capital/financial account, official reserve transactions, and errors and omissions must be zero. In practice, and as we saw in Table 13.2, errors and omissions are small. Analytically then (but not in actual accounts), we can ignore the errors and omissions. This gives us:

$$\text{Current Account} + \text{Capital/Financial Account} + \text{Official Reserve Transactions} = 0 \tag{13.7}$$

This is the analytical application of "things add up" for the balance of payments accounts. We have also seen that the current account contains the trade balance and the capital account contains foreign savings. So Equation 13.7 is similar to Equations 13.5 and 13.6 of our open-economy macroeconomic accounts. However, it is more inclusive than those accounts and allows for official reserve transactions.

What does Equation 13.7 tell us? There are many ways of going about describing this, but perhaps the easiest is to recognize that, if two of the items in Equation 13.7 have the same sign (positive or negative), then the third must have the opposite sign (negative or positive). To be more specific, we can state that:

- If the current and capital/financial accounts are both positive (negative), then official reserve transactions must be negative (positive).
- If the current and official reserve transaction accounts are both positive (negative), then the capital/financial account must be negative (positive).
- If the capital/financial and official reserve transaction accounts are both positive (negative), then the current account must be negative (positive).

Let's examine two cases of this with reference to the first of these bullet points. Suppose that the current and capital/financial accounts were both positive. This roughly means that Mexico is selling more goods, services, and assets in the private realm from the Rest of the World than it is buying. The official transactions must make up for the difference. The central bank must buy additional assets to generate an offsetting expenditure with a negative entry and bring the overall balance of payments back to zero.

Alternatively, suppose that the current and capital/financial accounts were both negative. This roughly means that Mexico is buying more goods, services, and assets in the private realm from the Rest of the World than it is selling. Again, the official transactions must make up for the difference. The central bank must sell additional assets to generate an offsetting receipt with a positive entry and bring the overall balance of payments back to zero.

Another way to look at Equation 13.7 is in terms of financing current account deficits. This often has relevance to countries in deficit positions and is a focal point for many types of analysis. Perhaps Mexico has a negative goods and services trade balance that is not offset by income and transfer receipts. Consequently, there is a current account deficit. Perhaps, however, the capital/financial account, even with a positive balance, is insufficient to finance the current account deficit. The central bank must step in to sell assets and generate additional receipts. As we will see in subsequent chapters, this entails drawing down foreign exchange reserves. There is a limit to central banks' abilities to do this, however, because foreign exchange reserves cannot fall below zero. That is why, in some instances, a current account deficit with an insufficient capital account surplus draws so much attention: it can precipitate a crisis.

The balance of payments accounts are thus an important *diagnostic tool* for international economists.[13] They help to identify patterns of relationships of the country in question with the rest of the world that might not be sustainable. For example, in the case just described, an international economist might begin considering potential corrective measures. The current account deficit, for example, may need to be suppressed through increases in government tax revenues that allow an increase in government savings.

GLOBAL IMBALANCES

The discussion in this chapter on open-economy and balance of payments accounts helps to provide a window onto one of the most central aspects of the current world economy. There is a tradition in international economics that suggests that it is natural for developed countries to have capital/financial account deficits or outflows and for developing countries to have capital/financial account surpluses or inflows. As a result, developing countries would receive net inflows of capital that would yield relatively high rates of return, the capital being supplied from developed countries where rates of return are relatively low. This reflects the fact that, at early stages of development, the need for capital is high, whereas domestic saving is low. As development proceeds, the need for capital slowly declines, whereas domestic saving slowly increases.[14]

Let's examine whether this proposition holds in the current world economy. We do this from the developed country perspective first, considering the United States. Figure 13.3 plots the capital/financial and official reserves account transactions of the U.S. balance of payments from 1960 to 2008.[15] These are the two accounts that involve the exchange of assets. Between 1960 and 1983, the United States was not a significant borrower (positive entries) or a significant lender (negative entries). Beginning in 1984, however, and in contraindication to the developed country as lender story just described, the United States began to *borrow* from abroad on the capital/financial account as part of the Reagan Administration's expansive fiscal policies and consequent decline of U.S. government savings. The concurrent expansion of government deficits and current account deficits became known as the "twin deficits." This borrowing began to decline in 1989.

A second episode of foreign borrowing on the capital/financial account began in 1993. Unlike the decade of the 1980s, this was due to a collapse of household savings rather than government savings. Beginning in 2001, an entirely new episode of foreign

[13] James (1996) stated that "analyzing the origins of balance of payments problems (can) provide a tool for diagnosing more wide-ranging economic difficulties. The balance of payments (act) as a fever thermometer" (p. 124).

[14] This theoretical framework predicting net capital flows from the developed to the developing world is *highly idealized*, with a number of intervening factors inhibiting the idealized flows. These include political risk, default risk, differences in levels of human capital and technology, and differences in institutional quality. These points were emphasized by Lucas (1990).

[15] Note that Figure 13.3 plots reserve account *transactions* or flows, not the holdings or stocks of foreign reserves.

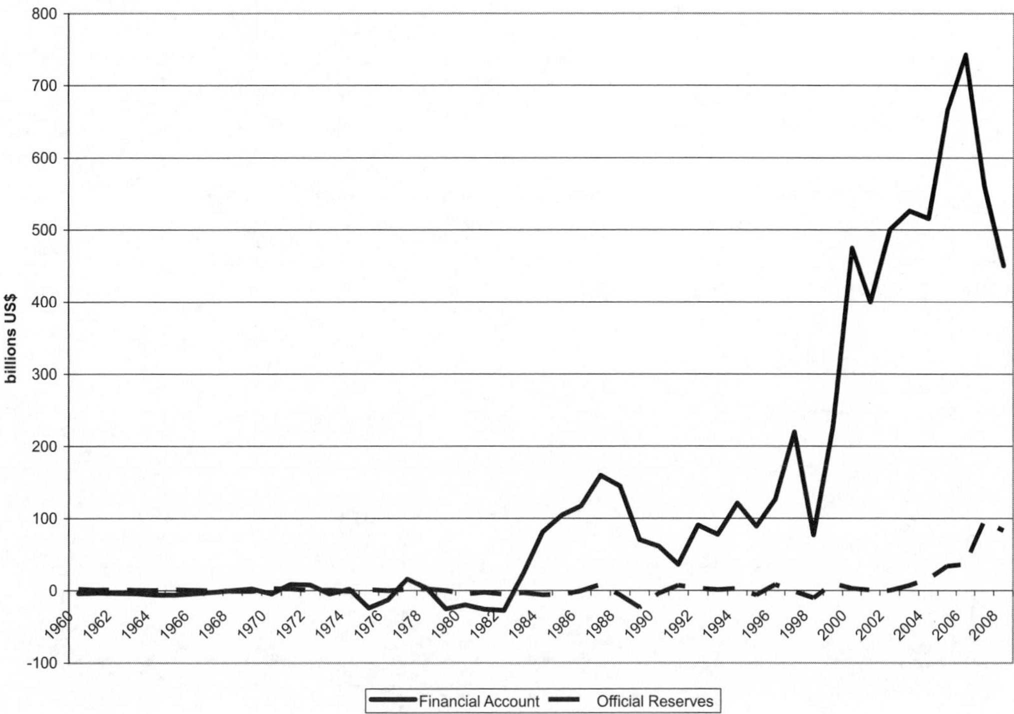

Figure 13.3. United States Capital/Financial and Official Reserves Account Transactions, 1960 to 2008 (billions of US$). *Source:* United States Bureau of Economic Analysis

borrowing on the capital/financial account began on a much larger scale, reaching a peak of nearly $800 billion in 2006.[16] This was the result of a deficit of domestic savings as a whole (both household and government), wars in Afghanistan and Iraq, and government tax cuts. In 2006, foreign borrowing on the official reserves account also began. Rather than being a source of capital for the developing world, the United States became a capital sink.

Figure 13.4 repeats Figure 13.3 for the case of China from 1982 to 2008.[17] It paints a very different picture. Both the capital/financial and official reserves accounts are in relative balance until the mid-1990s. At that point in time, the current/financial account moves into slight surplus, whereas the official reserve account moves into slight deficit. These accounts return to balance in 1999 and 2000, but a new episode opens up beginning in 2001. The current/capital account moves into slight surplus, but the official reserves balance begins to move into larger deficit realms that reach $460 billion in 2007. What we observe here is the official lending by China to the rest of the world (including the United States). Private inflows of capital into China (reaching $110 billion in 2004) are more than offset by official outflows of capital from China as

[16] *The Economist* (2005) reported that "the growing imbalances are weakening America's economy, not only because of the extra foreign debt the country has taken on, but because of the domestic toll of being the world's consumer of last resort. America is saving too little and not investing enough in productive assets, especially in the export sector" (p. 24).

[17] Note that, like Figure 13.3, Figure 13.4 plots reserve account *transactions* or flows, not the holdings or stocks of foreign reserves.

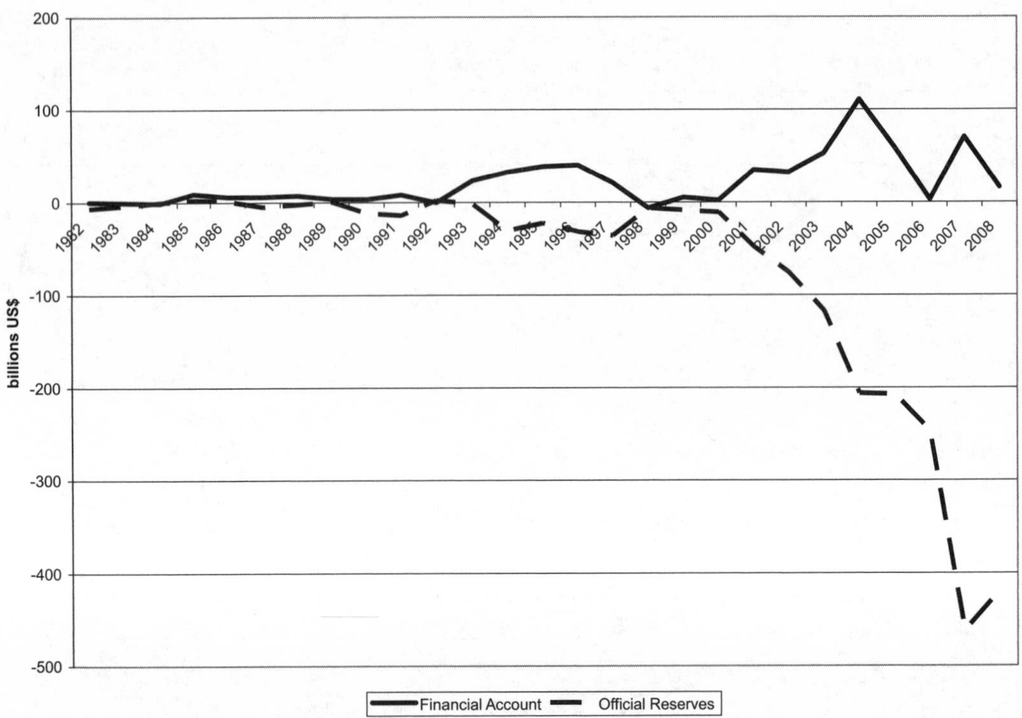

Figure 13.4. China Capital/Financial and Official Reserves Account Transactions, 1982 to 2008 (billions of US$). *Source:* International Monetary Fund, International Financial Statistics

the country built up foreign reserves in contraindication to the developing country as borrower story previously described.[18]

So here we have an interesting paradox in the modern world economy. Economic intuition suggests that developed countries will be sources of capital and developing countries will be capital destinations. But simple analysis of the United States and China balance of payments accounts shows that this is not currently the case. In fact, we have large *global imbalances* in savings and investment flows, imbalances that *The Economist* (2005) referred to as the "Great Thrift Shift." Taming these global imbalances is one of the most pressing current challenges for global economic policymakers.[19]

CONCLUSION

Chapter 1 discussed four realms of the world economy: international trade, international production, international finance, and international economic development. In this chapter, we have used accounting schemes to develop linkages among three of the realms: international trade (the exchange of goods and services), international production (foreign direct investment), and international finance (the exchange of assets). These linkages were present in the open-economy accounts as well as in the balance of payments accounts. The key insight is that current account deficits and surpluses have a counterpart in capital/financial account surpluses and deficits, respectively. The

[18] *The Economist* (2005) reported that "Between 2000 and 2004, China's national savings rate rose by an extraordinary 12 percentage points to 50% of GDP" (p. 4). At the time of this writing (mid-2010), China's foreign exchange reserve holdings have reached approximately $2.5 trillion.

[19] On the link between global balances and an open trade regime, see Wolf (2008).

trade balance is one major component of the current account. Foreign savings in the form of direct and portfolio investment is one major component of the capital/financial account. The open-economy and balance of payments accounts can both be used as diagnostic tools for the assessment of the sustainability of current economic conditions in the country in question. They can also be used to analyze imbalances of savings among the countries of the world.

REVIEW EXERCISES

1. In Figure 1.4 of Chapter 1, we emphasized connections among the four windows on the world economy: international trade, international production, international finance, and international development. Looking back on this chapter, please identify where in the open-economy accounts and balance of payments accounts connections appear among the first three of these windows: trade, production (FDI), and finance.
2. Looking at the open-economy circular flow diagram of Figure 13.2, please explain how an increase in government expenditures, G, without any increase in tax revenues, T, would tend to impact the trade balance. You will need to use one of the fundamental equations to answer this question.
3. Repeat the exercise of Question 2 for an increase in household consumption, C, without any increase in income, Y.
4. Consider the global imbalances issue discussed in this chapter. Given your understanding of the issue, try to suggest policies that might address it. You are just at the beginning of your exploration of international finance, but try to be as detailed as you can in your policy suggestions.
5. Using the open-economy macroeconomic model of the appendix, graphically analyze an increase in either tax revenues or the entire $S_H(Y)$ relationship. To do this, use a diagram like that of Figures 13.5 and 13.6.

FURTHER READING AND WEB RESOURCES

A concise review of balance of payments accounts can be found in Cumby and Levich (1992) and High (2009). A much more thorough and complete introduction is available in the IMF's (2009) *Balance of Payments and International Investment Position Manual.* At nearly 400 pages, this document goes a long way to answering detailed questions about balance of payments accounts and is available online. Both open-economy accounts and balance of payments data are available from the International Monetary Fund's publication *International Financial Statistics.* Most important is the annual *Yearbook* in this series. The IFS is also available in an online version to which many libraries have subscribed. It is not user-friendly, but nevertheless is an important source for standardized data. See the website of the International Monetary Fund at www.imf.org.

APPENDIX A: ACCOUNTING MATRICES

In many instances, international and development economists arrange open-economy accounts in the form of *an accounting matrix.*[20] This process begins with Figure 13.2,

[20] See, for example, Reinert and Roland-Holst (1997). These authors advocated for the accounting matrix approach, arguing that "it represents a comprehensive and consistent framework for developing databases for rigorous

Table 13.3. An open-economy accounting matrix

	Firm	Household	Capital	Government	ROW
Firm		C	I	G	E
Household	Y				
Capital		S_H		S_G	S_F
Government		T			
ROW	Z				

presented earlier. In setting up accounting matrices, we need to abide by four rules: (1) the number of accounts composes the dimensions of the square matrix; (2) expenditures or payments are recorded down the columns of the matrix; (3) receipts or incomes are recorded across the rows of the matrix; and (4) the row and column sums of the matrix are equal. Because Figure 13.2 has five accounts, it translates into a matrix with five rows and columns. Such a matrix is presented in Table 13.3.

To fill in Table 13.3, we can either record expenditures down columns or receipts across rows. Let us record expenditures down columns and leave it to you to check that recording receipts across rows gives us the same result. The Firm has two expenditures: income, Y, accruing to the Household and imports, Z, accruing to the Rest of the World. We record these down the first column. The Household has three expenditures: consumption, C, accruing to the Firm; household savings, S_H, accruing to Capital; and taxes, T, accruing to the Government. We record these down the second column. Capital has a single expenditure, I, accruing to the Firm, and we record this in the third column. The Government has two expenditures: government spending, G, accruing to the Firm, and government savings, S_G, accruing to Capital. We record these down the fourth column. Finally, the Rest of the World has two expenditures: exports, E, accruing to the Firm, and foreign savings, S_F, accruing to Capital. We record these down the fifth column.

We can gain insights into open economies by applying the fourth rule of accounting matrices to Table 13.3. The rule states that the row and column sums of the accounting matrix are equal. Applying this rule gives us the following set of accounting identity equations:

$$Y + Z = C + I + G + E \tag{13.8}$$

$$C + S_H + T = Y \tag{13.9}$$

$$I = S_H + S_G + S_F \tag{13.10}$$

$$G + S_G = T \tag{13.11}$$

$$E + S_F = Z \tag{13.12}$$

Equation 13.8 can be rearranged to give the standard national income equation from introductory macroeconomics:

$$Y = C + I + G + (E - Z) \tag{13.13}$$

economic methods" and that "it helps in the reconciliation of the numerous data sources to complete the detailed picture of economywide activity" (p. 117).

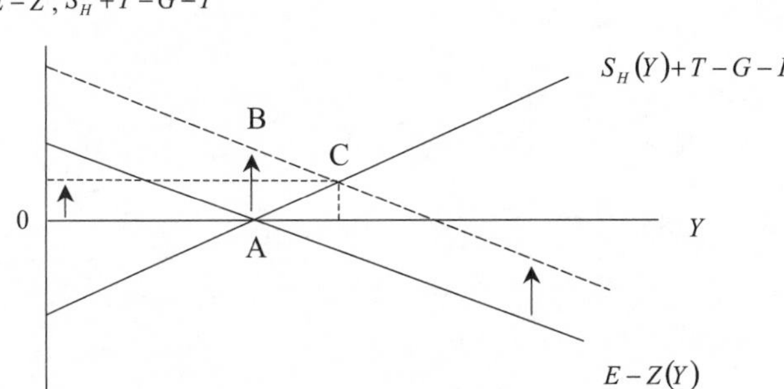

Figure 13.5. An Open-Economy, Macroeconomic Model and an Increase in Export Demand

Equations 13.10 and 13.12 can be rearranged to give the fundamental accounting equation discussed earlier in this chapter:

$$I - (S_H + S_G) = S_F = Z - E \tag{13.5a}$$

Or:

$$(S_H + S_G) - I = -S_F = E - Z \tag{13.6a}$$

The accounting matrix of Table 13.3 contains all of the information on open-economy macroeconomics accounts in a succinct form. We will next consider how to move from the open-economy accounts of Equations 13.8 to 13.12 to a simple, open-economy, macroeconomic model.

APPENDIX B: AN OPEN-ECONOMY MODEL

An open-economy model can be derived from the fundamental accounting equations of this chapter.[21] We begin with Equation 13.6a. Combining this with the government income-expenditure identity in Equation 13.11 gives us:

$$S_H + T - G - I = E - Z \tag{13.14}$$

Keynesian thinking in macroeconomics suggests that household savings (S_G) increases with the level of income (Y).[22] Experience also shows that imports (Z) increase with the level of income. We will denote these responses in functional form as $S_H(Y)$ and $Z(Y)$ where both S_H and Z respond positively to Y. If these two relationships are linear, and the other variables in this equation are independent of income (i.e., exogenous), we have the graphs depicted in Figure 13.5.

Figure 13.5 depicts a situation in which the trade balance is initially zero. Suppose that, from this initial position, there is an *increase in export demand.* This shifts the $E - Z(Y)$ curve upward by the amount of the increase in export demand from point A to point B. At point B, however, the trade surplus exceeds the net of domestic savings over domestic investment. The only way for the fundamental accounting equation to be restored is via an increase in Y. As Y increases, both S_H and Z increase. The

[21] See chapter 3 of Dornbusch (1988).

[22] This goes back to Keynes (1935) who stated: "The fundamental psychological law... is that men are disposed, as a rule and on the average, to increase their consumption as their income increases, *but not by as much as the increase in their income*" (p. 96, emphasis added).

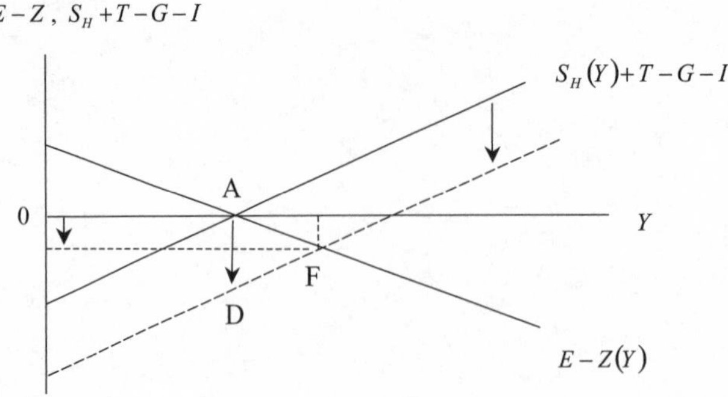

Figure 13.6. An Increase in Government Spending or Investment

former increases the net of domestic savings over domestic investment (a movement from A to C), whereas the latter reduces the trade surplus (a movement from B to C). The fundamental accounting equation and macroeconomic equilibrium are restored at point C.[23]

Next, consider Figure 13.6. We begin at the same initial equilibrium as in Figure 13.5 at point A. Suppose that, from this initial position, there is an *increase in government spending or investment.* This shifts the $S_H(Y) + T - G - I$ curve downward by the amount of the increase in government spending or investment from point A to point D. At point D, however, the net of domestic savings over domestic investment (now negative) is below the trade surplus (still at zero). The only way for the fundamental accounting equation to be restored is via an increase in Y. As Y increases, both S_H and Z increase. The former increases the net of domestic savings over domestic investment (a movement from D to F), whereas the latter reduces the trade surplus (a movement from A to F). The fundamental accounting equation and macroeconomic equilibrium are restored at point F, characterized by a trade deficit.[24]

Finally, we can have *an increase in either tax revenues or the entire $S_H(Y)$ relationship.* This shifts the $S_H(Y) + T - G - I$ curve upward rather than downward as in Figure 13.6 and is left as an exercise for the reader (see Review Exercise 5).

REFERENCES

Cumby, R. and R. Levich (1992) "Balance of Payments," in P. Newman, M. Milgate, and J. Eatwell (eds.), *The New Palgrave Dictionary of Money and Finance, Vol. 1*, Macmillan, 113–120.

Dornbusch, R. (1988) *Open Economy Macroeconomics*, Basic Books.

The Economist (2002) "Special Report: The IMF," September 28.

The Economist (2005) "The Great Thrift Shift," September 24.

Goldin, I. and K.A. Reinert (2005) "Capital Flows and Development: A Survey," *Journal of International Trade and Economic Development*, 14:4, 453–481.

High, J. (2009) "Balance of Payments," in K.A. Reinert, R.S. Rajan, A.J. Glass, and L.S. Davis (eds.), *The Princeton Encyclopedia of the World Economy*, Princeton University Press, 102–107.

International Monetary Fund (2009) *Balance of Payments and International Investment Position Manual.*

[23] As emphasized by Dornbusch (1988), the trade surplus at point C is smaller than it was at B.

[24] Governments cannot use a fiscal stimulus in an open economy without moving the economy into a trade deficit. This is one of the limitations on domestic policy independence placed by globalization.

James, H. (1996) *International Monetary Cooperation since Bretton Woods*, Oxford University Press.

Keynes, J.M. (1935) *The General Theory of Employment, Interest and Money*, Harcourt Brace.

Krugman, P. (1996) *Pop Internationalism*, MIT Press.

Lucas, R.E. (1990) "Why Doesn't Capital Flow from Rich to Poor Countries?" *American Economic Review*, 80:2, 92–96.

Reinert, K.A. and D.W. Roland-Holst (1997) "Social Accounting Matrices," in J.F. Francois and K.A. Reinert (eds.) *Applied Methods for Trade Policy Analysis*, Cambridge University Press, 94–121.

Wolf, M. (2008) "Global Imbalances Threaten the Survival of Liberal Trade," *Financial Times*, December 2.

14 Exchange Rates and Purchasing Power Parity

For U.S. companies with large trade and investment exposures to Western Europe, the year 2000 was a very difficult time. During that year, the euro fell in value from just under US$1.00 to approximately $0.80. U.S.-based firms such as Compaq, IBM, Intel, Polaroid, Microsoft, Baxter International, Heinz, Caterpillar, Dow Chemical, Dupont, and TRW all suffered as a result. Why? Their euro sales were worth less in dollar terms, and dollar terms mattered. One Wall Street analyst estimated that the fall of the euro in 2000 shaved 3 percent off total Standard and Poor 500 operating profits in the third quarter alone. The president of TRW lamented, "If I could report in euros, we would be having a bang-up year."[1] Unfortunately, this was not possible.

In 2003, the euro increased in value. This was good news for U.S.-based firms selling in the euro area, but bad news for EU-based firms selling in the United States and reporting profits in euros. Volkswagen, for example, attributed a €1 billion fall in profits to the strengthened euro.[2] One way or another, changing exchange rates affect firms engaged in international production.

Exchange rates matter, and they matter in many different ways to many different participants in the world economy. Much of this section of the book, focusing on the third window on the world economy, international finance, is directly or indirectly concerned with exchange rates. Indeed, this and the next two chapters are exclusively devoted to developing your understanding of exchange rates. In this chapter, we begin with two important exchange rate definitions. These are the **nominal exchange rate** and the **real exchange rate**. Next, we develop a first model of exchange rate determination: the **purchasing power parity model** (PPP model). Having developed this model, we relate it to our definition of the real exchange rate.

We then turn to the relationship of exchange rates and trade flows. Finally, we consider the difference between **spot rates** and **forward rates** and how this difference can, at times, be used by firms to hedge **exchange rate exposure**. The real exchange rate definition and the PPP model utilize the notion of overall **price levels** in an economy. For those who are not familiar with this idea, price levels are discussed in a first appendix to this chapter. A second appendix considers an extension of the PPP model in the form of the **monetary approach to exchange rate determination**.

As you conclude this chapter, you will have an understanding of one model of exchange rates: the PPP model. As you will see, this model has validity in helping to predict the *long-run* trends in nominal exchange rates. We also need a model to help predict *short-run* trends in nominal exchange rates; this is the central task of Chapters 15 and 16.

Analytical elements for this chapter:

Countries, *currencies*, and *financial assets*.

THE NOMINAL EXCHANGE RATE

Our discussion of exchange rates is placed within a particular context in order to make the concepts more concrete. Exchange rates are defined in terms of a home and a foreign country. In this chapter, we usually take Mexico as our *home* country and the

[1] See Tully (2000) and McMurray (2000).
[2] See *The Economist* (2004a).

Table 14.1 Nominal exchange rates, April 14, 2010 (per U.S. dollar)

Country or region	Currency	Nominal exchange rate	Nominal exchange rate 1 Year earlier
Argentina	Peso	3.88	3.68
Brazil	Real	1.74	2.17
Canada	Dollar	1.00	1.21
Chile	Peso	515	577
China	Yuan	6.83	6.84
Euro Zone	Euro	0.73	0.76
Indonesia	Rupiah	9,013	11,110
Japan	Yen	93.4	99.4
Mexico	Peso	12.2	13.1
Pakistan	Rupee	83.9	80.7
Russia	Ruble	29.0	33.4
South Africa	Rand	7.34	9.01
Thailand	Baht	32.3	35.7
Turkey	Lira	1.48	1.58
United Kingdom	Pound	0.65	0.67

Source: www.economist.com

United States as our *foreign* country.[3] Our first exchange rate definition is the **nominal exchange rate.** The nominal exchange rate is the home-country currency price of a foreign currency. It is expressed as the number of units of the local or home currency that are required to buy a unit of the foreign currency. The Mexican currency is the *Mexican peso*, which we express simply as the *peso*. The U.S. currency is the *U.S. dollar*, which we express simply as the *dollar*. Therefore, the nominal exchange rate is defined as:

$$e = \frac{pesos}{dollar} \tag{14.1}$$

which is in the form of:

$$e = \frac{home\ currency}{foreign\ currency} \tag{14.2}$$

As implied in these equations, we use the symbol e to denote the nominal exchange rate. Nominal exchange rates for a sample of 15 countries are presented in Table 14.1 for April 2010 and for one year earlier.

Let's examine the nominal exchange rate a little more closely. Suppose that, for some reason, e were to increase. What would this mean for the value of the peso? The increase in e implies that it takes *more* pesos to purchase a dollar. This, in turn, implies that the value of the peso has *fallen* (the peso *depreciates*). The opposite is the case when e falls. When e falls, it takes *fewer* pesos to buy a dollar, and this implies that the value of the peso has *increased* (the peso *appreciates*). Because these relationships are very important, we put them in a box for you to remember:

$e \uparrow \Rightarrow$ value of the home currency (peso) *falls* or *depreciates*
$e \downarrow \Rightarrow$ value of the home currency (peso) *rises* or *appreciates*

[3] Readers in the United States, please be careful here. The United States is the *foreign* country.

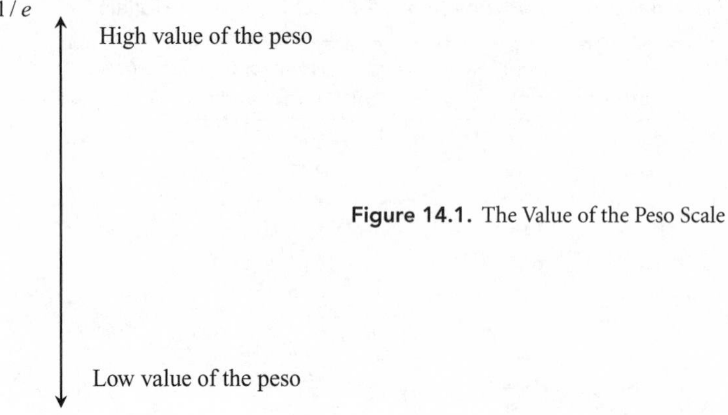

Figure 14.1. The Value of the Peso Scale

Let's consider a couple of the exchange rates in Table 14.1. Between April 2009 and April 2010, for example, the exchange rate of the Brazilian real to the U.S. dollar decreased from 2.17 to 1.74 reais per dollar.[4] This means that it took fewer reais to buy a dollar in 2010 than in 2009. Consequently, the value of the real increased. Consider next the Pakistani rupee. Between April 2009 and April 2010 the Pakistani rupee price of the U.S. dollar increased from 80.7 to 83.9. It took more rupees to buy a dollar in 2010 than in 2009, so the value of the rupee decreased.

As you can see in the preceding box and the examples of the Brazilian real and Pakistani rupee, *e* and the value of the peso are *inversely* related. For this reason, *e* is often graphed as its *inverse*, which is equal to the *value* of the peso or home currency. This inverted scale is presented in Figure 14.1. In this figure, a movement up the scale indicates a fall in *e* and a rise in the value of the peso. A movement down the scale indicates a rise in *e* and a fall in the value of the peso. Make sure you are comfortable with this inverse scale before continuing with the remainder of the chapter. It is important to emphasize that the definition of the nominal exchange rate depends on the choice of the home country. Consider another example. If Japan is our home country, we might be interested in the $\frac{yen}{euro}$ nominal exchange rate. But if the euro zone is our home country, we would instead consider the $\frac{yen}{euro}$ nominal exchange rate. For this reason, we always need to pause for a moment to make sure we express the nominal exchange rate in the correct way and to ensure that we understand how our research sources are expressing it. Otherwise, we can make some significant mistakes.

As a final example of a nominal exchange rate, let's maintain Japan as our home country but consider the $\frac{yen}{dollar}$ rate. This is plotted for the years 1960 to 2009 in Figure 14.2. As you see in this figure, for the period of time from 1960 to 1970, the nominal rate did not move at all. In fact, it was *fixed* at 360 yen per dollar for this decade.[5] Beginning in 1971, the exchange rate became flexible and began to decline as the yen strengthened against the U.S. dollar or the dollar weakened against the yen. There were periods of volatility within a general strengthening of the yen up until the 1990s. Then the volatility took place within a range of approximately 100 to 130 yen per dollar through 2009.

Our discussion of exchange rates so far has been in terms of two currencies at a time. However, in most cases, a country has significant economic relationships with more than one foreign country, so more than one nominal exchange rate becomes relevant.

[4] The plural of "real" is "reais."

[5] We will consider the difference between fixed and flexible exchange rates in detail in Chapters 15 and 16.

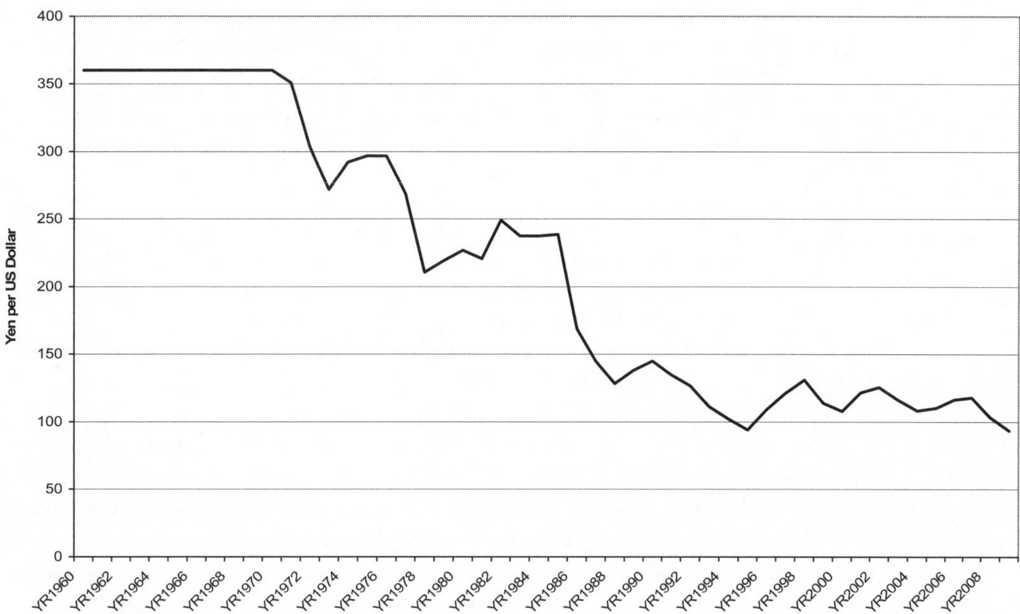

Figure 14.2. The Yen/Dollar Nominal Exchange Rate, 1960 to 2009. *Source:* World Bank, World Development Indicators

This leads us to consider **the effective exchange rate.**[6] To understand this, let's turn back to Mexico and its relationships to the United States and the European Union. Mexico's effective exchange rate (e^{eff}) would be:

$$e^{eff} = a_{US}e_{dollar} + a_{EU}e_{euro} \tag{14.3}$$

Here, e_{dollar} and e_{euro} are the $\frac{peso}{dollar}$ and the $\frac{peso}{euro}$ nominal exchange rates, respectively. The terms a_{US} and a_{EU} are weights that sum to one and determine how much the two nominal exchange rates affect e^{eff} as they change in value. The standard means of determining the weights in Equation 14.3 is via bilateral trade volumes typically measured as the sum of imports and exports to the United States and the European Union, respectively, as a proportion of Mexico's total imports and exports. Recognizing the increasing role of financial relationships in the world economy, however, there has been increased consideration given to asset-related determination of the weights. But the key thing for you to understand is that the effective exchange rate is a means of generalizing the two-country nominal exchange rate for Mexico or any other country across a number of relevant partner countries.

As it turns out, the nominal exchange rate is not the only type of exchange rate that we need to understand in international economics. Just as important is the real exchange rate. Let's consider it next.

THE REAL EXCHANGE RATE

Along with the nominal exchange rate, it is also important to understand a second exchange rate definition, namely the **real exchange rate**. Recall that the nominal exchange rate measures the relative price of two countries' currencies. Another way

[6] The origin of the effective exchange rate is Black (1976), but see also Chin (2009).

Table 14.2 Changes in the real exchange rate

Change	Intuition	Effect in "*re*" equation
P^{US} increases	U.S. goods increase in price. Therefore, it takes more Mexican goods to buy a unit of U.S. goods. The real value of the peso has fallen.	Because it is in the numerator, the increase in P^{US} increases the value of *re*.
P^{M} increases	Mexican goods increase in price. Therefore, it takes fewer Mexican goods to buy a unit of U.S. goods. The real value of the peso has risen.	Because it is in the denominator, the increase in P^{M} decreases the value of *re*.
e increases	It takes more Mexican pesos to buy U.S. dollars. The real value of the peso has fallen.	The increase in *e* increases the value of *re*.

to state this is that it measures the rate at which two countries' currencies trade against each other. In contrast, the real exchange rate measures the rate at which two countries' *goods* trade against each other. Let's distinguish the real exchange rate from the nominal exchange rate in a second box:

> *Nominal exchange rate:* The rate at which two countries' *currencies* trade against each other.
>
> *Real exchange rate:* The rate at which two countries' *goods* trade against each other.

The real exchange rate makes use of the **price levels** in the two countries under consideration. P^M is the overall price level in Mexico (the home country), and P^{US} is the overall price level in the United States (the foreign country). These can be considered to be an average of all the prices in the economy in question. If you are not familiar with the concept of price levels, please see the first appendix to this chapter before continuing with the remainder of this section. If you are already familiar with the price level concept, please continue.

The real exchange rate definition, denoted *re*, is as follows:

$$re = e \times \frac{P^{US}}{P^{M}} \tag{14.4}$$

which is in the form of:

$$re = e \times \frac{P^{foreign}}{P^{home}} \tag{14.5}$$

We have stated that *re* measures the rate at which the two countries' goods trade against each other. More specifically, it measures the amount of Mexican goods that trade against U.S. goods. A formal demonstration of this is provided in the first appendix to this chapter. Here, we show intuitively that this definition makes sense. We do so with the help of Table 14.2.

Suppose that the price level in the United States (P^{US}) rises. It now takes more Mexican goods to purchase U.S. goods. Therefore, there has been a *fall* in the *real* value of the peso. Alternatively, suppose that the price level in Mexico (P^M) rises. It now takes fewer Mexican goods to purchase U.S. goods. Therefore, there has been a *rise* in the *real* value of the peso. Finally, suppose that the nominal exchange rate (e) increases. It now takes more Mexican pesos to buy a U.S. dollar and, therefore, more Mexican goods to buy U.S. goods. There has been a *fall* in the *real* value of the peso. These are the changes presented in Table 14.2.

Given a long-term move in exchange rate arrangements in the world economy toward more flexibility in nominal exchange rates, one can generalize that changes in these nominal exchange rates tend to explain more of the changes in real exchange rates than do changes in price levels. Further, because many nominal exchange rates are rather volatile, so too are real exchange rates.[7]

Finally, just as there was an effective exchange rate for the nominal exchange rate, so is there a **real effective exchange rate** (REER) for the real exchange rate. This multicountry measure would be:

$$re^{eff} = a_{US}re_{dollar} + a_{EU}re_{euro} \tag{14.6}$$

Here the real exchange rates of the peso against the U.S. dollar and the euro are weighted as in Equation 14.3. The REER gives a measure of the rate at which Mexico's goods trade against a number of relevant partners. As such, it is a very important measure in international finance.

We now have an understanding of both nominal and real exchange rates. Public and private analysts keep track of both of these types of exchange rates for countries of interest because they provide different perspectives on the exchange of goods, services, and assets among the countries of the world economy.

PURCHASING POWER PARITY

Closely related to the definition of the real exchange rate is a model of exchange rate determination known as **purchasing power parity** (PPP). The PPP approach to exchange rates begins with the hypothesis that *the nominal exchange rate will adjust so that the purchasing power of a currency will be the same in every country.* This hypothesis is also worth putting in a box:

> **PPP hypothesis:** The nominal exchange rate will adjust so that the purchasing power of a currency will be the same in every country.

Let's explore the implications of this hypothesis. The purchasing power of a currency in a given country is inversely related to the price level in that country. For example, the purchasing power of the peso in Mexico can be expressed as $\frac{1}{P^M}$. The higher the price level in Mexico, the lower the purchasing power of the peso there. The purchasing power of the peso in the United States is a bit more complicated. First, we need the rate at which a peso can be exchanged into dollars. This is $\frac{1}{e}$. Second, we need the purchasing power of a dollar in the United States. This is $\frac{1}{P^{US}}$. Putting these together, we have the purchasing power of a peso in the United States as $(\frac{1}{e}) \times (\frac{1}{P^{US}})$. Now, we can state the PPP hypothesis as follows:

$$\frac{1}{P^M} = \frac{1}{e} \times \frac{1}{P^{US}} \tag{14.7}$$

[7] See Popper (2009), for example.

This equation can be rearranged to give us[8]:

$$e = \frac{P^M}{P^{US}} \tag{14.8}$$

which is in the form of:

$$e = \frac{P^{home}}{P^{foreign}} \tag{14.9}$$

What do Equations 14.8 and 14.9 mean? Suppose that the price level in Mexico, P^M in the numerator, were to increase. According to the PPP model, *e* would therefore increase. The value of the peso would consequently move down the scale in Figure 14.1. Alternatively, suppose that the price level in the United States, P^{US} in the denominator, were to increase. According to the PPP model *e* would decrease. In this case, the value of the peso would move up the scale in Figure 14.1. In this way, the nominal value of the peso adjusts to changes in its real purchasing power in the two countries. Although this makes a great deal of sense, the restrictiveness of the PPP model can be seen when we re-express it in a third equation. We obtain this equation by multiplying both sides of the Equation 14.8 by $(\frac{P^{US}}{P^M})$. This give us:

$$e\frac{P^{US}}{P^M} = 1 \tag{14.10}$$

If we compare Equation 14.10 of the PPP model with Equations 14.4 and 14.5 of the real exchange rate, we can see here that the PPP model is a *special case* of the real exchange rate. More specifically, the PPP theory implies that the real exchange rate is *fixed at unity*. That is, there will not be any change in the real exchange rate. It turns out that real exchange rates *do* change, a humorous case of which is presented in the accompanying box. If the PPP theory implies that real exchange rates do not change, and yet we observe real exchange rates varying in the real world, there must be important elements of the real world that the PPP theory ignores. In fact, some important elements come readily to mind.

Underlying the PPP idea is the assumption that all goods entering into the price levels of both countries are internationally *traded*. It is the traded nature of all the goods in the price levels of both countries that contributes to the strong relationship between price levels and nominal exchange rates expressed in the PPP equations. In fact, however, many goods are *nontraded*. For example, a large part of most economies consists of locally supplied services such as many kinds of cleaning, repairs, and food preparation. These services are not typically traded. The presence of such nontraded goods weakens the PPP relationship.[9] So does the fact that, as discussed in Chapter 1, currency trading is dominated by asset considerations rather than trade considerations.

[8] This equation is known as the "absolute version" of PPP. The "relative version" used in most empirical studies can be stated as: $\%\Delta e = \%\Delta P^M - \%\Delta P^{US}$. In this equation, Δ stands for "change in." This equation relates the percentage change in the nominal exchange rate to the inflation rate difference between the home and foreign country. See, for example, Froot and Rogoff (1996) and chapter 3 of Sarno and Taylor (2002).

[9] As Schnabl (2001) stated: "The more traded, or fewer non-traded goods, are included in the price index, the better the approximation of exchange rates by PPP would be" (p. 37). We will use the concept of nontraded goods in our analysis of structural adjustment in Chapter 24.

The Big Mac Index

In 1986, *The Economist* began to publish an annual test of the PPP theory of exchange rates based on an unusual measure of price levels around the world. This "Big Mac index" measures price levels using just one good, the McDonald's Big Mac hamburger. *The Economist* (2007) described its efforts as follows: "The Big Mac index is based on the theory of purchasing power parity (PPP), according to which exchange rates should adjust to equalize the price of a basket of goods and services around the world. Our basket is a burger: a McDonald's Big Mac." Calculations of this index are given in the accompanying table.

	Big Mac Prices				
Country	In Local Currency	In Dollars	Implied PPP	Actual 2009 exchange rate	Local currency over(+)/ under (–) valuation (%)
United States	$3.54	3.54	–	–	–
Argentina	Peso 11.50	3.30	3.25	3.49	–7
Brazil	Real 8.02	3.45	2.27	2.32	–2
Britain	£2.29	3.30	1.55[a]	1.44[a]	–7
Canada	C$ 4.16	3.36	1.18	1.24	–5
Chile	Peso 1,550	2.51	438	617	–29
China	Yuan 12.5	1.83	3.53	6.84	–48
Euro Area	€3.42	4.38	1.04[a]	1.28[a]	24
Indonesia	Rupiah 19,800	1.74	5,593	11,380	–51
Japan	¥290	3.23	81.9	89.8	–9
Mexico	Peso 33.0	2.30	9.32	14.4	–35
Philippines	Peso 98.0	2.07	27.7	47.4	–42
Russia	Ruble 62.0	1.73	17.5	35.7	–51
South Africa	Rand 16.95	1.66	4.79	10.2	–53
South Korea	Won 3,300	2.39	932	1,380	–32
Thailand	Baht 62.0	1.77	17.5	35.0	–50
Turkey	Lire 5.15	3.13	1.45	1.64	–12

[a] Dollars per pound and per euro. *Note:* The exchange rates may differ from those of Table 14.1, because the latter are more recent.

The Economist first measures the local currency price of Big Macs. These are given in the second column of the table. Next, *The Economist* converts these local currency prices into U.S. dollar terms using nominal exchange rates. These U.S. dollar prices are given in the third column. Dividing each of these U.S. dollar prices by $3.54 (the U.S. price of a Big Mac) gives the implied PPP of the dollar presented in the fourth column. The fifth column presents the actual year 2009 exchange rate. Comparing this to the purchasing power parities gives the degree of overvaluation or undervaluation of the currency according to the Big Mac index. For example, the Euro Area's implied PPP is 1.04, but its actual exchange rate is 1.28. This indicates that the euro is overvalued by 24 percent.

Should we take the Big Mac index seriously? *The Economist* (2000) gleefully noted that "several academic studies have concluded that the Big Mac index is surprisingly accurate in tracking exchange rates over the long term." One of these studies was Ong (1997), and a more recent study is Pakko and Pollard (2003). And if you are not a burger fan, *The Economist* (2004b) introduced a Starbuck's Tall Latte Index, so there is a PPP index for every taste.

There is one more serious issue embedded in the Big Mac index, and that is the case of China, shown to have an undervalued currency by nearly 50 percent in the preceding table. Given concerns over the bilateral trade deficit of the United States with China, this sort of data can have political implications. It is important to keep in mind though the issue of nontradable goods mentioned previously. As noted by Yang (2004), the estimated undervaluation would be less if the nontradable sector in China were better accounted for in the Big Mac index. This point was also made by Parsley and Wei (2007).

Sources: The Economist (2000, 2004b, 2007, 2009), Ong (1997), Pakko and Pollard (2003), Parsley and Wei (2007), and Yang (2004)

Does this imply that the PPP theory is useless? No. It is best to use the following interpretation. The real exchange rate equation captures reality at any point in time; the PPP relationship never holds exactly. The PPP equation, however, give us a sense of a *long-term tendency* toward which nominal exchange rates move *absent other changes.*[10] And, indeed, these PPP equations are in the backs of the minds of currency traders. Before exchange rates have the chance to move fully toward the PPP relationship, however, other changes invariably intervene. This necessitates alternative models of exchange rate determination more appropriate for the *short term* that we consider in Chapters 15 and 16.

EXCHANGE RATES AND TRADE FLOWS

Changes in e, and therefore in the value of the peso, have an impact on trade flows that is important for you to understand. To see this, we consider the case of Mexico's imports and exports. World prices (P^W) are typically in U.S. dollar terms, and Mexican prices (P^M) are in peso terms. The relationship between the Mexican peso and world dollar prices of Mexico's import (Z) goods can be expressed as:

$$P_Z^M = e \times P_Z^W \tag{14.11}$$

P_Z^W is in dollar terms. Multiplying it by e gives us P_Z^M in peso terms. Now, suppose that e were to increase (the value of the peso falls). This movement down the scale in Figure 14.1 increases the peso price of the imported good in Mexico. Following the "law of demand," import demand consequently decreases.[11] Next, suppose e were to decrease (the value of the peso rises). This movement up the scale in Figure 14.1 decreases the peso price of the imported good in Mexico. Import demand consequently increases.

Next, consider the case of Mexico's exports. The relationship between the peso and dollar prices of Mexico's exported (E) goods can be expressed as:

$$P_E^M = e \times P_E^W \tag{14.12}$$

In this equation, P_E^M is the price of Mexican export goods. For a given P_E^M, if e were to increase (the value of the peso falls), P_E^W will fall to maintain equality. The movement down the inverse scale in Figure 14.1 would consequently cause a fall in the world price

[10] For example, Sarno and Taylor (2002) concluded that "The main conclusion emerging from the recent literature on testing the validity of the PPP hypothesis appears to be that PPP might be viewed as a valid long-run international parity condition when applied to bilateral exchange rates among major industrialized countries" (p. 87).

[11] This is similar to the way an increase in the world price of rice would decrease Japan's rice imports in Figure 2.4 in Chapter 2.

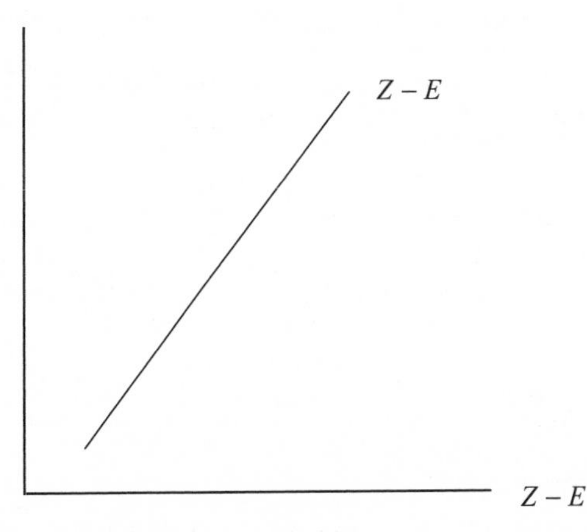

Figure 14.3. The Value of the Peso and Mexico's Trade Deficit

of Mexico's exports. This increases foreign demand for Mexico's goods, and Mexico's exports consequently increase.[12] Next, suppose that e were to decrease (the value of the peso rises). This movement up the inverse scale in Figure 14.1 increases the world price of Mexico's exports, and export demand would consequently decrease.[13]

What we have seen here is that, as the nominal exchange rate increases or the value of the peso falls, imports decrease and exports increase. We can represent these relationships as one between the value of the peso and the trade deficit, $Z - E$. This is done in Figure 14.3. As you can see, there is a *positive* relationship between the value of the peso and the trade deficit. We use this relationship in the remaining chapters of the book in this section on international finance.[14]

The relationship between exchange rates and trade flows is important in its own right as a link between the international trade and international finance windows on the world economy. Therefore, it is one example of the double-headed arrow between the international trade and international finance boxes illustrated in Figure 1.4 of Chapter 1. Further, however, we use Figure 14.3 in a model of exchange rates to be developed in the next two chapters.

HEDGING AND FOREIGN EXCHANGE DERIVATIVES

In Part I of this book, we considered the possibility of firms entering foreign markets via exports. In Part II of this book, on international production, we considered the possibility of firms entering foreign markets via contracting and **foreign direct investment**. If the sales from any of these market-entry strategies are not denominated in the currencies of the firms' home-base countries, issues of **exchange rate exposure** arise. For example, in the introduction to this chapter, we mentioned the impact of a fall in the value of the euro on the dollar value of U.S.-based firms' revenues and the rise of

[12] Alternatively, P_E^W can be thought of as the price of Mexican exports in dollar terms. Multiplying it by e gives us P_E^M in peso terms. Now, suppose that e were to increase (the value of the peso falls). This increases the peso price of the export good in Mexico, and export supply in Mexico consequently increases because Mexican firms now have more of an incentive in peso terms to export. This is similar to the way an increase in the world price of rice would increase Vietnam's exports in Figure 2.4 in Chapter 2.

[13] For a discussion of this process as it has actually affected Mexican exporters, see Malkin (2004).

[14] The graph in Figure 14.3 is not necessarily linear. We draw it that way for simplicity's sake.

Table 14.3 Foreign exchange derivatives

Derivative type	Explanation
Forward contracts	Two parties agree on a foreign exchange transaction to take place at a specified, future date.
Foreign exchange swaps	Two parties exchange currencies for a specified length of time, after which the currency exchange is reversed.
Currency swaps	Two parties exchange interest payments in different currencies for a specified period of time and then exchange principals at a specified maturity date.
Options	A party purchases the right to exchange one currency for another at a specified, future date and at a specified rate.

the value of the euro on the euro value of EU-based firms' revenues. Let's take a closer look at this exposure problem.

Suppose that the €/US$ exchange rate is currently at a value of 1.00. Suppose also that a U.S. firm is expecting euro revenues of €1.0 million. Given the current exchange rate, known as a **spot rate**, the U.S. firm might be expecting dollar revenues of US$1.0 million. Suppose, however, that the euro weakens, and the spot rate moves to $e = 1.25$ (a dollar value of the euro of $0.80). It now takes more euros to purchase a dollar, and the dollar revenues shrink to $800,000. Is there anything the firm can do to overcome this exposure? Possibly, yes, and this brings us to the issue of hedging and foreign exchange derivatives.

The most reliable source of data on foreign exchange derivatives is the Bank of International Settlements (BIS). The BIS distinguishes three categories of foreign exchange derivatives: forwards and foreign exchange swaps, currency swaps, and options. These categories, with forwards and foreign exchange swaps broken out, are defined in Table 14.3. The important thing to notice about each derivative type in this table is that there is a time element involved, an expectation about the future that involves some degree of uncertainty.

A semiannual time series available from the BIS is presented in Figure 14.4 for mid-1998 to mid-2009. Here we see an evolution of foreign exchange derivatives from just under US$20 trillion to a peak of more than $60 trillion in 2008 and to below $50 trillion in 2009. You can also see that most of the derivatives consist of forwards and foreign exchange swaps, with currency swaps and options playing smaller roles. This has been the case throughout the series presented in this figure.

Foreign exchange derivatives are financial instruments that have the effect of "locking in" a forward exchange rate. How can they play a role in hedging exchange rate exposure? Let's get a sense of this by looking at the most fundamental derivative, the **forward rate**. Forward rates are the rates of current contracts for "forward" transactions in currencies, usually for one, three, or six months in the future. If the forward rate of the euro (€/US$) is exactly the same as the spot rate, the euro is said to be "flat." If the forward rate of the euro is above the spot rate, the euro is said to be at a "forward discount." Finally, if the forward rate of the euro is below the spot rate, the euro is said to be at a "forward premium."

Suppose now that we again begin with the exchange rate (€/US$) being currently at a value of 1.00 and that a U.S. firm is expecting euro revenues of €1.0 million in six

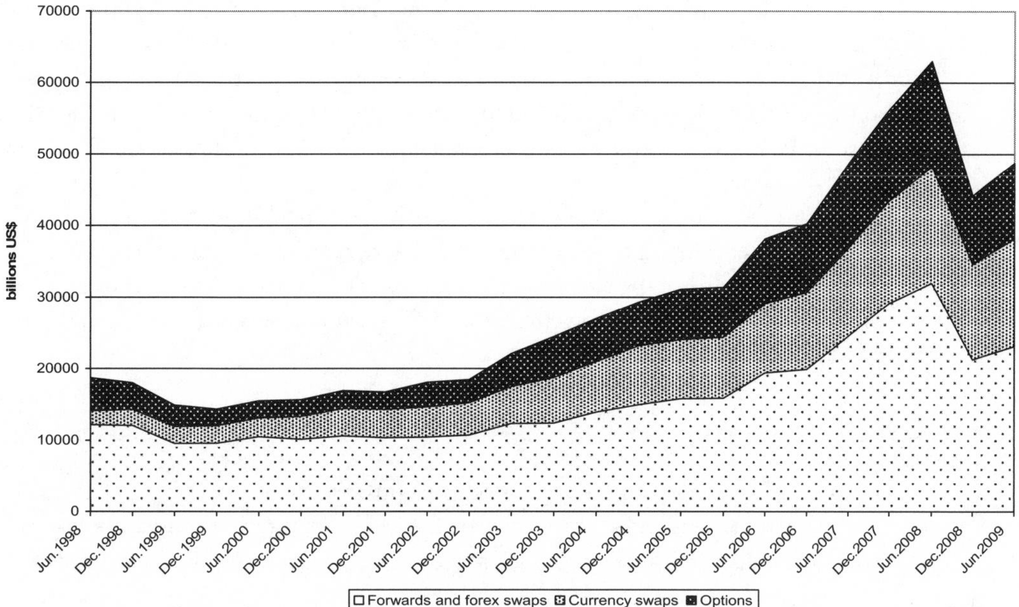

Figure 14.4. Foreign Exchange Derivatives. *Source:* Bank for International Settlements

month's time. Suppose also, though, that the euro is at a six-month forward discount of 1.11. The U.S. firm could take out a forward contract and, at that future time, convert the euro revenue into $900,900 of dollar revenue. Would this be a smart move? If the firm knew with certainty that the future spot rate were to be 1.25 as in the above example, it certainly would be. With the forward contract, the firm would earn $900,900 rather than $800,000. If the future spot rate were actually to be below 1.11, though, it would not. The firm could have earned more than $900,900 without the forward contract.

As becomes apparent even in this simple example, hedging exchange rate exposure requires that firms have expectations or forecasts of future spot rates that they can compare with forward rates. Such forecasts range from the simple (e.g., those based on PPP projections discussed in this chapter) to the complex (e.g., multivariate econometric analysis) and can be either performed in-house or contracted out to a forecasting service. Whatever the approach taken to exchange rate exposure, it is an ever-present problem for those firms engaging in foreign market entry. Indeed, foreign exchange exposure is a key link between the realms of international finance and international production illustrated in Figure 1.4 of Chapter 1.

CONCLUSION

The nominal exchange rate is the relative price of two currencies and is expressed as the number of units of a home currency required to buy a unit of a foreign currency. Another way of stating this is that the nominal exchange rates express the number of units of a home currency trading against a unit of a foreign currency. In contrast, the real exchange rate measures the rate at which two countries' goods trade against each other. The real exchange rate uses the price levels of home and foreign countries to adjust the nominal exchange rate.

The purchasing power parity model of exchange rate determination begins with the idea that *the nominal exchange rate will adjust so that the purchasing power of a currency will be the same in every country.* The PPP model is a restricted version of the real exchange rate definition and applies only in the long run. An extension of the PPP model into the monetary approach to exchange rates is given in the second appendix at the end of this chapter.

Home-country imports have a direct or positive relationship with the value of the currency. Home-country exports, on the other hand, have an inverse or negative relationship with the value of the currency. A country's trade deficit has a direct or positive relationship with the value of the currency. In these ways, the realms of international trade and international finance are linked.

REVIEW EXERCISES

1. Use supply and demand diagrams such as those we used in Chapter 2 to demonstrate why the relationships between the value of the peso and imports and exports illustrated in Figure 14.3 make sense. In doing so, keep in mind that $P^M = eP^W$.
2. Explain the *intuition* of how each of the following changes affect the real exchange rate, re : a fall in P^M, a fall in P^{US}, and a fall in e. In each case, describe the impact of the change on the rate at which Mexican goods trade against U.S. goods.
3. Use the PPP model of exchange rate determination to predict the impact on the nominal exchange rate of the following changes: a fall in P^M and a fall in P^{US}.
4. As shown in Table 14.1, the spot nominal exchange rate for the Canadian dollar was 1.00 in April 2010. What happened to the value of the Canadian dollar during the previous year? What would have to be true of the forward rate for the Canadian dollar to be at a forward premium? A forward discount?

FURTHER READING AND WEB RESOURCES

A good source for the material of this chapter at a slightly more advanced level is Melvin (2003). More advanced treatments are in Hallwood and MacDonald (2000) and Sarno and Taylor (2002). For a review of the real exchange rate, see Popper (2009), and for a review of effective exchange rates, see Chin (2009). For reviews of the PPP model, see Dornbusch (1992) and Froot and Rogoff (1996). A recent discussion of *The Economist* Big Mac Index is given in Pakko and Pollard (2003), and a similar application of PPP analysis to the video game market is given in Cox (2008).

Exchange rate data are available from the International Monetary Fund's publication *International Financial Statistics.* Most important is the annual *Yearbook* in this series. The IFS is also available in an online version to which many libraries have subscribed. It is not user-friendly, but nevertheless is an important source for standardized data. See the website of the International Monetary Fund at www.imf.org.

APPENDIX A: PRICE LEVELS AND THE PPP

In this chapter, we use the concept of price levels in the definition of the real exchange rate and in the purchasing power parity model of exchange rate determination. The purpose of this appendix is to introduce you to the concept of price levels. We do this with reference to a macroeconomic variable defined in Chapter 13, namely income or Y. Recall that, given the simple assumptions of Chapter 13, Y is equal to both the nominal gross domestic product (GDP) and the nominal gross national income (GNI).

Now, suppose that we observed this flow in two years, year 1 and year 2. Suppose also that $Y_2 > Y_1$ or that total nominal income/output is greater in year 2 than in year 1. From this fact, can we conclude that a greater *quantity* of goods and services is produced in this economy in year 2 than in year 1? No, we cannot. It may be that $Y_2 > Y_1$ simply reflects increases in *prices* between year 1 and year 2. The problem we face here is to separate the increase in Y into the part due to an increase in the number of goods and services and the part due to an increase in the prices of goods and services.

In practice, the division of Y into price and quantity components is accomplished through a slightly complex application of *index numbers*. For our purposes here, however, we are going to take a more simple approach. Let's assume that only *one type* of good or service is produced in the economy. Its price is P. Let a lower case y represent the total *quantity* of this good produced in the economy. Whereas Y is known as *nominal* output or income, y is known as *real* output or income. The relationship between nominal and real output or income is given by: $Y = P \times y$. The price level, P, can therefore be calculated as the ratio of nominal to real output or income: $P = \frac{Y}{y}$. This measure of the price level is known as the GDP price deflator. This is the price level measure used in this chapter.

The real exchange rate equation, involving price levels from two countries, is:

$$re = e \times \frac{P^{US}}{P^{M}}$$

To see that this equation actually measures the rate at which Mexico's goods trade against U.S. goods, we can rewrite it as follows:

$$re = \frac{pesos}{dollar} \times \frac{\frac{dollars}{U.S.\ goods}}{\frac{pesos}{Mexican\ goods}}$$

Next, let's rewrite the above equation as follows:

$$re = \frac{pesos}{dollar} \times \frac{dollars}{U.S.\ goods} \times \frac{Mexican\ goods}{pesos} = \frac{Mexican\ goods}{U.S.\ goods} \tag{14.13}$$

As you can see in this last equation, the real exchange rate indeed represents the rate at which Mexican goods trade against U.S. goods.

APPENDIX B: THE MONETARY APPROACH TO EXCHANGE RATE DETERMINATION

There is an approach to monetary theory known as *monetarism*.[15] At the center of this approach we find the *quantity theory of money* expressed as the *equation of exchange*:

$$MV = Py \tag{14.14}$$

[15] The monetarist paradigm has a very long intellectual history. For a review, see De Long (2000).

In this equation, M is the money stock, V is the velocity of money, and P is the overall price level of the economy measured here as the GDP deflator defined in the previous appendix, and y is real output or GDP, also defined in the previous appendix.

Equation 14.14 is an identity that always holds true as a definition. Monetarist thinking adds two assumptions to this equation. The first assumption is that the velocity of money is stable. That is, any changes taking place in V take place very slowly over time.[16] The second assumption is that, in the long run, y is determined by the supply side of the economy, especially the availability of factors of production and the operation of these factor markets. Given these two assumptions, any changes in the stock of money will translate into changes in the price level in the long run. Deviations in this relationship would be due to incremental changes in real output or velocity.

This long-run monetarist relationship can be combined with the long-run purchasing power parity (PPP) relationship of Equation 14.8:

$$e = \frac{P^M}{P^{US}} \tag{14.8}$$

First, we solve the equation of exchange in Equation 14.14 for the price level, once for Mexico and a second time for the United States:

$$P = \frac{MV}{y} \tag{14.15}$$

Substituting these into the real exchange rate equation, we get:

$$e = \frac{\dfrac{M^M V^M}{y^M}}{\dfrac{M^{US} V^{US}}{y^{US}}} = \left(\frac{M^M}{M^{US}}\right)\left(\frac{y^{US}}{y^M}\right)\left(\frac{V^M}{V^{US}}\right) \tag{14.16}$$

Equation 14.16 represents the **monetary approach to exchange rate determination**. Here, the nominal exchange rate is determined primarily by the money stock ratio, secondarily by the real output ratio, and finally by the velocity ratio.[17] Because PPP has validity only in the long run, the monetary approach to exchange rate determination also can only have validity in the long run. There is some evidence for this.[18] The approach can also be helpful in understanding exchange rates during periods of hyperinflation in which the home-country money stock and price level are increasing very rapidly.

REFERENCES

Black, S.W. (1976) "Multilateral and Bilateral Measures of Effective Exchange Rates in a World Model of Traded Goods," *Journal of Political Economy*, 84:3, 615–622.

[16] Empirically, this assumption has proved to not always hold and composes a weak spot of monetarist theory.

[17] This is the absolute version of the monetary approach to exchange rate determination. The relative approach would be $\%\Delta e = (\%\Delta M^M - \%\Delta M^{US}) + (\%\Delta y^{US} - \%\Delta y^M)$ on the assumption that velocity is stable (not a good assumption). In this equation, Δ stands for "change in."

[18] See, for example, Rapach and Wohar (2002). Sarno and Taylor (2002) state that "One finding which does ... seem to have some validity, is that the monetary model does resurface in a number of empirical studies as a *long-run* equilibrium condition. ... This finding itself is not, of course, completely robust, but it occurs with sufficient regularity in the empirical literature as to suggest that we may be observing the emergence of a stylized fact" (p. 137).

Chin, M. (2009) "Effective Exchange Rates," in K.A. Reinert, R.S. Rajan, A.J. Glass, and L.S. Davis (eds.), *The Princeton Encyclopedia of the World Economy*, Princeton University Press, 337–339.

Cox, J. (2008) "Purchasing Power Parity and Cultural Convergence: Evidence from the Global Video Games Market," *Journal of Cultural Economics*, 32:3, 201–214.

De Long, J.B. (2000) "The Triumph of Monetarism?" *Journal of Economic Perspectives*, 14:1, 83–94.

Dornbusch, R. (1992) "Purchasing Power Parity," in D. Newman, M. Milgate, and J. Eatwell (eds.), *The New Palgrave Dictionary of Money and Finance*, Macmillan, 236–244.

The Economist (2000) "Big Mac Currencies," April 29.

The Economist (2004a) "Currency Hedging," February 21.

The Economist (2004b) "The Starbuck's Index: Burgers or Beans?" January 15.

The Economist (2007) "The Big Mac Index," February 1.

The Economist (2009) "Big Mac Index," February 4.

Froot, K.A. and K. Rogoff (1996) "Perspectives on PPP and Long-Run Real Exchange Rates," in G.M. Grossman and K. Rogoff (eds.), *Handbook of International Economics*, Vol. 3, North Holland, 1647–1688.

Hallwood, C.P. and R. MacDonald (2000) *International Money and Finance*, Wiley-Blackwell.

Malkin, E. (2004) "Peso's Rise Pressuring Mexican Exporters," *New York Times*, February 8.

McMurray, S. (2000) "The Lost Art of Hedging," *Institutional Investor*, 34:12, 63–69.

Melvin, M. (2003) *International Money and Finance*, Addison-Wesley.

Ong, L.L. (1997) "Burgernomics: The Economics of the Big Mac Standard," *Journal of International Money and Finance*, 16:6, 865–878.

Pakko, M.R. and P.S. Pollard (2003) "Burgernomics: A Big Mac (TM) Guide to Purchasing Power Parity," *Federal Reserve of St. Louis Review*, 85:6, 9–27.

Parsley, D.C. and S.-J. Wei (2007) "A Prism into the PPP Puzzles: The Micro-Foundations of Big Mac Real Exchange Rates," *Economic Journal*, 117:523, 1336–1356.

Popper, H. (2009) "Real Exchange Rate," in K.A. Reinert, R.S. Rajan, A.J. Glass, and L.S. Davis (eds.), *The Princeton Encyclopedia of the World Economy*, Princeton University Press, 955–957.

Rapach, D.E. and M.E. Wohar (2002) "Testing the Monetary Model of Exchange Rate Determination: New Evidence from a Century of Data," *Journal of International Economics*, 58:2, 359–385.

Sarno, L. and M.P. Taylor (2002) *The Economics of Exchange Rates*, Cambridge University Press.

Schnabl, G. (2001) "Purchasing Power Parity and the Yen/Dollar Exchange Rate," *The World Economy*, 24:1, 31–50.

Tully, K. (2000) "Feeling Over-Exposed," *Corporate Finance*, 194, 47.

Yang, J. (2004) "Nontradables and the Valuation of the RMB: An Evaluation of the Big Mac Index," *China Economic Review*, 15:3, 353–359.

15 Flexible Exchange Rates

In 1998, a student was in my office complaining about increases in tuition payments. Naively, I said, "But tuition did not increase very much this past year." The student responded: "In Canadian dollars it has!" My mistake. The forces of supply and demand in currency markets determine the exchange rate of the Canadian dollar to the U.S. dollar (the nominal rate). This is one example of a **flexible** or **floating exchange rate regime**. The Canadian dollar began the decade of the 1990s at 1.651 per U.S. dollar. By 1998, it was trading at 2.155 per U.S. dollar.[1] In dollar value terms, this was a fall from 61 U.S. cents to 46 U.S. cents. With an income in Canadian dollars, this student's family was having a difficult time making payments for tuition in the United States.

What makes a flexible exchange rate move one way or another? In this chapter, we help you answer this question by developing a model of how the *nominal* exchange rate is determined in currency markets. To begin, we consider a *trade-based* model in which the nominal exchange rate is determined by currency transactions arising from imports and exports. We then extend this model to account for the exchange of *assets*. This **assets-based approach** to exchange rate determination is a more modern, and sophisticated, model of exchange rate determination. It will give you a picture of how the current and capital accounts interact in determining the value of currencies.

In Chapter 14, we also developed a model of exchange rate determination, the **purchasing power parity model**. Recall that this model was best interpreted as a model applying to the *long run*. The models we develop in this chapter, however, are best applied in the *short run* to describe the week-to-week or month-to-month movements in flexible exchange rates among the countries of the world.

Analytical elements for this chapter:

Countries, *currencies*, and *financial assets*.

A TRADE-BASED MODEL

In Chapter 13, we used the circular flow diagram to develop open-economy accounts. In doing this, we came up with an important relationship, namely:

$$\text{Foreign Savings} = \text{Trade Deficit} \tag{15.1}$$

This relationship was one part of the **fundamental accounting equations** developed in that chapter.

What we need to do in this chapter is to rewrite the relationship of Equation 15.1 in terms of symbols introduced in Figure 13.2 of Chapter 13. These were S_F (foreign savings), Z (imports), and E (exports). The rewritten relationship is:

$$S_F = (Z - E) \tag{15.2}$$

We will use this relationship to create a model of nominal exchange rate determination. We begin in this section with a *trade-based model*. In building our model, we maintain Mexico as our home country and the United States as our foreign country, as we did in Chapter 14.

[1] Recall from Chapter 14 that, in April 2010, the Canadian dollar was valued at exactly 1.00 per U.S. dollar, a significant increase in value. Perhaps the student should think about another graduate degree in the United States!

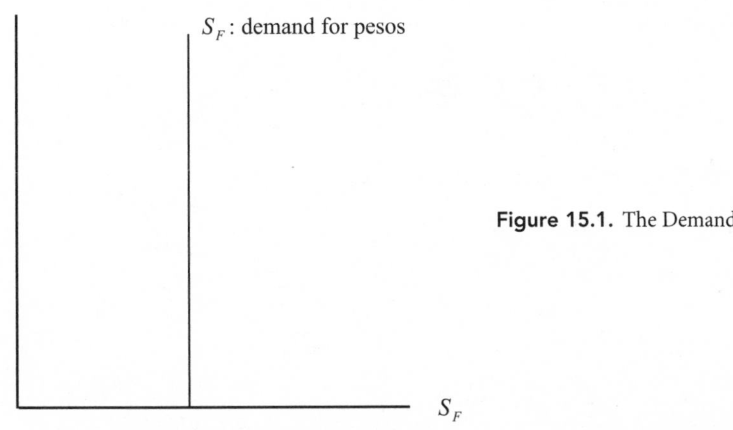

Figure 15.1. The Demand for Pesos

S_F is foreign savings. This is savings supplied by U.S. residents who buy Mexican assets. Consequently, S_F is a *demand for pesos* (or supply of dollars) by the United States. In our trade-based model, this demand for pesos is invariant with respect to the value of the peso. This gives us the *perfectly inelastic* demand for pesos curve represented in Figure 15.1.[2]

$Z - E$ is the trade deficit. The trade deficit is a net demand for U.S. goods by Mexico. It is therefore a *supply of pesos* (or demand for dollars) by Mexico. Before examining this supply side of the peso market, let's summarize what we have stated here for you to remember:

S_F (foreign savings) $\Leftrightarrow$ *demand* for pesos (supply of dollars)
$Z - E$ (trade deficit) $\Leftrightarrow$ *supply* of pesos (demand for dollars)

In Chapter 14, we showed that Z has a positive relationship to the value of the peso and that E has a negative relationship to the value of the peso. Because Z and E have positive and negative relationships, respectively, to the value of the peso, $Z - E$ has a positive relationship to the value of the peso. As the value of the peso increases, the trade deficit expands. This upward-sloping supply of pesos graph is represented in Figure 15.2. As you can see, there is a *positive* relationship between the value of the peso and the trade deficit and therefore between the value of the peso and the supply of pesos.

Our next step in constructing a trade-based model of exchange rate determination is to combine the demand for pesos with the supply of pesos, as in Figure 15.3.[3] We also need to specify the way in which the exchange rate adjusts. In this chapter, we are considering the case of a *flexible exchange rate regime.* This is the case where e can vary in response to excess supply of or excess demand for pesos. In the case of flexible exchange rates, we also need to introduce some terminology for changes in e. These

[2] Recall from introductory microeconomics that elasticities are ratios of percentage changes between two economic variables. The term *perfectly inelastic* means that the value of the elasticity is zero. That is, there is no response of one economic variable to another. In this particular case the percentage change in S_F is zero no matter what the percentage change in $1/e$ happens to be.

[3] Trade surpluses can arise in Figure 15.3 by placing the 0 value toward the middle of the horizontal axis rather than at its left end.

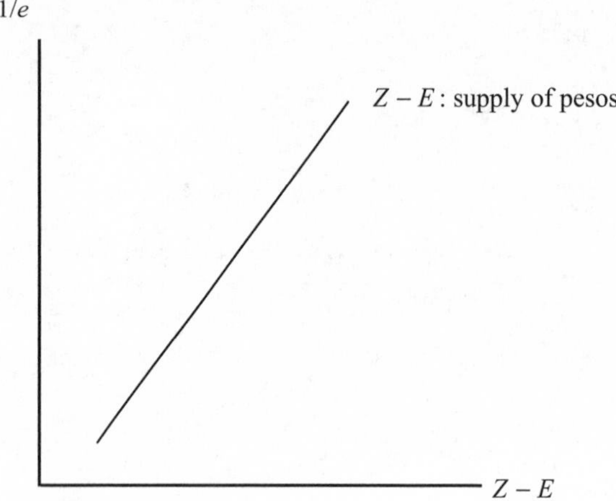

Figure 15.2. The Supply of Pesos.

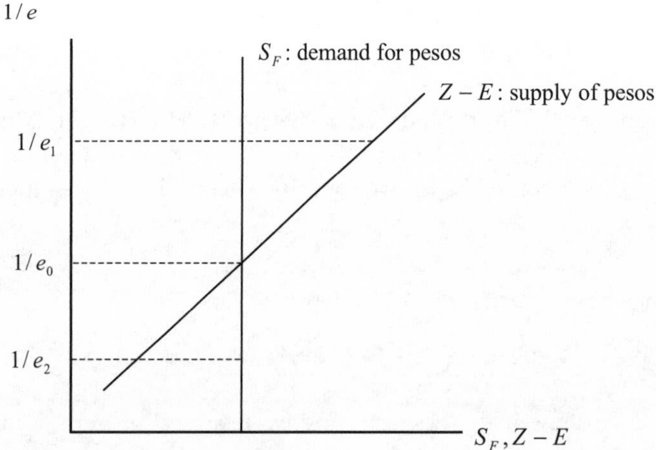

Figure 15.3. The Peso Market

definitions are given in Table 15.1. As shown in this table, under a flexible exchange rate regime, an increase in e or a fall in the value of the peso is called a **depreciation** of the peso. A decrease in e or a rise in the value of the peso is called an **appreciation** of the peso.[4] With this terminology in hand, we can begin to address Figure 15.3.

Under our assumption of a flexible exchange rate regime, let's consider three alternative values of the peso in Figure 15.3. The first of these is $1/e_1$. At $1/e_1$, we can see that the supply of pesos along $Z - E$ exceeds the demand for pesos along S_F. In other words, there is an *excess supply* of pesos. The presence of an excess supply of pesos has the effect of reducing the value of the peso or causing a depreciation of the peso. As the peso depreciates, the trade deficit falls, and it is this fall in the trade deficit that brings the supply and demand of pesos into equality. Next, consider $1/e_2$. At $1/e_2$, we can see that the demand for pesos exceeds the supply of pesos. In other words, there is an *excess demand* for pesos. The presence of an excess demand for pesos has the effect of increasing the value of the peso or causing an appreciation of the peso. As the peso

[4] We will consider alternative exchange rate regimes in Chapter 16, where we will expand Table 15.1 .

Table 15.1. Exchange rate terminology

Case	e	Value of Peso	Term
Flexible e	↑	↓	Depreciation
Flexible e	↓	↑	Appreciation

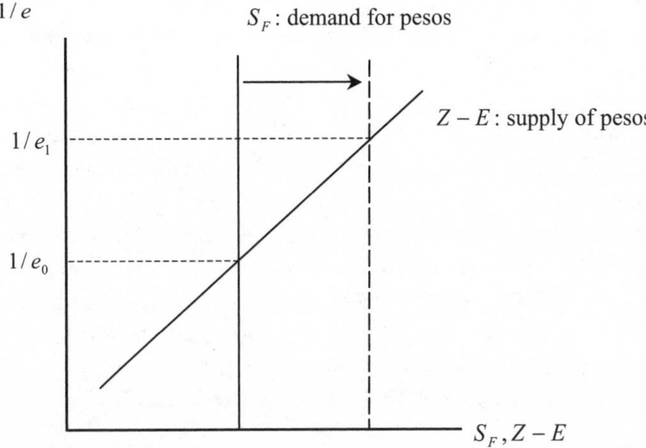

Figure 15.4. Capital Inflows and the Peso Market

appreciates, the trade deficit rises, and the rise in the trade deficit brings the supply and demand of pesos into equality.

Finally, consider $1/e_0$. Here the demand for and supply of pesos are exactly the same. For this reason, $1/e_0$ is the equilibrium value of the peso, and e_0 is the equilibrium nominal exchange rate. The adjustment of the value of the peso ensures that the trade deficit equals foreign savings.

We can use the trade-based model of Figure 15.3 to analyze one aspect of increased global financial integration, namely the possibility of *capital inflows*.[5] We do this in Figure 15.4. Here we begin in equilibrium in the market for pesos with an equilibrium value of the peso of $1/e_0$. From this initial equilibrium, an inflow of capital in the form of foreign savings shifts the S_F curve to the right. At the equilibrium value of the peso, $1/e_0$, the demand for pesos represented by S_F exceeds the supply of pesos represented by $Z - E$. Given this excess demand for pesos, the value of the peso will begin to increase toward $1/e_1$. That is, there will be an appreciation of the peso (see Table 15.1). As this occurs, the trade deficit will expand along the $Z - E$ graph, and the supply of pesos will therefore increase to meet the demand at $1/e_1$.

Of course, this process can (and does) go in reverse. We could just as easily examine capital outflows in Figure 15.4 to see how they contribute to a depreciation of the peso. Capital outflows contribute to the crises we will examine in Chapter 18.

The preceding model of exchange rate determination is trade-based in the sense that only trade flows respond to a change in the value of the peso. In the next section, we allow foreign savings to adjust to changes in the value of the peso, leading us to an

[5] A thorough analysis of capital inflows can be found in chapter 15 of Montiel (2003).

assets-based model. Theory is not everything, however. For a view from a trading desk, see the accompanying box.

Theory and Practice

Professor Richard Lyons, currently Dean of the Haas School of Business at the University of California Berkeley, is an expert on exchange rate theory. He was in for a surprise when he was invited by a friend to experience currency trading first-hand:

"A friend of mine who trades spot foreign exchange for a large bank invited me to spend a few days at his side. That was ten years ago. At the time I considered myself an expert, having written my thesis on exchange rates. I thought I had a handle on how it worked. I thought wrong. As I sat there my friend traded furiously, all day long, racking up over \$1 billion in trades each day (\$US). This was a world where the standard trade was \$10 million, and a \$1 million trade was a 'skinny one.' Despite my belief that exchange rates depend on macroeconomics, only rarely was news of this type his primary concern. Most of the time he was reading tea leaves that were, at least to me, not so clear. The pace was furious – a quote every 5 or 10 seconds, a trade every minute or two, and continual decisions about what position to hold. Needless to say, there was little time for chat. It was clear my understanding was incomplete when he looked over, in the midst of his fury, and asked me 'What should I do?' I laughed. Nervously."

Source: Lyons (2001)

AN ASSETS-BASED MODEL

The **assets approach** to exchange rate determination views foreign currency transactions as arising from the buying and selling of foreign currency–denominated *assets*, rather than just from trade flows.[6] In other words, it focuses on foreign savings rather than on the trade deficit in the $S_F = (Z - E)$ relationship. To introduce this approach into our model, pretend that you are a Mexican investor, deciding on the allocation of your wealth portfolio between two assets: a peso-denominated asset and a dollar-denominated asset. To make things simple, we take both assets to be open-ended mutual funds with fixed domestic-currency prices.[7] As with all investors, you will allocate your portfolio with an eye to the rates of return of the alternative assets. Let's consider each asset in turn.

In the case of peso-denominated assets, the return you obtain is simply the interest rate. We denote this rate of interest as r_M. Thus *the total expected return on the peso-denominated asset,* R_M^e, is simply:

$$R_M^e = r_M \tag{15.3}$$

Because you are a Mexican investor, dollar-denominated assets are a bit more complicated. There are two things you must consider. The first is the interest payment on

[6] The assets approach to exchange rate determination is sometimes referred to as the *portfolio balance model* (see Chapter 4 of Sarno and Taylor, 2002). An early source on this model is Branson and Henderson (1985). See also Chapter 6 of Isard (1995).

[7] Because additional shares of open-ended mutual funds are issued on demand, their supply curves are horizontal. Changes in demand therefore do not affect their prices. Readers in the United States, please be careful. You are pretending to be a Mexican investor, not a U.S. investor.

the dollar-denominated assets. This rate of interest we denote r_{US}. The second consideration is the exchange rate. To see this, suppose that the initial exchange rate is $e_1 = 1.0$. Suppose also that, at this exchange rate, you purchase a dollar-denominated asset worth \$1,000. This asset is worth 1,000 pesos. Now suppose that the peso depreciates so that the new exchange rate is $e_2 = 1.1$. With this change, the \$1,000 asset has increased in value to 1,100 pesos. Depreciation of the peso causes the foreign asset's value to increase in terms of the peso. You have experienced a **capital gain** in peso terms. This, along with interest payments, is what investors (including you) are looking for.

At any point in time, the current exchange rate is at a value e. Also, at any point in time, you have your *expectation* of what the exchange rate will be in the future. We denote this *expected exchange rate* as e^e. Therefore, your *expected rate of depreciation of the peso* is given by:

$$\frac{(e^e - e)}{e}$$

Finally, your expected total rate of return on dollar-denominated assets is the sum of the interest rate and the expected rate of depreciation of the peso. We denote this *total expected rate of return on dollar-denominated assets* as R^e_{US}. This is given as follows:

$$R^e_{US} = r_{US} + \frac{(e^e - e)}{e} \tag{15.4}$$

This relationship tells us that your total expected rate of return on dollar-denominated assets is composed of the interest rate plus the expected rate of depreciation of the peso.

We now have expressions for your total expected return on both peso- and dollar-denominated assets. Next, we need to think about how you will allocate your portfolio between these two asset types. To help us along, we are going to consider three alternative possibilities.

The first possibility is that $R^e_M > R^e_{US}$. That is, the expected total rate of return on peso-denominated assets exceeds the expected total rate of return on dollar-denominated assets. What will you do in this case? Because peso-denominated assets offer a higher expected rate of return, you will *reallocate* your portfolio toward these assets, selling dollars and buying pesos in the process.

The second possibility is that $R^e_M < R^e_{US}$. That is, the expected total rate of return on dollar-denominated assets exceeds the expected total rate of return on peso-denominated assets. In this case, you will reallocate your portfolio toward dollar-denominated assets, buying dollars and selling pesos in the process.

The third possibility is that $R^e_M = R^e_{US}$. In this case, there is no reason or incentive for you to reallocate your portfolio. You would gain nothing by doing so. Time to relax!

As we have just seen, whenever R^e_M and R^e_{US} are not equal, there will be reason for you to reallocate your portfolio between dollar-denominated and peso-denominated assets. These reallocations cause the buying of one currency and the selling of another. *Equilibrium* in the foreign exchange market, in the sense that there is no reason for you (or any other investors) to reallocate your portfolio, requires that $R^e_M = R^e_{US}$. This entails that Equations 15.3 and 15.4 are equal to one another:

$$r_M = r_{US} + \frac{(e^e - e)}{e} \tag{15.5}$$

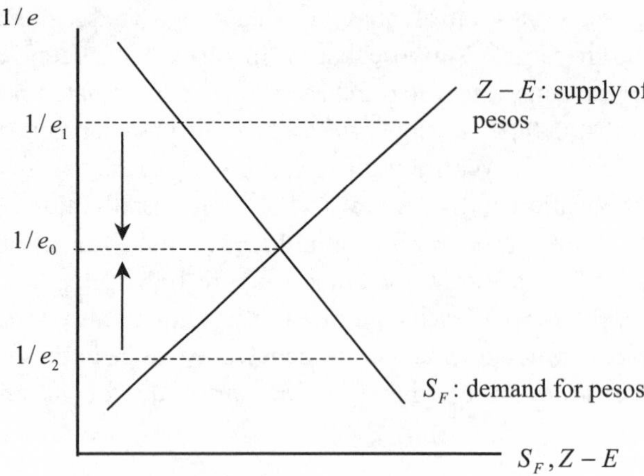

Figure 15.5. An Assets-Based View of the Peso Market

This equation is known as the **interest rate parity condition.**[8] It states that equilibrium in the foreign exchange market requires that the interest rate on peso deposits equals the interest rate on dollar deposits plus the expected rate of peso depreciation. Because it is one of the most important relationships in international finance, we have put it in a box to help you remember[9]:

Interest Rate Parity Condition

$$r_M = r_{US} + \frac{(e^e - e)}{e} \quad \text{Mexico/United States}$$

$$r_H = r_F + \frac{(e^e - e)}{e} \quad \text{Home/Foreign}$$

We are now going to incorporate the interest rate parity condition into a new version of Figure 15.3, the peso market. We begin by focusing on the role of the value of the peso in the interest rate parity condition. Suppose that, initially, we are in equilibrium so that $R_M^e = R_{US}^e$. Next suppose the value of the peso increases or e falls. *For a given expected future exchange rate* (e^e), the total expected rate of return on the dollar-denominated asset, R_{US}^e, increases because, as e falls, $\frac{(e^e-e)}{e}$ increases in value. Because now $R_{US}^e > R_M^e$, you, along with other investors from all other countries, would sell peso-denominated assets and buy dollar-denominated assets. S_F, the asset-based demand for pesos consequently declines. Therefore, we have shown that, for a given e^e, as e falls (and $1/e$ rises), S_F falls. This gives us the *downward-sloping* demand curve for pesos presented in Figure 15.5.

[8] Technically, this condition is known as the *uncovered interest parity condition* or UIP. The term *uncovered* refers to the fact that it assumes that investors are not making use of forward exchange markets. When investors do make use of these forward markets, the *covered interest parity condition* (CIP) comes into play. We consider the difference further in a box below.

[9] In practice, violations of the interest parity condition can arise in the form of what is known as the *carry trade.* Here a currency trade borrows in a low interest rate country to purchase foreign exchange in a high interest rate country hoping to earn returns *above* that described by the interest rate parity condition. This activity was significant from 2002 through the beginning of the 2007 crisis. See *The Economist* (2009) and Adams (2009).

To understand the adjustment process in this expanded view of the peso market, let's again consider three alternative values of the peso. The first of these is $1/e_1$. At $1/e_1$, we can see that the supply of pesos exceeds the demand for pesos. Given this surplus or excess supply of pesos, the value of the peso falls. The fall in the value of the peso (rise in e) does two things:

1. The trade deficit falls as Z decreases and E increases. This decreases the supply of pesos.
2. Foreign saving rises as the expected rate of depreciation of the peso and, therefore, the expected total rate of return on dollar-denominated assets falls. Investors move into the peso-denominated asset, and this increases the demand for pesos.[10]

Both of these changes bring the peso market toward equilibrium. Next, consider the value of the peso $1/e_2$. At $1/e_2$, we can see that the demand for pesos exceeds the supply of pesos. Given this shortage or excess demand for pesos, the value of the peso rises. The rise in the value of the peso (fall in e) does two things:

1. The trade deficit rises as Z increases and E decreases. This increases the supply of pesos.
2. Foreign savings falls as the expected rate of depreciation of the peso and, therefore, the expected total rate of return on dollar-denominated assets rises. Investors move out of the peso-denominated asset into the dollar-denominated asset, and this decreases the demand for pesos.[11]

Finally, at e_0, the demand for and supply of pesos are equal. The peso market is in equilibrium.

Recall from Chapter 1 that the volume of foreign exchange transactions vastly exceeds the volume of trade transactions. This points to the weakness of the trade-based model of exchange rate determination and to the relative strength of the assets-based approach. This fact was effectively described by Montiel (2003):

> The important fact is that the demand for foreign exchange and supply of foreign exchange that arise from the buying and selling of financial assets are much larger than those that arise from the buying of goods and services. The implication of this situation is that, for the exchange market to be in equilibrium, agents have to be willing to hold the existing composition of their portfolios between assets dominated in foreign exchange and assets dominated in domestic currency. The nominal exchange rate must adjust to make it so. (p. 355)

We have shown how this is so, but we still have some distance to go to fully appreciate the assets-based model of exchange rate determination. An important, remaining issue is the role of changes in interest rates and shifts of expectations in the model. We next turn to these interesting and important factors.

INTEREST RATES, EXPECTATIONS, AND EXCHANGE RATES

To appreciate the role of interest rates and expectations in the determination of flexible exchange rates, we need to return to the interest rate parity condition of Equation 15.5.

[10] It is important to remember that this effect is *for a given* e^e.
[11] Again, it is important to remember that this effect is *for a given* e^e.

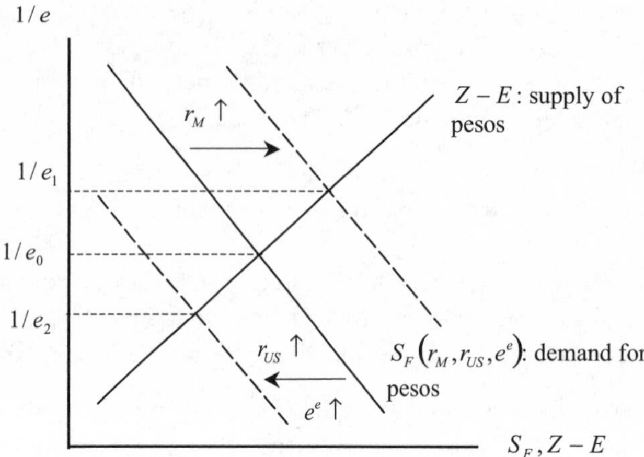

Figure 15.6. Interest Rates and the Peso Market

Note that, in this equation, an increase in r_M increases the total expected rate of return on peso-denominated assets, and an increase in r_{US} increases the total expected rate of return on dollar-denominated assets. Both of these changes will impact the peso market. To understand how this occurs, we need to recognize the role of r_M and r_{US} as variables that *shift the demand for peso curve.* This is done in Figure 15.6.[12]

We begin in equilibrium in Figure 15.6 with the value of the peso equal to $1/e_0$. From this initial equilibrium, suppose that r_M increases. This increases the total expected rate of return on peso-denominated assets. There is an *increase in demand for pesos,* which shifts the demand curve to the right and raises the value of the peso to $1/e_1$. This is an interest rate-caused capital inflow that expands the trade deficit via the exchange rate. An increase in the Mexican (home-country) interest rate causes an appreciation of the Mexican (home-country) currency in a flexible exchange rate regime.

Next, suppose that r_{US} increases. This increases the total expected rate of return on dollar-denominated assets. There is a *decrease in demand for pesos,* which shifts the demand curve to the left and lowers the value of the peso to $1/e_2$. This is an interest rate-caused capital outflow that contracts the trade deficit via the exchange rate. An increase in the U.S. (foreign-country) interest rate causes a depreciation of the Mexican (home-country) currency in a flexible exchange rate regime. For a more complete discussion of monetary policies and their link to exchange rates via interest rates, see the appendix.

A final remaining issue in the assets-based model of exchange rate determination is a *change in expectations.* The interest rate parity condition involves expectations about future exchange rates. These expectations are formed in the minds of investors and are therefore subjective. Suppose, for example, that the expected future exchange rate, e^e, were to increase in the minds of investors. Let's consider the effect of this change in Figure 15.6. Just like an increase in r_{US}, this would increase the total expected rate of return on dollar-denominated assets. There is a consequent decrease in demand for pesos, which shifts the demand curve to the left and lowers the value of the peso to $1/e_2$.

[12] As a general principle, when a relevant explanatory variable is not on the axis of a graph, changes in that variable *shift* the graph. This was true, for example, of nonprice variables affecting supply and demand in Chapter 2 on absolute advantage, as well as the non-relative-wage variables affecting emigration supply and immigration demand in Chapter 12.

This is an expectations-caused capital outflow, which contracts the trade deficit via the exchange rate. An increase in the expected future exchange rate for Mexico's (home-country's) currency causes a depreciation of Mexico's (the home-country's) currency in a flexible exchange rate regime.

Covered vs. Uncovered Interest Rate Parity

The interest rate parity condition introduced in this chapter is one of the most important relationships in international finance. In practice, this relationship comes in two varieties: uncovered interest rate parity (UIP) and covered interest rate parity (CIP). The variety we have been working with in this chapter is the UIP. In terms of home/foreign countries, we express it as:

$$r_H = r_F + \frac{(e^e - e)}{e}$$

That is, the home-country interest rate equals the foreign-country interest rate plus the rate of depreciation of the home-country currency.

CIP is expressed in terms of something we discussed in Chapter 14, namely the **forward rate**. The CIP is expressed as:

$$r_H = r_F + \frac{(e^f - e)}{e}$$

where e^f is the forward rate of the home-country currency and the expression $\frac{(e^f - e)}{e}$ is the *forward discount rate.*

In actual practice, forward rate traders do make use of interest rates and spot exchange rates in the transactions on forward markets. Consequently, CIP is considered to hold nearly exactly. The question is whether the UIP relationship also holds, and investigations into this issue typically compare expected and forward rates. If UIP is to hold, expected rates should be very close to forward rates. There is evidence that this is the case at time horizons of longer than one year. Deviations of expected and forward rates are sometimes interpreted in terms of *risk discounts* and *risk premia* (depending on the direction) in the UIP relationship, reflecting the extra returns demanded by investors when holding assets denominated in a particular currency.

Sources: Sarno and Taylor (2002) and Chinn (2006, 2009)

An important point here is that, in a number of circumstances, expectations can change rapidly. Furthermore, they can change rapidly in response to noneconomic (e.g., political) events. As we will discuss further in Chapter 18 on crises, changes in expectations can be *self-fulfilling* in foreign exchange markets. This causes a certain amount of instability, a continual difficulty for countries around the world. We mentioned in Chapter 14 that much of the volatility in real exchange rates is due to volatility in nominal exchange rates. In turn, much of the volatility in nominal (and therefore real) exchange rates is due to changes in expectations.

The above insights concerning interest rates and expectations are very important for your understanding of how currency markets operate in flexible exchange rate regimes. For this reason, we summarize them in Table 15.2. So that you might generalize these insights, this table is in terms of a home and foreign country rather than in terms of Mexico and the United States. Please take a close look at this table. The accompanying

Table 15.2. Changes in currency markets

Change	Effect on S_F curve	Effect on value of home currency (1/*e*)	Term
Increase in home-country interest rate	Shifts to right	Increases	Appreciation
Increase in foreign-country interest rate	Shifts to left	Decreases	Depreciation
Increase in expected future home-country exchange rate	Shifts to left	Decreases	Depreciation

box on types of interest rate parity conditions also considers the empirical role of expectations in the interest parity condition.

CONCLUSION

The purchasing power parity model of exchange rate determination that we considered in Chapter 14 applies only in the long run. In order to understand the short-run behavior of nominal exchange rates, we have the trade-based and asset-based models. The trade-based model focuses on the response of $(Z - E)$ to changes in the nominal exchange rate, whereas the assets-based model focuses on the response of *both* $(Z - E)$ *and* S_F to changes in the nominal exchange rate. The assets-based model is expressed as the interest rate parity condition. Expected future exchange rates play an important role in this condition and hence in the determination of nominal exchange rates. This makes flexible exchange rates, our focus in this chapter, very volatile in practice. We take up alternatives to flexible exchange rates in Chapter 16.

REVIEW EXERCISES

1. As we will discuss in some detail in Chapter 19, in 1999, the European Union introduced a common currency known as the euro. Take the EU as your home country and the United States as your foreign country. In this case, $e = \frac{euros}{dollar}$. Set up the equivalent of Figure 15.5 to show the determination of *e*. Next, use three additional diagrams to show the impacts on *e* of the following changes: a fall in the euro interest rate; a fall in the dollar interest rate; and a fall in the expected value of the exchange rate (e^e). In each case, *explain the intuition of your result.*
2. In Chapter 14, we discussed the links between trade flows and the nominal exchange rate. All other things constant, what would an *increase* in a home country's interest rate tend to do to its exports, imports, and trade deficit? Explain the intuition of your answer.
3. In Chapter 14, we discussed the links between trade flows and the nominal exchange rate. All other things constant, what would a *decrease* in a home country's interest rate tend to do to its exports, imports, and trade deficit? Explain the intuition of your answer.
4. For Appendix readers only. For the euro example of Question 1 above, set up the equivalent of Figure 15.9. Next, show the impacts in this figure of a contractionary monetary policy in the EU and a contractionary monetary policy in the United States. In each case, *explain the intuition of your results.*

FURTHER READING AND WEB RESOURCES

An introduction to exchange rate economics can be found in Isard (1995), and a more advanced treatment can be found in Sarno and Taylor (2002). The assets approach to exchange rate determination is discussed in Branson and Henderson (1985), in chapter 6 of Isard (1995), and in Chinn (2009). Monetary theory, taken up in the appendix, was effectively reviewed many years ago by Harris (1981). Finally, an important source in international macroeconomics is Montiel (2003).

Exchange rate data are available from the International Monetary Fund's publication *International Financial Statistics.* Most important is the annual *Yearbook* in this series. The IFS is also available in an online version to which many libraries have subscribed. It is not user-friendly, but nevertheless is an important source for standardized data. See the website of the International Monetary Fund at www.imf.org.

APPENDIX: MONETARY POLICIES AND THE NOMINAL EXCHANGE RATE

Some readers of this book will be familiar with the macroeconomic topic of monetary policies from a course on macroeconomics. If this is the case for you, you will be able to extend our analysis of this chapter to an understanding of the link between monetary policies, interest rates, and exchange rates. This is the purpose of this appendix.

In December 1935, the British economist John Maynard Keynes finished writing his *General Theory of Employment, Interest and Money.* Among other things, this book proposed a new theory of **money demand** that we utilize here.[13] Keynes' theory of money demand will help you understand where the interest rates in the interest parity condition come from and then to understand the impact of monetary policies on exchange rates.

To begin, we need to define some notation. M^D denotes **money demand** in the country in question. This is the amount of money households want to hold at any particular time. M^S denotes money supply in the country in question, and this value is determined by the monetary authority (central bank or treasury) of the country. We need to ask ourselves why households want to hold money. One obvious reason is that they hold money in order to conduct the economic transactions of everyday life. Keynes and other economists hypothesized that these transaction demands for money would increase as the income of the economy increased. As in Chapter 13, we denote this income as Y. M^D is related *positively* to Y. However, like all economic decisions, holding money has opportunity costs associated with it. When a household holds money, it forgoes the interest it could be earning if the money were put into an interest-bearing deposit. Unlike his predecessors, Keynes hypothesized that M^D would therefore be *negatively* related to the interest rate. The higher the interest rate, the more households would economize on money holdings, and the less money they would hold.

We want to summarize the above considerations in a *money demand function.* This function is as follows:

$$M^D = L(Y, r) \tag{15.6}$$

[13] An excellent overview of monetary theory can be found in Harris (1981). Harris discusses Keynes' contribution to money demand theory in chapter 9 of his book. As Skidelsky (1992, chapter 14) notes, this theory was first developed in lectures Keynes gave in the Autumn of 1933.

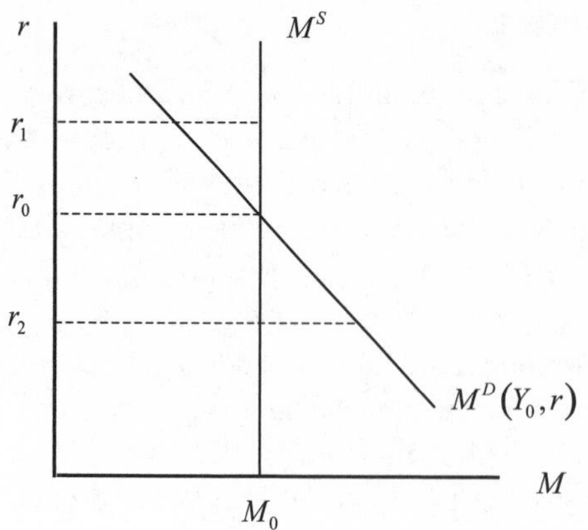

Figure 15.7. The Money Market

Money demand in Equation 15.6 is a function of income and the interest rate. The function itself is usually denoted as L (), where L stands for *liquidity*. To be in possession of money is to be financially liquid. As we described above, theory tells us that $\frac{\Delta M^D}{\Delta Y}$ is positive, whereas $\frac{\Delta M^D}{\Delta r}$ is negative.[14] Money demand is positively related to income but negatively related to the interest rate.

As we mentioned previously, we will assume that the money supply, M^S, is set by the central bank or treasury of the country in question. Although the money-supply process is not this straightforward in the real world, we will ignore any complications here in order to focus on our primary objective in this chapter: exchange rate determination.[15] We want to bring money demand and money supply into a single diagram. This diagram has money on the horizontal axis and the interest rate on the vertical axis and is depicted in Figure 15.7.

The money supply does not vary with the rate of interest. Therefore, the M^S curve is vertical. Money demand varies inversely with the rate of interest. This gives the negative slope to the M^D curve in the diagram. The position of the M^D curve, that is, how far to the left or right it lies in the diagram, depends on the level of income. The M^D curve in Figure 15.7 has been drawn for an initial income level, Y_0. Given this income level and the initial money supply, $M^S = M_0$, the interest rate is r_0. If the interest rate were to be above r_0 at r_1, there would be *excess supply* of money. This would put downward pressure on the interest rate. As the interest rate falls, the opportunity cost of holding money would also fall, increasing money demand to meet money supply. If the interest rate were to be below r_0 at r_2, there would be *excess demand* for money. This would put upward pressure on the interest rate. As the interest rate rises, the opportunity cost of holding money would also rise, decreasing money demand to meet money supply.

Figure 15.7 gives us a description of the equilibrium in the money market. Let's try to determine whether it provides any intuitive explanations of the link between monetary policy and the interest rate. Suppose that the central bank of the country decided to engage in an *expansionary monetary policy* by increasing M^S. This change is depicted

[14] As elsewhere in this book, " Δ " denotes "change in."

[15] It is often the case that, instead of targeting M^S as suggested in our diagrams, monetary authorities target an interest rate. For example, the U.S. Federal Reserve often targets an overnight bank rate. However, in achieving the target interest rate, the monetary authority usually conducts open market operations (the buying or selling of government debt), which has the effect of changing the money supply as indicated in our diagrams.

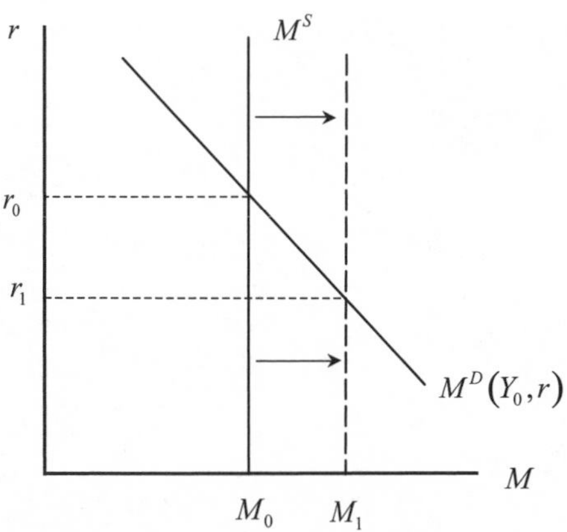

Figure 15.8. An Expansionary Monetary Policy

in Figure 15.8. The increase in the money supply shifts the M^S curve to the right. At the original interest rate, r_0, money supply exceeds money demand. The excess supply of money puts downward pressure on the interest rate. As the interest rate falls, the opportunity cost of holding money falls, and the demand for money increases. The economy moves to a new equilibrium in the money market at a lower interest rate, r_1, and a higher quantity of money, M_1. As we observe in the real world, an expansionary monetary policy is associated with a lower interest rate. Similarly, a contractionary monetary policy is associated with a decrease in the money supply and an increase in the interest rate.

In this chapter, we developed a model of exchange rate determination that viewed currency markets being affected by assets allocations (Figures 15.5 and 15.6). In this model, interest rates in Mexico and the United States played primary roles in determining the nominal exchange rate. In this appendix, we have developed a model of interest rate determination based on the money market of the economy. We next want to bring all of the elements together to understand how monetary policy affects exchange rates. To do this, we combine Figure 15.5 with two versions of Figure 15.7, one for the Mexican money market and a second for the U.S. money market. This is done in Figure 15.9.

The top diagram in Figure 15.9 depicts the equilibrium in the U.S. money market, which determines the interest rate on the dollar. The bottom diagram of Figure 15.9 depicts the equilibrium in the Mexican money market, which determines the interest rate on the peso. The dollar interest rate r_{US}, the peso interest rate r_M, and the expected rate of peso depreciation e^e all help to determine the position of the demand for peso line in the middle diagram. These three diagrams together give us a sense that monetary policies help to determine exchange rates. Our next task is to use the three diagrams in Figure 15.9 to analyze the impacts of changes in monetary policies on the value of the peso. To begin this exploration, we are going to consider an expansionary monetary policy in Mexico. We will then turn to an expansionary monetary policy in the United States.

The case of *expansionary monetary policy in Mexico* is presented in Figure 15.10. In the Mexican money market diagram, the increase in the money supply causes an excess supply of pesos at the initial interest rate. In order to clear the peso market, the interest rate falls to r_{M1}, increasing the demand for pesos to equal the increased supply. The lower interest rate on pesos means that the expected total rate of return on

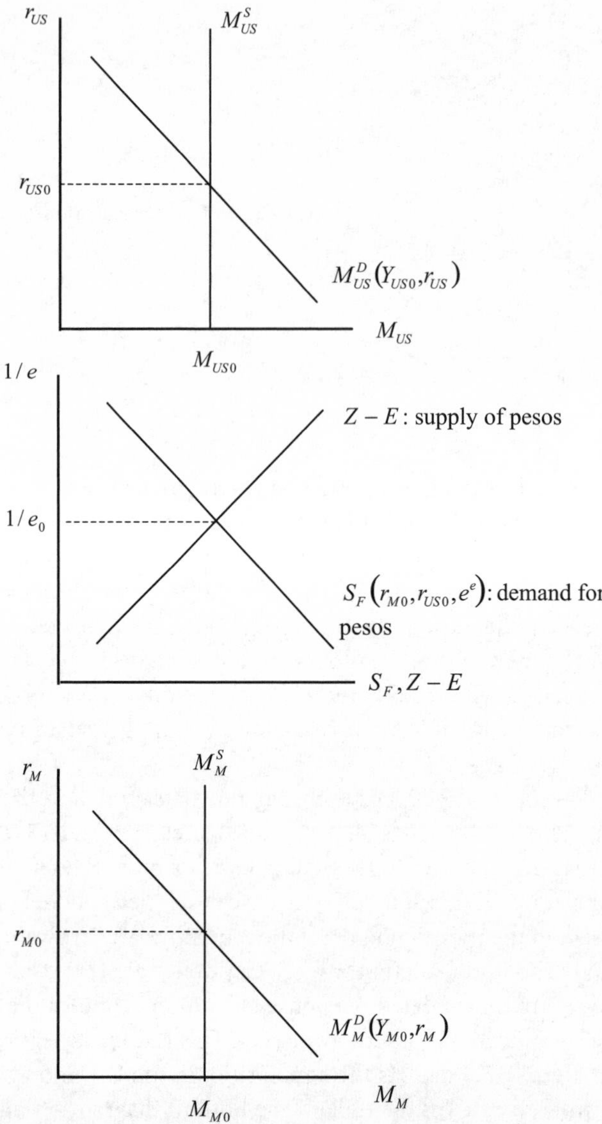

Figure 15.9. Money Markets and Exchange Rate Determination

peso-denominated assets is now less than the expected total rate of return on dollar-denominated assets. Investors sell pesos and buy dollars, which causes the demand for pesos graph S_F to move to the left to S_{F1}. As a result of this decrease in the demand for pesos, the value of the peso falls. In other words, there is a depreciation of the Mexican peso.

The case of *expansionary monetary policy in the United States* is presented in Figure 15.11. In the U.S. money market diagram, the increase in the money supply causes an excess supply of dollars at the initial interest rate. In order to clear the dollar market, the interest rate falls to r_{US1}, increasing the demand for dollars to equal the increased supply. The lower interest rate on dollar deposits means that the expected total rate of return on dollar-denominated assets is now less than the expected total rate of return

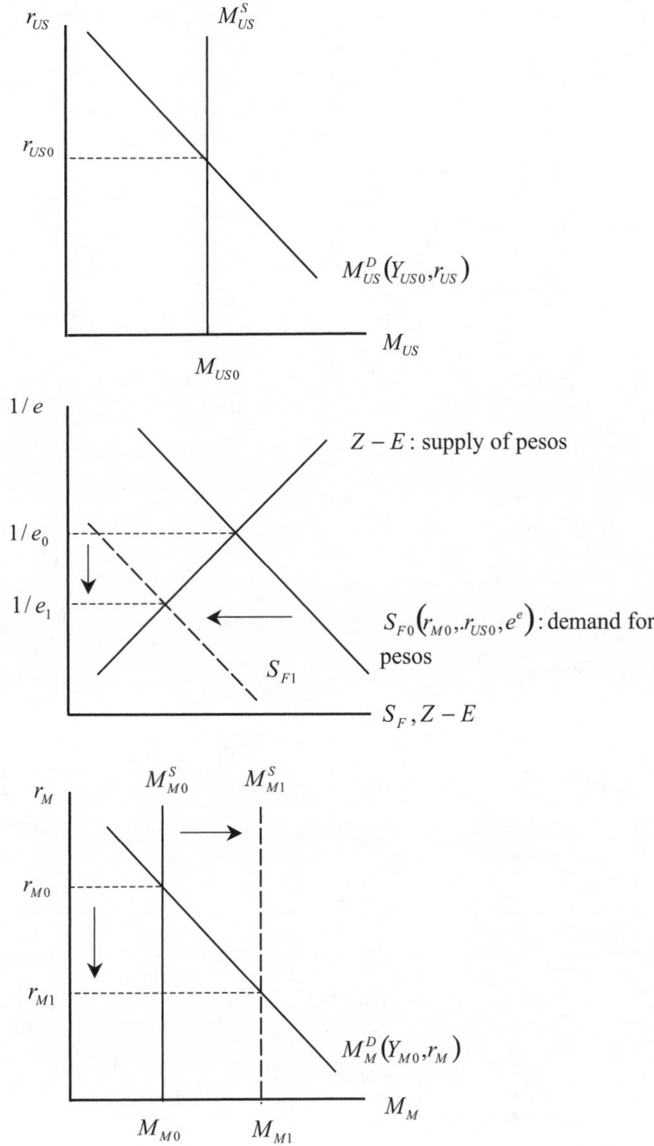

Figure 15.10. Expansionary Monetary Policy in Mexico (the Home Country)

on peso-denominated assets. Investors sell dollars and buy pesos, which causes the demand for pesos graph S_F to move to the right to S_{F1}. As a result of this increase in the demand for pesos, the value of the peso rises. In other words, there is an appreciation of the Mexican peso.

As we have shown here, monetary policies affect interest rates and exchange rates. In Chapter 14, we saw that exchange rates affect trade flows. Monetary policies, then, can affect trade flows. Take the case of an expansionary monetary policy in Mexico, the home country. An increase in the money supply in the home country causes a depreciation of the home-country currency, the peso. This involves a movement down the value of the peso scale. This tends to cause the trade deficit to contract or the trade surplus to expand.

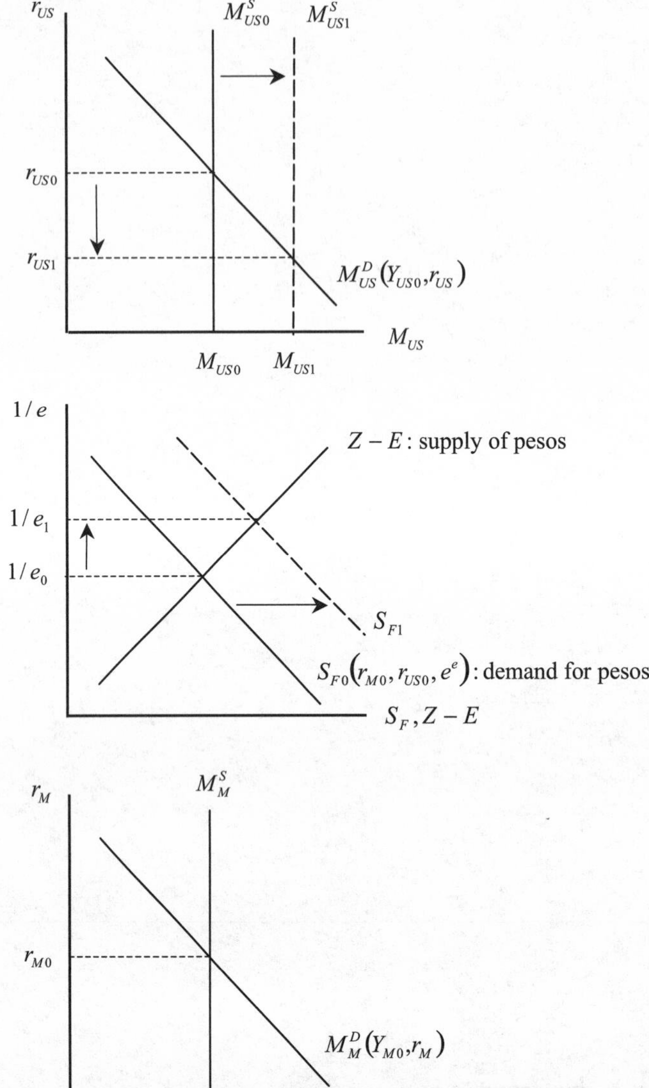

Figure 15.11. Expansionary Monetary Policy in the United States (the Foreign Country)

On the other hand, an expansionary monetary policy tends to encourage investment due to a lower cost of capital that is implied by the lower domestic interest rate. Any increase in investment would appear as the downward shift of the $S_H(Y) + T - G - I$ graph in Figure 13.6 of Chapter 13. As was shown there, this tends to *increase* the trade deficit. The impact of monetary policy on the trade balance, then, depends on the relative strengths of the exchange rate and investment effects.

REFERENCES

Adams, C. (2009) "Carry Trade," in K.A. Reinert, R.S. Rajan, A.J. Glass, and L.S. Davis (eds.), *The Princeton Encyclopedia of the World Economy*, Princeton University Press, 166–169.

Branson, W.H. and D.W. Henderson (1985) "The Specification and Influence of Asset Markets," in R. Jones and P.B. Kenen (eds.) *Handbook of International Economics*, North-Holland, 749–805.

Chinn, M.D. (2006) "The (Partial) Rehabilitation of Interest Parity: Longer Horizons, Alternative Explanations and Emerging Markets," *Journal of International Money and Finance*, 25:1, 7–21.

Chinn, M.D. (2009) "Interest Parity Conditions," in K.A. Reinert, R.S. Rajan, A.J. Glass, and L.S. Davis (eds.), *The Princeton Encyclopedia of the World Economy*, Princeton University Press, 649–653.

The Economist (2009) "Buttonwood: Bucking the Trend," April 30.

Harris, L. (1981) *Monetary Theory*, McGraw-Hill.

Isard, P. (1995) *Exchange Rate Economics*, Cambridge University Press.

Keynes, J.M. (1936) *The General Theory of Employment, Interest, and Money*, Harcourt, Brace and Company.

Lyons, R.K. (2001) *The Microstructure Approach to Exchange Rates*, MIT Press.

Montiel, P.J. (2003) *Macroeconomics in Emerging Markets*, Cambridge University Press.

Sarno, L. and M.P. Taylor (2002) *The Economics of Exchange Rates*, Cambridge University Press.

Skidelsky, R. (1992) *John Maynard Keynes: The Economist as Savior 1920–1937*, Macmillan.

16 Fixed Exchange Rates

In Chapter 15, we analyzed the case of flexible exchange rates. But not all exchange rates are flexible. Consider the case of Poland. In 1990, Poland had a fixed exchange rate, with the zloty pegged to the U.S. dollar. However, inadequate foreign reserves forced a change. In 1991, the Polish government set up a crawling peg, but expanded the peg to include a "basket" or collection of a number of currencies, including the U.S. dollar. The crawling peg involved a monthly devaluation against the currency basket at a rate of 1.8 percent. This too proved unworkable at times, and larger devaluations were required in 1992 and 1993. In 1995, the Polish government changed the crawling *peg* to a crawling *band* against the currency basket of $\pm$ 7.0 percent. This band was widened to $\pm$ 10.0 percent and then to $\pm$ 12.5 percent in 1998. In 1999, the currency basket was changed to reflect the introduction of the European Union euro. Finally, in 2000, the zloty began to float.[1]

We cannot get too far in understanding such complicated economic histories as that of Poland without understanding *nonflexible* exchange rate regimes, including fixed exchange rates. Developing such an understanding is the purpose of this chapter. We begin by defining a number of alternative exchange rate regimes, placing them on a continuum between "fixed" and "flexible." Next, we focus on the case of fixed exchange rates and examine the various ways that balance of payments adjustment can occur under this regime. We then consider the role of interest rates and credibility in maintaining fixed exchange rate regimes. Finally, we consider what has come to be known as the impossible trinity in the field of international finance. An appendix discusses monetary policies under fixed exchange rate regimes. As such, it follows on the appendix of Chapter 15.

> Analytical elements for this chapter:
>
> *Countries*, *currencies*, and *financial assets.*

ALTERNATIVE EXCHANGE RATE REGIMES

The model of exchange rate determination we developed in Chapter 15 assumed that the nominal exchange rate is perfectly flexible. However, in reality, there is a *menu* of exchange rate arrangements from which a country can choose. This menu is presented in Table 16.1.[2] As you can see in this table, in 2008, 40 countries pursued a **floating** or **flexible exchange rate regime**, in which the monetary authority (central bank or treasury) did not intervene to influence the market value of the nominal exchange rate, allowing it to be determined by the play of market forces. Forty-four countries maintained a **managed floating regime**, in which the monetary authority may have intervened by buying and/or selling its currency to influence the nominal exchange rate in some way.[3] Two countries used **crawling bands**, in which the monetary authorities intervened to maintain the nominal exchange rate in a band around a central rate, and

[1] See Kokoszczyński (2001).

[2] Levy-Yeyati and Sturzenegger (2005) distinguished the de jure exchange rate regimes reported to the International Monetary Fund from de facto regimes used in practice. For some countries, these diverge in significant ways. Table 16.1 reports the de facto regimes determined by the IMF. Husain, Mody, and Rogoff (2005) caution that de facto classifications can vary widely depending on the methodology used, so the classification of Table 16.1 might not be definitive. Indeed, we rely on a different classification in Table 16.2.

[3] Whereas pure floats are referred to as "clean floats," managed floats are known as "dirty" floats.

Table 16.1. Exchange rate arrangements, 2008

Arrangement	Description	Number of countries
Flexible or (clean) float	The exchange rate is market determined.	40
Managed (dirty) float	The exchange rate is primarily market determined, but the country's monetary authority intervenes in the currency market to influence the movements of the exchange rate.	44
Crawling bands	The country's monetary authority intervenes to maintain the exchange rate in a band around a central rate, and these bands are periodically adjusted.	2
Crawling pegs	The exchange rate is fixed in value to another currency or to a "basket" of other currencies, but adjusted periodically by small amounts.	8
Fixed	The exchange rate is fixed in value to another currency or to a "basket" of other currencies.	71
Currency board	The exchange rate is fixed in value to another currency, and domestic currency is fully backed by reserves of this foreign currency.	13
No separate legal tender	The legal tender of the country is a currency of another country.	10

Source: International Monetary Fund, www.imf.org

these bands were periodically adjusted. Eight countries employed **crawling pegs**. Here, the nominal exchange rate was fixed in value to another currency or to a "basket" or collection of other currencies, but adjusted periodically by small amounts.

Seventy-one countries pursued **fixed exchange rates** or fixed pegs, in which monetary authorities adopted a policy goal of keeping the nominal exchange rate at a fixed value in terms of another currency or in terms of a "basket" of other currencies.[4] Additionally, 13 countries pursued an extreme form of fixed exchange rate known as a **currency board**. Here, the monetary authority is required to fully back up the domestic currency with reserves of the foreign currency to which the domestic currency is pegged. Finally, 10 (usually very small) countries went even a step further and maintained no independent currency whatsoever.

One issue that has arisen in the analysis of exchange rate regimes is their *durability* or ability to persist over time without a necessary change or transition to another regime. The regime characterization of Table 16.1 is a snapshot in time. A more thorough analysis based on a more sophisticated conception of regime change (that due to Reinhart and Rogoff, 2004) for the 1975–2001 time period is presented in Table 16.2. The average durability of all regimes across all countries is just over 11 years. We see in this table that, for all countries, pegged exchange rates are quite durable, with an average duration of 23 years. But for emerging markets, the average durability of pegs is only 8 years, a significant difference. Emerging markets are that subset of developing countries that are experiencing higher levels of growth and thus have access to international capital flows. As has been pointed out by many observers, these capital

[4] A peg against a currency basket or a "basket peg" uses a weighted average of a collection of other important currencies as the pegged value. This was the case in the Polish example given in the introduction.

Table 16.2. The durability of exchange rate regimes, 1975–2001 (years)

Countries	All regimes	Pegs	Intermediate	Floats
All countries	11.4	23.2	18.4	14.3
Advanced countries	19.4	46.0	26.8	88.0
Emerging markets	8.6	8.4	16.5	11.0
Developing	10.7	27.3	16.2	5.5

Source: Husain, Mody, and Rogoff (2005) based on Reinhart and Rogoff (2004)

flows can be quite volatile.[5] This, as we see later, can make pegged exchange rates unstable. As can also be seen in this table, free floats are very durable in advanced countries but much less so in developing and emerging countries. This is due to problems with volatility in the latter sets of countries.

The overall conclusion we can take from Table 16.2 is that there is probably no "one size fits all" exchange rate regime that works for all countries in the world economy. Indeed, as has been pointed out by many observers (e.g., Montiel, 2003, Chapter 18), the durability of exchange rate regimes can depend on other "fundamentals," such as low inflation, prudential financial regulation, and capital account policies. Nevertheless, the choice of exchange rate regime is a very important decision for a country. In this chapter, we try to get of sense of why this is so by contrasting the case of fixed or pegged rates with the flexible rates we discussed in Chapter 15. In doing so, we get a sense of both the strengths and weaknesses of fixed exchange rate regimes.[6]

A MODEL OF FIXED EXCHANGE RATES

In contrast to the case of the flexible or floating exchange rate regime, we consider the polar opposite case of a fixed exchange rate regime. As in Chapter 15, Mexico is designated our home country, and the United States is designated our foreign country. The currency market we focus on is again the peso market, and we include the asset considerations of Chapter 15. Although the peso began floating in 1995, in previous years, it had indeed been fixed against the U.S. dollar.[7] For your convenience, our balance of payments table of Chapter 13 is reproduced here as Table 16.3. We refer to the balance of payments in the discussion that follows.

Before beginning, we need to establish some terminology and, in so doing, expand Table 15.1. This is done in Table 16.4. The first two rows of Table 16.4 repeat the flexible exchange rate terminology of Chapter 15. The third and fourth rows introduce new terminology for the fixed exchange rate regime. Let's consider them one at a time. Under a fixed exchange rate regime, when the Mexican government raises e and thereby decreases the value of the peso, there is said to be a **devaluation** of the peso. This contrasts with a market-driven, upward movement in e under a flexible exchange rate regime, known as a **depreciation**. Under a fixed exchange rate regime, when the Mexican government lowers e and thereby increases the value of the peso, there is said to be a **revaluation** of the peso. This contrasts with a market-driven, downward

[5] See Kaminsky, Reinhart, and Végh (2003) and Goldin and Reinert (2005).

[6] A thorough empirical investigation into exchange rate regime choice can be found in Levy-Yeyati, Sturzenegger, and Reggio (2010). These researchers consider both economic and political determinants. One interesting result in their research is that "whereas financial integration tends to foster flexible regimes among industrialized countries…, it increases the propensity to peg among non-industrialized countries" (p. 660).

[7] See Chapter 18, Crises and Responses.

Table 16.3. Mexican balance of payments, 2007 (billions of U.S. dollars)

Item	Gross	Net	Major balance
Current Account			
1. Goods exports	271.9		
2. Goods imports	−281.9		
3. Goods trade balance		−10.0	
4. Service exports	17.6		
5. Service imports	−24.1		
6. Goods and services trade balance		−16.5	
7. Net income		−18.3	
8. Net transfers		26.4	
9. Current account balance			−8.4
Capital/Financial Account			
10. Direct investment		18.8	
11. Portfolio investment		11.3	
12. Other investment		−10.6	
13. Capital/financial account balance			19.5
Official Reserve Transactions			
14. Official reserves balance			−10.3
Errors and Omissions			
15. Errors and omissions			−0.8
Overall Balance			
16. Overall balance			0

Source: International Monetary Fund, International Financial Statistics

Table 16.4. Exchange rate terminology revisited

Case	e	Value of peso	Term
Flexible *e*	↑	↓	Depreciation
Flexible *e*	↓	↑	Appreciation
Fixed *e*	↑	↓	Devaluation
Fixed *e*	↓	↑	Revaluation

movement in *e* under a flexible exchange rate regime, known as an **appreciation**. In practice, devaluations are much more common than revaluations.

There is some additional terminology we need to understand in the case of a fixed exchange rate regime, and we will address this with the help of Figure 16.1. This diagram represents the peso market as we developed it in Chapter 15. Suppose that e_0 represents the equilibrium exchange rate under a flexible exchange rate regime. This is where the supply of pesos given by the trade deficit equals the demand for pesos given by foreign savings.[8] In terms of the balance of payments accounts of Table 16.3, the supply of pesos is the negative of item 6, the goods and services trade balance. It excludes net income (item 7) and net transfers (item 8). The demand for pesos relates to item 13, the capital/financial account balance. The demand for pesos illustrated in Figure 16.1

[8] As mentioned in Chapter 15, trade surpluses can be handled in this diagram by the placement of the zero value toward the middle of the horizontal axis rather than at the left endpoint.

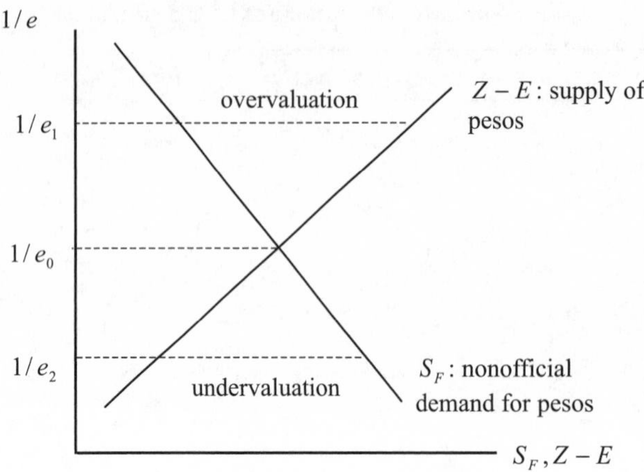

Figure 16.1. The Peso Market

is therefore the *nonofficial* capital account balance. This excludes the actions of central banks (item 14), which we discuss later.

Suppose that the Mexican government chooses to fix the exchange rate at e_1. The value of the peso, $1/e_1$, is therefore above the equilibrium value of the peso, $1/e_0$. This situation is known as an **overvaluation** of the peso. Note that an overvaluation of the peso implies an excess supply of pesos or an excess demand for dollars. How can this be sustained? There must be some additional demand for pesos or supply of dollars. As we see in Table 16.3, this can come from three sources: positive net income (item 7), positive net transfers (item 8), and positive net official reserve transactions (item 14).[9] Let's examine the last of these in some detail. If e is fixed at e_1, there is an excess nonofficial supply of pesos or demand for dollars. Mexico's central bank can address this by selling its holdings of dollars (buying pesos). In this process of *drawing down foreign reserves*, the central bank helps to eliminate the excess supply of pesos or demand for dollars. It is for this reason that we often find countries with overvalued currencies drawing down their foreign reserves. We explore the limits of this process in Chapters 18 and 24 on crises and structural adjustment, respectively.

Next, suppose that the Mexican government chose to fix the exchange rate at e_2. The value of the peso, $1/e_2$, is therefore below the equilibrium value of the peso, $1/e_0$. This situation is known as an **undervaluation** of the peso. Note that an undervaluation of the peso implies an excess demand for pesos or an excess supply of dollars. This situation can be sustained via some additional supply of pesos or demand for dollars. As we see in Table 16.3, this can come from negative net income (item 7), negative net transfers (item 8), and negative net official reserve transactions (item 14). Again, it is worthwhile to examine the last of these in some detail. Mexico's central bank can address the excess demand for pesos or supply of dollars by buying dollars (selling pesos). In this process of *building up foreign reserves*, the central bank helps to eliminate the excess demand for pesos or supply of dollars.[10] The case of China is described in the accompanying box.

[9] It is helpful to view positive entries in the balance of payments as (net) demands for pesos or supply of dollars. Here we ignore errors and omissions.

[10] Some development economists have argued that it is a good idea to maintain a slightly undervalued currency to keep trade deficits at manageable levels and to accumulate foreign reserves for future emergencies. Rodrik (2008) went a step further to identify an undervalued currency as an effective development policy that overcomes market failures in tradable sectors of developing-country economies.

The conclusion we reach here, which coincides with experience, is that central banks in countries with undervalued currencies tend to draw down foreign exchange reserves, whereas central banks in countries with undervalued currencies tend to build up foreign reserves. Let's summarize this in a box to help you remember:

Overvaluation $\Rightarrow$ Excess supply of pesos (demand for dollars) $\Rightarrow$ Central bank draws down foreign reserves

Undervaluation $\Rightarrow$ Excess demand for pesos (supply of dollars) $\Rightarrow$ Central bank builds up foreign reserves

Is China's Currency Undervalued?

In Chapter 13 we noted that China has experienced a dramatic expansion of negative official reserve transactions to approximately negative US$400 billion in 2008. Along with this process, China has accumulated $2.6 trillion dollars of foreign reserves as of late 2010. Given our discussion so far in this chapter, these are the sorts of things we associate with an undervalued currency. We also see from Figure 16.1 that an undervalued currency tends to suppress a trade deficit or enhance a trade surplus, again characteristics of the Chinese economy.

But is the Chinese currency (the Renminbi [RMB]) undervalued? A great deal of policy discussion has gone into this question. Makin (2007), for example, attributes RMB undervaluation not only to China's trade surplus, but also to the trade deficit of the United States. More controversially, Nobel Laureate Paul Krugman (2010) has called for the United States to impose a 25 percent surcharge (tariff) an all imports from China.

Estimates with regard to the extent of China's undervaluation vary widely. Goldstein and Lardy (2009) estimate an undervaluation of approximately 20 percent, whereas estimates of Subramanian (2010), based on a purchasing power parity (PPP) methodology discussed in Chapter 14, suggest a higher figure of approximately 30 percent. Whatever the correct percentage, it is clear that the Chinese economy can be described by the undervaluation situation depicted in Figure 16.1. The transition process for the Chinese economy toward an equilibrium exchange rate is one of the more important issues in the world economy at the current time. Some progress in this direction began in June 2010 when the Chinese government introduced more flexibility but limited the daily movement of the RMB to ± 0.5 percent on a single day.

Sources: Makin (2007), Goldstein and Lardy (2009), Krugman (2010), and Subramanian (2010)

INTEREST RATES AND EXCHANGE RATES

There is another approach to maintaining fixed exchange rates by affecting the *equilibrium* rate e_0. This approach is best analyzed using the **interest rate parity condition** from Chapter 15:

$$r_M = r_{US} + \frac{(e^e - e)}{e} \tag{16.1}$$

Suppose that the Mexican government successfully ensures that a *fixed* rate e_3 is an equilibrium rate. What must be the relationship between e_3 and e^e? A moment of

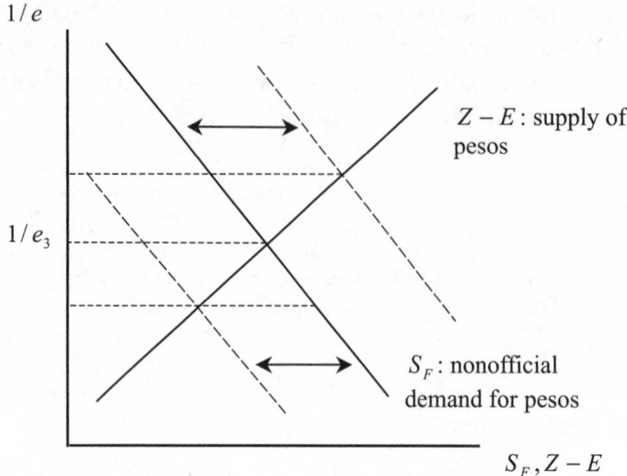

Figure 16.2. An Equilibrium Fixed Exchange Rate

thought tells us that if e_3 is both a *fixed* and an *equilibrium* rate, then e_3 *must equal* e^e. This causes a change in our interest rate parity condition. Because $e^e = e$, $(e^e - e)$ is zero, and therefore:

$$r_M = r_{US} \tag{16.2}$$

This relationship tells us that, for the Mexican government to maintain a fixed, equilibrium exchange rate, it must ensure that its interest rate equals that in the United States. Another way of looking at this is shown in Figure 16.2. By increasing or decreasing r_M into equality with r_{US}, the Mexican government can move the S_F graph to the left or right until the equilibrium e and e_3 are identical. For example, suppose that initially $r_M = r_{US}$, and this allows for a fixed exchange rate e_3. Next, suppose that the U.S. government *increases* r_{US} so that $r_M < r_{US}$. This shifts the demand for pesos graph to the left. In order to maintain the fixed e_3, the Mexican government will need to increase r_M, moving the demand for pesos graph back to its original position. Similarly, if from the initial equilibrium, the U.S. government were to *decrease* r_{US} so that $r_M > r_{US}$, this would shift the demand for pesos graph to the right. Here, in order to maintain the fixed e_3, the Mexican government will need to decrease r_M, moving the demand for pesos graph back to its original position.[11]

We have gained an important insight here into the operation of fixed exchange rate regimes. Let's summarize it in a box to help you remember:

> If a home country wants to maintain an *equilibrium* fixed exchange rate, it must set its interest rate equal to that prevailing in the foreign country whose currency serves as a peg for the home-country currency.

The real world is a complex place, and in practice, fixed exchange rates are maintained with combinations of net income, net transfers, official reserve transactions, and interest rates. That is, *both* Figure 16.1 and Figure 16.2 are relevant. We discuss this for the well-known case of the Brazil's exchange rate crisis in 1998–1999 in the accompanying box.

[11] For the role of monetary policies in this process, please see the appendix to this chapter.

However, one principle is always operable. The farther a fixed exchange rate is from the equilibrium exchange rate, the more difficult it is to maintain for an extended period of time. This principle brings us to the issue of the credibility of fixed exchange rates.

Defending the Brazilian *Real*, 1998–1999

In October 1998, Brazilian citizens reelected Fernando Henrique Cardoso to a second term as president. In the months preceding the election, however, Brazilian monetary authorities were engaged in an intense struggle with international investors to maintain a crawling peg of the Brazilian real against the U.S. dollar. By September 1998, interest rates had reached 40 percent. Despite this strong measure, however, foreign reserves had been drawn down from nearly US$75 billion to US$50 billion. Brazil began to talk to the International Monetary Fund (IMF) about a support package to maintain investor confidence in the face of a fiscal deficit of almost 8 percent of gross domestic product (GDP) and a current account deficit of approximately 4 percent of GDP.

Shortly after taking office, and in close consultation with the IMF, Cardoso's economic team drew up a package of budget cuts and tax increases. In November, an official agreement with the IMF worth US$41.5 billion was announced, and Cardoso's government denied that it would abandon the crawling peg. In December, the government also denied that it would abandon its central bank president Gustavo Franco, whose job it was to defend the real.

In mid-January 1999, Gustavo Franco resigned, and the real was devalued. Two days later, the real was allowed to float. It very quickly lost almost a third of its value.

Sources: The Economist (1998a, 1998b, and 1998c)

THE ROLE OF CREDIBILITY

Our discussion of interest rates and fixed exchange rates has been based on the expected rate of depreciation being zero in Equation 16.2. In Chapter 15, however, we noted that expectations regarding the future exchange rate can be volatile and subject to a host of economic and political events. For example, if a fixed exchange rate comes under pressure from an incipient fall in demand (shift of S_F to the left), this pressure must be alleviated via an increase in the domestic or home-country interest rate. There are two difficulties here, however. First, increases in interest rates are recessionary in that they suppress domestic investment. Second, increases in interest rates can potentially wreak havoc in fragile domestic financial systems, particularly when capital can leave the country in the form of capital flight. This point has been summarized by Montiel (2003):

> The currency should be in a strong position to resist speculative attack and the currency peg should be sustainable.... When the real exchange rate is not misaligned..., the financial sector is strong, the public sector does not have a large stock of domestic currency debt, and the economy is growing rapidly. Alternatively, if the currency appears to be overvalued, the domestic financial sector is weak, the public sector's solvency is precarious and it has a large stock of short-term domestic debt, and/or the economy is in recession, the prospects for a successful speculative attack would tend to be strong. (p. 364)

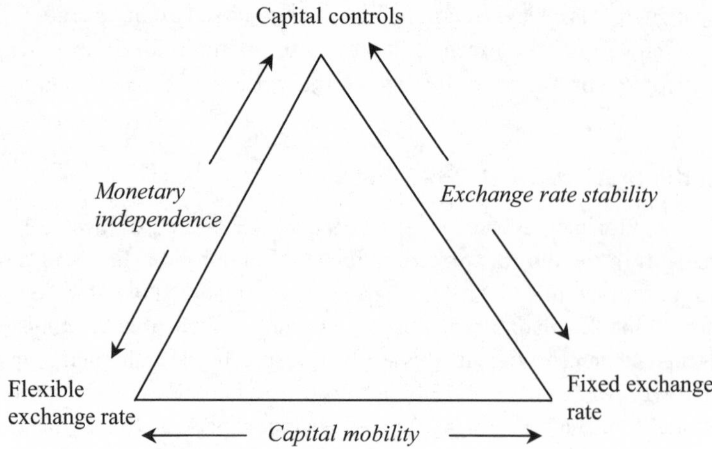

Figure 16.3. The Impossible Trinity

The reason for this is that investors know what the potentially negative impacts of an interest rate can be, and this information feeds back into expectations. If investors begin to question the willingness and ability of the home-country government to defend the fixed peg with interest rate increases, the expected rate of depreciation again becomes positive and the peg is no longer credible. This process operates in some of the crises we consider in Chapter 18 and contributes to the lack of durability of pegs in emerging markets that we saw in Table 16.2.

THE IMPOSSIBLE TRINITY

Our discussions in this chapter lead up to a concept in international finance that has received a lot of attention lately. It is known as the **impossible trinity.**[12] The impossible trinity recognizes that, in the realm of international finance, countries would ideally like to pursue three desired objectives (the trinity):

1. *Monetary independence*, or the ability to conduct an independent monetary policy with an eye to stabilizing the domestic macroeconomic policy.
2. *Exchange rate stability*, or the ability to avoid destabilizing volatility in the nominal exchange rate.
3. *Capital mobility*, or the ability to take advantage of flows on the direct and portfolio capital accounts from foreign savings.

As it turns out, however, countries must sacrifice one of the above desired objectives in order to achieve the other two. The impossible trinity, illustrated in Figure 16.3, helps to explain why this is the case. We develop your understanding of this figure in three steps.

First, suppose a country wants to maintain both capital mobility and exchange rate stability. These two objectives appear as italicized terms in Figure 16.3 associated with

[12] It also goes by the name of the "policy trilemma." The term *trilemma* is not one you will find in a dictionary. The term *dilemma* refers to a necessary choice between *two* undesirable alternatives. The term *trilemma*, then, refers to a necessary choice among *three* undesirable alternatives in the form of lost desirable policies.

the bottom and right-hand sides of the triangle. Arrows from these two terms converge in the lower right-hand corner of the triangle on the policy regime of fixed exchange rate. This indicates that the only way to maintain both capital mobility and exchange rate stability is to pursue a fixed exchange rate regime. The desired objective that the country must give up is the one on the side of the triangle opposite of the fixed exchange rate corner, namely, monetary independence. As you have seen above in this chapter, if a country wants to maintain its fixed exchange rate as an equilibrium rate, it must adjust its interest rate to that in the country to which its currency is pegged. Because, as is discussed further in the appendix, interest rates are set via monetary policy, *in maintaining capital mobility and exchange rate stability, the country must sacrifice its independent monetary policy.*

Second, suppose a country wants to maintain both capital mobility and monetary independence. These two objectives appear as italicized terms in Figure 16.3 associated with the bottom and left-hand sides of the triangle. Arrows from these two terms converge in the lower left-hand corner of the triangle on the policy regime of flexible exchange rate. This indicates that the only way to maintain both capital mobility and monetary independence is to allow the currency to float. The desired objective that the country must give up is the one on the side of the triangle opposite the flexible exchange rate corner, namely, exchange rate stability. As you saw in Chapter 15, changes in foreign interest rates and in expectations will, in the face of a given monetary policy in the country, alter the flexible, nominal exchange rate. Because in practice such movements in flexible exchange rates can be large, we see that *in maintaining capital mobility and monetary independence, the country must sacrifice exchange rate stability.*[13]

We should mention here that there are possible intermediate positions between these first two cases. With capital mobility, a country can in practice achieve a mix of some monetary independence and some exchange rate stability through the use of the intermediate regimes of managed floats, crawling bands, and crawling pegs described in Table 16.1. What these countries *cannot* achieve is *both* full monetary independence *and* full exchange rate stability.[14]

Third, suppose a country wants to maintain both monetary independence and exchange rate stability. These two objectives appear as italicized terms in Figure 16.3 associated with the left-hand and right-hand sides of the triangle. Arrows from these two terms converge at the apex of the triangle on the policy regime of capital controls. This indicates that the only way to maintain both monetary independence and exchange rate stability is to restrict transactions on the capital account of the balance of payments in order to suppress the portfolio considerations we discussed in this and the previous chapter. The desired objective that the country must give up is the one on the side of the triangle opposite the capital control corner, namely, capital mobility. In order to *maintain monetary independence and exchange rate stability, the country must sacrifice capital mobility.*

Economic analysis often helps to highlight tradeoffs among alternatives. Here we have highlighted some central tradeoffs among policies facing each country in the

[13] But see Calvo and Mishkin (2003) on the challenges of building monetary policy credibility even in flexible exchange rate regimes.

[14] The role of these intermediate regimes was emphasized by Frankel (1999).

world economy. As with economic tradeoffs in general, there are opportunity costs of any choice. In the realm of international finance, countries must give up one desired objective (monetary independence, exchange rate stability, or capital mobility) to attain the other two. To assume otherwise in policy deliberations is wishful thinking.

CURRENCY BOARDS

The volatility of currency values through the crises of the late 1990s led some observers to suggest the use of **currency boards** to stabilize exchange rates.[15] Currency boards are a fixed exchange rate regime with two characteristics. First, the fixed rate is presented as an inviolable commitment with legal backing in domestic legislation. Second, the central bank serving as the currency board fully backs up its base money (cash and commercial bank reserves) with foreign reserves and stands ready to exchange the domestic currency and the foreign currency in either direction in response to any such request. As you saw in Table 16.1, 13 countries of the world utilized currency boards in 2008. The most well-known case of a currency board was Argentina, which introduced a currency board to help stabilize the country's economy after a period of hyperinflation in the late 1980s.

Currency boards are effective ways to establish sound currencies and to limit excessive money creation that can fuel **inflation**. It is not clear, however, how useful currency boards are in the long run for all but the smaller and most open economies. In the case of Argentina, a larger and less open economy, the currency board was introduced as part of the *Plan Convertibilidad* (or Convertibility Plan) in 1991, which also included a set of fiscal and structural reforms. One assessment of the currency board arrangement through 1996 used the term "miracle" and hailed it as "the most successful program in the last half-century" (Kiguel and Nogués, 1998, p. 143). Indeed, between 1991 and 1995, annual inflation fell from 170 percent to 0 percent. However, a dangerous process of **deflation** began to occur in 1998, and without an independent monetary policy, the Argentine government was helpless to address it.

Argentina's real troubles began in July 2001 when it was required to significantly increase interest rates on its Treasury bills in order to attract investors. By December 2001, the situation had become dire. Despite ongoing talks with the IMF and limits on cash withdrawals within the country, all eyes began to focus on the country's US$135 billion public debt, and speculation grew that a devaluation was imminent, despite (typical) denials by President Fernando De la Rua. Indeed, the debt default came immediately in 2002, and the government began to prepare for a devaluation. Initially, the government attempted a 30 percent devaluation, adjusting the peg from 1.0 to 1.4 pesos per U.S. dollar. By June 2002, however, it had reached nearly 4.0 to the dollar, later appreciating back to approximately 3.5 to the dollar. Because most debt in the country was denominated in U.S. dollars, devaluation immediately increased the peso value of debt. In the aftermath of the currency board's demise, GDP shrank by more in percentage terms than in the United States during the Great Depression, and poverty exploded.

Given this history, it seems that the usefulness of currency boards is not universal but rather is limited to certain small and very open economies. In terms of the impossible

[15] See Enoch and Gulde (1998) and Ghosh, Gulde, and Wolf (2000).

trinity, these boards constitute an unusual commitment to remain in the lower right-hand corner of Figure 16.3 and to forsake any possibility of an independent monetary policy.

CONCLUSION

Although Chapter 15 considered the case of freely floating or flexible exchange rates, this is only one of a number of possible exchange rate regimes. Other alternatives include managed floating, crawling pegs, adjustable pegs, fixed exchange rates, and currency boards. The current chapter focused on fixed exchange rates, with a quick look at currency boards. Governments can maintain overvalued exchange rates through positive net income receipts, positive net transfers, and positive net official reserve transactions (drawing down foreign reserves). These provide the requisite extra demand for the home-country currency. Alternatively, governments can raise the domestic interest rate to increase the equilibrium value of the currency so that it is no longer overvalued. Governments can maintain undervalued exchange rates through negative net income receipts, negative net transfers, and negative net official reserve transactions (building up foreign reserves). These provide the requisite extra supply for the currency. Alternatively, the government can lower the domestic interest rate to decrease the equilibrium value of the currency so that it is no longer undervalued.

An overvalued exchange rate is not always sustainable. The home-country central bank can run out of foreign reserves to sell. We take up the complications of such situations in Chapter 18 on crises and responses and in Chapter 24 on structural adjustment.

Every country faces the impossible trinity in which it must sacrifice one desired objective (monetary independence, exchange rate stability, or capital mobility) to attain the other two. This reality puts significant constraints on possible policies available to countries to address the (often stormy) realities of international finance.

REVIEW EXERCISES

1. Until January 2002, the Argentine peso was pegged on a one-to-one basis against the U.S. dollar in an arrangement known as a *currency board.* Suppose that, to begin with, this exchange rate is an equilibrium rate. Next, using a diagram such as Figure 16.2, show how Argentina can respond to a decrease in the interest rate on the U.S. dollar.
2. Suppose that a country has a fixed exchange rate and that, over the past few years, it has been quickly accumulating foreign reserves. What does this tell you about the value of the pegged currency? Why?
3. Given what you have read in this book up to this point, can you say anything about the desirability of the three policy regime corners in the impossible trinity diagram of Figure 16.3? Please explain your reasoning.
4. For Appendix readers only. For the preceding example, set up the equivalent of Figure 16.4. Next, show the actions required on the part of the Mexican monetary authority in response to a decrease in income in Mexico, a decrease in income in the United States, and a contractionary monetary policy in the United States. In each case, *explain the intuition of your results.*

FURTHER READING AND WEB RESOURCES

On the classification of exchange rate regimes, see Corden (2002) and Reinhart and Rogoff (2004). A thorough review of the process of maintaining a fixed exchange rate regime is given in chapter 18 of Montiel (2003). On the impossible trinity, see Siklos (2009), and on currency boards, see Slavov (2009). For sources on the political economy of fixed exchange rate regimes, see Obstfeld and Rogoff (1995), Garber and Svensson (1995), Calvo and Mishkin (2003), and Levy-Yeyati, Sturzenegger, and Reggio (2010).

The International Monetary Fund's classification of exchange rate regimes is given on their web page entitled "Classification of Exchange Rate Arrangements and Monetary Frameworks." At the time of this writing, it can be found here: http://www.imf.org/external/np/mfd/er/index.asp.

APPENDIX: MONETARY POLICIES

As mentioned in the appendix to Chapter 15, some readers of this book will be familiar with monetary policies from a course on macroeconomics. If this is the case for you, the present appendix will explain to you the monetary consequences of fixed exchange rate regimes. We begin with a collection of diagrams presented in the appendix to Chapter 15. This collection of diagrams is presented in Figure 16.4. The top diagram of this figure depicts equilibrium in the U.S. money market and determines the interest rate on the dollar. The bottom diagram depicts equilibrium in the Mexican money market and determines the interest rate on the peso. The middle diagram depicts the peso market, e_0 being an equilibrium fixed exchange rate. As discussed in this chapter, an equilibrium fixed exchange rate requires $r_M = r_{US}$. Let's examine some implications of this requirement.

First, let's suppose that income in Mexico (Y_M) increased. What would be the implication of this? An increase in income in Mexico would tend to increase the demand for pesos. This would shift the Mexican money demand curve in Figure 16.4 to the right, which, in turn, would tend to increase r_M. This would shift the demand for pesos graph to the right in the center diagram, increasing the value of the peso. In order to prevent this peso appreciation, the Mexican central bank would need to increase the supply of pesos, selling them in the peso market. This will shift the M_M^S curve to the right until r_M falls back to its original level and e is maintained at e_0.

Second, let's suppose that income in the United States (Y_{US}) increased. What would be the implication of this change? An increase in income in the United States would tend to increase the demand for U.S. dollars. This would shift the U.S. money demand curve in Figure 16.4 to the right, which, in turn, would tend to increase r_{US}. This would shift the demand for pesos graph to the left in the center diagram, decreasing the value of the peso. In order to prevent this depreciation, the central bank would need to decrease the supply of pesos, buying them in the peso market. This will shift the M_M^S curve to the left until r_M increases to match the increase in r_{US}. This is the only way to maintain e at e_0.

Finally, let's consider an increase in money supply in the United States. An increase in M_{US}^S would decrease r_{US}. Just like the increase in Mexican income, this would lead to an increase in the value of the peso. In order to prevent this appreciation, the Mexican

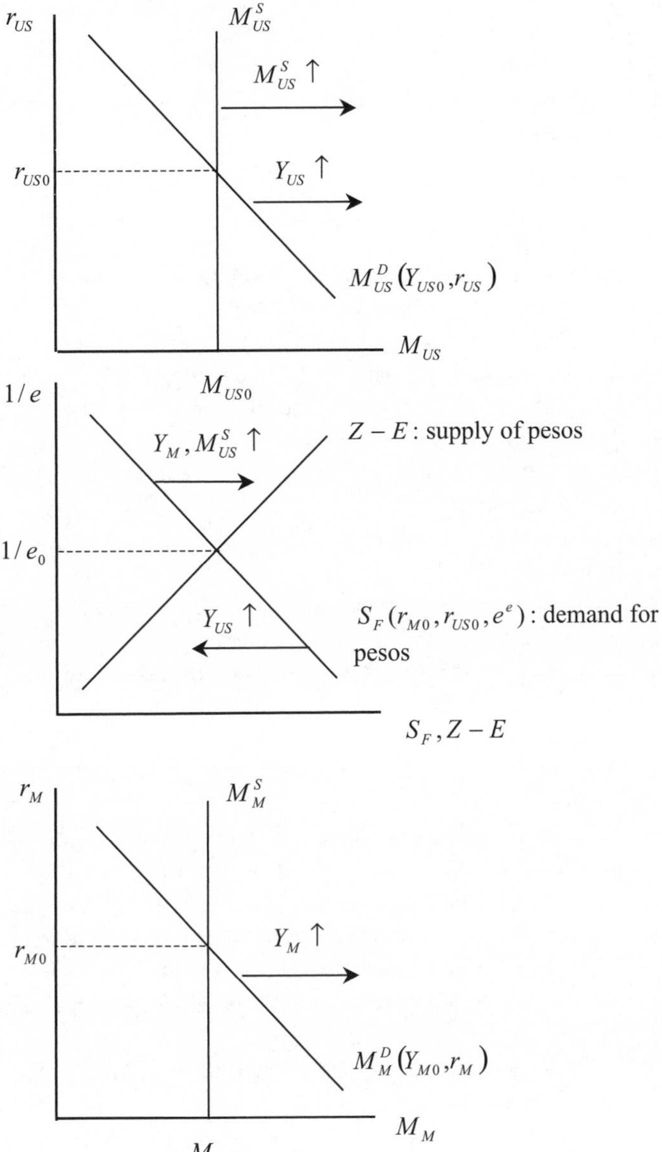

Figure 16.4. Money Markets and Fixed Exchange Rates

central bank would need to increase the supply of pesos, selling them in the peso market. This will shift the M_M^S curve to the right until r_M falls enough to meet the fall in r_{US}. This policy response will maintain e at e_0.

In each of the preceding three cases, the Mexican government must stand ready to buy and sell pesos at e_0 to meet any excess supply or demand for pesos and, thereby, maintain the fixed exchange rate. M_M^S is used to ensure that the exchange rate is fixed. Importantly, then, under a fixed exchange rate regime, a country cannot pursue monetary policy independently of the rest of the world, such as with an eye to stabilizing its own macroeconomy. Instead the monetary policy is committed to keeping the exchange rate fixed. This was *not* the case under the flexible or floating exchange rate policy. Under a flexible exchange rate regime, a country can pursue an independent monetary policy, but it gives up control of the exchange rate. Another way of expressing this is simply to say that *a country can control its interest rate or its exchange rate, but not both.* An integrated international financial system makes controlling both the interest rate and the exchange rate impossible.[16]

REFERENCES

Calvo, G.A. and F.S. Mishkin (2003) "The Mirage of Exchange Rate Regimes for Emerging Market Countries," *Journal of Economic Perspectives*, 17:4, 99–118.

Corden, W.M. (2002) *Too Sensational: On the Choice of Exchange Rate Regimes*, MIT Press.

The Economist (1998a) "Can Cardoso Use Financial Chaos to Reform Brazil?" September 26.

The Economist (1998b) "Cracking the Brazil Nuts," October 31.

The Economist (1998c) "Brazilian Jitters," December 19.

Enoch, C. and A.-M. Gulde (1998) "Are Currency Boards a Cure for All Monetary Problems?" *Finance and Development*, 35:4, 40–43.

Frankel (1999) *No Single Currency Regime Is Right for All Countries or At All Times*, Princeton Essays in International Finance No. 215.

Friedman, M. (1953) "The Case for Flexible Exchange Rates," in *Essays in Positive Economics*, University of Chicago Press, Chicago, 157–203.

Garber, P.M. and L.E.O. Svensson (1995) "The Operation and Collapse of Fixed Exchange Rate Regimes," in G.M. Grossman and K. Rogoff (eds.), *Handbook of International Economics*, Vol. 3, North-Holland, 1865–1911.

Ghosh, A., A.-M. Gulde, and H. Wolf (2000) "Currency Boards: More than a Quick Fix?" *Economic Policy*, 31, 269–321.

Goldin, I. and K.A. Reinert (2005) "Capital Flows and Development: A Survey," *Journal of International Trade and Economic Development*, 14:4, 453–481.

Goldstein, M. and N. Lardy (2009) *The Future of China's Exchange Rate Policy*, Policy Analyses in International Economics No. 97, Peterson Institute of International Economics.

Husain, A.M., A. Mody, and K.S. Rogoff (2005) "Exchange Rate Regime Durability and Performance in Developing versus Advanced Economies," *Journal of Monetary Economics*, 52:1, 35–64.

Kaminsky, G.L., C.M. Reinhart, and C.A. Végh (2003) "The Unholy Trinity of Financial Contagion," *Journal of Economic Perspectives*, 17:4, 51–74.

Kiguel, M. and J.J. Nogués (1998) "Restoring Growth and Price Stability in Argentina: Do Policies Make Miracles?" in H. Costin and H. Vanolli (eds.), *Economic Reform in Latin America*, Dryden, 125–144.

Kokoszczyñski, R. (2001) "From Fixed to Floating: Other Country Experiences: The Case of Poland," Paper presented at the International Monetary Fund seminar "Exchange Rate Regimes: Hard Peg or Free Floating?" Washington, DC.

Krugman, P. (2010) "Taking on China," *New York Times*, March 15.

Levy-Yeyati, E. and F. Sturzenegger (2005) "Classifying Exchange Rate Regimes: Deeds vs. Words," *European Economic Review*, 49:6, 1603–1635.

Levy-Yeyati, E., F. Sturzenegger, and I. Reggio (2010) "On the Endogeneity of Exchange Rate Regimes," *European Economic Review*, 54:5, 659–677.

[16] This is one reason why monetarists such as Milton Friedman support the use of flexible exchange rate regimes rather than fixed exchange rate regimes. See Friedman (1953).

Makin, A.J. (2007) "Does China's Huge External Surplus Imply an Undervalued Renminbi?" *China and World Economy*, 15:3, 89–102.

Montiel, P.J. (2003) *Macroeconomics in Emerging Markets*, Cambridge University Press.

Obstfeld, M. and K.S. Rogoff (1995) "The Mirage of Fixed Exchange Rates," *Journal of Economic Perspectives*, 9:4, 73–96.

Reinhart, C.M. and K.S. Rogoff (2004) "The Modern History of Exchange Rate Arrangements: A Reinterpretation," *Quarterly Journal of Economics*, 119:1, 1–48.

Rodrik, D. (2008) "The Real Exchange Rate and Economic Growth," *Brookings Papers on Economic Activity*, Fall, 365–412.

Siklos, P. (2009) "Impossible Trinity," in K.A. Reinert, R.S. Rajan, A.J. Glass, and L.S. Davis (eds.), *The Princeton Encyclopedia of the World Economy*, Princeton University Press, 619–622.

Slavov, S. (2009) "Currency Board Arrangement," in K.A. Reinert, R.S. Rajan, A.J. Glass, and L.S. Davis (eds.), *The Princeton Encyclopedia of the World Economy*, Princeton University Press, 240–243.

Subramanian, A. (2010) "New PPP-Based Estimates of Renminbi Undervaluation and Policy Implications," Policy Brief 10–8, Peterson Institute for International Economics.

17 The International Monetary Fund

In the history of global financial arrangements, the year 1941 stands as a turning point. In September of that year, the British economist John Maynard Keynes spent, as he wrote to his mother, "several days of peace writing a heavy memorandum on post-war international currency plans."[1] The result was a proposal for an International Clearing Union (ICU), an idea subsequently taken up by the British Treasury. Three months later and across the Atlantic, U.S. Treasury official Harry Dexter White wrote a proposal for an International Stabilization Fund (ISF), subsequently embraced wholeheartedly by U.S. Treasury Secretary Henry Morgenthau. These two proposals, which became known as the Keynes Plan and the White Plan, respectively, competed for prominence in the international deliberations over how to constitute the institutions of international finance after the end of the Second World War. The proposals were taken up at the Bretton Woods Conference in July 1944, with the White Plan gaining prominence. The result was the creation of the **International Monetary Fund** (IMF) and the International Bank for Reconstruction and Development (the World Bank). Neither Keynes nor White would live out the decade, both dying of heart attacks while the Fund and Bank were being established.[2]

In Chapter 7, you were introduced to the institutions of international trade in the form of the World Trade Organization. As a student of the world economy, you also need to be familiar with the IMF and World Bank. This chapter introduces you to the IMF, and Chapter 23 introduces you to the World Bank. Together, these two chapters will make you familiar with the basic "rules of the game" in international finance. We begin in this chapter with a brief history of international monetary arrangements during the twentieth century. This will allow you to place the IMF in the context of recent financial history. Next we turn to the actual operations of the IMF and the political economy of IMF lending. Finally, we make a preliminary assessment of the IMF and its role in the world economy. We take up the controversial role of the IMF in recent financial crises in Chapter 18.

Analytical elements for this chapter:

Countries, *currencies*, and *financial assets*.

SOME MONETARY HISTORY

Throughout the twentieth century, the countries of the world struggled with various arrangements for the conduct of international finance. None of these arrangements proved satisfactory. Over time, international economic policymakers attempted to set up one system after another, and, in each case, they were overtaken by events. In retrospect, we can see that the international financial system had a dynamic of its own, one much stronger than the institutional scaffolding temporarily built around it. As the most recent crisis that began in 2007 reminds us, this is also no doubt true today. In this section of the chapter, we briefly review some of the main events in the drama to give you an appreciation of the evolutionary power of international finance and to place the IMF in the context of this dynamic.

[1] Skidelsky (2000), pp. 202–203.

[2] On Keynes' contributions during this period, see Skidelsky (2000). On White, see chapter 7 of Skidelsky (2000) (including his alleged role as a Soviet agent) and Boughton (1998).

The Gold Standards

The decades from 1870 to 1914 were characterized by a highly integrated world economy that was supported by an international financial arrangement known as the **gold standard**. Under the gold standard, each country defined the value of its currency in terms of gold. Most countries also held gold as official reserves. Because the value of each currency was defined in terms of gold, the rates of exchange among the currencies were fixed. Thus the gold standard was one type of fixed exchange rate system.[3] When World War I began in 1914, the countries involved in that conflict suspended the convertibility of their currencies into gold. After the war, there was an attempt to return the international financial system back to "normal," that is, to rebuild the gold standard. Success in this endeavor was to prove elusive.

In 1922, there was an economic conference held in Genoa, Italy, that attempted to rebuild the pre-World War I gold standard. The new gold standard was different from the pre-war standard, however. There was a gold shortage at the time, and to address this problem, countries that were not important financial centers did not hold gold reserves. Instead, they held gold-convertible currencies, a practice utilized by a number of countries before the war. For this reason, the new gold standard was known as the **gold-exchange standard**. One goal of the gold-exchange standard was to set major rates at their pre-war levels. The most important rate was that of the British pound. In 1925, it was set to gold at the overvalued, pre-war rate of US$4.86 per pound.[4] This caused balance of payments problems (see Chapter 16) and market expectations of devaluation. At a systemwide level, each major rate was set to gold, ignoring the implied rates among the various currencies. As is often the case, the politics of the day prevailed over economic common sense.

The gold-exchange standard thus consisted of a set of center countries tied to gold and a set of periphery countries holding these center-country currencies as reserves. By 1930, nearly all the countries of the world had joined. The design of the system, however, held within it a significant incentive problem for the periphery countries. Suppose a periphery country expected that the foreign currency it held as reserves was going to be devalued against gold. It would be in the interest of this country to *sell* its reserves *before* the devaluation took place to preserve the value of its total reserves. This, in turn, would put even greater pressure on the value of the center currency. As mentioned previously, the British pound was set at an overvalued rate. In September 1931, there was a run on the pound, and this forced Britain to cut the pound's tie to gold. As the decade of the 1930s ensued, a system of separate currency areas evolved, and there was a combination of both fixed and floating rates. Austria and Germany also left the gold standard system in 1931, the United States in 1933, and France in 1936.

Many other countries subsequently cut their ties to gold. By 1937, no countries remained on the gold-exchange standard. Overall, the gold-exchange standard was not a success. Some international economists (most notably, Eichengreen, 1992) have even

[3] As students of the history of economic thought know, the operation of the gold standard was first described by Hume (1924, originally 1752). A more modern treatment can be found in McCloskey and Zecher (1976). For a complete historical assessment, see Eichengreen (1992).

[4] Keynes opposed this policy strenuously, famously calling the gold standard a "barbarous relic." In the same essay (1963, orig. 1923), he stated: "(Since) I feel no confidence that an old-fashioned gold standard will even give us the modicum of stability that it used to give, I reject the policy of restoring the gold standard on pre-war lines" (pp. 211–212). His observations here were to prove prescient.

seen it as a major contributor to the Great Depression.[5] During the unraveling of the system, countries engaged in a game of *competitive devaluation*, each trying to gain greater export competitiveness over other countries.[6] This breakdown in international economic cooperation helped to fuel the rise of nationalism and fascism that eventually erupted in World War II.

The Bretton Woods System

During World War II, the United States and Britain began to plan for the post-war economic system. As mentioned above, in the United States, the planning occurred at the U.S. Treasury under the direction of Harry Dexter White, whereas John Maynard Keynes took the lead at the British Treasury.[7] These individuals understood the contribution of the previous breakdown in the international economic system to the war, and they hoped to avoid the same mistake that was made after World War I. Also, however, White and Keynes were fighting for the relative positions of the countries they represented. In this competition, White and the U.S. Treasury had the upper hand, and White largely got his way during the 1944 Bretton Woods Conference.

The conference produced a plan for a new international financial system that became known as the **Bretton Woods system**. The essence of the system was an **adjustable gold peg.**[8] Under the Bretton Woods system, the U.S. dollar was to be pegged to gold at US$35 per ounce. The other countries of the world were to peg to the U.S. dollar or directly to gold. This placed the dollar at the center of the new international financial system, a role envisaged by White and the U.S. Treasury. The currency pegs were to remain fixed except under conditions that were termed *fundamental disequilibrium*. The concept of fundamental disequilibrium, however, was never carefully defined. The agreement also stipulated that countries were to make their currencies convertible to U.S. dollars as soon as possible, but this convertibility process did not happen quickly.

Views of the Bretton Woods Conference

The Bretton Woods Conference of July 1944 was unusual in the breadth of international representation and scope of work. The name of the conference derived from the New Hampshire resort where it took place. The 730 delegates from 45 countries were housed at the Mount Washington Hotel from July 1 to July 22, with British and U.S. delegations having begun work on June 23. Here are a few views of this extraordinary gathering.

Financial historian Harold James wrote: "The Bretton Woods conference wove consensus, harmony, and agreement as if under a magician's spell.... The participants met almost around the clock in overcrowded and acoustically unsuitable hotel rooms.

[5] In a usefully dense passage, Eichengreen (1992) stated: "The gold standard of the 1920s set the stage for the Depression of the 1930s by heightening the fragility of the international financial system. The gold standard was the mechanism transmitting the destabilizing impulse from the United States to the rest of the world. The gold standard magnified that initial destabilizing shock. It was the principal obstacle to offsetting action. It was the binding constraint preventing policymakers from averting the failure of banks and containing the spread of financial panic" (p. xi).

[6] Recall from Chapter 15 that a lower value of a currency gives a country's exporters an incentive to export.

[7] James (1996) reported that "Already weeks after the outbreak of war in 1939, Keynes was sending memoranda to President Roosevelt that included suggestions on how the postwar reconstruction of Europe might be handled better than after 1918" (p. 33).

[8] Keynes and the British government had advocated flexible rates, and White and the U.S. government had advocated fixed rates. The adjustable peg was the compromise between these two positions. See, for example, chapter 4 of Eichengreen (2008).

Gradually exhaustion set in. Keynes wrote: 'We have all of us worked every minute of our waking hours practically without intermission for what is now four weeks.... At one moment Harry White told me that at last even he was all in, not having been in bed for more than five hours a night for four consecutive weeks.' On July 19, 1944, Keynes collapsed with a mild heart attack."

Keynes biographer Robert Skidelsky wrote: "At Bretton Woods, the problems of peace were discussed in the shadow of war about to end. It was a war, moreover, which the Soviet Union was doing most to win, and this was reflected in the number of honorary posts its delegates were assigned. It was the first time Keynes had encountered the Commissars *en masse* since his visits to the Soviet Union in the late 1920s. He used the opportunity to try to persuade them to send the Bolshoi Ballet over to Covent Garden the following year. The Foreign Office took up the idea, but nothing came of it. There would be no Russian ballet in London till 1956. The reason, it turned out, was that the Russians had a well-founded fear of defections."

And finally, Keynes' wife, Lydia Keynes (née Lapakova), a former Russian ballerina herself, wrote: "the taps run all day, the windows do not close or open, the pipes mend and unmend and no one can get anywhere."

Sources: James (1996) and Skidelsky (2000)

The Bretton Woods system came into being in 1946, the year of Keynes' death. Like the gold-exchange standard, it contained the seeds of its own demise. Problems became apparent even by the end of the 1940s in the form of growing nonofficial balance of payments deficits of the United States. These deficits reflected official reserve transactions in support of expanding global dollar reserves.[9] Although the Bretton Woods agreements allowed par values to be defined either in gold or dollar terms, in practice, the dollar became the central measure of value. What was to be a revised gold standard became a de facto dollar standard.

The Belgian monetary economist Robert Triffin described the problem of expanding dollar reserves in his 1960 book *Gold and the Dollar Crisis.* This problem became known as the **Triffin dilemma**. The Triffin dilemma can be conceived of as a contradiction between the requirements of international *liquidity* and international *confidence.* The term *liquidity* refers to the ability to transform assets into currencies. With the dollar being the centerpiece of the system, international liquidity required a continual increase in the holdings of dollars as reserve assets. As dollar holdings of central banks expanded relative to U.S. official holdings of gold, however, international confidence would suffer. Could the United States back up an ever-expanding supply of dollars with a relatively constant amount of gold holdings? No, said Triffin. The requirements of international liquidity would compromise the requirements of international confidence, and a crisis was inevitable. This process is represented in Figure 17.1.

The first sign of trouble occurred during October 1960 when the London gold market price rose above US$35 to US$40 an ounce. At this time, there were calls for a change in the gold-dollar parity. U.S. President Kennedy would have none of this. In January of 1961, the Kennedy Administration pledged to maintain the US$35 per ounce convertibility. To support this position, the United States joined with other European countries and set up a *gold pool* in which their central banks would buy and sell gold to support the

[9] These official sales of dollars by the United States to the central banks of the world (a U.S. official reserve surplus) had its counterpart in a deficit on the sum of the U.S. current and nonofficial capital accounts. See Chapter 13.

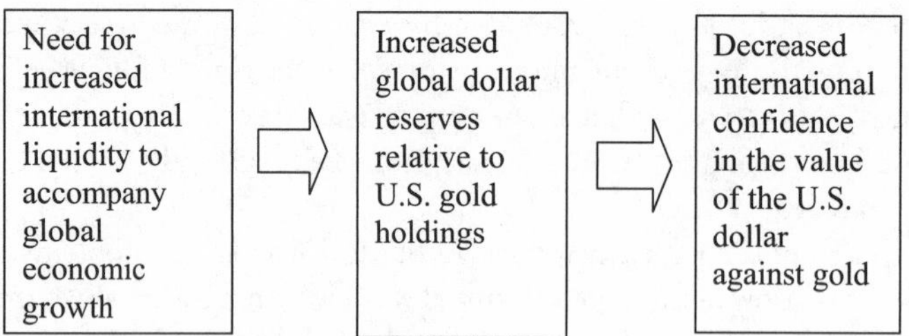

Figure 17.1. The Triffin Dilemma

US$35 price in the London market. Nevertheless, at the 1964 annual IMF meeting in Tokyo, representatives began to talk publicly about potential reforms in the international financial system. Specific attention was given to the creation of reserve asset alternatives to the U.S. dollar and gold. In 1965, the United States Treasury announced that it was ready to join in international discussions on potential reforms. The adamant stance of the Kennedy Administration gave way (after Kennedy's assassination) to a somewhat more flexible posture in the Johnson Administration. Meanwhile, the British pound was under pressure to devalue against the dollar. As it happened, the pound was devalued in November of 1967.

After the devaluation of the pound, President Johnson issued a statement recommitting the United States to the US$35 per ounce gold price. However, in the early months of 1968, the rush began. The London gold market was closed in mid-March, and central bank officials from around the world met at the Federal Reserve Board in Washington, DC. At this meeting, a two-tiered system was constructed. Official foreign exchange transactions were to be conducted at the old rate of US$35 per ounce. The rate in the London gold market, however, was allowed to float freely. The London price reached a high of US$43 in 1969 and then returned to US$35 in 1970. The Triffin dilemma was temporarily avoided.[10]

In early 1971, capital began to flow out of dollar assets and into German mark assets. The German Bundesbank cut its main interest rate to attempt to curb the purchase of marks. Canada had let its dollar begin to float in 1970. Germany and a few other European countries joined Canada in 1971. Thereafter, capital flowed out of dollar assets and into yen assets. In August 1971, U.S. Treasury Secretary John Connally proposed to President Nixon that the U.S. government close its "gold window," effectively suspending the convertibility of the U.S. dollar into gold. Nixon accepted this recommendation in an effort to force other countries to *revalue* against the U.S. dollar. On August 15, 1971, Nixon announced the close of the gold window, and with this announcement, the Bretton Woods adjustable peg system came to an end. This date remains a milestone in international financial history. What followed was a period of experimentation, often referred to as the "non-system," that continues to the present day.

[10] Eichengreen (2008) wrote: "The array of devices to which the Kennedy and Johnson administrations resorted became positively embarrassing. They acknowledged the severity of the dollar problem while displaying a willingness to address only the symptoms, not the causes. Dealing with the causes required reforming the international system in a way that diminished the dollar's reserve-currency role, something the United States was still unwilling to contemplate" (p. 127).

The Non-System

In December 1971, a two-day conference began in Washington, DC, that came to be known as the **Smithsonian Conference.** At this conference, several countries revalued their currencies against the dollar, and the gold price was raised to US$38 per ounce. Canada maintained its floating rate. The fact that it took the August closing of the gold window, a period of managed floating, and an international conference to introduce a small amount of adjustment into the adjustable peg system speaks to the failure of the Bretton Woods agreement as an effective system.

Actually, the Smithsonian Conference ignored the entire adjustment question and the Triffin dilemma, and this quickly became apparent. In June 1972, there appeared a large flow out of U.S. dollars into European currencies and the Japanese yen. These flows stabilized, but the new crisis reappeared in January 1973. During that month, the Swiss franc began to float. In February, there was pressure against the German mark, and there were closures of foreign exchange markets in both Europe and Japan. In February 1973, the United States announced a second devaluation of the dollar against gold to US$42. By this time, the Japanese yen, the Swiss franc, the Italian lira, the British pound, and the Canadian dollar were floating. By March, the German mark and the French franc, the Dutch guilder, the Belgian franc, and the Danish krone also began to float. The members of the IMF found themselves in violation of the Bretton Woods Articles of Agreement. The international financial system had crossed a threshold, although this was not fully appreciated at the time.[11]

During 1974 and 1975, the countries of the world went through nearly continuous consultation and disagreement in a process of accommodating their thinking to the new reality of floating rates. The French government, in particular, was skeptical of the long-term viability of the floating regime, whereas the U.S. government appeared reconciled to it. In November 1975, the heads of state of the United States, France, Germany, the United Kingdom, Italy, and Japan met at Château de Rambouillet outside of Paris. In a declaration, these heads of state proposed an amendment to the IMF's Articles of Agreement, developed at the Bretton Woods conference. This amendment restricted allowable exchange rate arrangements to (1) currencies fixed to anything *other than gold*, (2) cooperative arrangements for managed values among countries, and (3) floating. In January 1976, during an IMF meeting in Jamaica, the Articles of Agreement were indeed amended to reflect the Rambouillet Declaration. This became known as The Jamaica Agreement. The Jamaica Agreement institutionalized what had, in fact, already occurred.

THE OPERATION OF THE IMF

The IMF is an international financial organization comprising, at the time of this writing in 2011, of 187 member countries. Its purposes, as stipulated in its Articles of Agreement, are:

1. To promote international monetary cooperation
2. To facilitate the expansion of international trade

[11] For example, Solomon (1977) noted that "The move to generalized floating in March 1973 was widely regarded as a temporary departure from normality" (p. 267).

Table 17.1. Administrative structure of the IMF

Body	Composition	Function
Board of Governors	One Governor and one Alternate Governor for each member	Meets annually; highest decision-making body
Executive Board	24 Executive Directors plus Managing Director	Day-to-day operations; operates by consensus and voting
Managing Director		Head of Staff and Chair of Executive Board; responsible for staffing and general business
Deputy Managing Directors	First Deputy Managing Director and two other Deputy Managing Directors	Assist Managing Director
Staff	Citizens of member countries	Run departments

Source: www.imf.org

3. To promote exchange stability and a multilateral system of payments
4. To make temporary financial resources available to members under "adequate safeguards"
5. To reduce the duration and degree of international payments imbalances

The administrative structure of the IMF is summarized in Table 17.1. The IMF's major decision-making body is its Board of Governors, to which each member appoints a Governor and an Alternate Governor. Day-to-day business, however, rests in the hands of the Executive Board. This is composed of 24 Executive Directors plus the Managing Director. Large countries (including the United States, Japan, Germany, France, the United Kingdom, China, Russia, and Saudi Arabia) have their own representatives. The rest of the IMF's member countries are represented through constituencies. The Managing Director is appointed by the Executive Board and is traditionally a European (often French).[12] The Managing Director chairs the Executive Board and conducts the IMF's business. There are also currently three Deputy Managing Directors.

The IMF can be thought of as a sort of global credit union. Member country shares in this credit union are determined by its *quota system*. Members' quotas are their *subscriptions* to the IMF and reflect their relative sizes in the world economy. These quotas determine both the amount members can borrow from the IMF and their relative voting power. The higher a member's quota, the more it can borrow and the greater its voting power. A member pays one-fourth of its quota in widely accepted reserve currencies (U.S. dollar, British pound, euro, or yen) or in IMF **special drawing rights** (SDRs), a unit of account that came into being in 1969 and is a weighted average of these four currencies. The member pays the remaining three-quarters of the quota in its own national currency. A quota review in 2008 resulted in the quotas reported in Figure 17.2.[13] These percentages also determine voting power in the IMF.

[12] As indicated in Chapter 23, the President of the World Bank is traditionally a U.S. citizen.

[13] In general, quota reviews take place very five years, but there has been an agreement that the next quota review will be brought forward from 2013 to 2011. The reader should consult www.imf.org for these changes.

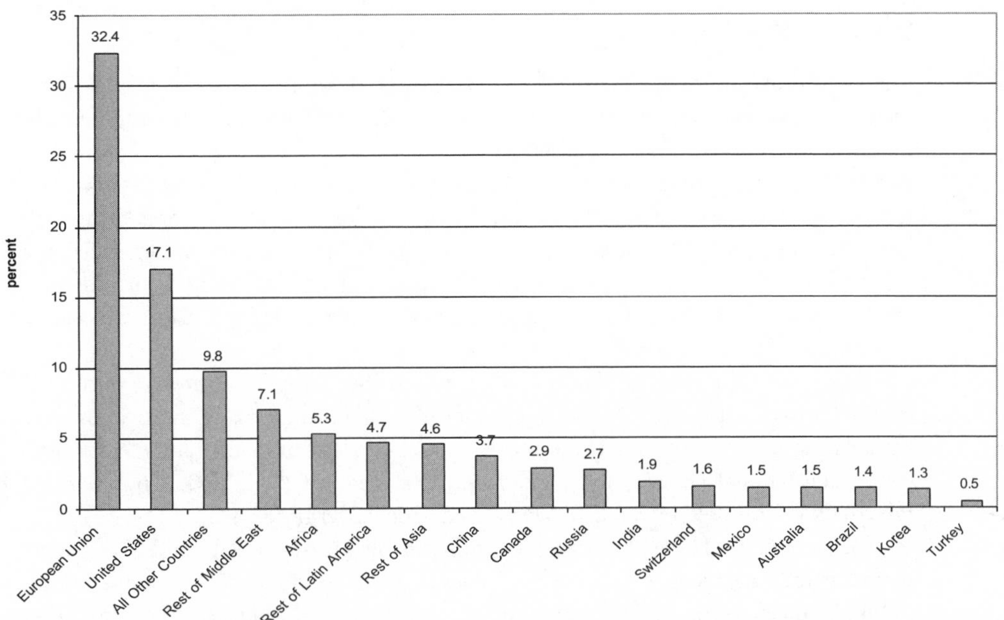

Figure 17.2. IMF Quotas as of 2008. *Source:* www.imf.org

In times of difficulty, an IMF member country gains access to the Fund's resources through a somewhat complex borrowing process. This process involves three stages, namely the reserve tranche, the credit tranche, and special or extended facilities. Let's consider each in turn.

If an IMF member faces balance of payments difficulties, it can automatically borrow 25 percent of its quota in the form of a *reserve tranche.*[14] The reserve tranche is considered to be part of the member country's own foreign reserves. Therefore, the reserve tranche is not actually part of the IMF lending process. It is automatic and free of the policy conditions described in the accompanying box.

The second source of IMF resources is in the form of *credit tranches*, each again set in 25 percent quota increments. There is a distinction here between a *lower credit tranche* or the first 25 percent of quota above the reserve tranche and *upper credit tranches* beyond that. In the typical case, access to credit tranches is obtained through Stand-By Arrangements (SBAs). SBAs are designed to assist the member country with balance of payments issues during a time frame of approximately two years. Access to upper credit tranches is achieved by the member country's commitment to *policy conditions* set in negotiation with the IMF. These are set out in a letter of intent negotiated between the member country and the IMF. Generally speaking, the higher the credit tranche, the more carefully the IMF looks at the request and the more policy conditions applied. Conditionality is discussed further in the accompanying box.

[14] Vreeland (2003) noted that "The general view of the Fund is that the ebbs and flows of reserves due to trading-as-usual may lead to small balance of payments deficits, causing a government to draw on no more than 25 percent of its quota. Thus a member can freely draw on other countries' currency up to an amount equivalent to 25 percent of its quota whenever it faces a balance of payments shortfall" (p. 10). Nevertheless, the 25 percent rule is entirely arbitrary.

IMF Conditionality

The conditions imposed by the IMF on borrowers take a number of forms. These include prior actions, quantitative performance criteria (QPCs), and structural benchmarks. Prior actions consist of measures the borrowing country agrees to before loan approval. According to the IMF, prior actions "ensure that the program has the necessary foundation to succeed." They can include the removal of price controls or approval of a government budget. According to Copelovitch (2010), "prior actions are intended as a signal to the IMF and private markets that a borrower has made a firm 'upfront' or *ex ante* commitment to reforming its economic policies and resolving its financial problems" (p. 18).

QPCs are measurable conditions that need to be met before an approved amount of credit is actually disbursed. According to the IMF, QPCs can include "macroeconomic variables under the control of the authorities, such as some monetary and credit aggregates, international reserves, fiscal balances, or external borrowing." The number and type of QPCs imposed by the IMF have varied widely over time.

Finally, structural benchmarks are less-quantifiable measures that the IMF considers to be "critical to achieve program goals." These can address financial sector operations, public financial management, privatization of state-owned enterprises, or any other policy realms deemed important by IMF staff.

The economic and political analysis of the extent and qualities of IMF conditionality is an ongoing enterprise and is part of the analysis of the political economy of IMF lending discussed later.

Sources: Copelovitch (2010) and International Monetary Fund (2010)

The process behind such IMF lending is depicted in Figure 17.3. When the IMF lends to a member country, what actually happens is that this country *purchases* international reserves from the IMF using its own domestic currency reserves. The member country is then obliged to repay the IMF by *repurchasing* its own domestic currency reserves with international reserves. In this way, IMF lending is known as a "purchase-repurchase" arrangement. For standard credit tranches, the repurchase typically takes place in a three- to five-year time frame. No repurchase requirements are placed on the reserve tranche.

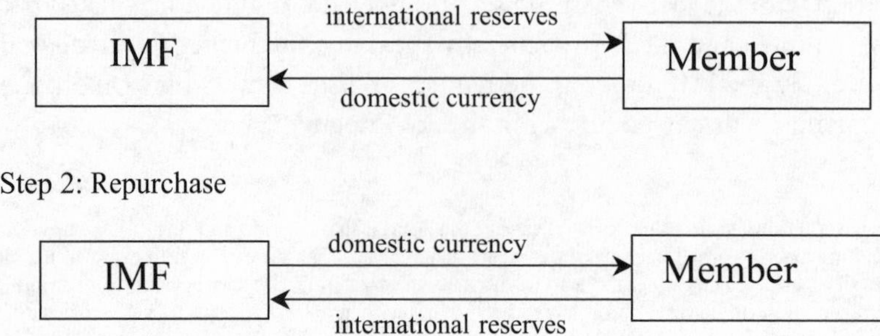

Figure 17.3. IMF Lending

Table 17.2. A selection of IMF facilities as of 2010

Category	Name	Year established	Purpose
Standard	Stand-By Arrangement (SBA)	1952	The standard IMF credit facility for balance of payments adjustment in middle-income countries over a two-year time horizon with repayment over a three- to five-year time period.
Special Nonconcessional	Extended Fund Facility (EFF)	1963	For balance of payments adjustment over a three-year time horizon with repayment over a 4- to 10-year period.
Special Nonconcessional	Flexible Credit Line (FCL)	2009	For balance of payments adjustment in countries with strong fundamentals over a one-year time horizon with repayment over a three- to five-year time period.
Special Nonconcessional	Emergency Assistance	1962 for natural disasters 1995 for civil conflict	Assistance for countries with natural disasters or civil conflict. Although generally nonconcessional, emergency assistance can be on concessional terms in some instances.
Special Concessional	Extended Credit Facility (ECF)	1986 as Structural Adjustment Facility 1987 as Enhanced Structural Adjustment Facility 1999 as Poverty Reduction and Growth Facility 2009 as ECF	Concessional financing to low-income countries to address medium-term balance of payments difficulties with repayment over a 10-year time period.
Special Concessional	Standby Credit Facility (SCF)	2008 as Exogenous Shocks Facility 2009 as SCF	Concessional financing to low-income countries to address short-term balance of payments difficulties with repayment over an eight-year time period.
Special Concessional	Rapid Credit Facility (RCF)	2010	Concessional financing to low-income countries with urgent balance of payments difficulties with repayment over a 10-year time period.

Source: www.imf.org

Beyond the credit tranches of IMF lending, the member country enters the realm of *special facilities* or *extended facilities*. Historically, these special facilities have changed rapidly in response to the vicissitudes of the world economy. Consequently, it is difficult to accurately catalogue them over time. Table 17.2 gives the picture in 2010. This table distinguishes among standard lending (the SBA), special nonconcessional lending, and special concessional lending. Nonconcessional lending involves a standard IMF charge in the purchase-repurchase agreement, whereas concessional lending reduces this charge below the standard rate.

Nonconcessional facilities currently include the Extended Fund Facility (EFF), the Flexible Credit Line (FCL), and Emergency Assistance. The EFF addresses more medium-term balance of payments adjustment, whereas the FCL is directed to short-term adjustment and has no conditions attached to its use. Emergency Assistance is usually (but not always) nonconcessional and is geared toward natural disasters and civil conflict.

Concessional lending includes the Extended Credit Facility (ECF), the Standby Credit Facility (SCF), and the Rapid Credit Facility (RCF). The Extended Credit Facility has a relatively long history in other guises (Structural Adjustment Facility, Enhanced Structural Adjustment Facility, and Poverty Reduction and Growth Facility). It is now the standard concessional financing of the IMF for medium-term balance of payments difficulties. The SCF was introduced in the wake of the 2007–2009 crisis and is geared toward short-term balance of payments difficulties. Finally, the RCF is the newest IMF facility and is meant to address the most urgent balance of payments crises in low-income countries.

In historical perspective, the preceding lending arrangements reflect the dominance achieved by the White Plan over the Keynes Plan at the Bretton Woods Conference. The Keynes plan had an ingenious feature in that it penalized both creditors and debtors symmetrically. This spread international adjustment responsibilities between *both* countries with balance of payments surpluses *and* countries with balance of payments deficits. This feature was not adopted in the final agreements, adjustment being the responsibility of the deficit countries.[15]

This discussion has focused on the disbursement of IMF resources, but where do these come from? The first and most traditional source of IMF resources is the quotas themselves. Additionally, the IMF can sell small portions of its large holdings of gold, as it did in 2010. More importantly, the IMF has standing bilateral and multilateral borrowing arrangements. The multilateral borrowing arrangements are more significant and are in the form of the General Arrangements to Borrow (GAB) and the New Arrangements to Borrow (NAB). These arrangements were significantly increased by major players in 2009 to set the Fund's total resources to US$750 billion. At the time of this writing in 2010, there are ongoing discussions to increase this further to US$1 trillion.[16]

A HISTORY OF IMF OPERATIONS

In its initial years, the IMF was nearly irrelevant, being pushed aside by the United States' own programs for post-war European reconstruction via the European Recovery Program and the Organization for European Economic Cooperation (see accompanying box). The IMF did play an advisory role to a series of European devaluations beginning in 1949 in the face of "fundamental disequilibria." Nevertheless, the *Financial Times* described the IMF in early 1956 as a "white elephant." The claim proved to be ill-timed. The Suez crisis of that year forced Britain to draw on its reserve and first credit tranches,

[15] See, for example, Buira (1995).
[16] See *Financial Times* (2010).

Japan drew on its reserve tranche in 1957, and between late 1956 through 1958, the IMF was involved in the policies that led to the convertibility of both the British pound and the French franc. This success was followed by a general increase in quotas of 50 percent in 1959. During these few years, SBAs described previously were made with many other countries, including many developing countries. The IMF had become an active institution with an increased membership due to de-colonization.

Limited Liquidity in the Early Years

One of the important functions of the IMF envisioned by its Bretton Woods originators was the provision of global liquidity. The Keynes Plan envisaged US$23 billion in total drawing rights. The White Plan, however, proposed total drawing rights of only US$5 billion. The resulting Articles of Agreement total set drawing rights at US$8.8 billion. By the time the IMF opened for business in 1947, post-war Europe's combined trade deficit was US$7.5 billion. As noted by Walter and Sen (2009), "By late 1947 it had become clear that the IMF's total resources were wholly inadequate" (p. 117). Given the size of Europe's deficit in relationship to the IMF's resources, the United States had to step in to fill the gap. Through 1951 and in response to the emerging Cold War, it provided US$13 billion in Marshall Plan aid to Europe, thus significantly supplementing IMF resources. Despite this infusion of liquidity that amounted to more than four times the total drawing rights of Europe, a number of European currencies had to be devalued in 1949.

Sources: Eichengreen (2008) and Walter and Sen (2009)

As described previously, the Bretton Woods system was one in which the U.S. dollar played the role of major reserve asset for member countries. We also described the difficulty of this arrangement, which first erupted on the London gold market in 1960. This "dollar problem" embodied in the Triffin dilemma (Figure 17.1) did not escape the notice of the IMF. Concerned about the United States' ability to defend the dollar and other major industrialized countries' abilities to maintain their parities, the IMF introduced the GAB in 1962. The GAB involved the central banks of 10 countries setting aside a US$6 billion pool to maintain the stability of the Bretton Woods system.[17] The countries involved became known as the Group of Ten, or G-10, and comprised a rich countries club of the world economy. The presence of such a club and its relationship with the IMF aroused suspicion on the part of countries not fortunate enough to be a member, especially the developing countries. Over time, the G-11 (including Switzerland) increased the GAB to US$23 billion, but as we mentioned previously, the GAB and NAB have recently been expanded to US$750 billion.

By 1965, facing the Triffin dilemma, the United States was in a position in which it faced two unappealing options: reduce the world supply of dollars to enhance international confidence by reducing international liquidity, or expand the world supply of dollars to enhance international liquidity by reducing international confidence. Other countries (particularly France) were objecting to the central role of the United States altogether. But where was the world to turn for a reserve asset? Back to gold? Between the 1964 and 1968 annual meetings of the IMF, discussions took place among major

[17] The countries were Belgium, Canada, France, Italy, Japan, the Netherlands, Sweden, the United Kingdom, the United States, and West Germany.

players, and the result was the creation of an entirely new reserve asset to supplement both gold and the dollar. This reserve asset was known as a **special drawing right** (SDR).

The SDR was "the first international currency to be created in the manner of a national paper currency – purely through a series of legal obligations to accept it on the part of members of the system" (James, 1996, p. 171) in the way envisaged by the Keynes Plan. The SDR came into being in 1969. Ironically, given its intended use to supplement gold and the dollar, its value was set in terms of gold at a value identical to the dollar (US$35 per ounce). In 1971, when the United States broke the gold–dollar link, the SDR was redefined in terms of a basket of five currencies: the dollar, the pound, the mark, the yen, and the franc. It is currently defined in terms of the dollar, the pound, the yen, and the euro and comprises the unit of account of the IMF.

Oil Shocks, Crises, and Adjustment

The oil price increases of 1973–1974 caused substantial balance of payments difficulties for many countries of the world. In 1974 and 1975, the IMF established special oil facilities. Using these, the IMF acted as an intermediary, borrowing the funds from oil-producing countries and lending them to oil-importing countries. Despite the presence of these facilities, the bulk of oil-producing country revenues were "recycled" to other countries by the *commercial* banking system. Recycled petrodollars via the commercial banking system allowed oil-importing countries to avoid IMF conditionality. Further, the commercial loans were often at negative real (inflation-adjusted) interest rates and were thus very attractive to borrowing countries.

Beginning in 1976, the IMF began to sound warnings about the sustainability of developing-country borrowing from the commercial banking system. Banks reacted with hostility to these warnings, arguing that the Fund had no place interfering with private transactions. However, as we shall see later, the Fund proved prescient on this issue.

The 1980s began with a significant increase in real interest rates and a significant decline in non-oil commodity prices. This increased the cost of borrowing and reduced export revenues. In 1982, the IMF calculated that U.S. banking system outstanding loans to Latin America represented approximately 100 percent of total bank capital: the IMF's concern in the latter half of the 1970s about the sustainability of developing-country borrowing had been justified. In 1982, in the face of capital flight, Mexico announced that it would stop servicing its foreign currency debt and nationalized its banking system.[18] Negotiations took place between the Mexican government, the IMF, the U.S. Federal Reserve Bank, and an Advisory Committee of New York banks. An agreement was established that involved the New York banks lending *additional* funds to Mexico. The New York banks complied under threat of additional regulation to address their inability to assess country risk.

The year 1982 also found debt crises beginning in Argentina and Brazil.[19] These and the Mexican crises were addressed by the IMF via a number of SBAs and other special

[18] The lack of foresight of the financial sector with regard to this event was noted by Krugman (1999): "As late as July 1982 the yield on Mexican bonds was slightly *less* than that on those of presumably safe borrowers like the World Bank, indicating that investors regarded the risk that Mexico would fail to pay on time as negligible" (p. 41).

[19] In the case of Argentina, the crisis ensued from an overvalued exchange rate, used as a "nominal anchor" to curb inflationary expenditures. In Brazil, rates of devaluation did not keep up with rates of inflation, causing an overvalued real exchange rate.

facilities throughout the 1980s, many of which fell apart and had to be renegotiated. As in the Mexican case, the New York banks had to be cajoled into releasing more funds. More systematically, in 1986 and 1987, the IMF introduced a Structural Adjustment Facility and an Enhanced Structural Adjustment Facility, respectively (the current ECF in Table 17.2). At the time, these facilities raised the total credit ceiling for member countries to 250 percent of quota.

Despite these efforts, international commercial banks began to withdraw credit from many of the developing countries of the world. The debt crisis became global. Within a few years of the outbreak of the crises, the phenomenon of *net capital outflows* appeared. This involved the capital/financial account payments of debtor countries *exceeding* capital/financial account receipts. The resulting capital/financial account deficits had their counterparts in current account surpluses: the developing countries were using trade surpluses to finance debt repayment. These surpluses were the result of increased exports and reduced domestic consumption. Poverty increased substantially, and much of the developing world, particularly Latin America and Africa, entered what came to be known as *the lost decade.*

Starting in the 1990s, private, nonbank capital began to flow to the developing countries in the form of foreign direct investment (FDI), portfolio investment, and commercial bank lending. The lost decade, however, remained lost. Furthermore, a number of highly indebted countries began to show increasing unpaid IMF obligations. In 1992, a Third Amendment to the Articles of Agreement allowed for suspension of voting rights in the face of large, unpaid obligations. This was hardly a sign of a well-functioning system of international adjustment.

Mexico underwent a second crisis in late 1994 and early 1995. In this instance, the IMF became involved after the U.S. Treasury made commitments from its Exchange Stabilization Fund. There were controversies within the Executive Board with regard to the IMF loan package, the largest to date, but the United States was able to apply pressure to push the package through.[20] In 1997, crises struck a number of Asian countries, most notably Thailand, Indonesia, South Korea, and Malaysia. In 1998, a crisis also hit Russia. In each of these cases, sharp depreciations of the currencies resulted. In the cases of Thailand, Indonesia, and South Korea, the IMF played substantial and controversial roles in addressing the crises. Loan packages were designed with accompanying conditionality agreements. A Supplementary Reserve Facility (SRF) was introduced to provide large volumes of high-interest, short-term loans to selected Asian countries.[21] During the Asian financial crisis, questions were raised about the appropriateness of the IMF's response and its advocacy of liberalizing capital accounts in the run-up to the crisis. IMF First Deputy Managing Director at that time, Stanley Fischer, was a particularly emphatic advocate of capital account liberalization within the Fund, but was forced to curtail his advocacy after the Asian crisis.[22]

The Russian economy was hit by a crisis in 1998, and the IMF responded. This was in the wake of "Western" economic and financial support (including from the IMF after Russia became a full member in 1992) that went back to the late 1980s. The purpose of this support had been to facilitate the transition in Russia from a communist system to a market democracy – a tall order! The IMF had begun large-scale lending in 1992

[20] See the detailed analysis of this in chapter 4 of Copelovitch (2010).
[21] The SRF has recently been discontinued and therefore does not appear in Table 17.2.
[22] For the advocacy position, see Fischer (1998). For an empirical analysis, see Joyce and Noy (2008).

to support Russia through an earlier crisis and to support the "reformers" in the new government that had formed in 1991. In mid-1992, the IMF mistakenly gave its support to a ruble zone in the former Soviet sphere, and the Fund appeared to be not up to the task of dispensing advice.[23]

The year 1995 found the IMF providing one of its largest loans ever to support the Russian economy. Although 1997 initially appeared to be a positive one for the Russian economy, oil prices and government revenues began to fall, the Asian crisis hit, and the government's debt service responsibilities began to exceed its resources. Foreign reserves began to fall precipitously, and the IMF was required to provide another large package, drawing on the GAB for the first time since 1978. That was not enough, and a full-fledged banking and currency crisis ensued, with a significant devaluation of the ruble. The IMF's role in Russia came under severe criticism. For example, Gould-Davies and Woods (1999) concluded that "the Fund failed on two counts: both in the narrower and immediate aim to stabilize, and in the long-term goal of fostering the right conditions for reform in Russia" (p. 19).

In 1998, the IMF also put together a package to support the Brazilian currency, the real, to attempt to prevent the Asian and Russian crises from spreading to Latin America. Despite these arrangements, Brazil was forced to devalue the real in 1999 (see box in Chapter 16). In 2001, a crisis in Argentina occurred despite IMF involvement, which resulted in an economic catastrophe for this country. The Argentine crisis involved the currency board discussed in Chapter 16. Although the IMF was initially skeptical of this exchange rate regime, it later became involved in supporting it. Some observers (e.g., Eichengreen, 2008) suggested that the IMF should have been more active in helping Argentina plot an exit strategy from this exchange rate arrangement rather than attempting to support it.[24]

Recent Changes

Recent years have witnessed a number of important changes at the IMF. In 1997, the GAB was supplemented by the NAB. This involved a subset of IMF members agreeing to lend further resources to the Fund in instances where quotas prove to be insufficient. In 1999, there was also a 45 percent increase in total quotas. However, the early 2000s found the IMF sinking into irrelevancy. As can be seen in Figure 17.4, the number of new arrangements the IMF concluded held fairly steady between 1990 and 2003. It then began to decline precipitously, to only eight in 2008. This was due to booming private capital markets and the buildup of foreign exchange reserves in some Asian countries, notably China and Korea. This proved difficult for the IMF because its operating budget depends on the charges it places on loans. Indeed, there were worries at the time that the IMF would need to begin laying off staff, and there was a commission put together (the Crockett commission after former Bank of International Settlements head Sir Andrew

[23] Controversial reformist Yegor Gaidar (1997) stated that "The scale of problems brought to life by the disintegration of a superpower, political in their nature, were beyond the competence and scope of the IMF" (p. 14).

[24] Eichengreen (2008) wrote: "The IMF's failure to push harder for modification of this rigid currency regime is harder to justify. The Fund had seen hard pegs come to grief in other countries. Unlike (other) cases . . . , it had programs with Argentina throughout this period. It was in continuous contact with the authorities and possessed detailed knowledge of their problems. . . . But it failed to push for a change in the regime while there was still time" (p. 207).

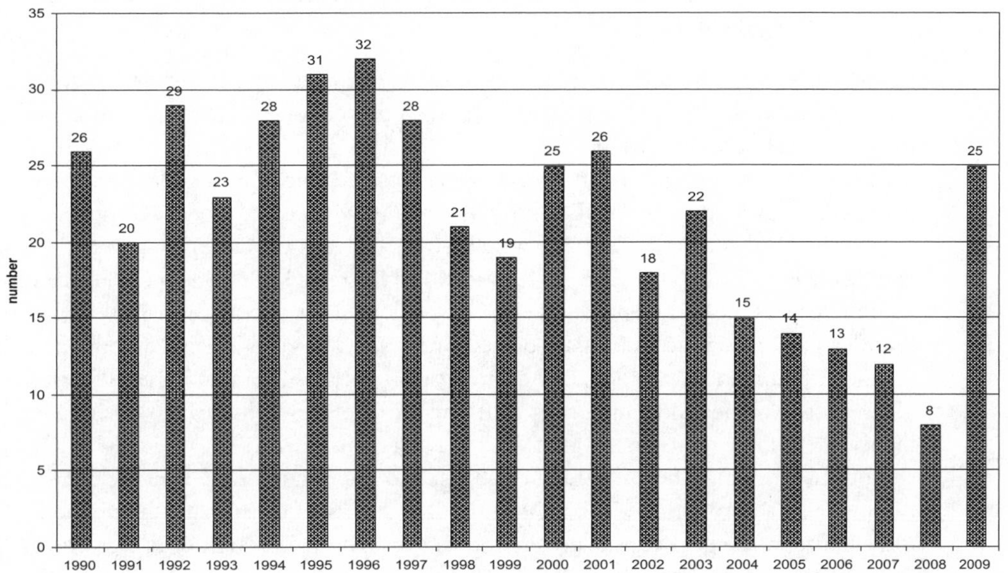

Figure 17.4. New Arrangements Approved, 1990–2009. *Source:* IMF Annual Reports, 2006–2009

Crockett) to make suggestions for how the IMF could continue some of its nonlending activities in the face of dwindling loan charge revenue.

The IMF was caught unaware by the crisis that began in 2007. The 2007 *World Economic Outlook*, the flagship publication of the IMF, stated: "Notwithstanding the recent bout of financial volatility, the world economy still looks well set for robust growth in 2007 and 2008" (p. xv). The year 2008, in particular, turned out to be different than the IMF expected. This crisis, however, gave renewed life to the IMF. Indeed, it is not clear what it would have done without the crisis! As can be seen in Figure 17.4, new IMF arrangements finally recovered in 2009 thanks to this financial event. Interestingly, a number of these loans were to European countries (Belarus, Iceland, Hungary, Latvia, Romania, and Ukraine) rather than to "typical" developing countries. In the face of the crisis, the IMF began to relax some of its conditionality requirements and changed its posture on capital controls.[25]

The year 2008 was also significant for the IMF in that its members agreed to institute a significant quota reform, resulting in the quotas reported in Figure 17.2 earlier. This quota reform involved the following elements: a new formula for calculating quotas, an additional "ad hoc" quota increase to selected countries that were "underrepresented" in the new quota formula, increasing the number of "basic votes" for low-income countries, and a decision to review quotas at a minimum of every five years. The new quota formula is a weighted average of gross domestic product (GDP), economic openness, economic variability, and level of international reserves. The entire quota reform package is one of the most important changes to occur at the IMF in some time.[26]

[25] We consider the capital control issue in Chapter 18.

[26] That said, it is not clear that the 2008 quota reform package addressed the critiques of Bird and Rowlands (2006), who pointed out that the quotas try to address too many functions at once: resource availability, access to resources, SDR distribution, and voting rights. They stated: "it is difficult to see how current problems can be overcome by simply modifying existing quota formulas. As currently constituted, quotas are being asked to do too much. One instrument will not achieve all the targets that it has been set" (pp. 169–170).

The IMF in Ethiopia

In 1996, the IMF announced a new, three-year loan to Ethiopia under its Enhanced Structural Adjustment Facility (ESAF). As part of this package, objectives were set for the 1997–1999 period in the areas of real GDP growth, inflation rate, current account deficit, and gross official foreign reserves. The second tranche of the loan was never delivered. According to the IMF, "the midterm review... could not be completed." Behind the scenes, however, conflicts were brewing between the Ethiopian government and the IMF. According to Wade (2001) and Nobel Laureate Joseph Stiglitz (2001), one major issue was the early repayment of a U.S. bank loan for aircraft brought to supply Ethiopian Airlines, a successful state-owned enterprise. The government lent Ethiopian Airlines the money to repay the loan. According to Stiglitz, "The transaction made perfect sense. In spite of the solid nature of its collateral (an airplane), Ethiopia was paying a far higher interest rate on its loan than it was receiving on its reserves."

Both the IMF and the U.S. Treasury objected to the nature of the loan repayment. Additionally, according to Wade (2001), the IMF began to insist that Ethiopia begin to liberalize its capital account despite the fact that the IMF's Articles of Agreement do not give it jurisdiction in this area. The Ethiopian government refused, and the IMF canceled the release of the second tranche of the 1997 ESAF. In late 1997, the Ethiopian government made contact with Stiglitz, then Chief Economist at the World Bank. Stiglitz visited Ethiopia, as did the then World Bank President James Wolfenson who, in turn, raised Ethiopia's case with then IMF Managing Director Michel Camdessus. As a consequence of these communications, a new ESAF was concluded in 1998.

In response to consultations with Ethiopia, the IMF expressed support of the government's economic management in 1999, but the ESAF was not extended that year. According to Wade (2001), IMF officials "saw themselves as having lost the argument the previous year due to the (illegitimate) intervention of the World Bank. They thought that the government had been let off the hook, and now they were going to bring it to heel by not agreeing to continue Ethiopia's ESAP status, even though the conditions had been fulfilled."

A new program was negotiated in 2000 under the Poverty Reduction and Growth Facility (PRGF) but was delayed until March 2001. In 2002, the IMF called Ethiopia's performance "commendable," and released a second tranche. However, the 2002 loan was followed by disagreements between the Ethiopian government and the Fund over privatization of state-owned enterprises.

Ethiopia has been involved with the IMF to the present time, with continued disagreements. For example, the IMF has recently provided the country with a number of loans under the Exogenous Shocks Facility (now part of the Standby Credit Facility in Table 17.2). Echoing a long-standing criticism of IMF conditionality, there has been concern raised over the government expenditure limits imposed in these recent loans (e.g., Molina 2009), particularly in light of the dire poverty prevalent in the country.

Sources: IMF, Stiglitz (2001), Wade (2001), and Molina (2009)

Finally, as mentioned previously, the IMF's resources have increased substantially. In the wake of the crisis that began in 2007, there was a growing recognition that the Fund's resources were woefully inadequate. Bilateral and multilateral (GAB and NAB, discussed previously) resources were increased to US$750 in 2009. This was to strengthen the IMF's role as *lender of last resort* (LOLR) in the global financial system

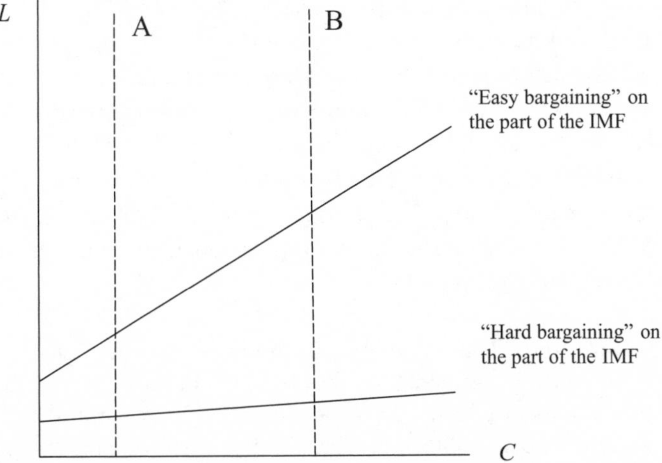

Figure 17.5. IMF Lending. *Source:* Vreeland (2003)

currently under great stress and therefore boost confidence among major financial players.[27]

THE POLITICAL ECONOMY OF IMF LENDING

The original conception of IMF lending was quite simple. A country (typically a developing country) develops balance of payments problems and is forced to approach the IMF for resources. It reluctantly proceeds through the lending process described in this chapter and takes on the associated conditionality conditions required by the IMF. The two relevant variables in the relationship between the member country and the IMF are value of loans (L) and number and strength of conditions (C). The member country was conceived of as wanting L to be high and C to be low. The negotiations proceed between the member country and the IMF in the space described in Figure 17.5. Figure 17.5 distinguishes between a "hard bargaining" line on the part of the IMF and an "easy bargaining" line. The former involves a lower level of L for a given level of C.

As Bird and Rowlands (2003) emphasized, seeking loans (L) from the IMF is a political decision on the part of a member country. As emphasized by Joyce (2006) and Bird (2008), member country governments are continually weighing the perceived (marginal) benefits and costs of being involved in an IMF program. A standard story assumes that a member country would like to be as far as possible to the left of either of these IMF bargaining positions. That is, they would prefer points along the vertical dashed line A than along the vertical dashed line B. This is because there is a sovereignty cost to any level of conditionality (C). There also can be threshold effects in that once a member country pays the sovereignty cost of an initial IMF loan and program, it is more likely to do so again.[28]

[27] It must be recognized that, by design, the IMF will never be a *true* lender of last resort. That possibility disappeared with the Keynes Plan. But it does play this role to some extent, and increasingly so given its extra resources. We return to this issue later.

[28] One way of thinking of this is that the sovereignty cost involves a significant fixed (as opposed to variable) component.

New thinking and evidence provided by Vreeland (2003) and Bird and Rowlands (2003) suggested that conditionality impacts might not be fully explained by sovereignty cost considerations. Instead, some member country governments might be interested in some significant amount of conditionality in order to push through reforms in the face of domestic political opposition. These country governments use IMF conditionality as a way of shifting the blame for unpopular reforms outside of the country to the "blue suits" of the IMF bureaucrats. That is, country governments might prefer points along the vertical dashed line B than along A. Some of these considerations were explained by Bird and Rowlands (2003) as follows:

> Do governments turn to the IMF in an attempt to import the superior reputation of the IMF for economic management? Are they trying to improve the credibility of policy reform by tying themselves into a Fund supported program, the signing of which signals a commitment to reform?... However, it may be unrealistic to view governments as being unified. They may be fragmented and represent fragile coalitions. This creates the possibility that one part of the government may seek to involve the IMF in order to strengthen its hand. Fund involvement may be sought in order to "tip the balance" in favor of economic reform. (p. 1260)

Importantly, perceived benefits and costs on the part of a member country can change significantly over time in response to a host of factors. Sometimes these changes occur in the middle of a loan program and lead a country to fail to meet agreed-to conditionality packages and seek additional tranches or programs. These "implementation failures" are often attributed to a "lack of political will" or "lack of ownership." But behind these failed cases are benefit-cost calculations of the member countries involved, and these are subject to political and economic analysis.[29]

These sorts of considerations give us some insight into the demand side of IMF loans, but what about the supply side? What determines whether the Fund will adopt the "easy bargaining" or "hard bargaining" positions in Figure 17.5? The work of Copelovitch (2010) suggests that one determining factor here is the size and composition of international capital flows. For example, he suggested that, in countries with strong ties to private capital sources in the G-5 countries (the United States, Japan, Germany, the United Kingdom, and France) such as commercial banks, the IMF tends to adopt an easier bargaining position with a larger L for a given C. In addition, when borrowing is in the form of bond finance as opposed to commercial bank lending or is by private borrowers (firms) rather than the central government, the staff of the IMF tends to promote larger loan size in order to overcome the collective action problems inherent in the potentially large number of bond holders.[30]

The importance of these insights is that IMF operations are not fully economic in character. As with the case of the World Trade Organization discussed in Chpater 7 and the World Bank discussed in Chapter 23, there is room for political scientists and other policy analysts outside of economics to make a contribution to our understanding of the IMF.

[29] See, for example, Joyce (2006) and Bird (2008). Joyce (2006) noted that "Blaming incomplete completion on a lack of political resolve misses the reasons for its absence" (p. 358).

[30] In these cases, "the Fund staff will... propose larger loans with more extensive conditionality, in an attempt to alleviate international creditors' concerns about a country's future ability to service its debt, and to convince them to 'bail in' rather than 'bail out' in response to an IMF loan" (Copelovitch, 2010, p. 289).

AN ASSESSMENT

In Chapter 16, we considered the impossible trinity (Figure 16.3). This concept identified three objectives that countries desire in the realm of international finance, namely, monetary independence, exchange rate stability, and capital mobility. In principle, only two of these three objectives are attainable at the same time. Given the history we considered in the present chapter, we can view the gold standard as a period of time in which monetary independence was sacrificed for exchange rate stability and capital mobility. The Bretton Woods system, on the other hand, was one in which there was an attempt to sacrifice capital mobility to achieve exchange rate stability and monetary independence. Eichengreen (2008) strongly defended the view that this change was necessitated by the expansion of democratic processes and interest representation, which demanded an expanded agenda for domestic monetary policy beyond maintaining exchange rate stability. This system did not work in the face of increasing capital mobility.

The IMF was originally designed to support the Bretton Woods system. It was therefore conceived of in an era of hoped-for limited capital mobility. John Maynard Keynes and Harry Dexter White could not anticipate the extent to which a resurgent momentum in international finance would weaken the role of capital controls in the system. With the end of the Bretton Woods era in 1971, the IMF needed to reinvent itself. It did so as a multilateral development institution (along with the World Bank), as well as a lender to emerging economies in crisis. Its lending shifted toward developing countries, and its involvement in what is called structural adjustment (considered in Chapter 24) increased substantially. It has played that role to the present time, supplemented most recently in the wake of the 1997 Asian crisis and the 2007–2009 financial crisis as an imperfect restorer of confidence.

Aspects of the international financial system are often assessed from the point of view of their contributions to providing *liquidity* and *adjustment*. In the realm of liquidity, the IMF never had the resources necessary to make a substantial contribution. In his initial Bretton Woods proposal, John Maynard Keynes envisioned a global central bank with an international currency, the *bancor*. This central bank would be responsible for regulating the expansion of international liquidity. This vision was never to come to fruition and still seems a long way off. Another way of stating this is that the IMF was never fully resourced to play the role of LOLR, mentioned earlier. It has therefore always played this role imperfectly.

In the realm of adjustment, Keynes's original Bretton Woods proposal distributed this requirement across deficit and surplus countries. This proposal was also discarded, and adjustment became solely the responsibility of deficit countries. Furthermore, as Dell (1981) emphasized a long time ago, deficit countries have been required to adjust *no matter what the source of the deficit*. Oil shocks, commodity price declines, and rapid, unforeseen changes in interest rates, which occur through no fault of the deficit (developing) countries, become events requiring conditionality and structural adjustment. At times, these requirements have appeared to violate the purposes of the IMF developed at Bretton Woods: to promote "the development of productive resources" and to achieve balance of payments adjustment "without resorting to measures destructive of national and international prosperity."[31]

[31] See also Dell (1983) on this era of conditionality.

Reform of the existing IMF framework could involve two things: (1) reconstituting it more along the lines of a world central bank, reaffirming the role of the SDR as a reserve asset, and giving the IMF independent responsibility for regulating world liquidity through dramatically expanded quotas and SDR management; and (2) redesigning adjustment mechanisms to spread responsibility over deficit and surplus countries. These changes are radical and would require a complete redrafting of the IMF's Articles of Agreement.[32]

CONCLUSION

During the twentieth century, the countries of the world struggled with three major transitions in financial arrangements: from a gold standard to a gold-exchange standard; from a gold-exchange standard to an adjustable gold peg (the Bretton Woods system); and from an adjustable gold peg to the current "non-system" in which the IMF attempts to stabilize a whole host of currency arrangements. The IMF has played a central, but imperfect role in managing the non-system. Its lending operations described in this chapter have been crucial in helping countries cope with balance of payments problems, but have also been very controversial both in appropriateness of conditionality and effectiveness.[33] We return to these issues in Chapter 18 on crises and Chapter 24 on structural adjustment. These two chapters give us some insight into how the IMF should adjust its conditionality packages in response to different national conditions and to systematic critiques.

We mentioned in Chapter 1 that data on international trade and international finance indicate that international finance is of an order of magnitude larger than trade. Despite its imperfect character, the IMF is a major player in the international finance realm, attempting to contribute to liquidity, adjustment, and stabilization. Having come back from the brink of irrelevancy in 2009, the IMF has quickly re-established its relevancy (and controversy) within the crisis-prone global financial system.

REVIEW EXERCISES

1. How did the gold-exchange standard differ from the gold standard? How did the adjustable gold peg (Bretton Woods) system differ from the gold-exchange standard?
2. Why are post–Bretton Woods monetary arrangements referred to as a "non-system"?
3. In the IMF credit arrangements, what distinguishes the upper credit tranches from the first credit tranche?
4. What is your reaction to the different visions of the Keynes Plan and the White Plan? If you had been a participant at the Bretton Woods Conference, which would you have supported?
5. Would you be in favor of expanding the role of the SDR to make it an international currency along the lines of Keynes' *bancor*?

[32] For proposals along these lines (as well as others), see Eichengreen (2010).

[33] Copelovitch (2010) noted that "virtually no one in today's global economy is happy with the IMF, and almost everyone has a proposal for how it should be reformed" (p. 4).

6. Choose an IMF member in which you have a special interest. Spend a little time perusing the "Country Information" section of the IMF website at www.imf.org. This can be found by clicking one of the major tabs along the top of the home page.

FURTHER READING AND WEB RESOURCES

For a concise introduction to the IMF, see Joyce (2009). An excellent and more extensive source is Copelovitch (2010). On the political economy of the global monetary system, see chapters 4 and 5 of Walter and Sen (2009). On the political economy of IMF lending, see both Vreeland (2003) and Copelovitch (2010). On alleged intellectual bias within the IMF, see Chwieroth (2007).

The reader with an interest in the material of this chapter would do well by consulting the concise and insightful book by Eichengreen (2008). A longer but now somewhat dated treatment can be found in James (1996). Solomon (1977) is also a very worthwhile insider's account of the Bretton Woods system, and Skidelsky's (2000) biography of Keynes is also an important look at the period of history that gave birth to the IMF.

Finally, an online chronology of events relevant to the IMF can be found here: http://www.imf.org/external/np/exr/chron/chron.asp.

REFERENCES

Bird, G. (2008) "The Implementation of IMF Programs: A Conceptual Framework," *Review of International Organizations*, 3:1, 41–64.

Bird, G. and D. Rowlands (2003) "Political Economy Influences within the Life-Cycle of IMF Programs," *World Economy*, 26:9, 1255–1278.

Bird, G. and D. Rowlands (2006) "IMF Quotas: Constructing an International Organization Using Inferior Building Blocks," *Review of International Organizations*, 1:2, 153–171.

Boughton, J.M. (1998) "Harry Dexter White and the International Monetary Fund," *Finance and Development*, 35:3, 39–41.

Buira, A. (1995) *Reflections on the International Monetary System*, Essays in International Finance, No. 195, Princeton University.

Chwieroth, J.M. (2007) "Testing and Measuring the Role of Ideas: The Case of Neoliberalism in the International Monetary Fund," *International Studies Quarterly*, 51:1, 5–30.

Copelovitch, M.S. (2010) *The International Monetary Fund in the Global Economy*, Cambridge University Press.

Dell, S. (1981) *On Being Grandmotherly: The Evolution of IMF Conditionality*, Essays in International Finance, No. 144, Princeton University.

Dell, S. (1983) "Stabilization: The Political Economy of Overkill," in J. Williamson (ed.), *IMF Conditionality*, Institute for International Economics, 17–45.

Eichengreen, B. (1992) *Golden Fetters: The Gold Standard and the Great Depression, 1919–1939*, Oxford University Press.

Eichengreen, B. (2008) *Globalizing Capital: A History of the International Monetary System*, Princeton University Press.

Eichengreen, B. (2010) "Out-of-the-Box Thoughts about the International Financial Architecture," *Journal of International Commerce, Economics and Policy*, 1:1, 1–20.

Fischer, S. (1998) "Capital-Account Liberalization and the Role of the IMF," in S. Fischer et al., *Should the IMF Pursue Capital-Account Convertibility?*, Princeton Essays in International Finance, 207, 1–10.

Financial Times (2010) "IMF Seeks $250bn to Boost Resources," July 18.

Gaidar, Y. (1997) "The IMF and Russia," *American Economic Review*, 87:2, 13–16.

Gould-Davies, N. and N. Woods (1999) "Russia and the IMF," *International Affairs*, 75:1, 1–21.

Hume, D. (1924) "On the Balance of Trade," A.E. Monroe (ed.), *Early Economic Thought*, Dover, 323–338 (originally published in 1752).

International Monetary Fund (2007) *World Economic Outlook: Spillovers and Cycles in the Global Economy*.

International Monetary Fund (2010) *IMF Conditionality Factsheet*.

James, H. (1996) *International Monetary Cooperation since Bretton Woods*, Oxford University Press.

Joyce, J. (2006) "Promises Made, Promises Broken: A Model of IMF Program Implementation," *Economics and Politics*, 18:3, 339–365.

Joyce, J. (2009) "International Monetary Fund," in K.A. Reinert, R.S. Rajan, A.J. Glass, and L.S. Davis (eds.), *The Princeton Encyclopedia of the World Economy*, Princeton University Press, 686–690.

Joyce, J. and I. Noy (2008) "The IMF and the Liberalization of Capital Flows," *Review of International Economics*, 16:3, 413–430.

Keynes, J.M. (1963) "Alternative Aims in Monetary Policy," in *Essays in Persuasion*, Norton, 186–212 (originally published in 1923).

Krugman, P. (1999) *The Return of Depression Economics*, Norton.

McCloskey, D.N. and J.R. Zecher (1976) "How the Gold Standard Worked, 1880–1913," in J.A. Frenkel and H.G. Johnson (eds.), *The Monetary Approach to the Balance of Payments*, University of Toronto Press, 357–385.

Molina, N. (2009) "IMF Emergency Loans for Low-Income Countries," *G-24 Policy Brief* 48.

Skidelsky, R. (2000) *John Maynard Keynes: Fighting for Freedom 1937–1946*, Viking.

Solomon, R. (1977) *The International Monetary System, 1945–1976*, Harper and Row.

Stiglitz, J. (2001) "Thanks for Nothing," *Atlantic Monthly*, October, 36–40.

Triffin, R. (1960) *Gold and the Dollar Crisis: The Future of Convertibility*, Yale University Press.

Vreeland, J.R. (2003) *The IMF and Economic Development*, Cambridge University Press.

Wade, R.H. (2001) "Capital and Revenge: The IMF and Ethiopia," *Challenge*, 44:5, 67–75.

Walter, A. and G. Sen (2009) *Analyzing the Global Political Economy*, Princeton University Press.

18 Crises and Responses

Mexico in 1994 and 1995. Thailand, Indonesia, the Philippines, Malaysia, and South Korea in 1997. Russia in 1998. Brazil in 1999. Argentina in 2001. The United States and the United Kingdom in 2007 to 2009. These are examples of recurrent **crises** that have recently plagued the world economy. At the time, each of these crises was described by some as unexpected, but as it turns out, there are good reasons to expect crises to occur with some regularity. Why? Unlike markets for most goods and services, financial markets are characterized by what economists term "imperfections." Because of these imperfections, we cannot be assured of economic or allocative efficiency in markets for financial products.[1] Furthermore, the imperfections tend to make financial markets somewhat unstable, with "booms" of one kind or another being followed by "busts." The purpose of this chapter is to help you understand why this is so and what role it has played in crises.

We begin by considering different types of crises. These include hyperinflation, balance of payments and currency crises, asset price deflation, banking crises, external debt crises, and domestic debt crises. This is followed by a brief consideration of contagion and systemic risk. We then consider the analysis of "old-fashioned" balance of payments and currency crises. This is followed by a consideration of the more "high tech" Asian crisis and the response of the International Monetary Fund (IMF). We take up the sub-prime crisis of 2007 to 2009, and finally, we discuss two proposals for addressing crises: the Basel standards and capital controls. A third proposal, exchange rate target zones, is considered in an appendix to the chapter. Having studied this chapter, you will be in a better position to assess much of the current debate on crises in the international financial system, an issue that will be with us for some time to come.

> Analytical elements for this chapter:
>
> *Countries*, *currencies*, and *financial assets*.

TYPES OF CRISES

It is often the case that the popular and financial presses use the word "crisis" or "financial crisis" without being more specific. This is somewhat unfortunate because financial crises come in different varieties. Being more specific about these types of crises is an important first step to understanding them. A summary of crisis types is presented in Table 18.1 and includes hyperinflation, balance of payments and currency crises, asset price deflation, banking crises, external debt crises, and domestic debt crises. These crisis types often occur in combination as opposed to in isolation. Let's briefly consider each type.

Hyperinflation is a period of rapid increase in the price level of a country, typically defined to be 40 percent or more annually. Periods of hyperinflation are associated with rapid expansions of the money supply.[2] As an example, Figure 18.1 presents the inflation rate for Zimbabwe during the years 1980 to 2005. Beginning in 1998, this began to increase rapidly, reaching nearly 400 percent in 2003. Official statistics of the World Bank and IMF on inflation in Zimbabwe end in 2005, but most estimates for

[1] The most fundamental imperfection in financial markets is *imperfect information*, particularly asymmetric information, where two parties to a financial transaction have different sets of information about factors relevant to the transaction. See Marks (2009).

[2] See the appendices to Chapter 14 on the relationship between monetary stocks and price levels.

Table 18.1 Types of crises

Crisis type	Characteristics	Examples
Hyperinflation	A rapid increase in the overall price level of a country, typically defined to be 40 percent or higher on an annual basis.	Zimbabwe, 1998–2009
Balance of payments and currency crises	A large devaluation or rapid depreciation in the value of a domestic currency in response to balance of payments difficulties.	Mexico, 1994–1995, and Brazil, 1999
Asset price deflation	A sustained and large decline in the prices of financial assets.	Japan, 1990, and United States, 2007–2009
Banking crises	The occurrence of bank runs and/or the merger, closure, or government takeover of banking institutions.	Argentina, 2001
External debt crises	Sovereign default on debt obligations to foreign creditors or substantial restructuring of this debt.	Mexico, 1982
Domestic debt crises	Sovereign default on debt obligations to domestic creditors or substantial restructuring of this debt.	Argentina, 1989

Sources: Eichengreen (1999) and Reinhart and Rogoff (2009)

subsequent years estimate it as reaching the tens of thousands in percentage terms in 2007 and billions in percentage terms in 2008. Consequently, Figure 18.1 hardly does justice to this episode of hyperinflation.[3] Indeed, the Zimbabwean government was forced to replace its currency with the U.S. dollar in 2009.

Balance of payments and currency crises consist of large devaluations or rapid depreciations in the value of domestic currencies. We considered the case of the 1999 Brazilian devaluation in Chapter 16 and consider the 1994–1995 currency crash in Mexico later in this chapter. As it turns out, periods of hyperinflation can contribute to currency crashes.[4] The reason for this is that, as significant degrees of inflation occur, asset owners move out of domestic currency–denominated assets into foreign currency–denominated assets in order to maintain the value of portfolios. This is a decrease in demand for the domestic currency relative to the foreign currency and puts downward pressure on the value of the domestic currency (upward pressure on the nominal exchange rate e as defined in Chapter 14). Because the foreign currency involved is often the U.S. dollar, this process is sometimes referred to as "dollarization." Reinhart and Rogoff (2009, chapter 12) showed that, once dollarization sets in, it is difficult to reverse, even after inflation levels have declined.

Asset price deflation involves a large and sustained decline in the prices of financial assets. This typically follows on an episode of large and sustained increases in asset prices, what is commonly referred to as **bubbles**. Formally, bubbles need to be defined in statistical terms, but their defining characteristics have been described by Vogel (2010) as follows:

> Generally, a bubble is considered to have developed when assets trade at prices that are far in excess of an estimate of the fundamental value of the asset, as determined from discounted expected future cash flows using current interest rates and typical long-run risk premiums associated with the asset class. Speculators, in such circumstances, are much more interested in profiting from trading in the asset than in its use or earnings capacity or true value. (p. 16)

[3] This forced Zimbabweans to turn to barter. See, for example, Dugger (2010).
[4] For empirical evidence of this, see chapter 12 of Reinhart and Rogoff (2009).

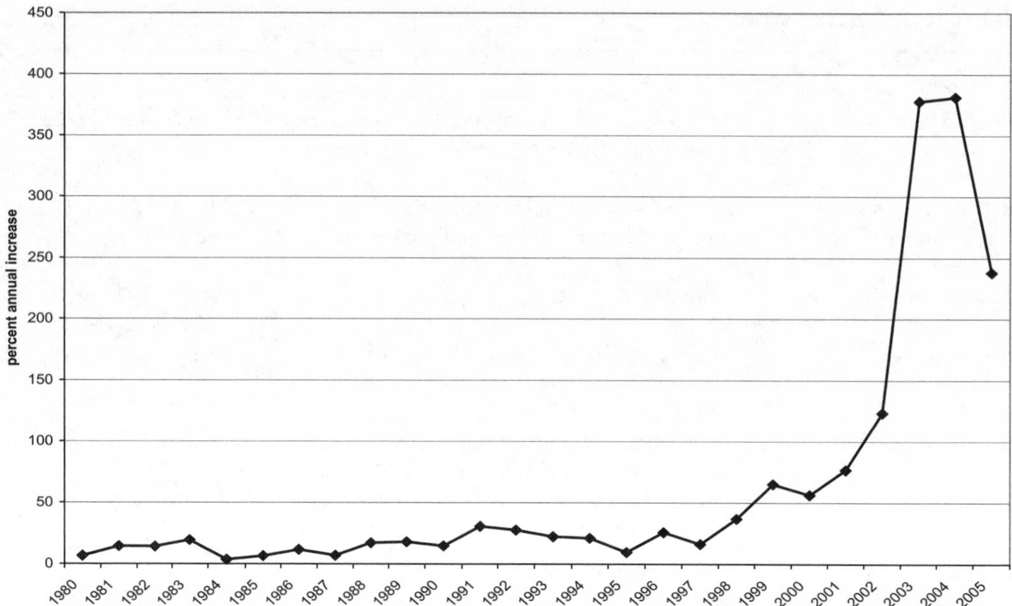

Figure 18.1. Inflation in Zimbabwe, 1980–2005 (% change in GDP price deflator). *Source:* World Bank, World Development Indicators Online. Note: 2005 is the last year for which either the World Bank or the International Monetary Fund report these data.

At the time of this writing, the world economy is recovering from a significant asset price deflation that took place between 2007 and 2009, and we discuss this crisis in more detail later. However, one of the classic cases of asset price deflation is that of Japan in 1990. Consider Figure 18.2. This shows the total values of equities and land in Japan between 1981 and 1992, land values being restricted to that of Tokyo. Both of these increased five-fold between 1981 and 1989. At the peak, the total land value of Japan (Tokyo plus the rest of the country) was estimated to be 20 percent of global wealth and five times that of the land value in the United States (Stone and Ziemba, 1993). As of 1989, most observers expected values to keep increasing, but as evident from Figure 18.2, they quickly declined as the bubble burst. Japan has been struggling to recover from the bursting of the 1989 bubble ever since, suffering two decades of slow growth and even deflation of goods and services prices.[5]

Banking crises involve the occurrence of bank runs, mergers, closures, or government takeover of banking institutions. As described by a number of observers in the accompanying box, the banking sector is a particularly fragile member of the global financial system.[6] This is due to what is known as *maturity transformation*, namely the role of banks in borrowing short term and lending long term, and it makes the

[5] Krugman (2010) wrote: "In the 1990s, Japan conducted a dress rehearsal for the crisis that struck much of the world in 2008. Runaway banks fueled a bubble in land prices; when the bubble burst, these banks were severely weakened, as were the balance sheets of everyone who had borrowed in the belief that land prices would stay high. The result was protracted economic weakness."

[6] This insight goes back at least as far as Diamond and Dybvig (1983). For a more recent source, see Bird and Rajan (2001).

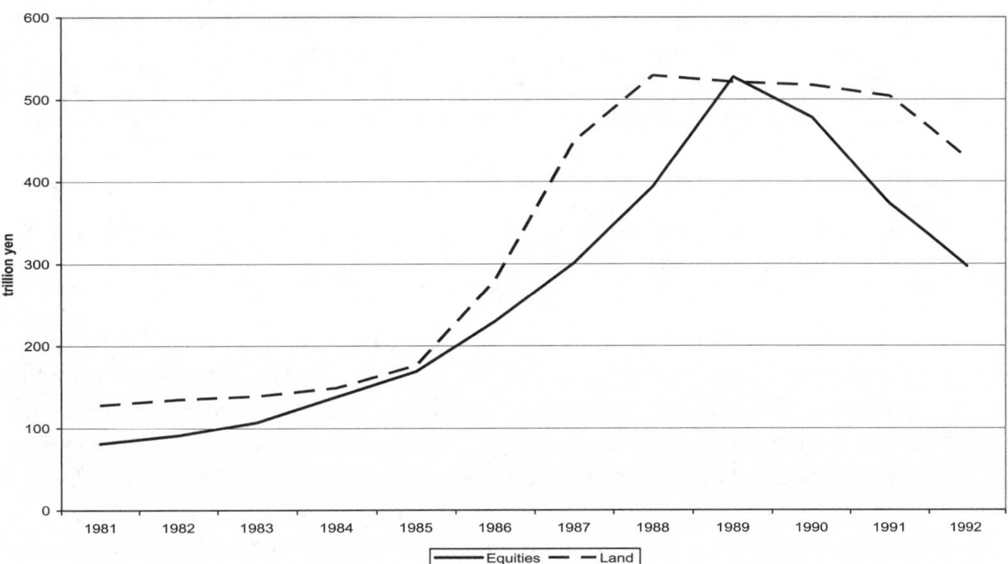

Figure 18.2. Asset Prices in Japan, 1981–1992 (¥ trillion). *Source:* Noguchi (1994). *Note:* the land value is only that of Tokyo.

banking sector prone to bank runs. For example, as described by Reinhart and Rogoff (2009):

> In normal times, banks hold liquid resources that are more than enough to handle any surges in deposit withdrawals. During a "run" on a bank, however, depositors lose confidence in the bank and withdraw en masse. As withdrawals mount, the bank is forced to liquidate assets under duress. Typically the prices received are "fire sale" prices, especially if the bank holds highly illiquid and idiosyncratic loans (such as those to local businesses about which it has better information than other investors). The problem of having to liquidate at fire sale prices can extend to a far broader range of assets during a systemic banking crisis.... Different banks often hold broadly similar portfolios of assets, and if all banks try to sell at once, the market can dry up completely. Assets that are relatively liquid during normal times can suddenly become highly illiquid just when the bank most needs them. (p. 144)

Views of the Banking Sector

Many observers have noted the particular fragility of the banking system in the world economy. Here are a few examples. The World Bank (2001) noted that "If finance is fragile, banking is the most fragile part" (p. 11). Dobson and Hufbauer (2001) noted that "Bank lending may be more prone to runs than portfolio capital, because banks themselves are highly leveraged, and they are relying on the borrower's balance sheet to ensure repayment" (p. 47). Crook (2003) wrote that "breakdowns in banking lie at the center of most financial crises. And banks are unusually effective at spreading financial distress, once it starts, from one place to another" (p. 11).

More recently, Kose et al. (2009) stated that "The procyclical and highly volatile nature of... short-term bank loans... can magnify the adverse impact of negative shocks on economic growth" (p. 38). Reinhart and Rogoff (2009) stated that "the aftermath of systemic banking crises involves a protracted and pronounced contraction in economic activity and puts significant strains on government resources" (p. xxix).

These few quotations give a flavor of the potential volatility of the banking sector and why it needs to be treated with caution in both national and international policymaking. Prudential regulation of the banking system is a high priority in trying to make crises less likely.

Sources: Crook (2003), Dobson and Hufbauer (2001), Kose et al. (2009), Reinhart and Rogoff (2009), World Bank (2001)

Research on the banking sector and its role in crises provides us with a number of insights.[7] First, banking crises are often set off by asset price deflation or the bursting of financial bubbles such as land prices, capital inflow surges, and financial sector liberalization, all of which can work in tandem with one another.[8] For example, all of these ingredients seem to have contributed to the recent 2007–2009 crisis. Second, historically, banking crises are quite common in both developed and developing countries. They are not limited to the developing world. Third, banking crises are usually followed by a protracted downturn in economic output and substantial fiscal costs.

External debt crises involve sovereign default on debt obligations to foreign creditors or the substantial restructuring of this debt. The classic case of this was Mexico in 1982, discussed in Chapter 17. Recall from that chapter that the decade of the 1980s began with a significant increase in real interest rates and a significant decline in non-oil commodity prices. These increased borrowing costs and reduced export revenues for many developing countries, including Mexico. In August 1982, in the face of capital flight, the Mexican government announced that it would stop servicing its foreign currency debt. Subsequently, both Argentina and Brazil entered into similar debt and balance of payments crises.

Research on external debt crises (e.g., Reinhart and Rogoff, 2009) suggests that (like banking crises) they tend to be set off by a previous period of large capital inflows. Recent debt default and debt restructuring have taken place in Africa (Côte d'Ivoire, 2000; Kenya, 2000; Nigeria, 2001 and 2004; Zimbabwe, 2000), Asia (Indonesia, 2000 and 2002; Myanmar, 2002), and Latin America (Argentina, 2001; Ecuador, 2008; Paraguay, 2003; Uruguay, 2003; Venezuela, 2004). But a broader time period, even only back to the 1970s, shows such episodes more widely dispersed to include Europe as well.

Domestic debt crises involve sovereign default on debt obligations to domestic creditors or substantial restructuring of this debt. As strongly emphasized by Reinhart and Rogoff (2009), this set of crises have not been well appreciated and well studied. As it turns out, levels of domestic debt help to explain a significant portion of external debt defaults and inflation crises. National governments default on external debt to help support domestic debt restructuring. They also have historically turned to inflation to reduce the real (price-adjusted) value of domestic debt obligations. As with banking crises and external debt crises, preceding inflows of capital are often a contributing factor.

We mentioned above that crises often occur in combinations. For example, Table 18.1 uses Argentina in 2001 as a case of a banking crisis, but much more was going on

[7] See, for example, Goldstein, Kaminsky, and Reinhart (2000), Kaminsky, Reinhart, and Végh (2003), and Reinhart and Rogoff (2009).

[8] The role of financial liberalization in banking crises was pointed out many years ago by Diaz-Alejandro (1985), but see also Bird and Rajan (2001).

in that country. The banking crisis was accompanied by a currency crisis (discussed in Chapter 16), the Argentine government defaulted on both its domestic and foreign debt, and there was deflation of some types of asset prices. Thus, although useful for sorting out different crisis types, the rows of Table 18.1 should not be seen as a set of isolated compartments. The real world of international finance is much more complicated than that.

CONTAGION AND SYSTEMIC RISK

It is sometimes the case that crises that begin in one country spread to other countries. This is called **contagion**. As expressed by Kaminsky, Reinhart, and Végh (2003), "some financial events . . . trigger an immediate and startling adverse chain reaction among countries within a region and in some cases across regions" (p. 51). These contagion episodes are sometimes given special names. For example, the spread of the 1994–1995 Mexican crisis to other countries in Latin America became known as the "tequila effect," and the spread of the 1997 crisis in Thailand to other countries in Asia became known as the "Asian flu." Contagion can make economic management even more difficult than it normally is.

The notion of a crisis "spreading" from one country to another is informal. More formally, we need to consider what exactly is transmitted across national boundaries. There are a variety of possibilities here and differing opinions among specialists in international finance. Some common identifiers include shifts in expectations and confidence ("herding" or "informational cascades"), asset prices ("financial linkage"), and capital flight ("sudden stops"). Contagion does not always occur in episodes where we might most expect it. For example, Kaminsky, Reinhart, and Végh (2003) noted the lack of contagion accompanying the 1999 devaluation of the Brazilian real, the 2001 demise of the Argentine currency board, and the 2001 devaluation of the Turkish lira. Brazil, Argentina, and Turkey are very large and important emerging markets, so the lack of contagion in these cases was notable.

Kaminsky, Reinhart, and Végh (2003) identified three causal factors that contribute to episodes of contagion: sudden stops in capital inflows, surprise announcements to financial markets, and highly leveraged financial institutions. Furthermore, Joyce and Nabar (2009) showed that sudden stops interact with banking sectors to cause banking crises. It therefore appears that sudden stops, banking crises, and contagion can all be related to one another. Country governments can help shield themselves from contagion through avoiding over-borrowing that can accompany pro-cyclical fiscal policy in open capital markets, continuous information sharing, prudential regulation of financial markets, and market-friendly capital controls, discussed later.

At times, contagion spreads so rapidly and to such an extent that it becomes global, affecting the entire world financial system. This is known as **systemic risk**. Unlike simple contagion, systemic risk is a rare event. It characterized the Great Depression of the 1930s, but it also characterized the 2007–2009 crisis that we discuss later. Goldin and Vogel (2010) strongly suggested that there has been an increase in systemic risk due to the process of financial globalization.[9] They sounded a note of alarm, stating "Global finance is the best understood and most institutionally developed of the global

[9] For example, they note that, by 2007, global derivatives trading had increased to "16 times global equity market capitalization and 10 times global gross domestic product" (p. 6).

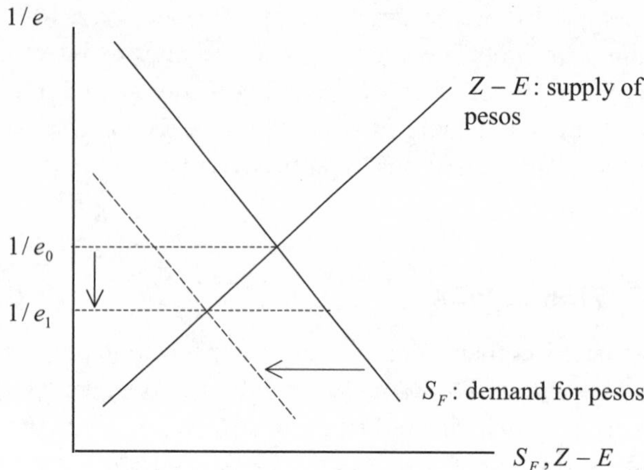

Figure 18.3. A Balance of Payments and Currency Crisis

governance regimes, yet these institutions failed to predict, prevent or understand the endemic systemic risks in the system, and they have yet to elicit the structural changes need to manage proactively future systemic risks" (p. 12). We return to these issues later in this chapter.

ANALYZING BALANCE OF PAYMENTS AND CURRENCY CRISES

Some observers have made a distinction between "old-fashioned" and "high-tech" crises.[10] A standard balance of payments and currency crisis is an example of an old-fashioned crisis. These have their roots in overvalued, fixed exchange rates and large current account deficits. For example, in Chapters 16 and 17, we mentioned the possibility of a balance of payments crisis ensuing when the capital account can no longer support a current account deficit. In this section, we want to return to our fixed exchange rate model of Chapter 16 to analyze the exchange rate dynamics behind such crises. As in Chapter 16, our home country is Mexico and our foreign country is the United States. The market for Mexican pesos is depicted in Figure 18.3. This diagram depicts an initial *equilibrium fixed exchange rate* at e_0, plotting the value of the peso ($1/e$) on the vertical axis, as in Chapters 14–16.[11]

In Figure 18.3, let's suppose that Mexico is successful in implementing an equilibrium exchange rate at e_0. Recall from Chapter 16 that this equilibrium exchange rate requires that $e^e = e_0$. That is, the expected future exchange rate must equal the equilibrium rate. This, in turn, requires that the interest rate on the peso must equal the interest rate on the U.S. dollar, or $r_M = r_{US}$. Next, suppose that we find Mexico in a position of a *current account deficit.* This was the actual case for Mexico in the early 1990s. For example, the current account deficit in Mexico was 8 percent of gross domestic product (GDP) in 1994. As we know from Chapter 13, such a current account deficit is always financed by a *capital account surplus.* In Mexico's case, in the early 1990s, the capital account surplus was primarily in the form of short-term portfolio investment, much of it denominated in dollars. When a large trade deficit is financed by an inflow of

[10] See, for example, chapter 1 of Eichengreen (1999).
[11] Mexico had adopted a fixed exchange rate regime in December 1987.

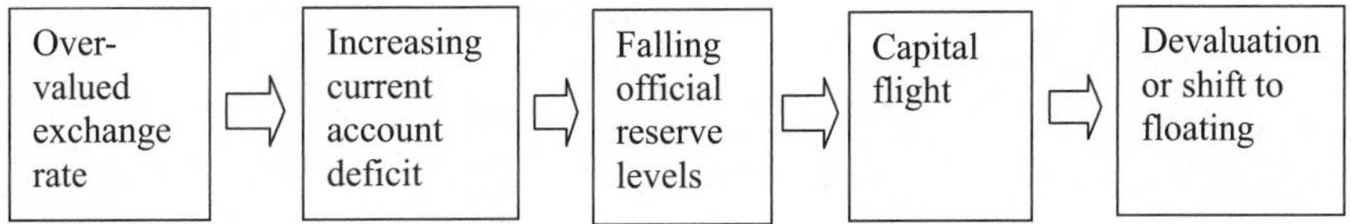

Figure 18.4. Balance of Payments and Currency Crises Revisited

short-term capital, trouble is in the air. That it was denominated in a foreign currency (U.S. dollars) made the trouble worse because any fall in the value of the home currency would inflate the domestic currency value of the debt. Many domestic investors were aware of these problems and began to sell pesos during 1994.

Let's pretend you are a Mexican investor. If you feel that the Mexican government will have to devalue the peso in order to suppress the trade deficit, then, in your mind, $e^e > e_0$. When this occurs, the interest rate parity condition comes back into play. If $r_M = r_{US}$ and $e^e > e_0$, then the following will be true:

$$r_M < r_{US} + \frac{(e^e - e)}{e} \tag{18.1}$$

On the left-hand side of inequality (18.1) is the expected total rate of return on peso-denominated assets. On the right-hand side is the expected total rate of return on dollar-denominated assets. Given that the expected total rate of return on dollar-denominated assets exceeds that of peso-denominated assets, you will adjust your portfolio, buying dollars and selling pesos. This is known as **capital flight**, and Mexican investors engaged in this type of portfolio reallocation during 1994.

This situation is depicted in Figure 18.3. The change in expectations shifts the demand for pesos graph to the left. At the original exchange rate e_0, the total expected return on dollar-denominated assets exceeds the total expected return on peso-denominated assets. The *equilibrium* value of the peso falls to $1/e_1$. In response to such changes, in December 1994, the Mexican government devalued the peso by 15 percent. Unfortunately, this proved to be too little and simply fueled speculation of further devaluations. The demand for pesos graph in Figure 18.3 shifted further to the left, and Mexico was forced to let the peso float. Beginning in February 1995, international investors began a sudden and massive portfolio shift out of peso-denominated assets, sending the peso into a deep fall.[12]

The severity of the capital flight from Mexico caused some observers to question the functioning of the international financial system. As Woodall (1995) put it at the time:

> There were many good reasons behind the run on the peso – political turbulence, a widening current-account deficit, a pre-election public spending spree and a lax monetary policy. But on their own they did not justify the scale of the capital outflow or of the depreciation of the peso; the markets simply lost their heads. (p. 18)

It is useful to summarize the preceding discussion with a second diagram, presented in Figure 18.4. Here we see that an overvalued exchange rate causes an increase in the current account deficit (capital account surplus) and a fall in official reserve levels.

[12] A basic and well-know article on balance of payments crises was presented in Krugman (1979). For more on the Mexican crisis, see Calvo and Mendoza (1996). An excellent and concise review of economic models of crises was presented in appendix B of Eichengreen (1999).

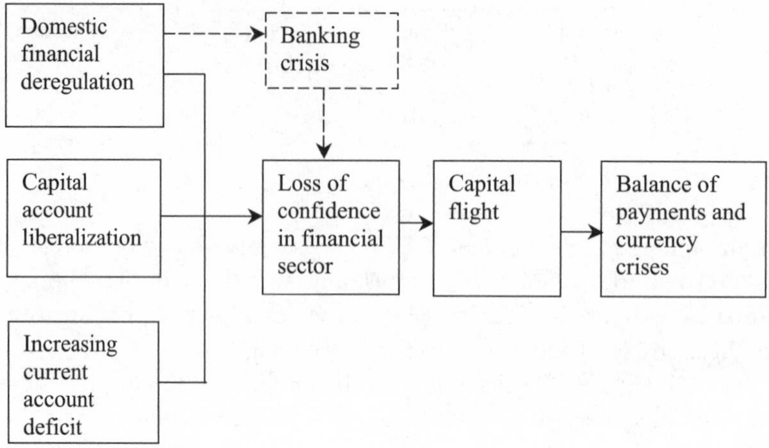

Figure 18.5. A "High-Tech" Balance of Payments Crisis. *Note:* The dashes around the banking crisis box suggest that this element might or might not be present in a particular instance.

As some point, expectations shift, causing capital flight. Eventually, despite strenuous denials, the government devalues the currency or shifts to floating.

The Mexican balance of payments crisis and currency crash should give us an appreciation of the delicacy of managing a fixed exchange rate regime. Although at the time, the crisis was contained by swift action on the part of the U.S. Treasury in supplying loans to Mexico, a similar set of crises began during the summer of 1997. This was the beginning of what now is known as the Asian crisis, which was more "high tech" than the Mexican crisis.

THE ASIAN CRISIS

Although high-tech crises typically include some elements of the balance of payments and currency crises described in Figures 18.3 and 18.4, they include some less-concrete factors as well. These crises combine current account deficits with weak financial sectors (especially in the banking system, as discussed previously) and/or inappropriate capital account liberalization.[13] The high-tech view of crises is summarized in Figure 18.5 and characterized the Asian crisis of 1997.

The Asian crisis began in Thailand, as described in the accompanying box. In some ways, the Thai crisis was similar to the Mexican crisis. It began with current account deficits amounting to nearly 8 percent of GDP under a fixed exchange rate regime. A devaluation of the baht took place in July 1997. Again, the markets lost their heads. Although most analysts expected that the baht would fall by 15 to 20 percent in value against the dollar, it fell by more than 50 percent. That said, the financial sector was more at the center of the Thai crisis than the Mexican crisis. This fact was well summarized by Reynolds et al. (2002):

> Briefly, the (Thai) crisis occurred when banks and financial companies . . . borrowed heavily on a short-term basis from banks in other countries (mainly in Japan and the United States) and made overly risky loans to finance the construction of commercial

[13] For example, in the case of the Asian crisis, Stiglitz (2002) stated that it "was, first and foremost, a crisis of the financial system" (p. 113).

> and residential units. When the demand for such units was not forthcoming as expected, a domino effect occurred: the real estate investors who borrowed defaulted, their lenders defaulted, and the banks were left with foreign-currency-denominated loans requiring payment. A subsequent foreign exchange crisis followed the collapse of the real estate market. (p. 237)

These characteristics are what led to the loss of confidence in the Asian financial sector, as depicted in Figure 18.5. In more general terms, domestic financial deregulation, capital account liberalization, and increasing current account deficits combine to eventually and suddenly cause a loss of confidence. This loss of confidence, in turn, causes capital flight, and balance of payments and currency crises ensue. As stated by Reinhart and Rogoff (2009), "Highly indebted governments, banks, or corporations can seem to be merrily rolling along for an extended period, when *bang!* – confidence collapses, lenders disappear, and a crisis hits" (p. 39).

The Baht Crisis

Until the summer of 1997, the Thai baht was pegged to the U.S. dollar. The Thai government set the rate at 25 baht per dollar. In June 1997, the baht came under pressure, and the Thai government attempted to support it through cooperative agreements with Asian central banks and controls on foreign-exchange transactions. The government's foreign reserves were approaching exhaustion, however. On July 2, these strategies failed, and the government attempted to devalue the baht in the face of a speculative attack. This strategy also failed, and the baht began to float. The Thai government contacted the IMF for assistance on July 27. In August 1997, the Thai government, under Prime Minister Chavalit Yongchaiyudh, accepted an International Monetary Fund (IMF) package worth US$17 billion.

In October 1997, the Thai finance minister resigned. In November Prime Minister Chavalit resigned. He was replaced by Chuan Leekpai. In December, the government closed nearly 60 financial companies that had been in very difficult financial conditions. The Thai economy, which had typically grown by more than 8 percent a year, plunged into a recession. The stock market plunged. By January 1998, the baht had fallen through the crucial barrier of 50 per U.S. dollar, less than half the value of its pegged rate.

Sources: The Economist (1997) and Mydans (1997a,b and 1998)

By the end of September 1999, the ensuing Asian crisis had spread to Malaysia and Indonesia. The Indonesian case was somewhat of a surprise because its current account deficit was less than 4 percent of GDP. From there, the crisis spread to the Philippines, Hong Kong, South Korea, and Taiwan. Only the Hong Kong dollar escaped devaluation.[14] Figure 18.6 plots the nominal exchange rates for four of these countries (Indonesia, South Korea, Philippines, and Thailand) for the years 1995 to 2005, normalized so that each exchange rate is 100 in 1995. You can see here that the largest decline in value occurred in Indonesia, where the nominal exchange rate increased by a factor of 4.5. The other three countries experienced increases of the nominal exchange rates of much less, but still substantial amounts of over 50 percent.

[14] This Asian crisis was later followed by the Russian ruble crisis of 1998 and the Brazilian real crisis of 1999. We considered the Brazilian crisis in a box in Chapter 16 and the Russian crisis in Chapter 17.

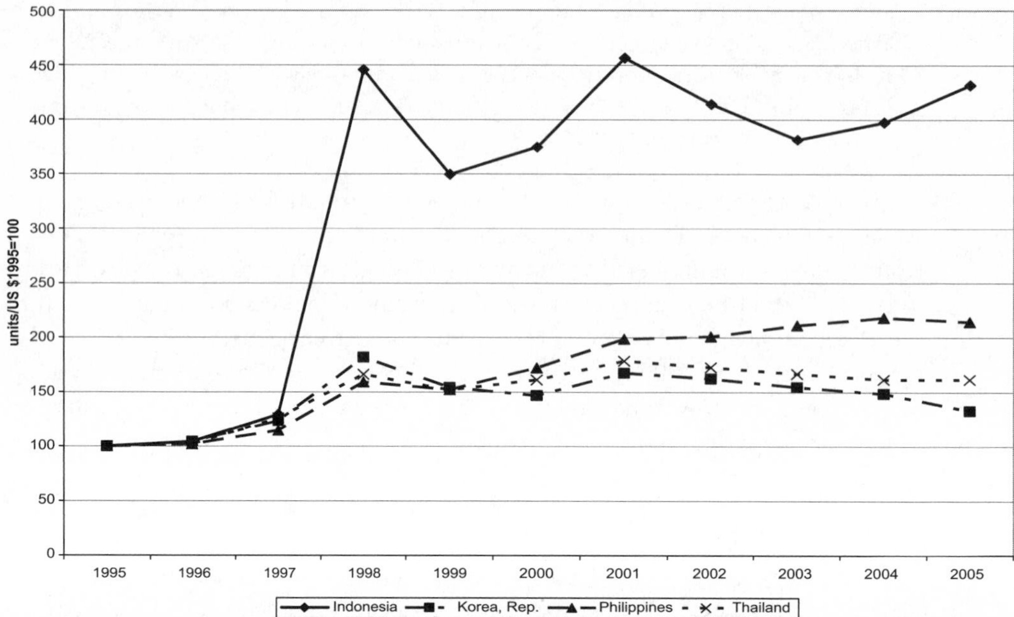

Figure 18.6. Nominal Exchange Rates of Four Asian Currencies, 1995–2005 (1995=100). *Source:* World Bank, World Development Indicators Online

What were some of the high-tech features of the Asian financial crisis? Here is a partial list[15]:

1. Financial firms in the region (including banks) had significant exposures in real estate and equities, and both of these markets began to deflate prior to the crisis. Thus asset price deflation was part of the Asian crisis.
2. Capital accounts had been liberalized to allow firms (including banks) to take on short-term foreign debt, including debt denominated in foreign currencies.[16] In two countries (Thailand and South Korea), capital account liberalization began with short-term debt, rather than long-term debt and FDI, as is more prudent.[17]
3. Banks were, in general, poorly regulated and supervised as the countries liberalized financial markets and the capital account. Indeed, banks were a crucial component of government industrial policies, which in some instances, supported systems of "crony" or "access" capitalism, rather than sound investment policies.
4. Due to previous confidence in fixed exchange rates, firms (including banks) were not in the practice of hedging their foreign exchange exposures in the manner we described in Chapter 14. This led them to very vulnerable positions by the eve of the crisis. When the crisis finally hit, their attempts to secure foreign exchange put extra downward pressure on the value of domestic currencies.

[15] For a fuller discussion, see appendix C of Eichengreen (1999).

[16] "Between 1990 and 1996, roughly 50 percent of net private portfolio capital inflows into Thailand took the form of short-term borrowing. Sixty-two percent of net capital inflows in South Korea consisted of short-term borrowing in the three years 1994–97, compared with 37 percent in 1990–93" (Eichengreen, 1999, p. 156).

[17] We take up these sequencing issues in earnest in Chapter 24.

These are some of the key aspects of the 1997 Asian crisis. As depicted in Figure 18.5, loss of confidence in the financial sectors of the countries involved was a central part of the evolution of the crisis, and the banking sector was a main culprit. Thus the warnings we presented previously with regard to the banking sector were a central part of the Asian crisis.

THE IMF RESPONSE

The IMF response to the 1997 Asian crisis and the 1999 Brazilian crises became a point of serious contention and debate. The case of Indonesia is discussed in the accompanying box. In simple form, we can characterize the IMF's policies as consisting of three elements: interest rate increases, fiscal austerity, and structural reforms. The IMF required that the afflicted economies increase their interest rates dramatically. Why? As we saw in Chapters 15 and 16 in our discussion of the interest rate parity condition, an increase in the domestic interest rate tends to increase the equilibrium value of a country's currency. The trouble with this policy as applied in Asia and Brazil was that increases in domestic interest rates also tend to suppress domestic investment and push debt-burdened firms (including banks) into default. This, in turn, fed into a sense of panic.[18] In the case of Brazil, the IMF insisted on interest rate increases after the real was allowed to float, despite the fact that its value had quickly stabilized. In doing so, it may have exacerbated the crisis.

As we discussed in Chapter 13, current account deficits can result from a lack of domestic savings ($S_H + S_G$ in terms of Figure 13.2). The IMF's fiscal austerity requirements were strategies to increase S_G. In the case of the Asian crisis, this strategy was probably misguided both economically and politically. The crises of Indonesia and other Asian countries were not the result of profligate governments. Rather, they generally involved excessive *private* borrowing. For this reason, some critics have alleged that the IMF inappropriately applied rescue packages designed for previous crises in Latin America to Indonesia and Thailand.

Structural reforms refer to economic policy changes outside the fiscal and monetary realms. For example, the IMF required Indonesia to close 16 banks and dismantle monopolies. Some economists saw these structural reforms as misguided. For instance, Krugman (1999) wrote that: "the sheer breadth of IMF demands, aside from raising suspicions that the United States was trying to use the crisis to impose its ideological vision on Asia, more or less guaranteed a prolonged period of wrangling between Asian governments and their rescuers, a period during which the crisis of confidence steadily worsened" (p. 116). In addition, the bank closures appear to have exacerbated depositor runs on other banks in a manner described earlier in this chapter.

Beyond these criticisms, however, a more fundamental point was at stake. In venturing into the realm of structural reforms, the IMF ventured beyond the scope of its past practices into what has traditionally been the purview of the World Bank (see Chapter 23). However, the IMF stood by its policies and claimed that they contributed to the recovery of the countries involved.[19] This reflected the thinking of the Washington Consensus, discussed in Chapter 23.

[18] Some prominent international economists (e.g., Jeffrey Sachs, Paul Krugman, and Joseph Stiglitz) considered that the increases in interest rates were a big mistake. Krugman and Stiglitz subsequently went on to win Nobel Prizes in economics. Consequently, their criticisms were hard to overlook in retrospect.

[19] See, for example, IMF (1999).

The Indonesian Crisis

One day in January 1998, the IMF's Managing Director, Michel Camdessus, met with Indonesian President Suharto to review the details of an IMF bailout package for Indonesia. Among the conditions stipulated by the IMF was the dismantling of monopolies in cloves and palm oil owned by Suharto associates. Another condition was that government food and energy subsidies be removed. As we discussed in Chapter 15, depreciation of a currency increases the domestic prices of traded goods such as food and energy. This, combined with attempts to remove subsidies and a very severe drought in Indonesia, drove up food and energy prices beyond the reach of millions of the Indonesian poor. Riots were the result, and these continued for nine months afterwards. Also contributing to this unrest was a widely distributed photograph of Camdessus hovering over Suharto with arms folded, an image that brought back bitter colonial memories.

Another component of the IMF's Indonesian program involved the closing of 16 insolvent banks. The IMF hoped that this move would restore confidence in the banking system. This seems not to have been the case. Critics alleged that the closing of these banks actually precipitated a banking panic. There was a run on remaining private banks as depositors withdrew funds and placed them in state-owned banks. IMF Chief Economist Stanley Fischer, however, denied that the closing of the banks had this effect. In his view, "the main culprits were President Suharto's illness . . . , perceptions that the government would not carry out the program, and excessive creation of liquidity by the central bank" (1998b, p. 24).

As it turned out, after receiving US$3 billion from the IMF, Indonesia reneged on its commitments. Some observers claim that Suharto never intended to abide by the agreement and that the IMF was naïve to not have recognized this. In April 1998, a new agreement was reached between the IMF and the Suharto government, and this agreement allowed for a total of US$40 billion of IMF loans to Indonesia. The funds, however, were to be delivered in billion-dollar installments based on Indonesia's progress in keeping its commitments. Food and fuel subsidies, however, were allowed to persist. In May 1998, continued rioting in Jakarta finally led to President Suharto stepping down after 32 years as President.

Sources: Fischer (1998b), Kristof (1998), and Sanger (1998)

THE SUB-PRIME CRISIS OF 2007–2009

Not all crises originate in developing countries. Indeed, the work of Reinhart and Rogoff (2009) suggests that, historically, the developed world is almost as likely as the developing world to experience financial crises of the sort described in Table 18.1. Further, the causes of crises in the developed world are not much different from those of the developing world: capital inflows, financial liberalization, asset price inflation, and over-borrowing. At the time of this writing in 2011, the world economy is trying to manage a crisis with origins in the *developed* world. This crisis emerged in the summer of 2007 in the United States but hit hard in the fall of 2008. The causes of this crisis were located in the U.S. economy and included an unprecedented housing price bubble (nearly doubling in real terms in the decade up to 2007), huge inflows of capital (financing a current account deficit of more than 6 percent of GDP), and a lack of prudential financial regulation (including overly sanguine Chairmen of the U.S. Federal

Reserve Alan Greenspan and Ben Bernanke).[20] The government-led interventions to address the crisis were huge. Alessandri and Haldane (2009) reported that in the United States, the United Kingdom, and the euro area, these were of the order of US$14 trillion, or *one-fourth of global GDP*.

With regard to the housing market in the United States, there developed a sub-prime mortgage market that even included mortgages known by the acronyms NINA (no income, no asset) and NINJA (no income, no job or asset). Sub-prime mortgages became bundled and resold in the form of mortgage-backed securities (MBS). Buyers of these securities were distributed around the world. The fact that there was pure speculation in the market was described by Vogel (2010):

> It was not unusual to see crowds and bidding frenzies whenever blocks of new housing units were opened for public sale. Many of these most aggressive buyers never intended to actually reside in the units; they were leveraged speculators taking advantage of easy credit and regulatory conditions and buying only with the intention of quickly flipping them to someone else at a higher price. For a number of years, this was a high-probability bet. (pp. 43–44)

In their analysis of this current crisis, Reinhart and Rogoff (2009) stated that "The U.S. conceit that its financial and regulatory system could withstand massive capital inflows on a sustained basis without any problems arguably laid the foundations for the global financial crisis of the late 2000s. . . . Outsized financial market returns were in fact greatly exaggerated by capital inflows, just as would be the case in emerging markets" (p. 212). Subsequent losses in housing mortgages were transmitted around the globe via a pyramid of financial instruments, including MBS. This was the result of banks taking loans that would traditionally have remained on their books, repackaging them in the form of asset-based securities, and trading these securities internationally.

In this way, a crisis related to new financial products originating in one country took on a global profile through systemic risk. Goldin and Vogel (2010) pointed to the rise of systemic risk as increasingly globalized finance outpaces institutional structures to manage it. They warned that "A fundamental regulator shift is nowhere in sight and no international supervisory body has done more than make vague recommendations about the radical structural . . . changes needed" (p. 10). These considerations suggest that crises will be with us for some time to come.

If the United States had entered into the 2007–2009 crisis in a strong fiscal position, its ability to stimulate the economy would have been stronger. Instead, it entered into the crisis from a position of fiscal weakness (recall our discussion in Chapter 13) due to a combination of tax cuts and expansions of defense spending. Consequently, its position is somewhat precarious. Asset price deflations (particularly in real estate) tend to persist for years, and the prospects of the fiscal situation improving are dim. That leaves its monetary policy as an additional policy tool, but interest rates are already quite low. It will be a difficult time for the U.S. economy.

[20] There was a very strong reluctance of the U.S. Federal Reserve (particularly under Chairman Alan Greenspan) to address the asset price bubble. In a now-famous speech he gave to the Economic Club of New York in 2002, Greenspan (2002) stated: "If the bursting of an asset bubble creates economic dislocation, then preventing bubbles might seem an attractive goal. But whether incipient bubbles can be detected in real time and whether, once detected, they can be defused without inadvertently precipitating still greater adverse consequences for the economy remain in doubt."

Table 18.2 The Basel Accords

Stage	Years of approval/ implementation	Components
Basel I	1988/1992	Proposed regulatory capital requirements of 8 percent.
Basel II	2004/2007	Introduced three pillars of bank regulation (minimum capital requirements, supervisory review, and disclosure for market discipline) and two tiers of capital. Effectively reduced the capital requirement and allowed asset measurements to be risk adjusted by banks' internal models.
Basel III	2010/2013–2018	Improved asset risk adjustment and increased capital requirements to 7 percent.

BASEL STANDARDS

In 1974, the central bank heads of the Group of 10 (G10) established the Basel Committee on Banking Supervision.[21] This was important because, as we have seen at various junctures in this chapter, the banking sector is a particularly fragile part of the global financial system. The Basel Committee resides at the Bank of International Settlements (BIS) and consists of representatives from central banks around the world. In 1988, the Committee introduced a banking capital measurement standard that became known as the Basel Capital Accord and, after some time, Basel I (see Table 18.2). Part of Basel I was a minimum capital standard of 8 percent, as well as a framework for measuring credit risk. Basel I also made a distinction between Tier I, or core banking capital, and Tier II, or supplementary capital. Tier I was to consist mostly of equity capital, whereas Tier II was to consist of reserves of various kinds.[22]

Beginning in 1999, the Basel Committee began to develop a revision of Basel I. In the process, it began to specify what became known as the three pillars of the Basel Capital Accord.[23] These three pillars are minimum capital requirements, supervisory review, and disclosure for market discipline. Basel II recognized that different asset classes involve different levels of risk and developed complex procedures for taking these risk differences into account in the first pillar. However, many observers thought that Basel II was far too flexible, with increased weight given to the second and third pillars but not to the first pillar. *The Economist* (2004) quipped that "bank regulators . . . have ended up committing themselves to almost nothing" and that "the central bankers might as well have stayed at home."

As the crisis of 2007–2009 testifies, Basel II was an utter failure. As noted by *The Economist* (2010), "the definition of Tier I capital was far too lax. Many of the equity-like instruments allowed were really debt. In effect, the fine print allowed banks' common equity, or 'core' Tier I, the purest and most flexible form of capital, to be as little as 2 percent of risk-adjusted assets" (p. 67). Further, leaving the risk adjustment process to banks' own internal models proved to be a mistake.

[21] The G10 includes Belgium, Canada, France, Germany, Italy, Japan, the Netherlands, Sweden, Switzerland, the United Kingdom, and the United States.

[22] Attention to bank capital standards was and is an important issue. As documented by Alessandri and Haldane (2009), banking-sector capital ratios in the United States and the United Kingdom fell by a factor of five in percentage terms during the twentieth century.

[23] Recall the three pillars of agricultural trade negotiations in the WTO from Chapter 7. These are quite different!

Having not succeeded in its mission, the Basel Committee began to try again, this time in the form of Basel III, announced in 2010. Tier I capital will be strictly limited to equity capital, the amount of this core capital required will be increased from 2 percent to 7 percent, and risk adjustment will be less determined by banks' internal models. Immediately, some leading commentators have questioned whether this is adequate. Indeed, Wolf (2010) dubbed the Basel III capital adequacy ratio as the "capital inadequacy ratio." He correctly pointed out that "this amount of equity is far below levels markets would impose if investors did not continue to expect governments to bail out creditors in a crisis." By some reckonings (e.g., *The Economist*, 2010), something on the order of 15 percent is necessary.

In December 2010 and January 2011, the Basel Committee set out specific standards for both Tier I and Tier II bank capital that, on initial examination, seem to strengthen standards significantly. The question is whether the incremental improvements pursued by the Basel Committee will prove to be sufficient to prevent further banking crises in the near future. Time will tell whether this is the case.

CAPITAL CONTROLS

In September 1997, a committee of the IMF made a recommendation to the Fund's Executive Board that the IMF take on as an explicit policy the full convertibility of the capital accounts of all its members. The IMF's Deputy Managing Director, Stanley Fischer, defended the proposal. Fischer (1998a) cited two arguments in support of capital account liberalization. First, he claimed, "it is an inevitable step on the path of development" (p. 2). Second, he claimed that "free capital movements facilitate an efficient allocation of savings and help channel resources into their most productive uses, thus increasing economic growth and welfare" (pp. 2–3). Both of these claims have proved to be unsubstantiated.

Coming in the wake of the Asian crisis, the timing of this defense was more than a bit awkward. More awkwardly still, a number of prominent international economists began to argue against the proposal. Jagdish Bhagwati (1998), Dani Rodrik (1998), Paul Krugman (1999), Barry Eichengreen (1999), and Joseph Stiglitz (2002) all strongly questioned the goal of capital account liberalization and called for capital controls of one kind or another. In the view of these economists, excessive borrowing within the short-term portfolio component of the capital account was a contributing factor to the Mexican and Asian crises. Further, they noted that financial capital is too prone to panics and manias to be trusted. Finally, they suggested that controls on the capital account do not appear to adversely affect the growth and development of countries with the controls (e.g., the People's Republic of China).

What is one to make of this disagreement? First, we must understand that there are different types of capital controls. At one end of the continuum are strict licensing systems, such as that in China. Here in order to convert the yuan into foreign currency, you have had to obtain a license from the government. This system is akin to the quotas some countries impose on trade flows in their current accounts (see Chapter 7). At the other end of the continuum are tax systems such as that used by Chile for a few years. Chile required that investments made in its country must be for a minimum of one year. It also required that 30 percent of the investment must be deposited with the central bank for that year. This is a much more liberal regime than China's. This sort of measure is known as a variable deposit requirement (VDR) or unremunerated reserve requirement (URR) and is akin to a tariff rather than a quota.[24]

Second, we must understand that different policies can be designed for different components of the capital account: direct investment, long-term portfolio investment, and short-term portfolio investment. Even opponents of full capital account liberalization acknowledge that controls on direct and long-term portfolio investment should be minimal. Their concern is with short-term assets used primarily for speculative purposes. For example, Chile regulated portfolio investment based on their risk levels. Finally, capital account liberalization is not an all-or-nothing proposition. It can (and should) be phased in gradually over time, allowing investors and domestic policymakers time to adjust to the changing regime.[25]

There is evidence that market-friendly, Chilean-style capital controls both curb the sort of market panics described in this chapter and shift the composition of capital account surpluses toward the long-term end of the asset spectrum. Consequently, countries employing them are better able to survive the panics that tend to spread from one country to another.[26] This is perhaps why even Stanley Fischer eventually acknowledged their appropriateness.[27] As summarized by Eichengreen (1999), "cautious steps in the direction of capital-account liberalization . . . should *not* extend to the removal of taxes on capital inflows" (p. 13, emphasis added).

To the surprise of many, after the 2007–2009 crisis, the IMF revisited capital controls and gave them an endorsement (Ostry et al., 2010). This study suggested that market-friendly capital controls can help countries cope with surges of capital inflows that can end in sudden stops and contribute to the kinds of crises discussed in this chapter. It endorsed many of the observations concerning capital controls discussed here. The 1997 position of the IMF on capital controls is now a thing of the past.

CONCLUSION

Financial crises come in many varieties, but these are varieties that can occur together. Hyperinflation, balance of payments and currency crises, asset price deflation, bank crises, external debt crises, and domestic debt crises can combine in ways in which one crisis makes another more likely and more sustained. Balance of payments and currency crises can put pressure on any entity that holds foreign currency-denominated debt that consequently increases in domestic currency value. If this includes banks, it can make a banking crisis more likely. If it includes the government, it can make default crises more likely. Balance of payments and currency crashes can worsen inflation by increasing the prices of trade goods, and asset price deflation can make banking crises more likely.

Fixed exchange rate regimes can be very fragile. In the face of large changes in the expected future exchange rate, a government can have a very difficult time supporting

[24] VDRs are flexible in three dimensions: percentage, minimum deposit period, and application to new versus existing credits. These flexibilities, as well as their market-friendly nature, make VDRs an attractive policy option.

[25] We take up the issue of phasing in Chapter 24 on "Structural Adjustment."

[26] See Massad (1998) and Eichengreen (1999).

[27] Fischer (2000) stated: "That is not to say . . . that countries should open their accounts prematurely: rather they need to ensure that their economies and the financial systems are sufficiently strong; and they may particularly want to avail themselves for some time of controls on short-term capital flows."

the fixed rate; at some point, it simply runs out of foreign reserves. Balance of payments crises can also occur as a result of capital flight. Weak financial (especially banking) systems add to the likelihood of high tech crises, where confidence in the financial system deteriorates. This is particularly true if the regulatory framework supporting the banking system is weak.

There are now new Basel Committee standards in the form of Basel III to hopefully make a systemic crisis like 2007–2009 less likely. The jury is still out on this. Market-friendly capital controls can also play a role and have been finally endorsed by the IMF. Better data on sovereign debt and asset prices can also help sound the alarm on future crises, but policymakers need to act in response to unsustainable debt levels and asset price bubbles. Unfortunately, in the case of asset price bubbles, central banks have been loathe to respond to curb their growth. Given this reluctance, the proposals of Reinhart and Rogoff (2009) and Eichengreen (2010) for an international financial regulatory organization (to replace the Basel Committee) are worth considering seriously.[28]

REVIEW EXERCISES

1. What is the key difference between "old-fashioned" and "high tech" crises?
2. In Chapter 16 we addressed fixed exchange rates. Policies to maintain fixed exchange rates fell into two categories. First, there were policies to address the excess demand or supply of the home country (official reserve transactions). Second, there were policies to change the equilibrium exchange rate (interest rate changes). Please answer the following questions with regard to the use of these policies in balance of payments crises.
   a. In a balance of payments crisis, what kind of official reserve transactions will be made?
   b. What are the limits of the official reserve transactions approach to resolving balance of payments crises?
   c. In a balance of payments crisis, what kind of interest rate policies will be used?
   d. What are the limits of the interest rate approach to resolving balance of payments crises?
3. The argument in favor of current account convertibility (free trade) is that it leads to gains from trade. Are there any reasons you can think of why we might not be able to extend this argument to the financial transactions of the capital account? Or to put it differently, are there any ways that financial markets differ from merchandise and service markets?
4. Take the crisis varieties in Table 18.1 and try to list the ways in which one can contribute to another.

FURTHER READING AND WEB RESOURCES

Readable and worthwhile reviews of crises can be found in Krugman (1999), Eichengreen (1999), and Reinhart and Rogoff (2009). For a more advanced treatment, see Allen and Gale (2007), and for the specific case of bubbles, see Vogel (2010). For a description of a more "sensible" way to conduct finance, see Bhidé (2010). The Alessandri and

[28] Eichengreen (2010) also proposed a Global Systemic Risk Facility that attempts to address some of the concerns raised by Goldin and Vogel (2010).

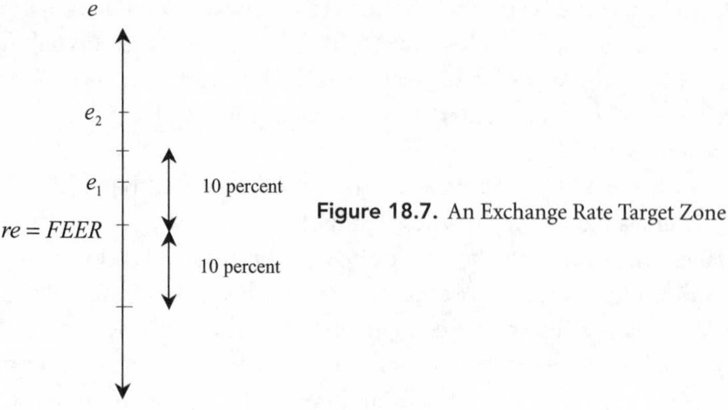

Figure 18.7. An Exchange Rate Target Zone

Haldane (2009) paper is very much worth a read for a historical perspective on the 2007–2009 bailout of the global financial system. The Basel Committee on Banking Supervision website can be found at http://www.bis.org/bcbs/index.htm.

APPENDIX: EXCHANGE RATE TARGET ZONES

The balance of payments and currency crises we described in this chapter are often associated with fixed exchange rate regimes. Why do countries adopt such regimes? As we mentioned in Chapter 16, it is because flexible exchange rate regimes are often volatile, and countries do not want to undergo the large changes in the home-currency prices of trade goods that come with these excessive exchange rate changes. This is sometimes referred to as "fear of floating."

Some international economists, notably John Williamson (1983, 1993), proposed to obtain the benefits of both fixed and floating exchange rate arrangements through the use of **exchange rate target zones.**[29] In Williamson's plan, the center of the target zone would be what he terms a **fundamental equilibrium exchange rate (FEER)**, which could be established by the IMF. Although it is not *exactly* the case, we can consider the FEER to be the purchasing power parity (PPP) rate defined in Chapter 14.[30] As we know, the nominal exchange rate need not equal the real exchange rate and, therefore, the FEER. Williamson terms "misalignments" situations in which $e \neq re = FEER$, and such misalignments can occur as a result of countries' monetary policies.

Around the FEER, Williamson advocated the use of a broad exchange rate band, on the order of $\pm\, 10$ percent. Over time, the FEER changes with movements in relative price levels. Therefore, in the target zone proposal, the central rate moves slowly over time, and the exchange rate band moves with it. Finally, Williamson proposed frequent (monthly) realignments of the nominal rate in situations of misalignment. For example, Figure 18.7 depicts an exchange rate target zone with a central rate of $re = FEER$ and 10 percent bands. The nominal rate e_1 is within the band, so no realignment is immediately necessary. The nominal rate e_2 is outside the upper band and calls for a nominal appreciation. As we saw in Chapter 15, this can be achieved through an increase in the domestic interest rate.

[29] See also *The Economist* (1993).

[30] "*Other things being equal*... one expects the nominal exchange rates consistent with long-run or fundamental equilibrium to change in accord with differential inflation, as posited by PPP theory" (Williamson, 1983, p. 14).

Does this proposal make sense? Holtham (1995) suggested that: "to the extent that the target zones are credible, their existence provides a focus from market expectations and tends to stabilize market movements" (p. 244). The key question though is whether the zones will be credible in practice. Obstfeld and Rogoff (1995) noted that even zones as large as ± 12 percent (and in one case ± 30 percent) failed to stem crises in the European Monetary System (see Chapter 19). They also suggested that a lack of credible "edges" to target zones may lead to destabilization within target zones. Nevertheless, the proposal is one that is often revisited in the wake of exchange rate crises.

REFERENCES

Alessandri, A. and A. Haldane (2009) "Banking on the State," Bank of England.

Allen, R. and D. Gale (2007) *Understanding Financial Crises*, Oxford University Press.

Bhagwati, J. (1998) "The Capital Myth," *Foreign Affairs*, May/June, 7–12.

Bhidé, A. (2010) *A Call for Judgment: Sensible Finance for a Dynamic Economy*, Oxford University Press.

Bird, G. and R.S. Rajan (2001) "Banks, Financial Liberalization and Financial Crises in Emerging Markets," *World Economy*, 24:7, 889–910.

Calvo, G.A. and E.G. Mendoza (1996) "Mexico's Balance-of-Payments Crisis: A Chronicle of a Death Foretold," *Journal of International Economics*, 41:3/4, 235–264.

Crook, C. (2003) "A Cruel Sea of Capital: A Survey of Global Finance," *The Economist*, May 3.

Diamond, D. and P.H. Dybvig (1983) "Bank Runs, Deposit Insurance and Liquidity," *Journal of Political Economy*, 91:3, 401–419.

Diaz-Alejandro, C. (1985) "Goodbye Financial Repression, Hello Financial Crash," *Journal of Development Economics*, 19:1–2, 1–24.

Dobson, W. and G.C. Hufbauer (2001) *World Capital Markets: Challenges to the G-10*, Institute for International Economics.

Dugger, C.W. (2010) "Zimbabwe Health Care, Paid with Peanuts," *New York Times*, December 18.

The Economist (1993) "The Way We Were," May 8.

The Economist (1997) "Lessons for Thailand, et al.," July 12.

The Economist (2004) "Bank Capital Adequacy: Basel Light," July 3.

The Economist (2010) "Reforming Banking: Base Camp Basel," January 23.

Eichengreen, B. (1999) *Towards a New Financial Architecture: A Practical Post-Asia Agenda*, Institute for International Economics.

Eichengreen, B. (2010) "Out-of-the-Box Thoughts about the International Financial Architecture," *Journal of International Commerce, Economics and Policy*, 1:1, 1–20.

Fischer, S. (1998a) "Capital-Account Liberalization and the Role of the IMF," in S. Fischer et al., *Should the IMF Pursue Capital-Account Convertibility?*, Princeton Essays in International Finance, 207, 1–10.

Fischer, S. (1998b) "Lessons from a Crisis," *The Economist*, October 3, 23–27.

Fischer, S. (2000) "Managing the International Monetary System," International Monetary Fund.

Goldin, I. and T. Vogel (2010) "Global Governance and Systemic Risk in the 21st Century: Lessons from the Financial Crisis," *Global Policy*, 1:1, 4–15.

Goldstein, M., G.K. Kaminsky, and C.M. Reinhart (2000) *Assessing Financial Vulnerability*, Institute for International Economics.

Greenspan, A. (2002) "Remarks by Chairman Alan Greenspan before the Economic Club of New York," U.S. Federal Reserve Board.

Holtham, G. (1995) "Managing the Exchange Rate System," in J. Michie and J. Grieve Smith (eds.), *Managing the Global Economy*, Oxford University Press, 232–251.

International Monetary Fund (1999) "The IMF's Response to the Asian Crisis."

Joyce, J.P. and M. Nabar (2009) "Sudden Stops, Banking Crises and Investment Collapses in Emerging Markets," *Journal of Development Economics*, 90:2: 314–322.

Kaminsky, G.L., C.M. Reinhart, and C.A. Végh (2003) "The Unholy Trinity of Financial Contagion," *Journal of Economic Perspectives*, 17:4, 51–74.

Kose, M.A., E. Prasad, K. Rogoff, and S.-J. Wei. (2009) "Financial Globalization: A Reappraisal," *IMF Staff Papers*, 56:1, 8–62.

Kristof, N.D. (1998) "Has the I.M.F. Cured or Harmed Asia? Dispute Rages after Months of Crisis," *New York Times*, April 23.

Krugman, P. (1979) "A Model of Balance of Payments Crises," *Journal of Money, Credit and Banking*, 11:3, 311–325.

Krugman, P. (1999) *The Return of Depression Economics*, Norton.

Krugman, P. (2010) "Things Could be Worse," *New York Times*, September 9.

Marks, S. (2009) "Asymmetric Information," in K.A. Reinert, R.S. Rajan, A.J. Glass, and L.S. Davis (eds.), *The Princeton Encyclopedia of the World Economy*, Princeton University Press, 89–94.

Massad, C. (1998) "The Liberalization of the Capital Account: Chile in the 1990s," in S. Fischer et al., *Should the IMF Pursue Capital-Account Convertibility?*, Princeton Essays in International Finance, 207, 34–46.

Mydans, S. (1997a) "Thai Prime Minister Falls Victim to Economic Crisis," *New York Times*, November 4.

Mydans, S. (1997b) "Economists Cheer Thailand's Tough Action on Ailing Finance Companies," *New York Times*, December 9.

Mydans, S. (1998) "Struggling Thailand Seeks Easier I.M.F. Terms," *New York Times*, January 9.

Noguchi, Y. (1994) "The 'Bubble' and Economic Policies in the 1980s," *Journal of Japanese Studies*, 20:2, 291–329.

Obstfeld, M. and K. Rogoff (1995) "The Mirage of Fixed Exchange Rates," *Journal of Economic Perspectives*, 9:4, 73–96.

Ostry, J.D., A.R. Ghosh, K. Habermeier, M. Chamon, M.S. Qureshi, and D.B.S. Reinhardt (2010) "Capital Inflows: The Role of Controls," International Monetary Fund.

Reinhart, C.M. and K.S. Rogoff (2009) *This Time Is Different: Eight Centuries of Financial Folly*, Princeton University Press.

Reynolds, S., R. Fowles, J. Gander, W. Kunaporntham, and S. Ratanakomut (2002) "Forecasting the Probability of Failure of Thailand's Financial Companies in the Asian Financial Crisis," *Economic Development and Cultural Change*, 51:1, 237–246.

Rodrik, D. (1998) "Who Needs Capital-Account Convertibility?" in S. Fischer et al., *Should the IMF Pursue Capital-Account Convertibility?*, Princeton Essays in International Finance, 207, 55–65.

Sanger, D.E. (1998) "IMF Role in World Economy Is Hotly Debated," *New York Times*, October 2.

Stiglitz, J.E. (2002) *Globalization and Its Discontents*, Norton, New York.

Stone, D. and W.T. Ziemba (1993) "Land and Stock Prices in Japan," *Journal of Economic Perspectives*, 7:3, 149–165.

Vogel, H.L. (2010) *Financial Market Bubbles and Crashes*, Cambridge University Press.

Williamson, J. (1983) *The Exchange Rate System*, Institute for International Economics, Washington, D.C.

Williamson, J. (1993) "Exchange Rate Management," *Economic Journal*, 103:416, 188–197.
Wolf, M. (2010) "Basel: The Mouse That Did Not Roar," *Financial Times*, September 14.
Woodall, P. (1995) "The World Economy: Who's in the Driving Seat?" *The Economist*, October 7.
World Bank (2001) *Finance for Growth: Policy Choices in a Volatile World*.

19 Monetary Unions

Imagine that you are a finance minister of a medium-sized country with extensive trade and investment relationships with fellow members of a **preferential trade agreement** (PTA) of the type discussed in Chapter 8. Imagine also that you have responsibility for determining the future exchange rate regime of your country. One option you have is a flexible exchange rate regime (a "clean" or "dirty" float). If you choose this option, however, your country might be buffeted by destabilizing changes in the nominal (and hence real) exchange rate. A second option you have is a fixed exchange rate (or crawling peg). If you choose this option, however, your country might eventually stumble into a balance of payments and currency crisis, as we discussed in Chapter 18. What should you do? There is no easy answer.

There is a third option available to you, one we mentioned briefly in Chapter 8 on PTAs. You and the other finance ministers in the PTA could agree to do away with all the exchange rates among your countries by becoming a **monetary union** with a common currency. This is not a panacea, because you and your colleagues would still need to decide on the exchange rate regime for the common currency against other major currencies. But at least you can avoid exchange rate instability with your major trade and investment partners. As it turns out, this policy was adopted as a goal by the countries of Western Europe in 1971 and was implemented in 1999. Monetary union has also been a living reality for the Communauté Financière Africaine (CFA) franc zone, a group of African countries with ties to France, and for the rand zone in Southern Africa. In this chapter, we first take up the case of the European Monetary Union (EMU), assessing both its planning and implementation. Next, we assess the EMU in light of the theory of **optimum currency areas** and discuss its potential adjustment problems and recent crisis. Finally, we briefly consider the cases of the CFA franc zone and the rand zone.

Analytical elements for this chapter:
Countries, currencies, and *financial assets.*

THE EUROPEAN MONETARY UNION AT A GLANCE

The European Monetary Union (EMU) is a monetary union among 17 countries (as of early 2011) in which the euro (€) serves as the shared currency. The euro is administered by the European Central Bank (ECB). The member countries are listed in Table 19.1. In 1999, there were only 11 members (Austria, Belgium, Finland, France, Germany, Ireland, Italy, Luxembourg, the Netherlands, Portugal, and Spain). Subsequently, accessions added Greece in 2001, Slovenia in 2007, Cyprus and Malta in 2008, and the Slovak Republic in 2009. Estonia joined in 2011.

During the initial years of the EMU, the euro was "invisible," used only as a unit of account and for electronic transactions. But beginning in 2002, it appeared "on the streets" in the form of notes and coins. The euro is therefore now legal tender in the EMU member countries for all types of transactions. It also plays a large role both in the European Union (EU) and the world economy, for example, as an important component of national governments' foreign reserves. Further, there are a number of mini-states and territories that use the euro as their legal tender.[1] Given the size of the

[1] For further information on the euro, see Salvatore (2009).

Table 19.1. EMU membership

Country	Year joined	Original currency	Central government debt as percent of GDP, year of entry	Central government debt as percent of GDP, 2008 or most recent
Original Members				
Austria	1999	Austrian schilling	66	65
Belgium	1999	Belgian franc	112	88
Finland	1999	Finnish markka	64	37 (2007)
France	1999	French franc	61	67 (2007)
Germany	1999	Deutsche mark	NA	41
Ireland	1999	Irish pound	49	27
Italy	1999	Italian lira	125	106
Luxembourg	1999	Luxembourg franc	NA	5
Netherlands	1999	Dutch guilder	58	43 (2007)
Portugal	1999	Portuguese escudo	61	76
Spain	1999	Spanish peseta	61	34
Subsequent Members				
Greece	2001	Greek drachma	126	114 (2007)
Slovenia	2007	Slovene tolar	NA	NA
Cyprus	2008	Cyprus pound	162 (2007)	162 (2007)
Malta	2008	Maltese lira	73 (2007)	73 (2007)
Slovak Republic	2009	Slovak koruna	37 (2008)	37
Estonia	2011	Estonian kroon	4 (2007)	4 (2007)

Sources: European Central Bank and World Bank, World Development Indicators Online

EMU (more than 300 million people), the bloc is also an important component of the world economy in its own right.

As we see later, there are two important EU members (the United Kingdom and Denmark) that *chose* not to join the EMU, utilizing an "opt out" provision of the Maastricht Treaty.[2] Table 19.1 lists the original currency of each EMU member country. It also lists the central government debt as a percent of gross domestic product (GDP) both for the year of entry and for the most recent year available. As we also see later, these debt levels have proved to be an important aspect of EMU history. Table 19.2 lists the EU members that are not members of the EMU and provides some information on their current exchange rate regime and readiness to join the EMU. With the exceptions of the United Kingdom and Denmark with their opt-outs, all EU members are expected to eventually join the EMU.

PLANNING THE EUROPEAN MONETARY UNION

The history of monetary integration in Europe has roots that go back to the immediate post–World War II period.[3] In Chapter 8, we discussed the evolution of the EU from 1951 through 2007. For your convenience, Table 8.3 of that chapter is reproduced here as Table 19.3. Issing (2008) noted that, after the formation of the European Economic Community (EEC) in 1958, "there were occasional suggestions that work should also

[2] Sweden's opt-out is considered to be de facto but not de jure.

[3] See chapter 1 of Gros and Thygesen (1992) and chapter 13 of Dinan (2010).

Table 19.2 In but out: Countries that are members of the EU but not the EMU

Country	Currency	Exchange rate regime	Status as of 2010
Bulgaria	Bulgarian lev	Pegged to euro	Not yet ready.
Czech Republic	Czech koruna	Floating	Not yet ready.
Denmark	Danish krone	Pegged to euro	Formal opt-out. Two referendums against joining.
Hungary	Hungarian forint	Floating	Not yet ready.
Latvia	Latvian lats	Pegged to euro	Nearly ready to join.
Lithuania	Lithuanian litas	Pegged to euro	Nearly ready to join.
Poland	Polish zloty	Floating	Not yet ready.
Romania	Romanian leu	Floating	Not yet ready.
Sweden	Swedish krona	Floating	Referendum against joining.
United Kingdom	British pound	Floating	Formal opt-out. A referendum would be a political necessity, and this would in all likelihood be against joining.

Sources: European Central Bank and *The Economist* (2009)

be undertaken towards monetary union" (p. 4). However, the real monetary union initiative began in 1970 when a commission chaired by the then Prime Minister of Luxembourg, Pierre Werner, issued a report providing a detailed plan for a step-by-step movement to an EMU by 1980. Some details regarding Pierre Werner are provided in the accompanying box. The European Council of Ministers of Economics and Finance (ECOFIN) endorsed the Werner Report in March 1971.

Werner's vision of an EMU by 1980 was not to come to pass. Recall from Chapter 17 that the early 1970s were characterized by the demise of the Bretton Woods system of global monetary arrangements. During 1971, key European currencies, including the German Deutsche mark, began to float, and U.S. President Nixon closed the "gold window," signaling an end to a monetary era. In response to this crisis, a year later, the members of the EEC decided to bind their exchange rates within 2.25 percent of each other. This became known as the "snake in a tunnel" or "snake." During 1972, however, the British pound came under pressure and was forced out of the snake. Later, the Danish krone also was forced to pull out of the snake. The French franc was forced out in 1974, re-entered in 1975, and was forced out again in 1976. Despite these difficulties, the "snake" continued through 1978, and this period of time represented one in which the EEC was attempting to deal with new, global monetary realities.[4] As we discussed in Chapter 17, this was not an easy task.

In 1977, European Commission President Roy Jenkins gave a lecture at the European University in Florence. In this lecture, he called for Europe to return to the Werner vision and adopt monetary union as a goal. As a result of this new impetus and other developments, negotiations began in earnest over the creation of a European Monetary System (EMS) in 1978. The EMS came into being as a fixed-rate system in 1979. In a very real sense, the EMS was an attempt to replicate the fixed-rate, Bretton Woods system

[4] See chapter 5 of Eichengreen (2008) for a history of the snake.

Table 19.3 The evolution of the European Union

Year	Initiative	Treaty	Members added
1951	European Coal and Steel Community	Treaty of Paris	Belgium France Germany Italy Luxembourg Netherlands
1958	European Economic Community	Treaty of Rome	
1973	Enlargement		Denmark Ireland United Kingdom
1981	Enlargement		Greece
1986	Enlargement		Portugal Spain
1992	European Union	Treaty on European Union (TEU) or the Maastricht Treaty	
1995	Enlargement		Austria Finland Sweden
1999	European Monetary Union		United Kingdom, Sweden, and Denmark not included
2002	Common EMU currency: the euro		United Kingdom, Sweden, and Denmark not included
2004	Enlargement		Cyprus Czech Republic Estonia Hungary Latvia Lithuania Malta Poland Slovakia Slovenia
2007	Enlargement		Bulgaria Romania
2007	EU Constitution	Lisbon Treaty	

Sources: Dinan (2010) and *europa.eu*

among the countries of Europe.[5] A new currency was created called the European currency unit (ECU), defined as a basket of European currencies. The ECU had a role equivalent to that initially hoped for special drawing rights (SDR) in the Bretton Woods system (see Chapter 17). Furthermore, the European Community acted in a role equivalent to the IMF, providing balance of payments credit to members.[6]

The original hope was that each country would peg their currency to the ECU, but this hope did not come to pass. Instead, in the 1980s, countries began to peg their

[5] See chapter 10 of James (1996).
[6] For example, this was the case during a 1983 French crisis.

currencies to the German mark.[7] The ECU continued only as a unit of account for official European Community business. In the early years of the EMS, there was a great deal of instability. A number of parity realignments were necessary with the French franc falling against the German mark. The latter was largely due to the expansive macroeconomic policies of the Socialist government of President François Mitterand. During a crisis in March 1983, Mitterand changed course in order to keep France within the EMS.[8] Thereafter, stability was restored with less frequent parity changes.

In 1988, the European Council called on then President of the European Commission, Jacques Delors, to study the steps required to move toward a monetary union. The subsequent Delors Report was issued in 1989. The report called for a single currency and an integrated system of European central banks. In 1991, a meeting of the European Community took place in the Dutch town of Maastricht. The Maastricht Treaty, agreed to at this meeting, was to serve as a constitution of the new European Union, or EU, replacing the Treaty of Rome. It was signed in 1992. Importantly for our purposes here, however, the Maastricht Treaty set 1999 as a target date for the EMU.

In 1994, as specified by the Maastricht Treaty, a European Monetary Institute (EMI) came into being. Its purpose was to plan for the future European System of Central Banks (ESCB) and to plot the course toward monetary integration. The EMI was to also monitor the progress of member countries toward meeting a set of *convergence criteria*. These criteria concerned price stability, levels of government deficits and debt, exchange rate targets, and interest rate targets. For example, government deficits (a flow) were required to be less than 3 percent of GDP, and government debts (a stock) were required to be less than 60 percent of GDP. These convergence criteria reflected the wishes of the German government.[9]

Pierre Werner

Pierre Werner was born in Luxembourg in 1913. Importantly, he grew up in a bilingual family, speaking both German and French. His professional life spanned the fields of law and economics. He studied Law at the University of Paris and Economics and Finance at the Paris École Libre de Sciences Politiques. Unlike many leading citizens of Luxembourg who fled the country, Werner spent the Second World War under German occupation, witnessing many horrors firsthand. As with many Western Europeans of this generation, Werner became passionate about European integration as an antidote to war. He was elected to the Luxembourg parliament in 1945 and befriended Jean Monnet, one of the architects of the European Community (EC) formed in 1958. To Werner, Monnet, and other leading integrationists of that era, "the central aim of European unity was to prevent war. Economic gain, though useful, was a secondary consideration" (*The Economist*, 2002b, p. 85).

[7] "Structurally, Germany... occupied within the EMS a situation analogous to that of the United States within the classical Bretton Woods par value system, and the deutsche mark constituted the European 'key currency'" (James, 1996, p. 482).

[8] The adjustment came under the guidance of Ministry of Economy Jacques Delors, who would later become a powerful President of the European Commission.

[9] Having experienced two periods of hyperinflation in the twentieth century, the German government and the German citizenry approached the EMU project with some caution. Issing (2008) wrote: "Without any doubt, a stable currency was to a very large extent the foundation that underpinned the economic reconstruction after the Second World War.... No wonder, then, that (Germans) saw little merit in the idea of abandoning their stable national currency" (p. 23). These considerations were also why the ECB was located in Frankfurt, home to the German central bank.

Werner became Prime Minister of Luxembourg in 1959 and remained in that post until 1974. He returned to that post in 1979, retiring from politics in 1984 to pursue a subsequent career in business. In 1993, he published his memoirs, entitled *Itinéraires Luxembourgeois et Europeens.*

Werner first floated the idea of a common European currency in a 1960 speech at Strasbourg. In 1969, the EC adopted the goal of monetary union and convened a High Level Group under Werner's chairmanship to develop a plan for an EC monetary union by 1980. The plan, which became known as the Werner Report, was circulated in 1970 and endorsed by the EC in 1971. Although not mentioning the adoption of a common currency per se, the Werner Report called for the "total and irreversible conversion of currencies, the elimination of fluctuation in exchange rates, the irrevocable fixing of parity rates and the complete liberation of capital accounts." A continued advocate of a common currency for Europe, however, Werner had to wait until January 2002 to witness the introduction of euro notes and coins. He died six months later.

Sources: Daily Telegraph (2002) and *The Economist* (2002b)

The evolution toward the EMU proved to be more difficult than envisioned in the Delors Report. In 1990, East and West Germany had reunified. This required unprecedented increases in public expenditure on the part of the German government. To prevent the German economy from expanding too quickly, the German central bank pursued a tight or restrictive monetary policy. This kept German interest rates high, caused international investors to favor mark-denominated assets over other European assets, and put downward pressure on the value of other European currencies. The EMS par-value system consequently came under pressure.

In addition, difficulties in ratification of the 1992 Maastricht Treaty ruffled investors' expectations. In particular, there were growing predictions of a "no" vote (proved to be incorrect) in the French referendum on Maastricht in 1992. In that very same month, pressure built against the British pound and Italian lira. Despite very large interventions by European central banks to support these currencies, they were forced outside of the EMS.[10] The French franc came under a second-round attack in 1993. In response to these events, the margins around the EMS parities were expanded from 2.25 percent to 15 percent.

The EMS crisis was certainly an inauspicious transition to European monetary integration. The British government, which subsequently opted out of the EMU, was particularly irritated by its forced exit from the EMS. That said, however, most EU leaders resolved to press on, and so they did. In 1995, EU members meeting in Madrid committed themselves to introducing the euro in January 1999. They also adopted the EMI's plan for monetary integration, despite widespread misgivings. After the Madrid meetings, the EMU project proceeded in large part by political faith, supplemented by technical competence in institutional design.[11]

[10] The pound and lira crises were preceded by crises of the Finish markka and the Swedish krone. Later, the Irish pound, the Portuguese escudo, and the Spanish peseta were also devalued. The franc peg survived thanks to intervention by the German Bundesbank.

[11] With regard to the political economy of the EMU, Walter and Sen (2009) argued that "it is difficult to avoid the conclusion that the strong commitment of France, Germany, and other European governments (left and right) to monetary union has much to do with the broader goal shared by political elites of promoting deeper political integration" (p. 138).

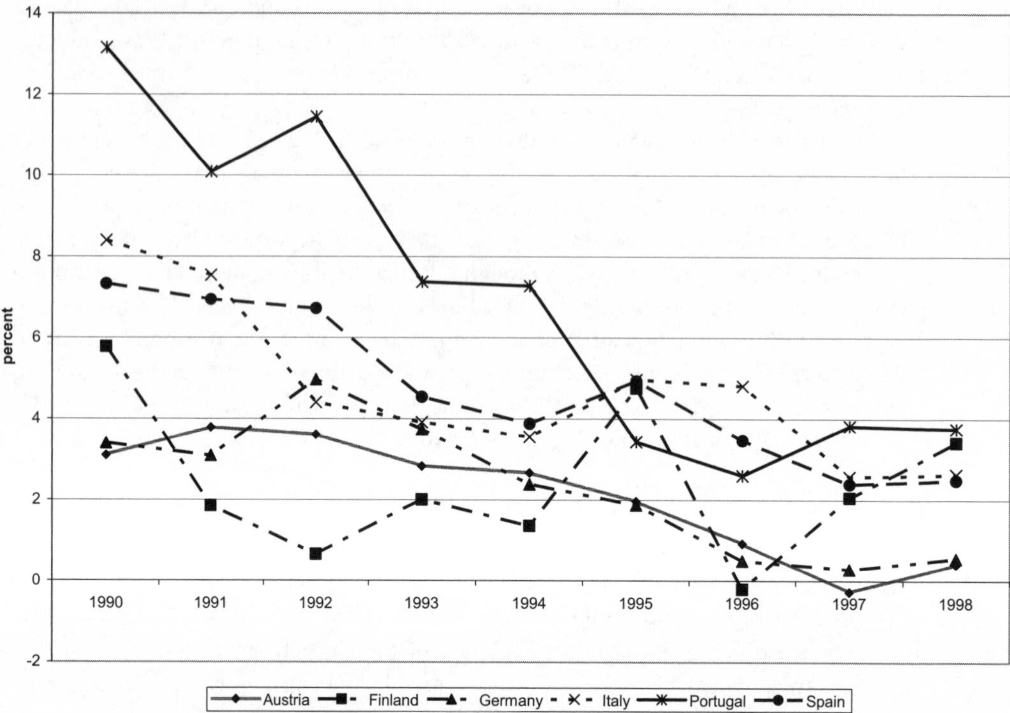

Figure 19.1. Inflation Rates (GDP Price Deflator) in Selected Euro Countries, 1990–1998 (percent). *Source:* World Bank, World Development Indicators Online

IMPLEMENTING THE EUROPEAN MONETARY UNION

The day of reckoning for the EMU came in May 1998, when the European Council met in Brussels to determine which countries were to take part in the EMU on January 1, 1999. Recall from earlier in this chapter that the first convergence criterion concerned price stability. Figure 19.1 plots inflation rates for the six countries ultimately included in the EMU, with the highest inflation rates in 1990 (Austria, Finland, Germany, Italy, Portugal, and Spain). As you can see in this figure, there was a significant degree of convergence in inflation rates between 1990 and 1998, a relatively short period of time. From the perspective of this first convergence criterion, then, prospects were good.

The second and third convergence criteria concerned central government deficits and debt. As it turned out, nearly all of the candidates for inclusion in the EMU had made significant progress in the area of government deficits, although in some cases this involved a bit of creative accounting. With regard to government debt levels, however, two countries stood out as *not* having met the convergence criterion: Belgium and Italy. As we saw in Table 19.1, these two countries had debts of 112 percent and 125 percent of GDP, respectively. No amount of creative accounting would move these statistics to the required 60 percent level!

In the event, the European Council chose to give Belgium and Italy a pass. As noted by Issing (2008), "For both of these countries, founder members of the European Economic Community and in every respect at the center of European integration, a major effort at interpretation and ultimately a political decision were required to enable their entry" (p. 16). In other words, a key convergence criterion was violated. As a result of this political decision, the original members of the EMU were Austria, Belgium,

Finland, France, Germany, Ireland, Italy, Luxembourg, the Netherlands, Portugal, and Spain. Greece was the one country that wanted to join but was not allowed. This decision was later reversed, and Greece joined in 2001 with a debt level of 126 percent of GDP, again violating the relevant convergence criterion. As mentioned previously, the United Kingdom, Denmark, and Sweden opted not to join. At the time, *The Economist* (1998b) summed up the situation as follows: "A striking feature of the single currency arrangements is that they make no provision, legal or practical, for any participant's withdrawal or expulsion. In this adventure, Europe has left itself no choice but to succeed" (p. 82).

The centerpiece of the EMU is the Frankfurt-based European Central Bank (ECB). The charter of the ECB was modeled on the German central bank, and the former national central banks are related to the ECB in a structure modeled quite closely on that of the Federal Reserve System of the United States. As specified in the Maastricht Treaty, the primary objective of the ECB in its monetary policy decisions is to maintain price stability within the EMU. The ECB is required to maintain annual increases in a Harmonized Index of Consumer Prices (HICP) at or below 2 percent. This is widely regarded as a very stringent rule, but one insisted on by the German central bank in the run-up to the EMU.[12] In the conduct of this objective, the ECB is to maintain independence from political influence.

The ECB is headed by a President with an eight-year, nonrenewable term. This proved difficult from the start. The European Council appoints the ECB President, and a battle ensued over who would initially fill this post. This inauspicious beginning of the ECB is discussed in the accompanying box. The European Council also appoints the ECB Vice President. The President, the Vice President, and four other individuals comprise the ECB Executive Board. The Executive Board is responsible for *implementing* monetary policy within the EMU. Issing (2008) described the Executive Board as the "operational decision-making body of the ECB" (p. 70).

The Executive Board plus the heads of EMU member central banks compose the ECB Governing Council. The Governing Council is responsible for *formulating* monetary policy within the EMU. There is also a General Council that adds the heads of the EU member central banks that are not part of the EMU. However, the four members of the Executive Board other than the President and the Vice President do not have the right to vote as part of the General Council. The General Council is an *administrative* body that is responsible for the work previously undertaken by the EMI, with a focus on accession processes.

The ECB actually plays two roles within the EU. This is illustrated in Figure 19.2. First, with regard to the EU, it is the centerpiece of the European Systems of Central Banks (ESCB). Originally, it had been assumed that all EU members would be members of the EMU, but we now know that it is not the case. So second, the ECB is the centerpiece of a subset of the ESCB that has become known as the Eurosystem, consisting of the central banks of EMU members and the ECB. Eventually, if and when all EU members join the EMU, the ESCB and the Eurosystem will be one and the same.[13]

[12] For more on the conduct of monetary policy within the EMU, see chapter 3 of Issing (2008). Issing noted that "With the Harmonized Index of Consumer Prices, Eurostat provided the most important indicator for the development of euro area prices on a timely basis" (p. 83). For a criticism on the 2 percent inflation ceiling, see Münchau (2011).

[13] Please note that many British politicians (known as "Eurosceptics") would want to make sure that such an event never occurs!

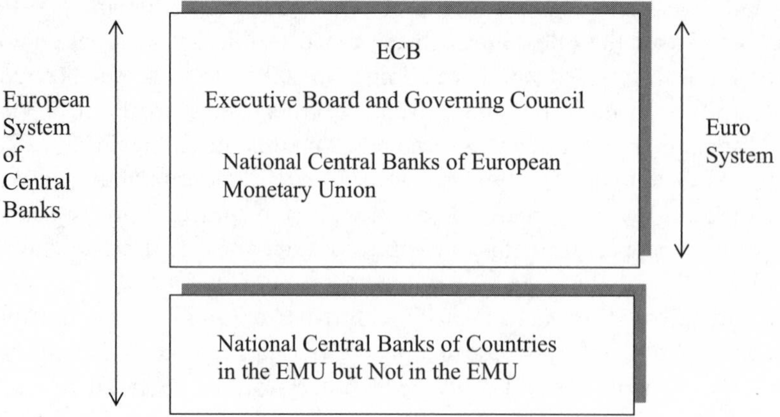

Figure 19.2. Organizational Structure of the ECB. *Source:* European Central Bank

Battles over ECB Head

The European Central Bank (ECB) had a rough start in the decision regarding who would head that body as President. Most members of the European Council favored Wim Duisenberg, a chain-smoking Dutch economist and former Chair of the EMI. French President Jacques Chirac, however, insisted on Jean-Claude Trichet, governor of the French central bank, despite the fact that Trichet had formerly endorsed Duisenberg! Finally, Duisenberg was appointed with the understanding that he would stand down during 2003 and that Trichet would then complete a full eight-year term. As Dinan (2010) stated: "To everyone's surprise, Chirac pursued this nakedly nationalistic position to the end." Because this arrangement was against both the letter and the spirit of ESCB statutes, the ECB had an unglamorous start.

Wim Duisenberg had been appointed as head of the European Monetary Institute in 1997, having previously served very successfully as head of the Dutch central bank. He took over at the helm of the ECB in 1999 and called on the European public to consider him their "Mr. Euro." But he ran into trouble in 2000 when he gave an interview to a newspaper in which he commented on the conditions under which the ECB might intervene to support the value of the euro. This comment violated a central banking taboo and resulted in calls for and rumors of his resignation.

Jean-Claude Trichet ran into his own troubles. During 2000, Trichet was caught up in the French financial scandals surrounding the bank Crédit Lyonnais. These issues related to his career at the helm of the French Treasury from 1987 to 1993 when he was responsible for the accounts of Crédit Lyonnais. He was cleared of wrongdoing in 2003 and eventually became head of the ECB during that year.

Trichet's term will expire in 2011. Political maneuvering over the new ECB head began in earnest in early 2011, with Axel Weber of Germany and Mario Draghi of Italy being the two most important candidates. In the end, Draghi (sometimes known as "Super Mario" after the video game) secured the nomination as the next ECB President.

Sources: Dinan (2010), Ewing and Castle (2011), and Sullivan (2000)

The euro was launched in January 1999. At that time, EMU member exchange rates became "irrevocably" locked, and monetary policy was transferred to the ECB. The value of the euro was initially set at 0.85 €/US$ or 1.18 US$/€ in a flexible exchange rate regime such as we discussed in Chapter 15.

In January 2002, the ECB introduced euro notes and coins and began the process of withdrawing old notes and coins from circulation. Amazingly, this huge logistical task was carried out with very few problems. Europe now had its common currency. As you can see in Figure 19.2, the euro's value initially fell against the U.S. dollar and the Japanese yen, despite predictions that it would appreciate. These falls continued through 2001. From 2001 through 2008, the euro strengthened against the yen and dollar, but with the onset of crises in selected euro countries (discussed later), the euro began to weaken again. Although some Europhiles interpret these movements as reflecting the strength or weakness of "Europe," it is really a sign of the workings of the flexible exchange rate regime between the EMU and the rest of the world.

In light of its history since 1999, EMU and its ECB have been a remarkable success. Monetary union on this scale is historically unprecedented, and much could have gone wrong in conducting this economic experiment. Issues have arisen with regard to the conduct of monetary policy, during both periods of economic prosperity and in downturns or crises, as well as with fiscal policies in member countries. We consider these issues in the next two sections on optimal currency areas and the recent crisis.

OPTIMUM CURRENCY AREAS AND ADJUSTMENT IN THE EMU

There is an idea in international economics that is important to our preceding discussion of the EMU. This is the notion of an **optimum currency area.**[14] An optimum currency area is a collection of countries characterized by the following:

1. Well-integrated factor markets
2. Well-integrated fiscal systems
3. Economic disturbances that affect each country in a symmetrical manner

Most observers, for example, agree that the United States constitutes an optimum currency area. Labor and physical capital are quite mobile among the states of the United States, and there is a great deal of integration of fiscal systems through the U.S. federal government. Finally, cycles of recession and recovery tend to affect each region of the United States in a somewhat symmetrical (albeit not equal) manner.

In the case of the EMU, there seems to be less evidence that it constitutes an optimum currency area.[15] First, despite the fact that the EMU is a subcomponent of the EU, which is, in turn, a common market (see Chapter 8), both labor and physical capital are less mobile among the countries of the EMU than in the United States. Second, the budget of the EU is relatively small in proportion to the size of the economies involved. This indicates a lack of fiscal integration of the EMU economy. Third, business cycles among the members of the EMU are somewhat asymmetrical with the potential of one country experiencing an expansion while another experiences a contraction.

[14] This line of thinking in international economics was started by Mundell (1961) and McKinnon (1963). For a more recent review, see Alesina and Barro (2002).

[15] For example, Issing (2008) concluded that "the euro area that was to be created on 1 January 1999 fell quite a long way short of meeting the conditions for an optimum currency area" (p. 49).

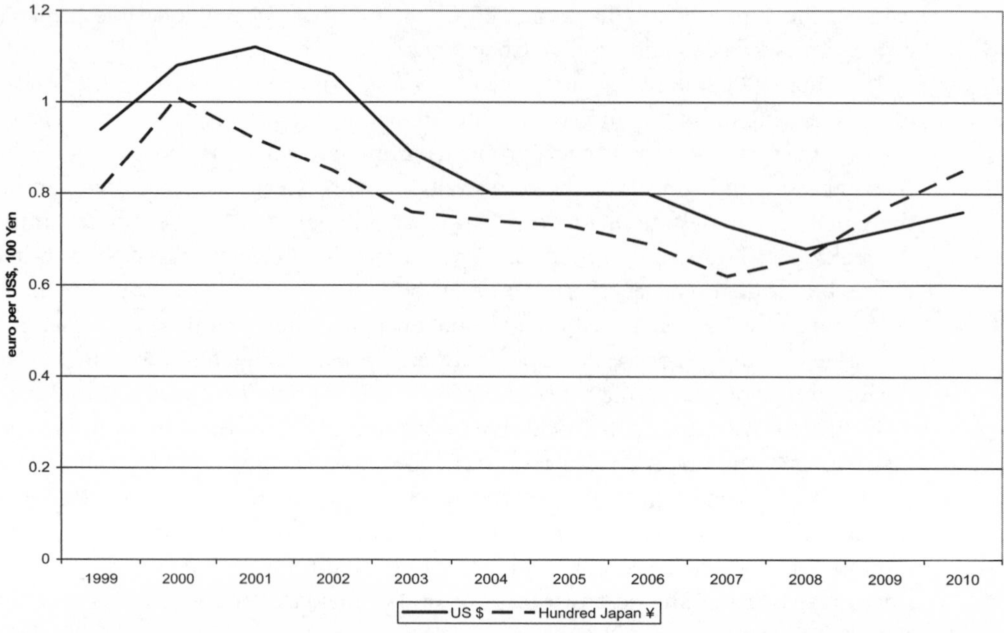

Figure 19.3. The Euro/US$ and Euro/100¥ Exchange Rates, 1999–2010. *Source:* www.oanda.com. *Note:* 2010 is through September.

The absence of an optimum currency area in the EMU leaves some room for worry over how economic adjustment will occur within it. In the face of a recession in one country, unemployment will rise. This rise in unemployment can be addressed in four ways:

1. An overall decline in wage rates leading to increases in quantity demanded for labor
2. Labor mobility out of areas of unemployment
3. Expansionary monetary policy (at the EU level)
4. Expansionary fiscal policies (at the member country level)

The first of these potential remedies, declining wages, can in principle address unemployment problems. We can appreciate this better by looking at the following equation for the foreign (U.S. dollar) real wage in EMU country i:

$$\text{Foreign currency wage for member } i = \frac{1}{e} x \frac{w_i}{P} \tag{19.1}$$

We can use Equation 19.1 to consider how EMU member country i can improve competitiveness in a downturn. Pre-EMU, it would have been able to increase its exchange rate e (devalue its currency), which would have decreased the foreign currency wage. With the EMU in place, however, that is not an option for an individual country. That leaves only an increase in the EMU-wide price level P or a decrease in the nominal wage w_i. But the ECB must ensure that the EMU-wide price level only increases by two percentage points a year. Any further decrease in the foreign currency wage therefore needs to come about by a decrease in the nominal wage. However, if there is one thing we know about EMU labor markets, it is that nominal wages tend to be downward inflexible.[16] So the first remedy is not likely to be of help.

The second remedy, labor mobility (migration out of the county experiencing a recession), could likewise help achieve adjustment. However, as we just mentioned, labor mobility within the EMU is not very strong overall.[17] The third potential remedy is the monetary policy of the ECB. Recall from above, however, that the ECB is required to maintain annual increases in a Harmonized Index of Consumer Prices (HICP) at or below 2 percent. It therefore has very little discretion to pursue other adjustment measures.[18]

The final potential remedy for unemployment is national fiscal policy, but this operates within two kinds of restraints. The first is the EU's Stability and Growth Pact. This Pact prescribes members to pursue balanced or surplus budgets during economic upswings and to limit deficits during downswings to 3 percent of GDP. Central government debt is also to be capped at 60 percent of GDP. Exceptions to the 3 percent rule exist for severe downturns.[19] The Stability and Growth Pact limits the extent to which the fiscal remedy for addressing unemployment can operate. But so do financial markets themselves. As EMU member countries issue government bonds to finance deficits, they are subject to differential interest rate spreads that reflect market expectations regarding the possibility of sovereign default. As we discuss later, these bond spreads played a role in the EMU crisis that began in 2009.

The ECB, naturally, defends the Stability and Growth Pact, stating some time ago that it "represents an important commitment to maintaining fiscal policies conducive to overall macroeconomic stability" (2001, p. 17). However, the truth of the matter is that the Pact has evolved into a soft constraint, with key EMU members such as Germany and France exceeding the 3 percent deficit threshold and countries let into the EMU vastly exceeding the 60 percent debt threshold.[20] A more central issue, however, is that the EMU is a monetary union but a fiscal disunion. There is no *central* fiscal authority to match the ECB. That will always place limits on how well the EMU can function.

The preceding considerations leave some observers worried about the future of the EMU as a less-than-optimal currency area. Early on, some researchers (e.g., Sheridan, 1999) predicted political problems as a result of the absence of economic adjustment mechanisms.[21] Even more pessimistic views (e.g., Feldstein, 1997) involve scenarios of war. Although the latter scenario is quite unlikely, the former proved to be prescient. Indeed, it now appears that managing policy conflicts within the EMU will be a prerequisite for its continued success.

[16] The ratio $\frac{w_i}{P}$ in Equation 19.1 represents what is known as the *real*, price-adjusted wage. *The Economist* (2009) noted that "workers have generally been reluctant to take wage cuts, at least in nominal terms, which has made real-wage adjustment slow" (p. 9).

[17] A key exception here is the case of Polish workers who have been willing to work in many other EU countries. But Poland is not yet an EMU member.

[18] ECB monetary policy is enacted using a "two-pillar strategy" of monetary targeting and inflation targeting. See Clausen and Donges (2001), European Central Bank (2001), and Issing (2008).

[19] For further fiscal issues regarding the EMU, see Ferguson and Kotlikoff (2000).

[20] *The Economist* (2009) wrote that the "stability and growth pact is now too full of holes to be a binding constraint on fiscal policy" (p. 15).

[21] Tsoukalis (1997) recognized this problem: "EMU could divide the EU; it could destabilize it politically, if new institutions do not enjoy the legitimacy which is necessary to carry their policies through; and it could create economically depressed countries and regions. These are the main risks" (p. 186).

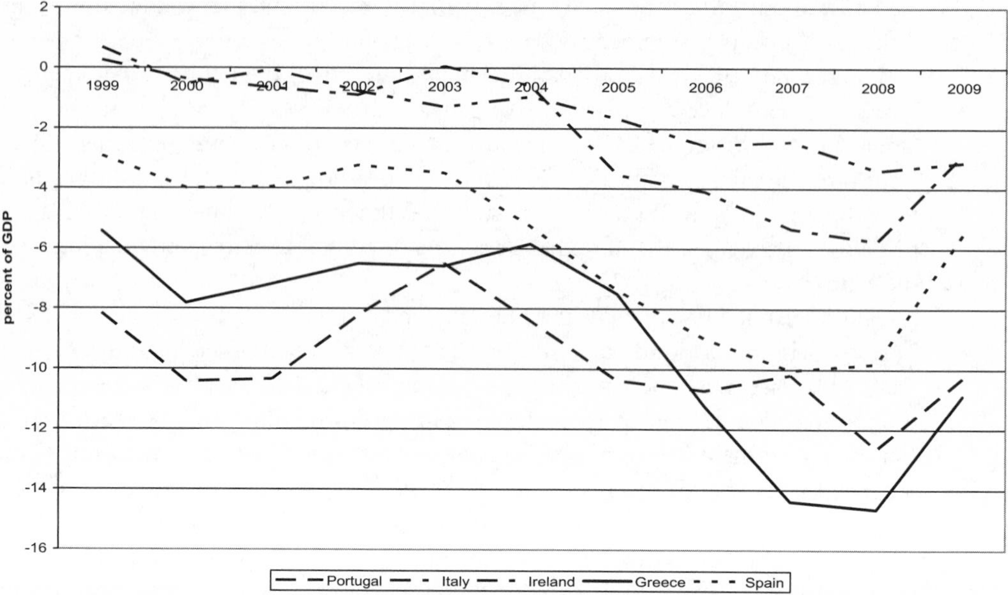

Figure 19.4. Current Account Balance in the PIIGS, 1999–2009 (percent of GDP). *Source:* World Bank, World Development Indicators Online

RECENT CRISES IN THE EMU

The year 2009 was a tough one for the world economy as a whole, but the 2007–2009 crisis discussed in Chapter 18 caused some particular difficulties in the EMU. These difficulties hit a subgroup of countries (Portugal, Italy, Ireland, Greece, and Spain) with the unfortunate acronym PIIGS. Recall from Chapter 18 that the 2007–2009 crisis had roots in a housing price bubble in the United States. As it happened, two of the PIIGS, Ireland and Spain, also experienced housing (and construction) booms that came to a rapid end in this crisis. Greece and Ireland became caught up in fiscal crises, and Portugal and Italy suffer from long-term fiscal weakness. The ramifications of these issues on external accounts can be seen in Figure 19.4, which reports their current account balances from 1999 to 2009. As you can see in this figure, all of these countries are experiencing long-term current account deficits, some (Portugal, Greece, and Spain) of large magnitudes relative to GDP.

These issues came to a head in mid-2010 when first Greece and then Ireland were caught up in market speculation of government or sovereign default of the kind we discussed in Chapter 18. Bond yield spreads widened, with Greece (at approximately 12 percent) and Ireland and Portugal (at approximately 6 percent) paying much higher rates than Germany (at approximately 2 percent) on new 10-year bond issues. To address the developing crisis that year, the EU set up the European Financial Stability Facility (EFSF) with funding of €440 billion to issue bond guarantees in order to help soothe the markets. The International Monetary Fund committed a further €250 billion to this endeavor. In the event, bond issues were successful, albeit at high interest rates. Even these efforts were not successful in addressing the case of Ireland. In late 2010, the EU and the IMF had to rescue the Irish economy with a €85 billion package, and all eyes fell on Spain as the next potential crisis.

The euro crisis is another reminder of the importance of our discussions in Chapter 18. It has also raised two other possibilities. First, there has been talk of centralized EMU bond issues, what have come to be known as "blue bonds" as opposed to sovereign "red bonds."[22] Second, there are renewed discussions of something we discussed in Chapter 17 on the IMF. That is whether adjustment in monetary systems should only be the responsibility of deficit countries (the PIIGS). There is also the possibility of adjustment coming from surplus countries (e.g., Germany and the Netherlands), as envisioned in the pre-Bretton Woods Keynes Plan discussed in Chapter 17. This model would suggest that increased spending in countries with current account surpluses could help the EMU function more coherently.

Some observers (e.g., *The Economist*, 2011) have suggested that defaults on sovereign debt within the EMU are inevitable, particularly in Greece, but also potentially in Ireland. The question is whether these two countries can work their way out of their public debt to reach sustainable levels and whether it might be wise to confront difficulties in this regard sooner rather than later through a debt write-down process. Politically, this will be very difficult to manage.

Finally, the crisis revealed cracks in the central project of the EU, namely political integration. For example, the idea of contributing to the EFSF did not sit well with the German public. Why should they "bail out" the profligate Greeks, for example? These sorts of political issues will be on the EMU and EU agenda for some time to come.

MONETARY UNIONS IN AFRICA

Outside of the EMU and what might be called mini-states, the only other examples of monetary union occur in Africa.[23] These are the Communauté Financière Africaine (CFA) franc zone in central and West Africa and the rand zone in southern Africa. Both are relatively longstanding, if not entirely stable. We consider each in turn.

The CFA franc zone is a complete and functioning monetary union among 14 member countries that have adopted the CFA franc as a common currency. It has been in existence since 1945, although a number of original members subsequently left to establish their own currencies. The CFA franc zone actually consists of two subunions, the West African Monetary Union (WAMU) and the Central African Monetary Area (CAMA), associated with the Central Bank for West African States and the Bank for Central African States, respectively. This longstanding monetary union was associated, at least until the mid-1980s, with economic performance no worse than and perhaps better than neighboring countries that utilized floating or managed floating exchange rate regimes.[24] As part of the monetary union, the Central Bank for West African States and the Bank for Central African States maintain a foreign exchange reserve pool in which they keep 65 percent of their reserves with the French Treasury, an arrangement that is clearly a legacy of the colonial past. The membership is listed in Table 19.4.

In the case of a completed monetary union, the issue of how to manage the relationship of the common currency to the rest of the world still remains. In the case of the CFA franc zone, this was resolved in 1948 by means of a fixed peg to the French

[22] Arguments for and against are presented in *The Economist* (2010).

[23] See Pomfret (2009). As we mentioned in Chapter 17, a proposed ruble zone in the former Soviet Union did not prove to be successful.

[24] See chapter 5 of Eichengreen (2008) and chapter 14 of James (1996).

Table 19.4 Members of the CFA franc zone

Member	Sub-zone	Former colonial power	Member since
Benin	West	France	1945
Burkina Faso	West	France	1945
Cameroon	Central	France	1945
Central African Republic	Central	France	1945
Chad	Central	France	1945
Côte d'Ivoire	West	France	1945
Equatorial Guinea	Central	Spain	1985
Gabon	Central	France	1945
Guinea-Bissau	West	Portugal	1997
Mali	West	France	1945, left 1962, rejoined 1984
Niger	West	France	1945
Republic of the Congo	Central	France	1945
Senegal	West	France	1945
Togo	West	France	1945

franc, the main trade partner. This management strategy proved workable up to the mid-1980s. Both controls on the capital accounts of member countries and the backing of the peg by the French Treasury helped to support the fixed rate.

Beginning in the early 1980s, the world prices of the main CFA export goods declined significantly, and the countries involved found themselves in balance of payments difficulties. With devaluation not a possibility, adjustment was attempted by contractionary macroeconomic policies aimed at reducing import demands and maintaining high interest rates. A number of CFA members began to turn to the IMF for assistance, some of them under the structural adjustment and enhanced structural adjustment facilities mentioned in Chapter 17. Following civil unrest in Cameroon and a withdrawal of support by French Prime Minister Edouard Balladur, both in 1993, a devaluation of 50 percent against the French franc was made in 1994.

With the launch of the euro in 1999, the franc peg became a euro peg at 656 CFA francs to the euro. This change made some economic sense because the EU is the CFA franc zone's main trading partner. The key question for the future of the zone is whether the CFA franc–euro peg can be maintained.[25] If the history of fixed exchange rate regimes is any guide, a further devaluation lies in the future.

One important lesson of the CFA franc zone experience is that a monetary union, despite resolving exchange rate difficulties among its members, still can involve difficulties in the relationship of the common currency with the rest of the world. The CFA opted for a fixed exchange rate regime, and this eventually led to exactly the sort of crises we discussed in Chapter 18. The history of the EMU also involved a number of crises. But as we discussed previously, in the end it opted for a flexible regime between its common currency and the rest of the world. Time will tell whether the CFA's fixed arrangement works in the long run.[26]

[25] For a fuller discussion of this issue, see *The Economist* (2002a).

[26] Of course, the CFA franc does have some flexibility as the euro changes in value against other major currencies, but this is somewhat more remote from the CFA member countries' perspective.

The rand zone, or Common Monetary Area (CMA), is a smaller endeavor than the CFA franc zone and includes South Africa, Lesotho, Namibia, and Swaziland.[27] The South African rand is legal tender in Lesotho and Namibia but not in Swaziland, and the South African central bank operates as lender of last resort for the other three countries of the zone.[28] The origins of the rand zone go back to the 1970s and, at one time, the zone also included Botswana as a member. Unlike the CFA franc, the rand floats against other major currencies. During the recent inflation crisis in Zimbabwe (see Chapter 18), there was talk of Zimbabwe joining the rand zone, but this has not (yet) occurred.

CONCLUSION

In a previous era of capital controls, it was possible to pursue an independent monetary policy within a fixed exchange rate system. Capital controls, however, have slowly and steadily been eroded, with only appropriate taxes on short-term flows possibly remaining in some cases. In such a world, countries can choose between floating with an independent monetary policy (inflation targeting) and fixing their currency's value without an independent monetary policy. At the end of his history of global monetary arrangements, Eichengreen (2008) concluded that "a floating exchange rate is not the best of all worlds. But it is at least a feasible one" (p. 232). But some groups of countries have pursued the rarer path of monetary union discussed in this chapter.

Monetary unions such as those discussed in this chapter are attempts to escape the limitations of both fixed and flexible exchange rate regimes. The EMU example has been a notable success, but the two African examples are even more longstanding. Having pursued monetary union, however, member countries face other limitations. As currency areas are generally less than optimal, adjustment is always a concern. So is the relationship between the currency of monetary union and other major currencies. Should the common currency float (as in the case of the EMU and rand zone) or be fixed (as in the case of the CFA franc)? These are issues that need to be addressed in any attempt at monetary union.

REVIEW EXERCISES

1. Imagine that, suddenly, the U.S. dollar was abolished and each state of the United States introduced its own currency (the Arizona, the Montana, the Wyoming, etc.). Would this alter economic life in the United States? How so? What problems would it entail?
2. Three European Union countries (the United Kingdom, Sweden, and Denmark) chose not to be part of the EMU. Can you think of any reasons why they would do so?
3. Have you or your classmates had any experiences with the euro or the CFA franc? What are they?
4. Do you have any ideas for how the adjustment problems and current crisis in the EMU could be better addressed?

[27] Adding Botswana to the rand zone gives the membership of the South African Customs Union (SACU).

[28] Grandes (2003) pointed out that the rand zone is actually a hybrid monetary union and currency board. See Chapter 16 on currency boards.

5. One region in which there are many discussions of monetary union is Latin America. Would the countries of Latin American qualify as an optimum currency area?

FURTHER READING AND WEB RESOURCES

An important and accessible source on the European Union is Dinan (2010). See in particular chapter 13 on the EMU. For a history of the EU, see Dinan (2004). For a discussion of the events leading up to the formation of the EMU, see *The Economist* (1998a), chapter 5 of Eichengreen (2008), and chapters 7 and 8 of Tsoukalis (1997). An advanced treatment can be found in chapter 18 of Hallwood and MacDonald (2000). An insider's account of the EMU, with numerous details on the conduct of monetary policy, is Issing (2008).

A useful website on the euro can be found within the European Union's website at www.europa.eu.int. The European Central Bank's website is www.ecb.int. The Brussels-based think tank Bruegal maintains a web site at www.bruegel.org. Giancarlo Corsetti maintains a euro homepage at www.eui.eu/RSCAS/Research/Eurohomepage.

REFERENCES

Alesina, A. and R.J. Barro (2002) "Currency Unions," *Quarterly Journal of Economics*, 117:2, 409–436.

Clausen, J.R. and J.B. Donges (2001) "European Monetary Policy: The Ongoing Debate on Conceptual Issues," *The World Economy*, 24:10, 1309–1326.

Daily Telegraph (2002) "Pierre Werner," June 27.

Dinan, D. (2004) *Europe Recast: A History of the European Union*, Lynne Rienner.

Dinan, D. (2010) *Ever Closer Union: An Introduction to European Integration*, Lynne Rienner.

The Economist (1998a) "A Survey of EMU," April 11.

The Economist (1998b) "Euro Brief: Eleven into One May Go," October 17, 81–82.

The Economist (1999) "Sailing in Choppy Waters," June 26, 83–84.

The Economist (2002a) "The CFA Franc and the Euro," February 9, 63–64.

The Economist (2002b) "Pierre Werner," July 6, 85.

The Economist (2009) "Holding Together: Special Report on the Euro Area," June 13.

The Economist (2010) "Fixing Europe's Single Currency," September 25.

The Economist (2011) "The Euro Areas Debt Crisis: Bite the Bullet," January 15.

Ewing, J. and S. Castle (2011) "Politics Will Determine the New ECB Head," *New York Times*, February 13.

Eichengreen, B. (2008) *Globalizing Capital: A History of the International Monetary System*, Princeton University Press.

European Central Bank (2001) *The Monetary Policy of the ECB*, Frankfurt.

Feldstein, M. (1997) "The EMU and International Conflict," *Foreign Affairs*, November/December, 60–73.

Ferguson, N. and L.S. Kotlikoff (2000) "The Degeneration of the EMU," *Foreign Affairs*, March/April, 110–121.

Grandes, M. (2003) "Macroeconomic Convergence in Southern Africa: The Rand Zone Experience," Working Paper 231, OECD Development Centre.

Gros, D. and N. Thygesen (1992) *European Monetary Integration*, Longman, London.

Hallwood, C.P. and R. MacDonald (2000) *International Money and Finance*, Blackwell, Oxford.

Issing, O. (2008) *The Birth of the Euro*, Cambridge University Press.

James, H. (1996) *International Monetary Cooperation since Bretton Woods*, Oxford University Press, Oxford.

McKinnon, R.I. (1963) "Optimum Currency Areas," *American Economic Review*, 53:4, 717–725.

Münchau, W. (2011) "Time to Get Real on Europe's Inflation Target," *Financial Times*, January 30.

Mundell, R.A. (1961) "A Theory of Optimum Currency Areas," *American Economic Review*, 51:4, 657–665.

Pomfret, R. (2009) "Common Currency," in K.A. Reinert, R.S. Rajan, A.J. Glass, and L.S. Davis (eds.), *The Princeton Encyclopedia of the World Economy*, Princeton University Press, 188–191.

Salvatore, D. (2009) "Euro," in K.A. Reinert, R.S. Rajan, A.J. Glass, and L.S. Davis (eds.), *The Princeton Encyclopedia of the World Economy*, Princeton University Press, 350–352.

Sheridan, J. (1999) "The Consequences of the Euro," *Challenge*, 42:1, 43–54.

Sullivan, R. (2000) "Duisenberg Tries to Rescue Reputation," *Financial Times*, October 20.

Tsoukalis, L. (1997) *The New European Economy Revisited*, Oxford University Press.

Walter, A. and G. Sen (2009) *Analyzing the Global Political Economy*, Princeton University Press.

IV INTERNATIONAL DEVELOPMENT

20 Development Concepts

I once spoke with a Ghanaian student who had just taken his first course in international economics. He held a well-known book on globalization in his hand (I won't say which one) and was waving it at me. "Professor," he asked with some agitation, "what does all this *really* mean for my country? We are going nowhere!" His question was a profound one, and it is shared by many, many individuals who have similar feelings about their countries' relationships to the world economy. It is a question that we begin to answer in this part of the book on the fourth window on the world economy, international development. Stated another way, the question is: what can globalization, be it via international trade, international production, or international finance, do for the well-being of individuals around the world, particularly in those places where measures of standards of living are low, where a significant number of people are deprived in some significant respects?

We address this question in the five chapters making up this part of the book, beginning with this chapter on *development concepts*. It may seem funny that we are dedicating an entire chapter to concepts. We did not have a chapter on *trade concepts*! But it is appropriate because the notion of development is close to our notion of what is good and desirable for people, and it therefore takes some preliminary sorting out.[1] So we begin by considering what we mean by development, taking up development as growth, development as human development, and development as structural change. Appendices to this chapter take up the relationship of gross domestic product and gross national income, as well as the Lorenz curve and Gini coefficient ratio, two measures of the degree of income inequality in an economy.

> Analytical elements for this chapter:
>
> *Countries*, *sectors*, and *factors*.

WHAT IS DEVELOPMENT?

Conceptions of development can differ dramatically among citizens, as well as among development researchers and practitioners. From an economic standpoint, the primary goal of international economic development is *the improvement of human well-being*. The dilemma we face, however, is that it is difficult to isolate a universal conception of human well-being, and without such a universal conception, there can be no single concept and measure of international development.[2] Conceptions of development can also change over time. Indeed, there is a tendency to fall into what Santiso (2006) called the "endless waltz of paradigms."[3] For these reason, conceptions of development tend to become multitudinous, as was noted by Arndt (1987) in a parody:

> Higher living standards. A rising per capita income. Increase in productive capacity. Mastery over nature. Freedom through control of man's environment. Economic

[1] This is why there is an emerging field of development ethics, described, for example, in Crocker (2008).

[2] As Szirmai (2005) emphasized, "development is unavoidably a normative concept involving very basic choices and values" (p. 9).

[3] As noted by Szirmai (2005), there is a *time element* inherent in this process: "A common characteristic of... recipes for development is their short-term perspective. Time and again, proposals have been put forward in order to achieve certain goals.... In the meantime, developments that take place irrespective of the fashion of the day are ignored or disregarded.... But when the immediate results are slow in materializing, disenchantment sets in. The issue disappears from the public eye, and new and more appealing solutions and catch-phrases emerge" (pp. 2–3). See also Adelman (2001).

> growth. But not mere growth, growth with equity. Elimination of poverty. Basic needs satisfaction. Catching up with developed countries in technology, wealth, power, status. Economic independence, self-reliance. Scope for self-fulfillment for all. Liberation, the means to human ascent. Development, in the vast literature on the subject appears to have come to encompass almost all facets of the good society, everyman's road to utopia. (p. 1)

We are going to try to give some more structure to the development concept than is contained in this quotation. To do so, we are going to consider three broad views of development: (1) development as growth, (2) development as human development, and (3) development as structural change. Development as growth views development as the sustained increase in either output per capita or income per capita. It is related to the conception of poverty as a deprivation of income. Development as human development views development as an increase in what individuals can achieve in the broadest sense of that word. It is related to another conception of poverty as deprivations of achievements of various kinds, namely education and health. Finally, development as structural change views development as involving significant alterations in patterns of production, consumption, and even social relations. Development as growth is the most common view of development, but development as human development and structural change have important roles to play as well. We begin with development as growth.

GROWTH

An early and persistent conception of international development is in terms of the sustained increase in either per capita production or per capita income, or in other words, growth. This concept begins with the circular flow diagram of Chapter 13 (Figure 13.2). In this diagram, **gross domestic product** (GDP) is the same as **gross national income** (GNI). In most countries, there is a difference between GDP and GNI, described in an appendix to this chapter. For the most part, we ignore this difference and work with GDP as our crucial variable. In the circular flow diagram, GDP or Y is divided by the total population to calculate GDP per capita or y. GDP per capita is an important measure of the *level* of economic development, and the growth rate of GDP per capita is an important measure of the *pace* of economic development over time.

Why is growth considered to be such a central indicator of development? Rodrik (2007) echoed much of the field when he stated that "Economic growth is the most powerful instrument for reducing poverty.... (N)othing has worked better than economic growth in enabling societies to improve the life chances of their members, including those at the very bottom" (p. 2). However, as Easterly (2001) commented, "We experts don't care about rising gross domestic product for its own sake. We care because it betters the lot of the poor and reduces the proportion of people who are poor. We care because richer people can eat more and buy more medicines for their babies" (p. 3). So it is not increases in GDP per capita per se that matter for development, but what can be done with them. This is an important point that we return to when we discuss human development.

Table 20.1 gives information on GDP per capita for 12 countries of the world for the year 2008. As we can see in Table 20.1, the range of GDP per capita among

Table 20.1. Development indicators for selected countries (2008 except where indicated)

	GDP per capita (U.S. dollars)	PPP GDP per capita (U.S. dollars)	Growth rate of GDP per capita (%)	Gini coefficient index (various years)	Life expectancy (years)	Adult literacy (%)	Human development index (0 to 1, 2007 throughout)
Ethiopia	321	869	7.9	30 (2005)	55	36 (2004)	0.414
Haiti	649	1,119	−0.8	60 (2001)	61	...	0.532
India	1,065	3,032	3.7	37 (2005)	64	63 (2006)	0.612
Indonesia	2,246	4,001	4.8	39 (2005)	71	92 (2006)	0.734
China	3,422	6,195	9.0	42 (2005)	73	91 (2000)	0.772
Costa Rica	6,565	11,250	1.2	49 (2007)	79	95 (2000)	0.854
Brazil	8,536	10,367	4.1	55 (2007)	72	90 (2007)	0.813
Turkey	9,881	14,068	−0.6	41 (2006)	72	89 (2007)	0.806
South Korea	19,162	26,875	2.0	...	80	...	0.937
Spain	35,000	32,995	−0.6	35 (2000)	81	98 (2007)	0.955
Japan	38,268	33,799	−1.1	...	83	...	0.960
United States	47,210	47,210	−0.5	41 (2000)	78	...	0.956

Note: The Gini coefficient ranges from 0 to 1. The Gini coefficient index ranges from 0 to 100.
Source: World Bank and United Nations Development Program

countries is significant. The average per capita income in Japan and the United States is approximately 150 times that in Ethiopia. From the perspective of development as the level of per capita GDP, we therefore would conclude that Japan and the United States are more than 150 times "more developed" than Ethiopia.

The growth perspective, based as it is on GDP per capita, has a few limitations that are important to recognize. These include:

1. Per capita GDP does not account for *factor income flows* among the countries of the world. This is the distinction between GDP and GNI that we take up in an appendix to this chapter.
2. Per capita GDP only includes market activities, and many activities in developing countries take place *outside the market.* For example, GNP does not include farmers' production of agricultural products for consumption within his or her family, but only the amount sold on the market.[4]
3. Per capita GDP does not account for certain *costs associated with development,* such as the use of nonrenewable resources, the loss of biodiversity, and pollution. Scholars and practitioners working in the field of *sustainable development* address this limitation.[5]
4. Per capita GDP is an average measure that *hides the distribution of income* among the households of a country. If income distribution becomes more unequal as per capita GDP increases, the level of well-being of the poorest groups in the country could fall. We discuss this issue later.
5. Per capita GDP is not always an accurate predictor of *human development.* It is not always well correlated with indicators of human development, such as levels

[4] Some development economists would point out that this exclusion is most relevant to the economic activities of women who tend to work more intensively in the home than do men. This is one aspect of what is knows as *gender and development.*

[5] See, for example, Hopwood, Mellor, and O'Brien (2005) and Pearce, Barbier, and Markandya (2000).

of education and health. As emphasized by Sen (1989) many years ago, "countries with high GDP per capita can nevertheless have astonishing low achievements in the quality of life" (p. 42). We discuss this issue later.

6. The nominal or currency exchange rates used to convert GDP into U.S. dollars for comparison among countries are misleading. A large part of economies consists of *nontraded goods.* Furthermore, a large part of nontraded goods consists of *services.* Services tend to be less expensive in developing countries, so a U.S. dollar buys more in developing countries than in developed countries.[6]

The solution to the last of the preceding problems lies in what is now called the *purchasing power parity* (PPP) methodology. This methodology is closely related to the purchasing power parity model of exchange rates that we developed in Chapter 14. The PPP methodology uses U.S. dollar prices to value all goods in all countries. This has the effect of increasing the GDP of developing countries. Table 20.1 presents PPP GDP per capita for the 12 countries we are using as examples. Note the following in this table. First, the PPP measures are larger than the standard measures for the first nine countries presented in the table. This reflects the cheaper nature of services and other nontraded goods in these countries relative to the United States. This helps us to understand how it is possible for individuals to survive in these countries with such low levels of GDP per capita. Some of these survival challenges are presented in the accompanying box.

Second, the PPP GDP per capita for the United States is identical to its GDP per capita because the same prices are used in both calculations. Third, the PPP GDP per capita is *lower* for Spain and Japan than their GDP per capita. This reflects the fact that their services and other nontraded goods are more expensive than in the United States. Incomes do not go as far in Spain and Japan as in the other countries listed in the table.

Surviving in Mexico City

Patrick Oster, a journalist residing in Mexico City, hired a woman by the name of Adelaida Bollo Andrade as a maid. He documented the quality of her life in his book *The Mexicans.* While working for the Oster family, Adelaida woke each morning at 5:00 a.m. This would allow her to catch the 6:00 a.m. bus to start her three-hour commute to work. Typically, the total daily commute of six hours would cost Adelaida one half of her daily wage. Her workday of eight hours was followed by her return commute. Because she and her family could not afford even a small refrigerator, there was an additional one-hour commute each day to the market. Adelaida was left with nine hours for cooking, cleaning, taking care of her family, and sleeping.

Adelaida's family lived in a cinder-block home of dimensions 15 × 24 feet with a corrugated metal roof and one window. There was one bed for the four children, which left the concrete floor for Adelaida and her husband to sleep on. Light came from a single, bare bulb hanging from the ceiling. Cooking was done on a three-burner gas stove.

[6] We mentioned nontraded goods in Chapter 14 in our assessment of the purchasing power parity model of exchange rate determination. We discuss this concept again in Chapter 24 on structural change and adjustment. One of the original attempts to examine the less expensive nature of services in developing economies was Bhagwati (1984).

Aside from an old kitchen table, the only other family possession was an old, black-and-white television donated to the family by their doctor. The family latrine consisted of a hole in the back yard.

The family's water supply was contaminated, and their food consisted of tortillas, beans, and coffee. These conditions contributed to frequent illnesses among Adelaida's children, including diarrhea, vomiting, and fevers. These illnesses would require Adelaida to go into debt to pay for doctor services.

Adelaida's difficult life is not in any way unusual for the residents of many large cities in developing countries. Lack of education, poor health, and difficult working conditions are the norm for the urban poor. The important challenge for governments, development organizations, and the private sector is to strategically improve these human lives in a broad-based way. It has proved, in many instances, to be a difficult challenge.

Source: Oster (1989)

Related to, but not always emphasized in, the per capita income measure is the question of the *distribution* of total income among the households of the economy. This is typically measured using the **Lorenz curve** and the **Gini coefficient**. Calculation of these measures is discussed in the second appendix to this chapter. The Gini coefficient ranges from the extreme of zero (perfect equality) to unity (perfect inequality). In practice, the coefficient ranges from approximately 0.25 (relatively low inequality) to 0.60 (relatively high inequality). The Gini coefficient *index* multiplies the Gini coefficient by 100 and therefore ranges from 0 to 100. Gini coefficient indices for the countries in our sample are presented in Table 20.1. The important point evident here is that income distribution is, to some extent, independent of the *level* of per capita income. A middle-income country such as Brazil can have a more unequal income distribution than a low-income country such as India. There is some evidence that equality of income can lead to a higher *growth rate* of total output. We return to this possibility in Chapter 21.

Deprivations in per capita GDP (and therefore of per capita GNI) are a central measure of **poverty**, namely poverty as income deprivation. The World Bank keeps estimates of both the *poor* and the *extremely poor.* The former are defined as those living below a US$2.00 per day poverty line (measured using PPP methods). The latter are defined as those living below a US$1.25 per day poverty line (again measured using PPP methods). The data that are available in this series appear in three-year increments and are presented in Figure 20.1.[7] We can see here that there is both good and bad news. The good news is that the number of *extremely poor* individuals is declining over time to a level below 1.5 billion. There is broad agreement in the field that most of this decline has been due to development processes in China. The bad news is that the number of *poor* is more or less constant and at a current value of 2.5 billion. The poverty challenge is therefore immense.

It is becoming clear that the relationship between distribution and poverty is more important then ever. With the movement of some large countries from low-income to middle-income status (e.g., India and Indonesia), the majority of the world's extremely poor reside in middle- rather than low-income countries.[8] Therefore, along with

[7] The longest tracking of world poverty is provided by Bourguinon and Morrisson (2002). These estimates cover the 1820–1992 period.

[8] See Sumner (2010), who places the figure at three-fourths of the world's extremely poor living in middle-income countries.

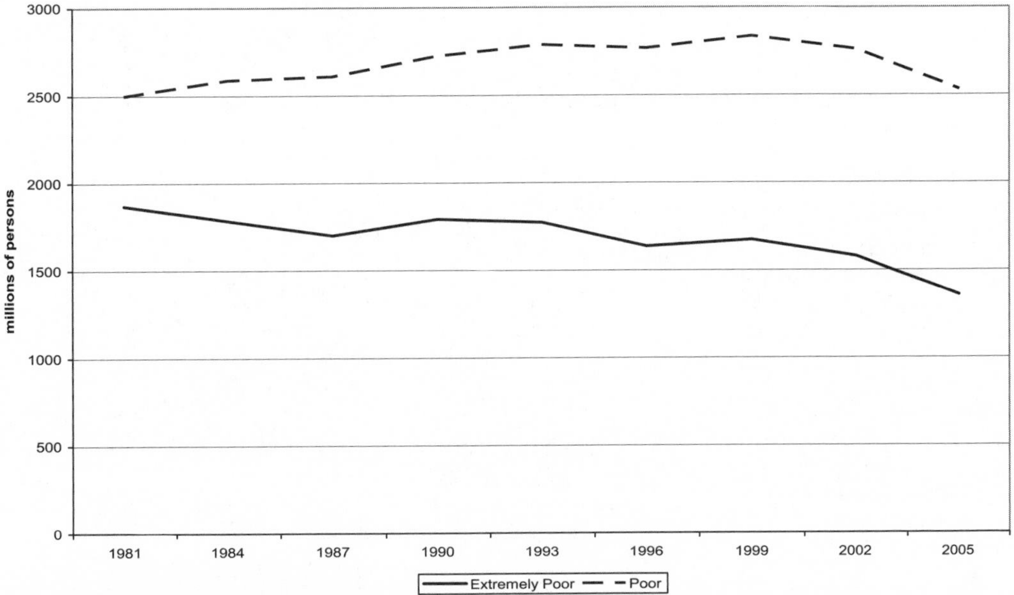

Figure 20.1. Recent Evolution of World Poverty (millions of persons). *Source:* World Bank, World Development Indicators Online

growth, it is often the distribution of income within middle-income countries that is important for alleviating poverty.

Analyzing the relationship between growth and poverty takes note of the fact that poverty reduction depends on initial inequality levels and changes in inequality, as well as growth itself. It also gives rise to what has come to be known as *pro-poor growth.*[9] This line of thinking considers what is known as the *growth elasticity of poverty*, namely the ratio of the percentage change in a poverty rate to the percentage change in a growth measure, such as GDP per capita. This elasticity can vary by country, time period, and region within a country and be influenced by a multitude of factors. But it is a first step in recognizing that the link between growth and poverty alleviation is not uniformly one-for-one, and it opens up a discussion on how to best increase the growth elasticity of poverty.

HUMAN DEVELOPMENT

We noted above that income per capita is not always valued for its own sake but for what it can achieve. This distinction between means (income) and ends (achievements) is one made most strongly in a conception of international development in terms of **human development**. One major source of the human development perspective was in the work of Nobel Laureate Amartya Sen, who once stated that "To broaden the limited lives into which the majority of human beings are willy-nilly imprisoned by force of circumstances is the major challenge of human development in the contemporary world" (1989, p. 55).[10] Sen's work inspired the United Nations Development Program

[9] See, for example, Cord (2007) and Kakwani and Pernia (2000).

[10] More formally, the human development perspective grew out of Sen's (1989) concepts of *capabilities* and their role in international development. Another major contributor to the capabilities concept was Nussbaum (2000).

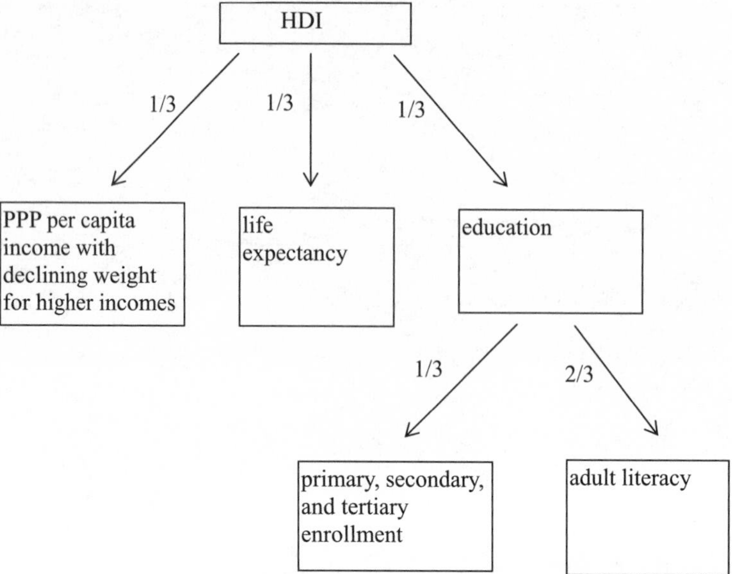

Figure 20.2. The Human Development Index

(UNDP) to take up the human development perspective in the form of an annual *Human Development Report* (HDR) that has been published since 1990. The first such report began with the following statement:

> People are the real wealth of a nation. The basic objective of development is to create an enabling environment for people to enjoy long, healthy and creative lives. (p. 9)

The human development perspective sees the growth of GDP or GNI per capita as an important but limited measure of the rate of economic development. For example, the 1995 HDR stated the following:

> The human development concept consistently asserts that growth is not the end of development – but the absence of growth often is. Economic growth is essential for human development. But to fully exploit the opportunities for improved well being that growth offers, it must be properly managed, for there is no automatic link between economic growth and human progress. (pp. 122–123)

The most fundamental contribution of the HDR was the introduction of the **human development index** (HDI). A brief description of its originator, Pakistani economist Mahbub ul Haq, is presented in the accompanying box. The HDI measures development as reflecting three important components: per capita income, health, and education. The construction of the HDI can be represented as in Figure 20.2. The HDI consists of equal, one-third components of per capita income, life expectancy, and education. The per capita income component is calculated in such a way that higher levels receive declining weights. Therefore, increases in per capita incomes are more important from low levels than from high levels.[11] Life expectancy is taken as an overall measure of

See also Alkire (2002). The term usually used in the human development perspective is *capabilities*, but we use the term *achievements* here.

[11] The way in which PPP per capita incomes were discounted at higher levels in the *Human Development Reports* changed in 1999, so that higher income levels were not discounted as severely as before. See UNDP (1999), "Technical Note," pp. 159–163.

health. Education is measured with one-third weight being given to primary, secondary, and tertiary enrollment and two-thirds weight being given to adult literacy. Thus there is more of an emphasis placed on educational *outcomes* than enrollment. HDI measures for our sample of countries, along with information on life expectancy and adult literacy, are presented in Table 20.1.

Mahbub ul Haq and the HDI

The Human Development Report and its human development index (HDI) were originally developed by the Pakistani development economist Mahbub ul Haq. ul Haq was educated at Cambridge, Yale, and Harvard Universities and worked at the World Bank. From 1982 to 1988, he was finance minister of Pakistan. He then moved to the United Nations Development Program and began to work on the human development paradigm. At his invitation, this work was done in collaboration with the Indian development economist Amartya Sen.

Sen recalled that "I did not, I must admit, initially see much merit in the HDI itself, which, as it happens, I was privileged to help him devise. I had expressed to Mahbub considerable skepticism about trying to focus on a crude index of this kind, attempting to catch in one simple number a complex reality about human development and deprivation.... In fact, the crudeness had not escaped Mahbub at all. He did not resist the argument that the HDI could not but be a very limited indicator of development. But after some initial hesitation, Mahbub persuaded himself that the dominance of GNP could not be broken by any set of tables.... 'We need a measure,' Mahbub explained to me, 'of the same level of vulgarity as the GNP – just one number – but a measure that is not as blind to social aspects of human lives as the GNP is.' Mahbub hoped that not only would the HDI be something of an improvement on, or at least a helpful supplement to, the GNP, but also that it would serve to broaden public interest in the other variables that are plentifully analyzed in the Human Development Reports.... Mahbub got this exactly right, I have to admit, and I am very glad that we did not manage to deflect him from seeking a crude measure. By skilful use of the attracting power of the HDI, Mahbub got readers to take an involved interest in the large class of systematic tables and detailed critical analyses presented in the Human Development Reports."

ul Haq was a long-time opponent of military spending in South Asia, seeing it as being at odds with human development in the region. However, when he died in 1998, he had just witnessed the revival of nuclear testing in India and Pakistan. And he missed the awarding of the Nobel Prize in Economics to his old friend, Amartya Sen, later that year.

Sources: The Economist (1998) and Sen (1999a)

There are two major points concerning human development to note in Table 20.1. First, achievements in health (life expectancy) and education (literacy) vary substantially. Just within this sample of countries, life expectancy varies by a range of nearly 30 years![12] Similarly, literacy rates vary between approximately 35 percent and nearly

[12] Two further points can be made here. First, low life expectancies have traditionally been associated with high rates of infant and child mortality (currently just under 10 million children per year). The exception to this rule is the HIV/AIDS crisis. Second, the HIV/AIDS crisis in some countries has caused life expectancies to begin declining rather than increasing.

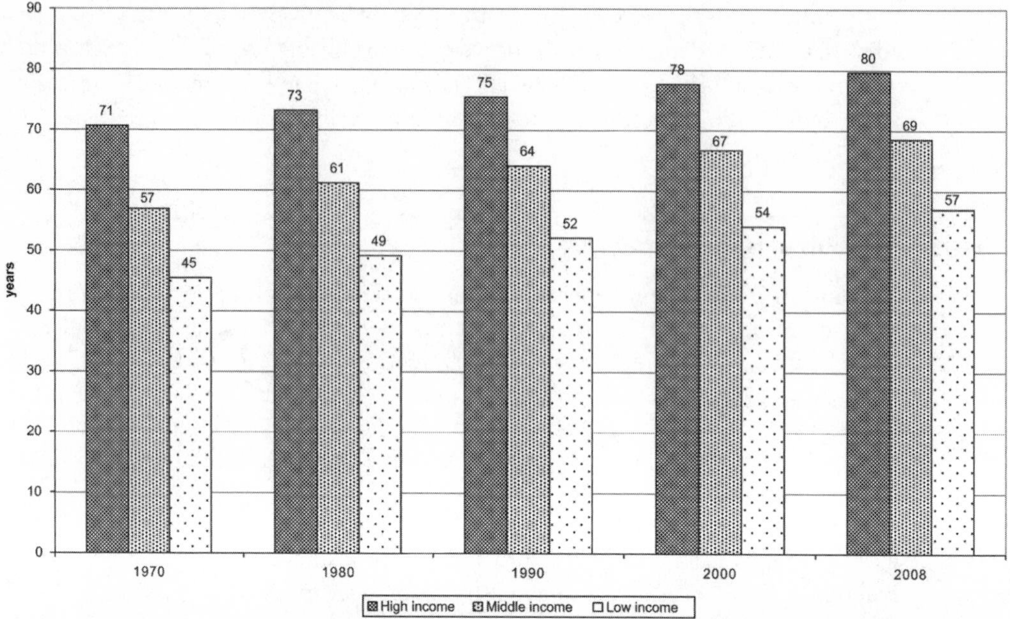

Figure 20.3. Life Expectancy in Low-, Middle-, and High-Income Countries (years). *Source:* World Bank, World Development Indicators Online

universal (just under 100 percent). These dramatically different levels of human development result in a wide range of HDIs reported in the last column of Table 20.1.

Second, although there is a positive correlation between GDP per capita and both life expectancy and adult literacy (and therefore the HDI), some important variation from the norm is possible. For example, Costa Rica has an average life expectancy and an adult literacy rate equivalent to that of the United States, despite its GDP per capita being only approximately 15 percent of the U.S. value (approximately 25 percent in PPP terms). Consequently, Costa Rica's HDI is above that of many other countries in its income group. These sorts of variations are better captured by the human development concept than the growth concept and point to the important role of health and educational *policy* in human development outcomes.

If there is a single-most important indicator of human development, it is perhaps life expectancy. Table 20.1 reports life expectancy for a single year, but it is instructive to consider how life expectancy has changed in recent decades. This is presented in Figure 20.3 for 1970–2008. The data are reported for low-, middle-, and high-income countries. We can see that the increases in life expectancy for these three groups of countries have been 12 years for low- and middle-income countries and 9 years for high-income countries. So, despite the disparities of Table 20.1, there is a general improvement of life expectancy over time in most instances. That is welcome news.

The HDI has been criticized in many instances for at least three reasons.[13] Some observers claim that its weighting scheme among per capita income, health, and education is arbitrary. This is certainly the case, but to be fair, the same could be said of the growth perspective, which assigns a weight of unity to per capita income alone.

[13] See, for example, Srinivasan (1994). A consideration and critique of *both* the growth *and* capabilities (achievements) perspectives can be found in Reinert (2011).

Table 20.2. Additional human development indices and their components

Index	Health	Education	Standard of living	Social exclusion
HDI	Life expectancy	Adult literacy rate and enrollment ratio	PPP income per capita	
GDI	Female and male life expectancy	Female and male adult literacy rate and female and male enrollment ratio	Female and male PPP income per capita	
HPI-1 (through 2009)	Probability of not surviving to age 40	Adult illiteracy rate	Deprivation as measured by lack of access to safe water, lack of access to health services, and underweight children	
HPI-2 (through 2009)	Probability of not surviving to age 60	Adult functional illiteracy rate	Percentage of population below poverty line, defined as 50 percent of median income	Long-term unemployment rate
MPI (beginning 2010)	Malnutrition and child mortality	Lack of years of schooling and enrollment	Deprivations in electricity, drinking water, sanitation, flooring, cooking fuel, and assets	

Source: United Nations Development Program and Alkire and Santos (2010)

The HDI has also been criticized for being "too political" in its assigning declining weights to higher per capita incomes. Finally, the HDI has been criticized for relying on measures for which data are unreliable.

In defense of the HDI, Streeten (1995) pointed out the following:

1. When there is an upward movement in the HDI, it almost always reflects an improvement in human well-being, something that is not always true of per capita income measures.
2. Closing gaps in HDIs among the countries of the world "is both more important and more feasible than reducing international income gaps" (p. 24).
3. The HDI registers (negatively) the potential impact of *over*-development in capturing the "diseases of affluence," such as circulatory disease and diabetes, that reduce the HDI through its health component.
4. The HDI, according to Streeten, is *appropriately* political in that "it focuses attention on important social sectors, policies, and achievements, which are not caught by the income measure" (p. 25).

Whatever our interpretation of the disagreements surrounding the HDI, we can at least state the following. Having the last three columns of Table 20.1 in front of us provides us with a little more information than the per capita GDP or GNI measures alone do. Because these columns of information are readily available and impact people's lives so directly, it is very useful to glance at them, along with the GDP measures, when assessing development levels among sets of countries. Additionally, as we discuss in Chapter 21, there are important feedbacks among the three components of the HDI that can be crucial mechanisms in development successes and failures.

In more recent years, the UNDP has introduced additional indices to supplement the HDI. These are summarized in Table 20.2. In 1996, it introduced the gender-related development index (GDI) and the gender-empowerment measure (GEM). The GDI adjusts the HDI downward to account for levels of gender inequality. For some countries, this makes a significant difference. In 1997, the UNDP introduced the human poverty indices 1 and 2 (HPI-1 and HPI-2), focusing on poverty in developing and developed countries, respectively. The former is especially relevant in capturing basic deprivations in education and health. In 2010, the HPI was replaced with the multidimensional poverty index (MPI) that attempts to capture multiple deprivations across health, education, and standards of living.[14]

The UNDP and its wide array of development measures are part of a set of Millennium Development Goals (MDGs) set by the United Nations in 2000. The deadline of the MDGs (2015) is rapidly approaching, and despite progress in a number of areas, it appears that most of the goals will not be met. The MDGs are discussed in the accompanying box.

Millennium Development Goals

In September 2000, members of the United Nations (UN) met in New York City for a Millennium Summit. At the Summit, the UN General Assembly adopted a resolution entitled the United Nations Millennium Declaration. The Declaration stated that: "the central challenge we face today is to ensure that globalization becomes a positive force for all the world's people." More specifically, UN members pledged to "spare no effort to free our fellow men, women and children from the abject and dehumanizing conditions of extreme poverty, to which more than a billion of them are currently subjected." In addition to endorsing a number of "fundamental values," UN members established a set of goals, which are now known as the Millennium Development Goals.

The first millennium development goal is to eradicate extreme poverty and hunger. It has two targets: to halve by 2015 the proportion of people whose income is less than US$1.25 a day (in PPP values) and to halve by 2015 the proportion of people who suffer from hunger. There is a good possibility that the first of these targets will be met due primarily to positive development in China, but it is likely that the second target will be missed. The second millennium goal is to achieve universal primary education for boys *and* girls by 2015. It now appears that this goal will not be met.

The third development goal, related to the second, is to promote gender equality and empower women. As measured by equity in education, this goal will probably not be reached. The fourth development goal is to reduce the under-five mortality rate with a target of two-thirds by 2015. It now seems that, despite substantial progress, this critical target will not be met.

The fifth development goal is to improve maternal health with a target of reducing the maternal mortality rate by three-fourths by 2015. The sixth development goal is to combat HIV/AIDS, malaria, and tuberculosis, and the seventh development goal is to ensure environmental sustainability. The last goal is to develop a "global partnership for development," a subject taken up in earnest at the 2002 Summit on Sustainable Development in Johannesburg, South Africa.

[14] See Alkire and Santos (2010).

As of 2005, the United Nations' own website on the Millennium Development Goals already acknowledged that "progress towards the goals has been mixed." A summit on the MDGs was held in 2010, and the accompanying report drew attention to the impacts of the 2007–2009 crisis in curbing progress on a few key goals. This was the case, for example, for halving the proportion of people who suffer from malnutrition. This is one area in which international finance and international development interact, and it points to the urgent need for crisis prevention, with a particular focus on systemic risk, discussed in Chapter 18.

Source: http://www.un.org/millenniumgoals

STRUCTURAL CHANGE

There is a third perspective on development that is an important complement to the growth and human development perspectives. This is development as **structural change**. This perspective was summarized by Davis (2009), who wrote that "Economic development is generally facilitated by a number of structural changes, including urbanization, the rise in the size of firms, the relative decline of the agricultural sector in terms of employment and output with expansion of manufacturing and services, the geographic expansion of markets, and increases in the diversity of goods produced and traded" (p. 277).

This line of thinking has its origins in the work of Nobel Laureate Simon Kuznets (1966). The basic notion of the structural change perspective in its economic application is that, as development proceeds, productive factors move out of lower productivity activities into higher productivity activities. This idea is more or less unassailable but has often applied in a particular, limited way. For example, a standard claim has been that development is a process of resources moving out of agriculture and into manufacturing. That is, development is a process of *industrialization* and *urbanization*. This limited application of the structural change perspective has led to a neglect of agriculture and rural development because these sectors are sometimes viewed as inherently unproductive, something we now know not to be true.[15] The limited application also ignored what happened to high-income countries as they developed in that it left out the important role of the service sector.

The truth is that, as development proceeds, the service sector expands. Eventually, even the manufacturing sector shrinks as this process unfolds. Szirmai (2005) captured this process well in the following statement[16]:

> It is striking how important the services sector has become in developing countries. Even in the 1950s, services were the largest sectors in terms of value added. Developing countries have not followed the classical sequence of shifts from agriculture to industry, followed by later shifts from industry to services. Rather, the service sector developed parallel to the industrial sector, as the shares of agriculture declined. (p. 110)

Why might this be so? Part of the answer lies in the fact that an increasingly productive subcomponent of the service sector is *producer services* that can supply both agricultural

[15] See, for example, Martin and Mitra (2001). Szirmai (2005) noted that "In the history of European industrialization, increases in agricultural productivity *preceded* industrialization" (p. 270, emphasis added).

[16] See also Francois and Hoekman (2010).

and manufacturing sectors with important inputs. This includes communications, transportation and logistics, and financial services at a general level, but many more specific producer services in practice. As was pointed out by Francois and Reinert (1996), producer services actually support productivity in manufacturing, including export manufacturing.[17]

Although it is important to account for the role of structural change as economies grow and develop, we need to do so outside of the simplistic "agriculture shrinks, manufacturing grows" perspective. The empirical reality is more complicated than that, with increases in agricultural productivity and an important role for services being part of the picture. Further, structural change can occur outside of the economic sphere, with particular social and political changes taking place. Although beyond the scope of this book and chapter, these potential sociopolitical changes are very important.[18]

CONCLUSION

From an economic standpoint, the primary goal of international economic development, as well as the trading of goods and services and the movement of capital in the world economy, is the improvement of human well-being. That is, at some level, the international development window explored here is more important than the international trade, production, and finance windows. However, it is hard to isolate a universally accepted conception of human well-being. Keeping in mind this limitation, this chapter investigated three complementary concepts of economic development, namely growth, human development, and structural change. The HDI indicator of human development represents a more comprehensive view of development than growth, but is not as universally acknowledged as a key indicator. Its advantage is that it expands the dimensionality of our thinking about development into the realms of health and education.

Whatever our measure of development, as we stressed in Chapter 1, levels of development differ in profound ways among the countries of the world. Our hope is that increased integration of countries via trade, production, and financial linkages would promote some convergence in levels of development, but this is not always the case.[19] We will spend the remainder of this book assessing these divergent outcomes. In doing so, you will perhaps develop you own partial answers to the question posed to me by the Ghanaian student mentioned at the beginning of this chapter.

REVIEW EXERCISES

1. In your opinion, is the GDP per capita or growth perspective a sufficient measure of economic development? Why or why not?
2. How can the PPP adjustment to income per capita change the ranking of countries' levels of economic development? Is this an important adjustment to make?
3. A controversial aspect to the human development index is its use of declining weights for per capita income. Do you agree with this adjustment? Why or why not?

[17] See also Francois and Woerz (2008).
[18] See chapters 11 and 12 of Szirmai (2005) for an effective review of these issues.
[19] On this point, see Goldin and Reinert (2007).

4. The human development index takes into account health and education as well as per capita income. Why might health and education be important considerations in the process of economic development?
5. Take some time to explore the UNDP's website at www.undp.org. Try to locate the human development indicators that are a part of the most recent *Human Development Report* (www.hdr.undp.org). Look up the indicators for a country in which you have an interest.

FURTHER READING AND WEB RESOURCES

A concise source on the material of this chapter is Davis (2009). Comprehensive texts in economic development include Cypher and Dietz (2004) and Szirmai (2005). Goldin and Reinert (2007) examine the relationship of a number of aspects of globalization to development and poverty alleviation. A popular but solid book on the poorest of the world is Collier (2007). Readers with an interest in the human development concept would benefit from a close reading of Sen (1987, 1989, and 1999b). Those readers with an interest in the HDI itself should turn to the United Nations Development Program's annual *Human Development Report*, particularly UNDP (2010), the 20th anniversary report. A more traditional annual review is the World Bank's *World Development Report*. Both of these reports are essential sources of data on developing countries.

The UNDP's website can be found at http://www.undp.org. Its *Human Development Report* series can be found at http://www.hdr.undp.org. The World Bank's *World Development Report* series can be found at http://www.worldbank.org/wdr.

APPENDIX A: GROSS DOMESTIC PRODUCT AND GROSS NATIONAL INCOME

There is an important distinction between gross domestic product (GDP) and gross national income (GNI).[20] GDP is defined as the value of goods and services produced within a country's borders. We will call this country Home and call its GDP Y^H_{GDP}. The distinction between GDP and GNI begins with the Home country's *factor payments*. This is the income from property in Home owned by foreign citizens and wages paid to foreign laborers working in Home. We will call the Home country's factor payments Y^H_{HF}. But the opposite flow is given by *factor income*. This is income from property in foreign countries owned by Home citizens and wages from Home workers in foreign countries. We will call the Home country's factor income Y^H_{FH}.

The difference between factor income and factor payments gives *net factor income* as follows:

$$\text{Home country's } \textit{net factor income} = Y^H_{FH} - Y^H_{HF} \tag{20.1}$$

We can then state the relationship between the Home country's GDP and GNI as follows:

$$\text{Home country's } \textit{gross national income} = Y^H_{GNI} = Y^H_{GDP} + \left(Y^H_{FH} - Y^H_{HF}\right) \tag{20.2}$$

[20] The term for *gross national income* used to be *gross national product* or GNP. The World Bank changed this terminology, however, and we follow that convention here.

In developing countries hosting multinational enterprises (see Chapter 22) that are repatriating a lot of profits, Y^H_{HF} is large, and consequently, $Y^H_{GDP} > Y^H_{GNI}$. But in developing countries with a large number of citizens working abroad (see Chapter 12), Y^H_{FH} is large, and consequently, $Y^H_{GNI} > Y^H_{GDP}$. The bottom line of these distinctions, however, is that GNI is a better measure of the income and purchasing power of the citizens of a country than GDP.[21] That said, researchers often rely on GDP because it fits neatly into growth models such as those we discuss in the next chapter.

If we define L^H to be the population of the Home country, per capita GDP and GNI in year i are:

$$\text{Per capita GDP in year } i = \left(\frac{Y^H_{GDP}}{L^H}\right)_i \tag{20.3}$$

$$\text{Per capita GNI in year } i = \left(\frac{Y^H_{GNI}}{L^H}\right)_i \tag{20.4}$$

To simplify a bit, let's drop the H superscripts and turn to the growth rates. The growth rate of per capita GDP between time periods 0 and 1 is given by:

$$g_{GDP} = \frac{\left(\frac{Y_{GDP}}{L}\right)_1 - \left(\frac{Y_{GDP}}{L}\right)_0}{\left(\frac{Y_{GDP}}{L}\right)_0} \times 100 \tag{20.5}$$

Finally, the growth rate of per capita GNI between time periods 0 and 1 is given by:

$$g_{GNI} = \frac{\left(\frac{Y_{GNI}}{L}\right)_1 - \left(\frac{Y_{GNI}}{L}\right)_0}{\left(\frac{Y_{GNI}}{L}\right)_0} \times 100 \tag{20.6}$$

From the growth perspective on development described in this chapter, the measurement and analysis of Equations 20.5 and 20.6 are the central problems to be confronted.

APPENDIX B: THE LORENZ CURVE AND GINI COEFFICIENT

The standard means of measuring income inequality based on the personal or household distribution of income is using the **Lorenz curve** and the associated **Gini coefficient.** The Lorenz curve is depicted in Figure 20.4. It relates *cumulative* percentage of income received (measured on the vertical axis) to the *cumulative* percentage of population (measured on the horizontal axis). The diagonal line in the figure is therefore the line of perfect equality, where each person receives the same income. Actual Lorenz curves, however, lie below the diagonal line, and the farther they are to the southeast corner of the box, the greater the level of inequality. The Gini coefficient is measured using the

[21] A further adjustment for transfers (e.g., aid and remittances) converts GNI into gross national disposable income (GNDI).

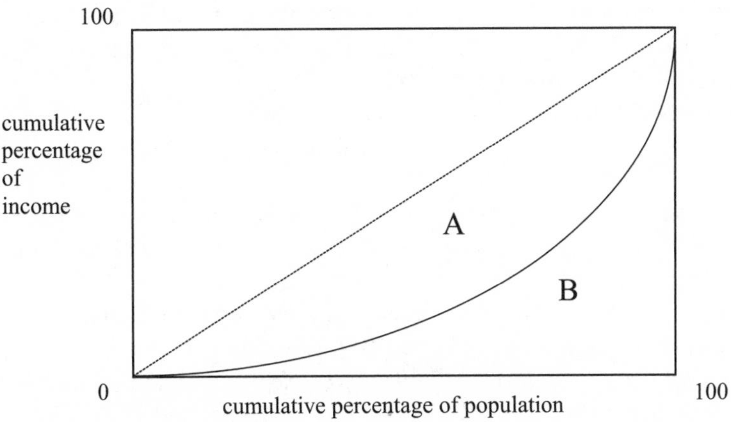

Figure 20.4. The Lorenz Curve

area between the diagonal and the actual Lorenz curve, area A, and the area under the diagonal, area A + B. It is measured as:

$$Gini\ coefficient = \frac{A}{A + B} \tag{20.7}$$

The greater is the area of A, the higher the value of Gini coefficient, and the greater the degree of inequality. In theory, Gini coefficients range from the extremes of zero (perfect equality) to unity (perfect inequality). In practice, the coefficient ranges from approximately 0.25 (relatively low inequality) to 0.60 (relatively high inequality). The Gini coefficient index (Gini coefficient multiplied by 100) is what is reported in Table 20.1.

REFERENCES

Adelman, I. (2001) "Fallacies in Development Theory and Their Implications for Policy," in G.M. Meier and J.E. Stiglitz (eds.), *Frontiers of Development Economics: The Future in Perspective*, Oxford University Press, 103–134.

Alkire, S. (2002) "Dimensions of Human Development," *World Development*, 30:2, 181–205.

Alkire, S. and M.E. Santos (2010) *Acute Multidimensional Poverty: A New Index for Developing Countries*, Human Development Research Paper 2010/11, United Nations Development Program.

Arndt, H.W. (1987) *Economic Development: The History of an Idea*, University of Chicago Press.

Bhagwati, J. (1984) "Why Are Services Cheaper in the Poor Countries?" *Economic Journal*, 94:374, 279–286.

Bourguignon, F. and C. Morrisson (2002) "Inequality among World Citizens: 1820–1992," *American Economic Review*, 92:4, 727–744.

Collier, P. (2007) *The Bottom Billion: Why the Poorest Countries Are Failing and What Can Be Done about It*, Oxford University Press.

Cord, L.J. (2007) "Overview," in T. Besley and L.J. Cord (eds.), *Delivering on the Promise of Pro-Poor Growth: Insights and Lessons from Country Experiences*, World Bank, 1–27.

Crocker, D.A. (2008) *Ethics of Global Development: Agency, Capability and Deliberative Democracy*, Cambridge University Press.

Cypher, J.M. and J.L. Dietz (2004) *The Process of Economic Development*, Routledge.

Davis, L. (2009) "Development," in K.A. Reinert, R.S. Rajan, A.J. Glass, and L.S. Davis (eds.), *The Princeton Encyclopedia of the World Economy*, Princeton University Press, 277–280.

Easterly, W. (2001) *The Elusive Quest for Growth*, MIT Press.

The Economist (1998) "Obituary: Mahbub ul Haq," July 25.

Francois, J.F. and B. Hoekman (2010) "Services Trade and Policy," *Journal of Economic Literature*, 48:3, 642–692.

Francois, J.F. and K.A. Reinert (1996) "The Role of Services in the Structure of Production and Trade: Stylized Facts from a Cross-Country Analysis," *Asia-Pacific Economic Review*, 2:1, 35–43.

Francois, J.F. and J. Woerz (2008) "Producer Services, Manufacturing Linkages, and Trade," *Journal of Industry, Competition and Trade*, 8:3–4, 199–229.

Goldin, I. and K.A. Reinert (2007) *Globalization for Development: Trade, Finance, Aid, Migration and Policy*, World Bank.

Hopwood, B., M. Mellor, and G. O'Brien (2005) "Sustainable Development: Mapping Different Approaches," *Sustainable Development*, 13:1, 38–52.

Kakwani, N. and E. Pernia (2000) "What is Pro-Poor Growth?" *Asian Development Review*, 18:1, 1–16.

Kuznets, S. (1966) *Modern Economic Growth: Rate, Structure, and Spread*, Yale University Press.

Martin, W. and D. Mitra (2001) "Productivity Growth and Convergence in Agriculture versus Manufacturing," *Economic Development and Cultural Change*, 49:2, 403–422.

Nussbaum, M.C. (2000) *Women and Development: A Capabilities Approach*, Cambridge University Press.

Oster, P. (1989) *The Mexicans: A Personal Portrait of a People*, Harper and Row.

Pearce, D., E. Barbier, and A. Markandya (2000) *Sustainable Development: Economics and Environment in the Third World*, Earthscan.

Reinert, K.A. (2011) "No Small Hope: The Basic Goods Imperative," *Review of Social Economy*, 69:1, 55–76.

Rodrik, D. (2007) *One Economics, Many Recipes: Globalization, Institutions and Economic Growth*, Princeton University Press.

Santiso, J. (2006) *Latin America's Political Economy of the Possible*, MIT Press.

Sen, A. (1987) *The Standard of Living*, Cambridge University Press.

Sen, A. (1989) "Development as Capability Expansion," *Journal of Development Planning*, 19, 41–58.

Sen, A. (1999a) "Mahbub ul Haq: The Courage and Creativity of His Ideas," *Journal of Asian Economics*, 10:1, 1–6.

Sen, A. (1999b) *Development as Freedom*, Knopf.

Srinivasan, T.N. (1994) "Human Development: A New Paradigm or Reinvention of the Wheel?" *American Economic Review*, 84:2, 238–243.

Streeten, P.P. (1995) *Thinking About Development*, Cambridge University Press.

Sumner, A. (2010) *Global Poverty and the New Bottom Billion: Three-Quarters of the World's Poor Live in Middle-Income Countries*, Institute of Development Studies.

Szirmai, A. (2005) *The Dynamics of Socio-Economic Development*, Cambridge University Press.

United Nations Development Program (1990) *Human Development Report 1990*.

United Nations Development Program (1995) *Human Development Report 1995*.

United Nations Development Program (1999) *Human Development Report 1999*.

United Nations Development Program (2010) *Human Development Report 2010*.

21 Growth and Development

In the last chapter, we mentioned a question posed to me by a Ghanaian student concerning the role of his country in the world economy. He said, "Professor, what does all this *really* mean for my country? We are going nowhere!" Indeed, although in the 1960s, per capita gross domestic product (GDP) in Ghana exceeded those of Malaysia and Thailand, by the 1990s, it had fallen significantly behind these countries. In 2000, around the time when this student asked me his question, per capita GDP in Ghana was only US$225, whereas those in Malaysia and Thailand were $4,030 and $1,968, respectively. Furthermore, Ghana's 2000 human development index (HDI) was only approximately 0.56, reflecting a relatively low life expectancy and unsatisfactory educational attainment. How could Ghana "get somewhere" rather than "go nowhere?"[1] What insights can we obtain into this possibility using the development as growth perspective? Finally, what roles might human capital, trade, and institutions play in this process? This chapter will help you answer these questions.

Economists are increasingly concerned with explanations of per capita GDP levels and their rates of growth. For such explanations, economists turn to what is known as **growth theory**. In this chapter, we consider two variants of growth theory: "old" growth theory and "new" growth theory.[2] In the case of new growth theory, we make an explicit link to the **human development** framework we discussed in Chapter 20. Next, we consider the inter-relationships among human capital, trade, institutions, and growth. For the interested reader, an appendix to the chapter presents some of the algebraic details of growth theory.

> Analytical elements for this chapter:
>
> *Countries* and *factors*.

OLD GROWTH THEORY

Why was Ghana's 2000 GDP per capita $225 rather than $1,225 or $10,225? An early attempt to answer this sort of question was provided by Nobel Laureate Robert Solow (1956) in what is now known as old growth theory.[3] Growth theory begins with what economists call a **production function**. In particular, it utilizes the **intensive production function** illustrated in Figure 21.1. The intensive production function relates two economic variables. The first is per capita GDP and is denoted by $y = \frac{Y}{L}$ where Y is GDP and L is the labor force/population.[4] The second is the capital-labor ratio and is denoted by $k = \frac{K}{L}$ where K is the total amount of physical capital.

Figure 21.1 indicates that there is a *positive* relationship between the capital-labor ratio and per capita GDP. For example, as the capital-labor ratio increases from k_1 to k_2 and each worker has more physical capital to work with, per capita GDP increases from y_1 to y_2. This is a process known as **capital deepening**. Figure 21.1 also indicates that the relationship between the capital-labor ratio and per capita GDP is decreasingly positive (the slope of the graph becomes flatter as k increases). This is the result of

[1] Unknowingly, my student was echoing concerns voiced by Easterly (2001, chapter 2).
[2] We can only touch the surface of this important area of research. Interested readers can pursue this subject further in Jones (2002).
[3] The Solow model replaced what was then called the Harrod-Domar model. See Sato (1964) and Easterly (1999).
[4] In more advanced models, the labor force and population can differ from one another.

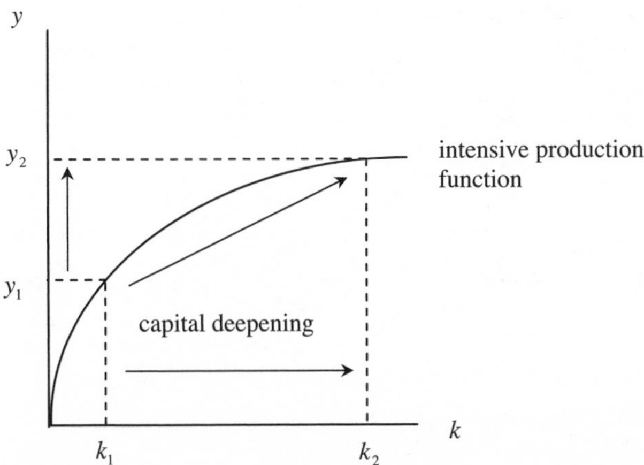

Figure 21.1. The Intensive Production Function and Capital Deepening

diminishing returns to labor and capital.[5] Consequently, increases in k at lower levels add more to per capita GDP than increases in k at higher levels.

Figure 21.1 indicates that increases in per capita income in a country such as Ghana can occur through capital deepening. There is, however, a set of other possible sources of increases in per capita income. This we refer to as *shift factors* because they shift the intensive production function, as in Figure 21.2. Originally, Solow had referred to this as *technological change*, but this turns out to be only one of the set of potential shift factors. In Solow's original analysis, technological change, involving a variable that does not appear on either axis of the intensive production function diagram, *shifts* the graph upward, as in Figure 21.2. For example, at a given capital-labor ratio, k_1, per capita income increases from y_1 to y_2.[6]

Figures 21.1 and 21.2 tell us some important things about increasing per capita incomes in Ghana or in any other county. Let's summarize them in a box:

> Increases in per capita incomes can come about through increases in the capital-labor ratio (capital deepening) or through other shift factors, such as improvements in technological efficiency.

How fast can increases in capital-labor ratios or other shift factors make economies grow? Table 21.1 presents some examples. In this table, Ghana has been added to the countries on which we reported in Chapter 20. As you see in Table 21.1, growth rates in GDP per capita can differ significantly among countries and over time. The variation recorded in this table alone ranges from −5 percent (Turkey in 1980) to 16 percent (China in 1970). It is important to keep in mind that when poor countries record negative growth rates, poverty is most likely increasing. In the case of Ghana, you can see that in 1990 and 2000, the growth rate was very low. In 2008, however, it had

[5] Diminishing returns to labor and capital appear as what is known as diminishing marginal products of labor and capital.

[6] The contrast between Figures 21.1 and 21.2 is one of many cases of the important difference in economics between a *movement along* a graph and a *shift of* a graph, respectively. When a variable on one of the two axes changes, there is a movement along a graph. When a variable *not* on one of the two axes changes, there is a shift of a graph. This was true of the demand and supply graphs in Chapter 2, for example, as well as for the emigration supply and immigration demand graphs in Chapter 12.

Table 21.1. Growth in GDP per capita (percent)

Country	GDP per capita, 2008	Growth rate in GDP per capita				
		1970	1980	1990	2000	2008
Ethiopia	321	NA	NA	−1	3	8
Haiti	649	NA	NA	NA	−1	−1
Ghana	713	7	−2	0	1	5
India	1,065	3	4	3	2	4
Indonesia	2,246	6	6	7	4	5
China	3,422	16	6	2	8	9
Costa Rica	6,565	5	−2	1	−1	1
Brazil	8,536	6	7	−6	3	4
Turkey	9,881	1	−5	7	5	−1
South Korea	19,162	6	−3	8	8	2
Spain	35,000	3	1	4	4	−1
Japan	38,268	9	2	5	3	−1
United States	47,210	−1	−1	1	3	0

Source: World Bank, World Development Indicators Online

increased to 5 percent. Also note that the 2008 GDP per capita recorded in the table was US$713, so some progress had been made since 2000.

We can use Figure 21.1 to understand some additional requirements for economic growth in Ghana based on capital deepening. To do this, however, we need to supplement it with some important relationships concerning Ghana's capital-labor ratio, k. Increases in k require increases in the capital stock that *more than offset* any increases in population. Increases in the capital stock, in turn, require investment. Finally, investment requires saving. The relationship between saving and investment was depicted in the circular flow diagram of Chapter 13. In particular, we are going to rely on Equations 13.1a,b from that chapter, reproduced here as:

$$I = (S_H + S_G) + S_F \tag{21.1a}$$

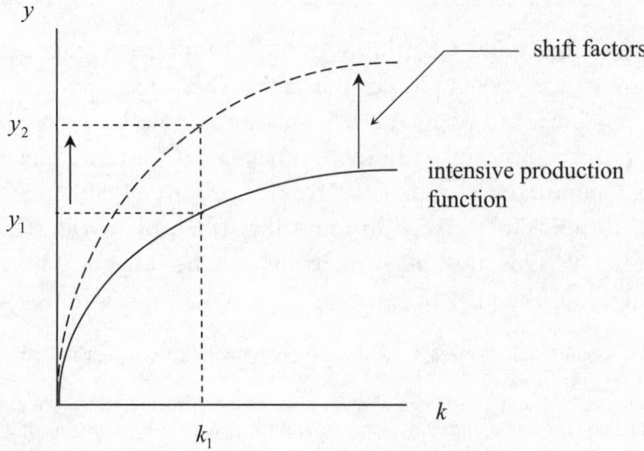

Figure 21.2. Technological Change in the Intensive Production Function

In words:

$$\text{Domestic Investment} = \text{Domestic Savings} + \text{Foreign Savings} \quad (21.1b)$$

How do these equations relate to our discussion in this chapter? Increases in GDP per capita through capital deepening require investment. Investment has two sources: domestic savings (household and government) and foreign savings. In the absence of shift factors such as technological improvements, increases in domestic and foreign savings are the only sources of growth in per capita incomes. As mentioned previously, these increases in savings must be large enough to increase the capital stock sufficiently so that it more than offsets any increase in population. If the increase in the capital stock is not large enough, k and y will fall due to population growth. This phenomenon sometimes goes by the ugly term *capital shallowing*.[7]

Let's return to the sources of savings in Ghana. Increasing household savings is often a matter of making institutions available to the households of the economy to facilitate savings. Importantly, these institutions should be as broad-based as possible, being accessible to rich and poor, rural and urban. Increasing government savings is a matter of decreasing government expenditures and increasing government tax revenues, moving the government budget toward surplus. An important caveat here is that some types of government expenditures (e.g., education) can positively affect the level of technology (see later discussion). Also, some government investments are *complementary* to private investments (see Chapter 24). Finally, increasing foreign savings, as we saw in Chapter 13, is a matter of increasing the capital/financial account surplus on the balance of payments. Here, it is important to pay attention to the form and magnitude of the capital/financial account surplus. As we discussed in Chapter 19 on crises, large capital account surpluses based on short-term investments are risky and could be damaging to Ghana in the long run.[8] But these sources of savings are key to increasing GDP per capita.

"Old" growth theory contributes greatly to our understanding of how per capita incomes are determined. It draws our attention to savings and shift factors such as technology as central variables that can be affected by various institutional and policy regimes among the countries of the world. It turns out, however, that this theory leaves a lot to be explained. This is represented in Figure 21.3. Here, in an initial year, we observe Ghana with a capital-labor ratio of k_1 and a per capita GDP of y_1. In a subsequent year, we observe a capital-labor ratio of k_2 and a per capita income of y_2. The double-headed arrow in Figure 21.3 indicates the amount of the unexplained growth in per capita incomes, which is known as the *Solow residual*.

In practice, these Solow residuals can be quite large. How can we begin to account for this unexplained growth? One explanation we have discussed already. As we showed in Figure 21.2, shift factors such as improvements of technology move the intensive production function graph upward. But technology is simply an *exogenous* parameter in our model. How is it determined in the real world? This is the question that "new" growth theory attempts to answer.[9]

[7] Recall that $k = \frac{K}{L}$, where K is the capital stock and L is the population assumed also to be equal to the labor force. The algebraic condition for investment to increase k is given in the appendix to this chapter.

[8] For a discussion of this, see also chapter 4 of Goldin and Reinert (2007).

[9] For example, years ago, *The Economist* (1992) assessed the "old" growth theory and concluded that it is "patently inadequate – so much so that its teachings have had virtually no influence on policy-makers" (p. 15). The theory

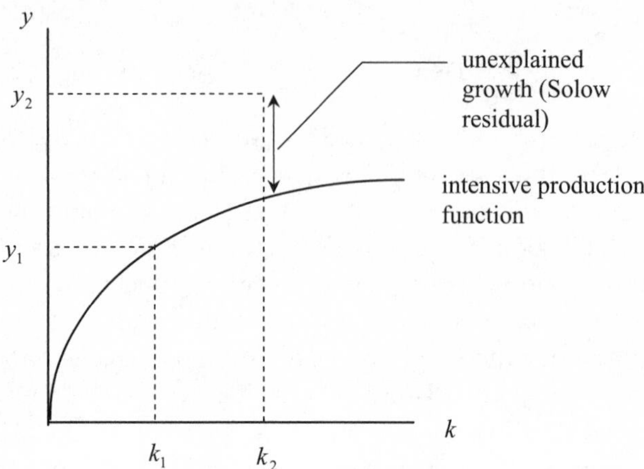

Figure 21.3. Unexplained Growth in Per Capita Incomes

NEW GROWTH THEORY AND HUMAN CAPITAL

It is easy to say the Ghana needs to improve its technical efficiency to help improve per capita income, but what does this entail? "Old" growth theory has little to say about this. "New" growth theory, however, provides us with some insights.[10] The models of the new growth theory are varied, and we cannot attempt a serious review of them here. Instead, we consider a single approach that helps us bring together the development as growth and development as human development perspectives considered in Chapter 20. A number of new growth theory models emphasize the role of a third factor of production in addition to labor and physical capital. This is **human capital**. Including this factor acknowledges that labor is more than just hours worked. It reflects skills, abilities, and education. In certain sectors, it might even reflect creativity. Because productive knowledge can be embodied in workers, there appears to be a positive link between human capital and technological efficiency. These considerations lead some economists to modify the intensive production function so that increases in human capital shift it upward (as in Figure 21.2) through a positive impact on technological efficiency.

Levels of human capital can vary significantly among countries as over time. Consider Figure 21.4. This takes adult literacy as a measure of human capital for a range of years and for five developing regions. Outside of sub-Saharan Africa, adult literacy rates are on significant upward trends. However, they vary significantly, from below 60 percent in South Asia to 90 percent in the Latin America/Caribbean and East Asia/Pacific regions. The view of new growth theory is that such differences can matter for technological efficiency and, therefore, GDP per capita.

In this intensive production function of new growth theory, technology is an *endogenous* variable that can be influenced by levels of human capital measured perhaps as literacy rates or years of education. The implication of this can be seen in Figure 21.5.

"supposes . . . that new technologies rain down from heaven as random scientific breakthroughs" (p. 16). This might be a bit harsh, but does point out the limits of old growth theory.

[10] The "new" growth theory traces its roots back to Romer (1986, 1990). See also Lucas (1988) and Romer (1994).

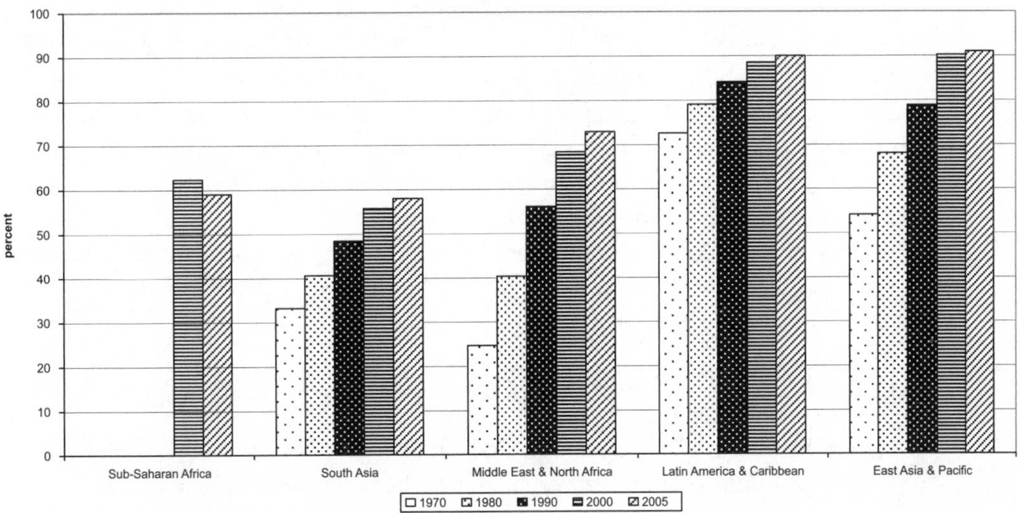

Figure 21.4. Adult Literacy Rates by Region (percent). *Source:* World Bank, World Development Indicators Online

In this figure, an increase in human capital from period 1 to period 2 shifts the intensive production function upwards. The amount of unexplained growth from Figure 21.3 (the Solow residual) declines, and changes in human capital are an important component in this decline.

Early attempts to address this possibility indicated that the human capital was important. For example, Mankiw, Romer, and Weil (1992) and Hall and Jones (1999) showed that including human capital in growth models can contribute to their ability to explain the variation in per capita incomes among the countries of the world. Subsequent work questioned the empirical importance of human capital as education in explaining development as growth. For example, Easterly (2001) noted that "the growth response to the dramatic educational expansion of the last four decades has been distinctly disappointing. If the incentives to invest in the future are not there, expanding education is worth little. . . . Creating skills where there exists no technology to use them is not going to foster economic growth" (p. 73).

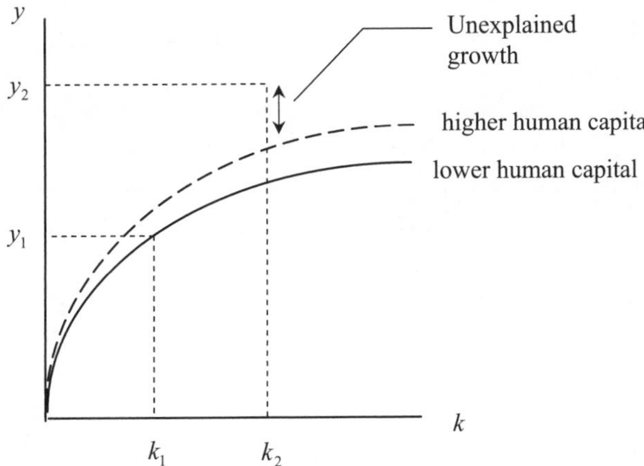

Figure 21.5. Human Capital and Unexplained Growth in Per Capita Incomes

Why did the seeming importance of human capital as education not show up as significant in empirical investigations? Krueger and Lindahl (2001) suggested that it is difficult to establish the role of education in growth due to *measurement errors.* Subsequent work by Cohen and Soto (2007) seems to have resolved the measurement error difficulties by establishing a nonlinear relationship between education (years of schooling in their study) and human capital. Once they do this, they find that education does indeed contribute to development as growth.

Further evidence on the importance of human capital in the form of education comes from research on the rate of return to education (RORE).[11] Standard results from this body of research suggest that:

1. The private/market RORE is generally higher than the rate of return on physical capital investments.
2. The private/market RORE is generally higher at lower levels of education.
3. The private/market RORE is generally higher at lower levels of GDP per capita.

There is also a body of research looking at female education that suggests that the human capital of girls and women is particularly important. For example, in a review, Schultz (2002) reported that "There is a substantial empirical literature suggesting that adding to a mother's schooling will have a larger beneficial effect on a child's health, schooling, and adult productivity than would adding to a father's schooling by the same amount" (p. 212).[12] Additional evidence of this kind is presented in Tembon and Fort (2008).

We also need to recognize that human capital can also include *health* components. Quite some time ago, in a review of growth theory, Pio (1994) advocated devoting "particular attention . . . to the role of human capital with an emphasis on the adjective human; that is to say, on the levels of health, education, and nutrition of the population and the implications of changes in such levels for long-term growth" (p. 278). He concluded that "the inclusion of a broader definition of human capital (encompassing health and nutrition as well as education) seems useful both in the construction of models and in their empirical verification" (p. 297).

Because of women's traditionally close relationship to children, it also turns out that the educational levels of women contribute positively and significantly to child health. The mediating factors here are hygiene, nutrition, and child-care factors. For this reason, beyond those discussed previously, focusing attention on women's education in developing countries is valuable.[13] Further, the work of Osmani and Sen (2003) and others indicates that women's deprivation in nutrition and health contributes to the ill health of offspring *both as children and as adults* through the pathway of fetal health. So even the health of adults (and consequently their capacity to work) depends on the health of their mothers as health outcomes are transmitted from one generation to another.

This discussion of human capital in both its education and health aspects in relation to growth suggests that there might be some important relationships among the three

[11] See, for example, Psacharopoulos (1994, 2006).

[12] Schultz (2002) also commented that "There are few instances in international quantitative social science research where the application of common statistical methods has yielded more consistent findings than in the area of gender returns to schooling" (p. 207).

[13] See for example the study of parental education and health in Brazil by Kassouf and Senauer (1996).

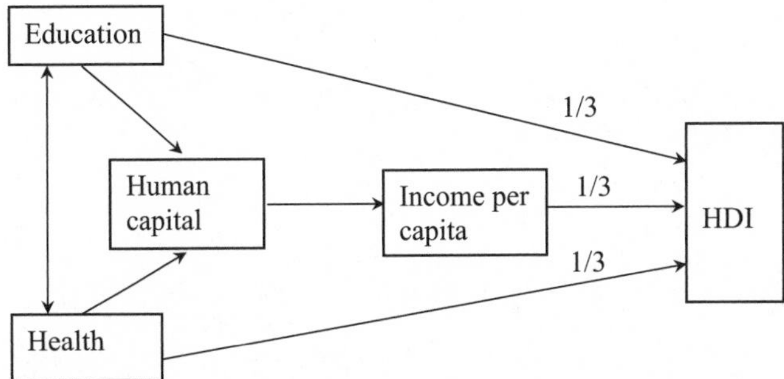

Figure 21.6. Education, Health, Growth, and Human Development

components of the human development index (HDI) presented in Chapter 20. This is illustrated in Figure 21.6. Here education has a *direct* impact on the HDI through its one-third weight. However, it also can have an *indirect* impact on the HDI via its impact on human capital and, thereby, on per capita GDP. Health also has a *direct* impact on the HDI through its one-third weight and an *indirect* impact on the HDI through human capital and per capita GDP. These indirect effects can be all the more powerful because, in addition, there is a two-way, positive interaction between education and health illustrated in Figure 21.6. Educated persons (particularly women) contribute to healthy children, and healthy children are more likely to become educated.

TRADE AND GROWTH

Many development economists and international trade economists have suggested that countries' openness to international trade has a positive impact on growth in per capita GDP and, therefore, on poverty alleviation and human development.[14] These researchers suggest that exports might be an important growth strategy for Ghana and other developing countries. This argument actually has a number of components.[15] First, increased exports can support increased employment and wage incomes, with the latter being reinvested in increases in human capital. Examples of this include clothing exports from Bangladesh and rice exports from Vietnam, both of which have been shown to have had these effects. Second, increased trade (both imports and exports) can in some circumstances improve competitive conditions in domestic markets.[16] Some studies have confirmed the importance of this effect in Mexico and India, for example. Third, and perhaps most importantly, exports can contribute to improved technological efficiency as a shift factor in the intensive production function diagram.

The notion here is that technological efficiency responds to two impulses. The first impulse is domestic innovation, which is positively affected by human capital accumulation in some new growth theory models. The second impulse is the absorption of new technology from the rest of the world.[17] It is thought that openness to trade, and exports in particular, facilitate this absorption of technology from abroad.[18] For

[14] See Dollar and Kraay (2004), for example. An alternative view is given in Rodríquez and Rodrik (2001). A thorough review of trade and poverty is provided by Winters, McCulloch, and McKay (2004).

[15] See, for example, chapter 3 of Goldin and Reinert (2007).

[16] This possibility is known as the *pro-competitive effects of trade.*

[17] See, for example, Romer (1993).

[18] For example, the World Bank (1999) claimed that "Trade can bring greater awareness of new and better ways of producing goods and services: exports contribute to this awareness through the information obtained from

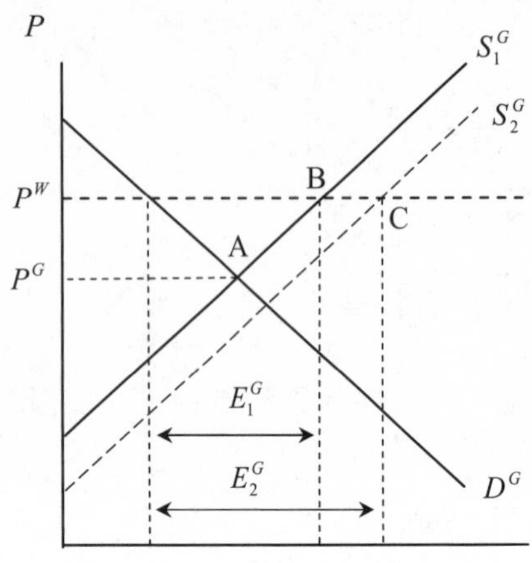

Figure 21.7. Export Externalities for Ghana

this reason, exports are sometimes seen as having a *positive externality* for the exporting country. That is, exports generate additional technology gains on the supply side of the economy.

The logic of export externalities is illustrated in Figure 21.7 in an absolute advantage diagram (see Chapter 2). P^G is Ghana's autarky price, and P^W is the world price. In the absence of a positive export externality, as the price increases from P^G to P^W in the movement from autarky to trade, quantity supplied increases from point A to point B, and exports of E_1^G appear. In the presence of export externalities, however, the process continues one step further. The initial export level, E_1^G, facilitates the absorption of technological knowledge from abroad, and the subsequent improvement in production technology makes possible an increase in supply or a shift in Ghana's supply curve from S_1^G to S_2^G.[19] Given P^W, Ghanaian firms move from point B to point C, and exports expand to E_2^G. In simplified form, this is how some international and development economists view the role of exports in the development process.

What is the evidence for the process depicted in Figure 21.7? The historical experience of East Asia, discussed in the accompanying box, is usually cited. More formally, early studies such as Sachs and Warner (1995) and Edwards (1998) deployed statistical techniques to show that the more open countries are to international trade, the faster their growth in per capita GDP. However, another study by Levin and Raut (1997) showed that these externalities are notably *absent* in the case of *primary product exports*, which characterize many developing countries, including Ghana. These initial studies were severely criticized by Rodríquez and Rodrik (2001), and subsequent revisits to the methodology of the studies (e.g., Wacziarg and Welch, 2008) show that such criticism had its merits. However, statistical analysis based on extended and improved indicators does seem to support the trade and growth link. The results of Wacziarg and Welch

buyers and suppliers" (p. 27). Similarly, Rodrigo (2001) noted that "By opening up a channel to the world market, trade... serves to promote specialization and sustain production tempos of goods in which learning effects are embodied; if constrained by domestic market size alone along with associated domestic business cycle uncertainty of demand, firms would be less willing to make the investments needed to capture gains from learning" (p. 90). For an example in the Uruguay software sector, see Kesidou and Szirmai (2008).

[19] Recall from Chapter 2 that reductions in input prices and improvements in technology shift the supply curve to the right, whereas increases in input prices and technology setbacks shift the supply curve to the left.

(2008), for example, suggest that openness to trade can increase investment and growth rates by more than 1 percent.[20]

Trade and Growth in East Asia

The large increases in per capita GDP in the countries of East Asia were one of the most notable successes of the world economy in the post–World War II era. One observation made about the East Asian economies is that the growth of per capita GDP was accompanied by a significant expansion of exports, especially in Japan, South Korea, and Taiwan. Some observers, especially those affiliated with the World Bank, concluded that the export promotion policies pursued by these economies explain a great deal of their growth and development successes. For example, this was the point of view expressed in a major World Bank report entitled *The East Asian Miracle: Economic Growth and Public Policy,* issued in 1993.

According to the World Bank, export promotion positively affects per capita incomes via *technology effects.* These can arise in a few ways. First, exports help firms to earn the foreign exchange necessary to purchase new equipment from abroad. This new equipment can embody a more sophisticated technology than the older equipment of the firm. Second, the presence of exports signals foreign firms that the country in question would be a good place in which to engage in export-oriented foreign direct investment (FDI). This FDI can bring with it new technology. Third, exports signal that the exporting firms are competitive and are therefore taken seriously in technology cross-licensing schemes. Thus the World Bank claimed that "the relationship between exports and productivity growth (arises) from exports' role in helping economies adopt and master international best-practice technologies" (p. 317).

Not all international economists agree with this interpretation. For example, Rodrik (1994) found this export-technology link to be unconvincing. His interpretation of the East Asian development experience was that exports were largely a *result,* not a cause, of successful development. He attributed the increases in per capita GDP to levels of education and the equal distributions of income and land. He stressed the role of these *initial conditions* in the subsequent economic development of East Asia. With regard to the role of exports in improving countries' technological capabilities, Rodrik (1994) stated that "whether export orientation generates spillovers and productivity benefits . . . is still unclear" (p. 48).

More generally, Rodrik (1999, chapter 2) demonstrated that there are many instances where high export-to-GDP ratios are associated with *low* rates of growth. He went further (1999, chapter 3) to demonstrate for a sample of 47 countries that increases in export-to-GDP ratios *followed* increases in investment-to-GDP ratios. The implication here is that exports were a *consequence* of East Asian growth rather than a cause of that growth.

Sources: World Bank (1993) and Rodrik (1994, 1999)

There are other caveats to the role of exports in economic growth. There is some agreement that the accumulation of human capital we discussed in the previous section is an important *prerequisite* to the absorption of technology from abroad.[21] Indeed,

[20] It is important to note that this overall result occurs within what Wacziarg and Welch (2008) describe as "considerable heterogeneity" in their country sample. For example, political instability can break the link between trade and growth. This opens up the way to institutional considerations taken up in the next section.

[21] For example, in its study of economic development of East Asia, the World Bank (1993) acknowledged that "Access to international best-practice technology and rapid formation of human capital supplement and

many statistical studies of the trade-growth link include educational measures, along with trade measures as explanatory variables. There has also been some empirical evidence to support the conclusion that human capital and *manufactured* exports interact positively in supporting the growth of per capita incomes. For example, the statistical analyses of Levin and Raut (1997) indicated that such interactions are significant. Levin and Raut's evidence showed that the contribution of human capital depends on the level of manufactured exports *and* the contribution of manufactured exports depends on the level of human capital. In this way, trade and education can contribute to increases in per capita GDP and, thereby, to the HDI both directly and indirectly. This interaction, however, is restricted to manufactured exports. Primary product exports do not necessarily generate the same effects. Finally, there is the additional role that institutions play, to which we next turn.[22]

INSTITUTIONS AND GROWTH

Although much attention has been given to the trade and growth possibility, increasing recognition has gone to the role of *institutions* in growth as an additional shift factor in the intensive production function diagram. This line of thinking goes back to the work of North (1990) and has a long history in economic thought, but has only more recently been taken up in modern growth theory and its associated empirical analysis. As we mentioned in Chapter 7 on the World Trade Organization, North defined institutions as "humanly devised constraints that shape human interaction" (p. 3). A less formal definition is as "the rules of the game." How can the rules of the game in a country affect economic growth?

Perhaps first and foremost, many developing countries had long histories as colonies of other (usually European) countries. In many instances, colonial institutions had a lasting impact. As North also emphasized, institutional change is "overwhelmingly incremental," and independence from a formal colonial power does not necessarily bring about the termination of colonial institutions, just the slow modification of them. This phenomenon is known as *path dependence*, the notion that a country's institutions are strongly influenced by its history. For example, the work of Bolt and Bezemer (2009) showed that variations in colonial education investments within sub-Saharan Africa help to explain human capital levels as far forward as 1995. They further show that colonial educational investments help to explain current institutional quality in the form of measures of democracy and constraints on the executive. Banerjee and Iyer (2005) showed similar results for colonial land tenure systems in India.[23]

But what are the relevant institutions from the perspective of growth? Table 21.2 presents some relevant institutional categories. The table begins with the *rule of law*

reinforce one another.... The externalities generated by *manufactured* exports in the high-performing Asian economies in the form of cheaper and more effective knowledge transfers would have undoubtedly been less productive had there been fewer skilled workers to facilitate their absorption" (pp. 320–321, emphasis added).

[22] Rodrik, Subramanian, and Trebbi (2004) made a relevant distinction. They wrote: "It may be useful to distinguish between 'moderate' and 'maximal' versions of this (trade and growth) view. Much of the economics profession would accept the hypothesis that trade can be an underlying source of growth once certain institutional pre-requisites have been fulfilled. But a more extreme perspective... is that trade/integration is the major determinant of whether poor countries grow or not" (p. 132).

[23] Institutional path dependence can even impact the export and growth linkage we discussed previously. As pointed out by Myint (2001), the export success of South Korea and Taiwan was in part due to the inheritance of rural and urban institutions from the (brutal) Japanese colonial period.

Table 21.2. Institutions and growth

Category	Elements	Relevance
Rule of law	Political representation Elections Independent judiciary Civil liberties Consistency	Prevents violent conflict and provides for legitimacy in political decision making
Property rights	Secure ownership or control of assets Right to returns on assets Asset distribution	Ensures that the use of productive assets will result in appropriable returns that will, in turn, provide incentives for further development and use
Contract enforcement	Contract design Escape clauses Recourse	Allows for parties to enter into long-term, productive arrangements with a minimum degree of certainty
Regulation	Prudential regulation of finance Macroeconomic management Health and safety regulation	Addresses well-known instance of market failure
Social insurance	Transfer payments Employment practices Traditional social arrangements	Ensures that market dislocations are managed so as not to impede human development

Sources: Rodrik (2007) and others

in the elements of political representation, elections, an independent judiciary, civil liberties, and consistency. The rule of law helps to prevent violent conflict and provides for legitimacy in political decision making. Clearly, conflict (either internal or external) involves productive asset destruction and is not good for growth. Issues of consistency in the rule of law are complex and under argument in the democracy and development research literature, but are clearly relevant.[24] For some time, the role of civil liberties in growth was unclear, but the work of Benyishay and Betancourt (2010) has shown that it does indeed matter.[25]

Property rights concerns the ownership of productive assets that are involved in the growth and development process. The relevant elements here include secure ownership or control of assets, the right to returns on these assets, and the distribution of the assets. As emphasized by Rodrik (2007, chapter 5) and many others, the private ownership (or at least control) of property has proven to be the best institutional arrangement for growth.[26] Economists tend to downplay the importance of the *distribution* of asset ownership or control, but this can be very important. For example, years ago Adelman (1980) stressed the importance of asset redistribution in Japan, South Korea, and Taiwan for their growth through export success. This point has been more recently made by Alesina and Rodrik (1994) and Birdsall and Londono (1998).

Contract enforcement is a third area of institutions for growth. Market systems rely on complex sets of contracts (both explicit and implicit), with varying degrees of inter-temporality. If the process of entering into and exiting from these contracts is

[24] For just one example, see Mansfield and Snyder (2005). But on the positive role of democratic processes in institutional development and growth, see chapter 5 of Rodrik (2007).

[25] This is in the form of personal autonomy and individual rights as measured by Freedom House.

[26] Rodrik (2007, chapter 5) rightly points out that "Formal property rights do not count for much if they do not confer control rights. By the same token, sufficiently strong control rights may do the trick even in the absence of formal property rights" (p. 156). This distinction is especially important in countries transitioning from formally socialist systems (e.g., Russia, China, and Ethiopia).

not regularized, confusion ensues. Relevant elements of contract enforcement include contract design, escape clauses for early exit, and legal recourse in the case of contract violation. As emphasized by Clague et al. (1999), "only countries where governments give private parties the capacity to make credible commitments that they could not otherwise make, and thereby achieve gains from trade that they could not otherwise obtain, achieve their economic potential" (p. 206).

Regulation is a fourth area of relevant institutions. Although the notion of regulation often has negative connotations, this area of government activity is actually essential for growth and development. Regulation's purpose is to address known market failures.[27] Important areas include the prudential regulation of finance to avoid the crises we discussed in Chapter 19, macroeconomic management, and basic health and safety regulation. As noted by Rodrik (2007), "the freer are the markets, the greater is the burden on the regulatory institutions" (p. 157). This is not to deny the possibility of over-regulation, but to recognize the importance of minimum regulatory requirements for sustained growth.

Finally, *social insurance* is an important institutional realm. This includes transfer payments, employment practices, and traditional (family and community) social arrangements. Traditional family and community social insurance systems tend to break down as growth and development proceed. This is one of the structural changes we mentioned in Chapter 20. As this occurs, they need to be replaced by other social insurance systems based on employment practices or transfer payments. Without these systems in place, the vicissitudes of the market system can undermine its effectiveness in allocating resources, improving technological efficiency, and accumulating physical and human capital.

What is the evidence on the role of institutions in economic growth? At one level, this is a silly question, because the entire classical literature on economics from Adam Smith on, as well as the entire early development economics literature, both addressed precisely this question.[28] But at another level, there has been a set of new quantitative studies of the role of institutions on growth, and taken as a whole, they indicated that institutions (in multiple dimensions) do matter. This appears to be true of the rule of law (e.g., Hall and Jones, 1999; Rodrik, Subramanian, and Trebbi, 2004; and Benyishay and Betancourt, 2010), property rights (e.g., Rodrik, Subramanian, and Trebbi, 2004), and contract enforcement (e.g., Clague et al., 1999), to name a few.

Despite this important and emerging evidence, the task of actually constructing effective institutions is difficult given the "overwhelmingly incremental" nature of institutional change. Further, there is the choice to be made between home-grown and imported institutions. As Rodrik (2007, chapter 5) emphasized, effective institutions are often hybrids between existing domestic institutions and imported institutions, often cobbled together in novel ways. So having established the importance of institutions, we need to be aware that approaches can vary from place to place but still have positive effects on growth. There is room for variety and experimentation.

This and the previous section allow us to supplement the box at the beginning of the chapter with the following:

[27] See, for example, chapters 2 and 3 of Acocella (2005).
[28] See chapter 3 of Szirmai (2005).

> Increases in per capita incomes can come about through increases in the capital-labor ratio (capital deepening) or through other shift factors such as improvements in technological efficiency, improvement in human development (education and health), export expansions, and improvements in institutional quality.

CONCLUSION

So what causes growth? It is clear that the accumulations of both physical and human capital are part of the story, but even with these two productive factors in the story, there is more to be explained. Trade and institutions are two other potentially important explanatory variables, with institutions probably being more important. Changing institutions is not easy, and there is no one formula for successful institutional design.

So what should Ghana do? We need to be careful in answering this question, because there is probably more than one potential answer. But it is difficult to imagine Ghana continuing to grow by neglecting human development and ignoring institutional development. And exports will no doubt help to some extent. It has become clear that treating the HDI as having three *independent* elements of per capita income, health, and education is limiting. Our discussion in the present chapter has shown that these three elements are *interdependent*, with it being possible for education and health to interact in positive ways to promote the growth in per capita incomes.

Another way to view the discussion of this chapter is by returning to Figure 1.4 in Chapter 1. This figure illustrated the presence of linkages among the realms of international trade, international production, international finance, and international development. We have shown that it is possible for two of these four realms to interact in a positive manner. The trade relationships of a country can result in the absorption of new technology, and this absorption can be facilitated by the accumulation of the appropriate types of human capital. There are also potentially positive (and negative) interactions between international production and international development, and we take up this subject in the next chapter.

REVIEW EXERCISES

1. Given the discussion of this chapter with regard to trade, education, health, and institutions, what policies do you think countries ought to pursue to ensure that international trade supports increases in per capita incomes?
2. Are there any connections you can find between the discussion of this chapter and that on international competition covered in Chapter 11? In particular, are there links between our discussion of education and Michael Porter's thinking about factor conditions?
3. The World Bank suggested that there are important externalities associated with exports. In general, such positive externalities call for subsidies on the part of governments. Given our discussion of the GATT/WTO system in Chapter 7, do you detect any problems with the use of *export subsidies*?
4. This is one of the few chapters in which we mentioned gender issues in our discussion. Are there any other aspects of the world economy in which gender

issues are important? How might these issues arise in the realms of international trade, international production, and international finance?

5. Consider a country with which you have some familiarity. Using Table 21.2 as a rough guide, what can you say about the institutional qualities of that country?

FURTHER READING AND WEB RESOURCES

Jones (2002) is a basic reference on the theory of economic growth. For a summary, see Rodrik (2003). Szirmai (2005) and Cypher and Dietz (2004) present the roles of education, health, and population in the growth and development processes in an accessible manner. The role of trade in growth and development is effectively reviewed by Bruton (1998) and in chapter 3 of Goldin and Reinert (2007). On the role of institutions in growth and development, see North (1990) and Rodrik (2007).

The Groningen Growth and Development Center at http://www.ggdc.net/ is a good source for data and research on growth and development. UNU-MERIT is an interesting research and training center jointly sponsored by the United Nations and Maastricht University. It focuses on technological change and innovation, with a website at http://www.merit.unu.edu/. Finally, an interesting journal related to the discussion of this chapter is *Innovations: Technology/Governance/Globalization.* See http://www.mitpressjournals.org/loi/itgg.

APPENDIX: GROWTH THEORY ALGEBRA

This appendix presents some of the algebra behind the growth theory presented in this chapter.

Growth theory begins with what economists call a **production function**:

$$Y = A \times F(L, K) \tag{21.2}$$

This equation presents what is known as the *aggregate* production function. In this equation, Y is total output and total income, L is the aggregate labor force, and K is the aggregate stock of physical capital. A refers to an *exogenous* measure of technology.

"Old" growth theory assumes that production takes place according to **constant returns to scale**. Constant returns to scale means that a doubling of both L and K will lead to a doubling of Y. More generally, multiplying both L and K by some constant θ will increase Y by that same factor. In other words,

$$\theta Y = A \times F(\theta L, \theta K) \tag{21.3}$$

Solow's growth model uses Equation 21.3 and introduces a little trick. The trick is to set θ equal to $1/L$. This gives us the following equation:

$$\frac{1}{L}Y = A \times F\left(\frac{1}{L}L, \frac{1}{L}K\right) \tag{21.4}$$

Equation 21.4 is a little confusing. To make sense of it, we are going to consider each of its terms in turn. Let's begin with the term on the left-hand side of the equation, $\frac{Y}{L}$. This we can interpret as *per capita GDP or income.* We are going to denote per capita income with a lower case y: $y = \frac{Y}{L}$. The second term, A, we have seen before. It is just our technology term. Inside the parentheses, we next encounter L/L. This term is equal to 1, a constant, and we can therefore ignore it. Finally, we have K/L. This is known at the *capital-labor ratio*. We denote the capital-labor ratio with a lower case k: $k = \frac{Y}{L}$. Given all of this, we can rewrite Equation 21.4 as follows:

$$y = A \times F(1, k) = A \times f(k) \tag{21.5}$$

This equation is the **intensive production function** used in this chapter.

New growth theory often works with a modified intensive production function of the form:

$$y = A(h) \times f(k) \tag{21.6}$$

where h is a measure of per capita human capital, $\frac{H}{L}$. Trade issues in new growth theory involve adding an additional variable to this equation, as follows:

$$y = A\,(h \times e_m) \times f(k) \tag{21.7}$$

where e_m is manufacturing exports' share in the gross national product. Note in Equation 21.7 that A is a function of the *product* of h and e_M. Therefore, the contribution of human capital depends on the level of manufactured exports, and the contribution of manufactured exports depends on the level of human capital.

Two important variables in the study of population and development are the *crude birth rate* (r_b) and the *crude death rate* (r_d). These measures are respectively defined as the number of live births and deaths per 1,000 population. Behind the crude birth rate is the *total fertility rate*, defined as the average number of children a woman will give birth to during her lifetime. The crude birth rate and crude death rate together determine the **natural rate of population growth** (a percentage measure), as follows[29]:

$$n = \frac{(r_b - r_d)}{10} \tag{21.8}$$

The natural rate of population growth discussed in this chapter is important because, along with the rate of growth of physical capital, $\frac{\Delta K}{K}$, it determines the level of the capital-labor ratio, k. This, in turn, determines the level of per capita income, y. More specifically, an increase in y will require that:

$$\frac{\Delta K}{K} \times 100 > n \tag{21.9}$$

The higher is the natural rate of population growth, the less likely this will be.

REFERENCES

Acocella, N. (2005) *Economic Policy in the Age of Globalization*, Cambridge University Press.

Adelman, I. (1980) "Income Distribution, Economic Development and Land Reform," *American Behavioral Scientist*, 23:3, 437–456.

Alesina, A. and D. Rodrik (1994) "Distributive Politics and Economic Growth," *Quarterly Journal of Economics*, 109:2, 465–490.

[29] The natural rate of population growth combines with the net migration rate to determine the *actual* rate of population growth.

Banerjee, A. and L. Iyer (2005) "History, Institutions, and Economic Performance: The Legacy of Colonial Land Tenure Systems in India," *American Economic Review*, 95:4, 1190–1213.

Benyishay, A. and R.R. Betancourt (2010) "Civil Liberties and Economic Development," *Journal of Institutional Economics*, 6:3, 281–304.

Birdsall, N. and J.L. Londono (1998) "No Tradeoff: Efficient Growth via More Equal Human Capital Accumulation," in N. Birdsall, C. Graham, and R.H. Sabot (eds.), *Beyond Tradeoffs: Market Reforms and Equitable Growth in Latin America*, Brookings Institution, 111–145.

Bolt, J. and D. Bezemer (2009) "Understanding Long-Run African Growth: Colonial Institutions or Colonial Education?" *Journal of Development Studies*, 45:1, 24–54.

Bruton, H.J. (1998) "A Reconsideration of Import Substitution," *Journal of Economic Literature*, 36:2, 903–936.

Clague, C., P. Keefer, S. Knack, and M. Olson (1999) "Contract Intensive Money: Contract Enforcement, Property Rights, and Economic Performance," *Journal of Economic Growth*, 4:2, 185–209.

Cohen, D. and M. Soto (2007) "Growth and Human Capital: Good Data, Good Results," *Journal of Economic Growth*, 12:1, 51–76.

Cypher, J.M. and J.L. Dietz (2004) *The Process of Economic Development*, Routledge.

Dollar, D. and A. Kraay (2004) "Trade, Growth, and Poverty," *Economic Journal*, 114:493, 22–49.

Easterly, W. (1999) "The Ghost of the Financing Gap: Testing the Growth Model Used in the International Financial Institutions," *Journal of Development Economics*, 60:2, 423–438.

Easterly, W. (2001) *The Elusive Quest for Growth*, MIT Press.

The Economist (1992) "Economic Growth: Explaining the Mystery," January 4.

The Economist (1996) "Economic Growth: The Poor and the Rich," May 25.

Edwards, S. (1998) "Openness, Productivity and Growth: What Do We Really Know?" *Economic Journal*, 108:447, 383–398.

Goldin, I. and K.A. Reinert (2007) *Globalization for Development: Trade, Finance, Aid, Migration and Policy*, World Bank.

Hall, R. and C.I. Jones (1999) "Why Do Some Countries Produce So Much More Output per Worker than Others?" *Quarterly Journal of Economics*, 114:1, 83–116.

Jones, C.I. (2002) *Introduction to Economic Growth*, Norton.

Kassouf, A.L. and B. Senauer (1996) "Direct and Indirect Effects of Parental Education on Malnutrition among Children in Brazil: A Full Income Approach," *Economic Development and Cultural Change*, 44:4, 817–838.

Kesidou, E. and A. Szirmai (2008) "Local Knowledge Spillovers, Innovation and Export Performance in Developing Countries: Empirical Evidence from the Uruguay Software Cluster," *European Journal of Development Research*, 20:2, 281–298.

Krueger, A.B. and M. Lindahl (2001) "Education for Growth: Why and for Whom?" *Journal of Economic Literature*, 39:4, 1101–1136.

Levin, A. and L. Raut (1997) "Complementarities between Exports and Human Capital in Economic Growth: Evidence from Semi-Industrialized Countries," *Economic Development and Cultural Change*, 46:1, 155–174.

Lucas, R.E. (1988) "On the Mechanics of Economic Development," *Journal of Monetary Economics*, 22:1, 3–42.

Mankiw, N.G., D. Romer, and D. Weil (1992) "A Contribution to the Empirics of Economic Growth," *Quarterly Journal of Economics*, 107:2, 407–438.

Mansfield, E.D. and J. Snyder (2005) *Electing to Fight: Why Emerging Democracies Go to War*, MIT Press.

Myint, H. (2001) "International Trade and the Domestic Institutional Framework," in G.M Meier and J.E. Stiglitz (eds.), *Frontiers of Development Economics: The Future in Perspective*, Oxford University Press, 520–528.

North, D.C. (1990) *Institutions, Institutional Change and Economic Performance*, Cambridge University Press.

Osmani, S. and A. Sen (2003) "The Hidden Penalties of Gender Inequality: Fetal Origins of Ill-Health," *Economics and Human Biology*, 1:1, 105–121.

Pio, A. (1994) "New Growth Theory and Old Development Problems," *Development Policy Review*, 12:3, 277–300.

Psacharopoulos, G. (1994) "Returns to Investment in Education: A Global Update," *World Development*, 22:9, 1325–1343.

Psacharopoulos, G. (2006) "The Value of Investment in Education: Theory, Evidence, and Policy," *Journal of Education Finance*, 32:2, 113–136.

Rodrigo, G.C. (2001) *Technology, Economic Growth and Crises in East Asia*, Edward Elgar.

Rodríquez, F. and D. Rodrik (2001) "Trade Policy and Economic Growth: A Skeptic's Guide to the Cross-National Evidence," in B. Bernanke and K.S. Rogoff (eds.), *Macroeconomics Annual 2000*, MIT Press, 261–325.

Rodrik, D. (1994) "King Kong Meets Godzilla: The World Bank and *The East Asian Miracle*," in A. Fishlow et al., *Miracle or Design: Lessons from the East Asian Experience*, Overseas Development Council, 13–53.

Rodrik, D. (1999) *The New Global Economy and Developing Countries: Making Openness Work*, Overseas Development Council.

Rodrik, D. (2003) "Introduction: What Do We Learn from Country Narratives?" in D. Rodrik (ed.), *In Search of Prosperity: Analytic Narratives on Economic Growth*, Princeton University Press, 1–19.

Rodrik, D. (2007) *One Economics, Many Recipes: Globalization, Institutions and Economic Growth*, Princeton University Press.

Rodrik, D., A. Subramanian, and F. Trebbi (2004) "Institutions Rule: The Primacy of Institutions over Geography and Integration in Economic Development," *Journal of Economic Growth*, 9:2, 131–165.

Romer, P. (1986) "Increasing Returns and Long-Run Growth," *Journal of Political Economy*, 94:5, 1002–1037.

Romer, P. (1990) "Endogenous Technological Change," *Journal of Political Economy*, 98:5, S71–S102.

Romer, P. (1993) "Two Strategies for Economic Development: Using Ideas and Producing Ideas," in L.H. Summers and S. Shah (eds.), *Proceedings of the World Bank Annual Conference on Development Economics 1992*, The World Bank, 63–91.

Romer, P. (1994) "The Origins of Endogenous Growth," *Journal of Economic Perspectives*, 8:1, 3–22.

Sachs, J. and A. Warner (1995) "Economic Reform and the Process of Global Integration," *Brookings Papers on Economic Activity*, 1, 1–118.

Sato, R. (1964) "The Harrod Domar Model vs. the Neoclassical Growth Model," *Economic Journal*, 74:294, 380–387.

Schultz, T.P. (2002) "Why Governments Should Invest More to Educate Girls," *World Development*, 30:2, 207–225.

Solow, R. (1956) "A Contribution to the Theory of Economic Growth," *Quarterly Journal of Economics*, 70:1, 65–94.

Szirmai, A. (2005) *The Dynamics of Socio-Economic Development*, Cambridge University Press.

Tembon, M. and L. Fort (2008) *Girls' Education in the 21st Century*, World Bank.
Winters, L.A., N. McCulloch, and A. McKay (2004) "Trade Liberalization and Poverty: The Evidence So Far," *Journal of Economic Literature*, 42:1, 72–115.
Wacziarg, R. and K.H. Welch (2008) "Trade Liberalization and Growth: New Evidence," *World Bank Economic Review*, 22:2, 187–231.
World Bank (1993) *The East Asian Miracle*, Oxford University Press.
World Bank (1994) *Adjustment in Africa*, Oxford University Press.
World Bank (1999) *World Development Report 1998/99*, Oxford University Press.

22 International Production and Development

Years ago, I attended a conference on the economies of Latin America that took place just outside the city of San José, Costa Rica. Before the conference began, I took a long walk through the neighborhoods surrounding the conference hotel. As I walked, I passed the factory gates of many foreign corporations that were operating in the area. During the conference, I spoke to a representative of the Costa Rican government. With some passion, she said, "Foreign firms are buying our companies! We are losing ownership of our economy!"

This statement made an impact on me, and on my return to the United States, I pulled an old book off my shelf written in 1987 by John Sheahan. Entitled *Patterns of Development in Latin America*, the book included a chapter on multinational enterprises (MNEs). I glanced through the chapter and came across this statement: "A particularly important concern is that foreign investment may foreclose opportunities for domestic investment and learning by . . . taking over existing domestic firms and eliminating independent national management" (p. 165). If she could have read this passage, I imagined the Costa Rican official would have said, "Exactly!" Or, more precisely, "¡Exactamente!"

And yet, as the years have passed since this conference, Costa Rica has continued to rely on **foreign direct investment** (FDI) as a central part of its development strategy. This was highlighted in the 1990s when the computer chip maker Intel decided to build a plant on the outskirts of San José, near where I had taken my walk. We discussed this plant in Chapter 10. This change in thinking has taken place in many developing countries, with initial dismay over the role of FDI in development given way to grudging acceptance or even to an outright embrace of this mode of international production.

What role does international production (via either contracting or FDI) play in international development? Is it a positive force or a negative force? What would your posture be if you were an economic official in the Costa Rican government? Or in the Ghanaian government? This chapter will help you to address these issues. We begin in the following section by considering how countries become desired destinations for international production and the role of institutions in this process. Next, we characterize the benefits and costs of hosting MNEs from a development perspective. We then describe the various policy stances that a host country can adopt toward inward FDI. Next, we consider the especially important issue of linkages between MNEs and host-country firms. Finally, we consider the issue of transfer pricing and the global institutional framework governing FDI practices and policies. An appendix presents the Organization for Economic Cooperation and Development's Guidelines for MNEs. Throughout the chapter, we explore the link between international production and international economic development illustrated in Figure 1.3 of Chapter 1.

Analytical elements for this chapter:

Countries, *sectors*, *tasks*, *firms*, and *factors*.

ATTRACTING INTERNATIONAL PRODUCTION

Recall from Chapter 1 (Figure 1.2) that FDI inflows are concentrated in high-income countries, with substantially smaller flows going to middle-income countries and almost no flows at all going to low-income countries. For example, in 2008, low-income countries received only 1 percent of global FDI. But even this 1 percent of the 2008 total was highly concentrated. Just three low-income countries – Vietnam, Ghana, and Yemen – received one-half of this 1 percent in 2008. These patterns raise a question, namely, what makes a developing country attractive to MNEs as a potential destination for international production in the form of contracting or FDI?

We know from Chapter 10 and our discussion of the OLI framework that *location advantages* matter for MNE choices. So we can rephrase our question in terms of what types of location advantages matter for developing countries to be able to attract international production. These could include domestic or adjacent markets for market-seeking FDI or particular types of resources for resource-seeking FDI. We also need to recognize, as emphasized by Caves (2007, chapter 9) that, when it comes to developing country locations, there are three distinct patterns of FDI: natural resource or resource-based FDI (e.g., petroleum, mining, rubber), domestic market-serving FDI, and export processing. The case of natural resource FDI is relatively straightforward: the MNE wants access to the resource and the host country government needs to manage this to share in the income for the benefit of the country.[1]

The cases of domestic market-serving and export-processing FDI require a bit more investigation, and it is here that *institutional issues* appear as a relevant factor. Recall that we discussed the role of institutions in growth and development processes in Chapter 21. As it turns out, these considerations can also be relevant for FDI inflows and contracting possibilities. To summarize, a significant number of new studies have demonstrated that institutional quality has a positive effect on FDI inflows. To mention just a few studies, Globerman and Shapiro (2002) found that a measure of good governance (combining a few categories in Table 21.2) matters for FDI inflows. The same was true of democracy, as studied in Li and Resnick (2003). Many institutional indicators were used in a sophisticated statistical analysis by Bénassy-Quéré, Coupet, and Mayer (2007), who also found that institutional quality supports FDI inflows.[2] Finally, measures of corruption are *negatively* related to FDI inflows, as shown by Zhao, Kim, and Du (2003) and others.

There is a particular dimension of institutional quality not emphasized in Chapter 21 that rises to the surface when considering the role of institutions in FDI flows. This is *intellectual property protection.* Recall from Chapter 9 that FDI is concentrated in sectors that are intensive in intellectual property (IP). This is because these firms avoid the contracting mode of foreign market entry due to *dissemination risk.* Actually, we were more specific than this in a box in Chapter 11. There we noted that both *switching* and *volume* effects were relevant. As dissemination risk decreases through increased IP protection, we should see a switch from FDI to contractual modes of entry, particularly that of licensing. In addition to the switching effect, however, there is a *volume effect.* That is, increased IP protection might increase the overall amount of international production through both contractual and FDI modes. Fink and Maskus (2005) found the IP effect on FDI to be largely confined to middle-income countries. But Nunnenkamp and Spatz (2004) found that IP protection does indeed matter for FDI flows across a large sample of countries.

[1] However, there can be perennial issues of corruption and mismanagement associated with natural resource rents. On the management of natural resource rents, see chapter 4 of Caves (2007).

[2] These authors controlled for the fact that institutional quality tends to increase with GDP per capita and captured the contribution of institutional quality independent of these increases.

Another means through which countries can attempt to increase FDI inflows is through bilateral investment treaties (BITs) or regional investment treaties (RITs). Sometimes these are jointly known as international investment agreements (IIAs). BITs are defined by the United Nations Conference on Trade and Development (UNCTAD) as "agreements between two countries for the reciprocal encouragement, promotion and protection of investments in each other's territories by companies based in either country."[3] BITs have grown rapidly over time, from approximately 400 in 1990 to approximately 2,600 in 2008. RITs are generally part of free trade areas (FTAs) or customs unions (CUs), discussed in Chapter 8. The use of BITs and RITs is a way for a host country to signal MNEs from signatory countries that it is committed to maintaining an institutional and legal environment favorable to the MNE operations. We can think of it as a means of enhancing L, or location advantages, in the OLI framework. These arrangements are occasionally criticized for being too favorable to MNEs, but are widely used nevertheless.

BENEFITS AND COSTS

If you were an economic official in the Costa Rican government trying to decide on your posture toward FDI in the development of your country, it might be a good idea to have some sense of *both* the benefits *and* costs that FDI might entail. We will discuss the benefits and costs with the help of Table 22.1. The items we consider are employment and wages, competition, education and training, technology, balance of payments, health and the environment, and culture.

Employment and wages. If a foreign firm engages in FDI in a home-country sector in which there is unemployment, it is possible for this FDI to increase the total number of jobs in that sector. This is a positive employment effect and constitutes a benefit of FDI. Such direct employment benefits can be supplemented by indirect employment benefits when local firms supply the foreign MNE with intermediate products, something we discuss later. It is also possible, in cases of acquisition, for a simple transfer of jobs from local to foreign firms to occur with no net increase in employment. Depending on one's point of view, this might be interpreted as a cost of FDI.

In addition to employment effects, there is accumulating evidence that MNEs often offer higher wages than domestic firms. This has been found in Mexico (Feenstra and Hanson, 1997), a set of African countries (te Velde and Morrissey, 2003), and Indonesia (Sjöholm and Lipsey, 2006), for example. These constitute another potential benefit of FDI.

Competition. If a foreign firm engages in FDI in a home-country sector characterized by imperfect competition, it is possible for the FDI to increase competition in the sector. As you learned in introductory microeconomics, an increase in competition tends to lower prices and increase quantities supplied through the erosion of market power. Because this benefits consumers, this positive competition effect constitutes a benefit of FDI. On the other hand, in cases where the foreign MNE possesses a large

[3] UNCTAD also reported that: "Treaties typically cover the following areas: scope and definition of investment, admission and establishment, national treatment, most-favored-nation treatment, fair and equitable treatment, compensation in the event of expropriation or damage to the investment, guarantees of free transfers of funds, and dispute settlement mechanisms, both state-state and investor-state."

Table 22.1. The benefits and costs of inward FDI

Item	Benefits	Costs
Employment and Wages	Generate direct and indirect increases in employment. Might offer higher wages.	Transfer jobs from home to foreign firms.
Competition	Promote competition by increasing the number of firms in an industry.	Retard competition in cases where the foreign firm has a large amount of market power.
Education and Training	Improve the education and training of host-country workers.	Restrict education and training to expatriate employees. Discriminate against host-country workers.
Technology	Transfer technology from developed to developing countries.	Technology employed might not be appropriate for the host-country economy.
Balance of Payments	Improve the import and export components of the current account. Improve the direct investment component of the capital/financial account.	Worsen the import component of the current account. Worsen the net factor receipt component of the capital/financial account.
Health and the Environment	Employ new technology that is more environmentally sound. Increase incomes and thereby make more resources available for the enforcement of existing environmental regulations.	Increase the amount of pollution and subject workers to unsafe workplaces.
Culture	Introduce progressive aspect of business culture in the areas of organizational development and human resource management.	Increase dominance of urban and Western culture over rural and non-Western culture.

Sources: Adapted from Dunning and Lundan (2008) and Hill (2009)

amount of market power itself compared with the host country firms, FDI could *worsen* competition. This would be a cost of FDI.

Education and Training. As we saw in Chapter 21, the accumulation of human capital via education and training is a crucial component of economic development. It is possible for foreign MNEs to provide education and training to host-country workers that were not available from domestic firms.[4] This provides benefits to the host-country economy as a whole. It is equally possible, however, for the foreign MNE to restrict education and training to its own transplanted employees and to even discriminate against host-country workers. Such discrimination would constitute a cost of FDI to the host country. Dunning and Lundan (2008) summarized the empirical evidence on the education and training issue, reporting that "the accumulated evidence suggests that, while the amount and character of training varies considerably between firms, as a general rule it is fairly narrowly focused on the specific needs of the investing enterprises, rather than on the wider economic and social goals of the countries in

[4] Dunning and Lundan (2008, chapter 13) included this possibility as one of the O, or ownership, advantages of MNEs in the OLI framework. They stated: "One of the key O-advantages which MNEs enjoy... is their ability to train and upgrade human resources, and to motivate their employees. They derive this advantage, in part at least, from their access to different labor market institutions and to their cross-border experiences in human resource management" (p. 444).

which they operate" (p. 445). For this reason, although MNEs probably do make a significant contribution, the overall human resource trajectory of a country remains the responsibility of the country government.

Technology. Many developing countries lack access to the technologies available in developed countries, and acquiring this technology is a key component of the development process.[5] Recall from Chapter 1 that MNEs account for approximately three-fourths of worldwide civilian research and development (R&D). Consequently, hosting MNEs is one way to gain access to that technology. There are two problems, however. First, MNEs will employ the technology that most suits their strategic needs, and these can differ from the development needs of the host country. For example, foreign MNEs might employ processes that are much more capital-intensive than would be desired on the basis of host-country employment considerations. Caves' (2007, chapter 9) relatively extensive review suggests that, although some MNEs adapt their technologies to local environments, this adaptation is not widespread or more than minimal. Second, as we discussed in Chapter 11, MNEs tend to concentrate their R&D in their home bases. That said, there are movements away from this traditional pattern of innovation in MNEs with the emergence of regional laboratories focused on at least the development aspect of R&D, if not applied research. For this reason, there is increasing reason to consider MNEs as potential sources of technology in some cases.

There is a presumption in much of the literature on FDI that MNEs provide positive "spillovers" in the form of technology upgrading to domestic firms in the host country. This line of thinking goes back to Caves (1974), who tested this possibility for Canada and Australia. The evidence of *generalized* technology spillovers, however, is somewhat mixed. A sample of evidence from developing countries is provided in Table 22.2. As can be seen here, most studies do find evidence of positive spillovers. However, as noted by Caves (2007), "demonstrated spillovers occur so as to suggest domestic firms must possess substantial competence before they can sup up spilled technology" (p. 221). This has led to an exploration of domestic preconditions (particularly human capital) that can make positive spillovers more likely.[6]

Balance of Payments. We presented the balance of payments accounts for Mexico in Table 13.2 of Chapter 13 as consisting of the current account and the capital/financial account. The process of FDI can affect a few of the components of both the current and capital/financial accounts. The setting up of a production facility in the host country causes an inflow (positive balance) in the direct investment component of the capital account (item 10) and thus tends to improve the balance of payments. Unless further expansion of the production facility occurs, this initial impact is a one-time-only effect. If the subsidiary experiences positive earnings, some of these earnings will be eventually repatriated to the MNE's home-base country. This causes an outflow (negative balance) on the net income component (item 7) of the current account.

[5] For example, Dunning and Lundan (2008) stated that "It is widely accepted that the ability to create, acquire, learn how to use and effectively deploy technological capacity is one of the key ingredients of economic success in virtually all societies. It is also acknowledged that, together with institutional reform, advances in product, production, information and organizational technology have accounted for much of the economic growth of nations over the past century" (p. 340).

[6] This general conclusion was also reached by Dunning and Lundan (2008, chapter 16). These authors stated that "while the . . . evidence strongly suggests that the benefits from linkages and spillovers should not be underestimated, the . . . evidence confirms that their benefit to the economy as a whole cannot be assumed as a matter of course" (p. 605).

Table 22.2. The potential spillover effects of FDI

Study	Country	Findings
Aitken and Harrison (1999)	Venezuela	Found two effects of FDI on local firms. First, a positive relationship between foreign equity and performance in plants with less than 50 workers. Second, negative spillovers from market-stealing effects. On net, evidence of only a small impact of FDI on plant productivity.
Arnold and Javorcik (2009)	Indonesia	Evidence of positive spillovers due to acquisition and restructuring of domestic firms. Foreign ownership leads to higher productivity and share of skilled workers.
Blalock and Gertler (2008)	Indonesia	Evidence of positive spillovers due to technology transfer to local suppliers and positive externality from these suppliers to other downstream buyers.
Blomström (1986)	Mexico	Evidence of positive spillovers due to increased competition.
Blomström and Persson (1983)	Mexico	Evidence of positive spillovers associated with increased technological efficiency.
Blomström and Sjöholm (1999)	Indonesia	Evidence of positive spillovers due to increased competition restricted to nonexporting, local firms.
Haddad and Harrison (1993)	Morocco	Although the dispersion of productivity levels is narrower in sectors with more foreign firms, no evidence of positive spillovers.
Kohpaiboon (2006)	Thailand	Foreign firms can either positively or negatively affect the productivity of local firms depending on the trade regime.
Kokko (1994)	Mexico	Potential positive spillovers were negatively related to productivity gaps between MNEs and domestic firm and differ among industries.
Kokko, Tansini, and Zejan (1996)	Uruguay	Little evidence of positive spillovers with only a small effect when the technology gap between local and foreign firms is small.
Kugler (2006)	Colombia	Evidence of spillovers to local upstream suppliers through diffusion of generic upstream suppliers.
Liu (2002)	China	Evidence of positive spillover effect on domestic sectors through technology transfers.
Marin and Bell (2006)	Argentina	Evidence of positive spillovers conditional on activity of MNE subsidiaries. Spillover effects depend on the local knowledge creation of subsidiaries.
Wei and Liu (2006)	China	Evidence of positive spillovers.

If the good produced by the MNE is sold domestically and replaces previously imported goods, the FDI will have the effect of making the goods and services trade balance component (item 6) of the current account more positive (less negative). However, the MNE might import a significant amount of intermediate products, and this would tend to make the goods and services trade balance component of the current account less positive (more negative). Finally, if the MNE exports the good it produces, this would tend to make the goods and services trade balance component of the current account more positive (less negative). Clearly, the net effect of all these balance of payments influences would need to be evaluated on a case-by-case basis.

Health and the Environment. Recently, a great deal attention has been focused on the impacts of MNEs on health and the environment. This relates to something known as the **pollution haven hypothesis**, the notion that MNEs locate environmentally damaging production in countries with lax environmental standards. The evidence to date suggests two things.[7] First, it is difficult to detect an overall pattern of FDI consistent with the pollution haven hypothesis. This is because there are so many other factors at play in FDI decisions. Second, though, it is clear that there are individual cases of pollution haven behavior. For example, in resource-extractive industries, certain (not all) MNEs have been grossly negligent. The accompanying box presents a brief discussion of the petroleum industry in the Ecuadorian Amazon region. A similar story applies to the petroleum industry in Nigeria discussed in Chapter 1.

The Petroleum Industry in the Ecuadorian Amazon

In the 1960s, Ecuador opened itself up to oil exploration, and in 1967, the U.S. MNE Texaco discovered the first commercially viable oil reserve in the Amazon region. Along with its local partner, Petroecuador, Texaco began to pump oil in 1972. Texaco was active in this manner until 1992, when its contract with Petroecuador expired. Thereafter, its operations were taken over by Petroecuador itself. Other U.S.-based MNEs operating in this region during the 1970s and 1980s included Occidental Petroleum, ARCO, Unocal, Conoco, and Mobil.

Texaco's operations included 350 wells and 1,000 open waste pits. Estimates vary widely, but it is clear that its operations involved substantial amounts of direct oil spillage and the release of toxic wastewater. Epidemiological studies also vary regarding the health effects of these spills, but there have been allegations of substantial impacts in the areas of cancers, birth defects, and spontaneous abortions. Less arguable are the large-scale dislocations of indigenous peoples (including the Cofan and Huaorani Indians) as a result of the oil exploration and pumping operations. For example, Kane (1996) reported:

> While I was in Toñampare a valve in an oil well near the Napo (River) broke, or was left open, and for two days and a night raw crude streamed into the river – at least 21,000 gallons and perhaps as many as 80,000, creating a slick that stretched from bank to bank for forty miles. Ecuador's downstream neighbors, Peru and Brazil, declared states of emergency, but Petroecuador shrugged off the problem. "It looks much worse than it is," an official said. "The water underneath is perfectly fine." Three weeks later the pipeline itself burst, in the Andean foothills that rise beyond the west bank of the Napo, and spilled another 32,000 gallons into the watershed. (p. 157)

Initially, the growing wrath of Ecuadorian environmentalists and indigenous peoples of Ecuador was directed against Texaco and resulted in the now-famous *Aguinda vs. Texaco* class action lawsuit of 1993. Texaco agreed to engage in some amount of environmental mitigation as a result of this lawsuit, but this was seen as too small a response. Texaco merged with Chevron in 2001, and Chevron consequently inherited this lawsuit. It was not uncommon for Chevron's attorneys to enter into court in Ecuador accompanied by armed guards, given the level of anger against them. Amazingly, at the time of this writing in 2010, the case is still ongoing and offers a sad, cautionary tale of the potential environmental impacts of some MNEs.

Sources: Kane (1996), Kelsh, Morimoto, and Lau (2009), and McAteer and Pulver (2009)

[7] For reviews, see chapter 10 of Dunning and Lundan (2008) and Copeland (2009).

Sometimes, MNEs have utilized production technologies in host countries that were banned in their home countries. For example, Standard Fruit, Dole Fruit, and Chiquita used the worm-killing chemical Dibromochloropropane (DBCP), known under its commercial name Nemagon, on their banana plantations even after its severe health impacts were well known. As a result, they subsequently had to cope with legal actions.[8] All of these cases involve significant costs to the host countries. Despite attention to such costs, it is possible for FDI to have environmental benefits for host countries. For example, MNEs can be involved in the development of new, environmentally friendly production processes and clean-up technologies.

Culture. MNEs serve as conduits of their home countries' national and business cultures. They also sometimes introduce new goods with cultural content into host countries. These activities can further the dominance of urban and Western culture over rural and non-Western culture and, in some developing host countries, exacerbate already existing tensions between these cultural/regional poles. In the case of resource-extraction activities, FDI can result in the dislocation of indigenous peoples. In these ways, FDI can impose significant cultural costs on host countries. More positively, however, MNEs can introduce progressive elements of business culture into their host countries. These might include new practices in the areas of organizational development and human resource management.

One would hope that, by assessing each of the items in Table 22.1, we could make a general statement about the degree to which FDI supports the process of international economic development. It appears, however, that this is not the case. Even some of the best minds that have focused on the issue do not agree on the matter. Consider the following. Rodrik (1999) was relatively *pessimistic* about the role of FDI in development, stating: "Absent hard evidence to the contrary, one dollar worth of FDI is worth no more (and no less) than a dollar of any other kind of investment" (p. 37). UNCTAD (1999) offered a somewhat *less pessimistic* view: "The role of FDI in countries' processes and efforts to meet development objectives can differ greatly across countries, depending on the nature of the economy and the government.... In a globalizing world economy, governments increasingly need to address the challenge of development in an open environment. FDI can play a role in meeting this challenge" (pp. 29 and 49). A somewhat *more enthusiastic* view was offered by Moran (1998): "The direct and indirect benefits from well-constructed FDI projects are substantially greater than commonly assumed, but they do not come easily" (p. 153).[9]

Can FDI generate net benefits for host countries? Yes. Does it always do so? No. The role that FDI plays in international economic development needs to be assessed on a case-by-case basis, with close attention being paid to the country characteristics, firm characteristic and strategy, and the national policy environment. Once these features have been carefully accounted for, we can begin to assess the benefits and costs of the FDI project under consideration. One of the purposes of the OECD Guidelines for MNEs presented in the appendix and discussed later is to tip the balance away from costs and toward benefits.

[8] See *The Economist* (1995), for example. This insecticide was banned in 1979 in the United States because it causes skin diseases, sterility, and birth defects. Despite this, it was used in Central American banana production through the 1980s and, in some cases, through the mid-1990s. Banana workers in Central America began to report many severe symptoms, including anencephaly, a malformation in which conceived fetuses fail to develop brains.

[9] See also chapter 4 of Goldin and Reinert (2007).

POLICY STANCES

As a Costa Rican economic official helping your country to host a foreign MNE, you want to minimize the costs and maximize the benefits of the FDI.[10] Attempts to achieve this are usually made through policy stances toward the MNE. These policies can be grouped into **ownership requirements** and **performance requirements**. Ownership requirements may be absolute, as in the case of foreign firms being excluded from certain sectors on national security grounds. Mexico has done this in its petroleum sector, for example. Alternatively, they may simply limit foreign ownership to a maximum specified amount. For example, China once limited foreign enterprises to joint ventures with Chinese firms in which the foreign firm could own a maximum of 50 percent of the venture.[11]

Performance requirements place controls on the *behavior* of the foreign firm in a number of areas. For example, a host country might require that the MNE maintain a minimum level of locally sourced intermediate inputs. This is known as a *local content requirement.* Other performance requirements can include requirements in the areas of training, technology transfer, exports, local research and development, and the hiring of local managers. These matters are usually settled in negotiations between the host-country government and the foreign MNE. Most East Asian countries have used performance requirements focused on local content and export performance. However, some Latin American countries (e.g., Argentina, Chile, Colombia, Mexico, and Venezuela) have significantly relaxed their performance requirements over time.

Many of the above requirements are also known as **trade-related investment measures** (TRIMs) and are listed in Table 22.3. The Marrakesh Agreement on Trade in Goods (see Chapter 7) included an Agreement on TRIMs, which prohibits some types of TRIMs in the case of goods. These include domestic content, trade balancing, foreign exchange balancing, and domestic sales requirements. Export performance requirements were *not* prohibited. Investment-related policies in services are covered under the General Agreement on Trade in Services (GATS) (again see Chapter 7). Some international economic policy experts are now calling for policies that would go beyond TRIMs to require the abandonment of all policies that discriminate between domestic and foreign firms. Others are critical of the Agreement on TRIMs itself.[12] We take up this issue later in a discussion of institutional considerations.

A number of countries also offer potential MNEs location incentives in the form of tax breaks. These policies often take the form of "customs-free zones" in which tax rates have been lowered. This was the case, for example, for Intel in Costa Rica. It is not clear that these policies are worthwhile in attracting FDI. They can result in excessive bidding wars among host countries and simply become transfers to the MNEs involved.[13]

Another policy stance toward hosting MNEs is to set up an **export processing zone** (EPZ). An EPZ is an area of the host country in which MNEs can locate and in which they

[10] In the case of Intel's new investment in Costa Rica, most of the items in Table 22.1 were benefits rather than costs. Intel was generating new employment and bringing new technology. It went so far as to assist the Costa Rican government in the education and training of future Intel workers. Its exports would generate foreign exchange. One significant potential cost, however, was in the environmental category in the form of toxic industrial waste. The solution to this problem was to re-export this waste back to the United States to be processed by U.S. companies.

[11] Recall the example of Beijing Jeep in Chapter 9.

[12] See, for example, chapter 5 of Lee (2006).

[13] See Hoekman and Saggi (2000).

Table 22.3. Types of trade-related investment measures

Measure	Explanation	Comment
Local content requirement	Requires that a certain amount of local input be used in production.	Prohibited by TRIMs
Trade-balancing requirement	Requires that imports be a certain proportion of exports.	Prohibited by TRIMs
Foreign exchange balancing requirement	Requires that use of foreign exchange for importing be a certain proportion of exports and the foreign exchange brought into the host country by the firm.	Prohibited by TRIMs
Domestic sales requirement	Requires that a proportion of output be sold locally.	Prohibited by TRIMs
Manufacturing requirement	Requires that certain products be manufactured locally.	
Manufacturing restriction	Prohibits the manufacturing of certain products in the host country.	
Export performance requirement	Requires that a certain share of output be exported.	Prohibited or discouraged by many BITs and RITs
Exchange restriction	Limits a firm's access to foreign exchange.	
Technology transfer requirement	Requires that certain technologies be transferred or that certain R&D functions be performed locally.	Prohibited or discouraged by many BITs and RITs
Licensing requirement	Requires that the foreign firm license certain technologies to local firms.	
Remittance restriction	Limits the right of the foreign firm to repatriate profits.	
Local equity requirement	Restricts the amount of a firm's equity that can be held by local investors.	Prohibited or discouraged by many BITs and RITs

Sources: Low and Subramanian (1996) and UNCTAD (2003)

enjoy, in return for exporting most or the whole of their output, favorable treatment in the areas of infrastructure, taxation, tariffs on imported intermediate goods, and labor costs. Caves (2007) noted that EPZs "are simply a device for bundling together many concessions" on the part of a host country (p. 261). EPZs have been a popular policy device and have been used in many countries around the world.[14] Table 22.4 gives a sense of the number and extent of EPZs, with 3,000 of them in existence in 2006. In most cases, EPZs involve relatively labor-intensive, "light" manufacturing, such as textiles, clothing, footwear, and electronics.

A number of studies have tried to assess EPZs from the benefit and cost framework of Table 22.1.[15] These studies show that in many (but not all) cases, the benefits do outweigh the costs. For example, Jayanthakumaran (2003) assessed EPZs in China, Indonesia, Malaysia, the Philippines, South Korea, and Sri Lanka. He concluded that the EPZs were an important source of employment in all six of these countries. Also, in all but the Philippines, the benefits outweighed the costs. In the case of the Philippines, the infrastructure costs of setting up the EPZ were too high for a net positive benefit. In the case of Costa Rica, Jenkins (2006) found that EPZs were very helpful in diversifying the industrial structure of the country and attracting FDI, but there were limitations in the extent to which firms formed linkages to local firms (see later discussion).

[14] See Schrank (2001) and Singa Boyenge (2007).

[15] See, for example, Johansson and Nilsson (1997), Schrank (2001), Jayanthakumaran (2003), and Jenkins (2006).

Table 22.4. Export processing zones

	1975	1986	1997	2002	2006
Number of countries with EPZs	25	47	93	116	130
Number of EPZs	79	176	845	3,000	3,000
Employment (millions)	NA	NA	23	43	66
Employment account for by China (millions)	NA	NA	18	30	40

Source: Singa Boyenge (2007)

It is not clear that the policy measures presented in Table 22.3 can always be counted on to shift the effects of hosting MNEs away from costs and toward benefits.[16] There is, however, accumulating evidence that net benefits can be gained by promoting *linkages* between foreign MNEs and host-country firms. These linkages are also important to securing the success of EPZs. It is therefore worth our while to examine linkage promotion in some detail.

PROMOTING LINKAGES

In Chapter 10, we considered the notion of a global production network (GPN). As we saw there, any MNE needs to decide what part of the GPN to undertake itself and what part to leave to other firms in buyer or supplier relationships. It is possible for MNEs to leave some parts of the upstream components of the GPN to other firms, but choose to buy from local firms in the country in which it is located. This is known as **backward linkages** to domestic suppliers.

Historically, backward linkages have been weak. For example, some time ago Battat, Frank, and Shen (1996) reported that U.S. MNEs operating for export assembly in Northern Mexico (known as *maquiladoras*) sourced only 2 percent of their inputs from Mexican firms. This was of concern from the Mexican point of view because the increased use of local firms as sources of intermediate product would increase their levels of employment and support their technological development. More recently, in the Costa Rican case, Jenkins (2006) demonstrated a reluctance of textile, clothing, and electronics MNEs to form backward linkages within that country. The increased role of MNEs in an economy without significant backward linkages results in what are termed "enclaves" with little connection to the rest of the economy and little contribution beyond direct employment effects. Traditionally, the means to avoid enclave FDI was via the local content requirements discussed in the previous section, but these are no longer allowed for WTO members.

Some new thinking in the area of facilitating backward linkages suggests that local content requirements should be replaced by efforts to support local suppliers in their efforts to secure contracts with foreign MNEs. If a foreign MNE can be induced to source inputs locally rather than importing them, the host country can gain a number of important benefits:

1. Employment can increase because the sourced inputs are new production.
2. The balance of payments can improve because the inputs will no longer be imported.

[16] Balasubramanyam (1991), however, made a case for local content and local equity requirement, and Moran (1998) made a case for export performance requirements.

3. Production technologies can be better adapted to local conditions.
4. The tangible and intangible assets we discussed in Chapter 10 can be, to some degree at least, passed from the foreign MNE to the local, host-country suppliers. Such a transfer can have significant benefits for *both* the foreign MNE *and* the local suppliers because, as we discussed in Chapter 11, local suppliers can coalesce into a spatial cluster that supports innovation and upgrading.[17]

The key policy question for developing countries is how to foster backward linkages between foreign MNEs and potential local suppliers. The linkage promotion process involves many players, including the government, the foreign MNEs, the local suppliers, professional organizations, commercial organizations, and academic institutions. The key role of the government is one of *coordination*, attempting to bridge the "information gaps" among the players. The government can do this in a number of different ways[18]:

1. In the realm of information, attempts can be made to provide a matching service between MNEs and local suppliers. This can be done by inviting the relevant players to linkage promotion forums.
2. In the realm of technology, efforts can be made to provide support in standards formation, materials testing, and patent registration. For example, these have been some of the functions of the Singapore Institute of Standards and Industrial Research. In addition, foreign MNEs can be invited to be involved in programs designed to upgrade local suppliers' technological capabilities.
3. In the realm of human resource development, efforts can be made to provide technical training and managerial training. For example, these have been some of the functions of the Taiwanese China Productivity Center.
4. In the area of finance, obstacles to access on the part of small firms can be removed. For example, this has been one of the functions of the Korean Technology Banking Corporation.

Efforts in these and other areas typically must be coordinated by a lead agency. In the case of Singapore, the Singapore Economic Development Board played this role. As mentioned in the introduction, in the case of Costa Rica, the Costa Rican Investment Board played this role. In the case of Ireland, a National Linkage Program under the direction of the Industrial Development Agency played this role. The Irish case is discussed in the accompanying box.

Fortunately, in recent years, MNEs themselves have developed an interest in forging backward linkages in some countries. For example, Intel, Toyota, and Volvo have developed programs for suppliers in some countries.[19] In some circumstances, then, host-country governments and MNEs can work together to support backward linkages.

[17] This last potential benefit was emphasized by Battat, Frank, and Shen (1996): "Rapid changes in design and technology have made it necessary to make more frequent modifications of inputs at all stages of production. In such cases, subcontracting based on a long-term consultative or networked relationship becomes more desirable.... While price competitiveness is still important, the ability of the supplier to react quickly to the manufacturer's changing design and production needs has often become an even more crucial factor than price. This form of backward linkage is of particular interest to developing countries because it makes the relationship between suppliers of inputs and the company purchasing the inputs more stable than the relationship between suppliers of off-the-shelf goods and the purchasers of such goods. This stability, in turn, helps suppliers to make better planning and technological decisions" (p. 5).

[18] See Battat, Frank, and Shen (1996), chapter 16 of Dunning and Lundan (2008), and UNCTAD (2001).

[19] For the case of Japanese MNEs in Thailand, see Moran (2001). On the Volvo case, see Ivarsson and Alvstam (2005).

Lessons from FDI in Ireland

A friend of mine, who grew up in Ireland in the 1970s, told me that, as a child and teenager, he had one major ambition: to emigrate. Even as of the mid-1980s, Ireland was recognized as a fairly poor country and was plagued with a number of serious difficulties: declining employment, high levels of emigration, and rapidly rising levels of debt. In the 1960s and 1970s, though, Ireland began a process of selectively attracting MNEs through tax holidays. During this time, the country also entered into the European Community (see Chapter 8).

Policy toward MNEs grew even stronger in the 1980s, when a number of government agencies and business incentive programs were created to attract MNEs into particular industrial clusters (e.g., electronics, chemicals, and pharmaceuticals), including in high-technology sectors. These policies proved to be successful, and by the mid-1990s, more than 1,000 foreign-based companies had established manufacturing facilities in the country. Included in these efforts was an EPZ strategy in the form of the Shannon Free Trade Zone (FTZ), which met with great success. Indeed, Buckley and Ruane (2006) noted that "Ireland is unusual in the extent to which it has consistently promoted export-platform inward investment in to the manufacturing sector for over four decades" (p. 1611). By the mid-2000s, MNEs accounted for approximately one-half of manufacturing employment in the country.

The government did not neglect the service sector, however. The positive outcome of the Shannon FTZ inspired the creation of the International Financial Services Center (IFSC) in Dublin in 1987. The establishment of the IFSC was an attempt at urban renewal in which a 75-acre dockside site in the heart of Dublin was converted into an attractive business center. It attracted hundreds of financial services firms. In coordinating efforts to support the IFSC, the Industrial Development Authority of Ireland (IDA Ireland) has played a key role. The government also supported the IFSC with a state-of-the-art telecommunications network and an educated workforce. World Bank data from that time demonstrated that Ireland spent a larger portion of its GDP on education (over 6 percent) than other EU countries except Denmark, Norway, and Sweden. Further, these educational efforts were tailored to emerging clusters, whether in manufacturing or services.

Ireland's economic growth rates during the decade of the 1990s were often on a par with those of East Asia, and in 1998 Ireland was one of the 11 countries of the EU selected for inclusion in the European Monetary Union (EMU). Success in hosting MNEs contributed significantly to these positive changes in the Irish economy. Emigration was no longer the prime goal of talented, young Irish citizens. However, as we discussed in Chapter 19, a real-estate boom and bust contributed to a banking crisis during the 2007–2009 period, severely compromising the Irish development model. Nevertheless, the decades-old, FDI and development policy of Ireland still holds out some lessons for other developing countries.

Sources: Buckley and Ruane (2006) and World Bank (1999)

TRANSFER PRICING

There is a common practice among MNEs that can, in some circumstances, be detrimental to the countries hosting them. This practice is known as **transfer pricing**. Transfer pricing problems arise from the fact that MNEs are global corporations, whereas tax systems are locally defined. MNEs can therefore adjust the *internal* pricing of their intra-firm trade to shift declared profits of subsidiaries to low-tax countries. The goal is to maximize the post-tax profits of the firm.[20]

Consider, for example, a vertically integrated MNE producing copper. Perhaps this MNE mines the copper in an African country and engages in some elementary processing of the ore in that country. The ore is then exported and is further processed in the MNE's home country. This is an example of intra-firm trade, discussed in Chapter 10. The price of the partially processed ore exported out of the African country is therefore an *intra*-firm price. Consequently, the firm can pay an artificially low price for the copper ore in the country, reducing its profits and tax obligations there. Given the administrative and enforcement resources, the African country could require the firm to pay world prices for the ore, but resources in many African countries are very scarce. MNEs also have the option of artificially inflating its costs in the African country. This is as simple as sending employees from the home base to the African country for a holiday and then recording the expenses as a cost.

The solution to the transfer-pricing problem is multifaceted. Dunning and Lundan (2008, chapter 17) provide a good review. Although unilateral policy options exist, "because there is competition for MNE activity between home and host countries, and between different host countries, the opportunities for MNEs to play one nation against another are enhanced without the establishment of supra-national institutions and harmonized inter-governmental action towards (transfer pricing)" (p. 633). Options include international guidelines and codes of conduct, international standardization of invoicing and customs procedures, global tax harmonization, negotiating and concluding international conventions, and the establishment of international arbitration procedures. For many developing countries, however, resources may need to be provided for them to effectively combat transfer-pricing abuses.

GOVERNING INTERNATIONAL PRODUCTION

As we have seen in Chapters 7 and 17, institutions governing international trade and international finance exist in the form of the World Trade Organization (WTO) and the International Monetary Fund (IMF). No such counterpart exists in the realm of international production. Two issues arise here: constraining the policies of host countries toward MNEs and constraining the behavior of the MNEs themselves. In the realm of the former, one organization that has promoted multinational approaches to FDI has been the Paris-based Organization for Economic Cooperation and Development (OECD). OECD-sponsored agreements include the 1961 Code of Liberalization of Capital Movements and the 1976 Declaration of International Investment and Multinational Enterprises. In 1991, the OECD tried to develop a comprehensive set of investment rules but failed.

In 1995, OECD ministers announced the beginning of a second effort, this time to develop a Multilateral Agreement on Investment (MAI). The purpose of the agreement was to liberalize the cross-border flows of FDI. It would have required host countries

[20] For early evidence on the presence of transfer pricing, see Grubert and Mutti (1991) and Bartelsman and Beetsma (2003). Both the United States and United Kingdom governments have investigated and fined selected MNEs for transfer pricing abuses.

to apply "national treatment" to all foreign firms. This would prevent host countries from implementing the ownership and performance requirements discussed earlier in this chapter. However, the OECD consisted at that time of fewer than 30, mostly high-income countries, and was hardly representative of WTO membership.[21] Consequently, despite a 140-page draft text, the hoped-for signing of the MAI in 1998 did not occur.

Despite the efforts by India and Malaysia to oppose the MAI, it would be a mistake to blame its failure on the reluctance of developing countries alone. France, Canada, the European Union, and the United States all advanced exceptions to the MAI draft text. Indeed, these exceptions exceeded the MAI draft text in page length. In addition, labor and environmental groups protested against the absence of standards in the draft MAI.

It is now clear that any further progress in this area should take place under the auspices of the WTO in future multilateral trade negotiations. The WTO possesses a number of advantages over the OECD. First, it has a much more representative membership in comparison to the OECD. Second, it is very experienced in developing and managing complicated negotiations and rules. Third, as discussed in Chapter 7, it has a dispute settlement mechanism already in place. Fourth, some argue that given the close links between trade and investment, the WTO is a natural venue. Fifth, because WTO negotiations include large numbers of issues simultaneously, there is more scope for compromises and tradeoffs between issues. Finally, if WTO members are unable to agree on a new investment framework, the option exists of developing a plurilateral agreement, which only a subset of members would sign.[22]

All of these considerations lead to the conclusion that, ideally, the institutional environment for FDI needs to be addressed by the WTO and its members in future negotiations. Whether this will indeed be the case remains to be seen, however. Although a working group on the issue was established at the 1996 WTO ministerial meeting in Singapore, it was not possible to establish a negotiating group at the 1999 ministerial in Seattle. Work on this issue then, has been confined to the working group. In a detailed review of this issue, Hoekman and Saggi (2000) saw no compelling reason for further negotiations in this area.

The second issue is the multilateral regulation of MNE conduct. Goldin and Reinert (2007, chapter 8) called for *de minimus*, binding constraints on MNE behavior, but this is not on the active international agenda at the moment.[23] A number of guidelines exist, such as the World Bank's Equator Principles, the Extractive Industries Transparency Initiative, and Publish What You Pay. But the most general guidelines are the OECD's Guidelines for Multinational Enterprises listed in the appendix to this chapter. These were developed in 1976, revised in 2000. An assessment of the 2000 revisions by Murray (2001) noted that the guidelines formed a useful complement to the core

[21] *The Economist* (1998) reported at that time that "Few developing countries seemed prepared to sign something they did not help to shape. Instead, the governments of developing countries increasingly see MAI as an exercise in neo-colonialism, designed to give rich-world investors the upper hand" (p. 81).

[22] The Marrakesh Agreement establishing the WTO contains an Annex 4 of plurilateral agreements to which members are not required to adhere. Graham (1996) wrote: "All of the nations that would sign an OECD agreement would presumably also sign such a plurilateral agreement, and some nations not party to the OECD agreement might sign on as well. In such a case, a plurilateral WTO agreement would definitely be preferable to an OECD-only agreement" (p. 104).

[23] These authors stated that "key areas to be addressed are forced labor, corruption, transfer pricing, and health and safety" (p. 238).

labor standards of the International Labor Organization and could serve as a point of reference for groups concerned with MNE behavior. At the time of this writing in 2010, the OECD has launched an effort to re-evaluate and update the guidelines.[24]

CONCLUSION

Imagining yourself as a Costa Rican government official, what do you take from this chapter? Most importantly, you understand that inward FDI into your country can *both* provide benefits *and* impose costs on a host country. These benefits and costs occur in the areas of employment, competition, education and training, technology, balance of payments, health and the environment, and culture. You can potentially manage the investment process through ownership and performance requirements. However, a more effective means of maximizing the benefits of inward FDI might be through the support of domestic suppliers linked to foreign MNEs in long-term relationships. The institutional structure governing the FDI process in the world economy is not well developed. Despite efforts on the part of the OECD to resolve this issue, it is really the WTO that would provide the best location for a multilateral or plurilateral agreement on investment. Such an agreement remains a possible future task for WTO members.

REVIEW EXERCISES

1. What institutional elements do you think would make it more likely for an MNE to locate in a particular country?
2. Table 22.1 lists a set of benefits and costs of hosting foreign MNEs in the areas of employment, competition, education and training, technology, balance of payments, health and the environment, and culture. Are there any additional benefits and costs that you think are important? Are there additional considerations that a host government should address before hosting foreign MNEs?
3. The Agreement on Trade-Related Investment Measures (TRIMs) of the Marrakesh Agreement requires WTO members to phase out local content requirements. Do you think this is a good idea? Why or why not?
4. Should there be multilateral agreements either constraining the behavior of governments toward MNEs or constraining the behavior of the MNEs themselves?

FURTHER READING AND WEB RESOURCES

An encyclopedic coverage of the material addressed in this chapter can be found in part III of Dunning and Lundan (2008), and more concise coverage is given in chapter 9 of Caves (2007). For a selection of articles on the overall topic of international business and government relations, see Grosse (2005). The OECD maintains a website at www.oecd.org. It provides materials on its activities in the area of international investment. The United Nations Conference on Trade and Development (UNCTAD) publishes an annual *World Investment Report*. This is a good place to turn for data on and discussion of FDI in the world economy. Their website is at http://www.unctad.org, and the *World Investment Report* is at http://www.unctad.org/wir/.

[24] The interested reader should consult www.oecd.org to follow progress on this effort.

APPENDIX: OECD GUIDELINES FOR MNES

The Organization for Economic Cooperation and Development (2001) has established the following voluntary guidelines for the operation of MNE. They state that any MNE should:

1. Contribute to economic, social, and environmental progress with a view to achieving sustainable development.
2. Respect the human rights of those affected by their activities consistent with the host government's international obligations and commitments.
3. Encourage local capacity building through close cooperation with the local community, including business interests, as well as developing the enterprise's activities in domestic and foreign markets, consistent with the need for sound commercial practice.
4. Encourage human capital formation, in particular by creating employment opportunities and facilitating training opportunities for employees.
5. Refrain from seeking or accepting exemptions not contemplated in the statutory or regulatory framework related to environmental, health, safety, labor, taxation, financial incentives, or other issues.
6. Support and uphold good corporate governance principles and develop and apply good corporate governance practices.
7. Develop and apply effective self-regulatory practices and management systems that foster a relationship of confidence and mutual trust between enterprises and the societies in which they operate.
8. Promote employee awareness of, and compliance with, company policies through appropriate dissemination of these policies, including through training programs.
9. Refrain from discriminatory or disciplinary action against employees who make bona fide reports to management or, as appropriate, to the competent public authorities, on practices that contravene the law, the Guidelines, or the enterprise's policies.
10. Encourage, where practicable, business partners, including suppliers and subcontractors, to apply principles of corporate conduct compatible with the Guidelines.
11. Abstain from any improper involvement in local political activities.

REFERENCES

Aitken, B.J. and A.E. Harrison (1999) "Do Domestic Firms Benefit from Direct Foreign Investment?" *American Economic Review*, 89:3, 605–618.

Arnold, J.M. and B.S. Javorcik (2009) "Gifted Kids or Pushy Parents? Foreign Direct Investment and Plant Productivity in Indonesia," *Journal of International Economics*, 79:1, 42–53.

Balasubramanyam, V.N. (1991) "Putting TRIMs to Good Use," *World Development*, 19:9, 1215–1224.

Bartelsman, E.J. and R.M.W.J. Beetsma (2003) "Why Pay More? Corporate Tax Avoidance through Transfer Pricing in OECD Countries," *Journal of Public Economics*, 87:9–10, 2225–2252.

Battat, J., I. Frank, and X. Shen (1996) *Suppliers to Multinationals: Linkage Programs to Strengthen Local Companies in Developing Countries*, Foreign Investment Advisory Service, World Bank.

Bénassy-Quéré, A., M. Coupet, and T. Mayer (2007) "Institutional Determinants of Foreign Direct Investment," *World Economy*, 30:5, 764–782.

Blalock, G. and P.J. Gertler (2008) "Welfare Gains from Foreign Direct Investment through Technology Transfer to Local Suppliers," *Journal of International Economics*, 74:2, 402–421.

Blomström, M. (1986) "Foreign Investment and Productive Efficiency: The Case of Mexico," *Journal of Industrial Economics*, 35:1, 97–110.

Blomström, M. and H. Persson (1983) "Foreign Investment and Spillover Efficiency in an Underdeveloped Economy: Evidence from the Mexican Manufacturing Industry," *World Development*, 11:6, 493–501.

Blomström, M. and F. Sjöholm (1999) "Technology Transfer and Spillovers: Does Local Participation with Multinationals Matter?" *European Economic Review*, 43:4–6, 915–923.

Buckley, P.J. and F. Ruane (2006) "Foreign Direct Investment in Ireland: Policy Implications for Emerging Economies," *World Economy*, 29:11, 1611–1628.

Caves, R.E. (1974) "Multinational Firms, Competition, and Productivity in Host-Country Markets," *Economica*, 41:162, 176–193.

Caves, R.S. (2007) *Multinational Enterprises and Economic Analysis*, Cambridge University Press.

Copeland, B.R. (2009) "Pollution Haven Hypothesis," in K.A. Reinert, R.S. Rajan, A.J. Glass, and L.S. Davis (eds.), *The Princeton Encyclopedia of the World Economy*, Princeton University Press, 924–929.

Dunning, J.H. and S.M. Lundan (2008) *Multinational Enterprises and the Global Economy*, Edward Elgar.

The Economist (1995) "The Cost of Bananas," September 16.

The Economist (1998) "The Sinking of the MAI," March 14.

Feenstra, R.C. and G.H. Hanson (1997), "Foreign Direct Investment and Relative Wages: Evidence from Mexico's Maquiladoras," *Journal of International Economics*, 42:3/4, 371–393.

Fink, C. and K.E. Maskus (2005) "Why We Study Intellectual Property Rights and What We Have Learned," in C. Fink and K.E. Maskus (eds.), *Intellectual Property and Development: Lessons from Recent Economic Research*, World Bank, 1–15.

Globerman, S. and D. Shapiro (2002) "Global Foreign Direct Investment Flows: The Role of Government Infrastructure," *World Development*, 30:11, 1899–1919.

Goldin, I. and K.A. Reinert (2007) *Globalization for Development: Trade, Finance, Aid, Migration and Policy*, World Bank.

Graham, E.M. (1996) *Global Corporations and National Governments*, Institute for International Economics.

Grosse, R. (ed.) (2005) *International Business and Government Relations in the 21st Century*, Cambridge University Press.

Grubert, H. and J. Mutti (1991) "Taxes, Tariffs and Transfer Pricing in Multinational Corporate Decision Making," *Review of Economics and Statistics*, 73:2, 285–293.

Haddad, M. and A. Harrison (1993) "Are There Positive Spillovers from Direct Foreign Investment? Evidence from Panel Data for Morocco," *Journal of Development Economics*, 42:1, 51–74.

Hill, C.W.L. (2009) *International Business: Competing in the Global Marketplace*, Irwin McGraw-Hill.

Hoekman, B. and K. Saggi (2000) "Assessing the Case for Extending WTO Disciplines on Investment-Related Policies," *Journal of Economic Integration*, 15:4, 629–653.

Ivarsson, I. and C.G. Alvstam (2005) "Technology Transfer from TNCs to Local Suppliers in Developing Countries: A Study of AB Volvo's Truck and Bus Plants in Brazil, China, India, and Mexico," *World Development*, 33:3, 1325–1344.

Jayanthakumaran, K. (2003) "Benefit-Cost Appraisals of Export Processing Zones: A Survey of the Literature," *Development Policy Review*, 21:1, 51–65.

Jenkins, M. (2006) "Sourcing Patterns of Firms in Export Processing Zones (EPZs): An Empirical Analysis of Firm-Level Determinants," *Journal of Business Research*, 59:3, 331–334.

Johansson, H. and L. Nilsson (1997) "Export Processing Zones as Catalysts," *World Development*, 25:12, 2115–2128.

Kane, J. (1996) *Savages*, Vintage.

Kelsh, M.A., L. Morimoto, and E. Lau (2009) "Cancer Mortality and Oil Production in the Amazon Region of Ecuador, 1990–2005," *International Archive of Occupational and Environmental Health*, 82:3, 381–395.

Kohpaiboon, A. (2006) "Foreign Direct Investment and Technology Spillovers: A Cross-Industry Analysis of Thai Manufacturing," *World Development*, 34:3, 541–556.

Kokko, A. (1994) "Technology, Market Characteristics, and Spillovers," *Journal of Development Economics*, 43:2, 279–293.

Kokko, A., R. Tansini, and M.C. Zehan (1996) "Local Technological Capability and Productivity Spillovers from FDI in the Uruguayan Manufacturing Sector," *Journal of Development Studies*, 32:4, 602–611.

Kugler, M. (2006) "Spillovers from Foreign Direct Investment: Within or between Industries?" *Journal of Development Economics*, 80:2, 444–477.

Lee, Y.S. (2006) *Reclaiming Development in the World Trading System*, Cambridge University Press.

Li, Q. and A. Resnick (2003) "Reversal of Fortunes: Democratic Institutions and Foreign Direct Inflows to Developing Countries," *International Organization*, 57:1, 175–211.

Liu, Z. (2002) "Foreign Direct Investment and Technology Spillover: Evidence from China," *Journal of Comparative Economics*, 30:3, 579–602.

Low, P. and A. Subramanian (1996) "Beyond TRIMs: A Case for Multilateral Action on Investment Rules and Competition Policy?" in W. Martin and L.A. Winters (eds.), *The Uruguay Round and the Developing Countries*, Cambridge University Press, 1996, 380–408.

Marin, A. and M. Bell (2006) "Technology Spillovers from Foreign Direct Investment (FDI): The Active Role of MNC Subsidiaries in Argentina in the 1990s," *Journal of Development Studies*, 42:4, 678–697.

McAteer, E. and S. Pulver (2009) "The Corporate Boomerang: Shareholder Transnational Advocacy Networks Targeting Oil Companies in the Ecuadorian Amazon," *Global Environmental Politics*, 9:1, 1–30.

Moran, T.H. (1998) *Foreign Direct Investment and Development*, Institute for International Economics.

Moran, T.H. (2001) *Parental Supervision: The New Paradigm for Foreign Direct Investment and Development*, Institute for International Economics.

Murray, J. (2001) "A New Phase in the Regulation of Multinational Enterprises: The Role of the OECD," *Industrial Law Journal*, 30:3, 255–270.

Nunnenkamp, P. and J. Spatz (2004) "Intellectual Property Rights and Foreign Direct Investment: A Disaggregated Analysis," *Review of World Economics*, 140:3, 393–414.

Organization for Economic Cooperation and Development (2001) *The OECD Guidelines for Multinational Enterprises: Text, Commentary and Clarifications.*

Rodrik, D. (1999) *The New Global Economy and Developing Countries: Making Openness Work*, Overseas Development Council.

Schrank, A. (2001) "Export Processing Zones: Free Market Islands or Bridges to Structural Transformation?" *Development Policy Review*, 19:2, 223–242.

Sheahan, J. (1987) *Patterns of Development in Latin America*, Princeton University Press.

Singa Boyenge, J.P. (2007) *ILO Database on Export Processing Zones*, International Labor Office.

Sjöholm, F. and R.E. Lipsey (2006) "Foreign Firms and Indonesian Manufacturing Wages: An Analysis with Panel Data," *Economic Development and Cultural Change*, 55:1, 201–221.

te Velde, D.W. and O. Morrissey (2003) "Do Workers in Africa Get a Wage Premium If Employed in Firms Owned by Foreigners?" *Journal of African Economies*, 12:1, 41–73.

United Nations Conference on Trade and Development (1999) *World Investment Report.*

United Nations Conference on Trade and Development (2001) *World Investment Report.*

United Nations Conference on Trade and Development (2003) *Foreign Direct Investment and Performance Requirements: New Evidence from Selected Countries.*

Wei, Y. and X. Liu (2006) "Productivity Spillovers from R&D, Exports and FDI in China's Manufacturing Sector," *Journal of International Business Studies*, 37:4, 544–557.

World Bank (1999) *World Development Report 1998/99*, Washington, DC.

Zhao, J.H., S.H. Kim, and J. Du (2003) "The Impact of Corruption and Transparency on Foreign Direct Investment: An Empirical Analysis," *Management International Review*, 43:1, 41–62.

23 The World Bank

The late 1970s were a calamitous time for the Ghanaian economy: agricultural and industrial output stagnated, budget deficits and inflation rates increased substantially, a fixed exchange rate regime began to generate foreign exchange shortages, and Nigeria expelled one million Ghanaian citizens, sending them back to Ghana.[1] The political situation deteriorated as well. Flight Lieutenant Jerry Rawlings took power in a coup. Despite the military nature of the Rawlings regime, the International Monetary Fund (IMF) and the World Bank began negotiations with it in 1982. These negotiations led to an official recovery and adjustment program that began in 1983. This was the start of a long relationship between Ghana and both the IMF and World Bank, which lasts to this day. In the 1980s, Ghana became known as the World Bank's "star pupil," and Rawlings the father of Ghana's "economic miracle." But if Rawlings was the star pupil, what do we know about the teacher, the World Bank itself?

You have a good understanding of the IMF from reading Chapter 17. The World Bank sits across from the IMF on 19th Street in Washington, DC, housed in an architecturally stunning building with a giant atrium, peaceful café, and flowing water. As we mentioned in Chapters 7 and 17, both institutions grew out of the Bretton Woods Conference held in 1944 in the wake of World War II. In the present chapter, we take up the **World Bank**, or more precisely, the **World Bank Group**, in earnest. We begin in the following section by considering the early history of the World Bank and its administrative structure. We then consider the Bank's infrastructure project lending and poverty reduction lending phases. Next, we consider the shift of the Bank to a policy-based lending phase and the application of this approach to Ghana. Finally, we consider recent modifications to policy-based lending within the Bank under its recent presidents.

Along with the IMF, the World Bank is a controversial institution. Both of these organizations are targets of increasingly disruptive protests during their annual joint meetings by a host of groups dedicated to their "radical reform." I hope that this chapter provides you with a balanced, historical assessment of the Bank that is critical but informed and that it helps you to form your own opinions about this important institution.

> Analytical elements for this chapter:
>
> *Countries*, *currencies*, and *financial assets*.

EARLY HISTORY AND ADMINISTRATIVE STRUCTURE

In 1943, U.S. Treasury Secretary Henry Morgenthau proposed via memorandum a "United Nations Bank for Reconstruction and Development." As in the case of the U.S. proposal for the IMF discussed in Chapter 17, U.S. Treasury official Harry Dexter White was the main author. Some months later, in 1944, the British briefly responded to this proposal, and the two countries entered into the Bretton Woods conference in July of that year ready to discuss the creation of such a Bank. The Bretton Woods conference initially focused on the IMF, but in response to the concerns of countries damaged by

[1] You can view Ghana's difficulties through a growth lens in Figure 23.2 .

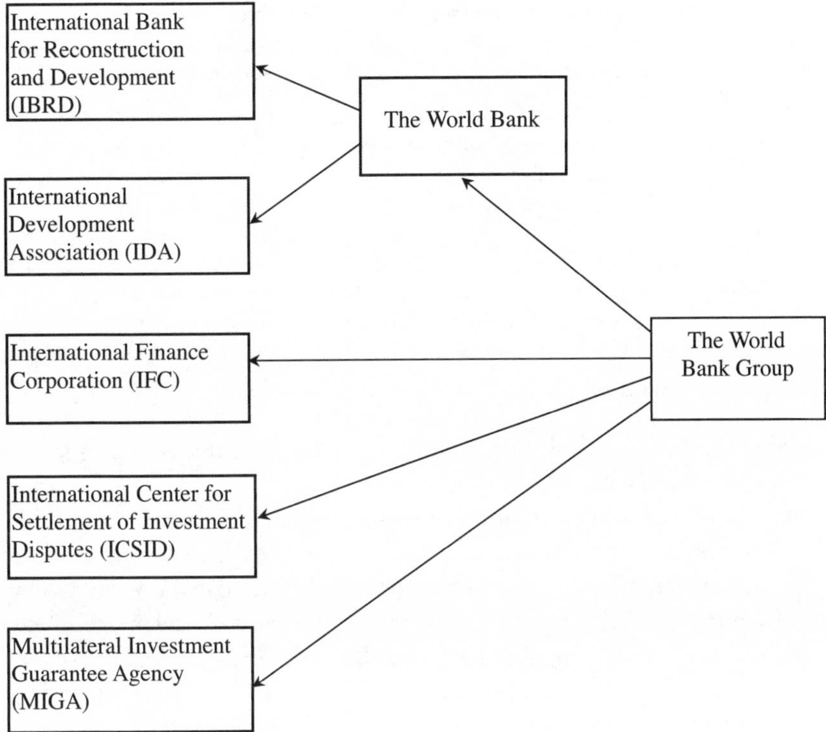

Figure 23.1. The Components of the World Bank Group

the war, as well as of developing countries, a group was finally constituted to work on the Bank under the supervision of John Maynard Keynes.[2]

The discussion at Bretton Woods focused on the relative roles of post-war reconstruction (emphasized by the European countries) and economic development (emphasized by the developing countries). The ensuing Articles of Agreement of the International Bank for Reconstruction and Development (IBRD) left room for both activities, although, as we shall see, attention was first given to reconstruction. The IBRD was the first of five components of what was later to be called the World Bank Group (see Figure 23.1).

IBRD membership is confined to countries that are already members of the IMF. Therefore, *IMF membership is a prerequisite for IBRD membership.* The capital stock of the Bank is based on members' subscription shares, which, in turn, are based on the members' quotas in the IMF. On joining the Bank, a member pays 10 percent of its subscription. The remaining 90 percent is "callable" by the Bank. The funds from which the Bank makes loans come from a number of sources: members' subscription shares, retained earnings on investments, bond issues, and loan repayments.[3] The main

[2] We mentioned Keynes' role in negotiating the IMF agreement in Chapter 17. We also utilized his theory of money demand in the appendices to Chapters 15 and 16. Keynes chaired the Bretton Woods commission that established the World Bank, whereas Harry Dexter White chaired the commission that established the IMF. Skidelsky (2000) noted: "White's aim in making Keynes chairman of the Bank Commission was to neutralize him.... If he could keep him occupied on Bank business, he would have no energy or time left for Fund business. The strategy worked" (p. 349).

[3] The fact that the IBRD borrows on world capital markets is one major characteristic distinguishing it from the IMF. Phillips (2009) noted that "despite the desire of the US administration to create an institution independent

Table 23.1. Administrative structure of the World Bank

Body	Composition	Function
Board of Governors	One Governor and one Alternate Governor for each member	Meets annually; highest decision-making body
Executive Board	25 Executive Directors plus President	Day-to-day operations; approve loans and bond issues
President	Traditionally U.S. citizen	Chair of Executive Board; responsible for staffing and general business
Vice President		Assists President
Advisor Council	Appointed by Board of Governors	Advises on general policy matters
Staff	Citizens of members	Run departments of Bank

Source: www.worldbank.org

source of funds, however, is bond issues. IBRD bonds achieved a "triple A" rating in the mid-1950s and have held this rating ever since.

The World Bank's organization and management are summarized in Table 23.1. As with the IMF, the Bank's major decision-making body is its Board of Governors, to which each member appoints a Governor and an Alternate Governor. An Executive Board, composed of 25 Executive Directors and the Bank President, conducts the day-to-day business of the Bank. Five Bank members with the largest capital shares appoint five of the Directors (France, Germany, Japan, the United Kingdom, and the United States). Governors representing various groups of other countries elect the remaining Directors. The President chairs the Executive Board and is ultimately subject to its control. The President has always been a U.S. citizen appointed by the executive branch of the U.S. government. A list of World Bank Presidents is presented in Table 23.2.[4] Recall from Chapter 17 that the Executive Director of the IMF has traditionally been a European. In staffing these two positions, then, the major Bretton Woods actors ensured their subsequent control of the Bretton Woods institutions (BWIs).

The World Bank has a plethora of Vice Presidents. These are structured around regions (Africa, East Asia and Pacific, Europe and Central Asia, Latin America and the Caribbean, Middle East and North Africa, South Asia), networks (financial and private sector development, human development, operations policy and country services, poverty reduction and economic management, and sustainable development), and a host of functions (e.g., external relations and development economics). Finally, the World Bank has over 10,000 staff members who work both in the head office in Washington, DC, as well as in over 100 country offices around the world.[5]

The IBRD opened in 1946 with an initial subscription capitalization of $10 billion.[6] The balance between reconstruction and development tilted quickly toward

of Wall Street, in the end Wall Street had to get involved and the first years of the new institution were preoccupied with persuading private lenders to support it" (p. 17).

[4] Mason and Asher (1973) noted that "once it was conceded that the president should be a US national, the task of finding a candidate acceptable at the highest levels of US government and in the US financial community inevitably devolved upon the executive branch of the US government" (p. 89). Paul Wolfensohn changed his citizenship from Australia to the United States in the hope of eventually becoming World Bank President. He succeeded.

[5] The number of World Bank staff often raises eyebrows. For example, in 2009, the World Bank's staff numbered just over 10,000, significantly above that of the IMF (2,500). But by way of comparison, its staffing level is less than that of the State of Wyoming in the United States (12,600 in 2009), a state with a population of only one half million.

[6] Keynes had died two months earlier.

Table 23.2. World Bank Presidents

President	Term	Comments
Eugene Meyer	1946	Financier and *Washington Post* publisher who only served six months as President.
John McCloy	1947–1949	Lawyer, banker, and member of the U.S. foreign policy establishment.
Eugene Black	1949–1963	Financier who served a very long term. During his tenure, the Bank became known as "Black's Bank."
George Woods	1963–1968	Financier who brought the Bank into the modern era, particularly with an increased use of economic analysis.
Robert McNamara	1968–1981	Industrialist and controversial U.S. Secretary of Defense during the Vietnam War who was responsible for a major reorganization and for a focus on policy-based lending.
Alden Clausen	1981–1986	Noted banker who introduced a new management committee into the Bank organization and changed its focus to policy-based lending.
Barber Conable	1986–1991	U.S. politician who increased funding for the Bank and leveraged Clausen's management committee into an advisory role.
Lewis Preston	1991–1995	Financier who emphasized the role of the private sector and established the Office of the Managing Director but was forced to resign due to ill health.
James Wolfensohn	1995–2005	Olympic fencer, concert cellist, and financier who was seen as either a transformational or polarizing leader. Originally an Australian citizen.
Paul Wolfowitz	2005–2007	Controversial figure who quickly became embroiled in conflicts with Bank staff and was forced to resign over preferential treatment given to a Bank staffer who was also a paramour.
Robert Zoellick	2007–2012	Capable lawyer and diplomat with substantial international trade experience.

Sources: Ayres (1983), Mason and Asher (1973), and Phillips (2009)

reconstruction. The first set of loans went to France, the Netherlands, Denmark, and Luxembourg. These loans were funded by the United States and were used primarily to purchase U.S. exports. The tilt toward reconstruction was soon offset by the introduction of the U.S. Marshall Plan and European Recovery Program, which surpassed the resources of the World Bank and IMF.[7] Subsequent to these programs, the IBRD made loans to Chile, Mexico, and Brazil. The Bank's first bond issue in 1947 quickly traded at a premium over the offer price. The IBRD was on its way to a respectable position in U.S. and world capital markets. In 1959, the Bank's subscription capital more than doubled to US$21 billion and currently stands at approximately US$275 billion.[8]

In 1956, the IBRD Executive Directors created the International Finance Corporation (IFC). This action followed nearly five years of discussion. In 1960, the Executive Directors followed up by creating the International Development Association (IDA). These two organizations became the second and third components of the World Bank Group

[7] Recall our discussion of this in Chapter 17.

[8] This was increased from US$190 billion in 2010. With regard to the IBRD's borrowing on capital markets, Gilbert and Vines (2009) noted that "the bank is able to borrow funds at rates lower than the London interbank offered rate because countries are reluctant to default on loans from an international institution, because the bank is able to provide additional lending to prevent default arising from inability to pay, and also because it has a buffer of 'callable capital' – money that member countries have an obligation to contribute if the bank were ever to get into financial difficulties" (p. 1174).

(see Figure 23.1). Importantly (and unfortunately from the standpoint of countries with small Bank shares), these institutions were not created via a process of international consultation as in the case of the IMF and IBRD.

The IFC is very different from the IBRD. IBRD loans require guarantee of repayment by borrowing country governments. This is not the case for the IFC, whose purpose is to encourage productive *private* enterprise in less developed countries, supplementing the activities of the IBRD. The IFC has its own staff, although some of these individuals also hold positions in the Bank. Membership in the IFC is contingent on membership in the Bank and, therefore, on membership in the IMF. Initially, the IFC encountered difficulties because, despite being limited to private projects, it was excluded from equity investments. This stipulation was later relaxed with an equity ceiling of 25 percent.[9]

The IDA can be seen as a "soft loan" version of the IBRD. The IDA and IBRD share staff and officers and together comprise what has come to be known as the World Bank (see Figure 23.1). Indeed, the IDA is often called a "fiction" because it is really a special fund or "window" of the World Bank. The official purpose of the IDA is to promote economic development and raise living standards by providing loans on terms that are significantly more flexible than the IBRD. More specifically, the IDA provides no-interest loans for long time periods (35–40 years) with significant grace periods (10 years).[10] In recent years, it has also provided grants. Unlike the IBRD, the IDA is primarily dependent on contributions from high-income member countries.

In 1966, the fourth member of the World Bank Group was added (see Figure 23.1). The International Center for Settlement of Investment Disputes (ICSID) provides arbitration between foreign investors and host-country governments. In previous years, the Bank had been called on to mediate in such disputes, and Bank officials thought that the presence and operation of the ICSID would support the flow of FDI into developing countries. The Administrative Council of the ICSID is chaired by the President of the World Bank and meets annually. Recall from Chapter 22 that many developing countries have concluded bilateral investment treaties (BITs) with other countries. Many of these BITs explicitly include advance consents to utilize the ICSID in the case of disputes. So do some preferential trade agreements (PTAs) with investment components, such as NAFTA and Mercosur.

In 1988, the final member of the World Bank Group was introduced. This was the Multilateral Investment Guarantee Agency (MIGA) (again, see Figure 23.1). The purpose of MIGA is to encourage the flow of FDI to developing countries, a process we analyzed in Chapter 22. To support this aim, MIGA engages in three kinds of activities. First, it issues guarantees against *noncommercial* risks in recipient member countries. Specifically, MIGA insures against transfer restriction, expropriation, breach of contract, and war and civil disturbance. Second, it engages in investment marketing through capacity building, information dissemination, and investment facilitation. Third, it provides a host of legal services to World Bank member countries to support

[9] In the 1990s, there was an effort to merge the IBRD and the IFC, but it was largely unsuccessful. Phillips (2009) noted that "The two institutions differ in objectives, culture and working methods. The IFC is impatient with the Bank's consensus-driven and academic style, and skeptical of the Bank's ability to promote the private sector. . . . On its side, the Bank stereotypes the IFC as narrow dealmakers" (p. 85). Here, Phillips uses the term "Bank" to refer to both the IBRD and IDA.

[10] As stated by Mason and Asher (1973): "Prior to the establishment of the IDA a number of poor countries to which the Bank had loaned extensively were considered to have about reached the limits of their ability to absorb and service foreign loans on Bank terms" (p. 117).

FDI. In this last function, MIGA engages in activities somewhat similar to that of the ICSID.[11]

With a current subscription capitalization of approximately $275 billion and over 10,000 staff, the World Bank Group has become a powerful institution in the world economy. Its main purpose is to productively transfer resources to its developing country members to enhance economic and human development. Given its role in development finance and its promotion of FDI and trade liberalization, it is fair to say that the World Bank is involved in all four of our windows on the world economy (see Figure 1.4 in Chapter 1), trying to promote positive linkages among them. The rest of this chapter is dedicated to your understanding of the history of the Bank's policies and the way it has attempted to influence development processes around the globe.

Infrastructure Project Lending and Poverty Alleviation Phases

In its early years, the IBRD directed its efforts toward large-scale infrastructure projects. This could be called its *infrastructure project lending phase.* The projects funded by the Bank included ports, railways, flood-control, power plants, roads, telecommunications facilities, and dams. Additionally, project lending was often accompanied by "program lending" (or "nonproject lending"), which helped to finance the importation of intermediate products necessary for infrastructure projects. Missing, however, was any significant lending in the social realm, such as for education, health, agricultural development, or urban planning. Some observers attributed this lack of attention to the social realm to a belief that large-scale infrastructure was a prerequisite for development, whereas others attributed it to a reluctance to disturb the capital markets with social-realm lending and, thereby, compromise the Bank's triple-A rating. There was also the observation on the part of the Bank that the large capital investments would be unlikely to be made by private capital, so the Bank should fill in the gap.

The project-lending phase of the Bank's operations was tempered to some extent in the 1960s. Subsequent to severe droughts in South Asia, the Bank began to pay more attention to agriculture in cooperation with the United Nations Food and Agriculture Organization (FAO). It even began to venture into education in cooperation with the United Nations Educational, Scientific and Cultural Organization (UNESCO). Nevertheless, "between fiscal years 1961 and 1965, 76.8 percent of all Bank lending was for electric power or transportation. Only 6 percent was for agricultural development, and a paltry 1 percent for social service investment" (Ayres, 1983, pp. 2–3).

In 1968, Robert McNamara took over as World Bank President, a position he held until 1981. The McNamara presidency coincided with a second phase for the World Bank, one we can call the *poverty alleviation phase.* McNamara gave a now-famous speech at the 1973 Board of Governors meeting in Kenya on this topic. The poverty alleviation phase was characterized by a focus on the eradication of absolute poverty (defined in terms of minimum incomes) through rural and urban development.[12] Within the Bank, these new ideas were operationalized via the concept of *redistribution*

[11] See Shihata (2009) for a comparison of MIGA and ICSID.

[12] Phillips (2009) commented on McNamara as follows: "McNamara is generally thought to have been the most successful president in terms of building organizational effectiveness. He combined a keen mind with rigorous attention to detail. . . . Despite his high-level background as US Defense Secretary and head of the Ford Motor Company, McNamara was also quite ascetic – he traveled economy class and tended to maintain a relatively low profile in his dealings with staff and the outside world, which built respect and trust, conditions needed in a transformational leader" (pp. 269–270).

with growth. This idea called for the harnessing of *new* sources of income to help the poor. It avoided any redistribution of *existing* incomes and assets. For example, World Bank projects did not address inequitable patterns of land ownership. In this sense, it was quite conservative and, in instances where asset redistribution was crucial to development, ineffectual.

In an important way, the redistribution with growth concept has persisted at the Bank to the present, although now it is called *pro-poor growth*, a concept we discussed in Chapter 20. For example, the World Bank used the concept of shared growth to analyze East Asian economies (World Bank, 1993). And in this case, too, it ignored the important role of asset distribution in the form of land and human capital in explaining East Asian success.[13] Nevertheless, at the time, the redistribution with growth concept did significantly affect patterns of Bank lending.

During the poverty alleviation phase, lending increased dramatically. World Bank staff increased, as did the proportion of the staff from developing countries. Subscription capital increased to $27 billion in 1971. Perhaps most importantly, especially after 1973, lending was channeled in new directions. Agriculture and rural development, education, health, and urban development all took on increasing importance, and none of these changes appeared to hurt the financial position of the Bank vis-à-vis the capital markets. In the case of rural development, the notion of "projects" changed, moving toward what was called *integrated rural development*.[14]

Integrated rural development involved constellations of activities focused on targeted regions of member countries. These activities included agricultural credit, roads, agricultural support services, irrigation, rural education, agricultural research and extension, and social services such as health clinics. The goal was to increase the productivity of the rural poor, but the targeted population was the small-scale, owner-operator farmer. Lending for integrated rural development had beneficial effects on these small-scale farmers, but ignored those who became known as "the poorest of the poor," namely, the rural landless agricultural workers.

Despite some limitations to alleviating absolute poverty among the landless, the integrated rural development strategy was a significant change from Bank agricultural lending under the infrastructure project-lending phase, which had primarily benefited the owners of large farms. To some development policy analysts (e.g., Paarlberg and Lipton, 1991), it is a strategy unfortunately absent from subsequent Bank lending. Indeed, Bank lending in the area of agriculture fell from approximately 20 percent of total lending in 1986 to only 4 percent in 2001, rising to just over 7 percent in 2007.[15] That said, the Bank subsequently did take some interest in land redistribution issues, as discussed in the accompanying box.

Land Redistribution in Brazil

In 1997, the World Bank made an interesting announcement. For the first time in a half-century of operations in Brazil, it had approved a US$90 million loan to support land reform. The project, *Cédula da Terra*, was aimed at 15,000 poor and landless farmers

[13] See, for example, Adelman (1980) and Rodrik (1994).
[14] See chapter 5 of Ayres (1983).
[15] See chapter 6 of Phillips (2009), for example. Phillips noted, however, that not all integrated rural development lending was effective.

in the northeastern states of the country. In announcing the loan, the Bank stated that: "The problems associated with Brazil's land tenure are one of the most important issues affecting rural poverty in the country." Most important, indeed. Brazil has one of the most highly skewed land distributions in the world. At the time, it was estimated that the top 5 percent of farms by size accounted for 70 percent of arable land, whereas the bottom 50 percent accounted for only 2 percent of arable land. The country had approximately 5 million landless peasants.

Embracing land reform was a serious break from World Bank traditions. This break was made possible by the fact that the *Cédula* project was "market-based." This term refers to a process in which landless peasants take out a loan, begin a negotiating process with landowners, and then purchase the land on the "open market." According to the World Bank, these transactions were to be facilitated by freely organized, local associations of landless peasants. There is evidence, however, that these associations were actually strongly influenced by state governments, local politicians, and even the landowners themselves. Consequently, prices paid by landless peasants reflected the peasants' weak bargaining position.

An independent assessment of the program commissioned by the Brazilian government found that almost one-third of the participating peasants were unaware that they had taken out a loan. One critic, Schwartzman (2000), claimed: "This is in reality not a 'market-based' land reform project at all, but a land reform project that devolves responsibility for land reform from the federal government to state governments – precisely those more susceptible to pressure and manipulation of local and regional elites."

Despite such criticisms, the World Bank pressed on with its market-based approach to land reform. In its own assessment, "First experiences confirm the expectation that beneficiaries are well capable of participating proactively in the project. Initial indications of impact in terms of family income and productivity are also highly encouraging." In late 2000, the Bank announced a continuation of the *Cédula* project in a second phase, supported by a US$200 million loan.

In 2001, the World Bank replaced the *Cédula* project with the *Crédito Funiário* project, jointly funded with the Brazilian government. This project still attempted to maintain community-level involvement, including that of agricultural worker organizations. According to the Bank, the *Cédula* and *Crédito Funiário* projects "demonstrate the viability of a large-scale community-based approach to land redistribution."

Sources: Childress and Muñoz (2008), Deininger and Binswanger (1999), Lindsay (2000), and Schwartzman (2000)

Under its poverty alleviation phase, the Bank also began to recognize the growing importance of urban areas in developing countries and, consequently, began to focus on urban poverty. The important areas of lending were affordable housing for the poor, small-scale enterprises, water supply, sewerage, transportation, and community services (e.g., health clinics and schools). The Bank has maintained an active loan portfolio in urban development up to the present, with poverty alleviation being one of many thematic areas within this lending category.

POLICY-BASED LENDING

During the late 1970s, at the same time that Flight Lieutenant Jerry J. Rawlings was establishing his control over Ghana, an important change was taking place at the

World Bank. As we mentioned previously, the World Bank President is traditionally a U.S. citizen appointed by the executive branch of the U.S. government. In 1981, the Reagan administration entered into office in the United States and replaced McNamara with A.W. Clausen, a banking executive. The Reagan administration took a dim view of the poverty alleviation phase of World Bank lending and, as the largest Bank donor, began to demand a change. With Clausen at the helm, the World Bank undertook a significant adjustment in its lending. In 1982, the year Bank negotiations began with Ghana, Clausen stated,[16]

> The World Bank . . . will remain a bank. And a very sound and prudent bank. It is not in the business of redistributing wealth from one set of countries to another set of countries. It is not the Robin Hood of the international financial set, nor the United Way of the development community. The World Bank is a hard headed, unsentimental institution that takes a very pragmatic . . . view of what it is trying to do.

This statement is inaccurate in its allegation that the goal of the Bank during its poverty alleviation phase was to redistribute wealth, but it captures well the sentiment of the change in Bank lending that took place.[17] Clausen introduced what has been called the *policy-based lending phase* of the Bank, which more or less persists up the present time. This third phase of Bank lending involved structural adjustment lending and policy conditionality. We consider each in turn.

Structural adjustment lending (SAL) began in 1980 under McNamara's presidency. It involved *nonproject* lending to support adjustment in the face of balance of payments and other macroeconomic difficulties.[18] In the words of an early SAL advocate:

> Structural adjustment lending is intended to assist governments to adopt necessary, though often politically difficult, policy and institutional reforms designed to improve the efficiency of resource use. By focusing on the policy and institutional reforms required to correct distortions in the pattern of incentives and to adapt each economy to the changed international price structure and trading opportunities, structural adjustment lending also helps create a more appropriate environment for the Bank's project lending. In this way, the two forms of assistance are complementary, not alternatives. (Stern, 1983, p. 89)

The Bank's SAL became controversial for a number of reasons. First, SAL began to encroach on the work of the IMF. Some argued that, in contrast to the IMF's fundamentally short-term and macroeconomic focus, the Bank's SAL had a medium-term and microeconomic focus. Others argued that this was too simplistic and that the real issue was in the different capabilities of the two institutions.[19] The potential for conflict between the two Bretton Woods institutions came to a head in 1988. The Bank approved

[16] Address to the Yomiuri International Economic Society, Tokyo. Quoted in Ayres (1983), p. 236. Phillips (2009) noted that "With Ronald Reagan came an ideology that viewed the Bank as an organ of global welfare, suspected of advancing the interests of socialism, and of being itself a typically incompetent public sector institution" (p. 33).

[17] Mosley, Harrigan, and Toye (1995) stated that "During the Clausen Presidency . . . , the McNamara interpretation of the world was largely swept aside"(pp. 23–24).

[18] We consider the economics of structural adjustment in some detail in Chapter 24.

[19] For example, Stern (1983) wrote that "although the Fund is effectively overseeing the management of the principal macroeconomic aggregates, it lacks the functional and sectoral specialists able to analyze in depth the long-term development implications of alternative macroeconomic strategies. Nor does the Fund have the frequent staff-government contacts afforded the Bank through its economic and sector missions and its extensive project work" (p. 106).

a large SAL package to Argentina in the absence of an agreement between this country and the IMF. This conflict led to a *concordat* or joint memorandum in 1989 delineating Bank and Fund roles.[20]

The second controversy over SAL related to bargaining over **conditionality**. Conditionality ties Bank lending to prescribed policy changes on the part of the recipient government. In actuality, World Bank loans always carried conditions. The change that occurred in the 1980s was that these conditions were broadened from the sectoral level to the macroeconomic level. As we discussed in Chapter 17, the IMF also imposes conditions on its loans. In contrast to IMF conditionality, Bank conditionality tends to be substantially more extensive. There were valid claims that the Bank demonstrated an inability to set priorities in its conditionality, with some loan agreements involving a hundred or more conditions. There also arose the *time-inconsistency problem*, in which loans were delivered based on conditionality pledges that were later not honored, leading to a complex, repeated bargaining game between the Bank and borrowing countries.[21]

Some observers have alleged that those countries in greatest need of SAL support were in the weakest bargaining position vis-à-vis the Bank and, therefore, accepted the greatest amount of requisite policy changes. However, the countries in greatest need of SAL were not necessarily those with the greatest need of policy reform because the need for support can be set off by changes in global economic conditions (e.g., export price declines) rather than by bad policies. Consequently, policy reform can be concentrated where it is not really needed.[22] There was the related issue of donor capture of the process, particularly in the case of the United States. For example, Kilby (2009) has presented evidence that conditionality has been imposed most strongly on recipient countries not aligned with the United States on foreign policy issues.[23]

A third concern was that the growth of SAL has come at the expense of rural development (e.g., Paarlberg and Lipton, 1991). An often-quoted fact is that approximately three-fourths of the world's poor people reside in rural areas. However, as mentioned above, during the SAL era, there was a *decline* in Bank lending for rural development. Consequently, the Bank's expertise and staffing in the areas of agriculture and rural development diminished. Ironically, the 2008 *World Development Report* of the Bank concluded that the rural sector was crucial for poverty alleviation. But as a result of the previous decades of neglect, the Bank was not in a position to do much about this.

A final criticism of the SAL program was that it tended to hurt the poor. This argument was bolstered by research sponsored by the United Nations Children's Fund (UNICEF) calling for "adjustment with a human face" or an attempt to offset adjustment's effects on the poor.[24] As a result of these and other critiques, the Bank began to pay attention to the effect of SAL and conditionality on the poor. Nevertheless, it

[20] One can also argue that the structural adjustment and enhanced structural adjustment facilities of the IMF encroached on the Bank's IDA. This point was made by Polak (1994). Polak offered a detailed analysis of the Bank-Fund conflict over Argentina, as well as a similar incident over Turkey.

[21] Later the Bank tried to address the time-inconsistency problem through a performance-based measure known as the Country Policy and Institutional Assessment (CPIA) formula. Unfortunately, the World Bank's Independent Evaluation Group later had harsh criticism of the CPIA. See World Bank (2010).

[22] This point was made by Mosley, Harrigan, and Toye (1995).

[23] For related studies on the effects of donor behavior in World Bank lending, see Dreher, Sturm, and Vreeland (2009) and Flores and Nooruddin (2009).

[24] See Cornia, Jolly, and Stewart (1987) and Stewart (1995).

would be an understatement to say that the two sides of this debate tended to talk past one another.

During the 1980s, the policy thinking of the Bank and Fund began to converge to a common set of conditions. As described in the accompanying box, these policy components became known in economic and international policy communities as the **Washington Consensus.** The Washington Consensus became intimately associated with the policy-based lending phase of the Bank and has been the subject of a great deal of controversy over its appropriateness that continues to this day.

The Washington Consensus

In 1990, John Williamson of the Institute for International Economics introduced a new term into the international economic policy lexicon. The new term was *Washington Consensus.* At the time, he was referring to the "lowest common denominator" of policy advice being offered by the World Bank and the IMF. According to Williamson, this common denominator consisted of 10 policy components:

1. Fiscal discipline
2. A redirection of government expenditures to primary health care, primary education, and infrastructure
3. Tax reform
4. Financial and interest rate liberalization
5. Competitive exchange rate
6. Trade liberalization
7. Liberalization of foreign direct investment
8. Privatization
9. Deregulation
10. Secure property rights

Since 1990, the term *Washington Consensus* has taken on a slightly different meaning. It has come to stand for "market fundamentalism," "neoliberal obsession," or "global laissez-faire." It has also become the target of many participants in the anti-globalization movement demonstrating at the annual Bank-Fund meetings, as well as of many in the global, nongovernmental organization community. Interestingly, Williamson himself is in disagreement with "market fundamentalism," stating "I would not subscribe to the view that such policies offer an effective agenda for reducing poverty." What, then, is Williamson's position?

First, Williamson now repudiates the financial and interest rate liberalization component included in the preceding list, recognizing that such liberalization can contribute to financial instability (see Chapters 18 and 24). Second, Williamson is opposed to the across-the-board liberalization of capital accounts. Third, Williamson is opposed to both the purely flexible exchange rate regimes and to currency boards, both (intriguingly) often advocated by supporters of "market fundamentalism." Instead, he supports exchange rate target zones discussed in the appendix to Chapter 18.

Fourth, with regard to the components of privatization and deregulation, his policy proposals are rather nuanced. He only favors privatization if it is carried out in a manner that prevents the transfer of formerly state-owned enterprises to a narrow group of elites, and he is indeed in favor of many types of government regulation. He only calls for the deregulation of entry and exit barriers, not the "rollback of the state" called for by many market fundamentalists.

As time went on, Washington Consensus thinking began to move into what were known as "second-generation reforms." Although the lists here varied, Rodrik (2007) identified 10 further elements: corporate governance, anticorruption, flexible labor markets, adherence to World Trade Organization disciplines, adherence to international financial codes and standards, capital account liberalization, nonintermediate exchange rate regimes (fixed or floating but not adjustable), independent central banks, social safety nets, and targeted poverty reduction. Thus, with the addition of these second-generation reforms, the to-do list for World Bank borrowers tended to double in size.

To put it mildly, doubts about the Washington Consensus quickly arose (e.g., Naím, 2000). It would be fair to say that many development economists (and some international economists) found it to be lacking as a development strategy. Even among international economists, there is disagreement about its appropriateness as a guide to effective policy. This became apparent when some countries such as China, Vietnam, and Bangladesh began to achieve substantial poverty reduction without having ticked off many of the boxes on the Washington Consensus list. For example, one World Bank official commented to me, "Our two new stars (China and Vietnam) are both communist dictatorships." That is something for Washington Consensus advocates to ponder.

Sources: Naím (2000), Rodrik (2007), and Williamson (1990, 2000)

The policy-based lending phase of the Bank was tempered by subsequent events, but never fully disappeared. From 1988 to 2005, the average number of conditions on Bank loans declined from approximately 55 to 10, but adjustment lending has continued to comprise approximately 30 percent of Bank lending since 2000.[25] That said, significant changes did occur with the 1995–2005 Wolfensohn presidency, discussed later.

CHALLENGES AND RESPONSES

The 1990s brought criticism of the World Bank from many different directions. Phillips (2009) captured the Bank's dilemma as follows:

> Liberal/left opposition groups wanted to curb the power of a crypto-capitalist institution and neo-conservative groups wanted to limit the power of a crypto-socialist institution. The liberal groups mounted their opposition on two principal grounds – the Bank's claimed inadequate attention to environmental issues, especially in large infrastructure projects, and its increasing focus on macro-economic reform through structural adjustment programs that, opponents claimed, undermined the interests of the recipient economies. The neo-conservative interests (opposed) public sector interventions in markets. (p. 25)

Let's consider some of these opposing critiques, beginning with the environment.

In 1973, Mason and Asher stated that "the IBRD has not . . . paid enough attention to the ecological or environmental effects of the projects it has financed" (p. 259). In retrospect, this was a prophetic statement. The environmental issue rose to the surface 10 years later. Bruce Rich, then an attorney with the Natural Resources Defense Council (later with the Environmental Defense Fund), launched an attack on the World Bank supported Polonoroeste project in Brazil. The term *Polonoroeste* stands for

[25] See chapter 6 of Phillips (2009). Structural adjustment lending was renamed development policy loans (DPL). For the Bank's own assessment of this era of lending, see World Bank (2005).

"North-West Regional Development Pole." Rich criticized the project on environmental grounds in articles and appearances before committees of the U.S. Congress. As a result of Rich's efforts, the project was canceled in 1986. This decision, and the new Bank Presidency of Barber Conable in 1986, launched a change in the Bank's policy toward the environment.[26]

Conable began to speak publicly on the Bank's role with regard to the environment in 1987. In Conable's (1989) words, "The Bank is now convinced that the pervasive nature of environmental issues dictates a new approach: integrating environmental management into economic policymaking at all levels of government, supplementing the traditional project-by-project approach" (p. 6). Conable committed the Bank to increasing its environmental staff, beginning a series of environmental issue papers, financing environmental programs, and involving grass-roots environmental organizations in the Bank's decision making. But the combined outrage of the left over both SAL and the environment proved a potent mix, contributing to the famous Fifty Years Is Enough campaign against the Bank that began in 1994.

On the political right, members of the U.S. Congress set up the International Financial Institutions Advisory Commission (IFIAC) that became known as the Meltzer Commission after its chair, Allan Meltzer. The Meltzer Commission's report was highly critical of the Bank, suggesting that it be substantially downsized, its lending to middle-income countries be phased out, and that it shift away from loans to grants.[27] Given the attacks from both sides of the political spectrum, the World Bank faced a difficult period.

Caught in this fray was the most prominent World Bank president since McNamara, Paul Wolfensohn. To address the concerns of the political right, he sponsored what was known as the Strategic Compact with the aim of making the Bank more efficient and less bureaucratic. To implement the Strategic Compact, he pushed through an internal reorganization of the Bank involving a number of elements, including matrix management, discussed in the context of multinational enterprises in Chapter 11.[28] Finally, he proposed a Comprehensive Development Framework (CDF) discussed in the accompanying box.

Wolfensohn's Comprehensive Development Framework

A few years after he assumed the presidency of the World Bank, Paul Wolfensohn proposed a Comprehensive Development Framework (CDF) that took into account a number of criticisms of the World Bank's adjustment lending phase and returned to some of the themes from its previous poverty alleviation phase. Initially, Wolfensohn argued that the development framework should be composed of:

[26] See Rich (1994), Steer (1996), and chapter 2 of Phillips (2009).

[27] Recall from Chapter 20 that most of the world's poor now reside in middle-income countries. In a *Financial Times* editorial related to the Commission's report, Meltzer (2000) wrote: "The World Bank is an overstaffed, ineffective, bureaucratic institution. Including its subsidiaries, it has about 12,000 employees, mostly dedicated professionals who are committed to development and poverty relief. Yet the Bank's record is fairly poor. By its own admission, half its projects are unsuccessful, and the failure rate is even higher in the poorest countries."

[28] For a thorough and ultimately critical review of this internal reorganization, see chapter 4 of Phillips (2009). The matrix structure had a network structure imposed on it, making it more complicated than the standard matrix approach to MNE management.

1. Good governance, including the free flow of information and commitments to fight corruption
2. Institutional elements such as the enforcement of contracts and the sound regulation of financial systems
3. Social inclusion policies directed toward girls and women, indigenous peoples, and the unemployed
4. Attention to the provision of public goods and infrastructure, including a renewed focus on rural and urban development
5. Environmental and human sustainability, which respects both biological and cultural conditions
6. Ownership and participation to develop strategies to which countries can buy into and commit themselves

Later, the CDF was condensed into four principles. First, development strategies should be comprehensive and shaped by a long-term vision. Second, each country should devise and direct its own development agenda based on citizen participation. Third, governments, donors, civil society, and the private sector should work together in partnership to carry out development strategies. Fourth, development performance should be evaluated on the basis of measurable results. Initially, the CDF was not warmly received by even the World Bank staff. But it did serve the purpose of reorienting the Bank from a thematic viewpoint in ways that eventually proved useful.

Sources: Wolfensohn (1998) and Phillips (2009)

One practical outcome of the criticisms levied at both the World Bank and the IMF was a new Poverty Reduction Strategy (PRS) initiative launched in 1999. From the World Bank's perspective, the PRS was closely related to Wofensohn's CDF described in the accompanying box. The Bank has adopted six principles to guide the PRS. These are that the strategies should be country-driven, results-oriented, comprehensive, prioritized, partnership-oriented, and long-term. The IMF, in turn, has supported the PRS with a Poverty Reduction and Growth Facility.[29]

Wolfensohn also was the first Bank president to raise the issue of corruption. This issue was taken up with vigor by his successor, Paul Wolfowitz, beginning in 2006. Unfortunately, Wolfowitz quickly lost the confidence of his staff as he was caught up in his own ethics scandal related to his treatment of a paramour within the staff.[30] Further, note was taken of the fact that corruption issues were raised with some countries (e.g., India) but not others (e.g., U.S. ally Pakistan). Indeed, Phillips (2009) reported that the United Kingdom Development Minister threatened to withhold its Bank contribution and the Chinese government threatened to cease borrowing from the Bank over this issue. In the end, Wolfowitz was forced to resign and was replaced by Robert Zoellick in 2007.

[29] As we saw in Chapter 17, this is now the IMF's Extended Credit Facility (ECF).

[30] The details of this episode are complicated, but revolve around the secondment arrangements of Ms. Shaha Riza to the U.S. State Department, which broke Bank rules. In an April 2007 letter to the *Financial Times*, 40 former senior staff members stated that Wolfowitz "has lost the trust and respect of Bank staff at all levels, provoked a rift among senior managers, developed tense relations with the Board, damaged his own credibility on good governance – his flagship issue, and alienated some key shareholders at a time when their support is essential for a successful replenishment of the resources needed to help the poorest countries, especially in Africa" (Kaji et al., 2007).

ENGAGING WITH GHANA

As stated previously, the advent of the policy-based lending phase of the World Bank coincided with the coming to power of the Rawlings regime in Ghana in the early 1980s. Initially, Rawlings and his government were anticapitalist and antimarket. However, economic conditions continued to worsen, and the Rawlings regime was losing credibility, even from the political left in Ghana. Further, the Ghanaian currency (the cedi) was fixed at such an overvalued rate (see Chapter 16) that most currency transactions were undertaken at black-market rates.

Eventually, a debate over economic policy emerged within the regime itself, and it was ultimately ready to take the plunge.[31] An Economic Recovery Program was negotiated with the World Bank in 1983. In 1983, a large de facto nominal devaluation was effected through import taxes and export subsidies,[32] but this was followed by an adjustment of the nominal rate itself from 2.75 cedi per U.S. dollar to 30 cedi per dollar. Further devaluations were to follow in 1984 (to 50 cedi per dollar), 1985 (to 60 cedi per dollar), and 1986 (90 cedi per dollar). Subsequently, the value of the cedi was market-determined. Import restrictions were reduced, especially after 1986, when the first official SAL program began.

Importantly, the Ghanaian government began to place an emphasis on revenue generation to address central government deficits. In 1985, the government formed a new National Revenue Secretariat. The purpose of this new unit was to broaden the tax base away from a previous emphasis on cocoa export taxes and to improve collection efficiency. Revenues as a percent of GDP responded significantly. Additionally, however, there were substantial layoffs of public-sector workers, particularly in state-owned enterprises, although retained public-sector workers were rewarded with raises.

The initial results of the SAL program were startling. As shown in Figure 23.2, both GDP growth and GDP per capita growth stabilized beginning in 1985. Inflation slowed and exports expanded. Subsequently, however, economic conditions began to take a turn for the worse. Inflows of FDI never appeared. Despite positive GDP growth, GDP per capita growth trended toward zero up to 1995. Inflation returned, and unemployment remained stuck at approximately 25 percent of the labor force. Worse still, both internal and external debt increased substantially to more than US$5 billion by 1995. In that year, a Ghanaian government budget statement lamented that: "We have hovered on the edge of recovery for too long, now threatening to relapse into the bleak decade that preceded the recovery program." In 1997, Finance Minister Kwame Peprah admitted that: "The same issues are still with us as they were in 1983 when we had to explain them to the people."[33]

In 1997, World Bank President James Wolfensohn visited Ghana to talk about progress in adjustment. His hosts complained about a lack of results, despite nearly

[31] As summarized by Kwesi Botchwey, the Secretary for Finance and Economic Planning at the time: "There were two options: We had to maneuver our way around the naiveties of leftism, which has a sort of disdain for any talk of financial discipline.... Moreover, we had to find a way between this naiveté and the crudities and rigidities and dogma of monetarism, which behaves as if once you set the monetary incentives everybody will do the right thing and the market will be perfect" (in Jebuni, 1995, p. 20).

[32] Years later, in 2001, Argentina was to use this same policy to offset an overvalued, fixed exchange rate in the form of a currency board discussed in Chapter 16.

[33] These two quotes are due to Ben Kwame Fred-Mensah and Asare Koti, respectively.

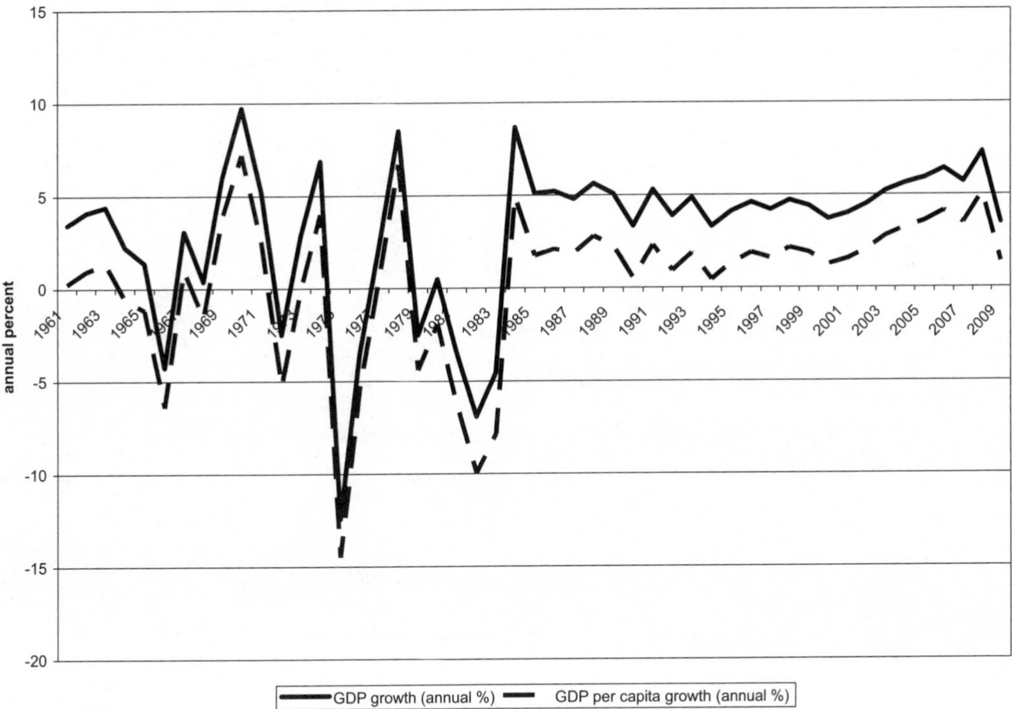

Figure 23.2. Growth Rates in GDP and GDP per Capita in Ghana, 1961–2009 (percent). *Source:* World Bank, World Development Indicators Online

15 years of hardship. Wolfensohn advised Jerry Rawlings and the Ghanaian government to cut government spending and fight corruption. This limited advice was a disappointment to all Ghanaians.

What were the missing ingredients holding Ghana back? Lall (1995) pointed out that structural adjustment programs in Africa often failed to emphasize human capital and, in particular, skill development. The World Bank (1984) itself had identified human capital and skills as a binding constraint on Ghana. Further disappointments emerged in the form of a distinct lack of formal sector employment, including little agricultural employment growth outside of export agriculture (cocoa, tuna, roses, and pineapples). Despite these limitations, however, the evidence presented by Aryeetey and McKay (2007) suggested that the growth of the 1990s contributed to significant decreases in poverty, along with declining fertility rates. Some of this was due to remittance inflows discussed in Chapter 12. The World Bank itself also changed course a bit, developing lending programs in the area of basic education with some significant short-term gains (World Bank, 2004).[34]

As a reflection of some of the difficulties Ghana continued to face, in 2004 it qualified for the World Bank/IMF Heavily Indebted Poor Countries (HIPC) initiative providing for debt relief. It is clear from Figure 23.2 that, since the involvement of the World Bank, much has improved for Ghana. On the other hand, as pointed out by Aryeetey and

[34] Similar positive short-term effects of World Bank lending in education appear more widely in Africa, but long-term effects are more problematic. See, for example, Bhaumik (2005). Mallick and Moore (2005) presented more positive results for the effects of Bank lending on growth, but noted that "it is possible that the positive impact of aid on growth may not hold in very poor countries" (p. 279).

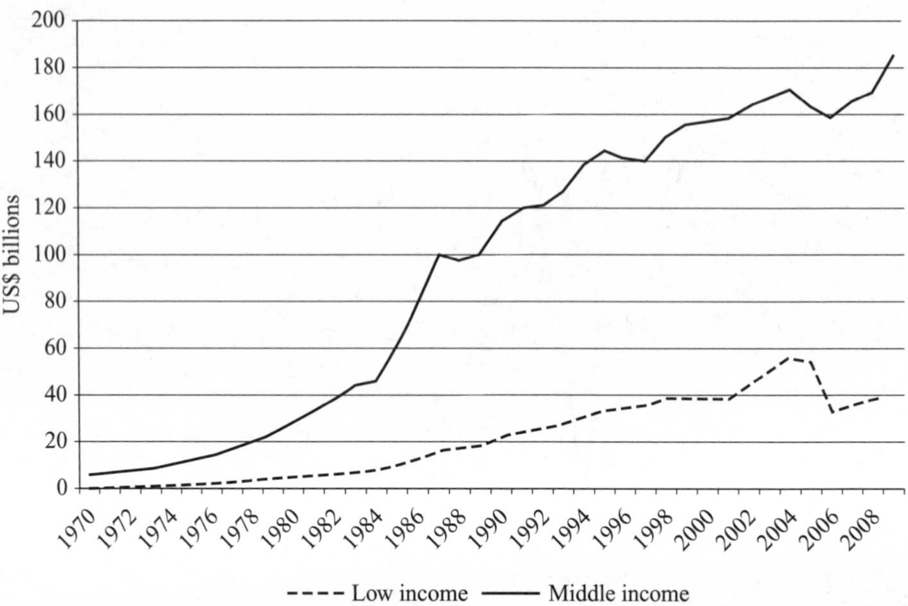

Figure 23.3. World Bank Loans and Grants to Low- and Middle-Income Countries, 1970–2009. *Source:* World Bank, World Development Indicators Online

McKay (2007), despite 20 years of a relatively stable economic environment, neither domestic nor foreign investment has responded significantly. And despite significant declines in poverty in the 1990s, poverty levels remain very high.[35] What we identified as pro-poor growth in Chapter 20 still remains somewhat elusive in Ghana.

RECENT SHIFTS

Recall from Chapter 17 that the 2007–2009 crisis had a big impact on IMF lending. A similar shift took place at the World Bank. As mentioned previously, the total capitalization of the Bank was increased in that year from US$190 to US$275. As had been the case at the IMF, voting shares at the Bank shifted in favor of some large emerging countries (e.g., Argentina, Brazil, China, India, Russia, and Vietnam). President Zoellick also introduced the theme "New World, New World Bank Group" in a report to the Board of Governors.[36] Along with this shift in emphasis toward emerging countries, there was an increase in proposed lending toward a set of middle-income countries and toward IBRD lending rather than IDA loans and grants. This followed a long-term pattern illustrated in Figure 23.3.[37]

With regard to the post-crisis year 2009, Wade (2010) suggested that most of the Bank's lending went to middle-income countries not badly hit by the 2007–2009 crisis (e.g., Indonesia, Brazil, Mexico, China, and Poland). This recent pattern of lending is accompanied by that of the IMF as discussed in Chapter 17, which is currently focused

[35] See Akologo (2006), who also raised doubts about how the HIPC funds were spent in Ghana. For previously expressed concerns, see *The Economist* (1996, 2002).

[36] For a critique of this and of Zoellick's leadership, see Wade (2010).

[37] For example, Phillips (2009) noted that "at the peak of the anti-poverty fight, in 2002, it was Turkey, a middle-income NATO member and prospective EU applicant, who alone received nearly 20% of the Bank's lending (no less than 30% of IBRD lending) in a series of major adjustment operations partly to support the Turkish banking system. This was more than double the entire Bank expenditure on what it defined as rural development!" (p. 141).

on Europe. It is true that most of the world's poor are now to be found in middle-income countries, but the question arises: given these emerging lending patterns, where do low-income countries (often badly hit by the crisis) turn for help? It is not clear that "New World, New Bank Group" has a good answer to this question.

CONCLUSION

Originally focused on the reconstruction of Europe after World War II, the World Bank Group quickly turned to the realm of economic development. In its early history, the Bank concentrated on infrastructure project lending. Then, under the McNamara presidency, it focused on poverty alleviation, including integrated rural development. In the 1980s, its direction shifted substantially to policy-based lending. In response to mounting criticism from both the political left and the political right, the Bank later recognized the importance of environmental sustainability, social inclusion, and participation, although implementation of these concerns remained a real issue. Most recently, it appears that the Bank is continuing its support of middle-income countries and neglecting low-income countries.

A central policy-based lending program in which the World Bank has been long involved is that of Ghana. This led to a stabilization of GDP growth and some significant poverty alleviation. However, Ghana still faces long-term problems in the area of employment generation and poverty alleviation that even the recent HIPC effort seems not to have fully addressed.

Because the structural adjustment policies of both the IMF and the World Bank have proved to be such a contentious issue in development debates, and because structural change and adjustment have wide implications for the development process, we turn to these issues in the next chapter.

REVIEW EXERCISES

1. The World Bank and the IMF are the two major institutions of international finance in the world economy. How do their missions and operations differ? Are there any areas in which these missions and operations work against each other?
2. How does the poverty alleviation phase of the World Bank differ from its previous infrastructure project lending phase? In what ways does the later policy-based lending phase represent a break with the poverty alleviation phase?
3. What is your assessment of Wolfensohn's Comprehensive Development Framework? Does it seem to support conceptions of growth and development discussed in Chapters 20 and 21?
4. If you were assigned the task of designing a development framework for the World Bank, what would it be?
5. If there is a World Bank member in which you have a special interest, spend a little time perusing the "Countries and Regions" section of the Bank's website at www.worldbank.org.

FURTHER READING AND WEB RESOURCES

For a concise introduction to the World Bank, see Gilbert and Vines (2009). For a discussion of the early history of the World Bank, there is no better source than Mason and Asher (1973). For the poverty alleviation phase, the reader should consult Ayres (1983). For the structural adjustment phase, see Mosley, Harrigan, and Toye (1995), and for the Wolfensohn era, see Mallaby (2004). A balanced view of the structural adjustment debate can also be found in Stewart (1995). For recent assessments of the Bank's operations, see Gilbert and Vines (2000), Phillips (2009), and Wade (2010). Finally, for a noted critique of longstanding World Bank (and IMF) lending, see Easterly (1999).

The World Bank maintains its main website at www.worldbank.org. It disseminates its own research through its journal, the *World Bank Research Observer*. You can view recent issues of this journal at www.wbro.oxfordjournals.org. The International Center for Settlement of Investment Disputes' website is at www.icsid.worldbank.org. The Multilateral Investment Guarantee Agency's website can be found at http://www.miga.org. The Bretton Woods Project monitors World Bank (and IMF) activities and provides a great deal of information on the World Bank from a critical perspective. You can access its website at www.brettonwoodsproject.org.

REFERENCES

Adelman, I. (1980) "Income Distribution, Economic Development and Land Reform," *American Behavioral Scientist*, 23:3, 437–456.

Akologo, S.Z. (2006) *Where Did Ghana's HIPC Funds Go?* World Bank.

Aryeetey, E. and A. McKay (2007) "Ghana: The Challenge of Translating Sustained Growth into Poverty Reduction," in T. Besley and L.J. Cord (eds.) *Delivering on the Promise of Pro-Poor Growth: Insights and Lessons from Country Experiences*, World Bank, 147–168.

Ayres, R.L. (1983) *Banking on the Poor: The World Bank and World Poverty*, MIT Press.

Bhaumik, S.K. (2005) "Does the World Bank Have Any Impact on Human Development of the Poorest Countries? Some Preliminary Evidence from Africa," *Economic Systems*, 29:4, 422–432.

Childress, M.A. and J.A. Muñoz (2008) *Brazil Land-Based Poverty Alleviation Project (Crédito Funiário)*, World Bank.

Conable, B. (1989) "Development and the Environment: A Global Balance," *Finance and Development*, 26:4, 2–4.

Cornia, G.A., R. Jolly, and F. Stewart (1987) *Adjustment with a Human Face*, Oxford University Press.

Deininger, K. and H. Binswanger (1999) "The Evolution of the World Bank's Land Policy: Principles, Experience, and Future Challenges," *World Bank Research Observer*, 14:2, 247–276.

Dreher, A., J.E. Sturm, and J.R. Vreeland (2009) "Development Aid and International Politics: Does Membership on the UN Security Council Influence World Bank Decisions?" *Journal of Development Economics*, 88:1, 1–18.

Easterly, W. (1999) "The Ghost of the Financing Gap: Testing the Growth Model Used in the International Financial Institutions," *Journal of Development Economics*, 60:2, 423–438.

The Economist (1996) "Investment in Africa: Primary Problems," November 9.

The Economist (2002) "Ghana as an Economic Model," April 27.

Flores, T.E. and I. Nooruddin (2009) "Financing the Peace: Evaluating World Bank Post-Conflict Assistance Programs," *Review of International Organizations*, 4:1, 1–27.

Gilbert, C.L. and D. Vines (eds.) (2000) *The World Bank: Structure and Policies*, Cambridge University Press.

Gilbert, C.L. and D. Vines (2009) "World Bank," in K.A. Reinert, R.S. Rajan, A.J. Glass and L.S. Davis (eds.), *The Princeton Encyclopedia of the World Economy*, Princeton University Press, 1174–1180.

Kaji, J. et al. (2007) "Letter to the Financial Times," *Financial Times*, April 22.

Jebuni, C.D. (1995) *Governance and Structural Adjustment in Ghana*, World Bank Private Sector Development Department, Occasional Paper No. 16.

Kilby, C. (2009) "The Political Economy of Conditionality: An Empirical Analysis of World Bank Loan Disbursements," *Journal of Development Economics*, 89:1, 51–61.

Lall, S. (1995) "Structural Adjustment and African Industry," *World Development*, 23:12, 2019–2031.

Lindsay, R. (2000) "Land Reform Returns to Center Stage in Brazil," *Washington Report on the Hemisphere*, 20:12.

Mallaby, S. (2004) *The World's Banker: A Story of Failed States, Financial Crises, and the Wealth and Poverty of Nations*, Yale University Press.

Mallick, S. and T. Moore (2005) "Impact of World Bank Lending in an Adjustment-Led Growth Model," *Economic Systems*, 29:4, 366–383.

Mason, E.S. and R.E. Asher (1973) *The World Bank since Bretton Woods*, Brookings.

Meltzer, A.H. (2000) "A Better Way to Help the World," *Financial Times*, April 28.

Mosley, P., J. Harrigan, and J.F. Toye (1995) *Aid and Power: The World Bank and Policy-Based Lending*, Routledge.

Naím, M. (2000) "Washington Consensus or Washington Confusion?" *Foreign Policy*, Spring, 86–103.

Paarlberg, R. and M. Lipton (1991) "Changing Missions at the World Bank," *World Policy Journal*, 8:3, 475–498.

Phillips, D.A. (2009) *Reforming the World Bank: Twenty Years of Trial and Error*, Cambridge University Press.

Polak, J.J. (1994) *The World Bank and the International Monetary Fund: A Changing Relationship*, Brookings.

Rich, B. (1994) *Mortgaging the Earth: The World Bank, Environmental Impoverishment, and the Crisis of Development*, Beacon Press.

Rodrik, D. (1994) "King Kong Meets Godzilla: The World Bank and *The East Asian Miracle*," in A. Fishlow et al., *Miracle or Design: Lessons from the East Asian Experience*, Overseas Development Council, 13–53.

Rodrik, D. (2006) "Goodbye Washington Consensus, Hello Washington Confusion? A Review of the World Bank's Economic Growth in the 1990s: Learning from a Decade of Reform," *Journal of Economic Literature*, 44:4, 973–987.

Rodrik, D. (2007) *One Economics, Many Recipes: Globalization, Institutions and Economic Growth*, Princeton University Press.

Schwartzman, S. (2000) "The World Bank and Land Reform in Brazil," Environmental Defense.

Shihata, I.F.I. (2009) "Towards Greater Depoliticization of Investment Disputes: The Role of ICSID and MIGA," in K.W. Lu, G. Verheyen, and S.M. Perera (eds.), *Investing with Confidence: Understanding Political Risk Management in the 21st Century*, World Bank, 2–35.

Skidelsky, R. (2000) *John Maynard Keynes: Fighting for Freedom 1937–1946*, Viking.

Steer, A. (1996) "Ten Principles of the New Environmentalism," *Finance and Development*, 33:4, 4–7.

Stern, E. (1983) "World Bank Financing of Structural Adjustment," in J. Williamson (ed.), *IMF Conditionality*, Institute for International Economics, 87–107.

Stewart, F. (1995) *Adjustment and Poverty: Options and Choices*, Routledge.

Wade, R. (2010) "The State of the World Bank," *Challenge*, 53:4, 43–67.
Williamson, J. (1990) "What Washington Means by Policy Reform," in J. Williamson (ed.), *Latin American Adjustment: How Much Has Happened?* Institute for International Economics, 5–38.
Williamson, J. (2000) "What Should the World Bank Think about the Washington Consensus?" *World Bank Research Observer*, 15:2, 251–64.
Wolfensohn, J. (1998) *The Other Crisis*, World Bank.
World Bank (1984) *Ghana: Policies and Program for Adjustment.*
World Bank (1993) *East Asian Miracle.*
World Bank (2004) *Books, Buildings, and Learning Outcomes: An Impact Evaluation of World Bank Support to Basic Education in Ghana.*
World Bank (2005) *Economic Growth in the 1990s: Learning from a Decade of Reform.*
World Bank (2010) *The World Bank's Country Policy and Institutional Assessment: An Evaluation.*

24 Structural Change and Adjustment

Let's recall a few things you learned in some previous chapters of this book. In Chapter 16, you learned that, in a fixed exchange rate regime, an overvalued domestic currency (Mexican peso or Ghanaian cedi) is associated with an excess demand for foreign currency (U.S. dollar or EU euro). This excess demand for foreign currency is often met by the central bank drawing down its foreign reserves. The drawing down process is not sustainable, however, and can result in a balance of payments crisis. In Chapter 17, you learned that, in most circumstances, the International Monetary Fund (IMF) stands ready to assist member countries in dealing with such balance of payments crises considered in Chapter 18. If this assistance involves the member country's moving into its upper credit tranches (which it almost always does), the IMF imposes policy conditionality on its loans. In Chapter 23, you learned that, beginning in the 1980s, the World Bank began structural adjustment lending (later called development policy lending) to countries facing balance of payments difficulties, also imposing policy conditionality in the process. You were introduced to the case of Ghana in that chapter.

As you have seen, then, for developing countries with balance of payments crises caused by fixed exchange rates or changes in global economic conditions, structural adjustment under the supervision of the IMF and World Bank is, for better or worse, often an inescapable reality. The effectiveness of these structural adjustment programs has been the source of a significant amount of disagreement among international economists. It is now time to tie the discussion of Chapters 16, 17, 18, and 23 together in a close examination of the structural adjustment process.

Before we begin this process, we consider the issue of structural change, one view of development introduced in Chapter 20, and introduce the distinction between traded goods and nontraded goods. This leads to a distinction between demand reduction and demand switching in structural adjustment processes. We then briefly consider the role of the traded goods sector in economic growth, as well as the order of economic liberalization. An appendix introduces the Rybczynski theorem of the Heckscher-Ohlin model of comparative advantage to help us understand structural change.

Analytical elements for this chapter:

Countries, *sectors*, *factors*, and *currencies*.

STRUCTURAL CHANGE

In Chapter 20, we briefly considered development through the lens of **structural change**. We noted that this lens was contributed by Nobel Laureate Simon Kuznets (1966). The basic notion of structural change is that, as development proceeds, productive factors move out of lower productivity activities into higher productivity activities. One limited application of this lens is to simply view development as the process of resources moving out of agriculture and into manufacturing. We noted, however, that this limited application ignores the important role of the service sector. We also noted that, as development proceeds, the service sector expands, partly due to the role of producer services.

Consider the data presented in Table 24.1. This presents gross domestic product (GDP) of low-, middle-, and high-income countries, split up between agriculture,

Table 24.1. Sectoral composition of GDP, selected years (% of GDP)

		1970	1980	1990	2000	2005
Low income	Agriculture		38	38	35	29
Low income	Manufacturing		12	12	11	12
Low income	Services		50	50	54	59
Middle income	Agriculture	25	20	18	11	10
Middle income	Manufacturing	24	26	23	22	21
Middle income	Services	51	54	59	67	69
High income	Agriculture	6	4	3	2	2
High income	Manufacturing				19	17
High income	Services				79	81

Source: World Bank, World Development Indicators Online

manufacturing, and services for years reported by the World Bank in its World Development Indicators. Not all years are available, but if we were to generalize from the data in this table, we can see that, as development proceeds, agriculture declines from approximately 40 percent of GDP to approximately 2 percent of GDP. Manufacturing initially increases from approximately 10 percent of GDP to approximately 25 percent of GDP and subsequently falls below 20 percent of GDP. Services increase from approximately 50 percent of GDP to approximately 80 percent of GDP.

One notable reason why agriculture declines as a percent of GDP is that of what is known as *Engel's Law*, named after a nineteenth-century statistician. Engel's law states that the income elasticity of demand for food is *less than one*, so for example, a 10 percent increase in income results in a *less than* 10 percent increase in demand for food.[1] A second reason why agriculture declines with economic growth is that it tends to be less capital intensive than manufacturing. As we saw in Chapter 21, growth involves an increase in the ratio of capital to labor, or capital deepening, and a key result of the Heckscher-Ohlin model of trade discussed in Chapter 5 (but not mentioned in that chapter) is that, as the capital-labor ratio increases (all else constant), labor-intensive sectors of the economy tend to shrink relative to capital-intensive sectors (the **Rybczynski theorem** discussed in the appendix). This can occur in the agricultural sector as capital deepening occurs.[2]

Finally, there is a tendency for the income elasticity of demand for services to be *greater than one*, so for example, a 10 percent increase in income results in a *more than* 10 percent increase in demand for services. Indeed, as noted by Szirmai (2005), service sectors appear to be expanding faster in contemporary developing countries than in developed countries in previous eras. All of these factors can work together to give rise to the pattern of structural change that appears in Table 24.1.[3]

There is a tradition in the analysis of the service sector that views it as inherently static, that is, not susceptible to productivity improvements. What is now known as *Baumol's law*, after Baumol (1986), suggests that the expansion of service sectors acts as a productivity drag on entire economies. But there is also emerging evidence of the importance of service sectors in productivity growth, of dynamism in key service

[1] Recall that the income elasticity of demand is the ratio of the percentage change in demand to the percentage change in income.

[2] But note, however, as we emphasized in Chapter 20, that the agriculture sector can experience significant productivity gains that have benefits for the manufacturing sector as well.

[3] These effects were discussed in Anderson (1987) and Szirmai (2005, chapter 8).

Table 24.2. Traded goods vs. nontraded goods

Good	Price determination	Consumption and production
Traded	Prices of traded goods are determined in world markets.	Domestic consumption and domestic production of traded goods can differ, causing a trade surplus or deficit.
Nontraded	Prices on nontraded goods are determined in domestic markets.	Domestic consumption and domestic production must be equal.

subsectors. As noted by Szirmai (2005), "though Baumol's law may hold for hairdressers and restaurants, it does not hold for mobile telecommunications, financial services or distance learning" (p. 272).[4] Increasingly, then, we need to view the service sector in a new light.

There is a particular treatment of the structure of economies that involves a distinction between traded and nontraded goods, and it has been applied to many problems in international economics, particularly structural adjustment. We consider this next.

TRADED AND NONTRADED GOODS

Imagine that you are an international economist advising the Ghanaian government on their approach to structural adjustment. You need to somehow simplify the complexities of the adjustment processes to clarify your own thinking and to communicate with government representatives. One useful first step is to distinguish between **traded goods** and **nontraded goods**. Recall that in Chapter 15 in our assessment of the PPP model of exchange rate determination, we said: "many goods are *nontraded*. For example, a large part of most economies consists of locally supplied services, such as many kinds of cleaning, repairs, and food preparation. These services are not typically traded." In the Ghanaian context, you might imagine the following:

Traded goods	Nontraded goods
Petroleum	Tailoring
Gold	Auto repair
Cocoa	Education
Food	Health services

There are two crucial things that you must understand about the difference between traded and nontraded goods. These are described in Table 24.2. First, the prices of traded goods are determined in world markets, whereas the prices of nontraded goods are determined in domestic markets. So, for Ghana, the price of petroleum is a world price denominated in U.S. dollars. The price of tailoring, on the other hand, is a domestic price, denominated in cedis. Second, for traded goods, domestic consumption and domestic production can differ in value, causing a trade surplus or deficit. However, domestic consumption and domestic production of nontraded goods must be exactly the same in value.

How does the distinction between traded and nontraded goods relate to the sectors discussed in the previous section: agriculture, manufacturing, and services? As it turns

[4] See also Francois and Reinert (1996), Francois and Woerz (2008), and Francois and Hoekman (2010).

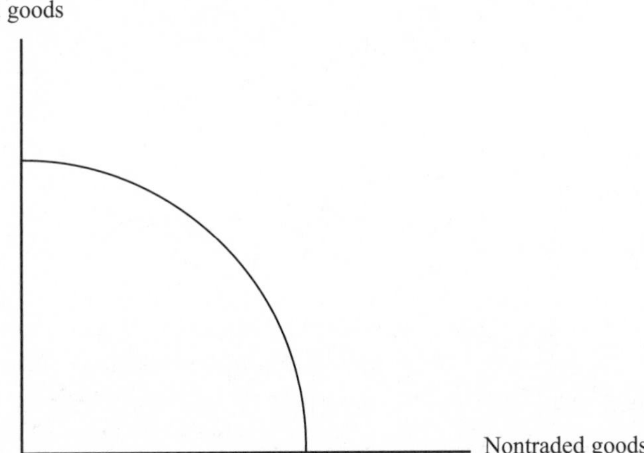

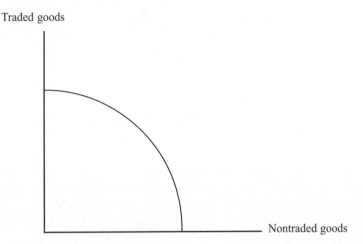

Figure 24.1. Ghana's PPF with Traded and Nontraded Goods

out, although each of these sectors is traded, services are in general less traded than agriculture and manufacturing. So nontraded goods include more service sub-sectors than traded goods, and traded goods include more agriculture and manufacturing sub-sectors than nontraded goods. Some researchers go so far as to *equate* nontraded goods with the service sector, but this is not entirely accurate.[5]

Having divided the Ghanaian economy into traded and nontraded goods, we can represent the supply side of this economy with a production possibilities frontier (PPF) as we did in Chapter 3 to discuss comparative advantage.[6] This is done in Figure 24.1. The production of traded goods as an aggregate entity (petroleum, gold, cocoa, food) is measured along the vertical axis, and the production of nontraded goods as an aggregate entity (tailoring, auto repair, education, health services) is measured along the horizontal axis. The PPF depicts the combinations of output of traded goods and nontraded goods that the economy can produce given its available resources and technology. The PPF is depicted as the concave line in this figure. Given the available resources and technology, Ghana can produce anywhere on or inside the PPF.

With these characteristics of traded and nontraded goods in mind, you are ready to be introduced to the concepts of internal and external balance. We do this in the following section.

INTERNAL AND EXTERNAL BALANCE

The concepts of **internal balance** and **external balance** relate directly to the PPF diagram we introduced in Figure 24.1, and we will use this PPF to help you understand them. We do this in Figure 24.2. In this figure, Ghana's production point is given by point *B*. Because the production point *B* is on the PPF rather than inside it, all of Ghana's resources are efficiently employed. This is what we mean by *internal balance*. In Figure 24.2, Ghana's consumption point is given by point *C* and is exactly the same point as point *B*. A dotted line proceeds to the left from points *B* and *C* to the vertical axis.

[5] Recall from Chapter 1 that a significant amount of world trade is composed of trade in services, and see Hoekman and Francois (2010).

[6] The PPF was introduced in the appendix to Chapter 3. If you need to, please review this appendix.

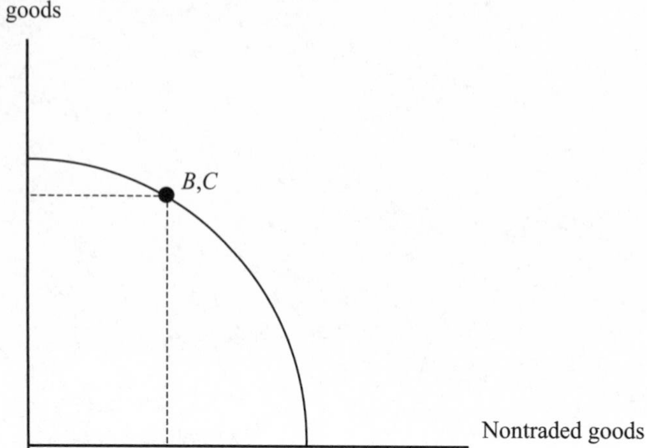

Figure 24.2. Internal and External Balance

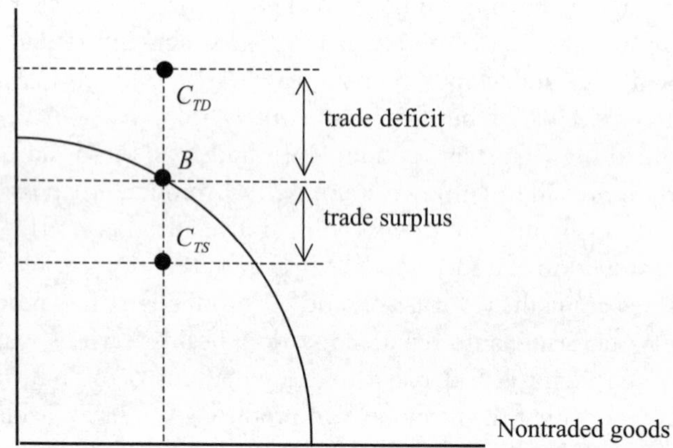

Figure 24.3. External Imbalances

This tells us that the consumption of tradable goods (point C) is exactly the same as the production of tradable goods (point B). Because consumption and production of tradable goods are the same, there is no trade deficit or trade surplus. This means that there is *external balance.*[7]

Let's summarize the internal balance and external balance concepts in a box:

Internal balance: all resources are efficiently employed.
External balance: consumption and production of tradable goods are equal.

Next consider Figure 24.3. As in Figure 24.2, the production point B is on the PPF. For this reason, there is internal balance. This figure also shows two consumption points, C_{TS} and C_{TD}. If consumption is at C_{TD}, the consumption of traded goods exceeds

[7] The concepts of internal and external balance were first presented by Salter (1959). A more recent discussion is included in chapter 1 of Corden (1986). See also Meade (1978).

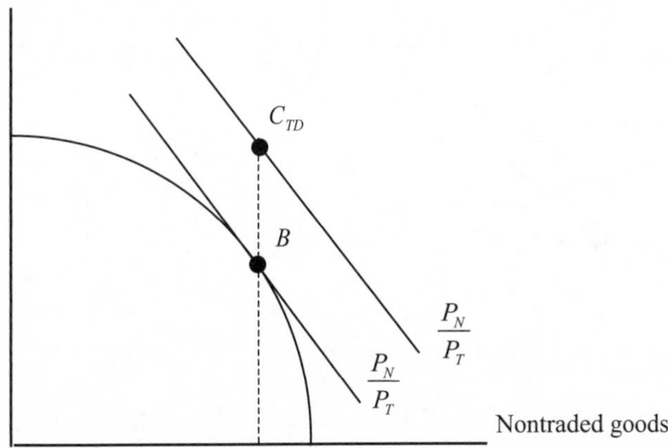

Figure 24.4. A Current Account Deficit

the production of traded goods along the vertical axis. This implies that Ghana has a *trade deficit* (*TD*). To simplify a bit, we interpret this trade deficit as a current account deficit.[8] Recall Equation 13.7 from Chapter 13, reproduced here:

$$\text{Current account} + \text{Capital/financial account} + \text{official reserve transactions} = 0 \tag{24.1}$$

As shown in this equation, if there is a current account deficit, there must be a capital/financial account surplus and/or an official reserves transactions surplus. These can come from positive direct or portfolio investment balances or from drawing down foreign reserves.

If consumption in Figure 24.3 is at C_{TS}, the production of traded goods exceeds the consumption of traded goods along the vertical axis. This implies that Ghana has a *trade surplus* (*TS*). Again, to simplify matters, we interpret this trade surplus as a current account surplus. If there is a current account surplus, we know that there must be a capital/financial account deficit and/or an official reserves transactions deficit. This can come from negative direct or portfolio investment balances or from building up foreign reserves. In contrast to Figure 24.2, in both the trade deficit and trade surplus cases depicted in Figure 24.3, there is *external imbalance.* As always, consumption and production of nontraded goods are the same, as we stated in Table 24.1. Therefore, point C is either directly above or directly below point B.

To understand some issues behind balance of payments adjustment, we will consider Ghana in an initial position of a trade (current account) deficit. This situation is depicted in Figure 24.4. Included in this figure are price ratio lines. As we discussed in Chapter 3, the price ratio line is tangent to the PPF at the point of production B.[9] We use P_T to denote the price of traded goods and P_N to denote the price of nontraded goods. A price ratio line with the same slope passes through the consumption point C_{TD}. This is to indicate that consumers as well as firms face the price ratio $\frac{P_N}{P_T}$. You can

[8] That is, we ignore net income and net transfers, items 7 and 8, in Table 13.2.

[9] As discussed in Chapter 3, this occurs with the conditions of full employment of resources, perfect competition in all markets, and profit-maximizing firms.

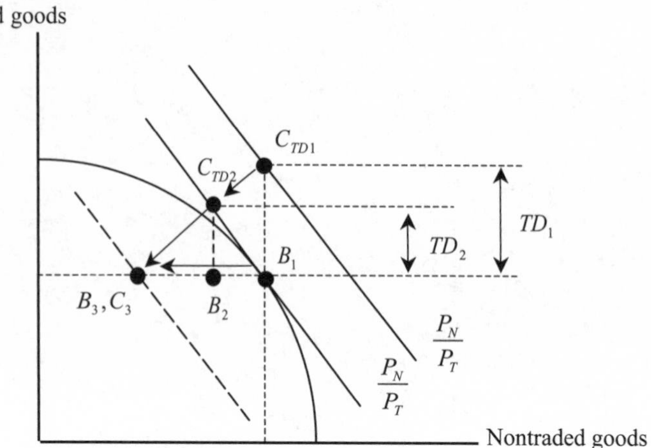

Figure 24.5. Adjustment via Demand Reduction

call this price ratio the "relative price of nontraded goods."[10] As stated previously, the vertical distance between B and C_{TD} is sustained by a capital/financial account surplus and/or an official reserves transactions surplus. Ghana has internal balance but external imbalance at points B and C_{TD} in Figure 24.4.

Difficulties in Figure 24.4 emerge if the inflows on the capital account begin to disappear or if reserves are drawn down too far. Suppose, for example, that direct and portfolio investment decline (foreign savings falls).[11] It is still possible for Ghana to maintain its current account deficit by drawing down its foreign reserves. This situation clearly is not sustainable, however. It can last only as long as the central bank has foreign reserves to sell. Eventually, the foreign reserves will be exhausted, and the country will face a balance of payments crisis of the kind we discussed in Chapter 18. How can Ghana adjust?

One possibility comes from recognizing that the external imbalance problem comes from the demand for tradable goods being too high. Recognizing this, Ghana could engage in **demand reduction** to reduce the demand for tradable goods. This policy is one that has often been suggested by the International Monetary Fund (IMF) and World Bank to developing countries in this situation. A significant limitation here is that *demand reductions typically cannot be confined to traded goods alone.* In most instances, demand falls for *both* traded *and* nontraded goods. An example of adjustment via demand reduction is depicted in Figure 24.5. We begin with consumption at C_{TD1} and production at B_1. The (unsustainable) current account deficit is at TD_1. Demand reduction consists of reducing the income households have for consumption. Under the reasonable assumption that both traded and nontraded goods are *normal goods*, as income falls, demands for both goods fall.[12]

[10] Recall from Chapter 14 that we defined the *real exchange rate* as $re = e \times \frac{p^{foreign}}{p^{home}}$. The relative price of nontraded goods turns out to be an approximation to the *inverse* of this real exchange rate. Why? Because we can rewrite $\frac{P_N}{P_T}$ as $\frac{P_N}{eP_T^W}$ where W denotes a world or foreign price.

[11] This could occur despite increases in Ghana's interest rate if foreign investors are changing their expectations or preferences with regard to portfolio allocations among countries.

[12] Recall that a *normal good* is one where there is a positive relationship between income and demand. This contrasts with an *inferior good*, where there is a negative relationship between income and demand, a rare case.

Suppose Ghana succeeds in reducing household incomes to the value of production at point B_1. Consumption would fall from C_{TD1} to C_{TD2}. The difficulty here is that there is *still a current account deficit* equal to TD_2, even though there is unemployment at the new production point B_2. Eliminating the trade deficit therefore requires reducing incomes *below* the value of production at point B_1, and this requires further unemployment. One scenario would involve maintaining the employment of resources in the traded goods sector and moving production and consumption to point B_3, C_3. Here, finally, the trade deficit has been eliminated. However, production is now far inside the PPF. Consequently, the demand reduction has caused a significant amount of unemployment. To put it another way, external balance adjustment via demand reduction has been achieved *at the expense of internal balance.*[13] Let's put this important result in a box:

Adjustment via demand reduction alone occurs at the expense of internal balance.

This is not a positive outcome for Ghana and leads us to consider whether there is anything else the country could do. As it turns out, in principle at least, a country can achieve external balance and maintain internal balance. The key here, as stated by Corden (1986), is: "If it is desired to attain two targets – external balance and internal balance – it is necessary to have *two* instruments. The (demand reduction) instrument is not enough.... The second instrument required is a **switching** policy" (pp. 9–10). In the typical case, the switching policy is implemented by a change in the **nominal exchange rate** defined in Chapter 14.

Remember from Chapter 14 that a devaluation or depreciation of the domestic currency ($e \uparrow$) causes an increase in the domestic (cedi) prices of both imports and exports. Therefore, if Ghana's currency (the cedi) were to be devalued or to depreciate, there would be an *increase* in the relative price of *tradable* goods or a *decrease* in the relative price of *nontradable* goods. The price lines in our PPF diagrams indicate the relative price of *nontradable* goods, so this line would become *flatter* when the cedi is loses value. This has two effects. First, it increases the incentive to produce traded goods. Second, it decreases the incentive to consume traded goods. Both of these effects tend to reduce the trade deficit. This is the process of moving down the $Z - E$ curve in Figure 14.3 in Chapter 14. The usefulness of a devaluation switching process can be seen in Figure 24.6.

As in Figure 24.5, Ghana begins in a position of a current account deficit measured by the vertical distance between C_{TD1} and B_1. The adjustment process, however, is different. There is demand reduction, but it is combined with the switching policy of devaluation. The devaluation or depreciation increases the cedi price of traded goods, and this lowers the relative price of nontraded goods, making the price line in the figure less steep. Ghanaian firms switch their production toward traded goods, and Ghanaian consumers switch their consumption away from traded goods. Production and consumption move to point B_2, C_2 where there is both external balance (no current account deficit) and internal balance (full employment). The lesson here is that

13 For the implications of demand reduction on socioeconomic outcomes, see Stewart (1995) and Gera (2007).

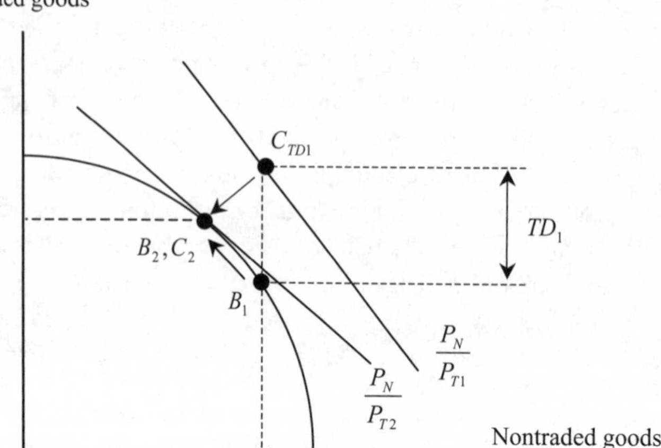

Figure 24.6. Adjustment via Demand Reduction and Switching

a successful adjustment program must combine both demand reduction and switching elements. This, too, deserves a box:

> In order to avoid internal imbalance (unemployment), a successful adjustment program must combine *both* demand reduction *and* switching elements.

The preceding discussion helps you to visualize certain processes that accompany countries' struggles to come to terms with a balance of payments crisis or other adjustment issue. It is important to understand that the correspondence of our graphical analysis to the actual experience of adjusting countries probably will not be complete. It is also important to note that we have said nothing about the *composition* of demand reduction. Is the country in question reducing military expenditures and industrial subsidies or is it reducing health and education expenditures? The answer to this question will have important economic and social consequences.[14] Finally, our model assumes that all things happen at once. In reality, policy changes occur over time, and the order in which they occur can be important. We take up the order of economic liberalization later in this chapter. Finally, as discussed in the accompanying box, there is a tradition in development economics, structuralism, that casts doubt on this adjustment process.

The Structuralist Critique

Structuralist economists have argued that we must account for the *structural diversity* of developing economies undergoing balance of payments crises and adjustment programs. For example, Taylor (1993) stated: "The real question is whether economic reform, or reconfiguration of the system to meet challenges posed by changes in both internal and external circumstances, is feasible in a given country's historical and institutional context" (pp. 43–44). Despite a diversity of views, we can identify some common structuralist arguments.

First, productive resources may not be mobile between sectors. In terms of the diagrams used in this chapter, inflexibilities can prevent productive resources from moving freely from the nontraded sector to the traded sector in a switching process. For example,

[14] See Stewart (1995) for a discussion of some of these issues.

urban workers in the nontraded sector might face a number of barriers (e.g., culture and family ties) to relocating to rural areas to increase the supply of agricultural products. Or gold production might simply be constrained by the capital stocks of mines. Consequently, the PPF in Figure 24.6 might look more like a rectangle than a normal PPF, and a nominal devaluation/depreciation will not shift production toward traded goods even as the relative price of nontraded goods falls.

Second, domestic production may be highly dependent on *imported intermediate and capital goods.* The devaluation/depreciation will raise the domestic prices of these traded goods. If the increase in the price of imported intermediate and capital goods puts them out of reach of domestic firms, production may decline and unemployment may occur, moving the economy inside the PPF. This is one kind of the "contractionary effects of devaluation" that have been discussed by structuralist economists

Third, demand reduction can include lost productive investments, including from reducing government expenditures. Some government expenditures, notably certain kinds of public investment (e.g., infrastructure, public utilities), may be necessary to support private investment and production. In the structuralist view, public and private investments are *complementary*, and a contraction of public investment can cause a subsequent contraction of private investment and, thereby, future productive potential as represented by the PPF. A similar story can be told with regard to productive investments in human capital, both education and health.

Fourth, adjustment often takes place under negative foreign savings (capital outflows or capital flight), as we discussed in Chapter 18. Consequently, it is *not* simply a matter of regaining external balance but of generating a trade or current account surplus to accommodate a capital/financial account deficit. Therefore, adjustments might need to proceed farther than we have assumed in our analysis here with potential structuralist syndromes becoming even stronger. Demand reduction is sharper, price increases of imported intermediate and capital goods are greater, and cuts in productive public investments are even more severe. Countries become caught in trade-surplus/low-growth traps with little future hope for poverty reduction.

Sources: Bacha (1987), Lipumba (1994), Tarp (1993), and Taylor (1993)

TRADED GOODS AND GROWTH

We have seen in this chapter that successful structural adjustment involves the increased production of traded goods, as in Figure 24.6. Recall also from Chapter 21 that there have been arguments made that, under some conditions, export expansions have additional benefits for growth of developing countries (see Figure 21.7). Finally, recall from Chapter 16 that there is evidence that at least one country with a dramatic export expansion, namely China, has had what appears to be a significantly undervalued currency, perhaps on the order of 20 to 30 percent (as of 2010). These considerations have been drawn together by some researchers (e.g., Gala, 2008, and Rodrik, 2008) to attempt to establish a relationship between the production of tradable goods, in developing countries and growth.

In its simplest form, the argument is that the production of traded goods involves positive growth externalities. Rodrik (2008) argued that "there is something 'special' about tradables in countries with low to medium incomes" and that the switching process discussed in this chapter can "foster desirable structural change and spur growth" (p. 370). We can visualize this argument in Figure 24.7. The increased production of

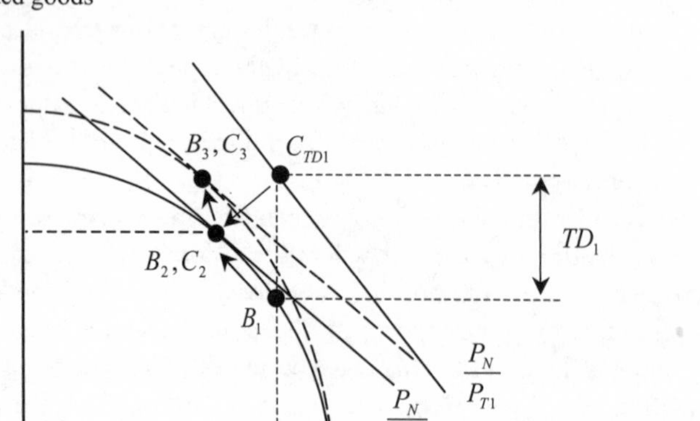

Figure 24.7. Adjustment via Demand Reduction and Switching Reconsidered

traded goods involved in the movement from point B_1 to point B_2 initiates the positive growth externalities, and this has the effect of shifting out the PPF along the traded goods axis. So instead of the economy coming to rest at point B_2, C_2, it can end up at a point along the new PPF such as B_3, C_3. This can involve welfare gains for the economy in question in that consumption is taking place on an expanded PPF.

Rodrik (2008) provided evidence of this sort of process for a number of countries, such as China, India, South Korea, Taiwan, Uganda, Tanzania, and Mexico. There have been criticisms of his methodology, but the study at least alerts us to the possibility of these sorts of effects. It also clearly cautions against pursuing overvalued currencies in developing countries, perhaps as a result of capital and foreign aid inflows.[15]

THE ORDER OF ECONOMIC LIBERALIZATION

As reflected in our discussions in Chapters 17 and 23, adjustment programs designed by the IMF and World Bank have been more complex than suggested by our demand reduction and demand switching analysis. Inspired by the Washington Consensus discussed in Chapter 23, including its appended second-generation reforms, adjustment programs have also included a number of kinds of market *liberalization*. For example, the two Bretton Woods institutions have had an abiding concern with reducing the welfare losses associated with import tariffs, import quotas, and export taxes, as discussed in Chapter 6. They have also called for *privatization* of state-owned enterprises.[16] For these reasons, structural adjustment programs have often included the following components:

1. Exchange rate depreciation or devaluation
2. Reductions in government expenditures, including reduction in public sector workforces, elimination of agricultural and industrial subsidies, and elimination of food and medical subsidies

[15] See, for example, Rajan and Subramanian (2011).

[16] Lin (2009) noted that "the objectives of the Washington Consensus were to eliminate government distortions and interventions in socialist and developing countries, and to set up a well-functioning market system" (p. 52). Sometimes researchers characterize structural adjustment programs of being composed of four "ations": stabilization, liberalization, deregulation, and privatization.

3. Wage controls to reduce demand and to prevent inflation
4. Elimination of import quotas and export taxes
5. Reduction of *ad valorem* tariffs to "moderate" levels of 10–15 percent
6. The privatization of state-owned enterprises
7. The liberalization of domestic financial markets

Historically, there has been a tendency for the IMF and World Bank to call for the implementation of the above components *all at once.* For example, this was the advice given to the "Southern Cone" countries of Chile, Argentina, and Uruguay in the late 1970s and early 1980s. In this instance, the results were not positive.[17] Subsequently, international economists have stressed that it is very important to pay attention to the *order of economic liberalization.*[18] There is evidence that failure to heed the warnings of the order of economic liberalization literature can significantly compromise the *sustainability* of adjustment policies. In particular, inadequate attention to the order of financial-sector liberalization can contribute to the crises we discussed in Chapter 18, particularly in the form of banking crises.

Suppose that Ghana or some other developing country faces emerging balance of payments difficulties such as that described in the previous sections. It is financing a current account deficit by selling foreign exchange reserves. The central government is running a deficit. Additionally, suppose that the government owns some enterprises on which it depends for some revenue (state-owned enterprises [SOEs]), the government restricts imports using a set of quotas, and the exchange rate is fixed. The question this country faces is how to order the steps it will take in alleviating the balance of payments crisis and securing sustainable adjustment. In what follows, we present one possible sequence and provide an accompanying rationale.

First *seek a means of securing central government revenue through a broad-based tax.* The government accounts are in deficit, and the government may be called upon to lower trade taxes and sell its SOEs, both of which will involve a loss of revenue sources. Alternative revenue sources must be found.[19] Possible sources are sales taxes, producer taxes, or value-added taxes. These should be *broad-based* and *set at low rates.* The increase in tax revenues will lower the government deficit, which will tend to narrow the gap between domestic investment and domestic savings that underlies the current account deficit. It will also position the government for further reforms without precipitating a fiscal crisis.

Second, *depreciate or devalue the exchange rate.* As we have stated a number of times now, reducing the value of the domestic currency begins a switching process and may even evoke some of the positive externalities of traded goods production discussed previously. Imports are reduced and exports can expand, the latter usually taking longer than the former. Both of these effects tend to reduce the current account deficit.[20]

[17] On the Southern Cone experience, Edwards (1984) wrote: "A decade after these reforms were first implemented, the evidence indicates that they were to a large extent a failure" (p. 1).

[18] See, for example, Edwards (1984), McKinnon (1993), part III of Lipumba (1994), and chapter 14 of Montiel (2003).

[19] McKinnon (1993) wrote that "the liberalizing government must quickly develop a regularized tax system for retrieving the revenue lost from giving up ownership of the means of production. . . . Until a full-fledged internal revenue service for collecting taxes from the private sector can be put in place, many industrial assets and most natural resources best remain government-owned as revenue sources for the public treasury" (pp. 4–5).

[20] For example, Lipumba (1994) was adamant that this switching policy must take place before trade liberalization. He was critical of cases in which the World Bank and the IMF suggested trade liberalization to African countries that had not adjusted their exchange rates. He noted that "exports take longer to respond to . . . a depreciation of the real exchange rate than imports. If countries are not willing to depreciate their currencies, it is irresponsible

To avoid exacerbating trade balance problems, an appropriate exchange rate should be established *before* trade liberalization occurs.

Third, *tariffy quotas on imports of consumer goods and remove quotas on imports of intermediate and capital goods.* In Chapter 6, we saw that a quota on imports of a good causes a *quota premium* equal to the amount by which the domestic price of the good increases above the world price as a result of the quota. It is possible for the government to set a tariff that maintains an excess of the domestic price over the world price equal to the previous quota premium. This is known as an *equivalent tariff.* The advantage of this *tariffication process* is that it converts quota rents into government revenue. This helps to alleviate the government's budget deficit. The removal of quotas on intermediate and capital goods will ensure that these goods are available to domestic producers. This will tend to lower the domestic prices of the goods, offsetting the effect of exchange rate depreciation and addressing structuralist concerns about declining production. Any tariffs on these goods should be set very low. Care should be taken to maintain existing government revenues from trade taxes despite the measures discussed previously.[21]

Fourth, *selectively begin to privatize SOEs.* With steps 1 to 3 complete, the government can begin to evaluate which SOEs to privatize and, just as important, how to privatize them. Issues of fair value, broad-based ownership, and competition are paramount here. For example, creating unregulated private monopolies owned by a few domestic or international agents will not increase welfare and promote development. As emphasized by Harberger (2001), an advocate of the Washington Consensus, countries must avoid the "excess of zeal" involved in privatization "right now, no matter to whom, no matter under what conditions" (p. 550). Unfortunately, such advice has not always been heeded.

Fifth, *liberalize the foreign direct investment component of the capital/financial account.*[22] As we discussed in Chapter 13, the capital account can be divided into direct investment and portfolio investment. As we stated in that chapter, direct investment involves ownership and control of physical capital, whereas portfolio investment reflects ownership alone of government bonds, corporate equities, corporate bonds, and bank deposits. Portfolio investment can be further broken down into long-term and short-term components. In general, portfolio investment (especially short-term portfolio investment) tends to be highly volatile, particularly commercial bank lending under the "other investment" component of the capital/financial account (item 12 in Table 13.2 of Chapter 13).

Given these considerations, it makes sense for a country to begin liberalization of the capital account with direct foreign investment. As we discussed in Chapters 9 and 10, foreign direct investment (FDI) is conducted as part of firms' strategic decisions regarding the construction of international value-added networks. In general, these decisions will not be taken lightly and are not as easily reversed as portfolio investment.

for them to liberalize imports" (p. 57). This point also has relevance for Latin America. For example, the effects of trade liberalization with an overvalued currency in Colombia in the early 1980s were reviewed by Urrutia (1998).

[21] Rodrik (1990) argued that "in general, a reduction in revenues from trade taxes must be avoided, *even* when it looks like alternative revenue sources may be available. In view of the fiscal crisis, it is probably better to *increase* overall revenues by implementing these alternatives than to have them substitute for reduced import duties" (p. 941). Urrutia (1998) noted that trade taxes in Colombia composed one-fourth of total central government revenue in the late 1980s, when trade policy reform began for a second time. Despite its adjustment success, Colombia has had to increase tariffs now and then in recent years to ensure adequate government revenues.

[22] Much of the early discussion on the order of economic liberalization concerned whether to first liberalize the current or capital accounts of the balance of payments. Edwards (1984) reviewed this literature and concluded that the capital account should be liberalized only *after* the current account is liberalized.

For this reason, it is with FDI that capital account liberalization should begin. Beyond that, countries should engage in what Eichengreen (1999) called "cautious steps in the direction of capital account liberalization," which "should not extend to the removal of taxes on capital inflows" (p 13).[23]

Sixth, in preparation for an eventual liberalization of the domestic financial industry and the capital account, *develop an effective system of bank regulation.* As emphasized by Eichengreen (1999), Reinhart and Rogoff (2009), and others, banks in developing countries both predominate in the provision of financial services and pose the most serious threat to financial stability due to their inherent instability.[24] The prevention of financial crises requires a well-developed system of banking supervision. This involves giving attention to capital adequacy requirements, auditing, loan policies, and degree of foreign borrowing. Until these systems are in place, financial sector liberalization is inadvisable.

As we mentioned previously, the whole question of the order of economic liberalization was raised after the unsatisfactory experience with the adjustment/liberalization process in the Southern Cone of Latin America during the late 1970s and early 1980s. Since that time, there have been many more examples of troubled adjustment/liberalization experiences. This includes privatization in Russia in the 1990s and financial sector liberalization in Hungary in the 2000s. One possible explanation for this unimpressive history is that failures to design order of economic liberalization strategies to the particularities of the countries involved has led to a lack of *sustainability* of the adjustment policies. This point was made over two decades ago by Rodrik (1990), who argued that, where a conflict between idealized adjustment policies and the economic and political sustainability of these policies exists, the idealized policies must be compromised.

For many developing countries, there is wisdom in proceeding through adjustment processes in a sequenced, step-by-step manner rather than in "shock therapy." As noted by Lin (2009), "the crucial issue in transition is to have a strategy of sequencing reforms that identifies the most pressing bottlenecks and concentrates resources on the relaxation of binding constraints, removing the suppression of incentives and inspiring people to improve performance to achieve a better life by their own efforts" (pp. 88–89). This, according to Lin, is the main lesson of the successful East Asian development experience.[25]

CONCLUSION

The growth and development process inherently involves structural change as resources naturally move into more productive sectors. This tends to involve a decline in agriculture as a percent of GDP, an initial expansion and then decline of manufacturing as a percent of GDP, and an expansion of the service sector as a percent of GDP. Productivity in all of these sectors is important, and both agriculture and many service sub-sectors have the potential for productivity increases.

[23] Recall the discussion in Chapter 18 on market-friendly capital controls in the form of variable deposit requirements (VDRs).

[24] See also Bird and Rajan (2001), Stiglitz (2000), and our discussion in Chapter 18.

[25] Interestingly, at the time of this writing in 2011, Justin Yifu Lin is the Chief Economist of the World Bank, having taken up the position in 2008.

The adjustment of developing economies to external factors in the world economy is an important and difficult process. An overvalued exchange rate is generally not sustainable, and consequently, external balance then needs to be restored. Achieving external balance by demand reduction alone will sacrifice internal balance (cause unemployment) and exacerbate poverty. Therefore, adjustment must also include demand switching achieved by a devaluation or depreciation of the domestic currency. The promotion of traded goods production via switching might entail extra benefits for growth.

Structuralists question whether the standard demand reduction/demand switching policies of the World Bank and IMF will work effectively in all cases, and their policy prescriptions call for measures to ensure that key productive investments are not sacrificed in demand reduction. Another group of international economists stress the order of economic liberalization in structural adjustment programs. Proper sequencing of reforms is necessary to maintain the sustainability of the adjustment process.

Whatever the specifics of structural adjustment programs, caution must be exercised not to sacrifice long-run growth and development on the altar of short-run adjustment. Productive human and physical capital must somehow be maintained for development to occur. Too often over the years, the World Bank and the IMF have forgotten this.

REVIEW EXERCISES

1. In our discussion of internal and external balance, we saw that a devaluation of a fixed exchange rate moves production in an economy toward traded goods. A revaluation of a fixed exchange rate, in contrast, would move production in an economy toward nontraded goods. Carefully explain the intuition of these results.
2. Structuralist economists maintain that resources are often not mobile among sectors of an economy. Consequently, PPFs tend to be nearly rectangular, and switching effects small. Can you think of any reasons why resources might not be mobile among sectors? Use a diagram like those presented in this chapter to show the ineffectiveness of switching policies in this case.
3. In Chapter 18 on Crises and Responses, we discussed capital controls. In this chapter, we have talked about how liberalization of the capital account should come after the liberalization of the current account. Suppose that you were advising a developing country on the liberalization of its capital account. What would you advise? How should the steps toward liberalization be sequenced?
4. In the antiglobalization movement, structural adjustment is often portrayed as *inherently* undesirable. In your opinion, are there elements of structural adjustment programs that do in fact appear necessary? If so, what are they?

FURTHER READING AND WEB RESOURCES

Chapter 1 of Corden (1986) provides a classic account of adjustment via demand reduction and switching policies. Another account is available in chapter 3 of Hossain and Chowdhury (1998). On the role of structural adjustment in economic development, important sources are Rodrik (1990), Stewart (1995), Tarp (1993), and Lin (2009). The

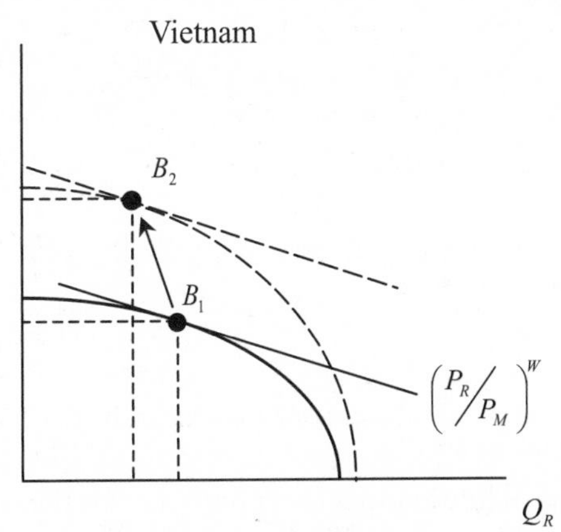

Figure 24.8. The Rybczynski Theorem in Vietnam

order of economic liberalization has been effectively discussed in Lipumba (1994), McKinnon (1993), chapter 14 of Montiel (2003), and Lin (2009).

APPENDIX: THE RYBCZYNSKI THEOREM

In Chapter 5, as part of our discussion of the political economy of trade, we introduced the Heckscher-Ohlin model of comparative advantage and its Stolper-Samuelson theorem. There is another theorem associated with the Heckscher-Ohlin model with relevance to structural change, namely the **Rybczynski theorem.**[26] We actually presented some results relevant to the Rybczynski theorem in the appendix to Chapter 9 on FDI and comparative advantage and in the appendix to Chapter 12 on migration and comparative advantage. The common denominator in these two appendices was the change in the amount of a *factor of production* (physical capital in Chapter 9 and labor in Chapter 12). The most important application of the Rybczysnki theorem for our purposes here is due to an increase in physical capital relative to labor in a process of capital deepening discussed in Chapter 21. This is presented in Figure 24.8.

The Rybczysnki theorem considers an increase in a factor of production under fixed world prices. Let's go back to our comparative advantage model of Chapter 3 and consider Vietnam producing rice (R) and motorcycles (M) at the world relative price of rice $(\frac{P_R}{P_M})^W$. If there is an increase in physical capital, then this favors the capital-intensive sector (motorcycles) over the labor-intensive sector (rice). The PPF consequently moves out more along the M axis than along the R axis in Figure 24.8.

For a given world price ratio, the production point moves from B_1 on the original PPF to B_2 on the new PPF. As we can see in the figure, this involves an increase in the production of motorcycles but a decrease in production of rice. The increase in physical capital via capital deepening results in a shift of the structure of the economy away from rice (the labor-intensive sector) and toward motorcycles (the capital-intensive sector). A process of capital shallowing, or an increase in labor, would have the opposite effect. This is the basic insight of the Rybczynski theorem.

[26] The Rybczynski theorem was presented in Rybczynski (1955).

REFERENCES

Anderson, K. (1987) "On Why Agriculture Declines with Economic Growth," *Agricultural Economics*, 1:3, 195–207.

Bacha, E.L. (1987) "IMF Conditionality: Conceptual Problems and Policy Alternatives," *World Development*, 15:12, 1457–1467.

Baumol, W.J. (1986) "Productivity Growth, Convergence and Welfare: What the Long Run Data Show," *American Economic Review*, 76:5, 1072–1086.

Bird, G. and R.S. Rajan (2001) "Banks, Financial Liberalization and Financial Crises in Emerging Markets," *World Economy*, 24:7, 889–910.

Corden, W.M. (1986) *Inflation, Exchange Rates, and the World Economy*, University of Chicago Press.

Edwards, S. (1984) *The Order of Liberalization of the External Sector of Developing Countries*, Essays in International Finance 156, Princeton University Press.

Eichengreen, B. (1999) *Towards a New International Financial Architecture: A Practical Post-Asia Agenda*, Institute for International Economics.

Francois, J.F. and K.A. Reinert (1996) "The Role of Services in the Structure of Production and Trade: Stylized Facts from a Cross-Country Analysis," *Asia-Pacific Economic Review*, 2:1, 35–43.

Francois, J.F. and B. Hoekman (2010) "Services Trade and Policy," *Journal of Economic Literature*, 48:3, 642–692.

Francois, J.F. and J. Woerz (2008) "Producer Services, Manufacturing Linkages, and Trade," *Journal of Industry, Competition and Trade*, 8:3–4, 199–229.

Gala, P. (2008) "Real Exchange Rate Levels and Economic Development: Theoretical Analysis and Econometric Evidence," *Cambridge Journal of Economics*, 32:2, 273–288.

Gera, N. (2007) "Impact of Structural Adjustment Programs on Overall Social Welfare in Pakistan," *South Asia Economic Journal*, 8:1, 39–64.

Harberger, A.C. (2001) "The View from the Trenches: Development Processes and Policies as Seen by a Working Professional," in G.M. Meier and J.E. Stiglitz (eds.), *Frontiers of Development Economics*, Oxford University Press, 541–561.

Hossain, A. and A. Chowdhury (1998) *Open-Economy Macroeconomics for Developing Countries*, Edward Elgar.

Kuznets, S. (1966) *Modern Economic Growth: Rate, Structure, and Spread*, Yale University Press.

Lin, J.Y. (2009) *Economic Development and Transition: Thought, Strategy, and Viability*, Cambridge University Press.

Lipumba, N.H.I. (1994) *Africa beyond Adjustment*, Overseas Development Council.

McKinnon, R.I. (1993) *The Order of Economic Liberalization*, Johns Hopkins University Press.

Meade, J.E. (1978) "The Meaning of 'Internal Balance,'" *Economic Journal*, 88:351, 423–435.

Montiel, P.J. (2003) *Macroeconomics in Emerging Markets*, Cambridge University Press.

Rajan, R.G. and A. Subramanian (2011) "Aid, Dutch Disease and Manufacturing Growth," *Journal of Development Economics.*

Reinhart, C.M. and K.S. Rogoff (2009) *This Time Is Different: Eight Centuries of Financial Folly*, Princeton University Press.

Rodrik, D. (1990) "How Should Structural Adjustment Programs Be Designed?" *World Development*, 18:7, 933–947.

Rodrik, D. (2008) "The Real Exchange Rate and Economic Growth," *Brookings Papers on Economic Activity*, Fall, 365–412.

Rybczynski, T.M. (1955) "Factor Endowment and Relative Commodity Prices," *Economica*, 22:88, 336–341.

Salter, W.E.G. (1959) "Internal and External Balance: The Role of Price and Expenditure Effects," *Economic Record*, 35:71, 226–238.

Stewart, F. (1995) *Adjustment and Poverty: Options and Choices*, Routledge.

Stiglitz, J. (2000) "Two Principles for the Next Round or, How to Bring Developing Countries in from the Cold," *World Economy*, 23:4, 437–454.

Szirmai, A. (2005) *The Dynamics of Socio-Economic Development*, Cambridge University Press.

Tarp, F. (1993) *Stabilization and Structural Adjustment*, Routledge.

Taylor, L. (1993) "Stabilization, Adjustment, and Reform," in L. Taylor (ed.), *The Rocky Road to Reform*, MIT Press, 39–94.

Urrutia, M. (1998) "Economic Reform in Colombia," in H. Costin and H. Vanolli (eds.), *Economic Reform in Latin America*, Dryden, 217–241.

Glossary

Absolute advantage. The possibility that, due to differences in supply conditions, one country can produce a product at a lower price than another country.

Adjustable gold peg. An international financial arrangement that was part of the Bretton Woods system. It involved pegging the U.S. dollar to gold at US$35 per ounce and allowing all other countries to either peg to the U.S. dollar or directly to gold. The currency pegs (other than the U.S. dollar) were to remain fixed except under conditions that were termed *fundamental disequilibrium.*

Appreciation. An increase in the value of a currency under a flexible or floating exchange rate regime.

Assets. Financial objects characterized by a monetary value that can change over time and making up individuals' and firms' wealth portfolios.

Assets-based approach. A model of exchange rate determination that views foreign exchange deposits as assets held as part of an overall wealth portfolio.

Asset price deflation. The rapid or substantial decline in the value of assets.

Autarky. A situation of national self-sufficiency in which a country does not import or export.

Backward linkages. The purchase of goods from local suppliers by foreign multinational enterprises.

Balance of payments. A detailed set of economic accounts focusing on the transactions between a country and the rest of the world. Two important sub-accounts are the current account and the capital/financial account.

Balance of payments and currency crises. Large devaluations or rapid depreciations of the value of domestic currencies.

Banking crises. The occurrence of bank runs, mergers, closures, or government takeovers of banking institutions.

Binding. A major GATT/WTO principle. As negotiations proceed through the rounds of trade talks, tariffs are bound at the agreed-upon level. They may not in general be increased in the future.

Brady Plan. A set of procedures proposed by U.S. Treasury Secretary Nicholas Brady and approved by the IMF in 1989. The Brady Plan allowed IMF and World Bank lending to be used by developing countries to buy back discounted international debt. It was a partial but important response to the developing country debt crisis that began in the 1980s.

Brain drain. The loss of highly educated or skilled citizens to emigration.

Bretton Woods system. An international financial system introduced at the Bretton Woods conference in 1944 involving an exchange rate arrangement known as the adjustable gold peg.

Bubbles. The rapid increase in asset prices above what is to be expected by the underlying productive value of the asset.

Capital/financial account. A subsection of the balance of payments recording transactions between a country and the world economy that involve the exchange of assets.

Capital deepening. An increase in the overall capital-labor ratio in a country.

Capital flight. A situation in which investors sell a country's assets and reallocate their portfolios towards other countries' assets. It tends to cause a capital account deficit for the country in question.

Capital gain (loss). An increase (decrease) in the price of an asset.

Change in demand. A shift of a demand curve due to a change in income, wealth, preferences, expectations, and prices of related goods.

Change in quantity demanded. A movement along a demand curve due to a change in the price of a good.

Change in quantity supplied. A movement along a supply curve due to a change in the price of the good.

Change in supply. A shift of the supply curve due to a change in technology or input prices.

Circular flow diagram. A graphical representation of the flow of incomes and expenditures in an economy. It involves firm, household, government, capital, and rest of the world accounts.

Closed economy. Similar to autarky. An economy that does not have any interactions with the world economy.

Comparative advantage. A situation in which a country's relative autarkic price ratio of one good in terms of another is lower than that of other countries in the world economy.

Competitive advantage. A situation in which a firm can sustain global, market competitiveness in a particular product niche.

Compulsory licensing. The production of off-patent medicines under the Agreement on Trade-Related Aspects of Intellectual Property Rights.

Conditionality. Policies pursued by the World Bank and International Monetary Fund in which loans are made only to countries that promise to institute a set of prescribed policy changes.

Constant returns to scale. A condition of production in which a doubling of all inputs leads to a doubling of output.

Consumer surplus. The benefit accruing to consumers from the fact that, in equilibrium, the consumers receive a price lower than their willingness to pay for lesser quantities.

Contagion. The spread of a financial crisis from one country to another.

Contracting. A mode of foreign market entry in which a home-country firm contracts a foreign-country firm to engage in production in the foreign country. Includes both licensing and franchising.

Crawling band. An exchange rate regime in which monetary authorities intervene to maintain the nominal exchange rate in a band of prescribed width around a central rate.

Crawling peg. An exchange rate regime in which a country fixes its nominal exchange rate in terms of another currency but changes this fixed rate gradually over time in small increments.

Crises. Any of a number of extreme difficulties faced by economies, including hyperinflation, balance of payments and currency crises, asset price deflation, banking crises, external debt crises, and domestic debt crises.

Currency board. A type of fixed exchange rate regime in which the monetary authority is required to fully back up the domestic currency with reserves of the foreign currency to which the domestic currency is pegged.

Current account. A subsection of the balance of payments recording nonofficial transactions between a country and the world economy that do not involve the exchange of assets.

Customs union. An agreement on the part of a set of countries to eliminate trade restrictions among themselves and adopt a common external tariff.

Deflation. A fall in the overall or aggregate price level in an economy.

Demand reduction. The decrease in domestic demand made in an attempt to move an economy toward external balance.

Depreciation. A decrease in the value of a currency under a flexible or floating exchange rate regime.

Devaluation. A decrease in the value of a currency under a fixed exchange rate regime.

Direct investment. An entry in the balance of payments that records the net inflows of foreign direct investment.

Dissemination risk. The possibility of a foreign-country partner firm obtaining technology or other know-how from a home-country firm and exploiting it for its own commercial advantage.

Domestic debt crises. The sovereign default on debt obligations to domestic creditors or the substantial restructuring of this debt.

Effective exchange rate. An exchange rate weighted across a country's trade partners.

Efficiency seeking. One motivation for foreign direct investment that involves the pursuit of firm-level economies in which intangible assets are spread over a greater number of international productive activities.

Endogenous protection. A body of trade theory that uses political considerations to explain the presence and level of barriers to trade, particularly tariffs.

European Community or European Union. A common market among European countries. The EC was established in 1958, the EU in 1992.

Exchange rate exposure. The loss of income denominated in a particular currency due to exchange rate changes.

Exchange rate target zone. An exchange rate arrangement proposed by John Williamson designed to obtain the benefits of both fixed and floating exchange rate agreements. The exchange rate target zone consists of a band around the fundamental equilibrium exchange rate (FEER) on the order of ± 10 percent.

Export processing zone. An area of a host country in which multinational enterprises can locate and in which they enjoy, in return for exporting the whole of their output, favorable treatment in the areas of infrastructure, taxation, tariffs on imported intermediate goods, and labor costs.

Export promotion. An economic development strategy promoted by the World Bank in which development occurs by encouraging export sectors.

Export subsidy. A subsidy to exports provided by the government of a country.

External balance. A situation in an economy in which trade (the current account) is balanced.

External debt crises. The sovereign default on debt obligations to foreign creditors or the substantial restructuring of this debt.

Financial intermediary. Financial institutions such as banks, mutual funds, and brokers that receive funds from savers and use these funds to make loans or buy assets, thereby placing the funds in the hands of investors.

Firm-level economies. Economies accruing to a firm from spreading the cost of firm-specific assets over larger numbers of production facilities, including production facilities in more than one country.

Firm-specific asset approach. An explanation of foreign direct investment based on the capabilities and resources possessed by a firm that contribute to its sustained competitiveness. The firm-specific assets can be tangible or intangible.

Fixed exchange rate regime. An exchange rate policy in which a country sets its nominal or currency exchange rate fixed in terms of another currency.

Flexible or floating exchange rate regime. An exchange rate policy in which a country allows the value of its currency to be determined by world currency markets.

Flexible manufacturing. A recent phase of manufacturing history in which information technology combines with machinery in a way to promote rapid switching among products and processes. Also known as "Toyotism."

Fordism. A middle stage in the history of manufacturing where the focus is on achieving economies of scale. Also known as "managerial capitalism."

Foreign direct investment or FDI. Occurs when a firm acquires shares in a foreign-based enterprise that exceeds a threshold of 10 percent, implying managerial influence over the foreign enterprise. Contrasts with portfolio investment. FDI may be horizontal, backward vertical, or forward vertical.

Foreign market entry. Sales on the part of a firm in a foreign country via trade, contractual, or foreign direct investment modes.

Foreign savings. An inflow of funds into an economy from the rest of the world. It occurs when foreign investors buy the assets of the economy in question.

Forward rate. The rates of current contracts for transactions in currencies that usually take place one, three, or six months in the future.

Fragmentation. The breaking up of a production process into a larger number of stages, particularly across national borders; used to explain vertical *intra*-industry trade.

Free trade area. An agreement on the part of a set of countries to *eliminate* trade restrictions among themselves. In contrast to a customs union, it does not involve a common external tariff.

Fundamental accounting equations. Derived from the circular flow diagram, it appears in two forms: the first is Domestic Investment – Domestic Savings = Foreign Savings = Trade Deficit. The second is Domestic Savings – Domestic Investment = Foreign Investment = Trade Balance.

Fundamental equilibrium exchange rate. An exchange rate concept developed by John Williamson. The FEER can be thought of as the purchasing power exchange rate, although this is not its exact definition. In Williamson's proposal, the FEER acts as the center point of an exchange rate target zone.

Gains from trade. Advantages that accrue to a country from engaging in importing and exporting relationships. In an absolute advantage framework, gains from trade are identified as a net gain between consumer and producer surplus effects. In a comparative advantage framework, gains from trade are identified as an increase in consumption of all goods.

GDP price deflator. A means of establishing a price level as the ratio of nominal to real gross domestic product.

General Agreement on Tariffs and Trade. Established in 1946, the GATT was to be part of an International Trade Organization. The ITO was never ratified, but the GATT and its Articles served as an international vehicle for trade relationships until 1995, when it became embodied in the Marrakesh Agreement establishing the World Trade Organization. As part of the Marrakesh Agreement, it is now known as GATT 1994.

General Agreement on Trade in Services. Part of the Marrakesh Agreement of 1994. Applies the GATT/WTO principles of nondiscrimination and national treatment to services.

Gini coefficient. A summary measure of the Lorenz curve that gives an overall value to the degree of income inequality. It varies between zero (perfect equality) and one (perfect inequality). The Gini coefficient index varies between zero and 100.

Global production network. A system of value chains linked together in buyer-supplier or ownership relationships across countries.

Gold standard. An international financial arrangement in existence from approximately 1870 to 1914. Under the gold standard, countries defined the value of their currencies in terms of gold and held gold as official reserves.

Gold-exchange standard. An international financial arrangement introduced in the 1920s to replace the gold standard. It consisted of a set of center countries tied to gold and a set of periphery countries tied to the center country currencies.

Gross domestic product. The value of all final goods and services produced within a country's borders during a year.

Gross national income. The value of all final goods and services produced by a country's factors of production (but not necessarily within the country's borders) during a year.

Growth. A sustained increase in per capita income over time.

Growth theory. In its "old" and "new" variants, growth theory is the explanation of economics of the sustained increase in per capita incomes over the long run. It is based on the intensive production function.

Grubel-Lloyd index. An index of the degree of *intra*-industry trade that varies between 0 and 100.

Heckscher-Ohlin model. A model of international trade based on differences in factor endowments among the countries of the world.

High-skilled migration. The movement of persons with significant education and/or training from one country to another.

Home base. The country in which a multinational enterprise is incorporated and holds its central administrative capabilities.

Human capital. Investments made in the education, training, and capabilities of a labor force.

Human development (index). A conception of economic development introduced by the United Nations Development Program that stresses health and education levels along with per capita income. The human development index (HDI) is reported in the annual *Human Development Report.*

Hyperinflation. A very large increase in the overall or aggregate price level in an economy on the order of 40 percent or more annually.

Import licenses. A right to import under a quota given either to domestic importers or foreign exporters.

Import substitution. A development strategy that attempts to replace previously imported goods with domestic production.

Impossible trinity. The inability of countries to obtain all three of monetary independence, exchange rate stability, and capital mobility.

Industrial capitalism. An early phase in the history of manufacturing in which the focus was on the procurement of industrial inputs on the part of colonial powers from their colonies in order to promote the manufactured exports of the colonial powers.

Inflation. A substantial increase in the overall or aggregate price level in an economy.

Intensive production function. A production function expressed on a per capita basis.

Interest rate parity condition. The equilibrium condition in the assets approach to the exchange rate determination model. It relates a country's interest rate to the expected rate of depreciation of its currency and the interest rate of another country. Appears in both "covered" and "uncovered" varieties.

Inter-industry trade. A pattern of trade in which a country *either* imports *or* exports in a given sector.

Internal balance. A situation in an economy in which all resources are fully employed.

Internalization. The process of taking a transaction along a value chain and bringing it within a firm.

International development. A concept with many meanings, including increases in per capita income, improvements in health and education, structural change, and institutional "modernization."

International finance. The exchange of assets among the countries of the world economy.

International Monetary Fund. A product of the Bretton Woods conference that functions as a global credit union for its member countries and supports the global monetary system.

International production. A production of a good or service with processes located in more than one country.

International trade. The exchange of goods and services among the countries of the world economy.

Intra-firm trade. Trade that takes place within a multinational enterprise.

Intra-industry trade. A pattern of trade in which a country *both* imports *and* exports in a given sector.

Jamaica Agreement. A 1976 amendment to the IMF's Articles of Agreement that allowed for floating exchange rates.

Knowledge capital. A particular type of firm-specific asset based on knowledge, such as intellectual property.

Lorenz curve. A graph relating the cumulative percentage of income to the cumulative percentage of households, the latter ranked from low to high income. It is a visual measure of income inequality.

Low-skilled migration. The movement of persons without significant education and/or training from one country to another.

Managed floating regime. An exchange rate regime in which a country allows its currency to float but intervenes in currency markets to affect its value when it determines that such intervention would be desirable.

Managerial capitalism. A middle stage in the history of manufacturing where the focus is on achieving economies of scale. Also known as "Fordism."

Market entry. The process of a home-country firm supplying a foreign market through exports, contracting, or foreign direct investment.

Market seeking. A motivation for foreign direct investment in which the multinational enterprise engages in FDI to better serve a foreign market.

Marrakesh Agreement. Signed in 1994, the Marrakesh Agreement concluded the Uruguay Round of trade talks began in 1986 and established the World Trade Organization.

Merchant capitalism. Part of the colonization efforts of the European powers during the sixteenth and seventeenth centuries that included state-supported trading companies such as the British East India Company, the Dutch East India Company, and the Royal African Company.

Migration. The movement of persons from one country to another, particularly outside of the country of residence.

Milieu. Related to a spatial cluster and including its firms, embedded knowledge, and institutional environment.

Monetary approach to exchange rate determination. A theory of long-run exchange rate determination based on purchasing power parity and the quantity theory of money.

Monetary union. A group of member countries in a common market all using a common currency. The most notable example is the European Monetary Union (EMU).

Money demand. The amount of money households want to hold at any particular time.

Money supply. The amount of money set in an economy by a central monetary authority such as a central bank or treasury.

Most favored nation. A principle of the GATT/WTO system in which each member must treat each other member as generously as its most-favored trading partner.

Multilateral environmental agreements. Agreements on any environmental issue negotiated and codified among a large number of countries.

Multilateral trade negotiations. Rounds of trade negotiations conducted under the auspices of the World Trade Organization and its predecessor, the GATT Secretariat.

Multinational enterprise. Also known as the multinational corporation or the transnational corporation. A firm with production, sales, and service operations in more than one country.

National treatment. A principle of the GATT/WTO system under which foreign goods within a country should be treated no less favorably than domestic goods with regard to tax policies.

Natural rate of population growth. An exogenous measure of the rate of population growth used in growth theory.

Net factor income. An item in the current account of the balance of payments. It records the difference between factor income and factor payments, both of which reflect income earned on physical capital.

Nominal exchange rate. The number of units of a country's currency that trade against a world currency such as the U.S. dollar or EU euro.

Nondiscrimination. A major GATT/WTO principle achieved via the sub-principles of most favored nation (MFN) and national treatment.

Nontariff measure. An import restraint or export policy other than a tariff. An import quota is one example.

Nontraded goods. Goods such as local services that are not imported or exported.

North American Free Trade Agreement. As the name implies, a free trade area among Canada, the United States, and Mexico.

Official reserves balance. The element of the capital account of the balance of payments that reflects the actions of the world's central banks.

OLI framework. A theory of the multinational enterprise based on ownership, location, and internalization advantages.

Open-economy accounts. The accounting identities derived from the firm, household, government, capital, and rest of the world accounts of the circular flow diagram.

Opportunity cost. What has to be given up to gain something. Along a production possibilities frontier, there is an opportunity cost of increasing the output of one good in the form of less production of another good.

Optimum currency area. A collection of countries characterized by well-integrated factor markets, well-integrated fiscal systems, and economic disturbances that affect each country in a symmetrical manner.

Overvaluation. Under a fixed exchange rate regime, a value of a home currency above its equilibrium value causing an excess supply of the home currency.

Ownership requirements. A limit placed on the degree of foreign ownership of firms by a country's government.

Performance requirements. A large host of measures placed on the performance of multinational enterprises by a government. A subset of these is known as trade-related investment measures.

Pollution haven hypothesis. The notion that multinational enterprises locate environmentally damaging processes in low-income countries.

Poverty. Significant deprivation in terms of income.

Preferential trade agreement. An agreement by a number of countries to grant preferential access to their markets to other members of the agreement. Examples include free trade areas and customs unions. Also called regional trade agreement.

Price level. A measure of the average or overall level of prices in a country. Includes the GDP price deflator and the consumer price index.

Producer surplus. The benefit accruing to producers from the fact that, in equilibrium, the producers receive a price higher than their willingness to accept for lesser quantities.

Product differentiation. The differentiation of one product from another along any dimension used to help explain horizontal *intra*-industry trade.

Product life-cycle theory. An early theory of the multinational enterprise (MNE) that viewed production as being confined to the home base of an MNE during the early phases of a product life cycle due to the need for technologically sophisticated production techniques. During later phases of the production cycle, as the production of the good becomes more routine and established, production can move to subsidiaries in foreign countries in order to take advantage of lower labor costs.

Production function. A mathematical relationship between the output of a firm, sector, or economy and inputs such as labor and physical capital.

Production possibilities frontier. A diagram that illustrates the constraints on production in general equilibrium imposed by scarce resources and technology. It shows all the combinations of two goods that a country can produce given its resources and technology.

Purchasing power parity model. A long-run model of exchange rate determination based on the notion that nominal exchanges rate will adjust so that the purchasing power of currencies will be the same in every country.

Quota. Usually applied to imports. A maximum amount of imports allowed by a government.

Quota premium. The increase in the domestic price of a good as a result of an import quota.

Quota rents. The income accruing to the holder of a right to import a good into a country.

Real effective exchange rate. A real exchange rate weighted across a country's trade partners.

Real exchange rate. The rate at which two countries' *goods* (not currencies) trade against each other. The real exchange rate adjusts the nominal exchange rate using the price levels in the two countries under consideration.

Regional trade agreement. An agreement by a number of countries to grant preferential access to their markets to other members of the agreement. Examples include free trade areas and customs unions. Also called preferential trade agreement.

Remittances. The flow of money from emigrants to their countries of origin.

Resource seeking. One of the motivations for foreign direct investment in which a multinational enterprise backward integrates into resource supply in a foreign country.

Revaluation. An increase in the value of a currency under a fixed exchange rate regime.

Rules of origin. A means to determine whether a product is from a partner country in a preferential trade agreement.

Rybczynski theorem. An element of trade theory that considers what happens to the sectoral structure of an economy as resource endowments change.

Smithsonian Conference. A conference that took place in Washington, DC, in December 1971 to attempt to repair the damaged adjustable gold peg system of the Bretton Woods system.

Spatial cluster. A collection of interrelated firms in a geographic area that engages in cooperative information sharing and, thereby, contributes to their collective efficiency and competitiveness.

Special drawing rights. An international currency administered by the IMF and introduced in 1969. It is currently defined in terms of a basket of three currencies: the U.S. dollar, the euro, and the yen.

Specific factors model. A model of trade theory that allows for factors of production that cannot move easily from one sector to another.

Spot rate. The current, nominal exchange rate between two currencies.

Stolper-Samuelson theorem. A result of international trade theory concerning the politics of trade. It states that an increase in the relative price of a commodity (e.g., as a result of trade) raises the return to the factor used intensively in the production of that good and lowers the return to the other factor.

Strategic asset seeking. A motivation for foreign direct investment in which the multinational enterprise wants to acquire productive assets as part of the *strategic game* among competitors in an industry.

Structural adjustment. The process of change in an economy that takes place in response to internal and/or external imbalances. It typically requires demand reduction and currency devaluation.

Structural adjustment lending. Nonproject lending of the World Bank to support adjustment in the face of balance of payments difficulties. Based on policy conditionality.

Structural change. The change in the sectoral composition of economies over time.

Switching. The use of a devaluation of a country's currency to move the economy toward external balance.

Systemic risk. The spread of a financial crisis among a large number of countries.

Tariff. A tax on imports that could be either in *ad valorem* or specific form.

Tariffication. The process of replacing quotas by equivalent tariffs.

Tariff rate quota. An import restraint involving two tariff levels: a lower tariff for levels of imports within the quota and a higher tariff for levels of imports above the quota.

Terms-of-trade effects. The effects of a country having an impact on the world prices of the merchandise and services it trades.

Toyotism. A recent phase of manufacturing history in which information technology combines with machinery in a way to promote rapid switching among products and processes. Also known as flexible manufacturing.

Trade creation. A potential outcome of a free trade area or a customs union in which imports switch from a high-cost source to a low-cost source.

Trade diversion. A potential outcome of a free trade area or a customs union in which imports switch from a low-cost source to a high-cost source.

Trade-related investment measures. A subset of performance requirements, including export requirements and domestic content requirements, some of which are now prohibited by the World Trade Organization.

Traded goods. Goods and services that can be imported or exported.

Transfer pricing. The manipulation of the prices of intra-firm trade by multinational enterprises to reduce their global tax payments.

Transparency. A major GATT/WTO principle prohibiting the use of quantitative restrictions on trade such as quotas.

Triffin dilemma. A critique of the gold-exchange standard developed by Robert Triffin. It involved a contradiction between the requirements of international liquidity and international confidence.

Undervaluation. Under a fixed exchange rate regime, a value of a home-country currency below its equilibrium value causing an excess demand for the currency.

Value chain. A series of value-added processes involved in the production of a good or service.

Washington Consensus. A term used to define a set of common policies adopted by the International Monetary Fund and the World Bank and imposed on developing countries through structural adjustment lending.

World Bank. An international organization founded in 1944 by the Bretton Woods Conference. It was originally designed to assist in the reconstruction of post-war Europe but quickly became a lender to developing countries in support of development projects and structural adjustment. The World Bank actually consists of the International Bank for Reconstruction and Development and the International Development Association.

World Bank Group. A collection of five organizations: the International Bank for Reconstruction and Development, the International Development Association, the International Finance Corporation, the International Center for Settlement of Investment Disputes, and the Multilateral Investment Guarantee Agency.

World Trade Organization. The WTO was established in 1995 as part of the Marrakesh Agreement ending the Uruguay Round of trade talks. It is an international organization with a legal foundation for managing world trading relationships.

Index